# STRATEGIC MANAGEMENT

## CASES

# NINTH EDITION

# STRATEGIC MANAGEMENT

## CASES

# FRED R. DAVID
*Francis Marion University*

Prentice
Hall

Upper Saddle River, New Jersey 07458

Library of Congress Cataloging-in-Publication Data

Library of Congress Cataloging-in-Publication Data

David, Fred R.
    Strategic management : cases / Fred R. David—9th ed.
        p. cm.
    Includes bibliographical references and index.
    ISBN 0-13-049795-9
    1. Strategic planning—Case studies.  I. Title.

    HD30.28 .D378 2002
    658.4'012—dc21

                                                                    2002034578

Acquisitions Editor: Michael Ablassmeir
Editor-in-Chief: Jeff Shelstad
Managing Editor (Editorial): Jennifer Glennon
Assistant Editor: Melanie Olsen
Senior Marketing Manager: Shannon Moore
Media Project Manager: Michele Faranda
Managing Editor (Production): Judy Leale
Production Editor: Marcela Maslanczuk
Production Assistant: Joseph DeProspero
Permissions Coordinator: Suzanne Grappi
Associate Director, Manufacturing: Vincent Scelta
Production Manager: Arnold Vila
Design Manager: Maria Lange
Designer: Steven Frim
Interior Design: Steven Frim/Donna Wickes
Cover Design: Steven Frim
Cover Illustration: Roger Allyn Lee/Superstock
Manager, Print Production: Christy Mahon
Composition: Black Dot Group
Cover Printer: Phoenix
Printer/Binder: R.R. Donnelley – Willard

Credits and acknowledgments borrowed from other sources and reproduced, with permission, in this textbook appear on appropriate page within text.

Pearson Education LTD.
Pearson Education Australia PTY, Limited
Pearson Education Singapore, Pte. Ltd
Pearson Education North Asia Ltd
Pearson Education, Canada, Ltd
Pearson Educación de Mexico, S.A. de C.V.
Pearson Education–Japan
Pearson Education Malaysia, Pte. Ltd

10 9 8 7 6 5 4 3 2 1
ISBN 0-13-049795-9

*To Joy, Forest, Byron, and Meredith—my wife and children—*
*for their encouragement and love.*

# CONTENTS

12 Selected – Need 10

# PREFACE

The global recession and war on terrorism has ushered in a radically different and more complex business world than it was just two years ago when the previous edition of this text was published. E-commerce has changed the nature of business to its core. Thousands of strategic alliances and partnerships were formed in 2000–2002. Hundreds of companies declared bankruptcy and interest rates fell to their lowest level in fifty years. Downsizing, rightsizing, reengineering, and countless divestitures, acquisitions, and liquidations permanently altered the corporate landscape. Thousands of firms globalized, and thousands more merged in the last two years. Thousands prospered, and yet thousands more failed. Many manufacturers became e-commerce suppliers, and many rival firms became partners. Long-held competitive advantages eroded, and new ones formed. Both the challenges and opportunities facing organizations of all sizes today are greater than ever.

Changes made in this ninth edition are aimed squarely at illustrating the effect of this new world order on strategic-management theory and practice. Changes in this edition are more substantial than changes made in the last four editions combined! To survive and prosper in the new millennium, organizations must build and sustain competitive advantage. This new edition provides up-to-date, state-of-the-art coverage of strategic-management concepts and techniques for achieving a competitive advantage.

Our mission in preparing the ninth edition of *Strategic Management* was "to create the most current, well-written business policy textbook on the market—a book that is exciting and valuable to both students and professors." To achieve this mission, every page has been revamped, updated, and improved. New strategic-management research and practice are incorporated throughout the chapters, and hundreds of new examples abound. There is a new Cohesion Case on American Airlines—2002. A wonderful selection of new cases include such companies as Royal Caribbean, Winn-Dixie, Coors, Hewlett-Packard Corporation, and Best Buy Company. The time basis for all cases included in this edition is 2002, representing the most up-to-date compilation of cases ever assembled in a business policy text.

I believe, along with scores of reviewers, that you will find this edition to be the best ever—and now the best business policy textbook available for communicating both the excitement and value of strategic management. The text is concise and exceptionally well organized. Now published in six different languages—English, Chinese, Spanish, Arabic, Indonesian, and Japanese—this text is perhaps the most widely used strategic-planning book in the world.

## SPECIAL NOTE TO PROFESSORS

This textbook meets all AACSB guidelines for the business policy and strategic management course at both the graduate and undergraduate levels. Previous editions of this text have been used at more than five hundred colleges and universities. Prentice Hall maintains a separate

Web site for this text at **www.prenhall.com/david**. The author maintains the Strategic Management Club Online Web site at **www.strategyclub.com**. These sites offer great content to both professors and students.

Although the structure of David's *Strategic Management,* 9th edition parallels the last, dramatic improvements have been made in readability, currentness, and coverage. In keeping with the mission "to become the most current, well-written business policy textbook on the market," every page has undergone rethinking and rewriting to streamline, update, and improve the caliber of presentation. A net result of this activity is that every chapter is shorter in length. New concepts and practices in strategic management are presented in a style that is clear, focused, and relevant.

## TIME-TESTED FEATURES

This edition continues many of the time-tested features and content that have made this text so successful over the last two decades. Trademarks of this text strengthened in this edition are as follows:

- The 2002 timeframe for cases offers the most current set in any business policy text on the market.
- The cases focus on well-known firms in the news making strategic changes. All cases are undisguised and most are exclusively written for this text to reflect current strategic-management problems and practices.
- The cases feature a great mix of small business, international, and not-for-profit firms organized conveniently by industry.
- All cases have been class tested to ensure that they are interesting, challenging, and effective for illustrating strategic-management concepts.
- Almost all cases provide complete financial information about the firm and an organizational chart.
- Customized inclusion of cases to comprise a tailored text is available to meet the special needs of some professors.
- A split-paperback version including only cases is available.
- An outstanding ancillary package, including a comprehensive *Instructor's Manual* and an elaborate *Case Instructor's Manual,* is available. An extensive transparency package, color case videos, PowerPoint diskettes, and computerized test bank come free with adoption.

## NEW TO THIS EDITION

In addition to the special time-tested trademarks described above, this edition includes some exciting new features designed to position this text as the clear leader and best choice for teaching business policy and strategic management.

### Changes in the Cases

- Eight brand-new, yearend 2001 cases focusing on companies in the news appear exclusively for the first time in this text. The cases are:

  Winn-Dixie

  Coors

  Royal Caribbean

  Strictly Roots Natural Hair Salon

Best Buy Company
Hewlett-Packard
First State Bank of Roans Prairie
US Airways

- Thirty-three fully updated cases from the last edition are included as follows:

Reader's Digest Association
Reebok International
E*Trade
eBay
Amazon.com
Lockheed Martin Corporation
Dell Computer Corporation
Limited Brands
Wal-Mart Stores
Target Corporation
Mandalay Resort Group
Harrah's Entertainment
Wachovia Corporation
The Audubon Institute
Riverbanks Zoological Park and Botanical Garden
The Classic Car Club of America
Carnival Corporation
Southwest Airlines Co.
Central United Methodist Church
Elkins Lake Baptist Church
Harley-Davidson
Winnebago Industries
Avon Products
Revlon
UST
Pilgrim's Pride Corporation
H. J. Heinz Company
Hershey Foods Corporation
The Boeing Company
Stryker Corporation
Biomet
Playboy Enterprises
Nike

- The new mix of forty-one cases includes a nice balance of twenty-one service companies and twenty manufacturing companies
- The new mix of cases includes three purely e-commerce cases to support the new e-commerce theme. The cases are E*Trade, eBay, and Amazon.
- The new mix of cases includes eight small-business cases and six not-for-profit cases.
- The new mix of cases includes thirty-two "international" companies.

## ANCILLARY MATERIALS

- *Instructor's Resource CD-ROM.* Includes improved PowerPoint slides for both cases and concepts, offering professors easy lecture outlines for in-class presentations. Chapter headings and topics are highlighted on up to thirty PowerPoint slides per chapter. The *Instructor's Manual* and Test Manager Software are also included.

- *Case Instructor's Manual.* Provides a comprehensive teacher's note for all forty-one cases. The teachers' notes feature detailed analyses, classroom discussion questions with answers, an external and internal assessment, specific recommendations, strategy implementation material, and an epilogue for each case. Each teachers' note is also provided on a PowerPoint slide for convenience to the professor.

- *Instructor's Manual with Test Item File.* Provides lecture notes, teaching tips, answers to all end of chapter Experiential Exercises and Review Questions, additional Experiential Exercises not in the text, sample course syllabi, and a Test Item file with multiple-choice, true/false, and essay questions.

- *Twenty Color Case Video Segments.* To accompany the Cohesion Case, a color video prepared by American Airlines is available to adopters free of charge. Shown near the beginning of the course, the American Airlines video can arouse students' interest in studying the Cohesion Case and completing Experiential Exercises that apply chapter material to this case. In addition, a collection of nineteen other color case video segments is available free of charge. The segments average fifteen minutes each and were professionally prepared by firms used in cases in this text.

- *The Prentice Hall Companion Website.* www.prenhall.com/david features an interactive and exciting online student study guide. Students can access multiple-choice, true/false, and Internet-based essay questions that accompany each chapter in the text. Objective questions are scored online, and incorrect answers are keyed to the text for student review. Supplements are available for faculty download on the password–protected side of the Web site.

- *Standard Web CT—Free to Adoptors.* Standard Web CT, an online course from Prentice Hall, features Companion Website and *Test Manager Software* Content in an easy-to-use system. Developed by educators for educators and their students, this online content and tools feature the most advanced educational technology and instructional design available today. The rich set of materials, communication tools, and course management resources can be easily customized either to enhance a traditional course or to create the entire course online.

- *Printed and Computerized Test Bank.* The test bank for this text includes true/false questions, multiple-choice questions, and essay questions for the text chapters. Answers to all objective questions are provided. The test questions given in the *Instructor's Manual* are also available on computerized test software to facilitate preparing and grading tests.

- *Blackboard.* Easy to use, Blackboard's single template and tools make it easy to create, manage, and use on-line course materials. Instructors can create online courses using the Blackboard tools, which include design, communication, testing, and course management tools. For more information, please visit our Web site located at **http://www.prenhall.com/blackboard**.

- *CourseCompass.* This customizable, interactive online course management tool powered by Blackboard provides the most intuitive teaching and learning environment available. Instructor's can communicate with students, distribute course material, and access student progress online. For further information, please visit our Web site located at **http://www.prenhall.com/coursecompass**.

## SPECIAL NOTE TO STUDENTS

Welcome to business policy. This is a challenging and exciting course that will allow you to function as the owner or chief executive officer of different organizations. Your major task in this course will be to make strategic decisions and to justify those decisions through oral and written communication. Strategic decisions determine the future direction and competitive position of an enterprise for a long time. Decisions to expand geographically or to diversify are examples of strategic decisions.

Strategic decision making occurs in all types and sizes of organizations, from General Motors to a small hardware store. Many people's lives and jobs are affected by strategic decisions, so the stakes are very high. An organization's very survival is often at stake. The overall importance of strategic decisions makes this course especially exciting and challenging. You will be called on in business policy to demonstrate how your strategic decisions could be successfully implemented.

In this course, you can look forward to making strategic decisions both as an individual and as a member of a team. No matter how hard employees work, an organization is in real trouble if strategic decisions are not made effectively. Doing the right things (effectiveness) is more important than doing things right (efficiency). For example, Lucent Technologies was prosperous during the 1990s but ineffective strategies in the years 2000–2002 led to massive losses, the ouster of chief executive Richard McGinn, an SEC investigation, a debt-rating one notch above junk, and a battle to raise any turnaround capital. The number of bankruptcies increased 30 percent in 2001, including such well known companies as AMF Bowling, Polaroid cameras, Converse sneakers, Schwinn bicycles, Vlasic pickles, Colemen camping supplies, Chiquita bananas, Sunbeam appliances, Enron, and Burlington Industries. The Houston-based energy firm Enron is the largest U.S. company ever to file for Chapter 11 bankruptcy.

You will have the opportunity in this course to make actual strategic decisions, perhaps for the first time in your academic career. Do not hesitate to take a stand and defend specific strategies that you determine to be the best. The rationale for your strategic decisions will be more important than any actual decision, because no one knows for sure what the best strategy is for a particular organization at a given point in time. This fact accents the subjective, contingency nature of the strategic-management process.

Use the concepts and tools presented in this text, coupled with your own intuition, to recommend strategies that you can defend as being most appropriate for the organizations that you study. You will also need to integrate knowledge acquired in previous business courses. For this reason, business policy is often called a capstone course; you may want to keep this book for your personal library.

This text is practitioner-oriented and applications-oriented. It presents strategic-management concepts that will enable you to formulate, implement, and evaluate strategies in all kinds of profit and nonprofit organizations. The end-of-chapter Experiential Exercises allow you to apply what you've read in each chapter to the American Airlines Cohesion Case and to your own university.

Be sure to visit the Strategic Management Club Online Web site at **www.strategyclub. com**. The templates and links there will save you time in performing analyses and will make your work look professional. Work hard in policy this semester and have fun. Good luck!

## ACKNOWLEDGMENTS

Many persons have contributed time, energy, ideas, and suggestions for improving this text over nine editions. The strength of this text is largely attributed to the collective wisdom, work, and experiences of business policy professors, strategic management researchers, students, and practitioners. Names of particular individuals whose published research is referenced in the ninth edition of this text are listed alphabetically in the Name Index. To all individuals involved in making this text so popular and successful, I am indebted and thankful.

Many special persons and reviewers contributed valuable material and suggestions for this edition. I would like to thank my colleagues and friends at Auburn University, Mississippi State University, East Carolina University, and Francis Marion University. These are universities where I have served on the management faculty. Scores of students and professors at these schools shaped development of this text. I would like to thank the following reviewers who contributed valuable suggestions over the years for this text:

Anthony F. Chelte, Western New England College
Leyland M. Lucas, Rutgers University
Joshua D. Martin, Temple University
Bob D. Cutler, Cleveland State University
Cathleen Folker, University of Nebraska–Lincoln
Jeffrey J. Bailey, University of Idaho
David Dawley, Florida State University
J. Michael Geringer, California State University
Evgeny A. Lapshin, Tomsk State Pedagogical University, Russia

Individuals who develop cases for the North American Case Research Association Meeting, the Midwest Society for Case Research Meeting, the Eastern Casewriters Association Meeting, the European Case Research Association Meeting, and Harvard Case Services are vitally important for continued progress in the field of strategic management. From a research perspective, writing business policy cases represents a valuable scholarly activity among faculty. Extensive research is required to structure business policy cases in a way that exposes strategic issues, decisions, and behavior. Pedagogically, business policy cases are essential for students in learning how to apply concepts, evaluate situations, formulate strategies, and resolve implementation problems. Without a continuous stream of updated business policy cases, the strategic management course and discipline would lose much of their energy and excitement.

The following individuals wrote cases that were selected for inclusion in this text. These persons helped develop the most current compilation of cases ever assembled in a business policy text:

M. Jill Austin, Middle Tennessee State University
Allen Badel, The Union Institute
Robert Barrett, Francis Marion University
Henry Beam, Western Michigan University
Eugene Bland, Francis Marion University
Donald Bumpass, Sam Houston University
Jim Camerius, Northern Michigan University
Maria Cruz-Batista, Francis Marion University
Forest David, Mississippi State University
Satish Deshpande, Western Michigan University
Mary Dittman, Francis Marion University
Sandy Durant, Francis Marion University
Ronald Earl, Sam Houston State University
Todd Ellison, Francis Marion University
Will Eskridge, Francis Marion University
Caroline Fisher, Loyola University, New Orleans

Margie Goodson, Francis Marion University

Christie Haney, Sam Houston State University

James Harbin, East Texas State University

Lenessa Hawkins, Francis Marion University

Marilyn Helms, Dalton State College

Brian Kinard, Mississippi University

Gerald Kohers, Sam Houston State University

Kay Lawrimore-Belanger, Francis Marion University

John Marcis, Coastal Carolina University

Bill Middlebrook, SW Texas State University

Valeric Muehsam, Sam Houston University

Paul Reed, Sam Houston State University

John Ross, Southwest Texas State University

Carlisle Sampson, Francis Marion University

Nicole Seminario, Francis Marion University

Amit Shah, Frostburg State University

Robert Shane, Francis Marion University

Matthew Sonfield, Hofstra University

Charles Sterrett, Frostburg State University

Carolyn Stokes, Francis Marion University

John Urbanski, Francis Marion University
Stephanie Wilhelm, Francis Marion University
Anthony Williams, Sam Houston State University

Scores of Prentice Hall employees and salespersons have worked diligently behind the scenes to make this text a leader in the business policy market. I appreciate the continued hard work of all those persons.

I especially appreciate the wonderful work completed by the ninth edition ancillary authors as follows:

Bruce Barringer, *Instructor's Manual*
    University of Central Florida
Forest David, *Case Instructor's Manual*
    Mississippi State University
Amit Shah, *Test Manager Software and Companion Website Content*
    Frostburg State University
Tony Chelte, *PowerPoint Electronic and Overhead Color Transparencies*
    Western New England College
Forest David, *Case PowerPoints*
    Mississippi State University

I also want to thank you, the reader, for investing the time and effort it took you to read and study this text. As we have entered the new millennium, this book will help you to formulate, implement, and evaluate strategies for organizations with which you become associated. I hope you come to share my enthusiasm for the rich subject area of strategic management and for the systematic learning approach taken in this text.

Finally, I want to welcome and invite your suggestions, ideas, thoughts, and comments and questions regarding any part of this text or the ancillary materials. Please call me at 843-669-6960, fax me at 843-661-1432, e-mail me at Fdavid@Fmarion.edu. or write me at the School of Business, Francis Marion University, Florence, South Carolina 29501. I sincerely appreciate and need your input to continually improve this text in future editions. Drawing my attention to specific errors or deficiencies in coverage or exposition will especially be appreciated.

Thank you for using this text.

*Fred R. David*

| | STOCK SYMBOL | STOCK EXCHANGE | TELEPHONE NUMBER | HEADQUARTERS ADDRESS | WEB PAGE ADDRESS |
|---|---|---|---|---|---|
| **NINTH EDITION SERVICE COMPANY CASES** | | | | | |
| **AIRLINES** | | | | | |
| 1. Southwest Airlines | LUV | NY | 214-792-4908 | 2702 Love Field Dallas, TX 75235 | www.iflyswa.com www.southwest.com |
| 2. US Airways | U | NY | 703-872-5009 | 2345 Crystal Drive Arlington, VA 22227 | www.usairways.com |
| **INTERNET COMPANIES** | | | | | |
| 3. E*Trade | ET | NY | 650-331-6000 888-772-3477 | 4500 Bohannon Dr. Menlo Park, CA 94025 | www.etrade.com |
| 4. eBay | EBAY | NASD | 408-558-7400 | 2005 Hamilton Ave. San Jose, CA 95125 | www.ebay.com |
| 5. Amazon | AMZN | NASD | 206-622-2335 | 1516 2nd Avenue Seattle, WA 98101 | www.amazon.com |
| **RETAILERS** | | | | | |
| 6. Limited Brands | LTD | NY | 614-415-7000 | 3 Limited Parkway Columbus, Ohio 43216 | www.limited.com |
| 7. Wal-Mart Stores, Inc. | WMT | NY | 501-273-4000 501-277-6921 | 702 SW Eighth St. Bentonville, Arkansas 72716-8611 | www.wal-mart.com |
| 8. Target Corporation | TGT | NY | 612-370-6948 | 777 Nicollet Mall Minneapolis, Minnesota 55402-2055 | www.target.com |
| 9. Best Buy Company | BBY | NY | 952-947-2422 | Eden Prairie, Minnesota | www.bestbuy.com |
| **HOTEL AND GAMING** | | | | | |
| 10. Mandalay Resort Group | MBG | NY | 702-734-0410 702-632-7777 | 3950 Las Vegas Blvd. Las Vegas, NV 89119 | www.mandalay resortgroup.com |
| 11. Harrah's Entertainment | HET | NY | 901-762-8600 702-407-6000 | 1023 Cherry Road Memphis, TN 38117 | www.harrahs.com |
| **BANKS** | | | | | |
| 12. Wachovia | WB | NY | 704-374-6565 | 1 Wachovia Center Charlotte, NC 28288-0570 | www.wachovia.com |
| 13. First State Bank of Roans Prairie | N/A | N/A | 936-395-2141 | Roans Prairie, TX | N/A |
| **ZOOS** | | | | | |
| 14. Audubon Nature Institute | N/A | N/A | 504-861-2537 | 6500 Magazine Street New Orleans, LA 70118 | www.audubon institute.org |
| 15. Riverbanks Zoo | N/A | N/A | 803-779-8717 | Riverbanks Society PO Box 1060 Columbia, SC 29202 | www.riverbanks.org |

*Continued*

| | STOCK SYMBOL | STOCK EXCHANGE | TELEPHONE NUMBER | HEADQUARTERS ADDRESS | WEB PAGE ADDRESS |
|---|---|---|---|---|---|
| **CRUISE LINES** | | | | | |
| 16. Carnival Corp. | CCL | NY | 800-438-6744 305-599-2600 | 3655 N.W. 87th Ave. Miami, FL 33178 | www.carnivalcorp.com |
| 17. Royal Caribbean | RCL | NY | 305-539-6000 | 1050 Caribbean Way Miami, FL 33132 | www.royal caribbean.com |
| **CHURCHES** | | | | | |
| 18. Central United Methodist Church | N/A | N/A | 843-662-3218 | 225 W. Cheves St. Florence, SC 29501 | www.centralumcsc. web.com |
| 19. Elkins Lake Baptist Church | N/A | N/A | 409-295-7694 | Huntsville, Texas 77340 | www.elbc.org |
| **GROCERY CHAIN** | | | | | |
| 20. Winn-Dixie | WIN | NY | 904-783-5000 | P.O. Box B Jacksonville, FL 32203 | www.winndixie.com |
| **MOM AND POP BUSINESS** | | | | | |
| 21. Strictly Roots Natural Hair Salon | N/A | N/A | 713-529-5017 | Houston, Texas | www.strictly-roots. com |
| **NONPROFIT ORGANIZATION** | | | | | |
| 22. Classic Car Club of America | N/A | N/A | 847-390-0443 | 1645 Des Plaines River Rd. Suite 7 Des Plaines, IL 60018 | www.classiccarclub. org/ |

## NINTH EDITION MANUFACTURING COMPANY CASES

| | STOCK SYMBOL | STOCK EXCHANGE | TELEPHONE NUMBER | HEADQUARTERS ADDRESS | WEB PAGE ADDRESS |
|---|---|---|---|---|---|
| **TRANSPORTATION** | | | | | |
| 23. Harley-Davidson | HDI | NY | 414-342-4680 | 3700 W. Juneau Ave. Milwaukee, WI 53208 | www.harley-davidson.com |
| 24. Winnebago Industries | WGO | NY | 641-585-3535 | 605 W. Crystal Lake Rd. Forest City, Iowa 50436 | www.winnebagoind. com |
| **COSMETICS** | | | | | |
| 25. Avon Products Inc. | AVP | NY | 212-282-5000 | Avenue of the Americas New York, NY 10105-0196 | www.avon.com |
| 26. Revlon Inc. | REV | NY | 212-527-4000 | 625 Madison Ave. New York, NY 10022 | www.revlon.com |
| **FOOD** | | | | | |
| 27. Pilgrim's Pride Corp. | CHX | NY | 903-855-1000 | 110 South Texas St. Pittsburg, Texas 75686 | www.pilgrimspride. com |
| 28. H.J. Heinz Co. | HNZ | NY | 412-456-5700 | 600 Grant Street Pittsburg, PA 15219 | www.heinz.com |
| 29. Hershey Foods | HSY | NY | 717-534-6799 | 100 Crystal Drive Hershey, PA 17033 | www.hersheys.com |

*Continued*

# FRED DAVID'S STRATEGIC MANAGEMENT, NINTH ED., CASE COMPANIES

|  | STOCK SYMBOL | STOCK EXCHANGE | TELEPHONE NUMBER | HEADQUARTERS ADDRESS | WEB PAGE ADDRESS |
|---|---|---|---|---|---|
| **AEROSPACE** | | | | | |
| 30. Boeing | BA | NY | 206-655-2121 | 7755 E. Marginal Way S. Seattle, WA 98108 | www.boeing.com |
| 31. Lockheed Martin | LMT | NY | 800-934-3566 301-897-6000 | 6801 Rockledge Drive Bethesda, MD 20817 | www.lockheed martin.com |
| **COMPUTERS** | | | | | |
| 32. Dell Computer | DELL | NASD | 512-338-4400 | 1 Dell Way Round Rock, TX 78682 | www.dell.com |
| 33. Hewlett-Packard | HPQ | NY | 650-857-1501 | 3000 Hanover Street Palo Alto, CA 94304 | www.hewlett-packrd. com |
| **MEDICAL** | | | | | |
| 34. Stryker Corp. | SYK | NY | 616-385-2600 | 2775 Fairfield Rd. Kalamazoo, MI 49002 | www.strykercorp.com |
| 35. Biomet Inc. | BMET | NASD | 219-267-6639 | Airport Industrial Pk. Warsaw, Indiana 46581 | www.biomet.com |
| **MAGAZINES** | | | | | |
| 36. Playboy Enterprises | PLA | NY | 312-751-8000 | 680 N. Lake Shore Dr. Chicago, IL 60611 | www.playboy.com |
| 37. Reader's Digest Association | RDA | NY | 914-238-1000 | Reader's Digest Road Pleasantville, NY 10570-7000 | www.readersdigest. com |
| **FOOTWEAR** | | | | | |
| 38. Nike Inc. | NKE | NY | 503-671-6453 800-640-8007 | 1 Bowerman Dr. Beaverton, OR 97005 | www.nike.com |
| 39. Reebok | RBK | NY | 781-401-5000 | 100 Technology Center Dr. Stroughton, MA 02072 | www.reebok.com |
| **TOBACCO** | | | | | |
| 40. UST Inc. | UST | NY | 203-661-1100 | 100 W. Putnam Ave. Greenwich, CT 06830 | www.ustshareholder. com |
| **BREWERY** | | | | | |
| 41. Coors | RKY | NY | 800-642-6116 | 310 North 10th St. Golden, CO 80401 | www.coors.com |

# INTRODUCTION

# HOW TO ANALYZE A BUSINESS POLICY CASE

## OUTLINE

- What Is a Business Policy Case?
- Guidelines for Preparing Case Analyses
- Preparing a Case for Class Discussion
- Preparing a Written Case Analysis
- Making an Oral Presentation
- Fifty Tips for Success in Case Analysis

## OBJECTIVES

*After studying this chapter, you should be able to do the following:*

1. Describe the case method for learning strategic-management concepts.
2. Identify the steps in preparing a comprehensive written case analysis.
3. Describe how to give an effective oral case analysis presentation.
4. Discuss fifty tips for doing case analysis.

## NOTABLE QUOTES

The essential fact that makes the case method an educational experience of the greatest power is that it makes the student an active rather than a passive participant.

WALLACE B. DONHAM

Two heads are better than one.

UNKNOWN AUTHOR

Good writers do not turn in their first drafts. Ask someone else to read your written case analysis, and read it out loud to yourself. That way, you can find rough areas to clear up.

LAWRENCE JAUCH

One reaction frequently heard is, "I don't have enough information." In reality, strategists never have enough information because some information is not available and some is too costly.

WILLIAM GLUECK

I keep six honest serving men. They taught me all I know. Their names are What, Why, When, How, Where, and Who.

RUDYARD KIPLING

Don't recommend anything you would not be prepared to do yourself if you were in the decision maker's shoes.

A. J. STRICKLAND III

A picture is worth a thousand words.

UNKNOWN AUTHOR

The purpose of this section is to help you analyze business policy cases. Guidelines for preparing written and oral case analyses are given, and suggestions for preparing cases for class discussion are presented. Steps to follow in preparing case analyses are provided. Guidelines for making an oral presentation are described.

## WHAT IS A BUSINESS POLICY CASE?

A *business policy case* describes an organization's external and internal condition and raises issues concerning the firm's mission, strategies, objectives, and policies. Most of the information in a business policy case is established fact, but some information may be opinions, judgments, and beliefs. Business policy cases are more comprehensive than those you may have studied in other courses. They generally include a description of related management, marketing, finance/accounting, production/operations, R&D, computer information systems, and natural environment issues. A business policy case puts the reader on the scene of the action by describing a firm's situation at some point in time. Business policy cases are written to give you practice applying strategic-management concepts. The case method for studying strategic management is often called *learning by doing*.

## GUIDELINES FOR PREPARING CASE ANALYSES

### The Need for Practicality

There is no such thing as a complete case, and no case ever gives you all the information you need to conduct analyses and make recommendations. Likewise, in the business world, strategists never have all the information they need to make decisions: information may be unavailable or too costly to obtain, or it may take too much time to obtain. So in preparing business policy cases, do what strategists do every day—make reasonable assumptions about unknowns, state assumptions clearly, perform appropriate analyses, and make decisions. *Be practical*. For example, in performing a pro forma financial analysis, make reasonable assumptions, state them appropriately, and proceed to show what impact your recommendations are expected to have on the organization's financial position. Avoid saying, "I don't have enough information." You can always supplement the information provided in a case with Internet and library research.

## The Need for Justification

The most important part of analyzing cases is not what strategies you recommend, but rather how you support your decisions and how you propose that they be implemented. There is no single best solution or one right answer to a case, so give ample justification for your recommendations. This is important. In the business world, strategists usually do not know if their decisions are right until resources have been allocated and consumed. Then it is often too late to reverse a decision. This cold fact accents the need for careful integration of intuition and analysis in preparing business policy case analyses.

## The Need for Realism

Avoid recommending a course of action beyond an organization's means. *Be realistic*. No organization can possibly pursue all the strategies that could potentially benefit the firm. Estimate how much capital will be required to implement what you recommended. Determine whether debt, stock, or a combination of debt and stock could be used to obtain the capital. Make sure your recommendations are feasible. Do not prepare a case analysis that omits all arguments and information not supportive of your recommendations. Rather, present the major advantages and disadvantages of several feasible alternatives. Try not to exaggerate, stereotype, prejudge, or overdramatize. Strive to demonstrate that your interpretation of the evidence is reasonable and objective.

## The Need for Specificity

Do not make broad generalizations such as "The company should pursue a market penetration strategy." *Be specific* by telling *what, why, when, how, where,* and *who.* Failure to use specifics is the single major shortcoming of most oral and written case analyses. For example, in an internal audit say, "The firm's current ratio fell from 2.2 in 2002 to 1.3 in 2003, and this is considered to be a major weakness," instead of, "The firm's financial condition is bad." Rather than concluding from a Strategic Position and Action Evaluation (SPACE) Matrix that a firm should be defensive, be more specific, saying, "The firm should consider closing three plants, laying off 280 employees, and divesting itself of its chemical division, for a net savings of $20.2 million in 2003." Use ratios, percentages, numbers, and dollar estimates. Businesspeople dislike generalities and vagueness.

## The Need for Originality

Do not necessarily recommend the course of action that the firm plans to take or actually undertook, even if those actions resulted in improved revenues and earnings. The aim of case analysis is for you to consider all the facts and information relevant to the organization at the time, to generate feasible alternative strategies, to choose among those alternatives, and to defend your recommendations. Put yourself back in time to the point when strategic decisions were being made by the firm's strategists. Based on the information available then, what would you have done? Support your position with charts, graphs, ratios, analyses, and the like—not a revelation from the library. You can become a good strategist by thinking through situations, making management assessments, and proposing plans yourself. *Be original*. Compare and contrast what you recommend versus what the company plans to do or did.

## The Need to Contribute

Strategy formulation, implementation, and evaluation decisions are commonly made by a group of individuals rather than by a single person. Therefore, your professor may divide the class into three- or four-person teams and ask you to prepare written or oral case analyses.

Members of a strategic-management team, in class or in the business world, differ on their aversion to risk, their concern for short-run versus long-run benefits, their attitudes toward social responsibility, and their views concerning globalization. There are no perfect people, so there are no perfect strategies. Be open-minded to others' views. *Be a good listener and a good contributor*.

## PREPARING A CASE FOR CLASS DISCUSSION

Your professor may ask you to prepare a case for class discussion. Preparing a case for class discussion means that you need to read the case before class, make notes regarding the organization's external opportunities/threats and internal strengths/weaknesses, perform appropriate analyses, and come to class prepared to offer and defend some specific recommendations.

### The Case Method Versus Lecture Approach

The case method of teaching is radically different from the traditional lecture approach, in which little or no preparation is needed by students before class. The *case method* involves a classroom situation in which students do most of the talking; your professor facilitates discussion by asking questions and encouraging student interaction regarding ideas, analyses, and recommendations. Be prepared for a discussion along the lines of "What would you do, why would you do it, when would you do it, and how would you do it?" Prepare answers to the following types of questions:

- What are the firm's most important external opportunities and threats?
- What are the organization's major strengths and weaknesses?
- How would you describe the organization's financial condition?
- What are the firm's existing strategies and objectives?
- Who are the firm's competitors, and what are their strategies?
- What objectives and strategies do you recommend for this organization? Explain your reasoning. How does what you recommend compare to what the company plans?
- How could the organization best implement what you recommend? What implementation problems do you envision? How could the firm avoid or solve those problems?

### The Cross-Examination

Do not hesitate to take a stand on the issues and to support your position with objective analyses and outside research. Strive to apply strategic-management concepts and tools in preparing your case for class discussion. Seek defensible arguments and positions. Support opinions and judgments with facts, reasons, and evidence. Crunch the numbers before class! Be willing to describe your recommendations to the class without fear of disapproval. Respect the ideas of others, but be willing to go against the majority opinion when you can justify a better position.

Business policy case analysis gives you the opportunity to learn more about yourself, your colleagues, strategic management, and the decision-making process in organizations. The rewards of this experience will depend on the effort you put forth, so do a good job. Discussing business policy cases in class is exciting and challenging. Expect views counter to those you present. Different students will place emphasis on different aspects of an organization's situation and submit different recommendations for scrutiny and rebuttal. Cross-examination discussions commonly arise, just as they occur in a real business organization. Avoid being a silent observer.

## PREPARING A WRITTEN CASE ANALYSIS

In addition to asking you to prepare a case for class discussion, your professor may ask you to prepare a written case analysis. Preparing a written case analysis is similar to preparing a case for class discussion, except written reports are generally more structured and more detailed. There is no ironclad procedure for preparing a written case analysis because cases differ in focus; the type, size, and complexity of the organizations being analyzed also vary.

When writing a strategic-management report or case analysis, avoid using jargon, vague or redundant words, acronyms, abbreviations, sexist language, and ethnic or racial slurs. And watch your spelling! Use short sentences and paragraphs and simple words and phrases. Use quite a few subheadings. Arrange issues and ideas from the most important to the least important. Arrange recommendations from the least controversial to the most controversial. Use the active voice rather than the passive voice for all verbs; for example, say, "Our team recommends that the company diversify," rather than, "It is recommended by our team to diversify." Use many examples to add specificity and clarity. Tables, figures, pie charts, bar charts, time lines, and other kinds of exhibits help communicate important points and ideas. Sometimes a picture *is* worth a thousand words.

### The Executive Summary

Your professor may ask you to focus the written case analysis on a particular aspect of the strategic-management process, such as (1) to identify and evaluate the organization's existing mission, objectives, and strategies; or (2) to propose and defend specific recommendations for the company; or (3) to develop an industry analysis by describing the competitors, products, selling techniques, and market conditions in a given industry. These types of written reports are sometimes called *executive summaries*. An executive summary usually ranges from three to five pages of text in length, plus exhibits.

### The Comprehensive Written Analysis

Your professor may ask you to prepare a *comprehensive written analysis*. This assignment requires you to apply the entire strategic-management process to the particular organization. When preparing a comprehensive written analysis, picture yourself as a consultant who has been asked by a company to conduct a study of its external and internal environment and to make specific recommendations for its future. Prepare exhibits to support your recommendations. Highlight exhibits with some discussion in the paper. Comprehensive written analyses are usually about ten pages in length, plus exhibits.

### Steps in Preparing a Comprehensive Written Analysis

In preparing a comprehensive written analysis, you could follow the steps outlined here, which correlate to the stages in the strategic-management process and the chapters in this text.

| | | |
|---|---|---|
| *Step* | *1* | Identify the firm's existing vision, mission, objectives, and strategies. |
| *Step* | *2* | Develop vision and mission statements for the organization. |
| *Step* | *3* | Identify the organization's external opportunities and threats. |
| *Step* | *4* | Construct a Competitive Profile Matrix (CPM). |
| *Step* | *5* | Construct an External Factor Evaluation (EFE) Matrix. |
| *Step* | *6* | Identify the organization's internal strengths and weaknesses. |
| *Step* | *7* | Construct an Internal Factor Evaluation (IFE) Matrix. |

*Step* 8 Prepare a Threats-Opportunities-Weaknesses-Strengths (TOWS) Matrix, Strategic Position and Action Evaluation (SPACE) Matrix, Boston Consulting Group (BCG) Matrix, Internal-External (IE) Matrix, Grand Strategy Matrix, and Quantitative Strategic Planning Matrix (QSPM) as appropriate. Give advantages and disadvantages of alternative strategies.

*Step* 9 Recommend specific strategies and long-term objectives. Show how much your recommendations will cost. Itemize these costs clearly for each projected year. Compare your recommendations to actual strategies planned by the company.

*Step* 10 Specify how your recommendations can be implemented and what results you can expect. Prepare forecasted ratios and pro forma financial statements. Present a timetable or agenda for action.

*Step* 11 Recommend specific annual objectives and policies.

*Step* 12 Recommend procedures for strategy review and evaluation.

## MAKING AN ORAL PRESENTATION

Your professor may ask you to prepare a business policy case analysis, individually or as a group, and present your analysis to the class. Oral presentations are usually graded on two parts: content and delivery. *Content* refers to the quality, quantity, correctness, and appropriateness of analyses presented, including such dimensions as logical flow through the presentation, coverage of major issues, use of specifics, avoidance of generalities, absence of mistakes, and feasibility of recommendations. *Delivery* includes such dimensions as audience attentiveness, clarity of visual aids, appropriate dress, persuasiveness of arguments, tone of voice, eye contact, and posture. Great ideas are of no value unless others can be convinced of their merit through clear communication. The guidelines presented here can help you make an effective oral presentation.

### Organizing the Presentation

Begin your presentation by introducing yourself and giving a clear outline of topics to be covered. If a team is presenting, specify the sequence of speakers and the areas each person will address. At the beginning of an oral presentation, try to capture your audience's interest and attention. You could do this by displaying some products made by the company, telling an interesting short story about the company, or sharing an experience you had that is related to the company, its products, or its services. You could develop or obtain a video to show at the beginning of class; you could visit a local distributor of the firm's products and tape a personal interview with the business owner or manager. A light or humorous introduction can be effective at the beginning of a presentation.

Be sure the setting of your presentation is well organized, with chairs, flip charts, a transparency projector, and whatever else you plan to use. Arrive at least fifteen minutes early at the classroom to organize the setting, and be sure your materials are ready to go. Make sure everyone can see your visual aids well.

### Controlling Your Voice

An effective rate of speaking ranges from 100 to 125 words per minute. Practice your presentation out loud to determine if you are going too fast. Individuals commonly speak too fast when nervous. Breathe deeply before and during the presentation to help yourself slow down. Have a cup of water available; pausing to take a drink will wet your throat, give you time to collect your thoughts, control your nervousness, slow you down, and signal to the audience a change in topic.

Avoid a monotone by placing emphasis on different words or sentences. Speak loudly and clearly, but don't shout. Silence can be used effectively to break a monotone voice. Stop at the end of each sentence, rather than running sentences together with *and* or *uh*.

## Managing Body Language

Be sure not to fold your arms, lean on the podium, put your hands in your pockets, or put your hands behind you. Keep a straight posture, with one foot slightly in front of the other. Do not turn your back to the audience; doing so is not only rude, but it also prevents your voice from projecting well. Avoid using too many hand gestures. On occasion, leave the podium or table and walk toward your audience, but do not walk around too much. Never block the audience's view of your visual aids.

Maintain good eye contact throughout the presentation. This is the best way to persuade your audience. There is nothing more reassuring to a speaker than to see members of the audience nod in agreement or smile. Try to look everyone in the eye at least once during your presentation, but focus more on individuals who look interested than on those who seem bored. Use humor and smiles as appropriate throughout your presentation to stay in touch with your audience. A presentation should never be dull!

## Speaking from Notes

Be sure not to read to your audience, because reading puts people to sleep. Perhaps worse than reading is memorizing. Do not try to memorize anything. Rather, practice using notes unobtrusively. Make sure your notes are written clearly so you will not flounder when trying to read your own writing. Include only main ideas on your note cards. Keep note cards on a podium or table if possible so that you won't drop them or get them out of order; walking with note cards tends to be distracting.

## Constructing Visual Aids

Make sure your visual aids are legible to individuals in the back of the room. Use color to highlight special items. Avoid putting complete sentences on visual aids; rather, use short phrases and then elaborate on issues orally as you make your presentation. Generally, there should be no more than four to six lines of text on each visual aid. Use clear headings and subheadings. Be careful about spelling and grammar; use a consistent style of lettering. Use masking tape or an easel for posters—do not hold posters in your hand. Transparencies and handouts are excellent aids; however, be careful not to use too many handouts or your audience may concentrate on them instead of you during the presentation.

## Answering Questions

It is best to field questions at the end of your presentation, rather than during the presentation itself. Encourage questions, and take your time to respond to each one. Answering questions can be persuasive because it involves you with the audience. If a team is giving the presentation, the audience should direct questions to a specific person. During the question-and-answer period, be polite, confident, and courteous. Avoid verbose responses. Do not get defensive with your answers, even if a hostile or confrontational question is asked. Staying calm during potentially disruptive situations, such as a cross-examination, reflects self-confidence, maturity, poise, and command of the particular company and its industry. Stand up throughout the question-and-answer period.

## FIFTY TIPS FOR SUCCESS IN CASE ANALYSIS

Business policy students who have used this text over eight editions offer you the following fifty tips for success in doing case analysis:

1. View your case analysis and presentation as a product that must have some competitive factor to differentiate it favorably from the case analyses of other students.
2. Prepare your case analysis far enough in advance of the due date to allow time for reflection and practice. Do not procrastinate.
3. Develop a mind-set of *why,* continually questioning your own and others' assumptions and assertions.
4. The best ideas are lost if not communicated to the reader, so as ideas develop, think of their most appropriate presentation.
5. Maintain a positive attitude about the class, working *with* problems rather than against them.
6. Keep in tune with your professor, and understand his or her values and expectations.
7. Since business policy is a capstone course, seek the help of professors in other specialty areas when necessary.
8. Other students will have strengths in functional areas that will complement your weaknesses, so develop a cooperative spirit that moderates competitiveness in group work.
9. Read your case frequently as work progresses so you don't overlook details.
10. When preparing a case analysis as a group, divide into separate teams to work on the external analysis and internal analysis. Each team should write its section as if it were to go into the paper; then give each group member a copy.
11. At the end of each group session, assign each member of the group a task to be completed for the next meeting.
12. Have a good sense of humor.
13. Capitalize on the strengths of each member of the group; volunteer your services in your areas of strength.
14. Set goals for yourself and your team; budget your time to attain them.
15. Become friends with the library.
16. Foster attitudes that encourage group participation and interaction. Do not be hasty to judge group members.
17. Be creative and innovative throughout the case analysis process.
18. Be prepared to work. There will be times when you will have to do more than your share. Accept it, and do what you have to do to move the team forward.
19. Think of your case analysis as if it were really happening; do not reduce case analysis to a mechanical process.
20. To uncover flaws in your analysis and to prepare the group for questions during an oral presentation, assign one person in the group to actively play the devil's advocate.
21. Do not schedule excessively long group meetings; two-hour sessions are about right.
22. A goal of case analysis is to improve your ability to think clearly in ambiguous and confusing situations; do not get frustrated that there is no single best answer.

23. Push your ideas hard enough to get them listened to, but then let up; listen to others and try to follow their lines of thinking; follow the flow of group discussion, recognizing when you need to get back on track; do not repeat yourself or others unless clarity or progress demands repetition.

24. Do not confuse symptoms with causes; do not develop conclusions and solutions prematurely; recognize that information may be misleading, conflicting, or wrong.

25. Work hard to develop the ability to formulate reasonable, consistent, and creative plans; put yourself in the strategist's position.

26. Develop confidence in using quantitative tools for analysis. They are not inherently difficult; it is just practice and familiarity you need.

27. Develop a case-writing style that is direct, assertive, and convincing; be concise, precise, fluent, and correct.

28. Have fun when at all possible. It is frustrating at times, but enjoy it while you can; it may be several years before you are playing CEO again.

29. Acquire a professional typist and proofreader. Do not perform either task alone.

30. Strive for excellence in writing and in the technical preparation of your case. Prepare nice charts, tables, diagrams, and graphs. Use color and unique pictures. No messy exhibits!

31. In group cases, do not allow personality differences to interfere. When they occur, they must be understood for what they are—and then put aside.

32. Do not forget that the objective is to learn; explore areas with which you are not familiar.

33. Pay attention to detail.

34. Think through alternative implications fully and realistically. The consequences of decisions are not always apparent. They often affect many different aspects of a firm's operations.

35. Get things written down (drafts) as soon as possible.

36. Read everything that other group members write, and comment on it in writing. This allows group input into all aspects of case preparation.

37. Provide answers to such fundamental questions as *what, when, where, why, who,* and *how.*

38. Adaptation and flexibility are keys to success; be creative and innovative.

39. Do not merely recite ratios or present figures. Rather, develop ideas and conclusions concerning the possible trends. Show the importance of these figures to the corporation.

40. Support reasoning and judgment with factual data whenever possible.

41. Neatness is a real plus; your case analysis should look professional.

42. Your analysis should be as detailed and specific as possible.

43. A picture speaks a thousand words, and a creative picture gets you an A in many classes.

44. Let someone else read and critique your paper several days before you turn it in.

45. Emphasize the Strategy Selection and Strategy Implementation sections. A common mistake is to spend too much time on the external or internal analysis parts of your paper. Always remember that the meat of the paper or presentation is the strategy selection and implementation sections.

46. Make special efforts to get to know your group members. This leads to more openness in the group and allows for more interchange of ideas. Put in the time and effort necessary to develop these relationships.

47. Be constructively critical of your group members' work. Do not dominate group discussions. Be a good listener and contributor.

48. Learn from past mistakes and deficiencies. Improve upon weak aspects of other case presentations.

49. Learn from the positive approaches and accomplishments of classmates.

50. Use the Strategic Management Club Online at **www.strategyclub.com**.

## MASTERING STRATEGY

*Mastering Strategy* is the first product in the *Mastering Business* series. It offers students an interactive, multimedia experience as they follow the people and issues of Cango, Inc., a small Internet startup. The text, video, and interactive exercises provide students an opportunity to simulate the strategic planning experience to and chart the future activities for Cango.

> Strategy has an impact across an entire organization, and the behaviors involved are often very subtle. Using this material really provides an opportunity to give an experiential approach to strategic concepts as applied in the business world. The videos and exercises demonstrate actual theories, practices and assumptions in daily operations. These are practical applications as faced in the real world, with real language, problems and relevant issues faced by modern companies.

> Students are drawn into a living, breathing, dynamic company and immediately get a feeling for strategy in operation, rather than in retrospect. This helps students assimilate their learning in a systemic manner as they move from watching the events unfold for the company to applying their own intuition about the problems and solutions. When they are on the mark, they see the results in the company's performance. If they are off the mark, they learn what they don't know and where they need to go back for a deeper understanding.

> —Helen Rothberg, Professor at the Marist College School
> of Management and co-author of the Strategy series

## THE MASTERING STRATEGY ENVIRONMENT

Students will learn strategy concepts within the context of Cango, Inc., a fictitious Internet company that focuses its efforts in the entertainment arena of the e-commerce world. The company began by retailing books on the Internet and has branched out to offer CDs, videos, MP3 files, and customized players. Cango employs mostly recent college graduates who are enthusiastic about working with an online business and its possibilities for expansion. Currently, Cango is experiencing great growth, but little profit.

Thus, Cango employees are always on the lookout for new ventures. The company is considering hosting streaming video, e-books and e-book readers, and partnerships with other firms. One example would be a film studio so that Cango can serve the needs of independent filmmakers and tap into the growing popularity of home video hardware and software.

The company's goals are to get bigger and better, and to someday make a significant profit. In *Mastering Strategy,* the firm transforms from a small, independent company to one listed on the NASDAQ through the Initial Public Offering (IPO) process. The firm's founder and the management team must deal with all the implications of this change, both within the company and in the context of the external world of investors, the board of directors, and potential competitors. Visit **www.prenhall.com/masteringbusiness** to find out more.

# STRATEGIC
# MANAGEMENT
## CASES

# SOUTHWEST AIRLINES CO.—2002

Amit Shah and Charles R. Sterrett
Frostburg State University

LUV

www.iflyswa.com

In the first week following the September 11, 2001, terrorist attacks, the shutdown of air travel, an exodus of travelers, and strict new security measures cost the airline industry close to $1 billion. Many major airlines responded by cutting their capacity by about 20 percent while tapping their lines of credit and hunting for more sources of cash. The airlines, their businesses already experiencing problems because of a sick economy, began to take desperate measures to avert disaster, and they lobbied the federal government for aid to rescue the industry. CEO Leo Mullins of Delta Air Lines stated, "The airline industry cannot be made the first (corporate) casualty of this war." A major question emerged: What would be the effect of the terrorist hijackings on the industry in both the short and long run, and, particularly, how would the "low price" companies such as Southwest Airlines be affected?

For eleven consecutive years (1991 through 2001), the Department of Transportation (DOT) *Air Travel Consumer Report* listed Southwest Airlines (tel. 214-792-4000 or 1-800-I-FLY-SWA) as among the top five of all major carriers for on-time performance, best baggage handling, and fewest customer complaints. In a highly competitive industry, all carriers continually strive to place first in any of these categories of the DOT report; Southwest is the only airline to ever hold the Triple Crown (first in all of the categories) for its annual performance. No other airline has earned the Triple Crown for even one month. In addition to this honor, Southwest is consistently among *Fortune* magazine's most admired companies (fourth in 2001), and it is also on the magazine's list of the one hundred best companies to work for. In September 1999, the *Wall Street Journal* also ranked Southwest among the top thirty companies on the basis of reputation—the only airline to make the cut. In addition to these achievements, Southwest continues to operate profitably; it made $625.2 million in net income on $5.6 billion in 2000 revenues. In an industry that historically has been awash in red ink, where airlines continually go in and out of bankruptcy or fail, Southwest has an enviable record of over twenty-eight consecutive years of operating at a profit. But, given the events of September 11 and the weeks that followed, could this record of success be sustained?

In their best-selling book *Nuts*, Kevin and Jackie Freiburg point to a company with people who are committed to working hard and having fun and who avoid following industry trends. The Freiburgs note that Southwest, based in Dallas, Texas, is a company which likes to keep prices at rock bottom; believes the customer comes second; runs recruiting ads that say, "Work at a place where wearing pants is optional"; paints its $30 million assets to look like killer whales and state flags; avoids trendy management programs; avoids formal, documented strategic planning; spends more time at planning parties than writing policies; and once settled a legal dispute by arm wrestling. Will this strategy and culture sustain the company through the rough years ahead?

(Note – If you are using the hardback *Strategic Management* textbook by Fred R. David, then refer to the External Issues part of the American Airlines Cohesion Case for additional information about Southwest Airlines.)

## HISTORY AND GROWTH OF SOUTHWEST AIRLINES

According to Southwest folklore, the airline was conceived in 1967 on a napkin when Rollin King, an investment adviser, met with his lawyer, Herb Kelleher, to discuss his idea for a low-fare, no-frills airline to fly between three of the major cities in Texas. At that time, King ran an unprofitable air charter service between small Texas cities. One day, his banker, John Parker, suggested that King concentrate on flying between the three biggest cities in the state. Parker suggested that the market was open for exploitation because he could never get a seat on the airlines currently flying between those cities, and besides, the fares were too high. King knew he couldn't compete with the airlines currently serving the cities, so he decided to start a bigger one. He put together a plan and a feasibility study, and then he went to see Kelleher. In that meeting, King scribbled three lines on a cocktail napkin; labeled the points Houston, Dallas, and San Antonio; and muttered, "Herb, let's start our own airline." Kelleher loosened his tie and knitted his brow before replying. "Rollin, you're crazy," he said. "Let's do it!" Kelleher completed the necessary paperwork to create Air Southwest Co. (later renamed Southwest Airlines). Then the two filed for approval with the FAA; and on February 20, 1968, the Texas Aeronautical Commission approved their plans to fly between the three cities.

The very next day, the upstart airline ran into stiff opposition from several of the major carriers then doing business in Texas. On February 21, 1968, these carriers—Braniff, Texas International, and Continental—blocked approval with a temporary restraining order. They argued that Texas didn't need another carrier. For the next three years, Southwest was unable to proceed while it fought legal battles with these airlines over the right to offer flights between the three cities. In 1971, however, Southwest won the right to fly and began to offer service with a total of three planes and about two hundred employees. The efforts to quash the airline led to unbridled enthusiasm for the airline by King, Kelleher, and the other employees, which became an important part of Southwest's culture.

The outlook for Southwest, however, remained bleak. The legal battles left the airline flat broke and deep in debt. In its first year of operation, it lost $3.7 million, and it did not earn a profit for the next year and a half. But in 1973, it turned its first profit—and it never looked back. By 1978, it was one of the most profitable airlines in the country.

In its early years, Southwest faced other legal battles. For example, in 1974 a new airport opened to serve the greater Dallas-Fort Worth area; but it was farther from downtown Dallas than Love Field, the airport that had previously served the area. Southwest was using Love Field and wanted to continue to do so. But competitors wanted Southwest to move to the new airport to share in the costs, and they began to pressure Congress to pass a law barring flights from Love Field to any airport outside of the state of Texas. Southwest was able to negotiate a compromise, known as the Wright amendment, that allowed flights from Love Field to airports in the four states bordering on Texas. The Wright amendment forced Southwest into a key part of its strategy: to become an interstate carrier.

Southwest grew steadily and by 1975 had expanded its operations to eight more cities in Texas. By the end of the 1970s, it dominated the Texas market. Its major appeal was to passengers who wanted low prices and frequent departures. In the 1980s and 1990s, Southwest continued to expand, and by 1993, it was serving thirty-four cities in fifteen states. Southwest slowly, but methodically, moved across the Southwestern states into California, the Midwest, and the Northwest. It added new destinations in Florida and the East Coast. With its low prices and no-frills approach, it quickly dominated the markets it entered. In some markets, after Southwest entered, competitors soon withdrew, allowing the airline to expand even faster than projected. For example, when Southwest entered the California market in 1990, it quickly became the second-largest player, with over 20 percent of the intrastate market. Several competitors soon abandoned the Los Angeles-San Francisco route because they were unable to match Southwest's $59 one-way fare. Before Southwest entered this market, fares had been as high as $186 one way.

California offers a good example of the real dilemma facing competing carriers, which often referred to Southwest as a "500 pound cockroach that was too big to stamp out." While airfares were dropping, passenger traffic increased dramatically. But competitors, such as American and US Airways, were losing money on several key route segments, even though they cut service drastically. In late 1994, United began to fight back by launching a low-cost, high-frequency shuttle service on the West Coast. But it found that even a shuttle could not win against Southwest in a head-to-head battle. So United repositioned its shuttle away from Southwest's routes and even abandoned some routes altogether. According to the DOT, eight airlines surrendered West Coast routes to Southwest; at the same time, one-way fares fell by over 30 percent to an average of $60, and traffic increased by almost 60 percent. The major problem for the larger airlines was the fact that many of these West Coast routes were critical for feeding traffic into their highly profitable transcontinental and transpacific routes, and Southwest was cutting into that market.

Southwest is currently the fourth largest domestic carrier in terms of customers boarded. The airline has transformed itself from a regional carrier operating out of Dallas into a truly national carrier. At yearend 2001, the airline served 58 cities in 30 states and operated more than 2,800 flights a day with its fleet of 355 Boeing 737s. In 2001, Southwest flew 44.5 billion revenue passenger miles (RPMs) compared with 42.2 billion RPMs in 2000. But most remarkable is its twenty-ninth year in a row of profitable operations, with total operating revenue in 2001 being $5.55 billion—a decrease of 1.7 percent over 2000. Operating income in 2001 fell by 38.2 percent in 2000. Net income fell by 18.2 percent from $625.2 million in 2000 to 511.1 million in 2001. However, Southwest was the only profitable U.S. airline in 2001. Financial statements are shown in Exhibits 1 and 2.

## MANAGEMENT

While Southwest was going through its traumatic beginnings, King and Kelleher realized they needed someone to run the company. King hired Lamar Muse, an executive who had airline experience, as CEO. Muse raised funding to keep the airline going and hired an experienced management team as company officers. He was able to purchase three brand new Boeing 737s at bargain-basement prices because Boeing had overproduced in a period when airlines were in a slump. Muse led the airline in its climb to profitability; but, in a dispute with the board, he was ousted in 1978. With Muse out, Kelleher moved into the top position, and he ran the airline until June 19, 2001. On that date, Mr. Kelleher was succeeded as CEO by Southwest's vice president and general counsel, James F. Parker, 54. Colleen C. Barrett, 56, who started her collaboration with Mr. Kelleher 34 years earlier as his legal secretary, would be president and chief operating officer. Mr. Kelleher is slated to remain as chairman for three years. Exhibit 3 shows the organizational chart of the company.

Mr. Parker has been the airline's top labor negotiator, making him well known to the company's employees, and, according to Mr. Kelleher, he has had a say in every important decision for a "long, long time." Ms. Barrett, the unsung hero of Southwest, has been the keeper and crusader of Southwest's culture, and she has successfully indoc-

# EXHIBIT 1    Operating Statistics for Southwest Airlines

Consolidated Highlights

| (in thousands except per-share amounts) | 2001 | 2000 | Change |
|---|---|---|---|
| Operating revenues | $5,555,174 | $5,649,560 | (1.7)% |
| Operating expenses | $4,924,052 | $4,628,415 | 6.4% |
| Operating income | $631,122 | $1,021,145 | (38.2)% |
| Operating margin | 11.4% | 18.1% | (6.7)pts. |
| Net income | $511,147 | $625,224* | (18.2)% |
| Net margin | 9.2% | 11.1%* | (1.9)pts. |
| Net income per share – basic | $0.67 | $0.84* | (20.2)% |
| Net income per share – diluted | $0.63 | $0.79* | (20.3)% |
| Stockholders' equity | $4,014,053 | $3,451,320 | 16.3% |
| Return on average stockholders' equity | 13.7% | 19.9% | (6.2)pts. |
| Stockholders' equity per common share outstanding | $5.24 | $4.53 | 15.7% |
| Revenue passengers carried | 64,446,773 | 63,678,261 | 1.2% |
| Revenue passenger miles (RPMs) (000s) | 44,493,916 | 42,215,162 | 5.4% |
| Available seat miles (ASMs) (000s) | 65,295,290 | 59,909,965 | 9.0% |
| Passenger load factor | 68.1% | 70.5% | (2.4)pts. |
| Passenger revenue yield per RPM | 12.09¢ | 12.95¢ | (6.6)% |
| Operating revenue yield per ASM | 8.51¢ | 9.43¢ | (9.8)% |
| Operating expenses per ASM | 7.54¢ | 7.73¢ | (2.5)% |
| Employees at yearend | 31,580 | 29,274 | 7.9% |

*Excludes cumulative effect of change in accounting principle of $22.1 million ($.03 per share)
Source: 2001 Annual Report, p. 2.

trinated thousands of new workers into Southwest's ways. Parker's plan as CEO is to stay with the blueprint—keep Southwest the low-cost, low-fare, no-frills airline it has always been. "There will be no change in our core philosophy and our basic business model," he says. It's a model he helped shape as general counsel for fifteen years.

Even though the airline has grown to 31,580 employees at yearend 2001, Southwest's management team drives home the feeling that all of its people are part of one big family. Southwest's Culture Committee, formerly headed by Colleen Barrett, devised unique ways to preserve Southwest's underdog background and can-do spirit. She constantly reinforced the company's message that employees should be treated like customers and continually celebrated workers who went above and beyond the call of duty. Barrett also regularly visited each of the company's stations to reiterate the airline's history and to motivate employees. As keeper of the company's culture, Barrett commemorated all employee birthdays and special events with cards signed, "Herb and Colleen." Employees know the culture and expect others to live up to it. Donna Conover, another long-time Southwest employee, who also understands and supports the company's culture, will succeed Barrett as president and COO.

## STRATEGY

Southwest's operation under Herb Kelleher has a number of characteristics that seem to contribute to its success. It has always been able to seize quickly a strategic opportunity whenever one arises. Other key factors are its conservative growth pattern, its cost-containment policy, and the commitment of its employees.

## EXHIBIT 2    Southwest Airlines Co. Consolidated Statement of Income

| *(in thousands, except per share amounts)* | Yearended December 31, | | |
|---|---|---|---|
| | *2001* | *2000* | *1999* |
| **OPERATING REVENUES:** | | | |
| Passenger | $5,378,702 | $5,467,965 | $4,562,616 |
| Freight | 91,270 | 110,742 | 102,990 |
| Other | 85,202 | 70,853 | 69,981 |
| Total operating revenues | 5,555,174 | 5,649,560 | 4,735,587 |
| **OPERATING EXPENSES:** | | | |
| Salaries, wages, and benefits | 1,856,288 | 1,683,689 | 1,455,237 |
| Fuel and oil | 770,515 | 804,426 | 492,415 |
| Maintenance materials and repairs | 397,505 | 378,470 | 367,606 |
| Agency commissions | 103,014 | 159,309 | 156,419 |
| Aircraft rentals | 192,110 | 196,328 | 199,740 |
| Landing fees and other rentals | 311,017 | 265,106 | 242,002 |
| Depreciation | 317,831 | 281,276 | 248,660 |
| Other operating expenses | 975,772 | 859,811 | 791,932 |
| Total operating expenses | 4,924,052 | 4,628,415 | 3,954,011 |
| **OPERATING INCOME** | 631,122 | 1,021,145 | 781,576 |
| **OTHER EXPENSES (INCOME):** | | | |
| Interest expense | 69,827 | 69,889 | 54,145 |
| Capitalized interest | (20,576) | (27,551) | (31,262) |
| Interest income | (42,562) | (40,072) | (25,200) |
| Other (gains) losses, net | (203,226) | 1,515 | 10,282 |
| Total other expenses (income) | (196,537) | 3,781 | 7,965 |
| **INCOME BEFORE INCOME TAXES AND CUMULATIVE EFFECT OF CHANGE IN ACCOUNTING PRINCIPLE** | 827,659 | 1,017,364 | 773,611 |
| **PROVISION FOR INCOME TAXES** | 316,512 | 392,140 | 299,233 |
| **INCOME BEFORE CUMULATIVE EFFECT OF CHANGE IN ACCOUNTING PRINCIPLE** | 511,147 | 625,22 | 474,378 |
| **CUMULATIVE EFFECT OF CHANGE IN ACCOUNTING PRINCIPLE, NET OF INCOME TAXES** | – | (22,131) | – |
| **NET INCOME** | $ 511,147 | $ 603,093 | $ 474,378 |
| **NET INCOME PER SHARE, BASIC BEFORE CUMULATIVE EFFECT OF CHANGE IN ACCOUNTING PRINCIPLE** | $.67 | $.84 | $.63 |
| **CUMULATIVE EFFECT OF CHANGE IN ACCOUNTING PRINCIPLE** | – | (.03) | – |
| **NET INCOME PER SHARE, BASIC** | $ .67 | $ .81 | $ .63 |
| **NET INCOME PER SHARE, DILUTED BEFORE CUMULATIVE EFFECT OF CHANGE IN ACCOUNTING PRINCIPLE** | $ .63 | $ .79 | $ .59 |
| **CUMULATIVE EFFECT OF CHANGE IN ACCOUNTING PRINCIPLE** | – | (.03) | – |
| **NET INCOME PER SHARE, DILUTED** | $ .63 | $ .76 | $ .59 |

*Source:* 2001 *Annual Report*, p. 9.

Kelleher always resisted attempts to expand too rapidly. His philosophy was to expand only when there were resources available to go into a new location with ten to twelve flights per day—not just one or two. For years, he also resisted the temptation to begin transcontinental operations or to get into a head-to-head battle with the major carriers on long-distance routes. But even with a conservative approach, Southwest expanded at a vigorous pace. Its debt has remained the lowest among U.S. carriers, and,

EXHIBIT 3    Southwest Organizational Chart

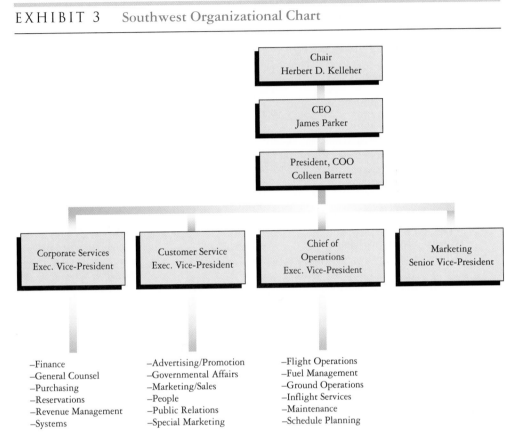

Source: Southwest Airlines Co. (February 1998).

with an A-rating, Southwest has the highest Standard & Poor's credit rating in the industry.

Southwest has made its mark by concentrating on flying large numbers of passengers on high frequency, short hops (usually one hour or less) at bargain fares. Southwest avoided the hub-and-spoke operations of its larger rivals, taking its passengers directly from city to city. Southwest also tends to avoid the more congested major airports in favor of smaller satellite fields. Kelleher revealed the niche strategy of Southwest when he noted that whereas other airlines set up hub-and-spoke systems in which passengers are shuttled to a few major hubs from which they are transferred to other planes going to their destinations, "we wound up with a unique market niche: We are the world's only short-haul, high-frequency, low-fare, point-to-point carrier. . . . We wound up with a market segment that is peculiarly ours, and everything about the airline has been adapted to serving that market segment in the most efficient and economical way possible." (See Exhibit 4.)

However, this strategy may be changing. Southwest has begun to introduce longer, nonstop trips on such routes as Baltimore, Maryland, to Las Vegas, Nevada (2,099 miles), and Austin, Texas, to Los Angeles, California (1,234 miles). Even one-stop trips are being added through central cities such as Nashville and Kansas City for coast-to-coast travel. The prospect of Southwest going long-haul on a grand scale is what "the

## EXHIBIT 4    Southwest Airlines Co. Consolidated Balance Sheet

| (in thousands, except per share amounts) | DECEMBER 31, 2001 | 2000 |
|---|---:|---:|
| **ASSETS** | | |
| Current assets: | | |
| Cash and cash equivalents | $ 2,279,861 | $ 522,995 |
| Accounts and other receivables | 71,283 | 138,070 |
| Inventories of parts and supplies, at cost | 70,561 | 80,564 |
| Deferred income taxes | 46,400 | 28,005 |
| Prepaid expenses and other current assets | 52,114 | 61,902 |
| Total current assets | 2,520,219 | 831,536 |
| Property and equipment, at cost: | | |
| Flight equipment | 7,534,119 | 6,831,913 |
| Ground property and equipment | 899,421 | 800,718 |
| Deposits on flight equipment purchase contracts | 468,154 | 335,164 |
| | 8,901,694 | 7,967,795 |
| Less allowance for depreciation | 2,456,207 | 2,148,070 |
| | 6,445,487 | 5,819,725 |
| Other assets | 31,435 | 18,311 |
| | $ 8,997,141 | $ 6,669,572 |
| **LIABILITIES AND STOCKHOLDERS' EQUITY** | | |
| Current liabilities: | | |
| Accounts payable | $ 504,831 | $ 312,716 |
| Accrued liabilities | 547,540 | 499,874 |
| Air traffic liability | 450,407 | 377,061 |
| Aircraft purchase obligations | 221,840 | – |
| Short-term borrowings | 475,000 | – |
| Current maturities of long-term debt | 39,567 | 108,752 |
| Total current liabilities | 2,239,185 | 1,298,403 |
| Long-term debt less current maturities | 1,327,158 | 760,992 |
| Deferred income taxes | 1,058,143 | 852,865 |
| Deferred gains from sale and leaseback of aircraft | 192,342 | 207,522 |
| Other deferred liabilities | 166,260 | 98,470 |
| Commitments and contingencies | | |
| Stockholders' equity: | | |
| Common stock, $1.00 par value: 2,000,000 shares authorized; 766,774 and 507,897 shares issued in 2001 and 2000, respectively | 766,774 | 507,897 |
| Capital in excess of par value | 50,409 | 103,780 |
| Retained earnings | 3,228,408 | 2,902,007 |
| Accumulated other comprehensive income (loss) | (31,538) | – |
| Treasury stock, at cost: 3,735 shares in 2000 | – | (62,364) |
| Total stockholders' equity | 4,014,053 | 3,451,320 |
| | $ 8,997,141 | $ 6,669,572 |

*Source:* 2001 *Annual Report,* p. 8.

genie [rivals] always hoped would not come out of the bottle," says analyst Kevin C. Murphy of Morgan Stanley Dean Witter. He believes that Southwest will continue its expansion and that it "will really rewrite the economics of the airline industry." This shifting strategy is downplayed by the fact that Southwest still flies about 80 percent of its flights on route that are shorter than 750 miles. "We're built for the short-haul markets, and we know that," says Chief Financial Officer Gary C. Kelly. Kelleher explains the jump into routes that are one-thousand-plus miles as a way to deal with the changes in the federal ticket tax in 1997 which was pushed by the bigger carriers. The incorporation of the new tax system replaced a percentage tax with a tax that included a flat, per-segment fee, which hits low-fare carriers harder.

Competitors believe that Southwest would have moved strongly into the long-haul flights market despite the altered tax requirements. "They've dug all the shallow holes," says Rona J. Dutta, senior vice president for planning at United Airlines, Inc. He also replies that the majors' low-fare units are increasing the competition in Southwest's core markets. Short-haul lines such as US Airways' MetroJet, Shuttle by United, and Delta Express may affect Southwest's profitability, but analysts say that with its lower costs and impressive balance sheet, Southwest should prevail.

Southwest continues to be the lowest-cost airline in its markets. Even when trying to match Southwest's cut-rate fares, the larger carriers could not do so without incurring substantial losses. Southwest's operating costs per available seat mile (the number of seats multiplied by the distance flown) average 15 to 25 percent below its rivals. One of the major factors in this enviable record is that all of its planes used to be of a single type—Boeing 737s—which dramatically lowered the company's cost of training, maintenance, and inventory. Because all Southwest crews know the 737 inside and out, they could substitute personnel rapidly from one flight to another in an emergency. In addition, Southwest recognized that planes only earn you money while they are in the air, so the company worked hard to achieve a faster turnaround time on the ground. Most airlines take up to one hour to unload passengers, clean and service the plane, and board new passengers. Southwest has a turnaround time for most flights of twenty minutes or less. Thorough knowledge of the 737 has helped in this achievement.

This ability to turn planes around rapidly, however, may now be jeopardized by the events after September 11. New government-mandated security procedures are expected to force airlines to spend as much as forty minutes or longer on the ground at each destination. This change will undoubtedly cause Southwest to incur added costs in its operations.

Southwest has also cut costs in the customer service area as well. Because its flights are usually one hour or less, it does not offer meals—only peanuts and drinks. Boarding passes are reusable plastic cards, and boarding time is saved since the airline has no assigned seating. The airline does not subscribe to any centralized reservation service. It will not even transfer baggage to other carriers: That is the passenger's responsibility. Even with this frugality, passengers do not seem to object, since the price is right.

Southwest has achieved a team spirit that others can only envy. One of the reasons for this team spirit is that the company truly believes that employees come first, not the customers. Southwest is known for providing its employees with tremendous amounts of information that will enable them to better understand the company, its mission, its customers, and its competition. Southwest believes that information is power. It is the resource that enables employees to do their jobs better. Armed with this knowledge, they are able to serve the customer better, and customers who deal with Southwest rarely get the runaround.

Even though unionized, Southwest has been able to negotiate flexible work rules that enabled it to meet the rapid turnaround schedules. It's not unusual for pilots to help flight attendants clean the airplanes or to help the ground crew load baggage.

Consequently, employee productivity is very high, and the airline is able to maintain a lean staff. In good times, Kelleher resisted the temptation to overhire, and he so avoided layoffs during lean times. Southwest has only laid off three people in twenty-five years— and it immediately hired them back. Even now, in the days after the attacks on September 11, 2001, as competitors announced job cuts of 20 percent, Southwest execs were scheming to cut costs in other ways. New plane deliveries were delayed, renovations to the company headquarters were scrapped—but layoffs were not considered. Said CEO Parker, "We are willing to suffer some damage, even to our stock price, to protect the jobs of our people." This employee retention policy has contributed to employees' feelings of security and a fierce sense of loyalty. The people of Southwest see themselves as crusaders whose mission is to give ordinary people the opportunity to fly.

Maximizing profitability is a major goal at Southwest. This leads to a drive to keep costs low and quality high. The airline's ideal service consists of safe, frequent, low-cost flights that get passengers to their destinations on time—and often closer to their destination than the major airlines do, because its competitors use larger airports farther from the cities. Southwest uses Dallas's Love Field, Houston Hobby airport, and Chicago's Midway, which are closer to their respective downtown areas, are less congested, and are, therefore, more convenient for the business traveler. This also helps Southwest's on-time performance.

In its marketing approach, Southwest always tries to set itself apart from the rest of the industry. It also played up its fun-loving, rebel reputation. In the early years, when the big airlines were trying to run Southwest out of business by undercutting its low fares, Southwest made its customers an unprecedented offer. In response to a Braniff ad offering a $13 fare to fly between Houston and Dallas, Southwest placed an ad that read, "Nobody's going to shoot Southwest Airlines out of the sky for a lousy $13." It then offered passengers the opportunity to purchase a ticket from Southwest for the same price, which was half the normal fare, or to buy a full-fare ticket for $26 and receive a bottle of premium whiskey along with it. The response was unprecedented. Southwest's planes were full and, for a short time, Southwest was one of the top liquor distributors in the state of Texas.

Southwest's ads always try to convince the customer that what the airline offers them is of real value to them. Southwest also believes it is in the business of making flying fun. With its ads, the company wants customers to know that when they fly Southwest, they'll have an experience unlike any other. Southwest promises safe, reliable, frequent, low-cost air transportation that is topped off with outstanding service. By keeping its promises, Southwest has earned extremely high credibility in every market it serves.

## e-BUSINESS

Southwest has been aggressively marketing its services on the Internet, and it was the first airline to establish a home page on the Web. When *Fortune* magazine asked the experts which businesses have Web sites that work, the answer they got was "not many." However, Southwest was one of ten cited as a business doing it right. In the Internet travel race, many observers think Southwest has lost the battle to a subsidiary of American Airlines, Travelocity. Yet while American has been getting most of the attention, Southwest has been getting the business. According to a Nielsen/NetRatings' survey, 13.8 percent of the people who visited Southwest's site booked a flight. The company's "look-to-book" ratio is twice that of Travelocity and higher than that of any traditional retailer on the Web. Southwest, it seems, has been a success in turning browsers into buyers. Southwest reports that approximately 30 percent of its passenger revenue is generated by online bookings. Southwest's cost per booking via the Internet is about $1; in comparison, the cost per booking via a travel agent is about $10.

Southwest's Web site has also been named the top ranking Web site for customer satisfaction among major travel sites according to research conducted by Harris Interactive. The Southwest site scored a rating of 8.62 out of 10, with its Web site attracting 4 million unique visitors during March 2001. In the June 11, 2001, issue of *InternetWeek*, Southwest's Web site was named as one of the top one hundred e-businesses in the United States, as determined by the publication's survey.

## COMPETITORS

Three of Southwest's major competitors are United Airlines, Delta Air Lines, and America West Airlines. Before September 11, 2001, United, with over ninety thousand employees, was one of Southwest's most formidable competitors, and it still remains so in many of Southwest's markets. United, the number two U.S. airline, flies over five hundred aircraft to about 140 locations in the United States and overseas. In addition, it operates United Express, which feeds passengers from regional carriers into the United system, and its United Shuttle provides over 450 short-haul flights between twenty cities in the western states. The latter service is one that has often put United into direct competition with Southwest.

Delta, the third largest U.S. carrier, has over sixty-three thousand employees. Delta flies to about 225 U.S. and foreign locations, and it is particularly strong throughout much of the southern tier of the United States, where two of its major hubs—Atlanta and Dallas-Fort Worth—are located. Delta has also built up a low-fare regional carrier service, Delta Express, and it has acquired a minority stake in three regional airlines which can feed passengers into its several hubs. Delta has begun to focus much of its attention on its transatlantic operations, but it remains a strong U.S. competitor and is intent on attracting more business traffic.

America West, the smallest of Southwest's competitors, has about eleven thousand employees. The airline serves 144 cities in the United States and seven foreign locations in Mexico and Canada. America West has strong positions in its hubs, Phoenix and Las Vegas. However, many of its locations put it into direct competition with Southwest. With Continental and Mesa Airlines, which have small stakes in America West, America West has formed alliances which give it access to another thirty-five destinations.

All of the competitors have come into head-to-head competition with Southwest on several occasions. Southwest always welcomed competition and firmly believes it can come out ahead in any of those situations. Kelleher, when asked about his thoughts on facing a competitor such as the United Shuttle head-on, stated, "I think its good to have some real competitive activity that gets your people stirred up and renews their vigor and their energy and their desire to win. I think that United's Shuttle assault on Southwest Airlines, which was a very direct assault, drew our people closer together and made them better as a consequence."

Long-haul success for Southwest will put pressure on the profits realized by its bigger competitors. The cost advantage for Southwest includes the rapid twenty-minute gate turnarounds; an efficient all-Boeing 737 fleet, including new 737-700s that can fly cross-country nonstop; and a more productive workforce. Even if longer flights increase the costs, Southwest still realizes a significant competitive advantage. Roberts, Roach & Associates Inc., an airline consultant in Hayward, California, says that Southwest has at least a 59 percent cost advantage over bigger rivals at flights of five hundred miles, as well as a 35 percent lead for flights at fifteen hundred miles. "It's a huge threat," says a rival airline executive. These long-haul flights will be a new focus for Southwest's higher-cost rivals. Already, according to an estimate by analyst Samuel C. Buttrick from Paine Webber, Inc., nonstop flights longer than one thousand miles account for more than 16 percent of Southwest's capacity.

But, all this may be changing, based on the events of September 11. One analyst at Atlanta-based Raymond James & Associates stated, "We're seeing a restructuring of the industry." US Airways' low-fare MetroJet service to Fort Lauderdale was shut down before Christmas 2001. Gone, too, is Delta's Delta Express low-fare service to that city. What's happening in Florida is just an example of what's happening elsewhere in the industry. AirTran CEO Joe Leonard said, "In our market, the eastern U.S., there are four thousand fewer flights today (October 25) than [on] September 10." During 2001, Southwest added service to West Palm Beach, Florida, and to Norfolk, Virginia, while discontinuing service to San Francisco.

Metrojet and Delta Express in the East and United's Shuttle in the West were launched to compete with Southwest. But they couldn't match Southwest and were thought to be marginally profitable at best. Now, MetroJet and United's Shuttle are phasing out, and Delta Express is grounding half its service, while Southwest hasn't cut it's schedule at all. Other major carriers are dropping or reducing regular flights to mid-size cities that weren't profitable enough. For passengers, the effect of schedule cutbacks will mean fewer flights to choose from and, possibly, fewer airline choices on routes they fly. This situation may open the door to low-fare carriers like Southwest that can make money in those locations.

Before the attacks on September 11, discount carriers were even beginning to make inroads with cost-conscious business travelers. The low-fare carriers were doing better because they don't rely on high business fares and don't offer the frills the major carriers offer. In 1994, revenues earned by low-fare carriers represented 5 percent of the $76 billion U.S. air travel market. By 2001, their share was 10 percent, according to Raymond James & Associates. Also, several of the nation's most important business markets are now home to successful low-fare airlines, such as JetBlue, AirTran, Frontier, and so on. Joe Leonard of AirTran says, "What's important now is staying power—the ability first of all to survive, see what happens, and act fast."

## THE FUTURE

Today, Southwest provides service to only fifty-eight cities, so there are tremendous opportunities for expansion. The problem: Where to go next? Over one hundred cities have asked the airline to begin service in their communities because of the positive impact the company has had when it began operations in a new location. The introduction of Southwest's low fares and frequent flights opens up the market and gives many more people the freedom to fly. But the events of September 11, as well as economic recession, have put all expansion plans on hold for the present.

Southwest continues to forge ahead in other ways. The airline introduced a new aircraft to the fleet in October 1997: the Boeing 737–700. Southwest was the launch customer for this aircraft, which is able to fly high, fast, and far and still be fuel-efficient. Southwest has purchased ninety-two of these aircraft, which require less maintenance time than the traditional 737s, but future purchases have been delayed to save costs in the current environment.

In 1997, Southwest Airlines added a twenty-four-hour emergency medical service for its customers for in-flight medical emergencies. The airline now has emergency room physicians on call twenty-four hours a day through a service called MedLink. MedLink can put a physician in contact with Southwest's flight attendants during a medical emergency. The physician can make diagnoses, advise treatments, and issue medical recommendations, including whether or not an emergency landing should be made. Southwest is the first major airline to make the medical service accessible by in-flight telephone.

Throughout it history, Southwest consistently followed a clearly defined purpose and a well-thought-out strategy: to make a profit, achieve job security for every employee, and make flying affordable for more people. Can Southwest continue to maintain this strategy? Will its position remain unassailable by competitors—especially with the growing presence of other low-fare carriers? What are the implications of expanding to longer-haul operations? Will Southwest begin to lose the distinguishing characteristics that were the hallmarks of its success? What will be the effects of September 11 and the shakeout occurring in the industry on Southwest? How should Southwest be prepared to respond to these events? And how about international routes—especially to Canada or Mexico, our NAFTA partners, where business travel is growing as a result of this treaty? Southwest certainly has come a long way from the little company with three aircraft that began operations in 1971. What's next?

# US AIRWAYS GROUP, INC.—2002

John C. Urbanski and Eugene M. Bland
Francis Marion University

U

www.usairways.com

The September 11, 2001, terrorist attacks on the United States had serious repercussions for the U.S. airline industry. Passenger traffic immediately dropped precipitously; not only did passengers cancel reservations and avoid air travel out of fear for their lives, but also the the U.S. government ordered the complete grounding of all nonmilitary aircraft for a period of several days. Additionally, the government completely shut down operations at Reagan International Airport in Washington, D.C., for an extended period of time.

A resulting major loss in revenue was experienced by all U.S. commercial passenger operations. Indeed, Midway Airlines, which had been in some significant financial difficulty for an extended period before these events, immediately and permanently ceased operations, going "belly-up." Some carriers, such as Southwest Airlines, were in a better financial position to weather this drastic revenue loss. Other carriers, in financial straits before September 11 due to a downturn in passenger travel, found themselves on the brink of disaster. US Airways was one of the most notable and vulnerable of these carriers.

## HISTORY

### Beginnings

US Airways began operation in western Pennsylvania in 1939 as All American Aviation, flying airmail service to smaller communities in western Pennsylvania and eastern Ohio. In 1949, the company changed its name to All American Airways and began operations as a passenger carrier with the acquisition of World War II surplus DC-3 aircraft, but it maintained regional service in Pennsylvania and Ohio. The company changed its name again in 1953 to Allegheny Airlines. For the next fifteen years, Allegheny remained a small regional carrier, but in 1968, combined with Lake Central Airlines, a small regional carrier serving Ohio, Indiana, and Missouri, the company began an expansion that would continue for the next twenty-odd years.

### Large-Scale Growth

Allegheny's growth consisted primarily of a continuing series of acquisitions of and mergers with smaller regional carriers whose service areas were roughly contiguous with that of its own existing service region. In 1972, Allegheny acquired Mohawk Airlines, thus allowing Allegheny to begin servicing New York State as well as New England. This made Allegheny the world's sixth-largest airline, measured by the total number of customers boarded. In 1979, after deregulation of the airline industry by the now defunct federal Civil Aeronautics Board (CAB), Allegheny initiated new, long-distance

(Note – If you are using the hardback *Strategic Management* textbook by Fred R. David, then refer to the External Issues part of the American Airlines Cohesion Case for additional information about Southwest Airlines.)

routes between cities in its current network and cities in Florida, California, Texas, Arizona, and Colorado. Allegheny changed its name to USAir to reflect its new national service orientation.

In 1987, in competition for a share of the West Coast market, USAir returned to its former growth formula, acquiring Pacific Southwest Airlines, based in San Diego, California, as a wholly-owned subsidiary of USAir. In addition to increasing the size of USAir's service area, this acquisition also provided a feeder system for many of USAir's transcontinental routes. In 1987, Piedmont Airlines, a large carrier serving the U.S. Mid-Atlantic region, also became a subsidiary of USAir, a reflection of USAir's continuing expansion into contiguous markets. In 1988, Pacific Southwest Airlines was merged into USAir.

In 1989, USAir made a quantum leap in the size of its service region, as well as in the nature of the airline's service area, by completing the acquisition of Piedmont and merging it into USAir. Not only was this the largest airline merger in history at the time, but with the assumption of Piedmont's international routes, it also transformed USAir into an international carrier. It also gave USAir control of Piedmont's major airport hubs in Charlotte, North Carolina, and Baltimore, Maryland.

## Expansion in the 1990s

Throughout the 1990s, USAir continued to expand. Service was instituted to Frankfurt, Germany, from USAir's major hubs in Pittsburgh and Charlotte, as well as to London, England, from Charlotte, Philadelphia, and Baltimore. USAir also initiated service to Rome, Italy, Munich, Germany, and Madrid, Spain, from its Philadelphia hub. Service area growth also continued with the expansion of shorter international routes serviced by US Airways Express to various destinations in the Caribbean basin and Canada. Caribbean expansion has continued into late 2001.

In 1992, USAir entered into a domestic marketing agreement with the then-named Trump Shuttle and purchased a minority position in that airline, which continued operations as the USAir Shuttle. The shuttle provided hourly service between New York-LaGuardia and Boston as well as between New York and Washington, D.C.-National, later renamed Reagan International. In 1998, USAir acquired the shuttle operation outright. During this period, USAir, now US Airways as a result of a name change in 1997, began the operation of MetroJet, a startup subsidiary designed to provide single-class low-fare service in the eastern United States.

Today, US Airways is the sixth-largest carrier in the United States and serves 204 locations in the United States, Europe, Canada, the Caribbean, and Mexico. In the past several years, however, the fiscal health of US Airways has been in steady decline. The company operated 472 aircraft at yearend 2001 as indicated in Exhibit 1.

The fortunes of most of the companies in the U.S. airline industry are tied closely to economic fluctuations, demand for air transportation being positively correlated to general economic conditions. With more available disposable income, people travel more. When the economy is expanding, businesses require their employees to travel more often in order to address organizational requirements. Airline operations are also sensitive to specific economic factors, such as fuel prices and labor activity, that addresses employee compensation issues. The U.S. and global economies in 2001–2002 have not done well.

## Recent Setbacks

Labor unrest and the threat of a work stoppage immediately upon expiration of the pilots' union contract in March 2000 resulted in a significant decline in US Airways

## EXHIBIT 1    US Airways' Aircaft at Yearend 2001

### A. US Airways Aircraft

| Type | Average Seat Capacity | Average Age (years) | Owned[1] | Leased[2] | Total |
|------|------|------|------|------|------|
| Airbus A330 | 266 | 1.4 | 9 | – | 9 |
| Boeing 767-200ER | 203 | 12.7 | 7 | 4 | 11 |
| Boeing 757-200 | 182 | 11.2 | 23 | 11 | 34 |
| Airbus A321 | 169 | 0.7 | 15 | 8 | 23 |
| Airbus A320 | 145 | 2.1 | 11 | 13 | 24 |
| Boeing 737-400 | 144 | 12.0 | 19 | 35 | 54 |
| McDonnell Douglas MD-80 | 141 | 19.3 | 11 | 3 | 14 |
| Boeing 737-300 | 126 | 14.8 | 11 | 74 | 85 |
| Airbus A319 | 120 | 1.9 | 22 | 44 | 66 |
| Fokker 100 | 97 | 11.1 | 21 | 1 | 22 |
|  |  | 9.1 | 149 | 193 | 342 |

[1]Of the owned aircraft, 127 were pledged as collateral for various secured financing arrangements.
[2]The terms of the leases expire between 2002 and 2023.

### B. US Airways' Regional Airline Aircraft

| Type | Seat Capacity | Average Age (years) | Owned | Leased[1] | Total |
|------|------|------|------|------|------|
| de Havilland Dash 8-300 | 50 | 10.0 | – | 8 | 8 |
| de Havilland Dash 8-100/200 | 37 | 10.4 | 26 | 73 | 99 |
| Dornier 328-110 | 32 | 6.3 | – | 25 | 25 |
|  |  | 9.6 | 26 | 106 | 132 |

[1]The terms of the leases expire between 2002 and 2009.
*Source:* US Airways 2001 *Form 10K,* p. 10 and 11.

ticket sales. In May 2000, a consolidation with United Airlines was proposed as a method both of reducing the operating costs of both carriers and of remaining competitive in the face of expansion into US Airways territory by other carriers. Fuel costs also continued to increase. For 2000, US Airways posted a net loss of $269 million, its first loss since 1994.

During 2001, the economy continued its cool-down. Despite a 12 percent increase in passenger traffic over the same period in 1999, rising costs caused US Airways to continue to lose money at an alarming rate. Losses for the first two quarters of 2001 totaled $196 million. To make matters worse, despite the approval of the European Union and despite the earlier acquisition of TWA by American Airlines, making it the world's largest carrier, the proposed consolidation of US Airways and United broke down in the face of likely opposition from the U.S. government. By August 2001, United had backed out of merger negotiations, and the proposed consolidation was a dead issue. Then at yearend 2001, US Airways posted a whopping $2.11 billion loss for the year. The company's yearend 2001 financial statements are provided in Exhibits 2 through 5.

EXHIBIT 2    US Airways Group, Inc., Consolidated Statements of Operations Year Ended December 31, (dollars in millions, except per share amounts)

| | 2001 | 2000 | 1999 |
|---|---|---|---|
| **Operating Revenues** | | | |
| Passenger transportation | $ 7,164 | $ 8,341 | $ 7,685 |
| Cargo and freight | 164 | 164 | 149 |
| Other | 960 | 764 | 761 |
| Total Operating Revenues | 8,288 | 9,269 | 8,595 |
| **Operating Expenses** | | | |
| Personnel costs | 3,726 | 3,637 | 3,380 |
| Aviation fuel | 1,103 | 1,284 | 727 |
| Aircraft rent | 573 | 519 | 480 |
| Other rent and landing fees | 449 | 448 | 430 |
| Aircraft maintenance | 532 | 504 | 499 |
| Other selling expenses | 368 | 419 | 379 |
| Depreciation and amortization | 392 | 369 | 341 |
| Commissions | 279 | 371 | 484 |
| Asset impairments and other special charges | 958 | – | 45 |
| Airline stabilization act grant | (320) | – | – |
| Other | 1,911 | 1,771 | 1,694 |
| Total Operating Expenses | 9,971 | 9,322 | 8,459 |
| Operating Income (Loss) | (1,683) | (53) | 136 |
| **Other Income (Expense)** | | | |
| Interest income | 61 | 76 | 66 |
| Interest expense | (297) | (251) | (193) |
| Interest capitalized | 18 | 33 | 38 |
| Merger termination fee | 50 | – | – |
| Gain on sale of investment | – | – | 274 |
| Other, net | (1) | (28) | 24 |
| Other Income (Expense), Net | (169) | (170) | 209 |
| Income (Loss) Before Income Taxes and Cumulative Effect of Accounting Change | (1,852) | (223) | 345 |
| Provision (Credit) for Income Taxes | 272 | (57) | 148 |
| Income (Loss) Before Cumulative Effect of Accounting Change | (2,124) | (166) | 197 |
| Cumulative Effect of Accounting Change, Net of Applicable Income Taxes of $5 Million and $63 Million, respectively | 7 | (103) | – |
| Net Income (Loss) | $ (2,117) | $ (269) | $ 197 |
| **Earnings (Loss) per Common Share** | | | |
| Basic | | | |
| Before Cumulative Effect of Accounting Change | $ (31.59) | $ (2.47) | $ 2.69 |
| Cumulative Effect of Accounting Change | $ 0.11 | $ (1.55) | $ – |
| Net Earnings (Loss) per Common Share | $ (31.48) | $ (4.02) | $ 2.69 |
| Diluted | | | |
| Before Cumulative Effect of Accounting Change | $ (31.59) | $ (2.47) | $ 2.64 |
| Cumulative Effect of Accounting Change | $ 0.11 | $ (1.55) | $ – |
| Net Earnings (Loss) per Common Share | $ (31.48) | $ (4.02) | $ 2.64 |
| **Shares Used for Computation (000)** | | | |
| Basic | 67,227 | 66,855 | 73,316 |
| Diluted | 67,227 | 66,855 | 74,603 |

*Source:* US Airways 2001 *Form 10K,* p. 37.

**EXHIBIT 3**    US Airways Group, Inc., Consolidated Balance Sheets December 31,
(dollars in millions, except per share amount)

| *Assets* | *2001* | *2000* |
|---|---|---|
| Current Assets | | |
| Cash | $ 36 | $ 40 |
| Cash equivalents | 557 | 503 |
| Short-term investments | 485 | 773 |
| Receivables, net | 281 | 331 |
| Materials and supplies, net | 209 | 249 |
| Deferred income taxes | – | 428 |
| Prepaid expenses and other | 207 | 268 |
| Total Current Assets | 1,775 | 2,592 |
| Property and Equipment | | |
| Flight equipment | 7,472 | 6,762 |
| Ground property and equipment | 1,211 | 1,148 |
| Less accumulated depreciation and amortization | (4,075) | (3,118) |
| | 4,608 | 4,792 |
| Purchase deposits for flight equipment | 85 | 197 |
| Total Property and Equipment | 4,693 | 4,989 |
| Other Assets | | |
| Goodwill, net | 531 | 551 |
| Pension assets | 411 | 401 |
| Other intangibles, net | 343 | 313 |
| Other assets, net | 272 | 281 |
| Total Other Assets | 1,557 | 1,546 |
| | $ 8,025 | $ 9,127 |
| *Liabilities and Stockholders' Equity (Deficit)* | | |
| Current Liabilities | | |
| Current maturities of long-term debt | $ 159 | $ 284 |
| Accounts payable | 625 | 538 |
| Traffic balances payable and unused tickets | 817 | 890 |
| Accured aircraft rent | 257 | 358 |
| Accrued salaries, wages and vacation | 372 | 324 |
| Other accrued expenses | 796 | 524 |
| Total Current Liabilities | 3,026 | 2,918 |
| Noncurrent Liabilities | | |
| Long-term debt, net of current maturities | 3,515 | 2,688 |
| Accrued aircraft rent | 293 | 182 |
| Deferred gains, net | 589 | 606 |
| Postretirement benefits other than pensions | 1,474 | 1,407 |
| Employee benefit liabilities and other | 1,743 | 1,684 |
| Total Noncurrent Liabilities | 7,614 | 6,567 |
| Commitments and Contingencies | | |
| Stockholders' Equity (Deficit) | | |
| Common Stock, par value $1 per share, issued 101,172,000 shares | 101 | 101 |
| Paid-in capital | 2,185 | 2,241 |
| Retained earnings (deficit) | (2,937) | (820) |
| Common Stock held in treasury, at cost, 33,584,000 shares and 34,166,000 shares, respectively | (1,749) | (1,807) |
| Deferred compensation | (62) | (75) |
| Accumulated other comprehensive income (loss), net of income tax effect | (153) | 2 |
| Total Stockholders' Equity (Deficit) | (2,615) | (358) |
| | $ 8,025 | $ 9,127 |

*Source:* US Airways 2001 *Form 10K*, p. 38.

EXHIBIT 4    US Airways Operating Segment Information
(in millions)

| | YEARENDED DECEMBER 31, | | |
|---|---|---|---|
| | 2001 | 2000 | 1999 |
| **Operating Revenues:** | | | |
| US Airways external | $ 7,220 | $8,295 | $7,764 |
| US Airways intersegment | 70 | 75 | 67 |
| US Airways Express external | 983 | 893 | 798 |
| US Airways Express intersegment | 61 | 47 | 33 |
| All Other | 85 | 81 | 33 |
| Intersegment elimination | (131) | (122) | (100) |
| | $ 8,288 | $9,269 | $8,595 |
| **Depreciation and amortization:** | | | |
| US Airways | $ 376 | $ 355 | $ 327 |
| US Airways Express | 16 | 14 | 14 |
| All Other | – | – | – |
| | $ 392 | $ 369 | $ 341 |
| **Interest income:** | | | |
| US Airways | $ 77 | $ 95 | $ 187 |
| US Airways Express | 1 | 2 | 2 |
| All Other | 125 | 146 | 96 |
| Intercompany elimination | (142) | (167) | (219) |
| | $ 61 | $ 76 | $ 66 |
| **Interest expense:** | | | |
| US Airways | $ 319 | $ 274 | $ 205 |
| US Airways Express | 4 | 4 | 4 |
| All Other | 83 | 102 | 173 |
| Intercompany elimination | (109) | (129) | (189) |
| | $ 297 | $ 251 | $ 193 |
| **Income (Loss) Before Income Taxes and** | | | |
| Cumulative Effect of Accounting Change: | $(1,860) | $ (349) | $ 18 |
| US Airways | (9) | 94 | 132 |
| US Airways Express | 17 | 32 | 195 |
| All Other | $(1,852) | $ (223) | $ 345 |
| **Capital Expenditures:** | | | |
| US Airways | $ 1,104 | $1,948 | $1,419 |
| US Airways Express | 23 | 12 | 10 |
| All Other | 8 | 18 | 19 |
| | $ 1,135 | $1,978 | $1,448 |
| **Assets:** | | | |
| US Airways | $ 6,999 | $7,768 | |
| US Airways Express | 169 | 162 | |
| All Other | 857 | 1,197 | |
| | $ 8,025 | $9,127 | |

*Source:* US Airways 2001 *Form 10K*, p. 63.

**EXHIBIT 5**   Selected US Airways Operating and Financial Statistics[1]

|  | 2001 | 2000[2] | 1999[2] |
|---|---|---|---|
| Revenue passengers (thousands)* | 56,114 | 60,636 | 57,397 |
| Total RPMs (millions)[3] | 45,979 | 47,065 | 41,878 |
| RPMs (millions)* | 45,948 | 47,012 | 41,793 |
| Total ASMs (millions)[4] | 66,744 | 66,919 | 59,925 |
| ASMs (millions)* | 66,704 | 66,851 | 59,815 |
| Passenger load factor*[5] | 68.9% | 70.3% | 69.9% |
| Break-even load factor[6] | 80.8% | 73.0% | 69.5% |
| Yield*[7] | 14.32¢ | 16.28¢ | 17.15¢ |
| Passenger revenue per ASM*[8] | 9.86¢ | 11.45¢ | 11.98¢ |
| Revenue per ASM[9] | 10.92¢ | 12.51¢ | 13.02¢ |
| Cost per ASM[10] | 12.46¢ | 12.72¢ | 12.99¢ |
| Average passenger journey (miles)* | 819 | 775 | 728 |
| Average stage length (miles)* | 667 | 633 | 604 |
| Cost of aviation fuel per gallon[11] | 86.28¢ | 95.76¢ | 58.61¢ |
| Cost of aviation fuel per gallon, excluding fuel taxes[12] | 80.09¢ | 89.11¢ | 52.41¢ |
| Gallons of aviation fuel consumed (millions) | 1,208 | 1,267 | 1,170 |
| Operating aircraft at yearend | 342 | 417 | 393 |
| Full-time equivalent employees at yearend | 35,232 | 43,467 | 42,016 |

*Scheduled service only (excludes charter service).

[1]Operating statistics include free frequent travelers and the related miles they flew. Unusual items (see Note 13 to US Airways' Notes to Consolidated Financial Statements for additional information) and revenues and expenses associated with US Airways' capacity purchase arrangements with certain affiliated airlines have been excluded from US Airways' financial results for purposes of financial statistical calculation and to provide better comparability between periods.

[2]Includes the activity of the former Shuttle on a pro forma basis as if it was merged into US Airways as of January 1, 1999. Also, effective January 1, 2000, US Airways changed its accounting policy related to Dividend Miles revenue recognition. The 1999 amount is presented on a pro forma basis to show what US Airways would have reported if the new accounting policy had been in effect in periods prior to 2000.

[3]Revenue Passenger Miles (RPMs)—revenue passengers multiplied by the number of miles they flew.

[4]Available Seat Miles (ASMs)—seats available multiplied by the number of miles flown (a measure of capacity).

[5]Percentage of aircraft seating capacity that is actually utilized (RPMs/ASMs).

[6]Percentage of aircraft seating capacity utilized that equates to US Airways breaking-even at the pretax income level.

[7]Passenger transportation revenue divided by RPMs.

[8]Passenger transportation revenue divided by ASMs (a measure of unit revenue).

[9]Total Operating Revenues divided by ASMs (a measure of unit revenue).

[10]Total Operating Expenses divided by ASMs (a measure of unit cost).

[11]Includes fuel taxes and transportation charges.

[12]Includes transportation charges (excludes fuel taxes).

*Source:* US Airways, 2001 *Form 10K,* pp. 29–30.

## STRATEGY

### Hub Operations

The hub system currently used by all major carriers other than Southwest ideally allows any airline to fly passengers to any destination on the globe. Rather than fly directly from an origination point A to destination B, as was the practice before airline deregulation, passengers fly from origination point A to the airline's hub and then transfer to another aircraft, which flies them to destination B (along with passengers from origination points C, D, E, etc.). The hub system also allows airlines to feed passengers from small markets into the carrier's transcontinental and international routes, thus allowing competition in these markets as well. In essence, with a strategically placed hub, any airline can compete for passengers flying on any route as long as there is space at the hub and destination terminals.

Hub size often varies substantially among carriers. Among the major carriers, US Airways suffers from two hub-related drawbacks. First, its hubs are smaller in capacity than those of other carriers, creating a bottleneck for the transfer of passengers and limiting the number of aircraft the hub can handle at any one time. As noted earlier, US Airways began addressing this shortcoming by expanding the facilities at several of its hubs. Second, and perhaps more telling, its hubs are bunched together geographically, being limited to several cities on the East Coast of the United States, specifically Boston, New York-LaGuardia, Pittsburgh, Philadelphia, Baltimore, Washington, D.C., and Charlotte. This East Coast concentration makes its route network more difficult to defend from competition. In contrast, Delta Airlines, one of US Airways main competitors, has the world's busiest hub in Atlanta, a major hub in Dallas/Fort Worth, another in Salt Lake City, and a smaller facility in Cinncinati.

## Load Factor

As a result of this hub system, the phrase *too much of a good thing* now applies to seat capacity of both individual airlines and the industry in general. There is a more than an ample supply of seats offered by numerous carriers, all of which serve a majority of the same routes. Fare prices fluctuate as with any commodity, and they affect the load factor, the percentage of filled seats on any given flight. Increase the load factor above breakeven (B/E), which is the expense required to fly the aircraft to a destination plus a portion of fixed costs, and profits result. Decrease the load factor and losses occur. Any small "twitch" in load factor, and the resultant financial effect can be critical to airlines, an industry which has traditionally operated on a 1 percent to 2 percent margin.

The primary goal of US Airways, as with most of its competitors, is to move "load factor" above the breakeven point into the profit range. This can be accomplished by raising the number of paying passengers per flight, by lowering operating costs or a portion of fixed costs and thus lowering the breakeven point, or some combination of both approaches.

Some type of fare war is the generally accepted method that is used to attempt increasing load capacity. The addition of a passenger does not have a significant effect on operating expenses, but it does significantly affect revenue. By offering the lowest priced fares to a destination, an airline hopes to lure customers from competitors—and even increase the amount of overall passenger traffic by attracting passengers who would not have considered air travel under a higher pricing structure. This allows the airline to significantly increase load capacity and to reach profitability. This also may be used to increase overall market share for any particular route, and in extreme form, it may often be used to drive the competition from the market, just as Southwest Airlines did in the West Coast market in the mid-1990s. Revenue may also be generated by increasing the service area or by increasing profitability on core routes to cover underperformance on other routes. Promotional "e-fares," available at the airline's Web site, offer significantly reduced fares for last minute travelers as a method of filling seats which would otherwise go unfilled. Airlines may also attempt to attract customers by increasing the levels of customer service significantly above that of competitors in areas such as overbooking, on-time arrivals, reductions in lost luggage, and other sensitive areas. US Airways continues to engage in fare reduction activity, both proactively and as a reaction to the fare reduction activities of its competitors. This is especially critical to US Airways due to the significantly increasing presence of its competitors in the company's regional market.

## Generic Solutions

Reducing operating expenses is not easily accomplished. Unlike other commodities, supply cannot be adjusted to demand. "Production" of seating cannot be curtailed, nor can excess inventory be warehoused until needed. A Boeing 767 cannot be "sized" to meet fluctuations in demand. It costs roughly as much to operate an aircraft carrying one passenger as it does one carrying a full load. Operating costs can often be addressed only by reducing the cost of a contributing factor, such as a reduction in fuel expense or payroll expenses, or by eliminating passenger amenities, such as meals. One attempt to match demand to supply, which has had limited success, is switching aircraft type to match route demand. Thus, a route using a 203-seat 767 but averaging only 100 passengers may switch to a 737, which has a lower operating expense but a maximum capacity approaching average demand. Operating costs may also be addressed through aircraft type. The carrier may limit the type of aircraft in its fleet, lowering costs through standardization in maintenance, flexibility in crew assignments, and reduced turnaround time; or it may purchase more efficient aircraft types, reducing expenditures for fuel or other costs.

## Current Restructuring

US Airways' current strategy is aimed at reducing operating expenses and increasing expansion of its international operation. Even though the company services international destinations, it is still primarily a regional carrier, albeit a larger one than it once was. Its expense structure, however, mirrors that of a large international carrier, while its revenues do not. After the collapse of the proposed merger with United and before the terrorist attacks of September 11, US Airways had already begun refocusing and restructuring activities in order to regain profitability. In an effort to match seat supply to route demand, the company reassigned regional-type aircraft to underperforming critical core routes to increase load factors. This type of aircraft offers great flexibility, since it has a smaller capacity, is significantly more efficient to operate, and has a shorter turnaround time than larger aircraft. The company's discretion in reassigning this type of aircraft is currently subject to restrictions. Under the existing labor agreement, use of this type of aircraft in the US Airways fleet was capped at seventy. As a result, many nontranscontinental-length routes are served by turboprop aircraft, which are not able to operate efficiently in routes with greater stage lengths. An increase in the use of regional jets would allow an increase in operating efficiency on these routes. At this time, US Airways has sixty regional jets in service.

As mentioned earlier, US Airways also entered into an agreement with Airbus to substantially modernize its fleet of major aircraft, ordering approximately four hundred Airbus A320 aircraft, with the first deliveries occurring in 1999. These aircraft replaced older Boeing 737s and 727s as well as variations of the DC-9 aircraft in the US Airways inventory. Compared to the aircraft being retired, the new-generation Airbus jets provide significantly increased fuel efficiency, have significantly lower maintenance costs, have longer operational ranges, and provide increased passenger amenities. This move to aircraft standardization also increased certain maintenance EOS, increased crew flexibility, and reduced crew training expenses. The company also ordered up to forty Airbus A330 wide-body aircraft for use in an expanded system of transatlantic routes. The acquisition of these aircraft offers the same advantages as the acquisition of the A320 aircraft. Both moves, however, create the paradox of increasing capacity in the face of a continued decline in demand. Due to the precarious financial position of the company, however, scheduled delivery of some A320 and A330 aircraft are being deferred from 2003–2006 until 2005–2009 in order to reduce debt and free cash.

US Airways is also addressing the reduction of overhead. Personnel costs represent the largest of US Airways expenses. To address these expenses, US Airways entered into labor contracts in 1999 and 2000 with several groups of employees. All contracts contained a parity clause, which ties employee compensation to the weighted average cost plus 1 percent of comparable positions in the four largest U.S. airlines, bringing compensation expenses to a more reasonable level. However, the company's operations and revenue structure still do not mirror that of these four airlines. In a related issue, as mentioned earlier, the company's labor contract with the Air Line Pilots Association (ALPA) capped the number of regional jets the company could use on its longer-leg regional routes. These jets are operated by several of the company's wholly-owned subsidiaries, such as US Airways Express and MetroJet. Pilots working for these subsidiaries are paid significantly less than their counterparts, who fly jet aircraft in US Airways' main fleet. The cap on the use of regional jet aircraft is an attempt to address this pay inequity issue. As business continued to decline in 2001, the company again began to address labor issues. It began attempts to gain salary concessions from several of its unions in order to further reduce labor overhead, and it began pressuring ALPA to abandon the current cap on use of regional-type jet aircraft. The terrorist attacks of September 11 resulted both in the layoff of approximately 25 percent (eleven thousand) of US Airways employees and a 23 percent cut in flight capacity. Both developments strengthened the company's negotiating position.

## International Operations

To take advantage of an annual increase in foreign travel to and from the United States over the past several years, US Airways also continued its efforts to increase its presence in the international arena, specifically in its service to western Europe. Although the concentration of its various hubs along the East Coast of the United States makes US Airways vulnerable to other regional low-cost competition, it does provide an ideal jumping-off point for transAtlantic flights, since the majority of passengers traveling between Europe and the United States begin or end their travel in the eastern United States. To support international expansion, the company addressed needs in several areas. As mentioned, it began acquiring a new generation of wide-bodied aircraft to facilitate long-haul international routes. In keeping with this hub's role as US Airway's primary international gateway, it also began a major upgrade of its international terminal at its Philadelphia hub. The company has also expanded the number of international destinations served, adding Amsterdam in the Netherlands and Brussels, Belgium, in 2001. US Airways also petitioned the U.S. Department of Transportation for authority to begin service to Heathrow Airport in London. The company currently serves Gatwick, another London-area facility. US Airways also continued expanding service to the Caribbean basin, another region conveniently served from the eastern United States. Even after September 11 and a 23 percent decline in service, US Airways announced service to new Caribbean destinations. The potential payoff from international expansion remains unclear; despite an 8 percent growth in international travel in 2000, a 1.3 percent decline in the first half of 2001 mirrored the decline in domestic travel. US Airway's domestic versus foreign revenues are given in Exhibit 6.

## COMPETITORS

Although US Airways is the sixth-largest airline in the United States at present, much of its competition comes from smaller regional carriers as well as from other majors. Southwest Airlines is one of the chief thorns in the side of US Airways. Southwest

EXHIBIT 6    Operating Revenues (based on revenue passenger miles and yield) in Principal Geographic Areas (in millions)

|  | 2001 | 2000 | 1999 | 1998 |
|---|---|---|---|---|
| United States | $ 7,449 | $ 8,524 | $ 8,006 | $ 8,143 |
| Foreign | 839 | 745 | 589 | 545 |
|  | $ 8,288 | $ 9,269 | $ 8,595 | $ 8,688 |

*Source:* SEC *Form 10K* for the yearend December 31, 2001, p. 63.

currently operates a fleet of 358 Boeing 737 aircraft, and it serves fifty-eight cities in various regions of the United States. In contrast to other major U.S. carriers, Southwest does not use the hub system: It prefers to fly direct routes, and it counts on its twenty-minute turnaround times to deliver high-frequency service between destinations. It is unclear, however, how drastically increased security measures at airports since the terrorist attack will affect this turnaround time.

Since 1990, when Southwest began a rapid expansion in the West Coast market, its operations have been a threat to US Airways as well as to other carriers. Using a combination of fare cuts of two-thirds or more as well as by adding flights to several major cities in northern and southern California, Southwest forced US Airways to essentially abandon its service on north-south California routes. Eventually, Southwest became the second-largest carrier in the California region, second only to United. In 1993, mistakenly believing that US Airways was about to abandon service from its Baltimore hub, Southwest aggressively entered this market. This became one of Southwest's fastest growing cities, and Southwest eventually surpassed US Airways in this market. US Airways had been cutting back service from its Baltimore hub, eliminating fifty-one of seventy-five mainline routes, including nonstop service to Florida. Since September 11, US Airways has also ceased operations of MetroJet, its express jet service. In addition to overlapping MetroJet's Baltimore operations, Southwest also overlapped MetroJet's services in New England cities such as Providence, Rhode Island. After the initial shock of the September 11 attack, most airlines reduced service on routes—or abandoned routes completely. Due to its strong financial position (its 33.3 percent debt-to-total capital ratio is the lowest in the industry), Southwest elected to maintain preattack levels of service, and it even drastically reduced ticket prices in order to attract leisure travel to make up for a decline in business travel. Expansion plans were temporarily halted, however, as Southwest delayed delivery of new aircraft. Additionally, Southwest was the only airline that was not forced to lay off employees after the attack. This strong financial position may allow Southwest to continue undercutting the fares of its more highly-leveraged competitors. Finally, although delivery has been delayed, Southwest had placed orders for Boeing 737-700 aircraft, extremely efficient versions of this type, which also have true transcontinental range. It has long been rumored that Southwest plans to inaugurate this type of service.

Delta Airlines, the third largest U.S. carrier, has two wholly owned subsidiaries, Delta Express and The Delta Connection, which consists of Comair, Atlantic Coast Airlines (ACA), and Atlantic Southeast Airlines (ASA). In 1996, Delta Express began direct competition with US Airways Shuttle, using a fleet of modern Boeing 737-800 aircraft to offer seventeen daily flights between NY-LaGuardia and Washington, D.C., and between NY-LaGuardia and Boston. The Delta Connection offers service out of

Delta hubs in Atlanta and Dallas/Fort Worth via ASA, Cincinnati and Orlando via Comair, as well as the New York and Boston hubs via ACA. These service areas considerably overlap many of the same destinations served by US Airways. Significantly, except for a few turboprop aircraft which are being phased out of ASA service, all Delta Connection subsidiaries exclusively operate some type of regional jet, a distinct advantage over the largely turboprop fleet operated over the same routes by US Airways Express. The large number of competitors in US Airways' region makes it difficult to achieve or exceed breakeven load factors on flights due to the sheer number of choices available to travelers. US Airways and Delta Airlines also compete for transcontinental passengers. Recently, Delta has increased its service to Philadelphia, US Airways' international gateway, and it has initiated international service to Brussels, a new destination for US Airways as well.

In addition to Southwest and Delta, the cumulative encroachment of other competitors into US Airways' service areas poses a substantial threat to the company's load factors, because it continues the saturation of an already crowded market with additional seats, as 82 percent of all US Airways flights are concentrated in the eastern U.S. region. Low-fare, no-frills startups such as JetBlue, Spirit Airlines, and AirTran Airways have collectively increased departures from East Coast facilities by 25 percent in the last quarter of 2000. JetBlue, backed by capital from George Soros, among others, competes for East Coast Florida service, flying between New York and several Florida destinations, all served by US Airways. JetBlue has taken a novel approach to no-frills service, exclusively operating brand new Airbus A320 aircraft, providing JetBlue with the same operating overhead that US Airways' upgraded fleet will provide. All aircraft in the JetBlue fleet are equipped with leather seating throughout the passenger cabin, and they provide seatback video screens which deliver twenty-four channels of DirecTV to all passengers. The cost includes blue corn nacho chips! JetBlue has also expanded service to a number of West Coast destinations, including cities in California and Washington, as well as several in mountain states such as Colorado and Utah. Recently, JetBlue placed an order for forty-eight more A320 aircraft, bringing its total fleet order to 131 aircraft. Interestingly, several of JetBlue's top management team had recently held similar positions with Southwest.

## THE FUTURE

After the September 11 attacks, the future of US Airways was questionable at best. All commercial flights originating from or terminating in the United States were suspended for several days. Reagan International Airport, a terminus for the US Airways shuttle, which operates 45 percent of its flights from this facility, was closed for a period of several weeks. The fear of flying caused passenger traffic to nose-dive; load factors plummeted, and the resulting steep drop in revenue placed additional burdens on an airline which had already been struggling financially. This was not helped by the crash of an American Airlines Airbus in November, which resulted in the loss of 250 lives. Although found not to be terrorist-related, this tragedy further eroded travelers' confidence. In addition to losses incurred during the first half of 2001, the company suffered a staggering net loss of $766 million for the third quarter of that year. Although load factors have significantly increased, they are still not at breakeven levels, due largely to the inability of the airline industry to lure back passengers. Especially critical was the further decline in business traffic, which comprises 50 percent of airline traffic but generates 65 percent of ticket revenue. An economy in recession requires less business travel; additionally, organizations began to use alternative strategies, such as teleconferencing,

Web-based conferencing, and sometimes travel by train and automobile, to reduce exposure of employees to further possible terrorist activity.

Some short-term solutions seemed to offer some relief. US Airways, as did most other airlines, laid off 24 percent of its employees to reduce payroll expenses. This resulted in a dramatic decrease in customer service, however, which was already a consumer flashpoint. Combined with slowdowns caused by increased security measures, this may have a further deleterious effect on air travel. US Airways also cut service by 23 percent. Routes were dropped and flights on many routes were consolidated to fill aircraft, which increased load factors but resulted in a decline in overall company revenues.

Short-term cash infusions were also available. US Airways was owed $50 million by United as a condition of their failed merger. The company raised $404 million of additional operating cash in November by the sale and leaseback of some aircraft. The U.S. government had passed legislation federalizing airport security operations, a move which relieved the airlines of this expense. Immediately after the terrorist attack, the U.S. Congress passed legislation providing $14 billion in aid to the airline industry. It is unclear, however, how this will help US Airways. Some of the package permits direct grants to airlines; however, the bulk of the package is in the form of loan packages which require the participating airlines to provide assets as loan collateral. With a leverage ratio of 92 percent, the second-highest in the airline industry, the company had little unencumbered assets to offer as collateral for these loans.

On November 27, 2001, Rakesh Gangwal, US Airways CEO, abruptly and unexpectedly resigned, ostensibly to pursue opportunities in venture capital investing. Gangwal's chief strengths were his attention to detail and a mastery of the airline industry's economics, critical requirements under the current conditions. Mr. Gangwal was immediately succeeded by Stephen Wolf, chairman of the airline, who had been CEO of the company before turning control over to Gangwal in 1998. Wolf's strengths, however, seemed to lie in deal making rather than in daily operations, and since at least 1987, he has had Gangwal present as his extremely capable number two man. Whether Wolf had the acumen to pull US Airways out of the morass without the help of Gangwal was a significant question for both company employees and the industry in general. At that moment, US Airways seemed to be rudderless—and continuing to lose altitude.

In August 2002, US Airways announced that they were filing Chapter 11 bankruptcy. A federal bankruptcy judge granted US Airways $75 million to continue flying through September 2002. Operations will continue as normal, however the airline didn't rule out flight cuts. US Airways expects to submit a reorganization plan by Dec. 31, 2002. (**www.usatoday.com**, August 13, 2002)

# E*TRADE GROUP, INC.—2002

**Sandra H. DuRant**
**Francis Marion University**

ET

www.etrade.com

The phrase *It's a small world after all* was coined years ago but never had quite the meaning it has today in the world of cyberspace. You can travel the world with the stroke of a key through the Internet and e-mail. The Internet can actually make money for you and let you "take it to the bank" without leaving your home if you invest wisely. This is every individual's fantasy, regardless of culture or country. E*Trade is a company that wants to make this fantasy a reality. E*Trade is a global leader in Internet online personal financial services. The company offers a full range of products that include investment and broker-age services, integrated banking, research capabilities, and educational and advisory ser-vices. E*Trade's banking service is currently the largest integrated online banking service in the world, with the largest Automated Teller Machine (ATM) network, and it offers a variety of financial services. E*Trade provides service twenty-four-hours a day, seven days a week through the Internet, direct modem access, automated telephone service, and live telephone support. E*Trade has 3,960 employees and is located in Menlo Park, California.

E*Trade has diversified significantly over the past two years and now offers extended trading hours for many exchanges around the world as well as direct interna-tional trades during trading hours. E*Trade has customers in 50 states and 119 coun-tries. It has established branded sites in eleven countries, including South Africa, Denmark, Korea, Japan, the United Kingdom, Sweden, Australia, New Zealand, Canada, Norway, and the United States.

## HISTORY

E*Trade was founded in 1983 by Bill Porter, a physicist and inventor, and it provided online quotes and trading services to Fidelity, Charles Schwab, and Quick & Reilly. These are the same companies E*Trade is now fighting for market share. Bill Porter began to wonder why, as an individual investor, he had to pay a broker hundreds of dol-lars for stock transactions. He had great foresight and envisioned the day when everyone would have a computer and invest through E*Trade. Bill Porter's foresight helped him fulfill his vision, and in 1992 E*Trade Securities, Inc., became one of the original all-electronic brokerage companies. E*Trade Securities, Inc., began offering online invest-ing services through America Online and CompuServe. In 1996, Bill Porter's dream became a reality when **www.etrade.com** was launched and the demand skyrocketed.

Porter appointed Christos Cotsakos as president and CEO of the company in 1996. Cotsakos brought over twenty years of senior level management experience with him to E*Trade. Prior to working at E*Trade, Cotsakos worked at FedEx and A.C. Nielsen, where he served as the former president, co-chief executive officer, and director. In the spring of 2001, E*Trade was ranked number three overall by Gomez Advisors Internet Brokers Scorecard for top Internet brokers. The Gomez Advisors Internet Brokers Scorecard results are based on a comprehensive review of the top fifty online brokerages across the nation in ten major categories and 150 different criteria.

## EXTERNAL FACTORS

### The Terrorist Attacks

On September 11, 2001, global investment activities of E*Trade and the entire online investment industry were greatly altered by the World Trade Center attack. The attack intensified a yearlong economic slowdown that began in the first quarter of 2000 and continued through 2001 with decreasing prices and downturns in the securities market. The attack shook the foundation of the American economy. The attack pushed the country into economic recession that extended far beyond the borders of the United States.

The World Trade Center attack resulted in a record one-day drop on September 17, 2001, of 684 points in the Dow Jones Industrial Average. The disaster was immediately felt around the globe, as signs of economic fallout became apparent. The federal government made a historical decision to close all airports in the United States for four days. The U.S. Congress and the federal government approved a $40 billion relief package to rebuild New York City and to bail out the airline industry. Wall Street was shut down for four days, the longest period of closure since the Depression.

The terrorist attacks caused a severe deterioration in global economic activity. The economic output loss in the United States is expected to exceed $50 billion. Gross Domestic Product (GDP) growth is expected to decline by 3 percent in the third quarter of 2001, which will be the first decline in the nation's GDP since the first quarter of 1993. The Federal Reserve lowered short-term interest rates a total of ten times in 2001 to stimulate the economy. The entire online brokerage industry has suffered decreasing profits due to declining trading volumes. This trend forced major players in the online brokerage industry, including E*Trade, to restructure their companies, to lay off employees, and to turn to diversification to enhance and expand their products and services. E*Trade is developing key strategic alliances to gain competitive advantages—with such companies as Yahoo!, AOL, Microsoft, AT&T, and CompuServe. E*Trade also has alliance agreements with industry leaders in the airline industry, the hotel industry, and the credit card industry to enhance product offerings and expand its client bases.

### Competitors

E*Trade and its major competitors are diversifying beyond domestic retail brokerage services by offering products and services that include initial public offerings, mutual fund offerings, banking services, global cross-border trading, institutional investing, and educational opportunities for customers. E*Trade's major competitors in the market are Charles Schwab, Fidelity Investments, TD Waterhouse, Ameritrade, Datek, and Harris Direct (formerly CSFBdirect). Charles Schwab is the largest broker in the industry, with 30 percent of the market share and revenues totaling almost $5.8 billion as of year-end 2000. Fidelity is ranked second, with a 20 percent market share. E*Trade increased its market share to 18 percent in 2000 and reported almost $2 billion in revenues, as indicated in Exhibit 1. However, by the period ending June 30, 2001, E*Trade reported a loss of $19 million. TD Waterhouse, Ameritrade, Datek, and Harris Direct collectively claim an additional 24 percent of the market share, and all other online brokerage firms represent the remaining 8 percent.

Established in 1974 and based in San Francisco, California, Charles Schwab Corporation is the largest broker in the industry. It is a full-service financial company that offers brokerage and trading services, investment planning services, a full range of financial products, and other related services. For the three months ending June 30, 2001, Charles Schwab reported a net income of $102 million and $1,071 billion in total revenues. Charles Schwab is publicly traded on the New York Stock Exchange (NYSE) under the ticker [SCH].

EXHIBIT 1    Industry Comparison of Major Competitors in 2000

| Broker | Market Share | Customer Accounts | Client Assets | Revenues* | Net Income* |
|---|---|---|---|---|---|
| Charles Schwab | 30% | 3,700,000 | $418,000,000,000 | $5,787,651 | $718,137 |
| Fidelity | 20% | 4,220,000 | $328,000,000,000 | $ N/A | $ N/A |
| E*Trade | 18% | 2,443,000 | $ 62,000,000,000 | $1,973,200 | $ 19,200 |
| TD Waterhouse | 11% | 1,728,000 | $118,000,000,000 | $1,575,415 | $210,316 |
| Ameritrade | 7% | 992,000 | $ 39,000,000,000 | $ 654,500 | $(13,600) |
| Datek | 3% | 457,000 | $ 15,000,000,000 | $ N/A | $ N/A |
| Harris Direct | 3% | 402,000 | $ 27,000,000,000 | $ 80,400 | $(10,800) |
| Others | 8% | 1,318,000 | $ 52,100,000,000 | – | – |

*Revenues and net income in thousands
Fidelity and Datek are privately held entities.
*Source:* "Industry Report," *Market Guide,* www.marketguide.com; annual reports and 10Ks of individual companies for the year 2000, www.freeedgar.com; *Market Research* (2000), www.infotechtrends.com.

Based in New York City, TD Waterhouse has operations in the United States, Canada, Australia, the United Kingdom, Hong Kong, and Australia. The company's primary markets are in Canada and the United States. TD Waterhouse has a worldwide global branch network that includes over 230 offices in Asia, Europe, and North America. TD Waterhouse is a provider of online investing and brokerage services. For the three months ending April 30, 2001, total revenues were $282 million, while net income totaled $6.5 million. TD Waterhouse is publicly traded on the New York Stock Exchange (NYSE) under the ticker of [TWE].

Located in Omaha, Nebraska, Ameritrade provides online brokerage services, an Internet-based personal financial management service, touch-tone telephone and market data, and research tools. For the month ended June 30, 2001, revenue was $120 million, and net income totaled $1 million. Ameritrade had plans to engage in an aggressive advertising and marketing campaign in 2001; however, the campaign is currently on hold. The campaign was intended to establish Ameritrade as the dominant brand in online trading. Ameritrade is publicly traded on the (NASDAQ) under the ticker [AMTD].

A comparison of commissions for the leading online brokerage firms is provided in Exhibit 2.

## Industry Outlook

The online brokerage industry is facing a consolidation trend that continues into 2002. Revenues and trading are steadily declining, creating a very volatile competitive environment. The unstable economy has caused investors to significantly limit or entirely discontinue their trading activities. Limited trading activity has caused an industrywide decline in revenues and forced online brokerage firms to restructure and diversify their business models to increase efficiency and profitability. Restructuring efforts have triggered staff reductions for most competitors, including Charles Schwab (with a reduction of 3,400 employees), Harris Direct (with a 10 percent reduction), Ameritrade (with a reduction of 1,991 employees), TD Waterhouse (with a reduction of 600 employees), and E*Trade (with a reduction of 360 contract workers).

E*Trade purchased E*Trade Bank as part of the company's business strategy, and the venture has been successful, with approximately 25 percent of net revenues now

---

EXHIBIT 2    Commission Comparison of
             Leading Online Brokerage
             Firms

| Company | Commission per 1,000 Shares (2001) |
|---|---|
| Ameritrade | $8.00 |
| Datek | $10.00 |
| TD Waterhouse | $12.00 |
| Fidelity | $15.00 |
| E*Trade | $15.00 |
| HarrisDirect | $20.00 |
| Charles Schwab | $30.00 |

*Source: "Investment Brokerage Industry Report," Market Guide,*
**www.marketguide.com**.

---

coming from banking-related operations. E*Trade's diversification into banking makes the company less susceptible to stock market fluctuations.

The gross annual revenue for financial services in 2002 is projected to be $400 billion, and only 10 percent of the total will come from online offerings. As diversification and consolidation efforts intensify industrywide, the remaining $360 billion represents a financial opportunity for the online brokerage industry in the form of increased customer accounts.

Legislation passed in March 2000 allows securities firms, insurance companies, and banks more flexibility when it comes to affiliating under one holding company. E*Trade is restructuring, continuing global expansion, pursuing consolidation opportunities, and diversifying its products and services. A major threat to the online brokerage industry is large banking firms such as Citigroup, which could enter the online banking and investments business. These firms have very large revenue bases, strong brand awareness, and loyal customers who are already clients of the online brokerage business.

## INTERNAL FACTORS

### Organizational Structure

E*Trade has successfully completed sixteen acquisitions as part of the company's global expansion strategy, resulting in a top-heavy executive team. E*Trade made the decision in 2001 to restructure the organization, and as part of this effort, numerous senior-level job titles were changed to lower status positions. The pay levels of affected employees, however, remained the same. The number of vice presidents dropped from 170 to 85 and the number of business managers decreased from 600 to approximately 300. A large number of top managers resigned following the change, as indicated by an 11 percent decrease in employees, from 4,440 at the peak to 3,960 at the end of June 2001. The new structure improved efficiencies of the company and reduced human resource costs through attrition. The new organization structure is shown in Exhibit 3.

E*Trade ranks third in market share, third in number of customers' accounts, and third in revenue base among Internet brokerages. E*Trade has acquired E*Trade Bank, E*Trade Mortgage, and E*Trade Access, which provides ATM services.

**EXHIBIT 3     E*Trade's Organization Chart**

```
                    ┌─────────────────────────┐
                    │  Chairman of the Board  │
                    │ Chief Executive Officer │
                    └─────────────────────────┘
                                │
                    ┌─────────────────────────┐
                    │      President and      │
                    │ Chief Operating Officer │
                    └─────────────────────────┘
                                │
     ┌──────────────┬───────────┴────────────┬──────────────┐
┌──────────┐  ┌──────────┐         ┌──────────┐  ┌──────────┐
│ CTO and  │  │ CTO and  │         │ CTO and  │  │ CTO and  │
│ Managing │  │ Managing │         │ Managing │  │ Managing │
│Director, │  │Director, │         │Director, │  │Director, │
│ Europe,  │  │  North   │         │  Latin   │  │  Asia–   │
│ Africa,  │  │ America  │         │ America  │  │ Pacific  │
│Middle East│  │          │         │          │  │          │
└──────────┘  └──────────┘         └──────────┘  └──────────┘
```

*Source:* E*Trade's 2001 *Annual Report.*

## Financial Condition

E*Trade has separated its financial services into four major segments: domestic retail brokerage, banking, global and institutional, and asset gathering and other. The financial information for both domestic retail brokerage and asset gathering and other are aggregated by management to form three reportable segments. The domestic retail brokerage category is comprised of E*Trade Securities, which offers Internet domestic retail brokerage services.

The banking category consists of the activities of the E*Trade Bank, which include E*Trade Access, a network of 9,600 Automatic Teller Machines; E*Trade Mortgage; and E*Trade Zone service center, a brokerage and planning service center located in New York.

Global and Institutional consists of TIR Holdings Limited, a service center for institutional investors; and also VERSUS Technologies, Inc., which provides both retail and institutional services and international affiliates that provide service to nondomestic retail investors.

The asset gathering and other category includes the mutual funds operations, e-Investing, Business Solutions Group (BSG), the money management delivery service, and the activities and product offerings generated from corporate operations. This category is aggregated into the domestic retail brokerage and other section.

E*Trade has diversified the company's operations from conventional online brokerage activities to reduce the company's overall risk and to have the ability to generate revenues from more than one activity.

Exhibit 4 contains extrapolated financial information on the three reportable financial segments and reveals the effect the economy has taken on E*Trade's bottom line.

E*Trade operates in the United States and in international markets, and it established geographic regions in 2001 that include North America; Latin America; Asia-Pacific; and Europe, Africa, and the Middle East. Each region has a general manager, whose objective is to provide seamless, localized, and integrated services to existing worldwide markets.

# EXHIBIT 4    E*Trade's Financial Services Segment Report (in millions)

| | Domestic Retail Brokerage & Other | Banking | Global and Institutional | Total |
|---|---|---|---|---|
| **Three Months Ended June 30, 2001:** | | | | |
| Interest income—net of interest expense | $   51,920 | $   38,286 | $   2,133 | $   92,339 |
| Noninterest revenue—net of provision for loan losses | 138,185 | 40,576 | 37,079 | 215,840 |
| Net revenues | $  190,105 | $   78,862 | $  39,212 | $  308,179 |
| Operating income (loss) | $(4,369) | $   22,373 | $ (10,547) | $7,457 |
| **Three Months Ended June 30, 2000:** | | | | |
| Interest income—net of interest expense | 59,192 | 32,395 | 1,963 | 93,550 |
| Noninterest revenue—net of provision for loan losses | 195,429 | 6,193 | 43,124 | 244,746 |
| Net revenues | $  254,621 | $   38,588 | $  45,087 | $  338,296 |
| Operating income (loss) | $   1,511 | $   3,365 | $  (6,507) | $   (1,631) |
| **Six Months Ended June 30, 2001:** | | | | |
| Interest income—net of interest expense | $  111,568 | $   74,605 | $   4,495 | $  190,668 |
| Noninterest revenue—net of provision for loan losses | 296,879 | 75,870 | 74,343 | 447,092 |
| Net revenues | $  408,447 | $  150,475 | $  78,838 | $  637,760 |
| Operating income (loss) | $  (12,550) | $   46,833 | $ (23,900) | $   10,383 |
| **Six Months Ended June 30, 2000:** | | | | |
| Interest income—net of interest expense | $  125,577 | $   61,699 | $   3,247 | $  190,523 |
| Noninterest revenue—net of provision for loan losses | 464,509 | 5,621 | 94,343 | 564,473 |
| Net revenues | $  590,086 | $   67,320 | $  97,590 | $  754,996 |
| Operating loss | $  (14,518) | $   (5,109) | $  (7,270) | $  (26,897) |
| **As of June 30, 2001:** | | | | |
| Segment assets | $6,184,821 | $12,690,075 | $425,275 | $19,300,171 |
| **As of September 30, 2000:** | | | | |
| Segment assets | $7,805,843 | $ 9,027,185 | $484,409 | $17,317,437 |

No single customer accounted for more than 10% of total revenues in the three and six months ended June 30, 2001, or 2000, respectively.
*Source:* "Security and Exchange Commission E*Trade *Quarterly Report* for the quarter ended June 30, 2001."

E*Trade's revenues increased 241 percent in 2001. E*Trade reported a net loss for 2001 of $241.5 million. Consolidated financial statements for E*Trade are listed as Exhibit 5 and Exhibit 6.

E*Trade had no debt until year 2000; but it obtained a term loan in 2001 of $17.2 million, and it renewed a $50 million line of credit that had no outstanding balance as of June 30, 2001. E*Trade repurchased 2.2 percent of the company's outstanding stock, or

# EXHIBIT 5    E*Trade's Annual Income Statements

| In Millions of U.S. Dollars (except for per share items) | 12 Months Ending 12/31/01 | 3 Months Ending 12/31/00 | 12 Months Ending 09/30/00 |
|---|---|---|---|
| Revenue | 1,891.2 | 536.3 | 1,865.5 |
| Other Revenue | 170.9 | 32.7 | 107.7 |
| **Total Revenue** | **2,062.1** | **569.0** | **1,973.2** |
| Cost of Revenue | 1,382.3 | 368.5 | 1,120.4 |
| **Gross Profit** | **508.8** | **167.8** | **745.1** |
| Selling/General/Administrative Expenses | 489.8 | 155.8 | 731.0 |
| Research & Development | 88.7 | 29.2 | 142.9 |
| Depreciation/Amortization | 43.1 | 7.8 | 22.8 |
| Interest Expense (Income), Net Operating | – | – | – |
| Unusual Expense (Income) | 244.1 | 0.8 | 36.4 |
| Other Operating Expenses | – | – | – |
| **Total Operating Expense** | **2,248.1** | **562.1** | **2,053.5** |
| **Operating Income** | **(186.0)** | **6.9** | **(80.3)** |
| Interest Expense, Net Non-Operating | (52.9) | (11.2) | (29.5) |
| Interest/Investment Income, Non-Operating | 22.2 | 7.1 | 17.2 |
| Interest Income (Expense), Net Non-Operating | (30.7) | (4.2) | (12.3) |
| Gain (Loss) on Sale of Assets | (56.0) | 3.5 | 199.6 |
| Other, Net | (37.6) | (3.1) | (2.5) |
| **Income Before Tax** | **(310.3)** | **3.2** | **104.4** |
| Income Tax | (39.9) | 1.9 | 85.5 |
| **Income After Tax** | **(270.3)** | **1.3** | **19.0** |
| Minority Interest | (0.5) | 0.1 | 0.2 |
| Equity In Affiliates | – | – | – |
| **Net Income Before Extra. Items** | **(270.8)** | **1.4** | **19.2** |
| Accounting Change | 0.0 | (0.1) | – |
| Discontinued Operations | – | – | – |
| Extraordinary Item | 29.3 | – | – |
| **Net Income** | **(241.5)** | **1.4** | **19.2** |
| Preferred Dividends | – | – | 0.0 |
| **Income Available to Common Excl. Extra. Items** | **(270.8)** | **1.4** | **19.2** |
| **Income Available to Common Incl. Extra. Items** | **(241.5)** | **1.4** | **19.2** |
| Basic/Primary Weighted Average Shares | 332.4 | 311.4 | 301.9 |
| **Basic/Primary EPS Excl. Extra. Items** | **(0.815)** | **0.005** | **0.063** |
| **Basic/Primary EPS Incl. Extra. Items** | **(0.727)** | **0.004** | **0.063** |
| Dilution Adjustment | 0.0 | 0.0 | 0.0 |
| Diluted Weighted Average Shares | 332.4 | 321.4 | 319.3 |
| **Diluted EPS Excl. Extra. Items** | **(0.815)** | **0.004** | **0.060** |
| **Diluted EPS Incl. Extra. Items** | **(0.727)** | **0.004** | **0.060** |
| Dividends per Share – Common Stock | 0.000 | 0.000 | 0.000 |
| Gross Dividens – Common Stock | 0.0 | 0.0 | 0.0 |
| Stock Based Compensation | – | – | 128.1 |
| Pro Forma Net Income | – | – | (108.9) |
| Pro Forma Basic EPS | – | – | (0.360) |
| Pro Forma Diluted EPS | – | – | (0.360) |
| Depreciation/Amortization, Supplemental | 52.9 | 11.2 | 29.5 |
| Total Special Items | 343.2 | 5.1 | (140.4) |
| **Normalized Income Before Tax** | **33.0** | **8.3** | **(36.0)** |
| Effect of Special Charge on Income Taxes | 0.0 | 3.0 | 0.0 |
| Income Taxes Excl. Impact of Special Items | (39.9) | 4.9 | 85.5 |
| **Normalized Income** | **72.9** | **3.4** | **(121.5)** |
| **Normalized Income Available to Common** | **72.4** | **3.5** | **(121.3)** |
| Basic Normalized EPS | 0.218 | 0.011 | (0.402) |
| Diluted Normalized EPS | 0.218 | 0.011 | (0.380) |

*Source:* http://www.investor.stockpoint.com.

## EXHIBIT 6    E*Trade's Annual Balance Sheet

| *In Millions of U.S. Dollars*<br>*(except for per share items)* | *As of 12/31/01* | *As of 12/31/00* | *As of 09/30/00* |
|---|---|---|---|
| Cash & Equivalents | 1,600.9 | 592.7 | 301.3 |
| Short Term Investments | – | – | – |
| Cash and Short Term Investments | 1,600.9 | 592.7 | 301.3 |
| Trade Accounts Receivable, Net | – | – | – |
| Other Receivables | 2,119.8 | 4,639.1 | 6,542.5 |
| Total Receivables, Net | 2,119.8 | 4,639.1 | 6,542.5 |
| Total Inventory | – | – | – |
| Prepaid Expenses | – | – | – |
| Other Current Assets | – | – | – |
| **Total Current Assets** | – | – | – |
| Property/Plant/Equipment—Gross | – | – | – |
| Accumulated Depreciation | – | – | (135.4) |
| Property/Plant/Equipment, Net | 331.7 | 368.4 | 334.3 |
| Goodwill, Net | 684.4 | 442.0 | 484.2 |
| Intangibles, Net | – | – | – |
| Long Term Investments | 4,725.2 | 6,151.8 | 5,173.8 |
| Other Long Term Assets | – | – | – |
| **Total Assets** | 18,205.9 | 17,741.1 | 17,317.4 |
| Accounts Payable | – | – | – |
| Accrued Expenses | – | – | – |
| Notes Payable/Short Term Debt | – | – | – |
| Current Port. LT Debt/Capital Leases | 760.3 | 650.0 | 650.0 |
| Other Current Liabilities | 2,606.1 | 4,226.1 | 6,055.5 |
| **Total Current Liabilities** | – | – | – |
| Long Term Debt | – | – | – |
| Capital Lease Obligations | – | – | – |
| **Total Long Term Debt** | – | – | – |
| **Total Debt** | 760.3 | 650.0 | 650.0 |
| Deferred Income Tax | – | – | – |
| Minority Interest | – | – | – |
| Other Liabilities | 12,322.8 | 10,410.3 | 8,283.4 |
| **Total Liabilities** | 16,627.2 | 15,995.1 | 15,460.6 |
| Redeemable Preferred Stock | – | – | – |
| Preferred Stock—Non Redeemable, Net | – | – | – |
| Common Stock | 3.5 | 3.1 | 3.1 |
| Additional Paid-In Capital | 2,072.7 | 1,827.4 | 1,814.6 |
| Retained Earnings (Accum. Deficit) | (247.1) | (5.6) | (6.9) |
| Treasury Stock—Common | – | – | – |
| Other Equity | (250.3) | (77.5) | 47.6 |
| **Total Equity** | 1,578.8 | 1,746.0 | 1,856.8 |
| **Total Liability & Shareholders' Equity** | 18,205.9 | 17,741.1 | 17,317.4 |
| Shares Outs.—Common Stock | 347.6 | 308.2 | 304.5 |
| **Total Common Shares Outstanding** | 347.6 | 308.2 | 304.5 |
| **Total Preferred Stock Shares Outs.** | – | – | – |
| Employees (actual figures) | – | – | 3,778.0 |
| Number of Common Shareholders (actual figures) | | | 2,118.0 |

*Source:* http://www.investor.stockpoint.com.

7.19 million shares of common stock, for $5.45 per share on August 20, 2001. Chairman and CEO Cotsakos personally purchased an additional two million shares on the same terms as the company. The strategic move was to increase the stock price and to restore confidence in the company's stock.

The key performance indicators used by E*Trade to measure financial performance are the increase or percentage change in new and active domestic brokerage accounts, new and active banking accounts, and new and active global and institutional accounts. Other key indicators are the cost per new account and the number of total domestic brokerage transactions, customer households, and assets in customer accounts. Instability and volatility of the market resulted in a drastic decrease of 78 percent in new domestic brokerage accounts, 21 percent in banking accounts, and 40 percent in global and institutional accounts as of June 30, 2000, when compared to the same period in June 30, 2001. Total new accounts also decreased by 71 percent, resulting in a 22 percent increase in the cost per new account during the same period.

As indicated in Exhibit 7, the decline in the number of new accounts resulted in a 38 percent decrease in domestic brokerage transactions from June 30, 2000, to June 30, 2001. The average commission per domestic brokerage transaction for new accounts also decreased, from $15.55 to $13.44, or 14 percent, primarily due to the severe decline in the value of publicly traded securities being held by E*Trade.

### EXHIBIT 7    E*Trade's Key Performance Indicators (Customer Accounts and Assets)

| | Three Months Ended June 30, | | | Six Months Ended June 30, | | |
| --- | --- | --- | --- | --- | --- | --- |
| | *2001* | *2000* | *Percentage Change* | *2001* | *2000* | *Percentage Change* |
| Net new domestic brokerage accounts | 65,610 | 270,708 | (76)% | 176,646 | 817,881 | (78)% |
| Net new banking accounts | 30,039 | 51,998 | (42)% | 72,187 | 91,947 | (21)% |
| Net new global and institutional accounts | 7,840 | 10,854 | (28)% | 20,768 | 34,413 | (40)% |
| Total net new accounts | 103,489 | 333,560 | (69)% | 269,601 | 944,241 | (71)% |
| Cost per new account | $232 | $291 | (20)% | $328 | $269 | 22% |
| Total domestic brokerage transactions | 7,148,235 | 10,491,288 | (32)% | 15,233,084 | 24,733,340 | (38)% |
| Daily average domestic brokerage transactions | 113,464 | 166,528 | (32)% | 121,865 | 196,296 | (38)% |
| Average commission per domestic brokerage transaction | $13.23 | $15.13 | (13)% | $13.44 | $15.55 | (14)% |
| Rebate income per domestic brokerage transaction | $2.06 | $1.79 | 15% | $2.36 | $1.92 | 23% |

| | *June 30, 2001* | *September 30, 2000* | *Percentage Change* |
| --- | --- | --- | --- |
| Active domestic brokerage accounts | 3,289,014 | 2,951,946 | 11% |
| Active banking accounts | 434,804 | 288,073 | 51% |
| Active global and institutional accounts | 104,792 | 75,416 | 39% |
| Total active accounts at period end | 3,828,610 | 3,315,435 | 15% |
| Total customer households end of period | 2,738,838 | Not Available | N/A |
| Average assets per household | $19,513 | Not Available | N/A |
| Total assets in domestic brokerage accounts | $44,553,710 | $59,901,277 | (26)% |
| Total deposits in banking accounts | 7,687,006 | 4,630,068 | 66% |
| Total assets in global and institutional accounts | 1,202,718 | 1,348,672 | (11)% |
| Total assets/deposits in customer accounts at period end | $53,443,434 | $65,880,017 | (19)% |

*Source:* Security and Exchange Commission E*Trade *Quarterly Report* for the quarter ended June 30, 2001.

E*Trade's total active accounts increased 15 percent, from September 30, 2000, to June 30, 2001, mainly from banking and global and institutional accounts, with an increase of 51 percent and 39 percent, respectively.

As a result of the declining number of customer accounts and the declining values of securities held by E*Trade, the company reported a net loss of $19.4 million on June 30, 2001.

### Marketing

E*Trade's marketing expenditures decreased 50 percent in the six months ending June 30, 2001. The expenditures primarily supported the cost of selling products in both the global and institutional business as well as the asset gathering and other segments. E*Trade has been cross-selling banking services to its active brokerage customers in an effort to use marketing resources more effectively. E*Trade made substantial investments in marketing efforts during the 2000 fiscal year to build a strong brand identity, and the company feels the decreased marketing expenditures will not significantly affect the company's competitive position during the economic downturn.

The marketing strategy for fiscal year 2002 is to focus on cross-selling the existing customer base to generate new banking and brokerage accounts, to sustain the existing accounts, to develop current customer households, and to review statistics, such as assets per household. The major thrust of the marketing campaign is to focus on the banking segment in order to capture a significant percentage of the projected growth in online banking.

Banking was the only segment that reported an increase in net revenues—123 percent—from June 30, 2000, to June 30, 2001. A report by Robertson Stephens Investment Bank predicted that the number of households banking online will be over 96.3 million by the year ending 2003, representing an annual growth rate of over 66 percent.

E*Trade has developed marketing partnership agreements with Delta Airlines, United Airlines, Northwest Airlines, and Trans World Airlines that allows E*Trade customers, who are also airline skymile members, to earn up to fifty thousand bonus miles each year by investing using E*Trade's online Web site. The bonus miles for the airline agreements are to be awarded based on the individual's investments. The bonus mile incentive is a tiered system and is based on the amount of an investment, ranging from a $1,000 deposit to a $50,000 deposit. E*Trade also has in place a marketing agreement with Marriott International and Hilton Hotels for similar bonus programs.

In the first six months of 2001, E*Trade acquired LoansDirect, Inc., an online mortgage originator, and WebStreet, Inc., an online brokerage firm. Also, E*Trade launched E*Trade Hong Kong and E*Trade Israel, and it opened E*Trade Center, a financial service superstore located in New York City that is designed to give consumers value-added financial services and educational content. Also in 2001, E*Trade extended an alliance with Target for twenty new E*Trade zones and over one thousand ATMs. E*Trade Mortgage was launched, and the company acquired fifteen thousand customer accounts in a transaction with Advanata National Bank, which has deposits valued at $389.7 million.

### CONCLUSION

E*Trade plans to continue its global expansion strategy of purchasing sites in the international market to grow its asset base. E*Trade should perhaps aggressively acquire smaller online brokerage companies during the economic downturn, which may be easy targets due to financial difficulties. Possible target companies include Ameritrade and Datek. Consolidation will add customer assets and accounts that can result in increased revenues. By purchasing smaller companies, E*Trade may ensure that the company maintains its rent among the top five major competitors. According to Jupiter Research, total online assets are predicated to grow from $1.5 trillion today to $5.4 trillion by 2005. This growth will be targeted by E*Trade through marketing and advertising campaigns as market conditions improve.

## REFERENCES

Ameritrade Inc., *Annual Report and 10K* (2000). www.freeedgar.com.

"Attack on America: Update on the Fallout in the U.S. Economy" (September 25, 2001). www.economy.com.

Charles Schwab, Inc., *Annual Report and 10K* (2000). www.freeedgar.com.

Datek Inc., *Annual Report and 10K* (2000). www.freeedgar.com.

DLJ Direct Inc., *Annual Report and 10K* (2000). www.freeedgar.com.

E*Trade Group Inc., *Annual Report and 10K* (2000). www.etrade.com.

Fidelity Inc., *Annual Report and 10K* (2000). www.freeedgar.com.

*Forbes* (October 1, 2001).

"Investment Brokerage Industry Report," *Market Guide*. www.marketguide.com.

"Market Research (2000)." www.infotrends.com.

*Security and Exchange Commission E*Trade 2001 Quarterly Filing*. www.hoovers.com.

"Reviews; Today in Reviews, Top of the Charts, The Week in Reviews" (September 21, 2001). www.pcworld.com.

"Scoreboard" (2001). www.Gomez.com.

TD Waterhouse Inc., *Annual Report and 10K* (2000). www.freeedgar.com.

*The Wall Street Journal* (October 2001).

# EBAY—2002

**Will Eskridge**
**Francis Marion University**

## EBAY

www.ebay.com

It is yearend 2001, and we are in the midst of a recession. The Gross Domestic Product for the third quarter shrank 1.1 percent, our first quarter of negative growth in ten years. The figure was negative again in the fourth quarter as well as the first quarter of 2002. Daily news headlines report job cuts and layoffs affecting virtually every industry. Since March 2001, the nation's workforce has shrunk by 887,000 jobs, or about 0.7 percent. The Dow Jones Industrial Average is down over 20 percent for the year to date, while the NASDAQ is down over 30 percent for the same period. The once golden tech sector, responsible for driving the stock market to heights never before seen, has not stumbled, but fallen. The irrational exuberance fueling the stock market in the 1998–1999 period has disappeared, and in its wake we find four-year-old companies, which, once upon a time, had valuations greater than bellweather companies like General Electric, but which are now wondering if they will survive. Not long ago, adding "dot-com" to the end of a corporate name and going public could turn people into multimillionaires overnight. Companies with little more than a plan and a dream were commanding some of the highest valuations on Wall Street. Today, those valuations seem like dreams, as investors are no longer willing to gamble on potential but instead are seeking companies making profits.

Nearly 1,000 Internet companies folded in 2000 and 2001. Companies such as Etoys and Pets.com no longer exist, while the vast majority of Internet companies have yet to make any profits. Amazon.com, arguably the most well-known company on the Internet, has yet to make a steady profit and has seen its market valuation decline from an unbelievably high $39 billion in December 1999 to $4.1 billion in November 2001.

The outlook for a recovery in the tech sector anytime soon seems bleak at best, and while most other dot-com companies continue to struggle, as one of the few Internet companies to make a profit, eBay seems to be the silver lining in a dark cloud. eBay owns and operates eBay.com, which, based upon the aggregate value of goods traded, is the world's largest and most popular online marketplace. eBay was the first company to bring the sale of goods via auction to the Internet, and it has proven to be a match made in new-economy heaven. eBay has established an Internet-based community of buyers and sellers who get together in an auction format to buy and sell items ranging from antiques, electronics, and collectibles to cars, boats, and real estate. Because the service is completely automated, it operates twenty-four hours a day, seven days a week.

## HISTORY

The eBay service was begun in September 1995 by Pierre Omidyar. Born in France and raised in the United States, Omidyar moved to the West Coast after graduating from college as a computer programmer. The business was started in his apartment as a means for his then-girlfriend, an avid Pez dispenser collector, to contact others who shared her interest in Pez dispensers. She complained that she found it difficult to find others who were willing to buy or sell. Omidyar's creation allowed her and other individuals to use the Internet for their Pez trading needs.

In the beginning, the original site, called Auction Web, made no promises or guarantees. Individuals logged on and bid for items, and the transactions occurred. At that time, there were no fees, no registrations, no security, few items, and little business—that is, until Omidyar made one very positive marketing decision. He listed his trading site on the National Center for Supercomputing Applications' What's Cool list—and the rest is history. After the listing was posted, business started to pick up, and in March 1996 the business turned a profit.

The business continued to grow, and in 1998 the company, now renamed eBay, went public. At the end of 1999, eBay had 10 million registered users, and by the end of 2000 the number had increased 125 percent to 22 million. During this expansion, the eBay community has become more diverse than ever, featuring homemakers, major corporations, and everyone in between. Users listed more than 265 million items on the site in 2000, up 104 percent from 1999. For 2001, eBay's revenues increased 74 percent to $748 million while their net income increased 87 percent to $90.5 million.

## HOW IT WORKS

Anyone can visit eBay and browse through the items listed for sale. However, if you wish to bid on items or list items for sale, you must register. The registration process is simple and quick: It takes less then five minutes, and once registered, you can immediately bid on or list items for sale. All buyers and sellers must be eighteen to bid on or list items.

Once registered, bidders can immediately search for specific items by category (there are generally more than eight thousand), and then they can click on individual items for detailed descriptions. The entire database can be queried by entering keywords that describe a desired item. eBay's search engine will locate all relevant items for sale and link the bidder to detailed descriptions. Each auction has a unique identifier that allows bidders to easily locate specific items.

eBay also provides highlights that alert bidders to certain types of auctions. For example, auctions that have started within the last twenty-four hours are highlighted with "New Today"; auctions that are ending on that day are highlighted with "Ending Today"; and those ending within three hours are highlighted under "Going Going Gone."

When the bidding on a particular auction has expired, eBay will determine if a bid exceeds the minimum asking price and the reserve price, if a reserve has been set. A seller can set a reserve price, the minimum that the seller will accept, which is usually higher than the minimum asking price. eBay will then notify both buyer and seller via e-mail, and the buyer and seller consummate the transaction independently of eBay. The buyer and seller agree upon and arrange for shipment and payment. eBay has no power to force the buyer and seller to complete the transaction, but it can ban either or both offending parties from trading on eBay in the future.

## VISION AND MISSION

eBay has no formal vision; however, the company states its mission as follows: "eBay's mission is to help practically anyone trade practically anything on earth."

The eBay mission statement obviously does not encompass the desirable characteristics of a corporate mission, and, as such, eBay should develop an appropriate formal mission statement. It could use its existing mission statement as a basis for its vision statement.

### Proposed eBay Mission Statement

eBay's mission is to be the world's most utilized and most profitable trading post. Hiring bright and talented employees who are dedicated to serving their customers and communities, eBay will provide the most technologically advanced, reliable, and secure trading platform available to individuals, business, and governments, while always striving to stay ahead of our competition.

As indicated in Exhibit 1, eBay appears to be functional in structure, which has worked very well thus far. Many companies are initially structured functionally, but if they experience any significant growth—and eBay certainly has—they outgrow this form of corporate structure. As eBay continues its massive global expansion, it is very possible it will need to restructure itself, possibly by geographic divisions.

## REVENUE

There is no charge for buyers to shop on eBay. Bidding is free, and revenue is derived from fees that sellers are charged for listing and selling items. Sellers pay a small placement fee to list items for sale, and placement fee rates are as follows:

- Insertion fees for regular, Reserve Price, and Dutch Auction listings.

| Minimum Bid, Opening Value, or Reserve Price | Insertion Fee |
| --- | --- |
| $0.01–$9.99 | $0.30 |
| $10.00–$24.99 | $0.55 |
| $25.00–$49.99 | $1.10 |
| $50.00–199.99 | $2.20 |
| $200.00 and up | $3.30 |

EXHIBIT 1    Corporate Structure

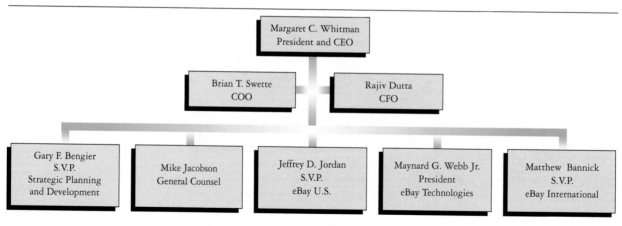

- Insertion fees for vehicles on eBay Motors:

| Item Category | Insertion Fee |
|---|---|
| Vehicles (Cars, Motorcycles, Other Vehicles) | $25.00 For a breakdown of all eBay Motors fees please *click here*. |

- Insertion fees for items covered by the Non-Binding Bid policy:

| Item Category | Insertion Fee |
|---|---|
| Real Estate | $50.00 Real Estate may be listed for an extended period (30 days) for an additional fixed fee of $50.00. |

- Additional Reserve Price Auction fee (**fully refunded if item sells**):

| Reserve Price | Reserve Price Auction Fee |
|---|---|
| $0.01–$24.99 | $0.50 |
| $25.00 and up | $1.00 |

Additional revenue from listings can come in a variety of ways. eBay offers sellers many ways to enhance their listings to attract bidders. Sellers can feature their auctions by paying additional incremental fees for various highlights. Available highlights and fee schedule are as follows:

| Fee | Highlight |
|---|---|
| $.10 | 10 day auction listing (longest time available) |
| $.25 | Sellers can have photos placed in the Gallery section |
| $2.00 | Bold font for heading |
| $5.00 | Highlight—eye-catching yellow band |
| $14.95 | Featured plus, featured within an eBay category |
| $19.95 | Feature the item in the Gallery section |
| $99.95 | "Featured auction," which allows the item to be rotated on the eBay homepage |

Finally, the seller pays eBay a commission if the seller is successful in selling his/her item(s). At the time of notification of a winning bid, eBay charges the seller a final value fee. Final value fees are shown below.

| Success Fee | Purchase Price |
|---|---|
| 5% | First $25.00 of the purchase price |
| 2.5% | Portion of the purchase price from $25.01 to $1,000.00 |
| 1.25% | Portion of the purchase price over $1,000.00 |
| $25.00 | Per vehicle |
| No Fee | Real Estate |

In the event that buyer and seller cannot complete the transaction, the seller can notify eBay to credit the fee. All invoices for placement fees, highlight fees, and successful selling fees are sent to sellers via e-mail on a monthly basis. Many sellers maintain a credit with eBay, and the account is charged shortly after an invoice is sent. At no time does eBay take possession of the merchandise or hold the receivable for the item. In contract to other Internet sites, the company does not enjoy revenue from advertisements. eBay sells no ad space on its site.

## THE EBAY COMMUNITY

In providing a place for trading of various items, eBay attempts to foster a sense of community among its users. CEO and President Whitman has stated that eBay began with commerce but quickly grew into a very large community. eBay users believe that this sense of community is what separates it from other Internet auction and retail sites, and eBay invests heavily in the programs that make users feel that their transactions and information are safe from Internet thieves and fraudulent users.

One method used to establish the reputations of users is eBay's Feedback Forum, which encourages users to record comments, both favorable and unfavorable, about the trading partners. All this feedback information is recorded and creates a feedback rating for a specific person. Naturally, too many negative comments will likely cause users to avoid transactions with the individual in question.

eBay users with favorable reputations will have a star next to their user identifications. This star is color-coded and indicates the amount of positive versus negative feedback that the user has received. Users may review a person's feedback profile prior to doing business with that person.

The Feedback Forum is a self-regulating system: The users police themselves. However, some users may be tempted to manipulate the system in order to discredit other users or to enhance their own reputations. eBay has several policies in place to prevent this, and the system has several automated features in place to detect and to prevent various forms of abuse.

Dealing with unknown individuals over the Internet can be a cause for concern for some and may cause many others to shy away from eBay. In order to ease user's fears, eBay has instituted what is called its Safe Harbor program, which provides trading guidelines and rules, provides information to help resolve disputes among users, and addresses and responds to misuse of the eBay system. Safe Harbor is composed of approximately twenty-eight individuals, a group that includes regular eBay employees and contract employees. These individuals investigate possible misuse of the system and will take appropriate action, which may include suspension from buying or selling on the site. Safe Harbor provides users with information to assist both with disputes over the quality of goods and with possible fraudulent activities. If fraudulent activities occur, eBay will usually suspend the offending party or parties from further eBay activity.

Because community plays such an important part in the eBay experience, the company has focused resources on its efforts to establish a community experience. The company believes that the eBay community is one of the strongest on the Internet. eBay offers a wide array of features that support the community, and these features solidify the eBay community and ensure its continued growth and loyalty. The company uses e-mail to provide users with category-specific chatrooms, the eBay café (a chatroom for the entire community), a bulletin board for feedback on new features, and announcements that cover new features and eBay news. Customer-support bulletin boards and an "items wanted" listing where users can post their requests for specific items are also provided.

Also available is *My eBay*, which gives users a report on recent activity. Users who have their own Web pages can post links to their homepage, and those without a Web site can use *About Me* to create a homepage free of charge.

The company also offers an insurance program for users. To qualify, a user must be a buyer in good standing or a seller with a Feedback Rating of zero or above. The insurance program provides coverage on qualified transactions if a winning bidder sends money to a seller and either does not receive the item or does not receive the item described on the site.

In June 1998, eBay donated 643,500 shares of common stock and established a fund called the eBay Foundation. eBay solicits input from users for worthwhile charities. Other unique promotions are held to support worthwhile causes. After the September 11 terrorist attacks, eBay started the Auction for America; items are donated by sellers to this site and eBay charges no fees, and the proceeds then go to the families of the victims. Examples of items donated are a Harley Davidson motorcycle signed by numerous celebrities who visited the *Tonight Show*. Also of interest was a U.S. flag signed by all the members of Congress; it is believed to be the first such mass signing since the time of the signing of the Declaration of Independence.

## CUSTOMER SUPPORT

eBay devotes significant resources to providing personalized, timely customer service and support. eBay offers customer support on a seven-days-a-week basis. Most customer support inquiries are handled via e-mail, with customer e-mail inquiries typically being answered within twenty-four hours after submission. In 2000, eBay continued its relationship with SatMetrix (formerly known as Customer Cast), an online customer satisfaction survey company, to help eBay understand and improve overall customer support. Overall customer satisfaction with eBay's support services has remained extremely high. eBay also offers an online tutorial for new eBay users. In 2000, eBay completed the relocation of all customer support personnel to its center in Salt Lake City, Utah.

## MARKETING

Historically, eBay relied on word of mouth to promote its Web site and occasionally has utilized links and sponsorships with other Web sites. Today, eBay employs a variety of methods to promote its brand and to attract potential buyers and sellers. Currently, eBay uses strategic purchases of online advertising to place advertisements in areas in which eBay believes it can reach its target audience. eBay also engages in a number of marketing activities in traditional media such as radio, broadcast as well as national and local TV advertising, print media, trade shows, and other events.

In March 1999, eBay expanded the scope of its preexisting strategic relationship with AOL. Under the amended agreement, eBay is given a prominent presence, featuring it as the preferred provider of online trading services on AOL's proprietary services (both domestic and international), including AOL.com, Digital Cities, ICQ, CompuServe (both domestic and international), and Netscape. eBay will pay $75 million over the four-year term of the contract. eBay has developed a co-branded version of its service for each AOL property, which prominently features each party's brand. AOL is entitled to all advertising revenue from the co-branded sites. The company also uses its site for brand advertising by offering a variety of eBay-branded merchandise that can be purchased through it's own online store, eBay Store.

## OPERATIONS PLATFORM

The eBay site operates on a software platform that was developed internally. This platform handles all aspects of the trading cycle, including e-mail notifications of when a bid is successful and when a bidder is outbid. The system sends daily reports to all active sellers and bidders on the status of eBay's auctions. In addition, the system also stores registration information, billing information, and credit card information for traders who use an open account balance. The software system is also the platform for all eBay chatroom and bulletin board information.

With the exception of once-a-week maintenance that takes a few hours, the system operates twenty-four hours a day, seven days a week. The eBay platform consists of Sun database servers running Oracle relational database management software. The company uses an outside load balancing system and has its own servers as back-up to reduce faults and outages. Outages do occasionally occur and are caused by a number of factors, including problems resulting from third party hardware and from software providers. eBay uses Resonate Inc.'s load balancing systems and its own redundant servers to provide for fault tolerance. The company's systems are vulnerable to attack from unauthorized persons.

The use rate of the eBay site has increased substantially during the last few years, and in fact, the increase has been not linear but exponential. As a result, the company is constantly adding to its infrastructure of software, hardware, and engineers. Because the entire eBay system operates on this platform, integrity and uptime are of the utmost importance. Any unscheduled or unanticipated downtime could severely harm current revenues and cause a ripple effect that could make users switch to competitive sites and thus affect long-term revenue.

## GROWTH

Growth as measured by several factors has increased exponentially over the past three years. As measured by registered users, merchandise sales, number of items listed, number of log-ons, and number of minutes on the site per user, the company is one of the most popular sites on the Web. By all measures, eBay is one of the most active and widely visited Internet sites. For the month of September 2001, eBay was the eighth most visited site on the Web, and the time spent per person on the site (1:45:05) is the most of any Web site—it is seven times higher than time spent on rival site Amazon (0:15:12).[1]

The following table shows the growth of registered users.

| Year | Number of Registered Users |
| --- | --- |
| 1996 | 41,000 |
| 1999 | 2.1 million |
| 2000 | 22 million |
| 2001 | 42.4 million |

Gross merchandise sales—that is, the dollar value of transactions between buyers and sellers—has increased from $5.4 billion in 2000 to $9.3 billion in 2001.

The number of items listed as available for bidding on the eBay site grew from 264.7 million in 2000 to 423.1 million in 2001. Gross revenue, gross profits, and net income all increased substantially from 2000 to 2001. Revenues have increased for twenty-eight consecutive quarters and have grown from $431.4 million in 2000 to $748.8 million in 2001. Gross profits have increased from $335.9 in 2000 to $614.0 million in 2001, while net income grew from $48.2 million at the end in 2000 to $90.4 million in 2001.

eBay is one of the few Internet companies to return a profit. Each year since eBay's IPO, it has experienced phenomenal growth in its sales, gross profits, and net profits. As a result, cash, working capital, total assets, and total stockholders' equity have all increased substantially. Acting as a facilitator and broker for individual traders keeps the company's business model a very profitable one.

## COMPETITION

The Internet has emerged as a global medium enabling millions of people worldwide to share information and to communicate and conduct electronic commerce transactions. According to Nua Internet Surveys, as of November 2000, more than 400 million people worldwide had access to the Internet either at home or at work. And according to Forrester Research, the total value of global e-commerce transactions in 2001 exceeded $1.2 trillion, up from approximately $657 billion in 2000.

Depending on the category of product, eBay currently or potentially competes with a number of companies serving particular categories of goods as well as those serving broader ranges of goods. The Internet is a new, rapidly evolving and intensely competitive area. eBay expects competition to intensify in the future insofar as the barriers to entry are relatively low, and current and new competitors can launch new sites at a nominal cost using commercially available software. eBay's broad-based competitors include the vast majority of traditional department and general merchandise stores as well as emerging online retailers. They include most prominently Wal-Mart, Kmart, Target, Sears, Macy's, JCPenney, Costco, Sam's Clubs as well as Amazon.com, Buy.com, AOL.com, Yahoo!shopping, and the Microsoft Network.

At the present time, eBay dominates the online auction business, having trounced its competition. More than two-thirds of all online auction revenues go to eBay. Yahoo!, Microsoft, and Amazon.com have made high-profile attempts to gain footholds in the online auction business. However, with the current global recession, those companies have been forced to look for ways to cut costs and trim unprofitable operations; as a result, all three have taken steps away from the auction business and shifted their focus into other areas.

Yahoo! operates localized versions of its Web site in twenty-four countries and has offices in the Asia/Pacific region, Europe, Latin America, and North America. Once seen as the chief rival to eBay, Yahoo! saw its listings plummet in January 2000 after it initiated a listing fee. According to independent estimates, Yahoo!'s listings dropped from more than 2 million to about two hundred thousand. Yahoo!'s annual sales for the year 2000 were $1.11 billion, more than double that of eBay. Only a tiny fraction of Yahoo!'s sales can be attributed to its online auction services. Twelve-month revenue growth is a negative 15.6 percent, compared to eBay's positive 79.1 percent, and the net income growth is (100) percent vs. 132.60 percent, respectively. Yahoo!'s gross profit margin, 88.25 percent, is only 1.5 percent lower than eBay's; however, Yahoo! has a net profit margin of (21.67) percent, while eBay's is 13.33 percent. Yahoo!'s current market capitalization, $9.5 billion, is approximately half of eBay's, at $18.2 billion. It is rather ironic that a little more than a year and a half ago, Yahoo! was worth $100 billion or so, and it was targeting eBay as a possible acquisition. It opted instead to develop its own online auction business.

The Seattle-based Amazon.com, which was locked in a battle with eBay for the title of "King of e-Commerce," has been scaling back its efforts in light of current economic conditions and its lack of market penetration. Amazon has cut staff in its online auction department and no longer has a manager solely dedicated to running auctions. Amazon.com has customers in all fifty states and more than 150 countries, with distribution facilities in New Castle, Delaware; Coffeyville, Kansas; Campbellsville and Lexington, Kentucky; Fernley, Nevada; Grand Forks, North Dakota; and Seattle in the United States; as well as in France, Germany, and the United Kingdom. An examination of the financial comparisons shows that Amazon's annual sales for year 2000 were approximately $2.76 billion, which is about 6.4 times eBay's gross sales revenue. Amazon has a significantly lower gross margin, 28.75 percent, and its net margin is (37.15) percent; eBay's gross is 89.91 percent, and its net margin is 13.33 percent. Amazon's twelve month revenue growth of 20.80 percent is approximately one-fourth of eBay's 79.10 percent.

Microsoft has scaled back its efforts to tackle the online auction industry, deciding instead to partner with eBay. In March 2001, eBay and Microsoft agreed to an alliance that is intended to supercharge eBay's Application Program Interface (API), extending it to Microsoft's legions of developers worldwide. Microsoft will also integrate eBay's marketplace into a number of its Web properties, including select MSN sites worldwide, CarPoint, bCentral, and WebTV.

At the present time, no one denies that eBay is the undisputed king of the online auction business—and quite possibly the best performing company in e-commerce and all of technology. In 2000 and 2001, eBay branched out from its traditional auction format. With the acquisition of Half.com and its adoption of the "Buy it Now" slogan, eBay has moved into the fixed price arena, and it has done so with great success. These moves into fixed pricing will make competition from Amazon.com and Yahoo! shopping more relevant than ever before.

The principal competitive factors for eBay include its ability to attract buyers, the volume of its transactions and the selection of goods, customer service, and brand recognition. With respect to eBay's online competition, additional competitive factors are community cohesion and interaction, system reliability, the reliability of delivery and payment, Web site convenience and accessibility, level of service fees, and the quality of search tools. Some current and potential competitors have longer company operating histories, larger customer bases, greater brand recognition in other businesses, and Internet spaces than eBay does. Some of these competitors also have significantly greater financial, marketing, technical, and other resources. As a result, eBay constantly monitors the activities of all competitors and adjusts its services to counter competitive activity. While eBay's rivals have been retrenching, the company has been expanding its own operations and cementing its dominant status in auctions.

## INTERNET FRAUD

Current laws regarding liability issues for online service providers remain vague and are still evolving. Although eBay only provides the platform in which individuals trade their merchandise, the company realizes that it may face potential liability for certain user conduct on its site. eBay understands that items such as alcohol, tobacco, firearms, and adult material are subject to certain local, state, and federal guidelines. The company also understands that it may be unable to prevent unlawful activity on its site and may be subject to penalties for the conduct of some of its users.

The company realizes that Internet fraud can severely damage its community atmosphere. Users will quickly abandon a community that is rife with fraud and dishonesty, and eBay has taken steps to prevent fraud and unlawful activity by implementing certain checks and balances during the registration process. The Safe Harbor program, customer service department, and Feedback Forum have been put in place to foster the sense of community that eBay holds important to successful trading. eBay is counting on the community at large to hold fraudulent and illegal activity to a minimum.

According to eBay, fewer than thirty auctions per million generate a possible fraud complaint, but the company wants to lower the number of complaints and eliminate the potential for an unhappy experience. In response to fraud concerns, the company has established a simpler escrow system, new rules preventing sellers from bidding on their own items, tougher ID checks, penalties if bidders do not complete transactions, and free buyer's insurance. The company's reputation could be severely damaged or it could be held liable for any illegal or fraudulent activity that occurs on its Web site. Even if found innocent, eBay could find that the costs of litigation might cause financial harm.

## GOVERNMENT REGULATION

Because eBay does not take possession of any of the items that are sold on its site or hold any receivables for merchandise sold, the company does not collect sales taxes associated with the transactions. The individual seller must conduct any tax requirements resulting from transactions. At present, sellers are not likely to collect and administer sales taxes. In the future, federal, state, and local governments may force the issue of sales tax collection and require compensation for such taxes. At that time, because eBay provides the platform for operation, the government may press eBay into some type of assistant or administrative role. This could conceivably add costs to operations without adding revenues.

Today, very few laws govern Internet sales. However, because Internet commerce is becoming more popular, it is very likely that within a few years, laws will be enacted to address user contracts, privacy, price structures, freedom of expression, security, and other areas. Additional costs may result from compliance.

## LEGAL PROCEEDINGS

Other third parties have from time to time claimed and may claim in the future that eBay is infringing on their past, current, or future intellectual property rights. eBay may become more vulnerable to such claims as laws such as the Digital Millennium Copyright Act are interpreted by the courts. eBay expects that it will increasingly be subject to infringement claims as the number of services and direct competitors grow. These claims, whether meritorious or not, could be time-consuming, result in costly litigation, cause service upgrade delays, require expensive changes in its methods of doing business, or could require eBay to enter into costly royalty or licensing agreements, if available. As a result, these claims could harm the business.

## ACQUISITIONS AND IMPROVEMENTS

During 2000, a number of improvements to the eBay trading platform were introduced. It acquired Half.com, a fixed-price, person-to-person trading Web site, where buyers and sellers can trade used books, CDs, movies, and video games at fixed prices that are less than the list price. Also, the launch of eBay Motors, in association with AutoTrader.com, created the Internet's largest auction-style Web site where consumers and dealers could buy and sell used cars. Furthermore, the eBay regional sites and the API and Developers Program, which allows other companies to use eBay content to drive their own businesses, are both new. The API provides three basic benefits. First, it allows eBay to be fully integrated into independent sites across the Internet. A new site will be able to use the eBay commerce engine to power its business, eliminating time and expense from the startup process. As a second benefit, the API will allow eBay and its commercial partners to more easily and rapidly add eBay's services to new devices, such as wireless telephones and handheld computers. Finally, the new platform interface will improve the user experience by allowing more companies to provide services to eBay users. The launch of electronic checks as a new payment option provides buyers and sellers with a means for faster transactions without returned checks, with no paperwork, and no charge-back risk. For eBay buyers, electronic checks combines the convenience of paper checks with the safety, convenience, and speed of electronic payments. For eBay sellers, electronic checks is a cost-effective alternative to paper checks and credit cards, in which payment is guaranteed. The launch of eBay Anywhere, a comprehensive mobile strategy, makes eBay accessible from any Internet-enabled mobile device. From WAP mobile phones to the latest PDAs, eBay Anywhere brings together leading technology companies, mobile carriers, portals, and hardware vendors with the goal of making eBay accessible to any user with a handheld Internet device. The launch of a new category called eBay Real Estate makes property transactions on eBay easier for buyers and sellers and provides a dedicated home for eBay's emerging real estate marketplace.

## INTERNATIONAL EXPANSION

To create a truly global trading platform, eBay is establishing a strong presence in countries whose populations generate the majority of the world's e-commerce revenue. In 2000, eBay entered four new markets: Japan, Canada, France, and Austria. In the first eight weeks of 2001, the company announced the launch of an Italian site and the acquisition of a controlling interest in Internet Auction, South Korea's largest auction-style Web site. eBay also announced the acquisition of iBazar, the pioneer in online auction-style trading in Europe. With the iBazar acquisition as well as the recent launches of sites in Ireland, Switzerland, New Zealand, Singapore, and its 20 percent stake in Mercado Libre (Latin America's leading auction site), eBay will have a strong leadership position in seventeen of the top twenty global markets, representing approximately 90 percent of the world's e-commerce dollars and a vast majority of the world's Internet users. In 2001, eBay's international revenues increased 294 percent to $114 million from $28.9 million the year before.

## FINANCIAL STATEMENTS

Income statements and balance sheets for 2000 and 2001 are provided in Exhibits 2 and 3, as well as some select financial ratios. The statements speak for themselves; eBay has experienced remarkable growth and is financially sound. In 2001, eBay again had record bottom-line profits, which were driven by record user growth, revenues, and gross merchandise sales.

eBay has identified two primary reporting segments: online trading services and offline, traditional auction services. The online trading services segment consists of the operations of eBay, Billpoint, alando.de.ag, and Half.com. The offine, traditional auction segment consists of the current operations of Butterfields and Kruse. eBay reports 2001 net revenues of $714 million and $34 million for online and offline, respectively.

## CONCLUSION

In a poor economy when virtually every Internet company is treading water or drowning, eBay is growing by leaps and bounds. eBay has managed to do what virtually no other Internet company has been able to do, and having done so under the current economic climate makes its accomplishment even more astounding. The business model is solid and eBay shows no signs of slowing down. eBay is the market leader in Internet auction

EXHIBIT 2    eBay Inc. Consolidated Statement of Income
(in thousands, except per share amounts)

| | Yearended December 31, | | |
|---|---|---|---|
| | *1999* | *2000* | *2001* |
| Net revenues | $224,724 | $431,424 | $748,821 |
| Cost of net revenues | 57,588 | 95,453 | 134,816 |
| Gross profit | 167,136 | 335,971 | 614,005 |
| Operating expenses: | | | |
| Sales and marketing | 96,239 | 166,767 | 253,474 |
| Product development | 24,847 | 55,863 | 75,288 |
| General and administrative | 43,919 | 73,027 | 105,784 |
| Payroll expense on employee stock options | – | 2,337 | 2,442 |
| Amortization of acquired intangible assets | 1,145 | 1,433 | 36,591 |
| Merger related costs | 4,359 | 1,550 | – |
| Total operating expenses | 170,509 | 300,977 | 473,579 |
| Income (loss) from operations | (3,373) | 34,994 | 140,426 |
| Interest and other income, net | 23,833 | 46,337 | 41,613 |
| Interest expense | (2,319) | (3,374) | (2,851) |
| Impairment of certain equity investments | – | – | (16,245) |
| Income before income taxes and minority interests | 18,141 | 77,957 | 162,943 |
| Provision for income taxes | (8,472) | (32,725) | (80,009) |
| Minority interests in consolidated companies | (102) | 3,062 | 7,514 |
| Net income | $ 9,567 | $ 48,294 | $ 90,448 |
| Net income per share: | | | |
| Basic | $ 0.04 | $ 0.19 | $ 0.34 |
| Diluted | $ 0.04 | $ 0.17 | $ 0.32 |
| Weighted average shares: | | | |
| Basic | 217,674 | 251,776 | 268,971 |
| Diluted | 273,033 | 280,346 | 280,595 |

*Source:* eBay's 2001 *Annual Report,* p. 62.

selling, and it operates in a rapidly expanding market. Driving the company's growth is the success eBay has had in moving overseas into Germany, Australia, and other markets. The company has seen its market grow from a site at which collectibles are traded to a marketplace for practical goods and services, which is certain to attract a larger audience. The gradual move into fixed-price trading may also prove to be huge for eBay, further expanding its appeal to the mainstream and attracting customers who might never have shopped on the auction site.

eBay is in a fantastic position to develop and to grow as a company. As the market leader with tremendous financial strength, it should take advantage of the current economic situation, and while others are forced to downsize and lay off employees, eBay can afford to seek out and hire the best and brightest individuals. eBay should also leverage its current brand recognition to further enhance and develop its position as a business-to-business trading platform, since the B2B (business to business) market is expected to account for $4.3 trillion in sales by 2005. At the heart of eBay's continued growth will be its continuous improvements and upgrades to its trading platform. Using the leading technologies to keep the platform reliable and dependable while maintaining the users feelings of security and trust will help ensure eBay's success for years to come.

**EXHIBIT 3**    eBay Inc. Consolidated Balance Sheet
(in thousands, except per share amounts)

|  | December 31, | |
| --- | ---: | ---: |
|  | *2000* | *2001* |
| **ASSETS** | | |
| Current assets: | | |
| Cash and cash equivalents | $  201,873 | $  523,969 |
| Short-term investments | 354,166 | 199,450 |
| Accounts receivable, net | 67,163 | 101,703 |
| Other current assets | 52,262 | 58,683 |
| Total current assets | 675,464 | 883,805 |
| Long-term investments | 218,197 | 286,998 |
| Restricted cash and investments | 126,390 | 129,614 |
| Property and equipment, net | 125,161 | 142,349 |
| Intangible assets, net | 13,063 | 198,639 |
| Deferred tax assets | 13,892 | 21,540 |
| Other assets | 10,236 | 15,584 |
|  | $1,182,403 | $1,678,529 |
| **LIABILITIES AND STOCKHOLDERS' EQUITY** | | |
| Current liabilities: | | |
| Accounts payable | $   31,725 | $    33,235 |
| Accrued expenses and other current liabilities | 66,697 | 94,593 |
| Deferred revenue and customer advances | 12,656 | 15,583 |
| Short-term debt | 15,272 | 16,111 |
| Income taxes payable | 11,092 | 20,617 |
| Total current liabilities | 137,442 | 180,139 |
| Long-term debt | 11,404 | 12,008 |
| Other liabilities | 6,549 | 19,493 |
| Minority interests | 13,248 | 37,751 |
| Total liabilities | 168,643 | 249,391 |
| Commitments and contingencies | | |
| Stockholders' equity: | | |
| Convertible Preferred Stock, $0.001 par value; 10,000 shares authorized; no shares issued or outstanding | – | – |
| Common Stock, $0.001 par value; 900,000 shares authorized; 269,250 and 277,259 shares issued and outstanding | 269 | 277 |
| Additional paid-in capital | 941,285 | 1,275,240 |
| Unearned stock-based compensation | (1,423) | (2,367) |
| Retained earnings | 74,504 | 164,633 |
| Accumulated other comprehensive loss | (875) | (8,645) |
| Total stockholders' equity | 1,013,760 | 1,429,138 |
|  | $1,182,403 | $1,678,529 |

*Source:* eBay's 2001 *Annual Report,* p. 61.

EXHIBIT 4    eBay Inc. Segment Information

|  | 2000 | | |
|---|---|---|---|
|  | Online | Offine | Consolidated |
| Net revenues from external customers . . . . . . . . . . . . . | $  391,952 | $  39,472 | $  431,424 |
| Operating income (loss), as adjusted . . . . . . . . . . . . . | 49,767 | (2,312) | 47,455 |
| Interest and other income and expense, net . . . . . . . . . | 45,642 | 695 | 46,337 |
| Interest expense . . . . . . . . . . . . . . . . . . . . . . . . . . . . | (1,071) | (2,303) | (3,374) |
| Amortization of certain non-cash items . . . . . . . . . . . . | (11,464) | (997) | (12,461) |
| Income (loss) before income taxes and minority interest and equity interest in partnership income . . . . . . . . . . . . . . . . . . . . . . . . . | $ 82,874 | $ (4,917) | $   77,957 |
| Total assets . . . . . . . . . . . . . . . . . . . . . . . . . | $1,084,909 | $ 97,494 | $1,182,403 |

|  | 2001 | | |
|---|---|---|---|
|  | Online | Offline | Consolidated |
| Net revenues from external customers . . . . . . . . . . . . . | $  714,405 | $  34,416 | $  748,821 |
| Operating income (loss), as adjusted . . . . . . . . . . . . . | 185,298 | (2,759) | 182,539 |
| Interest and other income and expense, net . . . . . . . . . | 42,208 | (595) | 41,613 |
| Impairment of certain equity investments . . . . . . . . . . . | (16,245) | – | (16,245) |
| Interest expense . . . . . . . . . . . . . . . . . . . . . . . . . . . . | (1,686) | (1,165) | (2,851) |
| Amortization of certain non-cash items . . . . . . . . . . . . | (41,772) | (341) | (42,113) |
| Income (loss) before income taxes and minority interest and equity interest in partnership income . . . . . . . . . . . . . . . . . . . . . . . . . | $  167,803 | $ (4,860) | $  162,943 |
| Total assets . . . . . . . . . . . . . . . . . . . . . . . . . | $1,588,913 | $ 89,616 | $1,678,529 |

|  | Yearended December 31, | | |
|---|---|---|---|
|  | 1999 | 2000 | 2001 |
| United States revenues . . . . . . . . . . . . . . . . . . . . . . . . | $  222,130 | $402,446 | $  634,659 |
| International revenues . . . . . . . . . . . . . . . . . . . . . . . . | 2,594 | 28,978 | 114,162 |
| Net revenues . . . . . . . . . . . . . . . . . . . . . . . . . . . . . . | $  224,724 | $431,424 | $  748,821 |

Source: eBay's 2001 Annual Report, p. 77.

---

## NOTES

[1]Nielson/Net Ratings Audience Measurement Service.

---

### EXHIBIT 5     eBay's Percentage Analysis

The following table sets forth, for the periods presented, certain data from our consolidated statement of income as a percentage of net revenues.

| | Yearended December 31, | | |
| --- | --- | --- | --- |
| | 1999 | 2000 | 2001 |
| Net revenues ................................... | 100.0% | 100.0% | 100.0% |
| Cost of net revenues............................. | 25.6 | 22.1 | 18.0 |
| Gross profit .............................. | 74.4 | 77.9 | 82.0 |
| Operating expenses: | | | |
| Sales and marketing........................... | 42.8 | 38.7 | 33.8 |
| Product development.......................... | 11.1 | 12.9 | 10.1 |
| General and administrative ..................... | 19.5 | 16.9 | 14.1 |
| Payroll expense on employee stock options........... | – | 0.5 | 0.3 |
| Amortization of acquired intangible assets........... | 0.5 | 0.3 | 4.9 |
| Merger related costs........................... | 1.9 | 0.4 | – |
| Total operating expenses ..................... | 75.8 | 69.7 | 63.2 |
| Income (loss) from operations...................... | (1.4) | 8.2 | 18.8 |
| Interest and other income, net .................... | 10.6 | 10.7 | 5.6 |
| Interest expense ................................ | (1.0) | (0.8) | (0.4) |
| Impairment of certain equity investments ............. | – | – | (2.2) |
| Income before income taxes and minority interests....... | 8.2 | 18.1 | 21.8 |
| Provision for income taxes ....................... | (3.8) | (7.6) | (10.7) |
| Minority interests in consolidated companies........... | (0.1) | 0.7 | 1.0 |
| Net income ................................... | 4.3% | 11.2% | 12.1% |

*Source:* eBay's 2001 *Annual Report,* p. 23.

EXHIBIT 6    eBay Operating Data: Net Revenues

| | 1999 | Percent Change | 2000 | Percent Change | 2001 |
|---|---|---|---|---|---|
| | | (in thousands, except percent changes) | | | |
| Online net revenues: | | | | | |
| Transactions .......................... | $179,895 | 94% | $348,174 | 73% | $602,671 |
| Third-party advertising ................... | 2,030 | 541% | 13,022 | 544% | 83,853 |
| End-to-end services and promotions .......... | 608 | 4,959% | 30,756 | (9)% | 27,881 |
| Total online net revenues ............... | 182,533 | 115% | $391,952 | 82% | 714,405 |
| Butterfields ......................... | 31,319 | (6)% | 29,405 | (14)% | 25,251 |
| Kruse ............................. | 10,872 | (7)% | 10,067 | (9)% | 9,165 |
| Total offline net revenues .............. | 42,191 | (6)% | 39,472 | (13)% | 34,416 |
| Total net revenues ..................... | $224,724 | 92% | $431,424 | 74% | $748,821 |
| U.S. net revenues ......................... | $222,130 | 81% | $402,446 | 58% | $634,659 |
| International net revenues .................... | 2,594 | 1,017% | 28,978 | 294% | 114.162 |
| Total net revenues ..................... | $224,724 | 92% | $431,424 | 74% | $748,821 |

| | 1999 | Percent Change | 2000 | Percent Change | 2001 |
|---|---|---|---|---|---|
| | | (in millions, except percent and per listing amounts) | | | |
| Supplemental Operating Data: | | | | | |
| Confirmed registered users at end of year ...... | 10.0 | 125% | 22.5 | 89% | 42.4 |
| Number of items listed ................... | 129.6 | 104% | 264.7 | 60% | 423.1 |
| Gross merchandise sales .................. | $ 2,805 | 93% | $ 5,422 | 72% | $ 9,319 |

*Source:* eBay's 2001 *Annual Report,* p. 24.

# AMAZON.COM, INC.—2002

**Margie Goodson**
**Francis Marion University**

AMZN

www.Amazon.com

September 11, 2001, began as just another ordinary day. There was a crispness in the air that always ushers in the fall season. No one could have predicted the events that would take place that day. The news resounded throughout the world. A plane had crashed into the World Trade Center in downtown Manhattan, New York, hitting one of the twin towers. Surely, it was a horrible accident. Then not many minutes later, another plane hit the remaining tower. Clearly, these events were no accident. Minutes later, news reports revealed that the Pentagon had also been struck by a hijacked plane. America was under attack by terrorists who had plotted against the country and had succeeded in violating a nation and a way of life. America would never be the same.

In mere seconds, thousands of lives were lost, and millions of dollars of property was damaged. Wall Street shut down for four days, the longest time ever. When the markets reopened on September 17, everyone waited to see how Wall Street would react. The first day saw a sputtering market that tried to rally only to close just above eight hundred by the session's end. The uncertainty of the market reflected the uncertainty felt by the United States—and the entire world. Could the American economy fight its way back from this destructive act? While digging among the rubble in recovery efforts and while waging a war on terrorism, could the American economy survive an almost certain recession? How long would the recession last? These are questions that all individuals as well as businesses in every sector of the economy will seek to answer in the days that lie ahead. It will be difficult for established companies that are viable and profitable to weather the rough days to come. It will be an even greater challenge for companies that are relatively new, unproven, and have not reached the realm of profitability. Amazon.com is one such company.

## HISTORY

Amazon.com, Inc. (Amazon) is an Internet-based company located in Seattle, Washington. The founder of the company as well as its president, CEO, and chairman is Jeff Bezos. While working as a senior vice president for DE Shaw & Company in 1994, Bezos was given an assignment: to find good Internet companies in which to invest. While Web surfing for the first time, he discovered a site showing that the number of Internet users was growing by 2,300 percent per month. Bezos began thinking of products and services that could be sold efficiently on the Web, and he developed a list of around twenty. Within two months, Jeff and his wife Mackenzie started a trip across America. While Mackenzie drove the Chevy Blazer, Jeff constructed a business plan on a laptop and contacted potential investors by cellular phone. Selling books was chosen as the market to pursue because there was no clear powerhouse in the market. The largest competitor was Barnes & Noble, Inc. with only 15 percent of the book-selling market in 1994.

Initially, Bezos wanted to call the company Cadabra, but after an acquaintance mistakenly thought that he was naming it "Cadaver," the search for a name began anew. The company was eventually named after the mightiest river in the world, the Amazon. The company's 2000 net income was negative $1.411 billion on revenues of $2.7 billion. Amazon shares were down 75 percent from their year high of more than $40 before September 11. As of October 3, they were down another 25 percent—at $6.08. Amazon's CEO, Jeff Bezos, predicted that the company would report its first operating profit in the fourth quarter of 2001. No one could have predicted the events of September 11 and the impact they would have on consumer confidence and spending.

In 1994, Amazon.com, Inc. was incorporated in the state of Washington. It would reincorporate in 1996 in the state of Delaware. Seattle was chosen as Amazon's headquarters because of the proximity to Ingram Book Group's warehouse and because of the population's noted computer expertise. In 1995, while operating out of a rented forty-five thousand square foot facility and using doors laid across sawhorses for desk space, Amazon started selling books exclusively online.

Amazon immediately enjoyed astounding growth rates. Sales for 1995, 1996, 1997, 1998, 1999, and 2000 were $.5, $16, $147, $610, $1,640 and $2,762.0 million, respectively. Amazon's 2001 financial statements are shown in Exhibits 1 and 2. Amazon's customer base increased from 180,000 in one hundred countries in 1996 to 20 million in 2000. The repeat purchase rate of existing customers rose from 44 percent in 1996 to 70 percent in 1999. The average spent per customer in 2000 was $134, up 19 percent over 1999.

In 1998, Amazon began expanding. Music and videos were added to the product mix. Within two months of the initial offering of these products, Amazon became the number one seller of books, music, and videos online. Further expansion followed in 1999. The company now also offers electronics and software, toys and video games, home improvements, electronic greeting cards, online auctions, DVDs, and a virtual mall called z-Shops. Amazon also operates the Internet Movie Database, a comprehensive source of information on movies and entertainment titles as well as crew and cast members. Presently, Amazon is organized into three operating segments: the U.S. books, music, and DVD/video segment; the early-stage businesses and other segment; and the international segment, consisting of sites focused in the United Kingdom, Germany, France, and Japan. Sales and Profit(Loss) information is listed in Exhibit 3.

During 2000, Amazon's Music store launched Bargain Music, Latin and Box Set stores, and a Music Accessories store. Amazon also created over thirty franchise stores for its DVD and Video stores, and it created and hosted official Web sites for a number of prominent films. In late 2000, Amazon launched a co-branded video and toy store with Toysrus.com. Amazon also has strategic partnerships with a drugstore; a deliverer of spoken audio over the Internet; an issuer of consumer credit cards; an auction site devoted to art, antiques, jewelry, and collectibles; a photography service; and an auto broker. All of these businesses operate in cyberspace. Also, Amazon has acquired businesses to produce e-commerce software and to establish a database to track customer demographic information and online buying habits. In August 2001, Amazon opened its new online computer store at a time when the PC business was at the industry's lowest point in years. In September 2001, the company introduced another new feature, a fully personalized store for every returning customer, with the launch of Your Store (**www.amazon.com/yourstore**). The site features each customer's name in a tab that contains selections from his or her favorite areas across the Amazon.com Web site. Bezos states, "At Amazon.com, we've always worked to put the customer at the center of his or her own shopping universe."

**EXHIBIT 1**    Amazon.com, Inc. Consolidated Balance Sheets (in thousands, except per-share data)

| | December 31, 2001 | December 31, 2000 |
|---|---|---|
| **ASSETS** | | |
| Current assets: | | |
| Cash and cash equivalents | $ 540,282 | $ 822,435 |
| Marketable securities | 456,303 | 278,087 |
| Inventories | 143,722 | 174,563 |
| Prepaid expenses and other current assets | 67,613 | 86,044 |
| Total current assets | 1,207,920 | 1,361,129 |
| Fixed assets, net | 271,751 | 366,416 |
| Goodwill, net | 45,367 | 158,990 |
| Other intangibles, net | 34,382 | 96,335 |
| Investments in equity-method investees | 10,387 | 52,073 |
| Other equity investments | 17,972 | 40,177 |
| Other assets | 49,768 | 60,049 |
| Total assets | $ 1,637,547 | $ 2,135,169 |
| **LIABILITIES AND STOCKHOLDERS' DEFICIT** | | |
| Current liabilities: | | |
| Accounts payable | $ 444,748 | $ 485,383 |
| Accrued expenses and other current liabilities | 305,064 | 272,683 |
| Unearned revenue | 87,978 | 131,117 |
| Interest payable | 68,632 | 69,196 |
| Current portion of long-term debt and other | 14,992 | 16,577 |
| Total current liabilities | 921,414 | 974,956 |
| Long-term debt and other | 2,156,133 | 2,127,464 |
| Commitments and contingencies | | |
| Stockholders' deficit: | | |
| Preferred stock, $0.01 par value: | | |
| Authorized shares—500,000 | | |
| Issued and outstanding shares—none | — | — |
| Common stock, $0.01 par value: | | |
| Authorized shares—5,000,000 | | |
| Issued and outstanding shares—373,218 and 357,140 shares, respectively | 3,732 | 3,571 |
| Additional paid-in capital | 1,462,769 | 1,338,303 |
| Deferred stock-based compensation | (9,853) | (13,448) |
| Accumulated other comprehensive loss | (36,070) | (2,376) |
| Accumulated deficit | (2,860,578) | (2,293,301) |
| Total stockholders' deficit | (1,440,000) | (967,251) |
| Total liabilities and stockholders' deficit | $ 1,637,547 | $ 2,135,169 |

*Source:* Amazon's 2001 *Annual Report,* p. 43.

## EXTERNAL ASSESSMENT

The number of Internet users is continuing to rise. At the end of 2000, about 370.8 million users worldwide accessed the Internet at least monthly. This number is expected to soar to 1.3 billion by 2005. The number of Web pages is expected to increase from

EXHIBIT 2    Amazon.com, Inc. Consolidated Statements of
Operations (in thousands, except per share data)

| | Years Ended December 31, | | |
|---|---|---|---|
| | 2001 | 2000 | 1999 |
| Net sales | $3,122,433 | $ 2,761,983 | $1,639,839 |
| Cost of sales | 2,323,875 | 2,106,206 | 1,349,194 |
| Gross profit | 798,558 | 655,777 | 290,645 |
| Operating expenses: | | | |
| Fulfillment | 374,250 | 414,509 | 237,312 |
| Marketing | 138,283 | 179,980 | 175,838 |
| Technology and content | 241,165 | 269,326 | 159,722 |
| General and administrative | 89,862 | 108,962 | 70,144 |
| Stock-based compensation | 4,637 | 24,797 | 30,618 |
| Amortization of goodwill and other intangibles | 181,033 | 321,772 | 214,694 |
| Restructuring-related and other | 181,585 | 200,311 | 8,072 |
| Total operating expenses | 1,210,815 | 1,519,657 | 896,400 |
| Loss from operations | (412,257) | (863,880) | (605,755) |
| Interest income | 29,103 | 40,821 | 45,451 |
| Interest expense | (139,232) | (130,921) | (84,566) |
| Other income (expense), net | (1,900) | (10,058) | 1,671 |
| Other gains (losses), net | (2,141) | (142,639) | — |
| Net interest expense and other | (114,170) | (242,797) | (37,444) |
| Loss before equity in losses of equity-method investees | (526,427) | (1,106,677) | (643,199) |
| Equity in losses of equity-method investees, net | (30,327) | (304,596) | (76,769) |
| Loss before change in accounting principle | $ (556,754) | $ (1,411,273) | $ (719,968) |
| Cumulative effect of change in accounting principle | (10,523) | — | — |
| Net loss | $ (567,277) | $ (1,411,273) | $ (719,968) |
| Basic and diluted loss per share: | | | |
| Prior to cumulative effect of change in accounting principle | $ (1.53) | $ (4.02) | $ (2.20) |
| Cumulative effect of change in accounting principle | (0.03) | — | — |
| | $ (1.56) | $ (4.02) | $ (2.20) |
| Shares used in computation of basic and diluted loss per share | 364,211 | 350,873 | 326,753 |

*Source:* Amazon's 2001 *Annual Report,* p. 44.

1.7 billion in 1999 to 8.0 billion in 2002. The United States accounts for more than one-half of the world's total number of Internet users; however, penetration is expected to increase in western Europe because of declines in access costs. Although 46 percent of the U.S. population is connected, there is still plenty of room for growth. Personal computer penetration in the United States rose from 42 percent in 1998 to 51 percent in 2000. A total of 98 million PCs were shipped in 1998, 114 million units were shipped in 1999 (up 23 percent), and 131 million units were shipped in 2000 (up 16 percent); and the number of units shipped rose to 139 million in 2001 (up 6 percent). The projections reflect a gradual slowing of the growth of PC shipments. While once dominated by males, Internet users are now almost equally divided between males and females. Internet users are more educated than the general population, with over 80 percent having at least some college experience. This percentage continues to fall as more people are acquiring access to the Internet using inexpensive computers and public access points, such as libraries and schools.

**EXHIBIT 3**    Amazon's Segment Financial Information (in billions)

| | U.S. Books, Music, DVD/Videos | U.S. Electronics, Tools, and Kitchen | International | Services |
|---|---|---|---|---|
| **NET SALES** | | | | |
| 2001 | $ 1.69 | $.547 | $.661 | $.225 |
| 2000 | 1.70 | .484 | .381 | .198 |
| 1999 | 1.31 | .151 | .168 | .013 |
| **GROSS PROFIT** | | | | |
| 2001 | $.453 | $.078 | $.141 | $.126 |
| 2000 | .417 | .045 | .077 | .116 |
| 1999 | .263 | −.020 | .036 | .012 |

*Source:* Amazon's 2001 *Annual Report,* pp. 22–24.

English is the predominant language used on Web sites. Australia, Canada, Ireland, New Zealand, South Africa, the United Kingdom, and the United States use English as a native language. The combined population and Gross Domestic Product of these countries are 322 million and $10.8 trillion, respectively.

Over 29 million people in the United States speak Spanish. That number is expected to grow to 40 million by 2010. Presently, the U.S. Hispanic market is estimated at $325 billion. Worldwide, 800 million people speak Spanish. Hispanics, both domestically and abroad, demonstrate high levels of brand loyalty.

Internet commerce, called e-commerce, is increasingly accepted. The e-commerce segment grew by over 125 percent in the year 2000. Online spending has been projected to exceed $428 billion in 2004, up from $60 billion in 2000 and just $10 billion in 1998.

E-commerce can be broken into four segments: (1) business-to-business (B2B), (2) business-to-consumer (B2C), (3) business-to-administration, and (4) customer-to-administration. The two most familiar are business-to-business and business-to-consumer commerce, during which products and services are exchanged via electronic networking systems instead of person-to-person. For example, at a checkout counter, an item is "scanned." That information is relayed to a computer system which, when the appropriate level has been sold, will order new supplies via Electronic Data Interchange (EDI). This is a form of business-to-business commerce and has been around since the 1960s. The U.S. Commerce Department projects that e-commerce will be the primary economic growth engine of the United States for the next one hundred years.

According to a study by the Boston Consulting Group, one based on a survey of European buyers, sellers, and supply-chain managers, the total volume of online transactions in Europe is expected to jump from an estimated $200 billion in 2000 to an estimated $3.1 trillion in 2004. Currently, online transactions in European countries are less than one-third of the number in the United States. Fifty-six percent of the companies surveyed expect online sales channels to enable them to increase revenues by 2004.

The B2C e-commerce segment is now experiencing rapid growth. As Internet use increases and as people grow more comfortable with ordering products online, more profit is made by businesses. Online B2C sales projected for 2004 are $428 billion, up from $60 billion in 2000 and just $10 billion in 1998. Business-to-business sales are projected to grow to $1.3 trillion by 2003, up from $251 billion in 2000.

Internet companies, including Amazon, continue to have a problem with people visiting and browsing but not buying. This is also a problem common to offline retailers. Web sites are being used to gather information about products, which is then used to purchase the product at offline locations or other Web sites. While it has been suggested that the major reason for not purchasing online is fear of the loss of private financial information, researchers have found that active online shoppers are not afraid. One of the reasons for this lack of fear is that credit card companies all but guarantee all online purchases and provide 100 percent coverage in the event that a consumer's card is misused online. Amazon also confronts this security issue by using encryption methods to encode transmitted data. In fact, the use of encryption is more secure than calling a business and giving a credit card number over an ordinary phone line.

As potential profits increase, more businesses want to come online. To paraphrase what a commercial states, "If you are not online, then you are not really in business." In today's business environment, three basic B2C structures exist: (1) traditional "brick and mortar," (2) completely online, or (3) "brick and click," a combination of the two. Amazon and E-bay, Inc. are examples of completely online businesses, while Barnes & Noble, Inc., Wal-Mart Stores, Inc., and Toys 'R' Us, Inc. are examples of the combination of "brick and mortar" and virtual. Each is offering products or services to the Internet user. Although Amazon is often considered to be the eight hundred pound gorilla of e-commerce, the Internet business market is still fragmented. It has been suggested that the "brick and click" segment of e-businesses use the Internet as another arm of their showroom to provide shoppers with product and inventory information. A retailer's Web site can be an incredibly powerful tool for driving offline sales. A lot of consumers like to research products online before purchasing them offline. Researchers have found that consumers will switch back and forth between online, offline, and a combination of the two depending upon which method serves them best for a particular purchase.

Researchers predict that sales of e-books will grow from $40 million in 2000 to $2.3 billion in 2005. People will increasingly download books from online bookstores and print them to a PC, personal digital assistant, or handheld e-book reader. E-books will not replace the traditional paper books, but they *will* provide consumers with a greater number of options. Another high growth area is that of auctions. It is predicted that consumer-to-consumer auctions will grow from $3 billion in 1999 to $6.4 billion in 2000—and to $15.1 billion in 2004. At the same time, according to predictions, B2C auction revenues will increase from $700 million in 1999 to a projected $1.1 billion in 2000—and $4.5 billion in 2004.

As the Internet becomes an increasingly essential part of people's lives, the government will begin to look at ways to evaluate and regulate online activity. The issue of Internet taxation has received much publicity. Currently, there is a ban on taxation of online purchases, and a bill was signed in November 2001 to extend the ban until Nov. 1, 2003. Losses attributed to nontaxation of the Internet have been estimated at $3.8 billion in 2000 and to be $12.4 billion in 2003. Many states are considering revising their tax codes to capture some of this potential revenue from Internet sales.

## Competitors

### Barnes & Noble

Amazon faces stiff and growing competition from established and growing Internet companies. Barnes & Noble, Inc. has been a classic comparative competitor for Amazon since Amazon's beginning. Barnes & Noble currently operates 908 bookstores and 978 video and entertainment software stores under several names: Barnes & Noble Booksellers, Bookstop, Bookstar, B. Dalton Booksellers, Doubleday Bookshops, and

Scribner's Bookstore. Touted as the world's largest bookseller, the company generated record sales of $4.4 billion in 2000, up 26 percent from the prior year. The company's principal business is the retail sale of trade books, mass-market paperbacks, children's books, off-price bargain books, and magazines. Sales of $2.797, $3.006, $3.486, and $4.375 billion were recorded for 1997, 1998, 1999, and 2000, respectively.

Located in high-traffic areas with convenient access to major commercial thoroughfares and ample parking, Barnes & Noble was the first bookseller to utilize the Superstore concept. The company has locations in forty-nine states and the District of Columbia as of February 3, 2001. The company has established a Web site, **http://www. barnesandnoble.com**, and is the exclusive bookseller on America Online. In November 2000, barnesandnoble.com merged with Fatbrain.com, Inc., the third largest online bookseller, which specialized in professional and technical titles for the corporate marketplace. In addition to books, B&N.com offers music, DVD/video, magazines, and related products. It also offers a large listing of rare and out-of-print books as well as an online selection of college textbooks and e-books. This segment saw a 65 percent increase in sales—to $320 million—in the fiscal year ending December 31, 2000.

## Wal-Mart

Wal-Mart Stores, Inc. is a Delaware corporation with headquarters based in Bentonville, Arkansas. In fiscal 2001, the company had a growth in revenues of more than $26 billion, representing a 16 percent increase in net sales. With net sales over $137.6, $165.0, and $191.3 billion, respectively, for fiscal years ending January 31, 1999, 2000, and 2001, the company is billed as the world's largest retailer. The founder was Sam M. Walton. Wal-Mart operates 1,736 discount stores, 888 Supercenters, 475 SAM's Clubs, and 19 Neighborhood Markets domestically. The company expects to open approximately 170 to 180 new Supercenters and 40 new Wal-Mart stores in the coming year. Wal-Mart has operating units in Argentina, Brazil, Canada, Germany, Mexico, South Korea, Mexico, Puerto Rico, and the United Kingdom. Wal-Mart is principally engaged in the operation of mass merchandising stores.

General operating hours domestically range from 7:00 A.M. to 11:00 P.M., six days a week, and from 10:00 A.M. to 8:00 P.M. on Sunday for discount stores and Supercenters. However, an increasing number of Wal-Mart discount stores and almost all of the Supercenters are open twenty-four hours each day.

Wal-Mart's Web site, **http://www.wal-mart.com**, was launched in late 1999. Wal-Mart has the second largest database in the world to track and predict customer purchases. Wal-Mart continues to enjoy great success with its physical retail outlets, and it appears to be focusing more on this core competency rather than on an expansion of its Internet presence. Amazon and Wal-Mart were in negotiation earlier this year, but no strategic partnership resulted from the talks.

## eBay

Ebay Inc. was formed as a sole proprietorship in 1995, and it was incorporated in California in 1996. EBay owns and operates eBay.com, which bills itself as the world's largest and most popular online marketplace. Its mission is to develop a global online trading platform that will help practically anyone buy or sell practically anything. Ebay, like Amazon, sells storefronts to businesses. The businesses pay both a fixed fee and in most cases a percentage of each item they sell. Ebay increases its sales without ever going to the expense of touching the product. The number of registered eBay users grew from approximately two million in 1998 to twenty-two million in December 2000, representing a 125 percent increase over 1999. In its attempt to establish a strong presence in countries that generate the majority of the world's e-commerce revenue, eBay entered four new markets in 2000; Japan, Canada, France, and Austria. Ebay also has introduced country-specific services for the United Kingdom, Australia, Germany, and Italy; and in February 2001, it acquired Internet Auction Company Ltd. of South Korea. The company believes its user base includes users located in over two hundred countries. For the year 2000, eBay reported net revenue of $431.4 million, a 92 percent increase over 1999. Online net revenues totaled $392 million, a 115 percent increase over 1999.

## INTERNAL ASSESSMENT

Amazon is committed to customer satisfaction. Jeff Bezos claims that the key to keeping customers is to give them what they want. Amazon has designed a system that is not only easy to use but also efficient. Amazon copyrighted the One-Click approach to online shopping. A customer can now shop in several areas throughout Amazon's entire domain without having to reregister or change virtual shopping carts. In addition, the company tracks customer purchases and preferences to personalize each customer's shopping experience. Also, the customer is allowed to participate in the review of some products. Thus, in the end, customers feels as if they are more a member of a community than just another customer.

Amazon, eBay, and many other Web sites joined together to boost charitable donations after the recent terrorist attack on the World Trade Center. Within hours of the incident, Amazon had a message of condolence posted on its site and instructions on how to give for the relief efforts. The Web site collected more than $30 million, with more than 70 percent of it going to the Red Cross.

Amazon has hired several well-established businesspeople from several major companies. These new employees' expertise range from computer software development to international distribution, credit management, and brand-name building. There was no organizational chart that could be found, but the chart in Exhibit 4 was constructed using the information found in Amazon's 2000 *Annual Report*.

Amazon currently has seven U.S. distribution centers and three European centers as well as numerous customer service centers. (See Exhibit 5.) The rationale is to ship 95 percent of all orders on the same day the order is received. By having more distribution

EXHIBIT 4    Amazon.com's Organization Chart

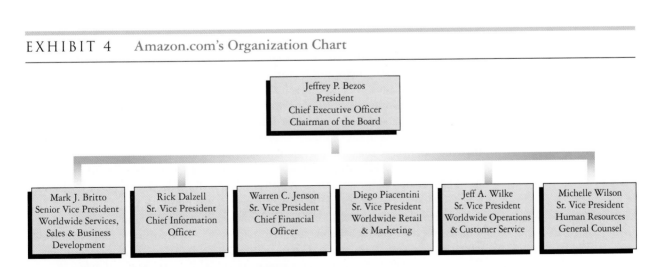

*Source:* Compiled from information obtained from Amazon.com's 2001 *Annual Report*.

**EXHIBIT 5   Amazon's Distribution Centers**

**DISTRIBUTION (FULFILLMENT) CENTERS**

1. Fernley, Nevada
2. Coffeyville, Kansas
3. Campbellsville, Kentucky
4. Lexington, Kentucky
5. New Castle, Delaware
6. Grand Forks, North Dakota
7. Seattle, Washington (seasonal)
8. United Kingdom
9. France
10. Germany
11. Japan (joint management with Nippon Express)

**CUSTOMER SERVICE CENTERS**

1. Tacoma, Washington
2. Huntington, West Virginia
3. Grand Forks, North Dakota
4. Slough, England
5. Regensburg, Germany
6. Sapporo, Japan
7. India (has outsourcing agreement with Daksh.com)

centers, the company can hold more accessible inventory and deliver merchandise in a reliable manner. Some criticism has been leveled against Amazon's management for not focusing on making a profit. The management response is that the focus is on the long term, not the short term, and that building a strong infrastructure is necessary to compete in today's ever-changing marketplace.

Amazon is also effective and resourceful with its promotions and advertisements. One of the first moves performed by the company was to initiate an Associates Program, allowing the company to establish exclusive contracts with owners of valuable cyberspace real estate. The program enables associated Web sites to make their products available to their respective audiences, with order fulfillment by Amazon. Amazon has currently enrolled 530,000 Web sites in the Associates Program. Amazon also has recently begun charging publishers and manufacturers to have books and other products promoted in specifically targeted e-mails to customers. This is an idea adapted from traditional retailers, which charge publishers for a special position or for a display in chain bookstores. The retailer sells the benefit of the extra attention to the publisher or manufacturer. This is a strategy that delivers a lot of cash to a business, because Amazon can track its customer's interests through its customized homepage, **www.amazon.com/yourstore**, which shows shoppers items they might want to buy based on previous visits. Consequently, Amazon can aim announcements at specific customers.

Amazon has also formed several strategic alliances that should strengthen its financial position. CEO Bezos states that Amazon has built a platform that not only allows the company to serve its customers extremely well but also allows it to serve the customers of other leading companies. Each one of its alliances is customized to make use of varying portions of Amazon's platform, which consists of its fulfillment technology, distribution centers, the customer service centers, and, of course, the customers themselves who are brought to the table. Bezos also states that many physical retailers have found that online business is a difficult business, just as physical retailing is a difficult business. They are choosing to align with an e-commerce company with a strong platform so that they can remain focused on their core competencies while providing a "best of the breed" online offering to their customers.

The partnership with Toys 'R' Us generated more than $125 million in sales of toys and video games in the fourth quarter of 2000. Amazon is eliminating a competitor to its online book selling operation by creating a site with Borders.com. This site will use Amazon's inventory, fulfillment, site content, and customer service.

In July 2001, AOL Time Warner invested $100 million in Amazon, and in exchange, Amazon's Platform Services Group agreed to develop and offer an enhanced online shopping experience for America Online users. The agreement also forbids AOL from increasing its holdings in Amazon beyond 5 percent for two years unless Amazon agrees to be acquired or if some other company attempts to take over the company. The agreement also forbids AOL from selling its 6.54 million shares for two years unless there is a material breach in certain commercial agreements. It is believed that this agreement allows Amazon to deliver technology to AOL to aid it in its battle with Microsoft.

Amazon also made a deal with Circuit City to allow in-store pickups of electronics equipment ordered at Amazon. In addition, Amazon announced a five-year alliance with Target Corp., which gives Target access to Amazon's technology and its customer base of 35 million people; in return, Amazon will receive sales commissions and annual fixed fees.

Amazon has an accumulated deficit and anticipates further losses resulting in significant indebtedness. Investors have expressed concern because of Amazon's inability to realize a steady profit. Analysts have stated that the company continues to expand its service offerings, and the company is looking for an increase in growth in its core business—the U.S. books, music, and video segment—that is barely growing. Another concern for analysts is that Amazon has to purchase some items (e.g., electronics) from distributors rather than from manufacturers. They argue that there is no positive contribution margin, and the more Amazon sells, the more it loses. One analyst went so far as to say Amazon may soon run out of money.

Amazon does not have a mission statement. The company's stated goal is "to put customer satisfaction first by using the Internet to transform product buying into the fastest, easiest, and most enjoyable shopping experience possible." Another universally accepted goal associated with Amazon is "to provide the largest selection of merchandise on Earth." These are not mission statements but instead could be considered vision statements.

## CONCLUSION

Amazon is a pioneer in the emerging B2C e-commerce market. By recognizing and taking advantage of the growing number of Internet users, the company has led the way in defining B2C e-commerce. But many opportunities and threats still lie ahead.

Should Amazon scale back its costs even further by decreasing the number of fulfillment centers or by seeking to make operations more efficient at each center? Should

Amazon continue its global expansion, or should it look at reducing its global presence? Has Amazon taken full advantage of the increasing Hispanic population? Should more strategic alliances with major brick and mortar retailers be formed? Can Amazon survive in the wake of an economic downturn, or will it merge with some other company such as AOL TimeWarner? Develop a three-year strategic plan for CEO Jeff Bezos.

## REFERENCES

www.amazon.com
www.thestreet.com
http://investor.stockpoint.com
http://dailynews.yahoo.com
www.forbes.com
www.marketwatch.com/news/yahoo
http://infotrac.galegroup.com/itw/
    infomamarc

www.bcg.com/new
www.thestandard.com
www.ecommercetimes.com
http://web6.infotrac.galegroup.com/itw
www.businessweek.com/reuters
www.msnbc.com/news
http://news.cnet.com/news

# LIMITED BRANDS—2002

**M. Jill Austin**
**Middle Tennessee State University**

LTD

www.limited.com

*Creating brands. Building value. Best talent. Best processes. Fewer, more dominant brands that understand their "best-at" and deliver it with consistency. Brands that, simply, know how to win. We'll concentrate on top stores, disciplined inventories, and tightly controlled expenses. We'll stay the course.*

This is Chairman and CEO Leslie Wexner's view of Limited Brands in 2002. For over thirty-six years, Wexner's Limited stores have achieved success by "breaking the rules" in the specialty retailing industry. Instead of offering a wide variety of types of clothing, the stores offer a limited assortment of sportswear in large quantities and in a variety of colors. In the mid-1990s, The Limited, Inc., made a strategic decision to develop strong brand associations for its stores. Today, the company has a number of store-brand leaders and in May 2002, changed its name to Limited Brands. Net sales from 2001 to 2001 decreased 7 percent to $9.36 billion. Operating income was $918 million in 2001, up from $866 million in 2000. 4,614 at yearend 2001, down from 5,129 in 2000.

## HISTORY

Leslie Wexner's mother and father both worked in retailing. His father worked for the Miller Wall specialty chain, and his mother was a buyer for Lazarus. When Wexner was fourteen, his parents opened their own specialty apparel store in Columbus, Ohio. After college and one year of law school, Wexner returned to work in his parents' store, where he planned to remain until he decided what he wanted to do with his life. He planned that his work in retail would be temporary, but he says he "got hooked."

In 1963, Wexner borrowed $10,000 from an aunt and a bank to open The Limited's first store. During its first year in operation, this store achieved sales of $157,000. His strategy was to provide a limited assortment of quality, fashionable sportswear at medium prices. The "limited" concept worked well, and by the late 1970s, Wexner began a twofold strategy of market development and product development. New stores were opened and acquired to appeal to women of different ages, different sizes, and different budget limits.

Throughout the 1980s, Wexner acquired a variety of businesses, including Lane Bryant, Victoria's Secret, Sizes Unlimited, Lerner, Henri Bendel, and Abercrombie & Fitch. Each of these stores was in financial trouble when acquired by Wexner. Wexner also started several store divisions during the 1980s. These included Express, Structure, Limited Too, and Cacique. Penhaligon's was acquired in 1990, and Galyan's Trading Company was acquired in 1995. Bath & Body Works was started by The Limited, Inc., in 1990. In May 1998, the company's Abercrombie & Fitch stores became an independent public company. Cacique stores closed in 1998, and Penhaligon's stores were sold in 1997.

In 1996, Wexner's Limited confronted its vulnerabilities. In response to the significant sales problems at Express, Wexner said, "We are fundamentally reinventing the business: sweeping change, greater discipline, more centralization, and a plan to build brands, not just business." This transition in thinking required each division to clearly define its fashion, advertising, price, and market position, and it required cooperation, not competition, among the division leaders. Wexner believes that retailing success in the future will be based on brand development.

## PRESENT CONDITIONS

The company continues to refine its store brands, spin off successful store brands as independent companies, and sell off less successful store brands. Limited Too was established as the independent company Too, Inc. in 1999, and The Limited, Inc. sold a majority interest in Gaylan's Trading Company that same year. In August 2001, the company sold its 653 Lane Bryant stores to Charming Shoppes, Inc. for $355 million. Remaining retail store brands will be remodeled, with approximately $350 million spent in 2001. The growth of The Limited, Inc. is shown in Exhibit 1.

Limited Brands continues to be successful in spite of significant problems at some of its retail divisions. Apparel division sales in 2001 were $3.811 billion, down 5 percent from 2001, but operating income for the apparel division was down 45 percent to $64 million. The vision and mission for Limited Brands continues to include growth and dominance in specialty retailing, as indicated in Exhibit 2 on page 68.

## BUSINESS STRUCTURE

Limited Brands operates as three separate business groups: Apparel, Intimate Brands, Inc. (85 percent owned by Limited Brands), and Other Retail Brands (Henri Bendel). Stores/operations included in each business group and net sales for each are shown in Exhibit 3 on page 69.

### Apparel Division

#### Limited Stores

This is the flagship division of the organization. Originally, merchandise in these stores was targeted to women between the ages of sixteen and twenty-five, but The Limited now focuses on twenty-something women who want modern, feminine, sophisticated sportswear. These stores sell medium-priced fashion clothing and accessories. Most of the 354 Limited stores are located in regional shopping centers or malls across the United States. The number of Limited stores has been reduced significantly in recent years; there were 778 Limited stores in 1990.

#### Express

The Express stores are the most profitable Limited apparel brand. The company describes its Express stores as being a "modern women's brand with international runway style" for women in their late teens and early twenties. Express added a lingerie department in 1999. Express stores are currently being remodeled with a modern look that the company calls the white store design. The 682 Express stores in operation are located mostly in shopping malls.

EXHIBIT 1     Limited Brands' Stores and Selling Square Feet
(a summary of stores and selling square feet by business follows)

| | End of Year | | | Change From | |
|---|---|---|---|---|---|
| | *Plan 2002* | *2001* | *2000* | *2002–2001* | *2001–2000* |
| **Express** | | | | | |
| Stores | 682 | 667 | 667 | 15 | – |
| Selling square feet | 4,400,000 | 4,280,000 | 4,288,000 | 120,000 | (8,000) |
| **Lerner New York** | | | | | |
| Stores | 504 | 522 | 560 | (18) | (38) |
| Selling square feet | 3,751,000 | 3,823,000 | 4,163,000 | (72,000) | (340,000) |
| **Limited Stores** | | | | | |
| Stores | 354 | 368 | 389 | (14) | (21) |
| Selling square feet | 2,244,000 | 2,313,000 | 2,445,000 | (69,000) | (132,000) |
| **Structure** | | | | | |
| Stores | 409 | 439 | 469 | (30) | (30) |
| Selling square feet | 1,673,000 | 1,774,000 | 1,885,000 | (101,000) | (111,000) |
| **Total apparel businesses** | | | | | |
| Stores | 1,949 | 1,996 | 2,085 | (47) | (89) |
| Selling square feet | 12,068,000 | 12,190,000 | 12,781,000 | (122,000) | (591,000) |
| **Victoria's Secret Stores** | | | | | |
| Stores | 1,017 | 1,002 | 958 | 15 | 44 |
| Selling square feet | 4,682,000 | 4,458,000 | 4,207,000 | 224,000 | 251,000 |
| **Bath & Body Works** | | | | | |
| Stores | 1,690 | 1,615 | 1,432 | 75 | 183 |
| Selling square feet | 3,710,000 | 3,463,000 | 3,039,000 | 247,000 | 424,000 |
| **Total Intimate Brands** | | | | | |
| Stores | 2,707 | 2,617 | 2,390 | 90 | 227 |
| Selling square feet | 8,392,000 | 7,921,000 | 7,246,000 | 471,000 | 675,000 |
| **Henri Bendel** | | | | | |
| Stores | 1 | 1 | 1 | – | – |
| Selling square feet | 35,000 | 35,000 | 35,000 | – | – |
| **Lane Bryant** | | | | | |
| Stores | – | – | 653 | – | (653) |
| Selling square feet | – | – | 3,162,000 | – | (3,162,000) |
| **Total retail businesses** | | | | | |
| Stores | 4,657 | 4,614 | 5,129 | 43 | (515) |
| Selling square feet | 20,495,000 | 20,146,000 | 23,224,000 | 349,000 | (3,078,000) |

*Source:* Limited Brands' 2001 *Annual Report,* p. 34.

## Lerner New York/New York & Company

This division offers "modern, city hip, and competitively priced fashion with an attitude." The store created a brand called New York & Company. In 2000, seventy-nine
Lerner New York stores were remodeled and renamed as New York & Company stores.
Presently, there are 504 Lerner/New York & Company stores in operation in malls and
shopping centers across the United States.

## Structure/Express Men's

Limited Brands began testing the market for men's fashions by offering Express for Men
in Express stores beginning in 1987. Sixty-nine Structure stores were opened in 1989,
and by the end of 2001, there were 409 stores. Structure stores were merged with

---

### EXHIBIT 2    Vision and Mission for Limited Brands

**VISION**

Create a "family of the world's best fashion brands."

**MISSION**

Limited Brands will focus on powerful and differentiated brands to create "sustained growth of shareholder value by focusing its time, talent, and capital on the highest return opportunities."

---

*Source:* Limited Brands, *Annual Report* (2000).

Express stores in 2001 and called Express Men's. The Express Men's stores stock good-quality, affordable clothing in the latest styles. The target customer is in his twenties and thirties and "urban, active, young, and creative." Only forty-five of the men's stores are currently side-by-side with Express stores, and a decision has not been made about whether the men's and women's stores will be combined in the same locations.

### Mast Industries

The business of this division is to arrange for the manufacture and import of women's clothing from around the world, and to wholesale this merchandise to Limited Brands stores and to other companies. This division delivers more than 100 million garments to Limited Brands each year. In 2001, purchases were made from thirty-one hundred suppliers, but no more than 5 percent of the items purchased came from any single manufacturer.

## Intimate Brands, Inc. (IBI)

### Victoria's Secret Stores

Victoria's Secret stores are the dominant intimate apparel store in the world. The stores were redecorated in the early 1990s in a Victorian parlor style and are currently undergoing another renovation to create an "upscale, modern, and sophisticated design" and a more "residential" look. Victoria's Secret bath and fragrance products are an increasingly important portion of store sales. In 2001, a new body/skin care collection called Body by Victoria was launched. There are 1,017 Victoria's Secret stores in the United States.

### Victoria's Secret Direct (Catalog/E-commerce)

Since its purchase by The Limited in 1982, the catalog has steadily increased its operations. Now the Victoria's Secret catalog is the dominant catalog for lingerie in the world. In 1996, the division established a phone center in Japan so that this market for mail order sales could be established. The company closed one of its three call centers in the United States in 2001. At the end of 1998, the company launched a Web site (http://www.VictoriasSecret.com) so consumers worldwide could shop online.

### Bath & Body Works

In response to demand by consumers for natural personal care products, The Limited opened six Bath & Body Works stores in 1990. These stores have a natural market atmosphere and sell a variety of personal care products. There are 1,690 Bath & Body

## EXHIBIT 3    Sales and Income Data (in millions)

| | 2001 | *2000 | 1999 | % Change 2001–2000 | % Change 2000–1999 |
|---|---|---|---|---|---|
| **Net Sales** | | | | | |
| Express | $ 1,542 | $ 1,594 | $ 1,367 | (3%) | 17% |
| Lerner New York | 940 | 1,025 | 1,001 | (8%) | 2% |
| Limited Stores | 618 | 673 | 704 | (8%) | (4%) |
| Structure | 502 | 569 | 607 | (12%) | (6%) |
| Other (principally Mast) | 209 | 158 | 108 | 32% | 46% |
| Total apparel businesses | $ 3,811 | $ 4,019 | $ 3,787 | (5%) | 6% |
| Victoria's Secret Stores | 2,403 | 2,339 | 2,122 | 3% | 10% |
| Bath & Body Works | 1,747 | 1,785 | 1,530 | (2%) | 17% |
| Victoria's Secret Direct | 869 | 962 | 956 | (10%) | 1% |
| Other | 2 | 31 | 24 | (94%) | 29% |
| Total Intimate Brands | $ 5,021 | $ 5,117 | $ 4,632 | (2%) | 10% |
| Henri Bendel | 36 | 39 | 38 | (8%) | 3% |
| Lane Bryant (through August 16, 2001) | 495 | 930 | 922 | nm | 1% |
| Galyan's (through August 31, 1999) | – | – | 165 | nm | nm |
| TOO (through August 23, 1999) | – | – | 222 | nm | nm |
| Total net sales | $ 9,363 | $ 10,105 | $ 9,766 | (7%) | 3% |
| **Operating Income** | | | | | |
| Apparel businesses | $ 64 | $ 116 | $ 79 | (45%) | 47% |
| Intimate Brands | 667 | 754 | 794 | (12%) | (5%) |
| Other | 17 | 6 | 34 | nm | nm |
| Subtotal | 748 | 876 | 907 | (15%) | (3%) |
| Special and nonrecurring items■ | 170 | (10) | 24 | nm | nm |
| Total operating income | $ 918 | $ 866 | $ 931 | 6% | (7%) |

*Fifty-three week fiscal year.
■Special and nonrecurring items:
 2001: a $170 million gain resulting from the sale of Lane Bryant, which relates to the "other" category.
 2000: a $10 million charge for Intimate Brands to close Bath & Body Works' nine stores in the United Kingdom.
 1999: (1) a $13 million charge for transaction costs related to the TOO spin-off; and (2) the reversal of a $37 million liability related to downsizing costs for Henri Bendel. These special items relate to the "Other" category.
nm = not meaningful

| | 2001 | 2000 | 1999 |
|---|---|---|---|
| **Comparable Store Sales** | | | |
| Express | (2%) | 15% | 5% |
| Lerner New York | (5%) | 4% | 12% |
| Limited Stores | (2%) | 5% | 5% |
| Structure | (8%) | (4%) | 4% |
| Total apparel businesses | (3%) | 8% | 7% |
| Victoria's Secret Stores | 0% | 5% | 12% |
| Bath & Body Works | (11%) | 1% | 11% |
| Total Intimate Brands | (5%) | 4% | 12% |
| Heuri Bendel | (6%) | (1%) | 7% |
| Lane Bryant (through August 16,2001) | 3% | 2% | 5% |
| Galyan's (through August 31, 1999) | – | – | 9% |
| TOO (through August 23, 1999) | – | – | 9% |
| Total comparable store sales | (4%) | 5% | 9% |

*Source:* Limited Brands 2001 *Annual Report,* p. 30.

Works stores. In 2000, Bath & Body Works held a 6 percent share of the $28 billion personal care market, and three of the company's fragrances were ranked among the top five U.S. fragrances. In 2001, the company closed its Bath & Body Works stores in the United Kingdom.

## Other Retail Businesses

### Henri Bendel

In 1985, The Limited purchased this upscale fashion store. The store offers the best in clothing and accessories from international designers. Prices are designed for "today's modern woman in her mid-thirties." This is the only upscale store owned by The Limited. The division was expanded to six stores in 1996, but the company closed five Henri Bendel stores in 1998. Currently, the New York store has high-profile parties to enhance its image, such as the party held for the *Charlie's Angels* film premiere in 2001.

## Center Functions

### The Limited Logistics Services

The Limited's distribution center is located in Columbus, Ohio. The center now has eight buildings and about 6.1 million square feet.

### The Limited Store Planning

This division is responsible for designing store layouts and developing merchandising techniques for all of The Limited's retail store divisions.

### The Limited Real Estate

This division handles store leases for the retail divisions. By the end of 1996, the total selling space of Limited Stores was 28.4 million square feet. Selling space decreased to 20.4 million square feet by the end of 2001.

### The Limited Design Services

This division manages the design of apparel and merchandise for the retail stores.

### The Limited Brand and Creative Services

The division works with the individual businesses and Wexner to create brands that have a distinctive character.

### The Limited Technology Services

This division handles the telecommunications and computing needs for the company.

## COMPETITION

The retail sale of women's clothing is a very competitive business. Competitors of Limited Brands include nationally, regionally, and locally owned department stores, specialty stores, and mail order catalog businesses. Some of Limited Brands' major competitors include Gap, American Eagle, Federated Department Stores, Dayton-Hudson, Dillard's, May Department Stores, Talbot's, Spiegel/Eddie Bauer, Nordstrom, Sears, and JCPenney.

Limited Brands is the number two apparel chain in the United States. The top fifteen apparel chains are shown in Exhibit 4. Other apparel retailers who were among the

EXHIBIT 4    Top Fifteen Apparel Chains (sales in thousands)

| Company (HQ) | Sales (000) | | % Change |
| --- | --- | --- | --- |
| | 2000 | 1999 | |
| Gap (San Francisco, Calif.) | $13,637,460 | $11,635,398 | +17.5% |
| Limited (Columbus, Ohio) | 10,104,606 | 9,723,334 | +3.5 |
| TJX (Framingham, Mass.) | 9,579,006 | 8,795,347 | +8.9 |
| Intimate Brands (Columbus, Ohio) | 5,117,199 | 4,510,836 | +13.4 |
| Spiegel/Eddie Bauer (Downers Grove, Ill.) | 3,724,778 | 3,414,703 | +9.1 |
| Ross Stores (Newark, Calif.) | 2,709,039 | 2,468,638 | +9.7 |
| Burlington Coat (Burlington, N.J.) | 2,226,183 | 1,988,500 | +13.1 |
| Charming Shoppes (Bensalem, Pa.) | 1,617,173 | 1,196,529 | +34.1 |
| Talbots (Hingham, Mass.) | 1,594,996 | 1,290,923 | +21.9 |
| Men's Wearhouse (Fremont, Calif.) | 1,333,501 | 1,186,748 | +12.4 |
| Goody's Family Clothing (Knoxville, Tenn.) | 1,250,604 | 1,180,930 | +5.9 |
| Abercrombie & Fitch (Reynoldsburg, Ohio) | 1,237,604 | 1,042,056 | +18.8 |
| Ann Taylor (New York, N.Y.) | 1,232,776 | 1,042,056 | +18.3 |
| SteinMart (Jacksonville, Fla.) | 1,206,624 | 1,034,561 | +16.6 |
| L.L. Bean (Freeport, Maine) | 1,100,000 | 1,050,000 | +4.8 |

top fifteen apparel chains for sales volume include The TJX Companies, Inc., Gap Inc., and Intimate Brands, Inc.

Two of Limited Brands' major competitors are discussed below.

## Gap Inc.

At the end of March 2001, Gap Inc. had 3,740 apparel stores in operation. Gap Inc. has several divisions that compete directly with Limited Brands stores. Gap Inc. (2,091 stores) sells casual sportswear items for both men and women. Banana Republic (408 stores) sells upscale casual wear. Old Navy Clothing Company, the company's fastest growing division (689 stores), sells budget-priced casual clothing. Casual and active wear for children is sold under the GapKids brand. Gap Inc. also operates 552 GapKids, Gap, and Banana Republic stores, primarily in Canada, Japan, Germany, the United Kingdom, and France. Financial information for Gap Inc. is shown in Exhibit 5.

EXHIBIT 5    Financial Information for Gap Inc.
             (in millions except per-share amount)

|                  | 1999 | 2000 |
|------------------|------|------|
| Gross revenue    | $11,635 | $13,673 |
| Net income       | 1,127.1 | 877.5 |
| Long-term debt   | 784.9 | 780.3 |
| Net worth        | $2,233.0 | $2,928.2 |
| Earnings per share | 1.26 | 1.00 |

Gap Inc. is currently facing some operational challenges. In 2000, six of the company's top managers left Gap for other positions, and beginning in 2001, CEO Drexler was handling additional responsibilities because of these resignations. Old Navy recently had merchandising problems and advertising problems. As a result, sales in the division suffered in 2001. A decision was made in 2000 to stock new merchandise less often in the stores so that clothing could be sold at full price for a longer period of time. In September 2000, Banana Republic managers launched the @Yourself concept; ministores are set up in major companies for a day and personal shoppers assist employees in making purchases. Gap Inc. also sells its merchandise online at **http://www.gap.com**.

## TJX Companies

TJX Companies is the largest off-price apparel chain in the United States. Target customers for TJX include middle-income women between the ages of twenty-five and fifty. Most TJX stores are located in strip shopping centers. At the end of July 2001, TJX Companies had 1,548 apparel stores in operation. The apparel division includes T.J. Maxx (661 stores), Marshalls (552 stores), Winners Apparel Ltd. (123 stores), Home Goods (99 stores), A.J. Wright (31 stores), and T.K. Maxx (82 stores). T.K. Maxx is an off-price apparel store located in the United Kingdom, and A.J. Wright is a Canadian off-price retailer. The company acquired Marshalls in 1995. Financial information for TJX Companies is shown in Exhibit 6.

## DEMOGRAPHIC AND SOCIETAL TRENDS

Generation Y (ages 10 to 24) is an increasingly important generation for apparel retailers. There are currently 31 million people who are between the ages 12 and 19, and this number is expected to increase to 34 million teens by 2010, making it the largest teen

EXHIBIT 6    Financial Information for TJX Companies
             (in millions except per-share amount)

|                  | 1999 | 2000 |
|------------------|------|------|
| Gross revenue    | $8,795.3 | $9,579.0 |
| Net income       | 526.8 | 538.1 |
| Long-term debt   | 319.4 | 319.4 |
| Net worth        | $1,119.2 | $1,218.7 |
| Earnings per share | 1.66 | 1.86 |

population in U.S. history. Another new target for retailers is the current "tween" age group of 7 to 12 years olds, who will be a part of the largest teenage population in 2010. Girls who are between the ages of 12 and 19 spent approximately $75 billion in 2000, with one-third of this spending in fashion. Gaining brand and store loyalty among these younger shoppers is essential for apparel retailers.

As women baby boomers reach their fifties, retailers and manufacturers of women's apparel have not provided for this group's needs. This large market group for women's apparel has found only youthful fashions and fads. As a result, large numbers of customers began staying away from the stores entirely or wound up purchasing fewer clothing items. In addition, many baby boomers consider retirement savings, college tuition, and mortgages to be a higher priority than spending for apparel. As more companies sell their items through the Internet, retail stores will have to learn how to contend with these competitors. Retailers in the apparel industry are likely to struggle.

Another trend affecting the apparel industry is the increasing acceptance of the casual workplace. Fewer dress work clothes are being sold, and those retailers that sell casual apparel have an easier time generating sales, especially in a slow economy. Adults are busy with work and family, so shopping is not the recreational activity it once was. More and more consumers see shopping as a chore, and retailers who make shopping easy on their customers are likely to have an advantage in the marketplace.

## ECONOMIC CONDITIONS

The U.S. economy saw slow growth in 2001, but consumer confidence began to decline as early as fall 2000. After the terrorist attacks on the World Trade Center in New York City and the Pentagon in September 2001, consumer confidence continued to falter. In 2001, retailing comprised one-third of the economy, and if the economy continues to slow, consumers will likely reduce their retailing expenditures.

Household debt has continued to increase since 1994. Consumers are likely to change their purchasing habits for items such as clothing so they can pay off credit card debt. The gap between rich and poor also continues to increase. The number of downscale shoppers is increasing. Because many adults owe significant debt for cars and homes and are unable to spend much money for apparel, they often purchase clothing at outlet malls or discount stores. Occasionally, however, the downscale shopper may want to indulge him- or herself by purchasing fashion items from specialty stores. Also, many of the women in the baby boom group spend their disposable income on items for their children and not on clothing for themselves.

Apparel retailers also have economic concerns. Several major retail chains have filed for reorganization under Chapter 11 bankruptcy laws, and many others have been unprofitable for years. It is difficult for retail chains to predict consumer spending patterns. In the past fifty years, apparel retailers have seen about sixteen different economic cycles. The longest cycle was six years, while the shortest was about a year. Since these cycles corresponded with the business cycle 60 percent of the time, it appears that apparel sales are likely to stay strong when the economy is good and will be significantly reduced when the economy is not growing.

Specialty retailers may have to take more gambles to gain a competitive advantage in this volatile industry. Specialty retailers have gained a competitive advantage in the past by taking a guess at fashion trends early and purchasing inventory to provide those trends to customers. If a specialty retailer purchases inventory for a fashion trend but cannot turn over the inventory, the store loses profit and cannot afford to take more risks. However, if it does not gamble by trying to keep up with fashion trends, it is impossible for it to make a profit when the economy turns around because the merchandise will be out-of-date.

## INTERNAL FACTORS FOR LIMITED BRANDS

### Marketing

Wexner believes that his company is "reinventing the specialty store business." Since The Limited retail store divisions sell different price ranges and styles of clothing and related goods, Wexner has created the effect of a department store in many malls by locating the stores in close proximity to one another. Wexner considers his stores as a collection of brands rather than a group of stores. He says, "When you think of yourself as a brand, you think more broadly. You think of the efficacy of the brand, the reputation, the integrity, the channels of distribution, whether that be in a store, a catalog, on television, or overseas." Brand building includes defining each store's image, fashion, advertising, price, and market position. In the past, Limited divisions copied each other's designs so that the only difference in some divisions was the price charged for the items sold. Design teams are now assigned to each business and the fashions are designed around narrowly defined brand positions for each division. Wexner believes this is "good for now [and] even better for the long run."

The Limited spent very little money on advertising campaigns in its first twenty years. Instead, the company relied on walk-in traffic in malls to sell its products. Currently, the only brands that are advertised in a meaningful way are Intimate Brands, Inc. stores, such as Victoria's Secret. Victoria's Secret first launched its Web site in December 1998. The television announcements during the Super Bowl in January 1999, which announced a live online fashion show, generated one million hits to the Web site. In 1999, the company created Limited Brand and Creative Services, a department that serves as an in-house advertising agency for The Limited's businesses. In December 2000, as part of the promotion for the new look at Victoria's Secret stores, spokesperson Gisele Bundchen modeled a $15 million ruby and diamond studded bra at the New York store. Express used print ads in fashion and women's magazines in 2001 to appeal to young women's renewed interest in denim fabric clothing. Approximately $359 million was spent on advertising and catalogs in 2000.

### Production

Limited Brands does not produce its own clothing, but it has a division that contracts for the manufacture of clothing. Mast Industries specializes in contracting for the production of high-quality, low-cost products. Much of the merchandise imported by Mast is marked with one of Limited Brands' own labels: The Limited, Victoria's Secret, Express, and NY & Co. Wexner believes that having private-label brands allows Limited Brands to keep merchandise inventory current and unique.

Limited Brands can also maintain control over its clothing supply through Mast Industries. Company managers try to maintain one-thousand-hour turnaround time between recognizing a new style and delivering the merchandise to stores. Mast can send high-resolution computer images of clothing designs by satellite to Far Eastern manufacturers. In addition, computer information that is collected from all individual stores is used to determine what needs to be produced in the Far East the next day. In a few days, the newly produced items arrive at the Columbus distribution center and are sent to the stores.

In 2000, Mast purchased merchandise from approximately thirty-one hundred different suppliers, but no more than 5 percent of Limited Brands' inventory was purchased from any single manufacturer. About half of Limited Brands' inventory is produced outside the United States. The coordination of work with so many factories made it difficult to ensure consistent quality. Two changes were made in 1995 in an effort to make sure the company's products were of consistent quality: Presidents of the store divisions have the responsibility for ensuring quality in their divisions, and individual store managers are not allowed to make significant sourcing decisions on their own.

## Management

Wexner has been a guiding force for the company since its beginning. His risk-taking style has concerned some investors, but his ability to create new marketing concepts has made Limited Brands the envy of other specialty retailers. Some critics suggest that Wexner is great at starting businesses but that he has not been as effective as a day-to-day leader of established businesses; they also think that he is a micromanager. The company uses a centralized process for planning, with Wexner leading the process. This leadership approach allows Wexner to remain involved in each store division, without being involved in every detail of division operations. After the company began its approach of considering store divisions as brands, Wexner started meeting with the top managers (president, marketing director, chief financial officer, head merchant, and head designer) of each store division on a monthly basis to make sure there is "agreement and alignment around core elements of the brand."

Limited Brands' managers hope to create a "family of the world's best fashion brands." According to Wexner, Limited Brands will achieve this vision by creating "sustained growth of shareholder value by focusing its time, talent, and capital on the highest return opportunities." Wexner is aggressive regarding Limited Brands' ability to compete in the specialty apparel industry of the future. He developed a campaign called WAR (Win at Retail) to motivate workers. Wexner says, "It is a war, and in wars people really do live and people do die." The plan was later named Must Win and is designed to improve store performance by motivating workers. The Must Win approach has had mixed results, demoralizing some workers, who are seated at meetings according to their weekly performance levels, while energizing others.

## Financial Condition

Note in Exhibit 7 that while Limited Brands' net sales decreased in 2001, the company's net income increased. The balance sheet (Exhibit 8) shows that the company's current assets and total assets increased in 2001 over 2000. However, the company's long-term debt decreased to $250 million in 2001.

## FUTURE OUTLOOK

Wexner says he is "determined to build a company of powerful, differentiated retail brands that maintain and strengthen our position as the world's dominant specialty retailer." His standard is that if a division does not have the potential to earn at least $1 billion in sales in the United States, Limited Brands should get out of that business. If a new concept works, Wexner is aggressive. He says, "Invent the concept. Prove it. Move forward fast." Some critics suggest that Wexner has the talent to identify unserved markets and create a marketing concept around those markets, but that he has not yet demonstrated the skill at reinventing mature businesses. Wexner responds, "My view is that whether you are turning around a business—that is, reconceptualizing it—or whether you are starting from scratch, your vision of what you are driving toward is the same."

The company's plans for the future include the following:

1. All of the company's Express stores will be remodeled by 2003.
2. Selling space will increase by 349,000 square feet in 2002.
3. During 2002, the company expects to close 43 underperforming stores.
4. The company leaders will continue to refocus the company through brand building.
5. The company plans to remodel a significant number of Victoria's Secret stores by 2003.

**EXHIBIT 7**    Consolidated Statements of Income
(in millions except per-share amount)

|  | 2001 | 2000 | 1999 |
|---|---|---|---|
| Net sales | $ 9,363 | $ 10,105 | $ 9,766 |
| Costs of goods sold, buying and occupancy | (6,110) | (6,668) | (6,443) |
| Gross income | 3,253 | 3,437 | 3,323 |
| General, administrative and store operating expenses | (2,505) | (2,561) | (2,416) |
| Special and nonrecurring items, net | 170 | (10) | 24 |
| Opetating income | 918 | 866 | 931 |
| Interest expense | (34) | (58) | (78) |
| Other income, net | 22 | 20 | 41 |
| Minority interest | (64) | (69) | (73) |
| Gains on sale of stock by investees | 62 | – | 11 |
| Income before income taxes | 904 | 759 | 832 |
| Income tax expense | 385 | 331 | 371 |
| Net income | $ 519 | $ 428 | $ 461 |
| Net income per share: |  |  |  |
| Basic | $ 1.21 | $ 1.00 | $ 1.05 |
| Diluted | $ 1.19 | $ 0.96 | $ 1.00 |

The following list presents some of the concerns that Wexner—and you—might consider:

1. Will the branding concept help Limited Brands to improve its market segmentation strategies?

2. Is locating stores in close proximity in malls a good idea for Limited Brands? Should the company locate some of its stores in strip-shopping centers?

3. Is Limited Brands' strategy of spending more money on print and television advertising a good one?

4. What is the likelihood of a continued downturn in the U.S. economy that negatively affects the women's apparel industry?

5. Will Wexner be able to turn around the Structure/Express Men's and Limited stores? What approach should he take in addition to concentrating on branding?

6. How serious are the potential problems Limited Brands could face in the future?

7. Should the company continue its strategy of developing a company and splitting it off as a separate company?

## REFERENCES

BARRETT, AMY. "To Reach the Unreachable Teen." *Business Week* (September 18, 2000).

BARRON, KELLY. "Limited Expectations." *Forbes* (March 5, 2001).

BERNER, ROBERT, and CHRISTOPHER PALMERI. "Just How Deep Are Those Teen Pockets?" *Business Week* (July 30, 2001).

D'INNOCENZIO, ANNE. "Turnaround at Express Attributed to Faster Pickup on Hot Trends." *Women's Wear Daily* (July 14, 1999).

EDELSON, SHARON. "Sisman: An Aggressive Plan for Advertising by Limited." *Women's Wear Daily* (June 2, 1999).

EXHIBIT 8    Consolidated Balance Sheets
(in millions excect per-share amounts)

| | February 2, 2002 | February 3, 2001 |
|---|---|---|
| **Assets** | | |
| Current assets | | |
|   Cash and equivalents | $ 1.375 | $ 564 |
|   Accounts receivable | 79 | 94 |
|   Inventories | 966 | 1,157 |
|   Other | 262 | 253 |
| Total current assets | 2,682 | 2,068 |
| Property and equipment, net | 1,359 | 1,395 |
| Deferred income taxes | 67 | 132 |
| Other assets | 611 | 493 |
| Total assets | $ 4,719 | $ 4,088 |
| Liabilities and Shareholders' Equity | | |
| **Current liabilities** | | |
|   Accounts payable | $ 245 | $ 273 |
|   Current portion of long-term debt | 150 | – |
|   Accrued expenses and other | 648 | 581 |
|   Income taxes | 276 | 146 |
| Total current liabilities | 1,319 | 1,000 |
| Long-term debt | 250 | 400 |
| Other long-term liabilities | 229 | 229 |
| Minority interest | 177 | 143 |
| Shareholders' equity | | |
|   Preferred stock – $1.00 par value; 10 shares authorized; none issued | – | – |
|   Common stock – $0.50 par value; 1,000 shares authorized; 432 shares issued in 2001 and 2000 | 216 | 216 |
|   Paid-in capital | 53 | 83 |
|   Retained earnings | 2,552 | 2,168 |
|   Less: treasury stock, at average cost; 3 shares in 2001 and 6 shares in 2000 | (77) | (151) |
| Total shareholders' equity | 2,744 | 2,316 |
| Total liabilities and shareholders' equity | $ 4,719 | $ 4,088 |

*Source:* Limited Brands 2001 *Annual Report,* p. 36.

GATLIN, GREG. "Limited, Mast Fined $500G Over Sleepwear." *The Boston Herald* (August 18, 2001).

GENTRY, CONNIE ROBBINS. "Fast Fashion." *Chain Store Age* (July 1, 2001).

GILL, PENNY. "Les Wexner: Unlimited Success Story." *Stores* (January 1993).

http://www.intimatebrands.com

http://www.limited.com

http://www.VictoriasSecret.com

MACHAN, DYAN. "Knowing Your Limits." *Forbes* (June 5, 1995).

QUICK, REBECCA. "Retail, Like War, Is Hell at the Limited." *The Wall Street Journal* (April 21, 1999).

SHEIN, ESTHER. "Intranet Logistics Goes High Fashion." *PC Week* (September 8, 1997).

THURSTON, KEN. "State of the Industry: Apparel Stores: New Merchandising and Marketing Strategies Account for Growth." *Chain Store Age State of the Industry Supplement* (August 1999).

THE LIMITED, INC. *Annual Reports* (1990, 1992, 1994, 1996, 1998).

# WAL-MART STORES, INC.—2002

**Amit Shah and Tyra Phipps**
**Frostburg State University**

WMT

www.walmart.com

On September 11, 2001, the United States fell victim to a homeland tragedy heretofore unparalleled in history. U.S. retailers reported declining sales as consumers stayed at home to watch the events being broadcast on television. According to Kurt Barnard, president of Barnard's Retail Consulting Group, customer traffic has begun to pick up; however, overall retail buying has remained down as consumer confidence continues to be shaken. The tragedy of September 11 has had a decidedly negative impact on the overall U.S. economy and its retail industries, including Wal-Mart, Inc.

Headquartered in Bentonville, Arkansas, Wal-Mart's sales rose from $191.3 billion in fiscal year 2001 to $217.7 billion in 2002. Net income rose from $6.3 billion to $6.7 billion during that period. For more than a decade, Wal-Mart has been on a roller coaster ride, growing by leaps and bounds as well as rolling over large competitors such as Kmart and thousands of small businesses. Financial statements are shown in Exhibit 1 and Exhibit 2. (Note: Wal-Mart's fiscal year ends January 31.)

In 1995, Wal-Mart ended a five-year battle with local leaders of Bennington, Vermont, and opened its first store in that state, thereby laying claim to having stores in all fifty states (see Exhibit 3). The Bennington store was Wal-Mart's 2,158th store. To get approval for this store, Wal-Mart abandoned its usual 200,000 square foot store near a major highway exit and instead located in a downtown building containing just fifty thousand square feet. Environmentalists in Vermont say the rural character of the state is endangered by "sprawl-mart development." Other chains, such as Ames and Kmart, have operated in Vermont for years, so some residents are mystified by the current controversy. Wal-Mart had established four stores in Vermont by the end of fiscal 2001.

Wal-Mart does not have a formal mission statement. When asked about Wal-Mart's lack of a mission, Public Relations Coordinator Kim Ellis recently replied, "We believe that our customers are most interested in other aspects of our business, and we are focused on meeting their basic consumer needs. If, in fact, we did have a formal mission statement, it would be something like this: "To provide quality products at an everyday low price and with extended customer service . . . always.'"

## HISTORY

No word better describes Wal-Mart than growth. In 1945, Sam Walton opened his first Ben Franklin franchise in Newport, Arkansas. Living in rural Bentonville, Arkansas, at the time, Walton, his wife Helen, and his brother Bud operated the nation's most successful Ben Franklin franchises. "We were a small chain," said Walton of his sixteen-store operation. "Things were running so smoothly [that] we even had time for our families." What more could a man want? A great deal, as it turned out.

Sam and Bud Walton could see that the variety store was gradually dying because supermarkets and discounters were developing. Far from being secure, Walton knew that

# EXHIBIT 1    Consolidated Statements of Income

| (Amounts in millions except per share data)<br>Fiscal years ended January 31, | 2002 | 2001 | 2000 |
|---|---|---|---|
| **Revenues** | | | |
| Net sales | $217,799 | $191,329 | $165,013 |
| Other income-net | 2,013 | 1,966 | 1,796 |
| | 219,812 | 193,295 | 166,809 |
| **Costs and Expenses** | | | |
| Cost of sales | 171,562 | 150,255 | 129,664 |
| Operating, selling and general and administrative expenses | 36,173 | 31,550 | 27,040 |
| **Interest Costs** | | | |
| Debt | 1,052 | 1,095 | 756 |
| Capital leases | 274 | 279 | 266 |
| | 209,061 | 183,179 | 157,726 |
| **Income Before Income Taxes, Minority Interest and** | | | |
| **Cumulative Effect of Accounting Change** | 10,751 | 10,116 | 9,083 |
| **Provision for Income Taxes** | | | |
| Current | 3,712 | 3,350 | 3,476 |
| Deferred | 185 | 342 | (138) |
| | 3,897 | 3,692 | 3,338 |
| **Income Before Minority Interest and** | | | |
| **Cumulative Effect of Accounting Change** | 6,854 | 6,424 | 5,745 |
| **Minority Interest** | (183) | (129) | (170) |
| **Income Before Cumulative Effect of Accounting Change** | 6,671 | 6,295 | 5,575 |
| Cumulative Effect of Accounting Change, net of tax benefit of $119 | – | – | (198) |
| **Net Income** | $ 6,671 | $ 6,295 | $ 5,377 |
| **Net Income Per Common Share:** | | | |
| **Basic Net Income Per Common Share:** | | | |
| Income before cumulative effect of accounting change | $ 1.49 | $ 1.41 | $ 1.25 |
| Cumulative effect of accounting change, net of tax | – | – | (0.04) |
| Net Income Per Common Share | $ 1.49 | $ 1.41 | $ 1.21 |
| Average Number of Common Shares | 4,465 | 4,465 | 4,451 |
| **Diluted Net Income Per Common Share:** | | | |
| Income before cumulative effect of accounting change | $ 1.49 | $ 1.40 | $ 1.25 |
| Cumulative effect of accounting change, net of tax | – | – | (0.04) |
| Net Income Per Common Share | $ 1.49 | $ 1.40 | $ 1.20 |
| Average Number of Common Shares | 4,481 | 4,484 | 4,474 |

Source: Wal-Mart's 2002 Annual Report.

he was under siege. He decided to counterattack. He first tried to convince the people in top management of Ben Franklin to enter discounting. After their refusal, Sam Walton made a quick trip around the country in search of ideas. He then began opening his own discount stores in small Arkansas towns like Bentonville and Rogers.

The company opened its first discount department store (Wal-Mart) in November 1962. The early stores had bare tile floors and pipe racks. Wal-Mart did not begin to revamp its image significantly until the mid-1970s, and growth in the early years was slow. However, once the company went public in 1970, sales began to increase rapidly. When it initially went public, one hundred shares of Wal-Mart stock would have cost $1,650. Now, those one hundred shares are worth over $11 million. Wal-Mart's stock was up 106 percent in 1999 and was named the number one stock on the Dow.

## EXHIBIT 2    Consolidated Balance Sheets

*(Amounts in millions)*

| January 31, | 2002 | 2001 |
|---|---|---|
| **Assets** | | |
| *Current Assets* | | |
| Cash and cash equivalents | $ 2,161 | $ 2,054 |
| Receivables | 2,000 | 1,768 |
| Inventories | | |
| At replacement cost | 22,749 | 21,644 |
| Less LIFO reserve | 135 | 202 |
| Inventories at LIFO cost | 22,614 | 21,442 |
| Prepaid expenses and other | 1,471 | 1,291 |
| **Total Current Assets** | 28,246 | 26,555 |
| *Property, Plant and Equipment, at Cost* | | |
| Land | 10,241 | 9,433 |
| Building and improvements | 28,527 | 24,537 |
| Fixtures and equipment | 14,135 | 12,964 |
| Transportation equipment | 1,089 | 879 |
| | 53,992 | 47,813 |
| Less accumulated depreciation | 11,436 | 10,196 |
| Net property, plant and equipment | 42,556 | 37,617 |
| *Property Under Capital Lease* | | |
| Property under capital lease | 4,626 | 4,620 |
| Less accumulated amortization | 1,432 | 1,303 |
| Net property under capital leases | 3,194 | 3,317 |
| *Other Assets and Deferred Charges* | | |
| Net goodwill and other acquired intangible assets | 8,595 | 9,059 |
| Other assets and deferred charges | 860 | 1,582 |
| **Total Assets** | $83,451 | $78,130 |
| **Liabilities and Shareholders' Equity** | | |
| *Current Liabilities* | | |
| Commercial paper | $    743 | $ 2,286 |
| Accounts payable | 15,617 | 15,092 |
| Accrued liabilities | 7,174 | 6,355 |
| Accrued income taxes | 1,343 | 841 |
| Long-term debt due within one year | 2,257 | 4,234 |
| Obligations under capital leases due within one year | 148 | 141 |
| **Total Current Liabilities** | 27,282 | 28,949 |
| Long-Term Debt | 15,687 | 12,501 |
| Long-Term Obligations Under Capital Leases | 3,045 | 3,154 |
| Deferred Income Taxes and Other | 1,128 | 1,043 |
| Minority Interest | 1,207 | 1,140 |
| *Shareholders' Equity* | | |
| Preferred stock ($0.10 par value; 100 shares authorized, none issued) | | |
| Common stock ($0.10 par value; 11,000 shares authorized, 4,453 and 4,470 issued and outstanding in 2002 and 2001, respectively) | 445 | 447 |
| Capital in excess of par value | 1,484 | 1,411 |
| Retained earnings | 34,441 | 30,169 |
| Other accumulated comprehensive income | (1,268) | (684) |
| **Total Shareholders' Equity** | 35,102 | 31,343 |
| **Total Liabilities and Shareholders' Equity** | 83,451 | $78,130 |

*Source:* Wal-Mart's 2002 *Annual Report.*

# EXHIBIT 3    Fiscal 2002 End-of-Year Store Count

| State | Discount Stores | Supercenters | SAM'S CLUBS | Neighborhood Markets | State | Discount Stores | Supercenters | SAM'S CLUBS | Neighborhood Markets |
|-------|------|------|------|------|-------|------|------|------|------|
| Alabama | 40 | 43 | 9 | 0 | Nebraska | 11 | 10 | 3 | 0 |
| Alaska | 6 | 0 | 3 | 0 | Nevada | 12 | 5 | 4 | 0 |
| Arizona | 26 | 14 | 9 | 0 | New Hampshire | 18 | 5 | 4 | 0 |
| Arkansas | 39 | 40 | 4 | 6 | New Jersey | 27 | 0 | 7 | 0 |
| California | 125 | 0 | 29 | 0 | New Mexico | 9 | 13 | 4 | 0 |
| Colorado | 20 | 22 | 12 | 0 | New York | 51 | 17 | 18 | 0 |
| Connecticut | 21 | 2 | 3 | 0 | North Carolina | 53 | 43 | 16 | 0 |
| Delaware | 3 | 3 | 1 | 0 | North Dakota | 8 | 0 | 2 | 0 |
| Florida | 78 | 69 | 35 | 0 | Ohio | 72 | 19 | 25 | 0 |
| Georgia | 44 | 53 | 18 | 0 | Oklahoma | 44 | 36 | 7 | 11 |
| Hawaii | 6 | 0 | 1 | 0 | Oregon | 23 | 3 | 0 | 0 |
| Idaho | 5 | 10 | 1 | 0 | Pennsylvania | 49 | 34 | 19 | 0 |
| Illinois | 83 | 30 | 27 | 0 | Rhade Island | 8 | 0 | 1 | 0 |
| Indiana | 44 | 39 | 14 | 0 | South Carolina | 25 | 34 | 9 | 0 |
| Iowa | 32 | 19 | 7 | 0 | South Dakota | 7 | 2 | 2 | 0 |
| Kansas | 32 | 19 | 6 | 0 | Tennessee | 40 | 49 | 15 | 0 |
| Kentucky | 35 | 39 | 5 | 0 | Texas | 129 | 135 | 64 | 14 |
| Louisiana | 37 | 43 | 11 | 0 | Utah | 8 | 11 | 6 | 0 |
| Maine | 15 | 5 | 3 | 0 | Vermont | 4 | 0 | 0 | 0 |
| Maryland | 28 | 4 | 11 | 0 | Virginia | 24 | 45 | 12 | 0 |
| Massachusetts | 38 | 1 | 3 | 0 | Washington | 29 | 3 | 2 | 0 |
| Michigan | 51 | 8 | 21 | 0 | West Virginia | 8 | 20 | 3 | 0 |
| Minnesota | 34 | 7 | 11 | 0 | Wisconsin | 50 | 13 | 11 | 0 |
| Mississippi | 27 | 34 | 5 | 0 | Wyoming | 3 | 6 | 2 | 0 |
| Missouri | 61 | 53 | 14 | 0 | U.S. Totals | 1647 | 1066 | 500 | 31 |
| Montana | 5 | 6 | 1 | 0 | | | | | |

## International/Worldwide

| Country | Discount Stores | Supercenters | SAM'S CLUBS | Neighborhood Markets | Country | Discount Stores | Supercenters | SAM'S CLUBS | Neighborhood Markets |
|---------|------|------|------|------|---------|------|------|------|------|
| Argentina | 0 | 11 | 0 | 0 | Mexico | 443† | 62 | 46 | 0 |
| Brazil | 0 | 12 | 8 | 2* | Puerto Rico | 9 | 1 | 7 | 0 |
| Canada | 196 | 0 | 0 | 0 | United Kingdom | 0 | 250‡ | 0 | 0 |
| China | 0 | 15 | 3 | 1 | International Totals: | 648 | 455 | 64 | 3 |
| Germany | 0 | 95 | 0 | 0 | Grand Totals | 2295 | 1521 | 564 | 34 |
| South Korea | 0 | 9 | 0 | 0 | | | | | |

*Brazil includes Todo Dia
†Mexico includes 106 Bodegas, 51 Suburbias, 44 Superamas, 242 VIPS
‡United Kingdom includes 244 ASDA stores, six Supercenters

Such retailers as Target, Venture, and Kmart provided the examples that Wal-Mart sought to emulate in its growth. The old Wal-Mart store colors, dark blue and white (too harsh), were dumped in favor of a three-tone combination of light beige, soft blue, and burnt orange. Carpeting, which had long been discarded on apparel sales floors, was put back. New racks were put into use that displayed the entire garment instead of only an outer edge.

In 1987, Wal-Mart implemented two new concepts: (1) Hypermarkets, which are two-hundred-thousand-square-foot stores that sell everything, including food; and (2) Supercenters, which are scaled-down supermarkets. Also in 1987, Walton named David Glass as the new chief executive officer (CEO), while he remained chairman of the board. In 2000, H. Lee Scott was named president and CEO of Wal-Mart Stores, Inc. Exhibit 4 specifies the current organizational structure of Wal-Mart and identifies the individuals holding top management positions within the organization.

Sam Walton died in 1992. Bud Walton died in 1995. Wal-Mart's 1995 *Annual Report* is dedicated to Bud. Sam Walton once said about Bud, "Of course, my number-one retail partner has been my brother, Bud. Bud's wise counsel and guidance kept us from many a mistake. Often, Bud would advise taking a different direction or maybe changing the timing. I soon learned to listen to him because he has exceptional judgment and a great deal of common sense."

EXHIBIT 4    Wal-Mart's Organizational Chart

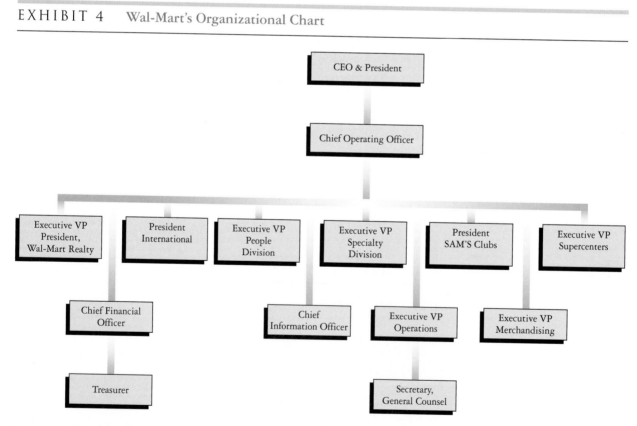

*Source:* **www.freeedgar.com.**

Wal-Mart's current president and CEO, H. Lee Scott, commends the past leadership and management standards set by Sam Walton. He states, "While our history is rich with success, there's no question that our best years are yet to come."

## DIVISIONS

### Wal-Mart Stores

Most Wal-Mart stores are located in towns of five thousand to twenty-five thousand. On occasion, smaller stores are built in communities of less than five thousand. As indicated in Exhibit 3 for fiscal 2002, Wal-Mart, Inc., currently operates domestically 1,647 Wal-Mart discount stores, 1,066 Supercenters, 500 SAM's Clubs, and 31 Neighborhood Markets. Most of Wal-Mart's $217.7 billion in fiscal 2002 sales came from Wal-Mart stores and Supercenters. Exhibit 5 provides a breakdown of net sales per division, while Exhibit 6 provides other pertinent financial data per division.

International sales accounted for approximately 28 percent of total company sales in fiscal 2002. This is up from 17 percent in fiscal 2001. For fiscal 2002, Wal-Mart operated internationally in 9 countries, with 648 discount stores, 455 Supercenters, and 64 SAM's Clubs.

Wal-Mart grouped its smaller discount stores, such as the one in Bennington, Vermont, into a new Hometown USA program. This strategy allows the company to give special attention to customers in smaller markets in rural America. Hometown USA consists of the stores that are less than 50,000 square feet and that are under one regional manager. The idea is to enable these stores to develop locally and with a different mix from the large prototypes. Although these stores represent Wal-Mart's heritage, they had become lost in the shuffle as the company opened 120,000 to 150,000 square foot stores.

Wal-Mart stores generally have thirty-six departments and offer a wide variety of merchandise, including apparel for women, girls, men, boys, and infants. Each store also carries curtains, fabrics and notions, shoes, housewares, hardware, electronics, home supplies, sporting goods, toys, cameras and supplies, health and beauty aids, pharmaceuticals, and jewelry. Nationally advertised merchandise accounts for a majority of sales of the stores. Wal-Mart has begun marketing limited lines of merchandise under the brand

EXHIBIT 5    Net Sales by Operating Segment

The Company and each of its operating segments had net sales (in millions) for the three fiscal years ended January 31, 2002 as follows:

| Fiscal Year | Wal-Mart Stores | SAM'S CLUB | International | Other | Total Company | Total Company Increase from Prior Fiscal Year |
|---|---|---|---|---|---|---|
| 2002 | $139,131 | $29,395 | $35,485 | $13,788 | $217,799 | 14% |
| 2001 | 121,889 | 26,798 | 32,100 | 10,542 | 191,329 | 16% |
| 2000 | 108,721 | 24,801 | 22,728 | 8,763 | 165,013 | 20% |

Our net sales grew by 14% in fiscal 2002 when compared with fiscal 2001. That increase resulted from our domestic and international expansion programs, and a domestic comparative store sales increase of 6% when compared with fiscal 2001. The sales increase of 16% in fiscal 2001, when compared with fiscal 2000, resulted from our domestic and international expansion programs, and a domestic comparative store sales increase of 5%. The Wal-Mart stores and SAM'S CLUB segments include domestic units only. Wal-Mart stores and SAM'S CLUBS located outside the United States are included in the International segment.

Source: Wal-Mart's 2002 Annual Report.

## EXHIBIT 6    Wal-Mart Segment Data

### A. Wal-Mart Stores Segment

| Fiscal year | Segment sales increase from prior fiscal year | Segment operating income (in billions) | Segment operating income increase from prior year | Operating income as a percentage of segment sales |
|---|---|---|---|---|
| 2002 | 14.1% | $ 10.3 | 6.0% | 7.4% |
| 2001 | 12.1% | 9.7 | 11.5% | 8.0% |
| 2000 | 14.0% | 8.7 | 20.2% | 8.0% |

The Wal-Mart Stores segment sales amounted to 63.9% of total Company sales in fiscal 2002, which compares to 63.7% and 65.9% in fiscal 2001 and 2000, respectively.

### B. SAM'S CLUB Segment

| Fiscal year | Segment sales increase from prior fiscal year | Segment operating income (in billions) | Segment operating income increase from prior year | Operating income as a percentage of segment sales |
|---|---|---|---|---|
| 2002 | 9.7% | $ 1,028 | 9.1% | 3.5% |
| 2001 | 8.1% | 942 | 10.8% | 3.5% |
| 2000 | 8.4% | 850 | 22.7% | 3.4% |

The SAM'S CLUB segment net sales amounted to 13.5% of total Company net sales in fiscal 2002, which compares to 14.0% and 15.0% in fiscal 2001 and 2000, respectively.

### C. International Segment

| Fiscal year | Segment sales increase from prior fiscal year | Segment operating income (in billions) | Segment operating income increase from prior year | Operating income as a percentage of segment sales |
|---|---|---|---|---|
| 2002 | 10.5% | $ 1,458 | 31.1% | 4.1% |
| 2001 | 41.2% | 1,112 | 36.1% | 3.5% |
| 2000 | 85.6% | 817 | 48.8% | 3.6% |

Our International segment is comprised of wholly-owned operations in Argentina, Canada, Germany, South Korea, Puerto Rico and the United Kingdom; operations through joint ventures in China; and operations through majority-owned subsidiaries in Brazil and Mexico. International sales accounted for approximately 16.3% of total Company sales in fiscal 2002 compared with 16.8% in fiscal 2001 and 13.8% in fiscal 2000.

### D. Other

| Fiscal year | Segment sales increase from prior fiscal year | Segment operating income (in billions) | Segment operating income increase from prior year | Operating income as a percentage of segment sales |
|---|---|---|---|---|
| 2002 | 30.8% | ($714) | (147.9%) | (5.2%) |
| 2001 | 20.3% | (288) | (9.5%) | (2.7%) |
| 2000 | 23.2% | (263) | 37.2% | (3.0%) |

Sales in the Other category comprise sales to third parties by the Company's wholly-owned subsidiary McLane Company, Inc., a whole-sale distributor. McLane offers a wide variety of grocery and non-grocery products, which it sells to a variety of retailers including the Company's Wal-Mart Stores and SAM'S CLUB segments. McLane's sales to other Wal-Mart companies are not included in the total sales of the Company.

*Source:* Wal-Mart's 2002 *Annual Report.*

name SAM's American Choice. The merchandise is carefully selected to ensure quality and must be made in the United States. Wal-Mart has also developed new apparel lines, such as the Kathie Lee career sportswear and dress collection, Basic Equipment sportswear, and McKids children's clothing.

## McLane's

McLane's is the nation's largest distributor of food and merchandise to convenience stores. McLane's offers a wide variety of grocery and nongrocery products, including perishable and nonperishable items. The nongrocery products consist primarily of tobacco products, merchandise, health and beauty aids, toys, and stationery. McLane's is a wholesale distributor that sells merchandise to a variety of retailers, including Wal-Mart stores, SAM's Clubs, and Supercenters.

## SAM's Clubs

SAM's Clubs are membership only, cash-and-carry operations. A financial service credit-card program (Discover Card) is available in all clubs. Qualified members include businesses and those individuals who are members of certain qualifying organizations, such as government and state employees and credit union members. Both business and individual members have an annual membership fee of $25 for the primary membership card. In addition, two individuals of the same household who don't qualify for the previously mentioned membership can establish an Advantage membership for $35 annually, and additional names can be added to this membership for $15 each.

SAM's offers bulk displays of name-brand merchandise, some soft goods, and institutional-size grocery items. SAM's Clubs usually offer over 3,500 items, which are used most often by the consumers they serve. Each SAM's also carries jewelry, sporting goods, toys, tires, stationery, and books. Most clubs have fresh-food departments, such as bakery, meat, and produce sections.

SAM's is a $26 billion business that is starting to grow again. The clubs were never designed to sell merchandise categories, but rather items, and because the number of items is limited to about two thousand for the wholesale part of the business, which is 60 to 65 percent of sales, and to one thousand to fifteen hundred for personal and individual use, it is very important for the items to be appropriate for the location. Also, the items have to come and go seasonally, so continuity by category is not appropriate. Thus, there is a problem for buyers who are item merchants and compete for space in the clubs.

At the end of fiscal 2002, Wal-Mart had a total of 500 domestic SAM's Clubs in operation. Sales for the Wal-Mart's SAM's Clubs segment increased by 9.7 percent in fiscal 2002, compared to fiscal 2001.

## Supercenters

Wal-Mart's Supercenters combine groceries with general merchandise, giving customers one-stop shopping. As evidenced by Exhibit 3, Wal-Mart operated 1,066 domestic Supercenters in fiscal 2002.

Supercenters constitute the company's fastest growing division, and management is extremely pleased with them. Currently, the limitation is distribution, and Wal-Mart is working hard to expand its food distribution capabilities. Most of the Supercenters replace Wal-Mart stores, so they had a jump-start on the general merchandise side of the store, while food has tended to build slowly. However, the company has gained market share more quickly than planned. Wal-Mart likes to locate Supercenters near the strongest food retailers so their facilities will "either get better or be run out of town."

The Wal-Mart Supercenter is one of the most important retail concepts on the landscape at this time. As with the discount stores, their real competitive impact comes not in the year they open but in the third year, because they have a maturation curve that's more like a Wal-Mart store than a food store. Also, the one-stop convenience aspect of the stores has such broad appeal that it is drawing a larger customer audience on a regular basis. Supercenters are continuing to get better in many categories and are attracting a higher-income audience, in addition to their traditional customers. Supercenters provide mart carts and are all on one floor, making the stores handicapped accessible. Wal-Mart's Supercenters average between 100,000 and 210,000 square feet of retail space. They usually employ between 200–550 associates, contingent upon store size and consumer needs. The company's broad assortments and everyday low prices are very compelling; extensive advertising is not needed. This represents an enormous saving over the competition. Furthermore, as Supercenters move more into food distribution, they gain a major cost advantage over Super Kmart and Super Target.

The Supercenters are designed with wider aisles, directory signs, departmental directories, and twenty-four-hour service. They are usually equipped with a customer service desk and scanning registers to provide more efficient checkout procedures.

## Neighborhood Markets

Wal-Mart's Neighborhood Markets first began operations in 1998 and are generally located in markets with Wal-Mart Supercenters. The Neighborhood Markets offer customers groceries, pharmaceuticals, and general merchandise. These Markets range from 42,000 to 55,000 square feet and usually employ 80 to 100 associates. They provide about 28,000 items to customers, including fresh produce, meats, and dairy items; one-hour photo processing; drive-through pharmacies; pet supplies; and household chemicals.

## International

As indicated in Exhibit 3, for fiscal 2002, the company had 196 Wal-Mart stores in Canada, 443 in Mexico, and 9 in Puerto Rico. Note that Wal-Mart also operated 455 Supercenters and 64 SAM's Clubs outside the United States as fiscal 2002 ended. Mexico is home to Wal-Mart's oldest and most extensive international operations. Wal-Mart de Mexico is strengthened by strong customer support, and the opening of several new stores in the near future is planned.

Wal-Mart has also reached a new market in South Korea; now there are nine Supercenters open there. Wal-Mart has recently bought the United Kingdom's number three supermarket, ASDA, for £6.7 billion ($11.19 billion) and is looking to grow ASDA in the United Kingdom and to expand further in continental Europe, including France. The United Kingdom market leader, Tesco, is trying to increase the scale of its operations internationally and recently revealed plans to have around two-hundred hypermarkets overseas by 2004, with more than £10 billion in annual sales from outside the United Kingdom.

Wal-Mart maintains a strategic competitive focus on global positioning. According to Bob L. Martin, president of the International Division, "We are a global brand name. To customers everywhere, [the name] means low cost, best value, and greatest selection of quality merchandise and highest standards of customer service. But the fact that International has grown to more than $12 billion in sales in less than seven years gives us an idea of how great the potential is."

Community involvement, responding to local needs, merchandise preferences, and buying locally are all hallmarks of the International Wal-Marts, just as they are in the United States.

## Distribution Centers

Wal-Mart has forty-three distribution centers nationwide, nine of which are grocery distribution centers and two of which are import distribution centers. Wal-Mart's distribution operations are highly automated. A typical Wal-Mart Discount Store has more than seventy thousand standard items in stock; Supercenters carry more than twenty thousand additional grocery items, a lot of which are perishable. So such items have to be ordered frequently. Associates use handheld computers that are linked by radio-frequency network to area stores. To place orders, each store wires merchandise requests to warehouses, which in turn either ship immediately or reorder. Wal-Mart computers are linked directly to over two hundred vendors, so deliveries are faster. Wal-Mart has one of the world's largest private satellite communication systems that enables it to control distribution. In addition, Wal-Mart has installed point-of-sale bar code scanning in all of its stores.

Wal-Mart owns a fleet of truck-tractors that can deliver goods to any store in thirty-eight to forty-eight hours from the time the order is placed. After trucks drop off merchandise, they frequently pick up merchandise from manufacturers on the way back to the distribution center. This back-haul rate averages over 60 percent and is yet another way Wal-Mart cuts costs.

With an information systems staff of twelve hundred and system links with about five thousand manufacturers, Wal-Mart leads the industry in information technology. This means Wal-Mart is dedicated to providing its associates with the technological tools they need to work smarter everyday. "With this technology, we're getting better, quicker, and more accurate information to manage and control every aspect of our business," said Randy Mott, senior vice president and chief information officer.

## WAL-MART.COM

Wal-Mart is in the retail business, which now includes Internet e-tailing. The Internet has interesting aspects and will definitely serve a growing market throughout the twenty-first century. Profits are not easily made over the Internet, and issues of cost of delivery, merchandise returns, and data security are top concerns prior to building business over the Internet. Wal-Mart moved into the Internet in 1996 with the introduction of Wal-Mart On-line, and then it relaunched the site on January 1, 2000, as **Wal-Mart.com**. Wal-Mart looks at Internet retailing as another store with possibility—but without walls.

**Wal-Mart.com**, with its headquarters located in the San Francisco Bay area, is a wholly owned subsidiary of Wal-Mart Stores, Inc. This location choice affords **Wal-Mart.com** access to the best pool of Internet executive and technical talent. The company was able to attract a top retail management talent in Jeanne Jackson as the CEO of **Wal-Mart.com**. This new venture combines the better of two worlds, technology and retailing, in order to provide customers easy access to more things at Wal-Mart twenty-four-hours a day and seven days a week. Its distinct purpose is to provide consumers with a convenient and rewarding online shopping experience. **Wal-Mart.com** will have a separate management team and board of directors. Ultimately, it might choose to go public; however, Wal-Mart Stores will retain a majority ownership of the new venture.

According to the information provided by the **Wal-Mart.com** Web site, Wal-Mart and AOL currently offer unlimited Internet access and e-mail to customers for a monthly charge of $9.94. This affords the global leader in retailing and the world's leading interactive services company a wide-ranging strategic alliance and a definite competitive advantage. As stated by H. Lee Scott in a December 1999 **Walmart.com** press release, "We are taking this step to benefit our customers. Millions of our customers will be enabled by this agreement to obtain affordable online offerings, and AOL's reach to more than 19 million households represents a significant opportunity for value-conscious Americans. This agreement is very consistent with our heritage. We are bringing a new form of shopping to people in small- to medium-sized communities across the country."

## OPERATIONS

Wal-Mart's expense structure, measured as a percentage of sales, continues to be among the lowest in the industry. Although Walton watched expenses, he rewarded sales managers handsomely. Sales figures are available to every employee at Wal-Mart. Monthly figures for each department are ranked and made available throughout the organization. Employees who do better than average get rewarded with raises, bonuses, and a pat on the back. Poor performers are only rarely fired, although demotions are possible.

All employees (called "associates") have a stake in the financial performance of the company. Store managers earn as much as $100,000 to $150,000 per year. Even part-time clerks qualify for profit-sharing and stock-purchase plans. Millionaires among Wal-Mart's middle managers are not uncommon. Executives frequently solicit ideas for improving the organization from employees and often put them to use.

Because Wal-Mart stock sold at thirty-five to forty times earnings—an almost incredible price—Walton presided over a sizable fortune before his death. The Walton family owns 39 percent of Wal-Mart stock. Family holdings are worth nearly $16 billion.

Continuing a Walton tradition, Wal-Mart invites over one hundred analysts and institutional investors to the field house at the University of Arkansas for its annual meeting in mid-June. During the day-and-a-half session, investors meet top executives as well as Wal-Mart district managers, buyers, and two hundred thousand hourly salespeople. Investors see a give-and-take meeting between buyers and district managers.

### Employee Benefits

Wal-Mart management takes pride in the ongoing development of its people. Training is seen as critical to outstanding performance, and new programs are often implemented in all areas of the company. The combination of grassroots meetings, the open-door policy, videos, printed material, classroom and home study, year-end management meetings, and on-the-job training has enabled employees to prepare themselves for advancement and added responsibilities.

Wal-Mart managers stay current with new developments and needed changes. Executives spend one week each year in hourly jobs in various stores. Walton himself once traveled at least three days per week, visiting competitors' stores and attending the opening of new stores, leading the Wal-Mart cheer, "Give me a W, give me an A. . . ."

Wal-Mart encourages employee stock purchases; about 8 percent of Wal-Mart stock is owned by employees. Under the Stock Purchase Plan, stock may be bought by two different methods. First, an amount is deducted from each employee's check, with a maximum of $62.50 per check. An additional 15 percent of the amount deducted is contributed by Wal-Mart (up to $1,800 of annual stock purchases). Second, a lump-sum purchase of up to $1,500 is allowed in April, with an additional 15 percent added by the company. Wal-Mart also offers an associate Stock Ownership Plan, with approximately four thousand management associates having stock options. Over four hundred thousand associates have chosen to take part in the Stock Purchase Plan, and another two hundred thousand have enrolled in a Direct Purchase Plan.

Wal-Mart has a corporate profit-sharing plan. The purposes of the profit-sharing plan are to furnish an incentive for increased efficiency, to provide progressive recognition of service, and to encourage careers with the company by Wal-Mart associates. This is a trustee-administered plan, which means that the company's contributions are made only out of net profits and are held by a trustee. The company from time to time contributes 10 percent of net profits to the trust.

Company contributions can be withdrawn only on termination. If employment with the company is terminated because of retirement, death, or permanent disability, the company contribution is fully vested (meaning the entire amount is nonforfeitable). If termination of employment occurs for any other reason, the amount that is nonforfeitable depends on the number of years of service with the company. After completion of the third year of service with the company, 20 percent of each participant's account is nonforfeitable for each subsequent year of service. After seven years of service, a participant's account is 100-percent vested.

## Predatory Pricing

Three independent pharmacies in Conway, Arkansas, recently filed a suit, claiming Wal-Mart was deliberately pricing products below cost to kill competition. Wal-Mart argued that it priced products below cost not to harm competitors but to meet or beat rivals' prices. Chancery Court Judge David L. Reynolds on October 11, 1996, found Wal-Mart guilty of predatory pricing and ordered the company to pay the pharmacies $286,407 in damages. The judge also forbade Wal-Mart from selling products below cost in Conway in the future.

Wal-Mart appealed the ruling to the Arkansas Supreme Court, which reversed and dismissed the case. It is Wal-Mart's policy that its store managers monitor the retail prices charged by competitors in their respective market areas and lower prices for highly competitive merchandise without regard to the cost of individual items. This price is frequently below Wal-Mart's cost of acquiring some of these products in highly competitive markets. The stated purpose of Wal-Mart's pricing policy is to "meet or beat" the retail prices contemporaneously charged by competitors for highly competitive, price-sensitive merchandise; to maintain "low-price leadership" in the local marketplace; and to "attract a disproportionate number of customers into a store to increase traffic."

The store's pricing practices with regard to specific articles did not violate the Arkansas Unfair Practices Act section prohibiting vendors from selling at or below their cost. The mere proof of below-cost sales was not sufficient to prove a violation of the act absent intent to destroy competition. There was no evidence showing exactly which individual items were sold below cost, the frequency of those sales, the duration of the sales, and to what extent the sales existed.

### Diversity Among Employees

Sam Walton was admittedly old-fashioned in many respects. Wal-Mart store policies reflect many of his values. For example, store policies forbid employees from dating other employees without the prior approval of the executive committee. Also, women are rarely found in management positions. Annual managers meetings include sessions in which wives are allowed to speak out about the problems of living with a Wal-Mart manager. No women can be found in the ranks of Wal-Mart's top management. Walton also resisted placing women on the board of directors; however, there are two women on the board at this time. Wal-Mart is an EEO/AA employer, but it has managed to get away with certain past discriminatory policies.

Wal-Mart has instituted several initiatives to increase the recruitment and promotion of women and minorities, including:

- A mentoring program encompassing more than 750 women and minority managers,
- A women's leadership group, in partnership with Herman Miller and ServiceMaster, to develop opportunities for high-potential female managers,
- Store internships during the summer for college students between their junior and senior years, with 70 percent being women or minorities.

### Philanthropy and Community Involvement

Exhibit 7 shows Wal-Mart's community involvement in fiscal 2002. Education is a primary beneficiary of Wal-Mart charitable giving. Some examples of its largesse follow.

- Each store awards a $1,000 college scholarship to a qualifying high school senior. More than $11 million in scholarships have been awarded since the program's inception.
- The company has made a major commitment to the United Negro College Fund. Wal-Mart pledged $1,000,000 to UNCF over a four-year period.
- The company sponsored the Competitive Edge Scholarship Fund. In 1993, Wal-Mart teamed up with participating vendor-partners to start the fund, which makes four-year scholarships—each worth $20,000—available to students pursuing technology-related college degrees.
- Since 1993, Wal-Mart and SAM's Clubs associates have raised more than $80 million in support of local United Way agencies.
- Wal-Mart Stores, Inc., is the number-one sponsor for the Children's Miracle Network (CMN) Telethon. Associates from all U.S. divisions of the company have helped raise more than $131 million for CMN since 1988. In 1998, Wal-Mart donated $27 million to CMN.
- In 1999, Community Matching Grants totaled more than $42 million from the Wal-Mart Foundation.

Wal-Mart's corporate citizenship extends well beyond U.S. borders and into every country in which the company operates.

### Marketing

The discount retailing business is seasonal to a certain extent. Generally, the highest volume of sales and net income occurs in the fourth fiscal quarter, and the lowest volume occurs during the first fiscal quarter. Wal-Mart draws customers into the store by radio and television advertising, monthly circulars, and weekly newspaper ads. Television

EXHIBIT 7    Community Involvement 2002

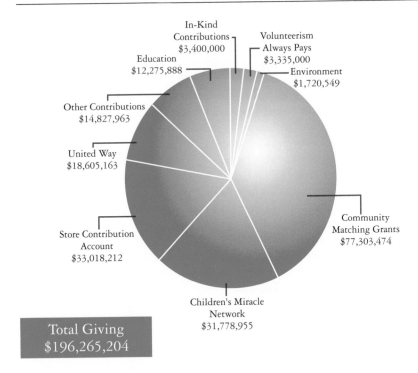

In-Kind
Contributions
$3,400,000

Volunteerism
Always Pays
$3,335,000

Education
$12,275,888

Environment
$1,720,549

Other Contributions
$14,827,963

United Way
$18,605,163

Community
Matching Grants
$77,303,474

Store Contribution
Account
$33,018,212

Children's Miracle
Network
$31,778,955

Total Giving
$196,265,204

*Source:* Wal-Mart's 2002 *Annual Report.*

advertising is used to convey an image of everyday low prices and quality merchandise. Radio is used to a lesser degree to promote specific products that are usually in high demand. Newspaper advertisements and monthly circulars are major contributors to the program, emphasizing deeply discounted items, and they are effective at luring customers into the stores.

Efforts are also made to discount corporate overhead. Visitors often mistake corporate headquarters for a warehouse because of its limited decor and "show." Wal-Mart executives share hotel rooms when traveling to reduce expenses. The company avoids spending money on consultants and marketing experts. Instead, decisions are made based on the intuitive judgments of managers and employees and on the assessment of strategies of other retail chains.

Wal-Mart censors some products. The company has banned recordings and removed magazines based on lyrics and graphics; it has also stopped marketing teen rock magazines. Wal-Mart advertises a "Buy American" policy in an effort to keep production at home. Consequently, Wal-Mart buyers are constantly seeking vendors in grass-roots America. In Tulsa, Zebco, the fishing equipment company, responded to Wal-Mart's challenge by bucking the trend toward overseas fishing tackle manufacturing. Zebco created more than two hundred U.S. jobs to assemble rods and to manufacture bait-and-cast reels. The company's bait-and-cast reels are the first to be manufactured in the United States in thirty years.

## COMPETITORS

Kmart is one of Wal-Mart's key competitors. However, compared to Wal-Mart, the scope of Kmart's problem becomes evident. Even though each company operates roughly the same number of stores (Kmart has 2001 discount stores and 104 Supercenters), Wal-Mart's sales are roughly four times Kmart's sales (almost $37 billion). Wal-Mart's discount stores are larger than Kmart's and produce sales of about $385 per square foot, compared to $236 per square foot for Kmart.

Should Wal-Mart, the price leader in discounting, choose to sacrifice $0.10 to $0.15 of its estimated earnings per share, it virtually could ensure that Kmart would not operate above the breakeven point. Kmart is in a capital-intensive battle with Wal-Mart, whose 1999 capital expenditures were nearly four times that of Kmart's. Kmart's capital resources for this battle are limited, and if its earnings fail to improve, it cannot stay in this capital-intensive race for long. When Kmart recently cut its dividend rate in half, management took a step in the right direction toward conserving its financial resources. The CEO's recommendation regarding the dividend payout will be a litmus test of the urgency with which management intends to apply the company's assets toward turning around the Kmart discount stores.

Supercenters are revolutionizing the discount store battlefield, just as tanks redefined trench warfare. Wal-Mart started 1995 with sixty-eight Supercenters but increased this number to 1,294 in fiscal 2001. The goal of each new store is to shatter the profit potential of at least one older Kmart discount store. This is the dusk of the discount store era, and improvements in the merchandising and systems of Kmart's discount stores might do little to forestall their decline.

Kmart had slowed its rollout of its Super Kmart Centers to allow more time to develop the staff and skills needed for these stores to achieve an adequate return. As the rollout reaccelerates, Wal-Mart is operating over 1,294 Supercenters worldwide, and retailing has changed greatly.

On a positive note, Kmart's board has been strengthened by new appointments who are steering the company; new management provides a fresh perspective for the company; new strategies are being implemented; same-store sales are strong; expenses are being reduced; and earnings should rise.

JCPenney and Sears responded to the reality of retail competition several years ago by offering consumers better values than before. They have succeeded in lifting their sales in both dollars and units. Kmart planned to take market share from them but was blocked. Kmart declared bankruptcy in 2001. By December 2000, Target operations consisted of 978 Target locations, 267 Mervyn's locations, and 64 Marshall Fields' locations through out the United States.

## FUTURE STRATEGIES

What strategies would you recommend to current CEO H. Lee Scott? How can Wal-Mart benefit from Internet retailing? How aggressively should Wal-Mart expand internationally and where? Should Wal-Mart get a foothold in Europe before competitors seize the initiative? Should Wal-Mart expand further in Mexico, the United States, or Canada? Should Wal-Mart make further acquisitions, like its Woolco acquisition in Canada? Is Wal-Mart's rate of growth of Supercenters too fast? What private label products should Wal-Mart consider developing? What can Wal-Mart do to improve its SAM's Clubs operations? Develop a three year strategic plan for CEO Lee Scott.

# TARGET CORPORATION—2002

Henry Beam
Western Michigan University

TGT

www.target.com

Target Corporation is the country's fourth largest general merchandise retailer, behind Wal-Mart, Kmart, and Sears Roebuck. Company revenues were $39.1 billion in 2001, a 7.7 percent increase over 2000. Earnings were $1.37 billion, an increase of 0.1 percent over 2000. Headquartered in Minneapolis, Minnesota, it caters to all income groups through three operating divisions: Mervyn's, Marshall Field's, and Target. Marshall Field's department stores are strong in the upper Midwest, controlling significant shares of the market in Detroit, Chicago, and Minneapolis. Target's upscale general merchandise discount stores are spread across the country and account for nearly 80 percent of the company's sales and profits. Mervyn's, with stores primarily in California, caters to lower-to-middle income shoppers. The Target division has been so successful that the company, formerly named Dayton Hudson, changed its name to Target Corporation in 2000. In addition, all department stores named Hudson's or Dayton's were renamed Marshall Field's. Reflecting the corporate emphasis on service, all divisions refer to their customers as guests.

Sometimes, a Target store will be located near a Mervyn's and a Marshall Field's department store, or both. A mall in Kalamazoo, Michigan, has a Marshall Field's and a Mervyn's, while less than a mile away there is a Target store in a shopping center. Despite such proximity of locations, Target Corporation has made little attempt to associate the divisions with each other in the eyes of consumers, many of whom aren't aware the three divisions are part of the same company.

## HISTORY

Joseph Hudson opened a men's clothing store in Detroit in 1873. Among his merchandising innovations were return privileges and price-marking in place of bargaining. By 1891, Hudson's was the largest retailer of men's clothing in America. When Hudson died in 1928, his four nephews took over and expanded the business. In 1928, Hudson's built a new building in downtown Detroit. The retailer eventually grew to twenty-five stories with forty-nine acres of floor space and exuded quality throughout. The Detroit store was closed in 1982 due to the steady economic decline which took place in downtown Detroit starting in the late 1950s. The store was demolished in 1998 to make room for a downtown Detroit redevelopment project.

In 1903, George Dayton, a former banker, opened his Dayton Dry Goods store in Minneapolis, where there was high foot traffic. Like Hudson, Dayton offered return privileges and liberal credit. His store expanded to a full-line department store that was twelve stories tall. After World War II, both companies saw that the future of retailing lay in the suburbs. In 1954, Hudson's built Northland at the northwest edge of Detroit, then the largest shopping center in the United States. Dayton's built the world's first fully enclosed shopping mall, Southdale, in Minneapolis in 1956. In an attempt to diversify, Dayton's opened its first Target discount store in 1962. After going public in 1966,

93

Dayton's grew through acquisitions. In 1969, it bought the family-owned Hudson's for stock, forming Dayton Hudson Corporation. In 1978, the company bought the California-based Mervyn's retail chain of forty-seven stores. Its last major acquisition came in 1990, when it bought Marshall Field's department stores, assuming $1 billion of debt in the process. Marshall Field's had grown out of a dry-goods business that was started in Chicago in 1852 by Potter Palmer. Marshall Field bought the store in 1865, the last year of the Civil War, and built it into one of Chicago's biggest retailers. His motto, "Give the lady what she wants," was a precursor of customer-oriented retailing. The original Marshall Field's store, located in downtown Chicago, was remodeled in 1992. It is the company's largest store and a major tourist attraction for visitors to Chicago. Marshall Field's 111 State Street apparel line is named for the store's Chicago street address.

Target Corporation's executive office provides leadership for all divisions and establishes the values under which those divisions operate. Each of the six operating divisions has its own CEO and president and is run like an independent business, even though the divisions are encouraged to share advances in technology and coordinate purchasing and financial management. An organization chart for the company and its operating divisions is given in Exhibit 1.

## DIVISIONS

### Target

At the end of 2001, the Target division consisted of 977 stores located in all forty-eight continental states as indicated in Exhibit 2. Target is an upscale discount retailer that provides good quality, family-oriented merchandise at attractive prices in a clean, spacious, and customer-friendly environment. Its motto is, "Expect more, pay less." A 1999 *Fortune* article on Target commented, "Going to Target is a cool experience, and everybody now considers it cool to save money. On the other hand, is it cool to save at Kmart, at Wal-Mart? I don't think so." Target offers innovative, well-designed merchandise at reasonable prices, such as Philips Kitchen Appliances, Calphalon cookware, Michael Graves designed small appliances, and Eddie Bauer camping gear.

Target stores, which average 125,000 square feet in size, are typically located in small, freestanding malls. Eight regional distribution centers process 90 percent of all freight for the stores. The objective of the distribution centers is to provide next-day service to all locations. Target invites evaluation from its customers on evaluation forms entitled "Be Our Guest Commentator" that are available at checkout counters.

EXHIBIT 1    Organization Chart for Target Corporation

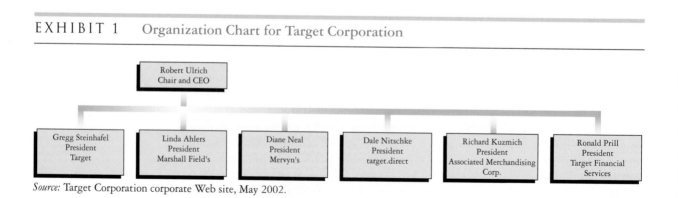

*Source:* Target Corporation corporate Web site, May 2002.

EXHIBIT 2    Number of Stores

|  | February 3, 2001 | Opened | Closed | February 2, 2002 |
|---|---|---|---|---|
| Target | 977 | 93 | 17 | 1,053 |
| Mervyn's | 266 | – | 2 | 264 |
| Marshall Field's | 64 | — | — | 64 |
| Total | 1,307 | 93 | 19 | 1,381 |

*Source:* Target's 2001 *Annual Report,* p. 20.

Target's micromarketing program has helped improve its merchandise assortments on a store-by-store basis. Micromarketing is Target's system for tailoring merchandise assortments to customers' needs in individual stores or markets, based on regional, climatic, demographic, and ethnic factors. This permits stores as close as fifteen miles apart to offer different merchandise mixes. The typical Target customer is a married woman with children, who is part of a two-wage-earner family with an average household income of $50,000. The average household income in the United States is $39,000. Over 80 percent of its customers have attended college. Target advertises through multipage inserts placed in local newspapers and television advertisements featuring the familiar red circular bull's eye symbol.

Target plans to continue opening stores in less penetrated markets, such as Boston, New York, and Philadelphia. But increasingly, Target is building new stores in more mature markets, such as Atlanta, Denver, Indianapolis, and Phoenix. Although the cost of a store site in these more densely populated regions is generally higher, so is the sales potential. Over the past five years, Target's square footage has grown at a compound annual rate of 10 percent and is expected to continue to grow at that rate for the next few years. In 2000, comparable store sales (stores open for more than a year) increased 2.4 percent. Shortly after Montgomery Ward's declared bankruptcy in 2000, Target announced plans to buy thirty-five former Ward's stores in prime locations across the country. Most of these former Ward stores are expected to reopen as Target stores in 2002.

In 1995, Target opened its first two supercenter stores (SuperTargets) in the Plains states. The stores are about 180,000 square feet in size, with a fourth of the space devoted to grocery items, including its own line of grocery products marketed under the Archer Farms label. Certain categories, such as health and beauty aids and paper products, link the grocery and general merchandise areas and facilitate crossover shopping. The stores also feature a Starbucks Coffee Shop. The company anticipates that it will operate more than two hundred SuperTarget stores by 2010. According to CEO Robert Ulrich, Super-Targets bring "fashion to food" and offer "a store that is attractive to our guests and as differentiated from our competition as are our discount stores."

## Marshall Field's

At the end of 2001, Marshall Field's operated sixty-four department stores in eight Midwestern states, as indicated in Exhibit 2. About half of the department stores are located in the major markets of Chicago, Detroit, and Minneapolis/St. Paul. Historically, they emphasized fashion leadership, quality merchandise, and superior customer service. Today, the stores offer strong national brands with competitive prices in men's and women's apparel, accessories, and home furnishings. The typical customer for the department stores is married, is female, is in her early forties, and has a median family income of $50,000. Over half have earned a college degree, and two-thirds hold white collar positions.

In 1996, Linda Ahlers became chairman and CEO of Marshall Field's, making her one of the highest ranking female executives in the United States. Under Ahlers, the division has emphasized selling more upscale merchandise, improving the look of the stores, and boosting customer service. In addition to building new stores in selected locations, such as the new two-hundred-thousand-square-foot store in the Rivertown Crossing Mall in Grand Rapids, Michigan, the division is also renovating some of its older stores. Target's 2000 *Annual Report* states, "We are committed to our department store heritage, providing superior guest service, fashion leadership and continued support of the communities we serve. Our vision to be 'The Best Store in Town' is unwavering and vital to our future success."

### Mervyn's

At the end of 2001, Mervyn's consisted of 266 stores, 124 of which were in California, as indicated in Exhibit 2. The remainder were spread across the western states, with a few in Michigan and Minnesota. Mervyn's is a moderately-priced family department store chain emphasizing brand-name and private-label casual apparel and home fashions that complement the offerings of Target and Marshall Field's. Its motto is "Big brands, small prices." Mervyn's typical customer is about forty years old, female, married with children, and working outside the home. Half its stores are located in regional malls, and the rest are freestanding or in neighborhood shopping centers.

While Mervyn's showed improved sales and profitability in 2000, performance in recent years has been disappointing. In 1995, Mervyn's embarked on a new strategy that included promoting more frequently, increasing the focus on national brands sold at promotional prices, refining merchandise assortments, and using a California theme with its merchandise and advertising. Like Target, Mervyn's advertises through weekly multi-page inserts in local newspapers.

### Direct Marketing and target.direct

The direct merchandising and electronic retailing division of Target Corporation is called target.direct. It was formed in 2000 by combining Target's e-commerce operation with its Rivertown Trading Company direct merchandising unit to create a single organization. This division consists of two separate, wholly owned subsidiaries of Target Corporation:

- Rivertown Trading Company, acquired in 1998, is the company's catalog and e-commerce subsidiary. It produces six retail catalogs, four of which also have their own Web sites. The two largest catalogs are *Wireless,* which offers an eclectic assortment of gifts and entertainment merchandise, and *Signals,* which was originally created to appeal to the public television audience. *Signals* offers a broad selection of gifts, including videos, art prints, distinctive jewelry, and creative toys.
- target.direct LLC is the e-commerce and catalog subsidiary that supports Target Stores, Marshall Field's, and Mervyn's California, each of which has its own Web site.

All catalogs and online shopping services can be accessed through Target Corporation's corporate Web site, **www.target.com**. All merchandise purchased at target.com may be returned to any Target store location.

## COMPETITION

Because its six divisions, taken together, compete across all major merchandising categories, Target Corporation faces a wide range of competitors. The largest division, Target, competes directly with "the marts": Kmart and Wal-Mart.

### Kmart

Kmart traces its roots to the S.S. Kresge Company, incorporated in 1912, which was originally a Michigan-based dime store chain. By the 1950s, Kresge had become one of the largest general retailers in the nation, with stores primarily in urban locations. The first Kmart was opened in 1962 in a suburb of Detroit after an extensive study of retailing trends made in 1958 by its future CEO, Harry B. Cunningham. The Kmart large-store format was so successful that the company concentrated on it, rapidly opening Kmarts from coast to coast and closing dime stores as they became unprofitable. In 1977, the company officially changed its name to Kmart Corporation. Kmart's stores are generally perceived as older, smaller, and less attractive than those of Wal-Mart and Target. In 1996, a program was begun to redesign some of its existing stores into Big Kmarts, which featured a grocery section, brighter decor, and an expanded selection of merchandise. It featured the popular Martha Stewart line of women's apparel, home furnishings, and lawn and garden products. In December 1999, Kmart started offering an initially free internet service through its **bluelight.com** Web site. Despite these changes, Kmart declared bankruptcy in 2001.

### Wal-Mart

Wal-Mart Stores is one of the best-known success stories in America. Sam Walton opened his first Wal-Mart store in Rogers, Arkansas, in 1962. Growth, slow at first, accelerated during the 1970s. Wal-Mart established highly automated distribution centers to reduce shipping time and implemented an advanced computer system to track inventory and to speed up checkout and reordering. Wal-Mart's motto is displayed on each of its stores: "We sell for less, satisfaction guaranteed."

Wal-Mart is the world's largest retailer, with sales in 2000 of $192 billion and net income of $6.3 billion. It operates 1,736 Wal-Mart stores, 888 Supercenters, and 475 SAM's Clubs in the United States. The average community served has about fifteen thousand people in it. Wal-Mart has over one thousand international stores, mostly discount stores in Canada and Mexico, where it is the largest retailer. It has also acquired or built stores in China, United Kingdom, Germany, South Korea, and South America in the past few years.

Wal-Mart plans to open about one hundred fifty new Supercenters in the United States every year for the next few years. Supercenters carry a full line of groceries as well as a moderate selection of soft and hard goods. At an average size of about one hundred eighty thousand square feet, these stores are more than twice as large as the company's traditional discount stores and significantly more profitable. Wal-Mart has overtaken Kroger to become the nation's largest seller of groceries.

In 1983, Wal-Mart entered the warehouse business with its membership-only SAM's Wholesale Clubs. Its only significant competitor in warehouse clubs is Costco Companies. SAM's Clubs-sales and net income figures are included with those of Wal-Mart. At the end of 2000, SAM's Clubs had sales of $27 billion, and Costco had sales of $32 billion.

Target, Marshall Field's, and Mervyn's also compete to some extent with large national retailers such as Penny's and Sears, as well as with regional department store chains such as Kohl's in the Midwest, Dillard Department Stores in the South, and May Department Stores in the East. Exhibit 3 gives sales and net income figures for the five largest general merchandise firms.

EXHIBIT 3    Sales and Net Income Data, Five Largest General
Merchandise Firms, 1997–2001 (in millions)

| Year | | Wal-Mart | Sears | Kmart | Target | Penny (J.C.) |
|------|------|------|------|------|------|------|
| 2001E | Sales | 216,000 | 41,600 | 37,300 | 39,800 | 31,950 |
| | Net Income | 6,885 | 1,375 | 215 | 1,390 | 95 |
| 2000 | Sales | 191,329 | 40,937 | 37,028 | 36,903 | 31,846 |
| | Net Income | 6,295 | 1,540 | 265 | 1,264 | 78 |
| 1999 | Sales | 165,013 | 41,071 | 35,925 | 33,702 | 31,391 |
| | Net Income | 5,709 | 1,482 | 683 | 1,185 | 465 |
| 1998 | Sales | 137,634 | 41,322 | 33,674 | 30,662 | 29,656 |
| | Net Income | 4,430 | 1,300 | 581 | 962 | 654 |
| 1997 | Sales | 117,958 | 41,296 | 32,183 | 27,487 | 29,618 |
| | Net Income | 3,526 | 1,303 | 298 | 775 | 839 |

*Source:* Value Line Investment Survey (August 3, 2001).

## FINANCIAL ASPECTS

Balance sheet and income statement data on Target Corporation are given in Exhibits 4 and 5. By-segment financial information is provided in Exhibit 6, and a percentage analysis is provided in Exhibit 7.

### Financial Services

Financial services, including the credit card operation, are becoming an important part of Target's growth. Over the past five years, pretax profits from financing grew at a compound annual rate of 17 percent. Each division has its own credit card. The transactions are handled through Target Corporation's wholly-owned Retailer's National Bank, chartered in 1994. The divisions will also take other credit cards, such as VISA and MasterCard. The Target credit card, called the Target Guest Card, has been very successful. Target has over eighteen million guest card accounts and expects the number to increase by 10 percent or more each year.

Target stores now provide access to integrated banking and to brokerage and investment planing services through its alliance with E*Trade, a leading online discount brokerage service. Exhibits 8-10 provides a by-state breakdown of the company's stores.

## CORPORATE SOCIAL RESPONSIBILITY

Target Corporation is considered a model corporate citizen by consumer groups. It has contributed 5 percent of its pretax profits to philanthropic purposes every year since 1946. (By contrast, most large corporations in the United States contribute about 1 percent.) In 2000, the three operating divisions and the Target Corporation Foundation (funded by the corporation) gave over $50 million to the arts, to education, and to social action causes across the United States. Major contributions were made to programs and projects that strengthen families, promote the economic independence of individuals, or help neighborhoods respond to key social and economic concerns. Target will also donate 1 percent of purchases made on the Target Guest Card to the school of the guest's choice.

EXHIBIT 4    Target's Consolidated Statements of Financial Position
(in millions)

| | February 2, 2002 | February 3, 2001 |
|---|---|---|
| **Assets** | | |
| Cash and cash equivalents | $   499 | $   356 |
| Accounts receivable (net of $261 million allowance) | 3,831 | – |
| Receivable-backed securities | – | 1,941 |
| Inventory | 4,449 | 4,248 |
| Other | 869 | 759 |
| Total current assets | 9,648 | 7,304 |
| Property and equipment | | |
| Land | 2,833 | 2,467 |
| Buildings and improvements | 10,103 | 8,596 |
| Fixtures and equipment | 4,290 | 3,848 |
| Construction-in-progress | 1,216 | 848 |
| Accumulated depreciation | (4,909) | (4,341) |
| Property and equipment, net | 13,533 | 11,418 |
| Other | 973 | 768 |
| **Total assets** | $24,154 | $19,490 |
| **Liabilities and shareholders' investment** | | |
| Accounts payable | $ 4,160 | $ 3,576 |
| Accrued liabilities | 1,566 | 1,507 |
| Income taxes payable | 423 | 361 |
| Current portion of long-term debt and notes payable | 905 | 857 |
| Total current liabilities | 7,054 | 6,301 |
| Long-term debt | 8,088 | 5,634 |
| Deferred Income taxes and other | 1,152 | 1,036 |
| Shareholders' investment | | |
| Common stock | 75 | 75 |
| Additional paid-in-capital | 1,098 | 902 |
| Retained earnings | 6,687 | 5,542 |
| Total shareholders' investment | 7,860 | 6,519 |
| **Total liabilities and shareholders' investment** | $24,154 | $19,490 |

*Source:* Target's 2001 *Annual Report,* p. 25.

## ROBERT ULRICH, CHAIR AND CEO

Robert Ulrich, Chair and CEO of Target Corporation since 1994, received a B.A. degree from the University of Michigan and completed the Stanford Executive Program at the Stanford University Graduate School of Business. His whole career has been with Target and its predecessor companies, starting as a merchandise trainee at Marshall Field's in 1967. Ulrich is a devotee of the arts and serves on the board of the Minneapolis Institute of Arts.

The company does not have a formal mission statement, but Mr. Ulrich's first letter to shareholders as chair set forth his vision and growth goals for Target:

*We are committed to serving our guests better than the competition with trend-right, high-quality merchandise at very competitive prices. We are committed to*

EXHIBIT 5    Target's Consolidated Results of Operations (millions, except per share data)

| | February 2, 2002 | February 3, 2001 | February 2, 2000 |
|---|---|---|---|
| Sales | $39,176 | $36,362 | $33,212 |
| Net credit revenues | 712 | 541 | 490 |
| Total revenues | 39,888 | 36,903 | 33,702 |
| Cost of sales | 27,246 | 25,295 | 23,029 |
| Selling, general and administrative expense | 8,420 | 7,900 | 7,231 |
| Credit expense | 463 | 290 | 259 |
| Depreciation and amortization | 1,079 | 940 | 854 |
| Interest expense | 464 | 425 | 393 |
| Earnings before income taxes and extraordinary items | 2,216 | 2,053 | 1,936 |
| Provision for income taxes | 842 | 789 | 751 |
| Net earnings before extraordinary items | 1,374 | 1,264 | 1,185 |
| Extraordinary charges from purchase and redemption of debt, net of tax | (6) | – | (41) |
| Net earnings | $ 1,368 | $ 1,264 | $ 1,144 |
| Earnings before extraordinary items | $ 1.52 | $ 1.40 | $ 1.32 |
| Extraordinary items | (.01) | – | (.04) |
| Basic earnings per share | $ 1.52 | $ 1.40 | $ 1.28 |
| Earnings before extraordinary items | $ 1.51 | $ 1.38 | $ 1.27 |
| Extraordinary items | (.01) | – | (.04) |
| Diluted earnings per share | $ 1.50 | $ 1.38 | $ 1.23 |
| Weighted average common shares outstanding: | | | |
| Basic | 901.5 | 903.5 | 882.6 |
| Diluted | 909.8 | 913.0 | 931.3 |

Source: Target's 2001 Annual Report, p. 24.

being a low-cost, high-quality distributor of merchandise through "boundary-less" functioning—through leverage resources, expertise, and economies across divisions. Our primary objective is to maximize shareholder value over time. We believe we will achieve a compound annual fully diluted earnings per share growth of 15 percent over time, while maintaining a prudent and flexible capital structure.

Target Corporation has adhered closely to this management philosophy during Ulrich's tenure as CEO. Wall Street liked what it saw, since the price of Target Corporation's stock, adjusted for splits, has risen by a factor of 5 over this period of time, largely due to accelerating growth in sales and earnings at the Target division. Nevertheless, some analysts think Target Corporation's performance would be even better if it divested itself of its underperforming Marshall Field's and Mervyn's units. Yet CEO Ulrich remains as committed as ever to keeping Mervyn's, stating in the 2000 Annual Report,

Target Corporation reflects our core belief that our three retail segments are far more similar than they are different, and that scale matters. Though our two smaller retail divisions represent 20 percent or less of the corporation today, we believe that their combined contribution to our overall strategy and financial performance remains important. As a result, we are taking steps to leverage the power of these brands and {to} strengthen their position in the marketplace.

# EXHIBIT 6    Target's Business Segment Comparisons (in millions)

| | 2001 | 2000 |
|---|---|---|
| **Revenues** | | |
| Target | $32,588 | $29,278 |
| Mervyn's | 4,038 | 4,152 |
| Marshall Field's | 2,829 | 3,011 |
| Other | 433 | 462 |
| Total revenues | $39,888 | $36,903 |
| **Pre-tax segment profit and earnings reconciliation** | | |
| Target | $ 2,546 | $ 2,223 |
| Mervyn's | 286 | 269 |
| Marshall Field's | 133 | 190 |
| Total pre-tax segment profit | $ 2,965 | $ 2,682 |
| LIFO provision (expense)/credit | (8) | (4) |
| Securitization adjustments: | | |
| Unusual items | (67) | – |
| Interest equivalent | (27) | (50) |
| Interest expense | (484) | (425) |
| Mainframe outsourcing | – | – |
| Real estate repositioning | – | – |
| Other | (183) | (150) |
| Earnings before Income taxes and extraordinary items | $ 2,216 | $ 2,053 |
| **Assets** | | |
| Target | $18,515 | $14,348 |
| Mervyn's | 2,379 | 2,270 |
| Marshall Field's | 2,284 | 2,114 |
| Other | 976 | 758 |
| Total assets | $24,154 | $19,490 |
| **Depreciation and amortization** | | |
| Target | $ 784 | $ 660 |
| Mervyn's | 126 | 131 |
| Marshall Field's | 135 | 133 |
| Other | 34 | 16 |
| Total depreciation and amortization | $ 1,079 | $ 940 |
| **Capital expenditures** | | |
| Target | $ 2,901 | $ 2,244 |
| Mervyn's | 104 | 106 |
| Marshall Field's | 125 | 143 |
| Other | 33 | 35 |
| Total capital expenditures | $ 3,163 | $ 2,528 |
| **Segment EBITDA** | | |
| Target | $ 3,330 | $ 2,883 |
| Mervyn's | 412 | 400 |
| Marshall Field's | 268 | 323 |
| Total segment EBITDA | $ 4,010 | $ 3,606 |
| **Net assets** | | |
| Target | $13,812 | $10,659 |
| Mervyn's | 1,868 | 1,928 |
| Marshall Field's | 1,764 | 1,749 |
| Other | 561 | 463 |
| Total net assets | $18,005 | $14,799 |

Source: Target's 2001 Annual Report, p. 35.

## EXHIBIT 7    Target's Percentage Analysis

**Revenues and Comparable-store Sales Growth**
(52-week basis)

|  | 2001 | | 2000 | |
|---|---|---|---|---|
|  | *Revenues* | *Comparable-Store Sales* | *Revenues* | *Comparable-Store Sales* |
| Target | 13.1% | 4.1% | 10.5% | 3.4% |
| Mervyn's | (1.7) | (1.5) | 0.2 | 0.3 |
| Marshall Field's | (4.8) | (5.7) | (3.3) | (4.0) |
| Total | 9.7% | 2.7% | 7.9% | 2.4% |

**Revenues per Square Foot***
(52-week basis)

|  | *2001* | *2000* | *1999* |
|---|---|---|---|
| Target | $274 | $268 | $264 |
| Mervyn's | 188 | 190 | 189 |
| Marshall Field's | 194 | 210 | 220 |

*Thirteen-month average retail square feet.

**Pre-tax Segment Profit and as a Percent of Revenues**

| *(millions)* | *Pre-tax Segment Profit* | | *As a Percent of Revenues* | |
|---|---|---|---|---|
|  | *2001* | *2000* | *2001* | *2000* |
| Target | $2,546 | $2,223 | 7.8% | 7.6% |
| Mervyn's | 286 | 269 | 7.1 | 6.5 |
| Marshall Field's | 133 | 190 | 4.7 | 6.3 |
| Total | $2,965 | $2,682 | 7.5% | 7.4% |
| Net earnings before extraordinary items | $1,374 | $1,264 | | |

**EBITDA and as a Percent of Revenues**

| *(millions)* | *EBITDA* | | *As a Percent of Revenues* | |
|---|---|---|---|---|
|  | *2001* | *2000* | *2001* | *2000* |
| Target | $3,330 | $2,883 | 10.2% | 9.8% |
| Mervyn's | 412 | 400 | 10.2 | 9.6 |
| Marshall Field's | 268 | 323 | 9.5 | 10.7 |
| Total segment EBITDA | $4,010 | $3,606 | 10.2% | 9.9% |

*Source:* Targets 2001 Annual Report, p. 17–18.

## EXHIBIT 8    Target's Year-end 2001 Store Count and Square Footage by State

| Density Group | Sq. Ft. per Thousand Population | No. of Stores | Retail Sq. Ft. (in thousands) | Density Group | Sq. Ft. per Thousand Population | No. of Stores | Retail Sq. Ft. (in thousands) |
|---|---|---|---|---|---|---|---|
| Minnesota | 1,485 | 59 | 7,366 | Ohio | 391 | 38 | 4,457 |
| Iowa | 811 | 19 | 2,383 | Wyoming | 370 | 2 | 184 |
| North Dakota | 786 | 4 | 505 | Tennessee | 363 | 19 | 2,091 |
| Anzona | 744 | 34 | 3,901 | Oragon | 346 | 11 | 1,199 |
| Nebraska | 733 | 10 | 1,263 | Delaware | 337 | 2 | 267 |
| Montana | 701 | 6 | 638 | **Group 3 total** | **404** | **141** | **16,393** |
| Nevada | 692 | 12 | 1,424 | North Carolina | 328 | 24 | 2,677 |
| Colorado | 691 | 25 | 3,023 | New Hampshire | 319 | 3 | 397 |
| Indiana | 623 | 34 | 3,815 | Kentucky | 315 | 12 | 1,280 |
| Wisconsin | 596 | 28 | 3,218 | New Jersey | 311 | 21 | 2,634 |
| **Group 1 total** | **801** | **231** | **27,536** | South Carolina | 295 | 10 | 1,197 |
| Utah | 574 | 8 | 1,304 | Oklahoma | 242 | 8 | 840 |
| Michigan | 550 | 50 | 5,493 | Alabama | 237 | 7 | 1,064 |
| California | 543 | 159 | 18,555 | Pennsylvania | 236 | 23 | 2,902 |
| Texas | 539 | 95 | 11,402 | Massachusetts | 228 | 11 | 1,454 |
| Washington | 527 | 28 | 3,147 | Connecticut | 190 | 5 | 648 |
| South Dakota | 517 | 4 | 393 | **Group 4 total** | **269** | **124** | **16,093** |
| Illinois | 506 | 53 | 6,329 | New York | 173 | 25 | 3,294 |
| Florida | 504 | 69 | 8,177 | Louisiana | 125 | 4 | 563 |
| Maryland | 496 | 22 | 2,645 | Rhode Island | 122 | 1 | 128 |
| Georgia | 485 | 33 | 4,034 | Maine | 98 | 1 | 125 |
| **Group 2 total** | **527** | **521** | **61,479** | Arkansas | 85 | 2 | 229 |
| Kansas | 475 | 10 | 1,285 | Mississippi | 83 | 2 | 239 |
| New Mexico | 473 | 8 | 871 | West Virginia | 68 | 1 | 124 |
| Virginia | 442 | 26 | 3,157 | Vermont | 0 | 0 | 0 |
| Missouri | 416 | 20 | 2,346 | **Group 5 total** | **139** | **35** | **4,702** |
| Idaho | 407 | 5 | 536 | **Total** | **445** | **1,053** | **125,203** |

## EXHIBIT 9    Mervyn's Store Count Year-end 2001

| | Retail Sq. Ft. (in thousands) | No. of Stores |
|---|---|---|
| California | 9,622 | 124 |
| Texas | 3,347 | 42 |
| Washington | 1,277 | 14 |
| Arizona | 1,203 | 15 |
| Michigan | 1,165 | 15 |
| Minnesota | 1,160 | 9 |
| Colorado | 855 | 11 |
| Utah | 754 | 8 |
| Oregon | 553 | 7 |
| Louisiana | 449 | 6 |
| Nevada | 422 | 6 |
| Oklahoma | 269 | 3 |
| New Mexico | 267 | 3 |
| Idaho | 82 | 1 |
| **Total** | **21,425** | **264** |

**EXHIBIT 10**    Marshall Field's Store Count Year-end 2001

|  | Retail Sq. Ft. (in thousands) | No. of Stores |
|---|---|---|
| Michigan | 4,825 | 21 |
| Illinois | 4,690 | 17 |
| Minnesota | 3,067 | 12 |
| Wisconsin | 817 | 5 |
| Ohio | 600 | 3 |
| North Dakota | 295 | 3 |
| Indiana | 244 | 2 |
| South Dakota | 100 | 1 |
| **Total** | 14,638 | 64 |

*Source:* Target's 2001 *Annual Report,* pp. 16 and 23.

## REFERENCES

BRANCH, SHELLY. "How Target Got Hot." *Fortune* (May 24, 1999): 168–174.

HELLIKER, KEVIN. "Sold on the Job: Retail Chains Offer a Lot of Opportunity, Young Managers Find." *The Wall Street Journal* (August 25, 1995): A1.

MAHONEY, TOM and LEONARD SLOANE. *The Great Merchants* (New York: Harper & Row, 1966).

# BEST BUY COMPANY, INC.—2002

**Alen Badal**
**The Union Institute**

BBY

www.bestbuy.com

Best Buy Company, Inc., with its headquarters in Eden Prairie, Minnesota (952-947-2422), achieved annual sales of $15.3 million in 2001, compared to $12.4 million in 2000, and a net income of over $395 million in 2001.[1] The company has been in existence for thirty-five years and is the largest electronics specialty retailer in the United States, with 420 Best Buy stores in forty-one states.[2] Best Buy markets such commodities as home office equipment, audio/video items, cameras, appliances, and music CDs.

On October 8, 2001, Best Buy created an Internet division to sell music by way of downloading digital files.[3] The site includes such music labels as EMI Group and AOL Time Warner. The company hopes to add more such sites that allow consumers to purchase an entire CD once they have downloaded a song, because such sites should enhance Best Buy's CD sales.[4] The new Internet division provides an opportunity to increase revenues without necessarily increasing warehousing, as a result of the division's ability to sell digital files. A further advantage comes from its ability to link Web page online CD sales with digital file downloads. Best Buy recently purchased a $40 million distribution center in the state of New York, estimated to be completed in the Spring of 2003.[5]

Best Buy envisioned the following strategic objectives for fiscal 2001:

1. Acquiring Musicland, which is a retailer of music and movies, in order to reach more consumers through four outlets (Sam Goody, On Cue, Suncoast, Media Play)
2. Acquiring Magnolia Hi-Fi, a retailer of high-end electronics, which offers a broader service center, loyal customers, and pricey product lines
3. International expansion into Canada in order to broaden Best Buy operations and offer Best Buy's product lines to Canada[6]

## HISTORY

One-stop electronics, CD, and appliance shopping, among others, best describes the specialty retailer Best Buy as prices are competitive and offerings comprehensive. Best Buy Company initially emerged when Richard Schulze tired of working for his father in the electronics distribution business.[7] In 1966, Schulze quit his father's business and, with a partner, founded a home/car stereo business in Minnesota which he named Sound of Music. The milestones of Best Buy Company, Inc., which emerged from Sound of Music, are displayed in Exhibit 1.

Many negative events in the United States recently have affected Best Buy in particular and the specialty retail industry in general. Such events have included the World Trade Center collapse in New York City and the cyclical employment layoffs that Silicon Valley (Northern California-Bay Area) experienced in 2001. Additionally, Montgomery Ward's, previously a direct competitor of Best Buy, has closed many locations, including locations in California, where Best Buy began emerging in the 1990s.

## EXHIBIT 1  Best Buy Company, Inc. Historical Timeline

- In 1971, Schulze bought out his Sound of Music partner and expanded the business.
- In the 1980s, Schulze expanded his target customer base to an older and more affluent base by adding appliances and VCRs to his product lines.
- In 1983, Schulze changed the business name to Best Buy and expanded the business by opening larger super-stores.
- In 1985, Best Buy went public.
- As a result of the booming demands in VCRs between 1984 and 1987, Best Buy expanded from eight stores to twenty-four and, as a result, sales increased from $29 million to $240 million.
- In 1988, Best Buy opened another sixteen stores and sales increased by 84 percent; however, Best Buy began feeling pressures from rival competitors, and as a result, profits began to decline.
- In 1989, Best Buy introduced the Concept II warehouse store format, where Schulze cut payroll by reducing sales staff by 33 percent and by taking employees off commission.
- In 1994, Best Buy introduced Concept III, which was a larger-store format.
- In 1995, Best Buy opened forty-seven more stores.
- In 1997, the company's earnings plunged due to large PC inventory on hand as a result of Intel's impact on the PC market.
- Also in 1997, Best Buy began selling CDs on the Internet; however, Best Buy realized it may be growing itself out of business and decided to slow expansion and abolish its "no money down, no monthly payment, and no interest" policy.
- In 1999, Best Buy entered New England with the introduction of its Concept IV stores, which included digital products and expositions of computer software and DVD products.
- Also in 1999, Best Buy formed a separate subsidiary for online operations and invested $10 million in an etown.com site, which was closed down in February 2001.
- In 2000, Best Buy began marketing personalized computers from Micron Electronics via kiosks in its stores.
- Also in 2000, Best Buy acquired a privately held chain of Magnolia Hi-Fi high-end audio/video stores.
- In 2001, Best Buy acquired Musicland Stores, which operated more than 1,300 Sam Goody, Suncoast, On Cue, and Media Play music retailers for approximately $377 million.
- Also in August 2001, Best Buy purchased Canada's largest computer and consumer electronics retailer, Future Shop, and it also announced that it would be expanding internationally. It projected that it would open some 65 Best Buy stores in Canada over a three to four year timeframe.

*Source:* Dow Jones Interactive.

Product innovations, such as the transition from the VCR to DVD players and personal computer upgrades to speedier processing, have affected the electronics industry. Best Buy has been affected by both: It benefitted by capitalizing on its sale of VCRs, but it had trouble adjusting to PC changes in the market.

## DIVISIONS

### Best Buy Company, Inc.

Best Buy Company, Inc. stores are located throughout the United States. Best Buy historically has increased its revenues at a compound yearly growth rate of 37 percent as a

EXHIBIT 2    Consolidated Statements of Income (in millions, except per-share data)

| | FISCAL YEARS ENDED FEBRUARY 28, | | |
|---|---|---|---|
| | *2001* | *2000* | *1999* |
| **Revenues** | | | |
| Net Sales | $15,326.6 | $12,494.0 | $10,077.9 |
| Other Income—net | 37.2 | 23.3 | 0.4 |
| | 15,363.8 | 12,517.3 | 10,078.3 |
| **Costs and Expenses** | | | |
| Cost of Sales | $12,100.1 | $ 9,991.1 | $ 8,171.7 |
| Selling, General, and Administrative Expenses | 2,454.8 | 1,854.2 | 1,463.3 |
| | 14,554.9 | 11,845.3 | 9,635.0 |
| **Taxes** | | | |
| Pretax Income | $ 641.5 | $ 562.5 | $ 364.9 |
| Income Taxes | 245.6 | 215.5 | 140.5 |
| **Net Income** | $ 395.8 | $ 347.1 | $ 224.4 |
| **Net Income Earnings Per Share** | $ 1.92 | $ 1.70 | $ 1.13 |

*Source:* Dow Jones Interactive.

result of expanding and opening new stores.[8] According to the annual letter written to shareholders and employees in 2001, the president writes, "We have an opportunity to continue our national Best Buy store growth for a number of years; we estimate that we will have blanketed the country with our yellow tag by fiscal 2005."

Best Buy has plans to open smaller stores of about thirty thousand square feet in smaller, developing markets.[9] Best Buy locations are generally much larger than these proposed smaller stores. Many of its locations are in open sections of a city, where they can be easily accessed and are visible to the general public from the highway or road. The general operating hours are Monday through Saturday from 10:00 A.M. to 9:00 P.M. and Sunday from 11:00 A.M. to 6:00 P.M. Best Buy floor plans are generally categorical, and music CDs are positioned near the checkout counters. The remaining square footage includes various departments, such as appliances, TV/VCR, and so on. As a convenience, return counters are housed near the entrance/exit doors. Stores typically include car audio installation centers, too.

Home office products continue to be the lead department in sales, followed by consumer electronics. Also, appliance sales decreased from 8 percent of total sales in 2000 to 7 percent in 2001, as noted in Exhibit 5. Moreover, while consumer electronics sales generally increased, other product sales decreased by 30 percent, falling from 10 percent to 7 percent of sales in 2001. Video sales impressively increased more than 25 percent between 2000 and 2001; the acquisitions of Musicland and Magnolia Hi-Fi may further have a positive impact on the consumer electronics categories, in general.

Best Buy and competitor Circuit City achieved nearly identical revenues in 1999. However, as Exhibit 6 indicates, Best Buy had some three hundred fewer locations in 1999 than did Circuit City. An increase in units was a result of the acquisitions Best Buy made in 2000 (Magnolia Hi-Fi) and 2001 (Musicland). Both Best Buy and Circuit City sell almost the same product lines; however, Circuit City plans to include home office products and high-profit electronics as a strategy to increase revenues.[10]

EXHIBIT 3    Consolidated Balance Sheet (in millions)

| | FEBRUARY 28, | | |
| --- | --- | --- | --- |
| | *2001* | *2000* | *1999* |
| **Current Assets** | | | |
| Cash and Cash Equivalent | $  746.9 | $  750.7 | $  785.8 |
| Receivables | 209.0 | 189.3 | 132.4 |
| Inventories | 1,766.9 | 1,183.7 | 1,046.4 |
| Other Current Asset | 205.8 | 114.8 | 98.5 |
| Total Current Assets | 2,928.7 | 2,238.5 | 2,063.1 |
| Gross Fixed Assets | 1,987.4 | 1,093.5 | 731.9 |
| Accumulated Depreciation | 543.2 | 395.4 | 308.3 |
| Net Fixed Assets | 1,444.2 | 698.1 | 423.6 |
| Other Noncurrent Assets | 81.4 | 58.8 | 25.8 |
| Total Noncurrent Assets | 1,911.0 | 756.9 | 449.4 |
| Total Assets | 4,839.6 | 2,995.3 | 2,512.5 |
| **Current Liabilities** | | | |
| Accounts Payable | $1,772.7 | $1,313.9 | $1,011.7 |
| Short-Term Debt | 114.9 | 15.8 | 30.1 |
| Other Current Liabilities | 827.0 | 455.3 | 345.1 |
| Total Current Liabilities | 2,714.7 | 1,785.0 | 1,386.9 |
| Long-Term Debt | 181.0 | 14.9 | 30.5 |
| Other Noncurrent Liabilities | 122.0 | 99.4 | 30.9 |
| Total Noncurrent Liabilities | 303.0 | 114.3 | 61.4 |
| Total Liabilities | 3,017.6 | 1,899.3 | 1,448.3 |
| Common Equity | 1,821.9 | 1,096.0 | 1,064.1 |
| Retained Earnings | 1,224.3 | 828.5 | 511.6 |
| Total Equity | 1,821.9 | 1,096.0 | 1,064.1 |
| Total Liabilities and Equity | 4,839.5 | 2,995.3 | 2,512.4 |

*Source:* Dow Jones Interactive.

Due to Best Buy's Concept II warehouse/store strategy in 1989, some suppliers pulled their products from Best Buy because sales staff was limited and selected suppliers required more sales staff assistance in order to sell their products.[11] Otherwise, almost all brand names and products are sold by Best Buy. Even with the reduction of sales staff, it is not difficult to obtain expert assistance should a shopper need help. A majority of Best Buy products are positioned in the store next to the exhibitions/floor models, and so they are easily accessible for consumers to pick up and then proceed to the checkout counter.

Best Buy Company does run television commercials and newspaper ads as forms of advertising. The products on display can be tested in the store, and descriptive product information is included on most price tags. Best Buy plans to open approximately forty stores per year and to increase online sales, too.[12] Best Buy currently has seven distribution centers (five leased, two owned), ranging from the entertainment software center, which is 245,000 square feet, to the Findlay, Ohio, distribution center, which is 808,000 square feet.[13]

EXHIBIT 4    Corporate Officers

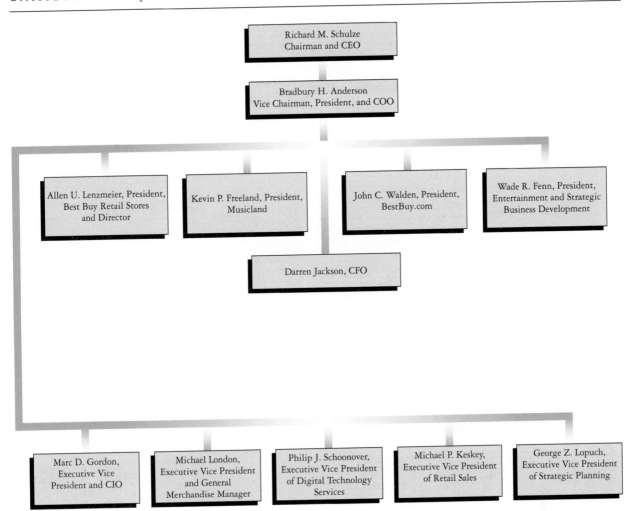

*Source:* Dow Jones Interactive.

## Musicland

Musicland is a retailer of music and videos and is based in Minneapolis; it includes 630 Sam Goody music stores, 200 On Cue stores, four hundred mall-based Suncoast stores, and 80 Media Play superstores.[14] As noted in Exhibit 7, Musicland achieved $1,891.8 million in sales in 1999 and employed 15,900 people.[15] Best Buy acquired Musicland Stores Corporation in the fourth quarter of 2001.[16] Cumulatively, the stores are expected to generate three hundred million shopping visits annually, including more female shoppers. The outlets primarily sell music CDs (most include listening stations), tapes, books, and videos. Depending on the location, all stores hold normal business hours, seven days a week. Additionally, Best Buy Company, Inc., acquired Magnolia Hi-Fi, based in Seattle, Washington, which sells high-end audio/video products.[17]

| EXHIBIT 5 | Best Buy Productions/ Operations (2000/2001 Sales) | |
|---|---|---|
| | 2000 | 2001 |
| | *% of Total* | |
| Home Office | 35 | 34 |
| Consumer Electronics | | |
|    Video | 17 | 22 |
|    Audio | 11 | 11 |
| Entertainment Software | 19 | 19 |
| Appliances | 08 | 07 |
| Other | 10 | 07 |
| Total | 100 | 100 |

*Source: Hoover's Handbook of American Business 2001 (2000 Sales);* Dow Jones Interactive (2001 Sales).

**EXHIBIT 6    Top Twenty Specialty Retailers (all figures in thousands)**

| | Revenues | | | No. of Units | | |
|---|---|---|---|---|---|---|
| | *2000* | *1999* | *% Change* | *2000* | *1999* | *% Change* |
| Best Buy | $15,326,552 | $12,494,023 | 22.7% | 1,741 | 357 | 387.7% |
| Gap | 13,673,460 | 11,635,398 | 17.5 | 3,676 | 3,018 | 21.8 |
| Circuit City Group | 12,959,028 | 12,614,390 | 2.7 | 636 | 658 | −3.3 |
| Office Depot | 11,569,696 | 10,272,060 | 12.6 | 1,020 | 939 | 8.6 |
| Toys 'R' Us | 11,332,000 | 11,862,000 | −4.5 | 1,586 | 1,548 | 2.5 |
| Staples | 10,673,671 | 8,936,671 | 19.4 | 1,305 | 1,129 | 15.6 |
| Limited Brands | 10,104,606 | 9,766,220 | 3.5 | 2,739 | 2,913 | −6.0 |
| TJX | 9,579,006 | 8,795,347 | 8.9 | 1,483 | 1,357 | 9.3 |
| CompUSA | 6,150,000 | 6,321,391 | −2.7 | 226 | 210 | 7.6 |
| OfficeMax | 5,156,392 | 4,847,022 | 6.4 | 995 | 946 | 5.2 |
| Intimate Brands | 5,117,199 | 4,632,029 | 10.5 | 2,390 | 2,110 | 13.3 |
| RadioShack | 4,794,700 | 4,126,200 | 16.2 | 7,100 | 7,050 | 0.7 |
| AutoZone | 4,482,696 | 4,116,392 | 8.9 | 2,915 | 2,711 | 7.5 |
| Barnes & Noble | 4,375,804 | 3,486,043 | 25.5 | 1,886 | 942 | 100.2 |
| Venator Group | 4,217,000 | 3,726,000 | 13.2 | 3,582 | 4,529 | −20.9 |
| Spiegel | 3,724,778 | 3,414,703 | 9.1 | 580 | 560 | 3.6 |
| Big Lots | 3,277,088 | 2,933,690 | 11.7 | 1,290 | 2,550 | −49.4 |
| Borders Group | 3,271,200 | 2,968,400 | 10.2 | 1,249 | 1,195 | 4.5 |
| Payless ShoeSource | 2,948,400 | 2,730,100 | 8.0 | 4,912 | 4,492 | 9.3 |
| Ross Stores | 2,709,039 | 2,468,638 | 9.7 | 409 | 378 | 8.2 |

*Source: STORES* magazine (**www.Stores.org**).

Sam Goody ("Goody got it!") competes well with music retailers when it comes to selling music. While retailers such as Wal-Mart and Target carry music CDs and tapes, Sam Goody stores market best-selling music favorites at relatively low prices, since they are a specialty music store. Shopping malls and other locations house Sam Goody stores.

On Cue stores sell music CDs, tapes, books, and movies. Suncoast stores sell music and DVDs, VHS videos, music, apparel, books, electronics, and software. Suncoast sells online, too (**www.suncoast.com**). Media Play superstores are akin to Suncoast retailers. Media Play superstores (45,000 square feet, on average) contain reading nooks and computer software and music; these stores typically draw more than 4.4 million consumers each month (**www.musicland.com/sg**).

## Magnolia Hi-Fi

Magnolia Hi-Fi is a specialized retailer of high-end electronics (**www.magnoliahifi.com**). Currently, there are thirteen stores located in Washington and Oregon, and there are two in northern California, where the average size of a store is 10,200 square feet. Each store generates about $8.4 million annually.[18] This trendy outlet contains product lines, such as Bose, and offers sales experts who are available to demonstrate products or to answer any technical questions a consumer may have. Furthermore, Magnolia Hi-Fi contains a fine in-house service department. Store hours are typically Monday through Friday from 10:00 A.M. to 9:00 P.M., Saturday from 10:00 A.M. to 8:00 P.M., and Sunday from 11:00 A.M. to 6:00 P.M.

The product lines generally are the same as Best Buy's; however, Magnolia Hi-Fi, due to its larger number of sales experts, contains higher-end models/products. The stores maintain an upscale clientele, whose questions and wants are specific, which are all features of a trendy Magnolia Hi-Fi store.

In summary, the Best Buy Company, Inc. business portfolio is unique in that all of its businesses typically include the same product lines, with minor deviations. All businesses to date are within the continental United States and Puerto Rico; however, plans to go international are being developed. Best Buy locations provide one-stop shopping for electronic needs, and the company finances purchases with its own label credit card. Best Buy appears relatively stable financially.

## INTERNATIONAL

Best Buy plans to expand internationally into Canada in 2003 with five stores (thirty thousand square feet, approximately), ultimately expanding to sixty to sixty-five Canadian locations.[19] The focus is to export American methods of conducting Best Buy business to Canada. To date, no other considerations to expand into other parts of the country or Mexico have been discussed; apparently, the focus is on Canadian markets. Furthermore, no plans to date have been discussed as to whether to include other businesses of Best Buy Company, Inc., such as Musicland, into Canadian markets.

EXHIBIT 7    Musicland Financials: 1997–1999

|  | 1997 | 1998 | 1999 |
|---|---|---|---|
| Sales ($ mil.) | 1,768.3 | 1,846.9 | 1,891.8 |
| Net Income ($ mil.) | 14.0 | 38.0 | 58.4 |
| Income as % of Sales | 0.8% | 2.1% | 3.1% |
| Employees | 16,400 | 15,600 | 15,900 |

*Source:* Hoover's Company Profile, 2001 (**web.Lexis-Nexis.com**).

## OPERATIONS

Best Buy stands strong financially, with annual sales of more than $15 million in 2001.[20] Furthermore, Best Buy's revenues in 1999 of $12,494 million were generated as a result of 357 store locations, whereas Circuit City achieved only marginally higher revenues by way of 658 locations (**www.Stores.org**). Nonetheless, Best Buy has achieved commendable results to date as it looks into further expansion.

Best Buy and its portfolio businesses, with the exception of Magnolia Hi-Fi, focus on delivering products to all customers. However, Musicland operations focus on tailoring to mostly middle class customers, while Magnolia Hi-Fi tailors to trendier, upscale customers who prefer service centers and support.

Approximately half (52 percent) of Sam Goody's customers are between the ages of 14 and 21, whereas 42 percent are 22 to 44 year olds (**www.musicland.com/sg**). Media Play attracts more families (children and parents) as a core customer base, and its median incomes range from $50,000 to $60,000 a year on average (**www.musicland.com/sg**).

On Cue attracts and focuses on the family type of customer, too, and its locations offer a pleasant environment, where families and their children can browse through book, movie, and music sections. The locations are generally located close to main shopping hubs; as a result, they provide an opportunity for families to visit On Cue locations while spending the day shopping (**www.musicland.com/sg**).

Suncoast's customer base has historically been 22–44 year olds, representing 56 percent of the customers; 45+ year olds represent 17 percent (**www.musicland.com/sg**). Suncoast specializes in movies and videos; as a result, customers are aware of selections and availability when shopping for those items. Specialty DVD outlets such as Suncoast still remain strong. Music specialty stores such as Sam Goody and On Cue will indirectly continue to compete with the likes of Kmart and Wal-Mart insofar as both carry a sufficient selection of music CDs; however, listening stations are not available in Target, Wal-Mart and Kmart stores.

## EMPLOYEES

Best Buy employees are noncommissioned hourly workers. They are not as technically proficient as Magnolia Hi-Fi employees, but they are knowledgeable enough to describe features of products to customers. Best Buy employees' level of electronic expertise ranges from novice to expert. They are generally educated on-the-job regarding products in their departments. Magnolia Hi-Fi employees are commission-based.

## SPECIALTY RETAIL INDUSTRY TRENDS

Best Buy today faces new challenges, such as a lack of consumer spending as a result of the World Trade Center attack in New York City. Additionally, the Internet as a way to obtain goods has simplified shopping for consumers. Online shoppers are expected to increase exponentially; it is expected that an estimated sixty million people will make at least one online purchase every three months in 2003.[21] The process of buying online is safe and reliable; consumers can often save or obtain incentives by shopping online. Retailers are able to offer their products at a minimal discount, as opposed to facilitating the products in stores. Furthermore, shopping over the Internet is available twenty-four hours a day, seven days a week. Typically, consumers physically visit stores and test/view products and then purchase online.

Best Buy's current market share within the specialty electronics industry is attractive insofar as it offers and sells a comprehensive product line, ranging from appliances to stereos to computers. Best Buy's earnings, as compared to its competitors, are strong, considering the number of Best Buy locations currently operating. With few competitors considering or having initiated overseas expansion, testing the international markets is a potentially viable option.

The "bigger is better" theory will continue to affect smaller specialty retailers and might eventually phase them out of the arena, since one-stop-shopping offered with supercenters allows consumers to save on and purchase products at one location. On the other hand, small specialty retailers like Magnolia Hi-Fi will continue to prosper insofar as a market does exist, one consisting of upper-class consumers who are interested in personal sales, service, and a technically knowledgeable workforce.

## COMPETITORS

Best Buy Company, Inc., is the number one electronics retailer in the United States, representing some 360 stores in some forty states.[22] Best Buy competes both directly and indirectly with many specialty retailers, such as Staples, Circuit City, Office Depot, CompUSA, and so on (**www.Stores.org**). Best Buy competes lean insofar as its revenues are impressive, especially considering the fact that it has fewer store locations than rival Circuit City or Office Depot.

Currently, Best Buy stands firmly as the leader, although Circuit City is attempting to capture the number one electronics specialty retailer position. Circuit City Group, which, with over 600 stores, has locations in virtually every state, is now focusing on satellite television systems and cellular telephones to make up for the PC sales deficit.[23] Also, Circuit City plans to phase out appliances and remodel stores to make space for home office products and high-profit electronics; it will also close six distribution centers.[24]

Sears store appliance departments have been successful in years past. The Good Guys Expedition stores have influenced Circuit City, causing it to revamp in much the same manner. Currently, The Good Guys does not sell appliances, which is the direction Circuit City is planning to go in. Circuit City has about 600 superstores, ranging from 9,500 to 43,000 square feet; and it has about 50 mall-based express stores, although it plans to add 30–50 more annually.[25]

Staples, Inc (locations average twenty-four thousand sq. ft.) stands as the second largest U.S. office products superstore behind Office Depot. Staples has more than eleven hundred stores in about forty states, and it internationally operates in Canada, Germany, the United Kingdom, the Netherlands, and Portugal.[26] Furthermore, Staples is looking to continue to open airport locations and superstores in suburban cities and to expand its online business services.[27] Staples primarily sells office products and furniture, which Best Buy succeeds in selling, and houses a copy center.

OfficeMax, Inc. currently has more than 950 stores in forty-nine states and has proposed to phase out computers and to market Gateway computers only.[28] OfficeMax is expanding in Japan, Mexico, and Brazil.[29] OfficeMax sells primarily office products and furniture and carries limited electronics, such as calculators; it also has a duplication center. OfficeMax competes directly with Best Buy in home office products, which, to date, is the highest achiever as a percent in sales for Best Buy.

Office Depot, Inc. currently has more than 950 stores in the United States and abroad too, which sell by way of a warehouse format and delivery system.[30] Office Depot sells via the Internet (**www.officedepot.com**). Office Depot sells computers and copying services, which primarily cater to small businesses; approximately one-third of its sales are achieved from small business sales.[31] Office Depot, Inc. plans to continue with superstore operations and to terminate smaller supply stores, office furniture businesses (Furniture at Work), and copy-printing service stores (Images).[32] This strategy will ultimately redirect revenues toward warehouse stores and possible additions abroad.

## THE FUTURE

1. What strategies would you recommend to CEO Richard M. Schulze?

2. Should Best Buy Company enter other international markets? Why or why not? If so, what should the timeline be? Which countries should be targeted?

3. Is the current global strategy to enter Canada appropriate? Why or why not?

4. Should Best Buy continue to expand in the United States and/or carry or eliminate products?

5. Considering Best Buy Company's current financial situation, should it consider acquiring other businesses? If so, which ones would be appropriate, and why?

6. What relative emphasis do you think Best Buy should place on its various divisions in terms of further growth? Why?

## ENDNOTES

[1] Dow Jones Interactive—available at http://ptg.djnr.com/ccroot/asp/cqs_exe_report.asp?mdnum=87128.

[2] Ibid.

[3] *The New York Times* (October 9, 2001), p. C12.

[4] Ibid.

[5] Dow Jones Interactive, op. cit.

[6] Lexis-Nexis Academic Universe-Document—available at http://web.lexis-nexis.com/universe...d5=8e5c496318500dff0b1db280bda1b20e.

[7] Dow Jones Interactive, op. cit.

[8] Lexis-Nexis Academic, op. cit.

[9] Ibid.

[10] *Hoover's Handbook of American Business* (2001).

[11] Dow Jones Interactive, op. cit.

[12] *Hoover's Handbook*, op cit.

[13] Best Buy Company, Inc., *10K Report* (web.lexis-nexis.com).

[14] Lexis-Nexis Academic, op. cit.

[15] *Hoover's 2001 Company Profile* (web.Lexis-Nexis.com).

[16] Best Buy, op. cit.

[17] Lexis-Nexis Academic, op. cit.

[18] Best Buy, op. cit.

[19] Lexis-Nexis Academic, op. cit.

[20] Dow Jones Interactive, op. cit.

[21] Standard & Poor's Industry Surveys (July 26, 2001).

[22] *Hoover's Handbook*, op. cit.

[23] Ibid.

[24] Ibid.

[25] Ibid.

[26] Ibid.

[27] Ibid.

[28] Ibid.

[29] Ibid.

[30] Ibid.

[31] Ibid.

[32] Ibid.

# MANDALAY RESORT GROUP—2002

**John K. Ross, III, Mike Keeffe, and Bill Middlebrook**
**Southwest Texas State University**

MBG

www.mandalayresortgroup.com

Las Vegas, the kingdom of glitz and glamour, was no more. Where once was heard the sounds of laughter and the clink of coins falling from slot machines, now only crickets could be heard on the strip. The terrorist attacks in New York and Washington on September 11, 2001, had cast a gloomy spell on the land of make-believe. The flights to Las Vegas, the colossal hotels/casinos, the bright lights, and the large crowds now became possible terrorist targets to be avoided.

On September 17, 2001, six days after the terrorist attacks, David Strow of the *Las Vegas Sun* reported that:

> *Resorts along the Las Vegas strip are considering layoffs and some are already cutting workers' hours as business slows down in response to Tuesday's terrorist attacks. This expected downturn is already causing one company to make a big change in its plans. This morning, Park Place Entertainment Corp. announced it is delaying a $475 million expansion at Caesars Palace. "We're just going day by day," said John Marz, vice president of marketing at Mandalay Resort Group. When asked if the company was considering layoffs, he said, "not that I know of."*

"Not that I know of." Suddenly, the lives of everyone associated with Mandalay Resort Group had been affected by what happened in New York and Washington, D.C. Within days, Mandalay had donated $1 million to aid families of the victims in New York and Washington, and by the end of the month it had laid off forty-five hundred employees (about 15 percent of the workforce in Nevada). What is going to happen to the tourist/entertainment industry—and more specifically to the Las Vegas gaming industry? How long will the effects last? What does Mandalay need to do to survive? What happens after the crisis is over? These and other tough questions are the ones to which management at Mandalay Resort had to respond—and respond quickly.

## MANDALAY RESORT GROUP

Mandalay Resort Group (hereafter Mandalay) describes itself as in the business of entertainment, and it has been one of the innovators in the theme resort concept that is popular in casino gaming. Its areas of operation are the extravagant vacation and convention centers of Las Vegas, Reno, and Laughlin, Nevada, as well as other locations in the United States and abroad. Historically, Mandalays' marketing of its products has been called "right out of the bargain basement" and has catered to "low rollers." Beginning with the opening of the Excalibur in 1990, Mandalay has broadened its market and now targets the middle-income gambler and family-oriented vacationer as well as the more upscale traveler and player.

Mandalay began in 1974, when partners William G. Bennett, an aggressive cost-cutter who ran furniture stores before entering the gaming industry in 1965, and William N. Pennington bought a small and unprofitable casino operation for $50,000. The partners were able to rejuvenate Circus Circus with fresh marketing, went public with a stock offering in October 1983, and experienced rapid growth and high profitability. Within the five-year period between 1993 and 1997, the average return on invested capital was 16.5 percent, and Mandalay generated over $1 billion in free cash flow. Today, Mandalay is one of the major players in the Las Vegas, Laughlin, and Reno markets in terms of both the square footage of casino space and the number of hotel rooms, and it has achieved this success despite the incredible growth in both markets. Casino gaming operations provide slightly less than one-half of total revenues, and that trend continued into 2002 (see Exhibit 1). On January 31, 2001, Mandalay reported a net income of $53.0 million on revenues of $2.46 billion.

## Mission

Mandalay currently does not seem to have a formally stated mission. No publicly stated vision statement is available; however, the continued development of the Mandalay Mile continues to be the core of Mandalay's future development. The Mandalay Mile consists of three interconnected gaming resorts in Las Vegas on 230 acres.

## OPERATIONS

Mandalay defines entertainment as pure play and fun, and it goes out of its way to see that customers have plenty of opportunities for both. Each Mandalay location has a distinctive personality, and the Mandalay corporate structure seems to allow each site to exploit that difference to its best advantage. Although Mandalay does not publish its organization chart, it appears that Mandalay Resort Group provides overall direction and strategic leadership as well as functional coordination in the areas of finance, accounting, human resources, legal issues, and marketing. Each resort, in turn, has its own functional structure that enables it to handle the specific activities required to successfully operate a large combined hotel, casino, and entertainment resort.

EXHIBIT 1    Mandalay's Revenues by Segment

|  | 2001 | 2000 | 1999 | 1998 |
|---|---|---|---|---|
| Casinos | 48.8% | 46.3% | 48.0% | 46.7% |
| Food & Beverage | 16.7 | 16.9 | 16.7 | 15.9 |
| Rooms | 23.6 | 26.0 | 24.0 | 24.4 |
| Other | 13.5 | 12.2 | 11.5 | 10.5 |
| Unconsolidated | 4.6 | 4.8 | 5.7 | 7.3 |
| Less: Complementary Allowances | 7.2 | 6.3 | 5.9 | 4.8 |

Note: 2001 column is for fiscal year ending 1-31-02.
*Source:* Mandalay Resort Group 10K (January 31, 1996–2002).

The largest hotel/casino—and the crown jewel of the Mandalay group—is Mandalay Bay, which was completed in the first quarter of 1999 and opened on March 2 of that year at an estimated cost of $950 million (excluding land). This is the third addition to the Mandalay Mile, a contiguous mile at the southern end of the Las Vegas strip that currently contains the Mandalay Bay, Excalibur, and Luxor resorts (see Exhibit 2 for

**EXHIBIT 2    The Las Vegas Strip**

**Las Vegas Blvd. "The Strip"**

**North/South Streets**
2. Decatur Boulevard
3. Valley View Boulevard
4. Rancho Drive
5. Martin Luther King Boulevard
6. Koval Lane
7. Paradise Road
8. Swenson Street
9. Maryland Parkway

**East/West Streets**
A. Charleston Boulevard
B. Sahara Avenue
C. Desert Inn Road
D. Spring Mountain Road
E. Karen Avenue
F. Flamingo Avenue
G. Harmon Avenue
H. Tropicana Avenue
I. Russel Road

Hotels, Casinos and Landmarks

1. Stratosphere
2. Bonanza Gifts
3. Holy Cow Brewery
4. Palace Station
5. Sahara
6. Circus Circus
7. Wet 'N Wild
8. Slots a Fun
9. Algiers
10. Las Vegas Hilton
11. Westward Ho
12. Riviera
13. Stardust
14. LV Convention Center
15. The New Frontier
16. Desert Inn – *Closed*
17. Fashion Show Mall
18. Treasure Island
19. Venetian
20. Casino Royale
21. Sands Expo Center
22. Harrah's
23. The Mirage
24. Imperial Palace
25. O'Shea's
26. Flamingo
27. Gold Coast
28. Rio
29. Caesars Palace
30. Barbary Coast
31. Bellagio
32. Bally's
33. Terrible's
34. Jockey Club
35. Paris
36. Helicopter Rides
37. Aladdin
38. Hard Rock
39. Boardwalk
40. Harley-Davidson Cafe
41. Polo Towers
42. Monte Carlo
43. Showcase Mall
44. The Orleans
45. Wild Wild West
46. New York-New York
47. MGM Grand
48. Howard Johnson's
49. Excalibur
50. Tropicana
51. San Remo
52. Luxor
53. Mandalay Bay
54. Four Seasons

Map courtesy Donrey Media Group, **http://www.lasvegas.com**, Copyright 2001.

a map of the Las Vegas "Strip" and the locations of the major hotel/casinos). All three themed hotels/casinos are connected by an elevated monorail system. Located next to the Luxor, Mandalay Bay aims for the upscale traveler and player and is styled as a South Seas adventure.

The Mandalay Bay hotel/casino contains a 43-story hotel/casino with over 3,700 rooms and an 11-acre aquatic environment. The aquatic environment contains a surfing beach, a swim-up shark tank, and a snorkeling reef. A Four Seasons Hotel with some 424 rooms complements the remainder of Mandalay Bay and strives for the high roller gamblers. Mandalay anticipates that the remainder of the "Masterplan Mile" will eventually consist of at least one additional casino resort, a convention center, and a number of stand-alone hotels and amusement centers. The planned convention center was placed on hold after the September 11 terrorist attacks.

Circus Circus-Las Vegas is the world of the Big Top, where live circus acts perform free every thirty minutes. Kids may cluster around video games while the adults migrate to nickel slot machines and dollar game tables. Located at the north end of the Vegas strip, Circus Circus-Las Vegas sits on 69 acres of land with 3,744 hotel rooms, shopping areas, two specialty restaurants, a buffet with seating for 1,200, fast-food shops, cocktail lounges, video arcades, and 109,000 square-feet of casino space, and it includes the Grand Slam Canyon, a five-acre glass enclosed theme park, including a four-loop roller coaster.

Luxor, an Egyptian-themed hotel and casino complex, opened on October 15, 1993, when 10,000 people entered to play the 2,245 slot and video poker games and 110 table games in the 120,000 square-foot casino in the hotel atrium (reported to be the world's largest). By the end of the opening weekend, 40,000 people per day were visiting the 30-story bronze pyramid that encases the hotel and entertainment facilities.

Luxor features a thirty-story pyramid and two new 22-story hotel towers, including 492 suites. It is connected to Excalibur by a climate-controlled skyway with moving walkways. Situated at the south end of the Las Vegas strip on a 64-acre site adjacent to Excalibur, Luxor features a food and entertainment area on three different levels beneath the hotel atrium. The pyramids' hotel rooms can be reached from the four corners of the building by state-of-the-art "inclinators" that travel at a 39-degree angle. Parking is available for nearly 3,200 vehicles, including a covered garage that contains approximately 1,800 spaces.

The Luxor underwent major renovations costing $323.3 million during fiscal 1997 and another $116.5 million in fiscal 1998. The resulting complex contains 4,425 hotel rooms, extensively renovated casino space, an additional 20,000 square-feet of convention area, an 800-seat buffet, a series of IMAX attractions, 5 theme restaurants, 7 cocktail lounges, and a variety of specialty shops. Mandalay expects to draw significant walk-in traffic to the newly refurbished Luxor, which is one of the principal components of the Masterplan Mile.

Located next to the Luxor, Excalibur is one of the first sights travelers see as they exit Interstate 15 (management was confident that the sight of a giant, colorful medieval castle would make a lasting impression on mainstream tourists and vacationing families arriving in Las Vegas). Guests cross a drawbridge that is over a moat and proceed onto a cobblestone walkway where multicolored spires, turrets, and battlements loom above. The castle walls are four 28-story hotel towers containing a total of 4,008 rooms. Inside is a medieval world complete with a Fantasy Faire inhabited by strolling jugglers, fire-eaters and acrobats, as well as a Royal Village complete with peasants, serfs, and ladies-in-waiting who wander around medieval theme shops. The 110,000 square-foot casino encompasses 2,442 slot machines, more than 89 game tables, a sports book, and a poker and keno area. There are 12 restaurants that are capable of feeding more than 20,000 people daily, and a 1000-seat amphitheater. Excalibur, which opened in June 1990, was built for $294 million and was primarily financed with internally generated funds. In fiscal yearend January 31, 2002 and January 31, 2001, Excalibur contributed 12 percent of the organization's revenues.

Situated between the two anchors on the Las Vegas strip are two smaller casinos owned and operated by Mandalay. The Silver City Casino and Slots-A-Fun primarily depend on the foot traffic along the strip for their gambling patrons. Combined, they offer more than 1,202 slot machines and 46 gaming tables on 34,900 square-feet of casino floor.

Mandalay owns and operates eleven properties in Nevada, one in Mississippi, a 50 percent ownership in three others, and a 53.5 percent ownership of MotorCity Casino in Detroit, Michigan (see Exhibit 3).

All of Mandalay's operations do well in the city of Las Vegas with a combined hotel room occupancy rate that has (until recently) remained above 90 percent. This has been due, in part, to low room rates (from $39 at Circus Circus-Las Vegas) and popular buffets. Each of the major properties contains large, inexpensive buffets that management believes make staying with Mandalay more attractive. As can be seen in Exhibit 4, the total earnings from each property continue to increase as the entire market for gaming

## EXHIBIT 3    Mandalay's Percent Revenue Data

| Properties | 2001 | 2000 |
|---|---|---|
| Las Vegas | | |
|   Mandalay Bay | 22 | 22 |
|   Circus Circus-Las Vegas | 15[1] | 18[1] |
|   Excalibur | 12 | 14 |
|   Luxor | 16 | 17 |
|   Slots-A-Fun and Silver City | | |
| Reno | | |
|   Circus Circus-Reno | | |
| Laughlin | | |
|   Colorado Bell | 7[2] | 8[2] |
|   Edgewater | | |
| Jean, Nevada | | |
|   Gold Strike | 3[3] | 4[3] |
|   Nevada Landing | | |
| Henderson, Nevada | | |
|   Railroad Pass | | |
| Tunica, Mississippi | | |
|   Gold Strike | 5 | 6 |
| 50% ownership: | | |
|   Silver Legacy, Reno, Nevada | | |
|   Monte Carlo, Las Vegas, Nevada | | |
|   Grand Victoria Riverboat Casino, Elgin, Illinois | | |
| MotorCity Casino, Detroit, Michigan | 13 | 2 |

[1]Combined with revenues from Circus Circus-Reno.
[2]Colorado Bell and Edgewater have been combined.
[3]Gold Strike and Nevada Landing have been combined.
Note: Revenues from Slots-A-Fun and Silver City, management fees, and other income were not separately reported.

EXHIBIT 4    Mandalay's Income by Property
(in millions)

|  | FYE 1/31/2002 | | | FYE 1/31/2001 | | |
|---|---|---|---|---|---|---|
|  | Operating Income | Depreciation | EBITDA | Operating Income | Depreciation | EBITDA |
| Mandalay Bay | $ 41.6 | $ 43.4 | $ 85.0 | $ 38.4 | $ 40.8 | $ 79.2 |
| Luxor | 74.9 | 33.8 | 108.7 | 85.9 | 37.3 | 123.2 |
| Excalibur | 67.6 | 17.9 | 85.5 | 79.0 | 16.9 | 95.9 |
| Circus Circus-Las Vegas | 39.8 | 23.0 | 62.8 | 47.7 | 23.6 | 71.3 |
| Gold Strike-Tunica | 11.0 | 12.8 | 23.8 | 19.4 | 12.8 | 32.2 |
| Colorado Belle/Edgewater | 10.5 | 11.5 | 22.0 | 13.6 | 11.3 | 24.9 |
| Circus Circus-Reno | 14.4 | 9.2 | 23.6 | 18.9 | 9.8 | 28.7 |
| Gold Strike properties | (55.6) | 10.2 | (45.4) | 7.7 | 10.4 | 18.1 |
| MotorCity Casino | 72.2 | 39.1 | 111.3 | 49.3 | 37.5 | 86.8 |
| Unconsolidated joint ventures | 107.1 | 6.5 | 113.6 | 108.5 | 6.5 | 115.0 |
| Other | (3.7) | 0.9 | (2.8) | (4.9) | 0.3 | (4.6) |
| Subtotal | 379.8 | 208.3 | 588.1 | 463.5 | 207.2 | 670.7 |
| Corporate expense | (28.7) | 7.7 | (21.0) | (32.0) | 10.8 | (21.2) |
| Total | $351.1 | $216.0 | $567.1 | $431.5 | $218.0 | $649.5 |

Source: Mandalay Group's 2001 Annual Report, p. 51.

continues to increase. As shown in Exhibit 5, room occupancy rates vary between 76 and 95 percent due to the building boom in Las Vegas, the higher room rates at some locations ($99 to $399 for special occasions at Mandalay Bay), and the consuming public's attraction to newer properties. Also note the continued rise in room rates reflecting the general trend in Las Vegas of generating more revenue from sources other than gaming (i.e., rooms, restaurants, shows, and other attractions).

EXHIBIT 5    Average Room Rates, Occupancy, and REVPAR[1]

|  | As of 1/31/2001 | | | As of 1/31/2002 | | |
|---|---|---|---|---|---|---|
|  | Avg. Rate | Occ.% | REVPAR | Avg. Rate | Occ.% | REVPAR |
| Mandalay Bay | $154 | 86% | $133 | $168 | 80% | $134 |
| Luxor | $ 98 | 93% | $ 92 | $ 98 | 83% | $ 81 |
| Excalibur | $ 70 | 94% | $ 66 | $ 70 | 92% | $ 64 |
| Circus Circus-Las Vegas | $ 57 | 95% | $ 54 | $ 55 | 89% | $ 49 |
| Circus Circus-Reno | $ 53 | 82% | $ 43 | $ 54 | 81% | $ 44 |
| Colorado Belle | $ 30 | 84% | $ 25 | $ 31 | 80% | $ 25 |
| Edgewater | $ 27 | 85% | $ 23 | $ 30 | 78% | $ 23 |
| Gold Strike-Tunica | $ 69 | 76% | $ 52 | $ 62 | 78% | $ 48 |
| Weighted Average-All | $ 79 | 89% | $ 70 | $ 81 | 83% | $ 67 |
| Weighted Average-Las Vegas | $ 93 | 92% | $ 85 | $ 95 | 86% | $ 82 |

[1]Revenue Per Available Room.
Source: Mandalay Report's 2001 Annual Report, p. 50.

The company's other big-top facility is Circus Circus-Reno. With the addition of Skyway Tower in 1985, this big top now offers a total of 1,605 hotel rooms, 60,600 square feet of casino, a buffet which can seat 700 people, shops, video arcades, cocktail lounges, midway games, and circus acts. Circus Circus-Reno had several marginal years, but it has become one of the leaders in the Reno market. Mandalay anticipates that recent remodeling, at a cost of $25.6 million, will increase this property's revenue-generating potential.

The Colorado Belle and The Edgewater Hotel are located in Laughlin, Nevada, on the banks of the Colorado River, a city 90 miles south of Las Vegas. The Colorado Belle, opened in 1987, features a huge paddle wheel riverboat replica, buffet, cocktail lounges, and shops. The Edgewater, acquired in 1983, has a southwestern motif, a 57,000 square-foot casino, a bowling center, a buffet, and cocktail lounges. Combined, these two properties contain 2,700 rooms and over 120,000 square-feet of casino. These two operations contributed 7 percent of the company's revenues in the year ending January 31, 2001, down from 21 percent in 1994. The extensive proliferation of casinos throughout the region, primarily on Indian land, and the development of megaresorts in Las Vegas, have seriously eroded outlying markets such as Laughlin.

Three properties purchased in 1995 and located in Jean and Henderson, Nevada, represent continuing investments by Mandalay in outlying markets. The Gold Strike and Nevada Landing service the I-15 market between Las Vegas and southern California. These properties have over 73,000 square-feet of casino space, 2,140 slot machines, and forty-two gaming tables combined. Each has limited hotel space (1,116 rooms total) and depends heavily on I-15 traffic. The Railroad Pass is considered a local casino and is dependent on Henderson residents as its market. This smaller casino contains only 395 slot machines and eleven gaming tables.

Gold Strike-Tunica (formally Circus Circus-Tunica) is a dockside casino located in Tunica, Mississippi. Opened in 1994 on twenty-four acres of land located along the Mississippi River, it lies approximately twenty miles south of Memphis.

## JOINT VENTURES

In Las Vegas, Mandalay joined with Mirage Resorts to build and operate the Monte Carlo, a hotel-casino with 3,002 rooms designed along the lines of the grand casinos of the Mediterranean. It is located on 46-acres (with 600 feet on the Las Vegas strip) between the New York-New York casino and the Bellagio; all three casinos are connected by monorail. The Monte Carlo features a 90,000 square-foot casino containing 2,221 slot machines and 95 gaming tables, along with a 550-seat bingo parlor, high-tech arcade rides, restaurants and buffets, a microbrewery, approximately 15,000 square feet of meeting and convention space and a 1,200 seat theater. Opened on June 21, 1996, the Monte Carlo generated $14.6 million as Mandalay's share in operating income for the first seven months of operation.

In Elgin, Illinois, Mandalay is in a 50 percent partnership with Hyatt Development Corporation in The Grand Victoria. Styled to resemble a Victorian riverboat, this floating casino and land-based entertainment complex includes some 36,000 square-feet of casino space, containing 977 slot machines and 56 gaming tables. The adjacent land-based complex contains two movie theaters, a 240 seat buffet, restaurants, and parking for approximately 2,000 vehicles. Built for a total of $112 million, The Grand Victoria returned all of Mandalay's initial investment.

The third joint venture is a 50 percent partnership with Eldorado Limited in the Silver Legacy. Opened in 1995, this casino is located between Circus Circus-Reno and the Eldorado Hotel and Casino on two city blocks in downtown Reno, Nevada. The Silver Legacy has 1,711 hotel rooms, 85,000 square-feet of casino, 2,275 slot machines, and 89 gaming tables. Management seems to believe that the Silver Legacy holds promise; however, the Reno market is suffering, and the opening of the Silver Legacy has cannibalized the Circus Circus-Reno market.

A final current joint venture is with the Atwater Casino Group to build and operate a hotel/casino in Detroit, Michigan. A temporary 75,000 square-foot casino was built under a plan agreed to by the city of Detroit. Future plans call for the construction of an approximately 800-room hotel, expansion of the gaming areas, the addition of new restaurants, more retail space, more convention space, and other amenities. Total costs are estimated at some $600 million, with Mandalay contributing 20 percent and the remainder being funded by debt with the joint venture. However, the Detroit City Council has not yet given final approval for the completion of this project. As anticipated in the construction of new gaming facilities outside of Las Vegas, a number of lawsuits have been filed that could delay or halt new construction.

Mandalay has achieved success through an aggressive growth strategy and a renovated corporate structure designed to enhance that growth. A strong cash position, innovative ideas, and attention to cost control have allowed Mandalay to satisfy the bottom line during a period when competitors were typically taking on large debt obligations to finance new projects. Yet the market is changing. Gambling of all kinds has spread across the country; no longer does the average individual need to go to Las Vegas or Atlantic City. Instead, gambling can be found as close as the local quick market (lottery), bingo hall, many Indian reservations, the Mississippi River, and of course on the Internet. There are now almost 300 casinos in Las Vegas alone, 60 in Colorado, and 160 in California. In order to maintain a competitive edge, Mandalay has continued to invest heavily in the renovation of existing properties (a strategy common to the entertainment/amusement industry), it continues to develop new projects, and it has shifted from a strategy dependent on gaming to one focusing as well on income from hotel, food, and entertainment.

## New Ventures

Mandalay owns a contiguous mile at the southern end of the Las Vegas strip, which is called the Masterplan Mile (or Mandalay Mile) and which currently contains the Excalibur, Luxor, and Mandalay Bay resorts. Located next to the Luxor, Mandalay Bay aims for the upscale traveler and player, and its presence enhances the destination resort value of all three properties. Mandalay anticipates that the remainder of the Masterplan Mile will eventually consist of at least one additional casino resort and a number of stand-alone hotels and amusement centers.

Mandalay also plans three other casino projects, provided all the necessary licenses and agreements can be obtained. In Detroit, Michigan, Mandalay has combined with the Atwater Casino Group in a joint venture to build a $600 million project. Negotiations with the city to develop the project have been completed; however, the remainder of the appropriate licenses will need to be obtained before construction begins.

Along the Mississippi Gulf, at the north end of St. Louis, Mandalay plans to construct a casino resort containing fifteen hundred rooms at an estimated cost of $225 million. Mandalay has received all of the necessary permits to begin construction; however, these approvals have been challenged in court, delaying the project.

Most of Mandalay's projects are being tailored to attract mainstream tourists and family vacationers. However, the addition of several joint ventures and the completion of the Masterplan Mile will also attract the more upscale customer.

## THE GAMING INDUSTRY

By 2001, the gaming industry had captured a large amount of the vacation/leisure time dollars spent in the United States. Gamblers lost over $58.2 billion on legal wagering in 1999 (up from $29.9 billion in 1992), including wagers at racetracks, bingo parlors, lotteries, and casinos. This figure does not include dollars spent on lodging, food, transportation, and other related expenditures associated with visits to gaming facilities. Casino gambling accounts for 40.6 percent of all legal gambling expenditures, still ahead of spending on second-place lotteries at 32.2 percent and third-place Indian reservations at 15.4 percent. The popularity of casino gambling may be credited to more frequent and somewhat higher pay-outs as compared to lotteries and racetracks; however, as winnings are recycled, the multiplier effect restores a high return to casino operators.

Geographic expansion has slowed considerably since no additional states have approved casino type gambling since 1993. Growth has occurred in developed locations, with Las Vegas, Nevada, and Atlantic City, New Jersey, leading the way. However, the Internet as a gaming venue has exploded.

Las Vegas remains the largest U.S. gaming market and one of the largest convention markets with more than 124,000 hotel rooms hosting more than 35.8 million visitors in 2000. By August 2001, Las Vegas had hosted over 24.3 million visitors, up 1 percent over the previous year. However, it can be anticipated that total visitation will be down for 2001 and may be down for 2002. Prior to the September 11 terrorist attacks, casino operators had been building to take advantage of this continued growth. Recent projects have included the Monte Carlo ($350 million), New York-New York ($350 million), Bellagio ($1.4 billion), Hilton Hotels ($750 million), Mandalay Bay ($950 million), Venetian ($1.4 billion), and Paris-Las Vegas ($760 million). Las Vegas hotel and casino capacity continued to expand when some 12,300 rooms opened in 1999, another 4,219 in 2000, 3,099 in 2001, 3,070 for 2002, and 3,761 expected for 2003. According to the Las Vegas Convention and Visitor Authority, Las Vegas is a destination market, with most visitors planning their trips more than a week in advance (81 percent), arriving by car (43 percent) or airplane (46 percent), and staying in a hotel (72 percent). Gamblers are typically return visitors (79 percent), averaging 2.2 trips per year because they like playing the slots (65 percent).

For Atlantic City, besides the geographical separation, the primary differences in the two markets reflect the different types of consumers frequenting these markets. While Las Vegas attracts overnight resort-seeking vacationers, Atlantic City's clientele is predominantly day-trippers traveling by automobile or bus. Gaming revenues are expected to continue to grow, and they reached $4.2 billion in 1999, up some 2 percent over 1998, split between twelve casinos/hotels currently operating. Growth in the Atlantic City area will be concentrated in the Marina section of town, where Mirage Resorts has entered into an agreement with the city to develop 150 acres of the Marina as a destination resort. This development will include a resort wholly owned by Mirage, a casino/hotel developed by Mandalay, and a complex developed by a joint venture with Mirage and Boyd Corp. Currently in Atlantic City, Donald Trump's gaming empire holds the largest market share with Trump Marina, Trump Plaza, and the Trump Taj Mahal (total market share is 29 percent). The next closest in market share is Bally's (12.1 percent), Caesar's (11.2 percent), Tropicana (9.9 percent), and Harrah's (9.5 percent).

## EXHIBIT 6 Mandalay Resort Group and Subsidiaries Consolidated Balance Sheets
(in thousands, except share data)

| | January 31, | |
|---|---:|---:|
| | *2002* | *2001* |
| **Assets** | | |
| Current assets | | |
|   Cash and cash equivalents | $ 105,905 | $ 105,941 |
|   Accounts receivable, net of allowance | 58,372 | 78,359 |
|   Income tax receivable | 18,089 | — |
|   Inventories | 30,555 | 31,180 |
|   Prepaid expenses | 40,848 | 40,986 |
|   Deferred income tax | 13,218 | 30,164 |
|     Total current assets | 266,987 | 286,630 |
| Property, equipment and leasehold interests, at cost, net | 3,049,812 | 3,236,824 |
| Other assets | | |
|   Excess of purchase price over fair market value of net assets acquired, net | 45,445 | 65,778 |
|   Investments in unconsolidated affiliates | 554,086 | 560,987 |
|   Other investments | 35,751 | 27,021 |
|   Deferred charges and other assets | 84,953 | 71,026 |
|     Total other assets | 720,235 | 724,812 |
|     Total assets | $4,037,034 | $4,248,266 |
| **Liabilities and Stockholders' Equity** | | |
| Current liabilities | | |
|   Current portion of long-term debt | $ 39,251 | $ 42,262 |
|   Accounts and contracts payable | | |
|     Trade | 33,473 | 37,275 |
|     Construction | 8,284 | 3,920 |
|   Accrued liabilities | | |
|     Salaries, wages and vacations | 52,680 | 51,866 |
|     Progressive jackpots | 11,556 | 11,334 |
|     Advance room deposits | 13,242 | 14,069 |
|     Interest | 58,592 | 53,122 |
|     Other | 92,163 | 82,827 |
|     Total current liabilities | 309,241 | 296,675 |
| Long-term debt, net of current portion | 2,482,087 | 2,623,597 |
| Other liabilities | | |
|   Deferred income tax | 199,478 | 235,763 |
|   Deferred gain | 28,339 | — |
|   Other long-term liabilities | 80,919 | 41,966 |
|     Total other liabilities | 308,736 | 277,729 |
|     Total liabilities | 3,100,064 | 3,198,001 |
| Commitments and contingent liabilities | | |
| Minority interest | (3,639) | (18,675) |
| Stockholders' equity | | |
|   Common stock $.01 2/3 par value | | |
|   Authorized–450,000,000 shares | | |
|   Issued—113,634,013 shares | 1,894 | 1,894 |
|   Preferred stock $.01 par value | | |
|   Authorized—75,000,000 shares | — | — |
|   Additional paid-in capital | 572,992 | 572,207 |
|   Retained earnings | 1,374,376 | 1,321,332 |
|   Accumulated other comprehensive loss | (21,902) | (6,804) |
|   Treasury stock (45,278,193 and 37,357,777 shares), at cost | (986,751) | (819,689) |
|     Total stockholders' equity | 940,609 | 1,068,940 |
| Total liabilities and stockholders' equity | $4,037,034 | $4,248,266 |

*Source:* Mandalay Group's 2001 *Annual Report,* p. 73.

There remain a number of smaller markets located around the United States, primarily in Mississippi, Louisiana, Illinois, Missouri, and Indiana. Each state has imposed various restrictions on the development of casino operations within the state. In Illinois, for example, where there are only ten gaming licenses available, growth opportunities and revenues have been severely restricted. In other states, such as Mississippi and Louisiana, revenues are up 7 percent and 6 percent, respectively, in riverboat operations. Native American casinos continue to be developed on federally controlled Indian land. These casinos are not publicly held but do tend to be managed by publicly held corporations. Overall, these other locations present a mix of opportunities and generally constitute only a small portion of overall gaming revenues.

## MAJOR INDUSTRY PLAYERS

Over the past several years, there have been numerous changes as mergers and acquisitions have reshaped the gaming industry. As of year-end 2000, the industry was a combination of corporations ranging from those engaged solely in gaming to multinational conglomerates. The largest competitors, in terms of revenues, combined multiple industries to generate both large revenues and substantial profits (see Exhibit 8). However, those engaged primarily in gaming could also be extremely profitable.

Park Place was founded from the separation of the lodging and gaming operations of Hilton Hotels in December 1998. Park Place merged with the Mississippi gaming operations of Grand Casinos, and then it bought Caesars from Starwood. Now it consists of a total of 29 casinos, 20 of which are located in the United States. Its latest venture is the Paris Las Vegas Casino & Resort located next to Bally's in Las Vegas. The Paris features a 50-story replica of the Eiffel Tower, 85,000 square-feet of casino space, 13 restaurants, and 130,000 square feet of convention space. Park Place is the largest casino operator in the world, with approximately 2 million square-feet of gaming space, 28,000 rooms, and revenues of $4.9 billion in 2000.

Harrah's Entertainment, Inc., is primarily engaged in the gaming industry, with casinos/hotels in Reno, Lake Tahoe, Las Vegas, and Laughlin, Nevada, as well as in Atlantic City, New Jersey; riverboats in Joliet, Illinois, Vicksburg and Tunica, Mississippi, Shreveport, Louisiana, and Kansas City, Kansas; two Indian casinos; and one casino in Auckland, New Zealand. In June 1998 Harrah's purchased the assets of Showboat and its operations in Atlantic City and Las Vegas, and in January 1999 it merged with Rio Hotel and Casino, Inc. In 2000, it sold the Showboat and purchased Players International. The resulting company now has a total of over 1,258,220 square-feet of casino space; 6,858 slot machines; 1,099 table games; 11,562 hotel rooms or suites; approximately 294,844 square feet of convention space; 86 restaurants; 30 snack bars; 11 showrooms; and four cabarets. Harrah's attempts to target the experienced gambler who likes to play in multiple markets by establishing strong brand names of consistent high quality.

MGM Mirage (formally known as the MGM Grand) owns and operates eighteen hotels casinos worldwide. These properties include the MGM Hotel and Casino; MGM Grand Australia; MGM Grand Detroit; the Bellagio in Las Vegas; the Beau Rivage in Biloxi, Mississippi; the Golden Nugget-Downtown in Las Vegas; the Mirage on the strip in Las Vegas; Treasure Island; Holiday Inn-Boardwalk; and the Golden Nugget-Laughlin. Additionally, it is a 50 percent owner of the Monte Carlo with Mandalay. The MGM Las Vegas is located on approximately 116 acres at the northeast corner of Las Vegas Boulevard across the street from New York-New York Hotel and Casino. The casino is approximately 171,500 square-feet in size, and it is one of the largest

EXHIBIT 7    Mandalay Resort Group and Subsidiaries Consolidated Statements of Income
(in thousands, except share data)

| | Year ended January 31, | | |
| | 2002 | 2001 | 2000 |
| --- | --- | --- | --- |
| Revenues | | | |
| Casino | $ 1,201,707 | $ 1,221,595 | $   925,499 |
| Rooms | 581,551 | 611,352 | 534,132 |
| Food and beverage | 410,276 | 418,081 | 346,647 |
| Other | 332,253 | 299,753 | 251,509 |
| Earnings of unconsolidated affiliates | 113,287 | 114,645 | 98,627 |
| | 2,639,074 | 2,665,426 | 2,156,414 |
| Less-complimentary allowances | (177,275) | (169,642) | (131,509) |
| | 2,461,799 | 2,495,784 | 2,024,905 |
| Costs and expenses | | | |
| Casino | 669,719 | 670,243 | 494,054 |
| Rooms | 197,300 | 203,352 | 189,419 |
| Food and beverage | 283,864 | 299,726 | 276,261 |
| Other | 219,358 | 200,236 | 170,654 |
| General and administrative | 417,149 | 409,603 | 339,455 |
| Corporate general and administrative | 20,981 | 21,153 | 22,464 |
| Depreciation and amortization | 216,001 | 217,984 | 178,301 |
| Operating lease rent | 32,185 | 40,121 | 25,994 |
| Preopening expenses | 2,155 | 1,832 | 49,134 |
| Impairment loss | 52,027 | — | — |
| Abandonment loss | — | — | 5,433 |
| | 2,110,739 | 2,064,250 | 1,751,169 |
| Income from operations | 351,060 | 431,534 | 273,736 |
| Other income (expense) | | | |
| Interest, dividends and other income | (1,163) | 8,339 | 2,369 |
| Guarantee fees from unconsolidated affiliate | 2,264 | 2,498 | 2,775 |
| Interest expense | (221,352) | (219,940) | (164,387) |
| Interest expense from unconsolidated affiliates | (8,451) | (11,293) | (11,085) |
| | (228,702) | (220,396) | (170,328) |
| Minority interest | (29,352) | (16,746) | (292) |
| Income before provision for income taxes | 93,006 | 194,392 | 103,116 |
| Provision for income taxes | 39,962 | 74,692 | 38,959 |
| Income before cumulative effect of change in accounting principle | 53,044 | 119,700 | 64,157 |
| Cumulative effect of change in accounting for preopening expenses, net of tax benefit of $11,843 | — | — | (21,994) |
| Net income | $    53,044 | $   119,700 | $    42,163 |
| Basic earnings per share: | | | |
| Income before cumulative effect of change in accounting principle | $        .73 | $       1.53 | $        .71 |
| Cumulative effect of change in accounting principle | — | — | (.24) |
| Net income | $        .73 | $       1.53 | $        .47 |
| Diluted earnings per share: | | | |
| Income before cumulative effect of change in accounting principle | $        .71 | $       1.50 | $        .70 |
| Cumulative effect of change in accounting principle | — | — | (.24) |
| Net income | $        .71 | $       1.50 | $        .46 |
| Average shares outstanding (basic) | 72,798,916 | 78,334,735 | 90,607,487 |
| Average shares outstanding (diluted) | 74,459,831 | 79,700,614 | 91,896,224 |

*Source:* 2001 *Annual Report,* p. 74.

EXHIBIT 8    Competitors (in millions)

|  | 2000 | 2000 | 1999 | 1999 |
|---|---|---|---|---|
|  | *Revenue* | *Net Income* | *Revenue* | *Net Income* |
| Park Place Entertainment | $4,896 | $143 | $3,176 | $136 |
| Harrah's Entertainment | 3,471 | (12.1) | 3,024 | 208 |
| MGM Mirage | 3,232 | 160 | 1,392.2 | 209 |
| Mandalay Resort Group | 2,050 | 42 | 1,479 | 85 |
| Trump Hotel and Casino | 933 | (29) | 973 | (149) |
| Aztar | 848 | 53 | 800 | 10 |

*Source:* Individual companies annual reports and 10Ks (1999–2000).

casinos in the world, with 3,669 slot machines and 157 table games. Through a wholly owned subsidiary, MGM owns and operates the MGM Grand Diamond Beach Hotel and a hotel/casino resort in Darwin, Australia. In March 1999, MGM and Primadonna Resorts, Inc., merged, resulting in ownership of New York-New York Hotel and Casino and three hotels casinos on the California/Nevada border. MGM also intends to construct and operate a destination resort hotel/casino, entertainment, and retail facility in Atlantic City on approximately thirty-five acres of land on the Atlantic City boardwalk.

## FUTURE CONSIDERATIONS

Mandalay was one of the innovators of the gaming resort concept and has continued to be a leader in that field. However, the mega-entertainment resort industry and the traditional casino gaming industry operate differently. In the past, consumers would visit a casino to experience the thrill of gambling. Now they not only gamble but also expect to be dazzled by enormous entertainment complexes that cost billions of dollars to build. The competition has continued to increase at the same time growth rates have been slowing.

For years, analysts have questioned the ability of the gaming industry to continue high growth in established markets as the industry matures. Through the 1970s and 1980s, the gaming industry experienced rapid growth. Through the 1990s, the industry began to experience a shake out of marginal competitors and a consolidation phase. Mandalay has been successful through this turmoil but now faces the task of maintaining high growth in a more mature industry severely impacted by the terrorist attacks of September 11, 2001.

## BIBLIOGRAPHY

"AGA Fact Sheets," American Gaming Association, retrieved October 17, 2001 from http://www.americangaming.org/casino_entertainment/aga_facts/.

Aztar Corp. *1997, 1998, 1999, and 2000 10K,* retrieved from EDGAR Data Base, http://www.sec.gov/Archives/edgar/data/.

"Economic Impacts of Casino Gaming in the United States," by Arthur Andersen for the American Gaming Association (May 1997).

Harrah's Entertainment, Inc. *1997, 1998, 1999, and 2000 10K,* retrieved from EDGAR Data Base, http://www.sec.gov/Archives/edgar/data/.

"Harrah's Survey of Casino Entertainment," Harrah's Entertainment, Inc. (1996).

Industry Surveys—Lodging and Gaming, *Standard & Poor's Industry Surveys* (June 19, 1997).

"ITT Board Rejects Hilton's Offer as Inadequate, Reaffirms Belief That ITT's Comprehensive Plan Is in the Best Interest of ITT Shareholders," press release (August 14, 1997).

ITT Corp. *1997 10K,* retrieved from EDGAR Data Base, **http://www.sec.gov/ Archives/edgar/data/**.

Mandalay Resort Group (formally Circus Circus), *Annual Report to Shareholders* (January 31, 1989; January 31, 1990; January 31, 1993; January 31, 1994; January 31, 1995; January 31, 1996; January 31, 1997; January 31, 1998; January 31, 1999; January 31, 2000; January 31, 2001).

MGM Mirage *1997, 1998, 1999, and 2000 10K,* retrieved from EDGAR Database, **http://www.sec.gov/Archives/ edgar/data/**.

Strow, David, "LV Casinos Look at Layoffs," *Las Vegas Sun* (September 17, 2001).

# HARRAH'S ENTERTAINMENT, INC.—2002

**Mary R. Dittman**
**Francis Marion University**

HET

www.harrahs.com

Harrah's Entertainment, Inc., is a $3.7 billion per year gaming company that operates twenty-one casinos in seventeen markets, including properties in Arizona, Illinois, Indiana, Kansas, Louisiana, Mississippi, Missouri, Nevada, New Jersey, and North Carolina. Harrah's is headquartered in Las Vegas, Nevada, and is one of the gaming industry's forerunners in customer-oriented database marketing.

## HISTORY

William F. Harrah founded Harrah's as a bingo parlor in Reno, Nevada, in 1937. Over the next thirty-two years, Harrah's grew into one of the nation's premier gaming establishments.

In 1973, Harrah's became the first casino to be listed on the New York Stock Exchange. In 1980, Holiday Inns, Inc., acquired Harrah's. In 1989, Holiday Inn announced the creation of a new spinoff company, The Promus Companies, Inc. In 1995, Promus spun off its Embassy Suites, Hampton Inn, and Homewood Suites brands; the remaining Harrah's brand was renamed Harrah's Entertainment, Inc., and it included Harrah's hotels and casinos, Harrah's assets, and a majority of the Promus headquarters and people.

In 1997 and 1998, Harrah's joined with the Cherokee Indians and the Prairie Band of Potawatomi Nation, respectively, to open tribal-run casinos in North Carolina and Kansas. Also in 1998, Harrah's purchased Showboat, Inc., which includes four properties in Atlantic City, East Chicago, Las Vegas, and Sydney, Australia. (Operation of this Australian property ceased in January 2000.) In 1999, Harrah's completed a merger with the Rio Hotel & Casino, a true destination resort in Las Vegas.

In March 2000, Harrah's acquired Players International, Inc., which contributed significantly to the company's 15 percent revenue growth over 1999. Players owned riverboat casinos in Missouri, Louisiana, and Illinois and a racetrack in Kentucky.

## EXTERNAL FACTORS

### Gaming Industry

The gaming industry reports revenues as GGR—Gross Gambling Revenue. GGR is the amount of money wagered less the winnings paid to the player. For example, a player goes to a casino intending to bet $100 in the slot machines. At the casino, he exchanges his $100 bill for one hundred $1.00 casino tokens. The player plays his tokens; he wins some bets and loses some bets. Because slot machines typically pay out $.90 for every $1.00 put into the machine, the player ends up with $90. He continues to bet each of his ninety $1.00 tokens and ends up with $81 (ninety bets with an expected value of $.90, or $90 \times .90 = 81$). He pockets the $81 and goes to a show at the casino's showroom. The player intended to spend $100 but actually spent only $19. The casino recognizes only $19 in revenue from the player.

In 1999, GGR for casinos was $22.6 billion. This was a 12.7 percent increase in revenues over 1998. The total gaming industry (including lotteries, bookmaking, and bingo) reported revenues of $58.2 billion in 1999 (up 6 percent from 1998).

Casinos' annual revenues from March 1999 through March 2000 are shown in Exhibit 1.

EXHIBIT 1    2000 Annual Casino Revenue by Market

| Casino Market | Annual Revenues |
|---|---|
| Las Vegas Strip | $   4.5 billion |
| Atlantic City, NJ | $   4.2 billion |
| Chicago Area (IL, IN) | $   1.8 billion |
| Connecticut Indian | $   1.6 billion |
| Tunica, MS | $   1   billion |
| Gulf Coast, MS | $   1   billion |
| Reno, NV | $817.7 million |
| Las Vegas—Downtown | $665   million |
| Bossier City/Shreveport, LA | $659.9 million |
| St. Louis Area (IL, MO) | $652   million |
| Lake Charles, LA | $561.4 million |
| Laughlin, NV | $539.3 million |
| Kansas City, MO | $512.7 million |
| Cincinnati Area (OH) | $472.4 million |
| Black Hawk/Central City (CO) | $448.1 million |
| Delaware Racetracks | $432.1 million |
| New Orleans, LA | $399.3 million |
| Southern IL/IN | $356.8 million |
| Council Bluffs, IA | $337.4 million |
| South Shore Lake Tahoe, NV | $323.5 million |
| Vicksburg, MS | $222   million |
| Quad Cities Area (IL, IA) | $181.6 million |
| Des Moines, IA | $149.8 million |
| Baton Rouge, LA | $149.2 million |
| Cripple Creek, CO | $126.4 million |
| Peoria, IL | $122.1 million |
| Coahoma, MS | $102.7 million |
| Dubuque, IA | $ 78.4 million |
| Greenville, MS | $ 73.5 million |
| Deadwood, SD | $ 49.7 million |
| Natchez, MS | $ 32.5 million |
| Caruthersville, MO | $ 23.7 million |
| St. Joseph, MO | $ 20.8 million |

Source: "Casino Markets by Annual Revenue", AGA Fact Sheet. www.americangaming.org.

The Nevada market constitutes 30.2 percent of the gaming industry's volume, while New Jersey represents 18.6 percent of the volume. The commercial casino industry employs more than 370,000 people with wages of more than $10.9 billion, and the industry contributed more than $3.5 billion in tax revenue in 2000. The industry is an important part of the economies of the eleven states where more than 425 commercial casinos are located.[1]

Residents of communities where commercial casinos are located overwhelmingly support the gaming industry. According to the 2001 AGA Survey of Casino Entertainment, an annual survey conducted by the American Gaming Association:

> *Metropolis, Ill., is one example of a local community that has been transformed with help from the casino industry. Home to Harrah's Metropolis Casino, the town received more than $6.5 million from riverboat casino taxes in 2000. This revenue has helped the small rural community upgrade its infrastructure and city utilities, as well as expand municipal services. The city recently completed a capital improvement plan for the next five years that includes projects such as construction of a new water filtration plant, development of a new industrial park, and completion of several parks and recreation projects. More than 88 percent of the funds to fulfill the plan objectives are expected to come from riverboat casino funds.[2]*

The gaming industry is also active in bringing attention to problem gaming. Much like alcohol companies that encourage consumers to drink responsibly, most casinos post the phone number for Gamblers Anonymous at every cashier's cage; many also offer free literature with information on problem gambling and how to get help. In the same spirit of involvement, the gaming industry is active against underage gambling; casinos will not permit minors to even stand in the gaming areas.

## Demographics

According to the 2000 State of the States: The AGA Survey of Casino Entertainment, the profile of the typical casino customer has remained consistent over the past several years.

The following factors seem to characterize the casino player market[3]:

- Casino players have a household income that is 19 percent higher than that of the U.S. population.
- The median age of casino players is similar to that of the U.S. population.
- Casino players are slightly less educated.
- Casino players are more likely to be white-collar workers.

Eighty-one percent of casino customers "always" or "usually" set a budget before visiting a casino. Exhibit 2 summarizes the differences between casino customers and the general population.

## Competition

The gaming industry boasts five major players (in descending order by 2000 reported revenues): Park Place Entertainment Corporation, MGM Mirage, Harrah's Entertainment, Mandalay Resort Group, and Trump Hotels and Casino Resorts. Exhibit 3 at the end of this section summarizes each competitor's 2000 revenues and net income.

Park Place Entertainment Corporation is the world's largest gaming company and owns the Hilton Hotel (including the Las Vegas Hilton and Flamingo Hilton) chain, Grand Casinos, Caesar's, the Bally's brand, and the Paris Hotel & Casino.

EXHIBIT 2    2001 Profile of U.S. Casino Customers

| Characteristic | U.S. Casino Customer | United States Population |
|---|---|---|
| Median Household Income | $50,453 | $42,343 |
| Median Age (adults 21 and older) | 46% | 45% |
| **Education** | | |
| No College | 45% | 48% |
| Some College | 27% | 30% |
| Bachelor's Degree | 17% | 16% |
| Post-Graduate Degree | 9% | 9% |
| **Employment** | | |
| White Collar | 47% | 41% |
| Blue Collar | 25% | 28% |
| Retired | 25% | 28% |
| Other | 15% | 18% |

*Source:* Andrea Lessani, "How Much Do You Want to Bet That the Internet Gambling Prohibition Act of 1997 Is Not the Most Effective Way to Tackle the Problems of Online Gambling?" The UCLA Online Institute for Cyberspace Law and Policy (May 1998), p. 1. **http://www.gseis.ucla.edu/iclp/hp.html**.

MGM Mirage owns the MGM, Mirage, Bellagio, New York-New York, Beau Rivage, Treasure Island, and Golden Nugget brands, and it holds a 50 percent ownership in the Monte Carlo (Las Vegas) with the Mandalay Resort Group. MGM Mirage had successful simultaneous opening of two major properties (Bellagio and Beau Rivage), while a difficult undertaking, signaled MGM Mirage's ability to grow and expand; Bellagio and Beau Rivage doubled the size of MGM Mirage.

Trump Hotels and Casino Resorts owns three properties in Atlantic City: the Trump Taj Mahal Casino Resort, the Trump Plaza Hotel & Casino, and the Trump Marina Hotel Casino. A fourth property, the Trump Hotel Casino, is located in Buffington Harbor, Indiana.

Mandalay Resort Group holds the Mandalay Bay, Luxor, Excalibur, and Circus Circus brands, as well as a 50 percent ownership of the Monte Carlo with MGM Mirage. Mandalay Resort Group was founded in 1974 as Circus Circus Enterprises. It holds properties in Nevada, Mississippi, and Illinois.

These figures include revenue from room, food and beverages, casinos, and other corporate sources of income. It is important to note that casinos report revenues from all income sources, while the gaming industry reports revenues as GGR (as described earlier).

EXHIBIT 3    2000 Revenues of Major Gaming Competitors

| Company | 2000 Revenue | 2000 Net Income |
|---|---|---|
| Park Place | $4,896,000,000 | $143,000,000 |
| MGM Mirage | 3,232,590,000 | 160,744,000 |
| Harrah's | 2,852,048,000 | (12,060,000) |
| Mandalay | 2,050,898,000 | 42,163,000 |
| Trump | 1,245,014,000 | (37,312,000) |

*Source:* **www.americangaming.org**

## Other Competition

The companies profiled make up slightly less than 50 percent of the gaming industry. There are many other, smaller competitors both domestically and internationally that make up the other half of the market. Since gaming could be considered part of the vast entertainment industry, hotels/casinos compete with the myriad of other entertainment venues: theme parks, resorts, theaters, cruise ships, and so on.

One potential source for intense gaming competition is the Internet. Both the state and federal governments have actively worked to regulate and even ban Internet gaming. Internet gaming is estimated to be a multibillion-dollar-per-year industry; however, there are four major concerns with this type of gaming:

1. The potential for fraud over the Internet
2. Children's access to gambling sites
3. State regulations that "lock out" commercial casinos from the Internet gaming industry
4. The need to preserve state revenues generated from legally enforced and state-run gambling operations.[4]

While the federal government does not yet ban Internet gaming, many states have passed laws regulating its use. For example, Nevada has become the first state to pass a law that specifically prohibits its residents from placing or accepting bets over the Internet.[5]

The commercial casino industry is one of the most heavily regulated industries in the United States. Not only do commercial casino companies have to meet strict state regulations, casinos also must adhere to numerous federal laws.

Members of the American Gaming Association have expressed concerns over Internet gambling because Internet gambling companies are not regulated for fairness and integrity, their revenues are not taxed equitably, and those who wager may not be protected or guaranteed the same quality gaming experience they might expect from a commercial casino company. The commercial casino industry does not seem to oppose Internet gambling because of a fear of competition. In fact, many casinos would like the opportunity to market their services over the Internet.

Over the past few years, many bills have been introduced into the U.S. Senate and the House of Representatives that would ban Internet gambling; however, these bills have consistently been defeated, including one in October 2001 that would have prohibited using credit cards to pay for Internet gambling. This bill was introduced as part of a bill designed to prevent money laundering by terrorists. While the anti-money laundering bill was passed, the final version of this legislation did not include provisions related to Internet gambling.

## Technology

Three major developments affect the gaming industry: player cards, slot technology and linked jackpots, and the Internet. The Internet was examined in the previous section; the following discussion focuses on player cards and slot technology/linked jackpots.

Most casinos offer a player card, which is similar to an airline's frequent flyer card. The card is inserted into the slot machine prior to play, or it is run through a scanner at certain table games (usually with a $25 betting minimum). The card tracks player demographics and playing habits. Each casino's card is valid at that casino's locations.

Players can earn cash, prizes, and complementary meals, rooms, and other amenities by racking up points on their player cards.

Gaming industry suppliers (such as International Game Technology) have been developing new types of slotlike games with such themes as Wheel of Fortune, the Addams Family, the Richard Petty Driving Experience, and I Dream of Jeannie. The goal of such suppliers is to keep players excited and satisfied. Sierra Design Group introduced the Raining Diamonds slot machine in July 2001. The machine not only pays out coins but also rewards customers with genuine diamond jewelry, which is secured in vaults in each machine. Harrah's Rio All-Suites Hotel & Casino in Las Vegas will be the first casino in the industry to offer players the opportunity to play the Raining Diamonds slot machine.

Other than the traditional spinning reel slot machines, there are a variety of new games on the market: video-based games, multigame machines (where the player can select from a variety of games), and interactive games. Linked jackpots (like the Megabucks jackpot) pool revenues from around a gaming area (like Megabucks, which pools revenues from all over Nevada) and then pay out millions in winnings. It is conceivable that a player who wins a linked jackpot could win millions of dollars just by spending $1 dollar in a slot machine.

## Economic and Government Concerns

Casino gambling has created thousands of jobs, a high percentage of which are held by minorities and women. The hundreds of millions of dollars in tax revenues that casinos pay to cities and states each year help lower taxes and pay for many basic civic needs. Casinos also lead to growth in other areas: retail, housing construction, restaurants, and other tourism venues.[6]

For these reasons, many states support gaming. In fact, Nevada residents pay no state income tax, and sales taxes are relatively low, thanks to the taxes paid by the gaming industry.

In the past, gaming benefited from consumers' growing recreational discretionary incomes. However, following the events of September 11, 2001, the industry may see a significant decline in revenues due to losses of jobs in many industries.

The events of September 11, 2001, will surely affect Harrah's revenues. Airline travel and destination travel has decreased both domestically and internationally since that date. Consumers may have concerns related to spending discretionary income on gaming. Many businesses are affected by the loss of jobs in the airline and travel sectors. Consumers who are still employed are also nervous about traveling and spending money "unwisely."

## INTERNAL CONDITION

In 2000, Harrah's experienced a significant setback in revenues due to the bankruptcy reorganizations for Harrah's New Orleans and National Airlines, of which Harrah's owns 40 percent and 48 percent, respectively.

### Divisions

The company owns twenty casinos in seventeen markets in ten states. Those markets are divided into four divisions: (1) western region, (2) central region, (3) eastern region, and (4) managed casinos and other.

#### Western Region

The western region includes northern Nevada (Reno and Lake Tahoe) and southern Nevada (Las Vegas and Laughlin). The significant increase in 1999 revenues is due to the acquisition of the Rio All-Suites Hotel & Casino in Las Vegas; however, all southern Nevada properties reported approximately a 10 percent increase in revenues that year.

In 2000, the Rio opened its new $32 million showroom complex which includes ten thousand feet of retail space, a hospitality center, and a state-of-the-art theater. This complex has not generated an increase in entertainment revenues and is the primary cause of the significant revenue shortfall in 2000. Lower table game revenue also contributed to the loss of revenue.

| (in millions) | 2001 | 2000 | 1999 | Percentage Increase/(Decrease) 01 vs. 00 | 00 vs. 99 |
|---|---|---|---|---|---|
| Casino revenues | $ 786.3 | $ 726.8 | $ 730.1 | (8.2)% | (0.5)% |
| Total revenues | 1,203.5 | 1,141.7 | 1,147.9 | (6.5)% | (0.6)% |
| Operating profit | 130.8 | 127.9 | 182.4 | (2.3)% | (29.9)% |
| Operating margin | 10.9% | 11.2% | 15.9% | (0.4) pts | (4.7) pts |

*Source:* www.americangaming.org

## Central Region

The central region includes properties in Chicago, Louisiana, Missouri, and Mississippi.

The significant increase in revenues in 2000 over 1999 are due to the acquisition of Players in March 2000; however, excluding this acquisition, revenues in the central region still increased approximately 14 percent in 2000 over 1999.

| (in millions) | 2001 | 2000 | 1999 | 1998 | Percentage Increase/Decrease 01 vs. 00 | 00 vs. 99 |
|---|---|---|---|---|---|---|
| Casino revenues | $1,698.0 | $1,381.6 | $ 970.9 | $661.9 | 22.9% | 42.3% |
| Total revenues | 1,707.6 | 1,453.9 | 1,020.1 | 702.7 | 22.6% | 43.0% |
| Operating profit | 361.4 | 304.8 | 201.8 | 121.0 | 18.6% | 51.0% |
| Operating margin | 21.2 | 21.0% | 19.8% | 17.2% | (0.7) pts | 1.2 pts |

*Source:* www.americangaming.org

## Eastern Region

The eastern region is composed of the Harrah's Atlantic City and Atlantic City Showboat properties.

| (in millions) | 2001 | 2000 | 1999 | 1998 | Percentage Increase/Decrease 01 vs. 00 | 00 vs. 99 |
|---|---|---|---|---|---|---|
| Casino revenues | $751.0 | $743.3 | $723.3 | $540.8 | 1.0% | 2.8% |
| Total revenues | 724.0 | 791.8 | 775.6 | 590.8 | 0.1% | 2.9% |
| Operating profit | 183.0 | 182.3 | 173.8 | 129.2 | 0.4% | 4.9% |
| Operating margin | 25.3 | 23.0% | 22.4% | 21.9% | 0.1 pts | 0.5 pts |

*Source:* www.americangaming.org

*Managed Casinos and Other*

This region includes Indian gaming partnerships, management fees from Harrah's New Orleans, and branding costs.

| (in millions) | 2001 | 2000 | 1999 | 1998 | Percentage Increase/Decrease 01 vs 00 | 00 vs 99 |
|---|---|---|---|---|---|---|
| Revenues | $69.0 | $78.5 | $77.9 | $65.5 | (12.1)% | 0.8% |
| Operating profit | 30.8 | 40.4 | 43.3 | 25.3 | (23.8)% | (6.7)% |

## Vision and Mission

Harrah's has developed a comprehensive Code of Commitment that addresses customers, employees, and communities. This Code of Commitment can be found in various Harrah's publications and on the company's Web site:

**A commitment to *our guests* to promote responsible gaming:**
- We do not cash welfare or unemployment checks.
- We have a process to honor the requests of customers who wish to be denied access to our casinos, and [to have] their access to credit, check-cashing, and casino promotions . . . restricted.
- We display toll-free helpline numbers for problem gambling in our ads, brochures, and signs, and we provide financial support for those helplines.
- We train our employees to understand the signs of problem gambling and empower them to provide customers with information describing how to get help.
- We emphasize to our employees that casino gaming is an appropriate activity for adults only, and [we] require them to be vigilant in their efforts to prevent individuals under the legal age from playing at our casinos.

**A commitment to *our employees* to treat them with respect and provide them opportunities to build satisfying careers:**
- We invest in our employees by providing excellent pay and valuable benefits, including health insurance and a retirement plan.
- We are committed to sharing our financial success through tuition reimbursement, on the job training, career development, and promotion from within.
- We actively seek and respond to employee opinions on all aspects of their jobs, from the quality of their supervisors to the quality of our casinos.

**A commitment to *our communities* to help make them vibrant places to live and work, and to market our casinos responsibly:**
- We conduct our business with honesty and integrity, consistent with the highest moral, legal, and ethical standards, complying with all applicable laws and regulations.
- We share our financial success with our communities by donating one percent of company profits to civic and charitable causes.
- We encourage our employees to volunteer in civic and charitable causes.
- We restrict the placement and content of our advertising and marketing materials.

All commercial casinos prohibit minor children from participating in gaming; in fact, children are not even allowed on the casino floor. Children are permitted to walk through the casino if escorted by an adult; however, if the child stops—even to watch the adult drop a quarter into a slot machine—casino security will ask the two of them to leave the gaming floor.

Harrah's is vigilant about protecting minor-age children from gaming activity. The company has a comprehensive Marketing and Advertising Code, which governs all aspects of marketing and advertising. This code includes such policies as:

1. Not using any cartoons, illustrations, entertainment figures, or toy figures to promote gaming that would appeal to minors.

2. Not advertising in media in which the majority of the audience is known to be under the legal gambling age.

3. Not printing the Harrah's name, logo, or brand marks on items or apparel intended for persons under the legal gambling age.

## Financial Data

Exhibits 4 and 5 contain Harrah's Income Statements and Balance Sheets, respectively.

## Marketing

The Communications Act of 1934 prohibited all television ads that showed gambling activity. This act only affected commercial casinos—lotteries, horse and dog tracks, and Indian casinos were allowed to advertise freely. In June 1999, the Supreme Court struck down the Communications Act with its decision in the case *Greater New Orleans Broadcast Association* v. *United States*.

Harrah's has an incredibly strong focus on marketing. The casino industry is highly competitive; there are billions of dollars at stake. Because Harrah's competes in the entertainment industry, its customers are purchasing "a good time." Therefore, service is of the utmost importance.

It is difficult to place a price on the product offered by the casino industry. In terms of room, food, and amenity pricing, Harrah's is competitive with—and in some cases, slightly below—competitive pricing. For example, a room at Bellagio in Las Vegas starts around $300 per night; a full-size suite at the Rio is well under $200 per night. At Harrah's Las Vegas, the room rates are approximately $150 per night.

One area of price that is of interest to gaming customers is the probability of winning. Harrah's (Las Vegas and Reno) hosts annual multimillion dollar slot tournaments. These tournaments are easy to compete in, take no skill, appeal to the customer's belief that "maybe that can happen to me, too," and help to generate traffic onto the casino floor. The slot machines are the major revenue generator at a casino, so generating more slot business usually means more revenue for the casino. The reputation of having loose slots draws more people in.

Harrah's has twenty locations. There are eight land-based properties:

- Harrah's Reno
- Harrah's Lake Tahoe
- Harrah's Las Vegas
- Harrah's Atlantic City
- Atlantic City Showboat
- Harrah's Laughlin (Nevada)
- Rio All-Suites Hotel & Casino (Las Vegas)
- Metropolis (Players property located in Metropolis, Illinois)

EXHIBIT 4    Consolidated Statements of Operations

| *(in thousands, except per-share amounts)* | Year Ended December 31, | | |
|---|---|---|---|
| | *2001* | *2000* | *1999* |
| Revenues | | | |
| Casino | $3,235,761 | $2,852,048 | $2,424,237 |
| Food and beverage | 532,115 | 480,757 | 429,684 |
| Rooms | 301,846 | 270,313 | 253,629 |
| Management fees | 64,842 | 66,398 | 75,890 |
| Other | 140,234 | 142,072 | 127,527 |
| Less: casino promotional allowances | (565,758) | (481,792) | (416,842) |
| Total revenues | 3,709,040 | 3,329,796 | 2,894,125 |
| Operating expenses | | | |
| Direct | | | |
| Casino | 1,528,106 | 1,354,268 | 1,124,254 |
| Food and beverage | 234,938 | 228,002 | 218,580 |
| Rooms | 78,085 | 67,800 | 66,818 |
| Depreciation and amortization | 285,773 | 236,082 | 193,599 |
| Write-downs, reserves and recoveries | | | |
| Reserves for New Orleans casino | 2,322 | 220,000 | – |
| Other | 20,176 | 6,106 | 2,235 |
| Project opening costs | 13,136 | 8,258 | 2,276 |
| Corporate expense | 52,746 | 50,472 | 42,748 |
| Headquarters relocation and reorganization costs | – | 2,983 | 10,274 |
| Equity in (income) losses of nonconsolidated affiliates | (148) | 57,935 | 43,467 |
| Venture restructuring costs | 2,524 | 400 | (322) |
| Amortization of intangible assets | 25,288 | 21,540 | 17,617 |
| Other | 885,129 | 793,212 | 691,542 |
| Total operating expenses | 3,128,075 | 3,047,058 | 2,413,088 |
| Income from operations | 580,965 | 282,738 | 481,037 |
| Interest expense, net of interest capitalized | (255,801) | (227,139) | (193,407) |
| (Losses) gains on interests in nonconsolidated affiliates | (5,040) | (41,626) | 59,824 |
| Other income, including interest income | 28,219 | 3,866 | 12,129 |
| Income before income taxes and minority interests | 348,343 | 17,839 | 359,583 |
| Provision for income taxes | (126,737) | (15,415) | (128,914) |
| Minority interests | (12,616) | (13,768) | (11,166) |
| Income (loss) before extraordinary losses | 208,990 | (11,344) | 219,503 |
| Extraordinary losses, net of tax benefit of $13, $388 and $5,990 | (23) | (716) | (11,033) |
| Net income (loss) | $ 208,967 | $ (12,060) | $ 208,470 |
| Earnings (loss) per share–basic | | | |
| Before extraordinary losses | $        1.84 | $      (0.09) | $        1.74 |
| Extraordinary losses, net | – | (0.01) | (0.09) |
| Net income (loss) | $        1.84 | $      (0.10) | $        1.65 |
| Earnings (loss) per share–diluted | | | |
| Before extraordinary losses | $        1.81 | $      (0.09) | $        1.71 |
| Extraordinary losses, net | – | (0.01) | (0.09) |
| Net income (loss) | $        1.81 | $      (0.10) | $        (1.62) |
| Weighted average common shares outstanding | 113,540 | 117,190 | 126,072 |
| Dilutive effect of stock compensation programs | 2,168 | – | 2,676 |
| Weighted average common and common equivalent shares outstanding | 115,708 | 117,190 | 128,748 |

*Source:* Harrah's Entertainment, Inc. *2001 Annual Report*

# EXHIBIT 5    Consolidated Balance Sheets

| | December 31, | |
|---|---|---|
| *(in thousands, except per-share amounts)* | *2001* | *2000* |
| **ASSETS** | | |
| Current assets | | |
| Cash and cash equivalents | $    361,470 | $    299,202 |
| Receivables, less allowance for doubtful accounts of $61,150 and $49,357 | 110,781 | 122,050 |
| Deferred income taxes | 45,319 | 35,126 |
| Income tax refunds receivable | 28,326 | 56,132 |
| Prepayments and other | 48,927 | 48,107 |
| Inventories | 22,875 | 22,816 |
| Total current assets | 617,698 | 583,433 |
| Land, buildings, riverboats and equipment | | |
| Land and land improvements | 766,401 | 705,393 |
| Buildings, riverboats and improvements | 3,200,493 | 2,652,867 |
| Furniture, fixtures and equipment | 1,208,706 | 974,233 |
| Construction in progress | 164,294 | 248,760 |
| | 5,339,894 | 4,581,253 |
| Less: accumulated depreciation | (1,280,564) | (1,084,884) |
| | 4,059,330 | 3,496,369 |
| Goodwill, net of accumulated amortization of $92,046 and $72,465 | 947,678 | 685,393 |
| Investments in and advances to nonconsolidated affiliates | 79,464 | 86,681 |
| Deferred costs, trademarks and other | 424,412 | 314,209 |
| | $ 6,128,582 | $ 5,166,085 |
| | | |
| **LIABILITIES AND STOCKHOLDERS' EQUITY** | | |
| Current liabilities | | |
| Accounts payable | $    123,428 | $    89,051 |
| Accrued expenses | 412,897 | 343,524 |
| Short-term debt | 31,000 | 215,000 |
| Current portion of long-term debt | 1,583 | 130,928 |
| Total current liabilities | 568,908 | 778,503 |
| Long-term debt | 3,719,443 | 2,835,846 |
| Deferred credits and other | 173,677 | 177,654 |
| Deferred income taxes | 261,119 | 85,650 |
| | 4,723,147 | 3,877,653 |
| Minority interests | 31,322 | 18,714 |
| Commitments and contingencies | | |
| Stockholders' equity | | |
| Common stock, $0.10 par value, authorized–360,000,000 shares, outstanding–112,322,143 and 115,952,394 shares (net of 28,977,890 and 22,030,805 shares held in treasury) | 11,232 | 11,595 |
| Capital surplus | 1,143,125 | 1,075,313 |
| Retained earnings | 248,098 | 224,251 |
| Accumulated other comprehensive loss | (1,449) | (1,036) |
| Deferred compensation related to restricted stock | (26,893) | (40,405) |
| | 1,374,113 | 1,269,718 |
| | $ 6,128,582 | $ 5,166,085 |

*Source:* Harrah's Entertainment, Inc. *2001 Annual Report*

There are eight riverboats:

- Harrah's Joliet (Illinois)
- Harrah's Vicksburg (Mississippi)
- Harrah's Tunica (Mississippi)
- Harrah's Shreveport (Louisiana)
- Harrah's North Kansas City (Missouri)
- Harrah's St. Louis-Riverport (Missouri)
- Showboat Mardi Gras (East Chicago)
- Harrah's Lake Charles (formerly Players) (Louisiana)

There are three Indian gaming properties:

- Harrah's Phoenix Ak-Chin Casino (Arizona)
- Harrah's Cherokee Smoky Mountains (North Carolina)
- Harrah's Prairie Band (Kansas)

These many locations allow Harrah's to attract many different people into the casinos. This diversification also means that Harrah's is not dependent on any one region for its customers, nor is it dependent on one area's economy. Half of the U.S. population lives within a three-hour drive of a Harrah's owned or managed property. This strength is important given the events of September 11, 2001. If customers are hesitant to fly to destinations, Harrah's may benefit from having many properties within driving distance.

Following the bankruptcy proceedings of National Airlines, Harrah's has partnered with America West airlines to offer package deals to customers for airfares. Harrah's has also joined the travel agents' Global Distribution System, which makes it easier for travel agents and customers using the Internet to book hotel reservations and access information about Harrah's hotels and casinos.

Harrah's is a master of promotion. From slot tournaments to Internet Web sites, and from art exhibits (Treasures of Russia at the Rio was replaced by the Titanic exhibit, which features artifacts recovered from the famed ship's resting place) to world-class

---

EXHIBIT 6    Organizational Chart

entertainers, Harrah's has a complete marketing program. Using the Total Rewards program, Harrah's has well over fifteen million customer names in its database. It uses these names and the corresponding demographic information to customize programs.

Harrah's has mastered targeted marketing. Not only does Harrah's talk to its customers, but the company also faithfully observes play patterns and conducts formal research. In fact, Harrah's surveys have formed the basis for research conducted by the Arthur Andersen Group for the American Gaming Association.

Harrah's Total Gold system, the predecessor of the Total Rewards player card, was introduced in 1997. The technology is patented, and it is the number one player card in Las Vegas and Atlantic City. In December 2000, *Information Week* and Cap Gemini Ernst & Young ranked the Total Rewards system number one among the top one hundred U.S. companies that use information technology to build customer relationships.

The customer database generated by the Total Rewards system allows Harrah's to focus on serving its market. Twenty-three percent of Harrah's Total Rewards play comes from multimarket play: from players who use their cards in more than one Harrah's casino. Harrah's can use the Total Rewards system to determine how much an Atlantic City customer plays in Las Vegas! Using this information, Harrah's placed a bank of the most popular slot machines from the Atlantic City property in the middle of Harrah's Las Vegas.

Total Rewards offers three tiers of membership: Total Gold, Total Platinum, and Total Diamond. The tiers helped generate an increase of $165 million in revenue from Platinum and Diamond level players in 2000. Also in 2000, the number of Platinum level players increased 124 percent over 1999, while the number of Diamond level players increased 118 percent.

Total Rewards allows customers to obtain discounts on shows, hotel rooms, food and beverages, as well as priority-customer status when making reservations, checking in, or making reservations for show seating.

## THE FUTURE

Harrah's focuses on four main strategies to grow its business:

1. More distribution
2. Quality products
3. Patented technology
4. Great service

Harrah's has focused on acquiring and building properties in key gaming markets. The addition of the Rio allows Harrah's to compete in the Las Vegas resort market, because the Rio is classified as a full-service resort (featuring a golf course, full-service spa and salon, meeting and convention facilities, a retail promenade, and a museum).

Although none of Harrah's properties are alike, they strive for consistency in the quality of the food, service, gaming, and accommodation experiences.

In 2001, Harrah's Entertainment won 216 awards in *Strictly Slots* magazine's annual "Best Of" customer ratings issue. The company was also the only gaming company to receive *Darwin* magazine's Darwin Fittest 50 award for its management of customer relationships.

Harrah's has received numerous patents for its Total Rewards system, which allows it to keep its customer database from its competitors. Harrah's uses the database to customize marketing plans and programs and to create brand loyalty to the Harrah's, Showboat, and Rio brand names. Since the launch of the Total Rewards program,

Harrah's has seen solid same-store sales growth and increases in cross-market play. Rio and Showboat had their own player cards, which have been merged into the Harrah's system, meaning that a Rio player may use his Play Rio card at Harrah's and Showboat, with the rewards system between the three casinos being standardized and equal.

Harrah's recognizes that it is competing in a service industry. The company has a three-tiered service strategy:

1. A regular Employee Opinion Poll that measures employee attitudes and expectations
2. Spotlight on Success—a type of mystery shopper program designed to reward excellent service and correct substandard service
3. The Target Player Satisfaction Survey, which surveys the experiences of target customers

## CONCLUSION

Harrah's Entertainment is focused, and it instills this focus in each employee: to become the undisputed leader in the casino entertainment industry. In the first quarter of 1998, Harrah's was the first casino to launch a national brand-image advertising campaign, with TV spots that aired during the Academy Awards. Harrah's has become one of the gaming industry's top competitors. While ranked third in revenues in 2000, the company is poised to grow its sales and increase its revenues and market share.

Harrah's faced numerous challenges in 2000, including the bankruptcy proceedings of the New Orleans casino property and National Airlines. The financial performance of the Rio property in Las Vegas also negatively affected revenues; however, Harrah's superior dedication to customer-oriented marketing and the top-notch management team's focus on healthy performance promise to help Harrah's overtake the competition.

Harrah's will likely face many financial challenges in the next five years due to the possible impending economic recession fueled by the events of September 11, 2001. Domestic consumers are reluctant to travel and to spend money on recreation, and international customers are more restricted in their travel to the United States. This potential recession may dramatically decrease Harrah's revenues.

## NOTES

1. "AGA Releases First Annual Survey of Casino Entertainment," press release from American Gaming Association (September 14, 1999). **www.americangaming.org**.
2. "2001 AGA Survey of Casino Entertainment." **www.americangaming.org**.
3. "2001 AGA Survey of Casino Entertainment." **www.americangaming.org**.
4. Lessani, Andrea, "How Much Do You Want to Bet That the Internet Gambling Prohibition Act of 1997 Is Not the Most Effective Way to Tackle the Problems of Online Gambling?" The UCLA Online Institute for Cyberspace Law and Policy (May 1998), p. 1. **http://www.gseis.ucla.edu/iclp/hp.html**.
5. "Economic Impacts of Casino Gaming in the United States," in the section entitled by "Overall Conclusions," prepared by Arthur Andersen Consulting Group for the American Gaming Association (December 1996). **www.americangaming.org**.
6. "Economic Impacts of Casino Gaming in the United States," in the section entitled "Macroeconomic Impacts of the Casino Gaming Industry," prepared by Arthur Andersen Consulting Group for the American Gaming Association (December 1996). **www.americangaming.org**.

# WACHOVIA CORPORATION—2002

**Fred R. David**
**Francis Marion University**

WB

www.wachovia.com

Wachovia Corporation, created through the September 1, 2001, merger of First Union and the former Wachovia, had assets of $330 billion and stockholders' equity of $28 billion at December 31, 2001. Wachovia is a leading provider of financial services to 20 million retail, brokerage, and corporate customers throughout the East Coast and the nation. Wachovia is the nation's fourth largest banking company based on assets and operates 2,800 full-service banking offices and 4,700 automated teller machines under the First Union and Wachovia names in 11 East Coast states and Washington, D.C. As the nation's fifth largest full-service retail broker dealer, based on client assets, the company offers full-service brokerage with offices in 49 states. Wachovia also provides global services through more than 30 international offices. Online banking and brokerage products and services are available through **wachovia.com** and **firstunion.com**.

## HISTORY OF FIRST UNION

Born as the brainchild of H. M. Victor in 1908, then named Union Bank, First Union has evolved from a hometown bank to the nation's sixth largest financial institution. Its growth has come largely from acquisitions, with the first one taking place in 1958 and many more since then. The company's corporate headquarters is conveniently located in Charlotte, North Carolina, which is also home to its fierce rival, Bank of America (formerly NationsBank), the fifth largest U.S. financial institution.

First Union is not just a bank. The easing of the Glass-Steagall Act facilitated strategic acquisitions, thus allowing First Union to involve itself in various overlapping industries, including but not limited to:

- Banking—commericial and retail.
- Asset management.
- Brokerage and security underwriting.
- Investment banking.
- Asset leasing.

By diversifying its operations, First Union has been able to reduce the overall risk to the company's shareholders. However, the growth and diversification has not come without tremendous costs. Due to poor planning, the 1998 Corestates merger was a near disaster. After the merger, First Union realized that many of the branches that had been added to its own branch network were in close proximity to the already existing First Union branches. So at great expense, many branches were closed, and many employees were laid off. A similar situation arose in 1998 with acquisition of the high-risk lender, The Money Store. First Union planned to eliminate a portion of the high-risk lending that had enabled The Money Store to carve a profitable niche for itself over the years. Following a great deal of effort to salvage the merger, First Union in 2000 announced that it would cease loan originations in that division. As the size of the acquisitions that First Union has undertaken has increased, its problems have also increased.

## OPERATIONAL OVERVIEW OF FIRST UNION

At the time of its merger with Wachovia, First Union was the sixth largest financial institution in the United States, and it has the third largest branch network, with 2,200 financial centers in eleven East Coast states and Washington, D.C. The company held the largest deposit share on the East Coast and was fifth nationally. First Union also had 375 full service brokerage offices nationwide, 160 home equity loan originators in 31 states, and 3,800 automated teller machines, the nation's sixth largest network.

In 2000, First Union announced the divestiture of its credit card and mortgage servicing portfolios. According to the company press release, the reason for the divestiture was absence of any potential to be a leading competitor in the marketplace. Considering that these divisions were both profitable, analysts especially questioned the divestiture of the credit card portfolio, since credit card usage is at an all-time high and is continuing to increase.

First Union was one of the most technologically advanced organizations in the financial industry. It was the first in its industry to design and implement a standardized data processing system across all of its holdings. As firms were acquired, they were converted to First Union's common system, named Emerald, which had enabled First Union to effectively introduce new product and service offerings. First Union had the third largest and fastest growing banking Internet channel, **www.firstunion.com**. In late 2000, the company had launched its Spanish Web site (**www.firstunion.com/spanish**) in an ongoing effort to meet the needs of this rapidly growing market segment. The Spanish Web site has been very successful.

In the third quarter of 2000, First Union became the first U.S.-based bank to join the Worldwide Automated Transaction Clearing House (WATCH). WATCH is a new electronic payment system that allows cross-border/multicurrency transactions. Prior to its introduction, these types of payments were very difficult to process due to unique local methods of handling these transactions. The company believed that joining WATCH allowed another value-added service to be offered to its existing customers with international dealings and possibly garner new business.

Wachovia was an excellent merger candidate. With its corporate headquarters located in Winston-Salem, North Carolina, and $74 billion in assets, Wachovia has a very prestigious and well-respected name. Wachovia would also make First Union the fourth largest U.S. financial institution. However, Wachovia and First Union already have significant overlap in their markets, so cannibalization could be an issue, as in the case of the Corestates merger. Merger with Wachovia further increased First Union's already dominant market share on the East Coast.

With 111 million American Internet users and a projected 45 percent annual growth rate through 2005, e-commerce is causing whole industries to redefine the businesses that they are in and also the way their businesses are conducted. The major shakedown in the dot-com market has already taken place, and many shell dot-coms are gone. But the fact remains that the Internet has transformed business and life as it is known today. First Union made a significant investment in the development of its online banking services very early on, and it has continued to keep up-to-date with technology as it changes. The result is a very user-friendly Internet-based financial medium that has been widely accepted by the company's customers and led it to develop into the third largest and fastest growing banking Internet Web site.

## EXHIBIT 1    Wachovia's Segment Financial Data

### A. GENERAL BANK

Selected Financial Data
*(Dollars in millions)*

| | 2001 | 2000 |
|---|---|---|
| Net interest income* | $5,151 | 4,382 |
| Fee and other income | 1,769 | 1,314 |
| Intersegment revenue | 114 | 100 |
| Total revenue* | 7,034 | 5,796 |
| Noninterest expense | 4,112 | 3,790 |
| Operating earnings | 1,616 | 1,179 |
| Economic profit | $1,165 | 762 |
| Risk adjusted return on capital | 38.44% | 33.01 |

Cash Overhead Efficieny Ratio *(Percent)*: 2000 64.4%, 2001 57.9%

Average Loans, Net *(In billions)*: 2000 $59.1, 2001 $75.8

Average Core Deposits *(In billions)*: 2000 $97.6, 2001 $111.1

*Tax equivalent.

The merger of First Union and the former Wachovia closed on September 1, 2001. Because this merger was accounted for as a purchase, prior periods have not been restated. Results in 2001 include four months of the former Wachovia.

### B. CAPITAL MANAGEMENT

Selected Financial Data
*(Dollars in millions)*

| | 2001 | 2000 |
|---|---|---|
| Net interest income* | $ 131 | 160 |
| Fee and other income | 2,819 | 2,820 |
| Intersegment revenue | (48) | (50) |
| Total revenue* | 2,902 | 2,930 |
| Noninterest expense | 2,399 | 2,342 |
| Operating earnings | 324 | 390 |
| Economic profit | $ 222 | 286 |
| Risk adjusted return on capital | 37.87% | 45.16 |

Total Assets Under Management *(In billions)*: 2000 $171, 2001 $226

Brokerage Client Assets *(In billions)*: 2000 $241, 2001 $274

Annuities Sales *(In billions)*: 2000 $3.5, 2001 $4.7

*Tax equivalent.

## INTERNAL OPERATIONS OF WACHOVIA

As indicated in Exhibit 1, Wachovia is divided into four major divisions: (1) General Bank, (2) Capital Management, (3) Wealth Management, and (4) Corporate and Investment Bank. Note that the Wealth Management division and the Corporate and Investment Bank division had lower revenues in 2001 than 2000.

As indicated in Exhibit 2, Wachovia is also divided into six geographic regions. Note that Wachovia has more branches in Florida than any other state.

Wachovia's 2001 Balance Sheet and Income statement are provided in Exhibits 3 and 4, respectively. Note in Exhibit 4 that Wachovia's net income increased to $1.61 billion in 2001 from $92 million in 2000.

## C. WEALTH MANAGEMENT

| Selected Financial Data (Dollars in millions) | 2001 | 2000 |
|---|---|---|
| Net interest income* | $246 | 190 |
| Fee and other income | 394 | 319 |
| Intersegment revenue | 1 | — |
| Total revenue* | 641 | 509 |
| Noninterest expense | 444 | 317 |
| Operating earnings | 127 | 126 |
| Economic profit | $ 94 | 102 |
| Risk adjusted return on capital | 52.27% | 75.54 |

*Tax equivalent.

**Assets Under Management** (In billions)

$53 (2000)  $78 (2001)

**Average Loans, Net** (In billions)

$4.2 (2000)  $5.7 (2001)

**Average Core Deposits** (In billions)

$5.7 (2000)  $7.3 (2001)

## D. CORPORATE AND INVESTMENT BANK

| Selected Financial Data (Dollars in millions) | 2001 | 2000 |
|---|---|---|
| Net interest income* | $2,075 | 1,674 |
| Fee and other income | 730 | 1,708 |
| Intersegment revenue | (56) | (49) |
| Total revenue* | 2,749 | 3,333 |
| Noninterest expense | 1,999 | 1,863 |
| Operating earnings | 265 | 829 |
| Economic profit | $ (320) | 277 |
| Risk adjusted return on capital | 7.07% | 16.73 |

*Tax equivalent.

**Capital Raised for Clients** (In billions)

$114 (2000)  $222 (2001)

**Equity Underwriting** Number of Transactions

32 (2000)  61 (2001)

**Investment Grade Debt** Number of Transactions

88 (2000)  128 (2001)

The merger of First Union and the former Wachovia closed on September 1, 2001. Because this merger was accounted for as a purchase, prior periods have not been restated. Results in 2001 include four months of the former Wachovia.

*Source:* Wachovia's 2001 *Annual Report*, pp. 8–9.

## CONCLUSION

The name "First Union" is being phased out slowly across the United States. Wachovia is closing hundreds of branches where the two banks are located close to one another. Wachovia is adopting the First Union computer operations systems but is keeping most of the Wachovia products.

Wachovia is changing rapidly daily. Develop a three-year strategic plan for the CEO of Wachovia, Mr. Kennedy Thompson.

EXHIBIT 2    Wachovia's Geographic Regions

## A. GENERAL BANKING REGIONS

**Atlantic Region**
New Jersey
Branches: 338
ATMs: 504

New York
Branches: 55
ATMs: 96

Connecticut
Branches: 86
ATMs: 121

**Mid-Atlantic Region**
Virginia
Branches: 354
ATMs: 537

Maryland
Branches: 77
ATMs: 111

Washington, D.C.
Branches: 27
ATMs: 59

**Carolinas Region**
North Carolina
Branches: 386
ATMs: 779

South Carolina
Branches: 171
ATMs: 331

**Georgia Region**
Georgia
Branches: 255
ATMs: 613

**PennDel Region**
Pennsylvania
Branches: 350
ATMs: 549

Delaware
Branches: 21
ATMs: 43

**Florida Region**
Florida
Branches: 691
ATMs: 919

## B. FOREIGN BRANCHES AND REPRESENTATIVE OFFICES

**International Branches**
Hong Kong, China
    (Restricted License Branch)
London, England
Tokyo, Japan
Seoul, South Korea
Taipei, Taiwan

**Representative Offices**
Buenos Aires, Argentina
Sydney, Australia
Sao Paulo, Brazil
Santiago, Chile
Beijing, China
Guangzhou, China

Hong Kong, China
Shanghai, China
Bogota, Colombia
Guayaquil, Ecuador
Cairo, Egypt
London, England
Paris, France
Frankfurt, Germany
Hamburg, Germany
Mumbai, India
Jakarta, Indonesia
Milan, Italy
Tokyo, Japan
Kuala Lumpur, Malaysia
Mexico City, Mexico

Panama City, Panama
Manila, Philippines
Singapore
Johannesburg, South
    Africa
Seoul, South Korea
Madrid, Spain
Taipei, Taiwan
Bangkok, Thailand
Istanbul, Turkey
Dubai, United Arab
    Emirates
San Diego, California

**Embassy and
    Government Banking
    Group**
Washington, D.C.

**International
    Processing Centers**
Charlotte, North Carolina
Los Angeles, California
Miami, Florida
New York, New York
Philadelphia, Pennsylvania

*Source:* Wachovia's 2001 *Annual Report*, p. 15.

EXHIBIT 3    Wachovia Corporation and Subsidiaries Consolidated Balance Sheets

| | December 31, | |
|---|---|---|
| *(in millions, except per-share data)* | *2001* | *2000* |
| **ASSETS** | | |
| Cash and due from banks | $ 13,919 | 9,906 |
| Interest-bearing bank balances | 6,875 | 3,239 |
| Federal funds sold and securities purchased under resale agreements | | |
|   (carrying amount of collateral held $7,207 at December 31, 2001, $2,287 repledged) | 13,919 | 11,240 |
|     Total cash and cash equivalents | 34,711 | 24,385 |
| Trading account assets | 25,386 | 21,630 |
| Securities (amortized cost $57,776 in 2001; $47,930 in 2000) | 58,467 | 47,603 |
| Investment securities (market value $1,728 in 2000) | – | 1,643 |
| Loans, net of unearned income ($9,694 in 2001; $6,482 in 2000) | 163,801 | 123,760 |
|   Allowance for loan losses | (2,995) | (1,722) |
|     Loans, net | 160,806 | 122,038 |
| Premises and equipment | 5,719 | 5,024 |
| Due from customers on acceptances | 745 | 874 |
| Goodwill and other intangible assets | 12,772 | 3,664 |
| Other assets | 31,846 | 27,309 |
|     Total assets | $330,452 | 254,170 |
| **LIABILITIES AND STOCKHOLDERS' EQUITY** | | |
| Deposits | | |
|   Noninterest-bearing deposits | 43,464 | 30,315 |
| Interest-bearing deposits | 143,989 | 112,353 |
|     Total deposits | 187,453 | 142,668 |
| Short-term borrowings | 44,385 | 39,446 |
| Bank acceptances outstanding | 762 | 880 |
| Trading account liabilities | 11,437 | 7,475 |
| Other liabilities | 16,227 | 12,545 |
| Long-term debt | 41,733 | 35,809 |
|     Total liabilities | 301,997 | 238,823 |
| **STOCKHOLDERS' EQUITY** | | |
| Preferred stock, Class A, 40 million shares, no par value; 10 million shares, | | |
|   no par value; none issued | — | — |
| Dividend Equalization Preferred shares, no par value, 96 million shares issued | | |
|   and outstanding in 2001 | 17 | — |
| Common stock, $3.33-1/3 par value; authorized 3 billion shares, outstanding | | |
|   1.362 billion shares in 2001; 980 million shares in 2000 | 4,539 | 3,267 |
| Paid-in capital | 17,911 | 6,272 |
| Retained earnings | 5,551 | 6,021 |
| Accumulated other comprehensive income, net | 437 | (213) |
|     Total stockholders' equity | 28,455 | 15,347 |
|     Total liabilities and stockholders' equity | $330,452 | 254,170 |

*Source:* Wachovia's 2001 *Annual Report*, p. 65.

# EXHIBIT 4  Wachovia Corporation and Subsidiaries Consolidated Statements of Income

| | Years Ended December 31, | | |
|---|---|---|---|
| (in millions, except per-share data) | 2001 | 2000 | 1999 |
| **INTEREST INCOME** | | | |
| Interest and fees on loans | $10,537 | 11,246 | 10,629 |
| Interest and dividends on securities | 3,534 | 3,903 | 3,098 |
| Trading account interest | 760 | 820 | 600 |
| Other interest income | 1,269 | 1,565 | 824 |
| Total interest income | 16,100 | 17,534 | 15,151 |
| **INTEREST EXPENSE** | | | |
| Interest on deposits | 4,744 | 5,269 | 4,054 |
| Interest on short-term borrowings | 1,736 | 2,536 | 2,019 |
| Interest on long-term debt | 1,845 | 2,292 | 1,626 |
| Total interest expense | 8,325 | 10,097 | 7,699 |
| Net interest income | 7,775 | 7,437 | 7,452 |
| Provision for loan losses | 1,947 | 1,736 | 692 |
| Net interest income after provision for loan losses | 5,828 | 5,701 | 6,760 |
| **FEE AND OTHER INCOME** | | | |
| Service charges and fees | 2,167 | 1,920 | 1,987 |
| Commissions | 1,568 | 1,591 | 1,014 |
| Fiduciary and asset management fees | 1,643 | 1,511 | 1,238 |
| Advisory, underwriting and other investment banking fees | 836 | 718 | 702 |
| Principal investing | (707) | 395 | 592 |
| Other income | 789 | 577 | 1,400 |
| Total fee and other income | 6,296 | 6,712 | 6,933 |
| **NONINTEREST EXPENSE** | | | |
| Salaries and employee benefits | 5,810 | 5,659 | 4,716 |
| Occupancy | 730 | 622 | 546 |
| Equipment | 879 | 870 | 793 |
| Advertising | 66 | 114 | 234 |
| Communications and supplies | 480 | 503 | 481 |
| Professional and consulting fees | 359 | 348 | 287 |
| Goodwill and other intangible amortization | 523 | 361 | 391 |
| Merger-related and restructuring charges | 106 | 2,190 | 404 |
| Sundry expense | 878 | 1,043 | 1,010 |
| Total noninterest expense | 9,831 | 11,710 | 8,862 |
| Income before income taxes and cumulative effect of a change in accounting principle | 2,293 | 703 | 4,831 |
| Income taxes | 674 | 565 | 1,608 |
| Income before cumulative effect of a change in accounting principle | 1,619 | 138 | 3,223 |
| Cumulative effect of a change in the accounting for beneficial interests, net of income taxes | — | (46) | — |
| Net income | 1,619 | 92 | 3,223 |
| Dividends on preferred stock | 6 | — | — |
| Net income available to common stockholders | $ 1,613 | 92 | 3,223 |
| **PER COMMON SHARE DATA** | | | |
| Basic | | | |
| Income before change in accounting principle | $1.47 | 0.12 | 3.35 |
| Net income | 1.47 | 0.07 | 3.35 |
| Diluted | | | |
| Income before change in accounting principle | 1.45 | 0.12 | 3.33 |
| Net income | 1.45 | 0.07 | 3.33 |
| Cash dividends | $ 0.96 | 1.92 | 1.88 |
| **AVERAGE SHARES** | | | |
| Basic | 1,096 | 971 | 959 |
| Diluted | 1,105 | 974 | 967 |

Source: Wachovia's 2001 Annual Report, p. 66.

# FIRST STATE BANK OF ROANS PRAIRIE—2002

**Paul Reed, Jason Gooch, and Gerald Kohers**
**Sam Houston State University**

## INTERNAL OPERATIONS

### Mission Statement

The current mission statement for First State Bank of Roans Prairie, Texas, is:

> *It is the goal of management and the Board of Directors of First State Bank of Roans Prairie to prosper while adhering to the "small town" ideals which have made it successful; the banker–customer relationship must be preserved. The bank desires to serve area residents by supplying all traditional banking services. New services with profit potential will be developed and offered as the area and economy evolves.*

### Operations

First State Bank of Roans Prairie (936-395-2141) is and has been since its establishment in 1903 owned and controlled by the Matthys family. Its only office is located in Roans Prairie, Texas (population less than 500). Under the leadership of the Matthys family, First State Bank of Roans Prairie pursues operational efficiencies by controlling overhead and employing technology in place of hiring additional employees. The bank currently employs ten people. This equates to one employee per $4.2 million in assets, and it compares to competitors' ratio of one employee per $2.7 million in assets (average of local competitors). This, however, is partly due to the low loan-to-deposit ratio of First State Bank.

### Products

First State Bank offers most of the basic banking services, such as:

- checking, savings, money markets, CDs.
- IRAs.
- auto, real estate, commercial, agriculture, and consumer loans (most customer requests are answered the same day for loans, etc.).

The bank does not offer ATM cards, credit or debit cards, trust department services, or Internet banking. It is lagging behind the industry in offering new products (ATMs have existed in some form for nearly twenty years). This may cause a loss of customers or missed opportunities for new customers in the future. However, the bank does have an advantage over the larger metropolitan banks and mortgage companies insofar as it is able to serve the rural real estate market and agricultural lines. This may be of particular importance as more and more people look to move from the urban areas into the rural areas. Additionally, there has been an increase of "weekenders" purchasing rural land for recreational purposes. These loans do not generally fit the molds of the metropolitan banks or the mortgage companies.

## Marketing

First State Bank has traditionally spent very little on advertising. Likewise, it has not solicited business in the past. Rather, it has relied on its reputation for providing superior service, low cost services, and its ability to react quickly to the needs of its customers.

This has worked well for the bank in the past. This is not to imply that the bank has not been actively involved in and supportive of the community. Furthermore, First State Bank has been successful in building and maintaining customer relationships.

## Finance

First State Bank's financial statements and performance ratios for 1998 to 2000 are provided in Exhibit 1. These statements reveal increases in total assets, loans, and deposits. Additionally, a comparison of First State Bank's two primary competitors is included in the comparison report in Exhibits 2 and 3. Notice that both competitors have higher net interest margins and noninterest income. This is primarily due to First State Bank's lower loan-to-deposit ratio. Additionally, large amounts of capital and undivided profits have contributed to First State Bank's low ROE (9 percent vs. 10.6 percent for peer banks with less than $100 million in assets).

## Management Style and Culture

First State Bank has created a strong culture based on customer loyalty. The employees are all very close and share a sense of companionship. This clearly is a major strength of the bank. However, it is something that has been very natural for the group and has been accomplished without coaching or training. The average length of employment for the ten employees is 9.7 years (the ranges run from five years to twenty years).

Although communication is not the greatest virtue among management people and the front lines, it does remain open. If a problem is severe enough, any employee feels that he or she can approach management to discuss such issues. Nonetheless, there is room for improvement for top-down and bottom-up communication.

The board of directors tends to resist making any changes to the organization. This explains why it has not offered some of the newer financial services. Furthermore, continuing to operate without a formal strategic plan may prevent management from having a clear vision of where the organization is and where it needs to position itself for the future.

## EXTERNAL ENVIRONMENT

### Industry Health

Fiscal year 2000 proved to be a record setting year for insured commercial banks. Commercial bank profits for the year were a record $71.7 billion. Full-year earnings were $9.9 billion (16.0 percent) higher than in 1999. The industry's return on assets (ROA) for 2000 was 1.31 percent, easily eclipsing the previous record of 1.23 percent set in 1998. Banks' return on equity (ROE) matched the all-time high of 15.34 percent reached in 1993. Large banks (assets greater than $100 million) experienced much of the improvement in profitability because noninterest income registered strong growth and noninterest expense growth was limited. Only 44.9 percent of banks reported higher ROAs in 2000 than in 1999. The average ROA at banks with less than $100 million in assets declined from 1.13 percent in 1999 to 1.01 percent in 2000. The decline would have been greater but for the rising proportion of banks operating as Subchapter S corporations. For the first time since 1991, more than 10 percent of commercial banks with

EXHIBIT 1    First State Bank of Roans Prairie Balance Sheet (dollar figures in thousands)

|  | December 31, 2000 | December 31, 1999 | December 31, 1998 |
|---|---|---|---|
| **ASSETS AND LIABILITIES** | | | |
| Total employees (full-time equivalent) | 10 | 10 | 10 |
| **Total assets** | $42,105 | $40,131 | $39,029 |
| Cash and due from depository institutions | 4,861 | 5,344 | 3,555 |
| Interest-bearing | 3,102 | 3,693 | 3,198 |
| *Securities* | 18,843 | 17,125 | 18,784 |
| Federal funds sold & reverse repurchase agreements | 700 | 2,300 | 3,450 |
| *Net loans & leases* | 16,694 | 14,539 | 12,480 |
| Loan loss allowance | 179 | 175 | 180 |
| Trading account assets | 0 | 0 | 0 |
| Bank premises and fixed assets | 381 | 398 | 345 |
| *Other real estate owned* | 0 | 14 | 9 |
| Goodwill and other intangibles | 0 | 0 | 0 |
| Mortgage servicing assets | 0 | 0 | 0 |
| All other assets | 626 | 411 | 406 |
| Total liabilities and capital | 42,105 | 40,131 | 39,029 |
| **Total liabilities** | 36,627 | 34,655 | 33,173 |
| *Total deposits* | 36,291 | 34,220 | 32,465 |
| Interest-bearing deposits | 31,894 | 29,944 | 28,629 |
| Deposits held in domestic offices | 36,291 | 34,220 | 32,465 |
| Percentage insured (estimated) | 95.78% | 95.99% | 96.79% |
| Federal funds purchased & repurchase agreements | 0 | 0 | 0 |
| Demand notes issued to U.S. Treasury | 0 | 0 | 0 |
| Trading liabilities | 0 | 0 | 0 |
| Other borrowed funds | 0 | 0 | 0 |
| Subordinated debt | 0 | 0 | 0 |
| All other liabilities | 336 | 435 | 708 |
| **Equity capital** | 5,478 | 5,476 | 5,856 |
| Perpetual preferred stock | 0 | 0 | 0 |
| Common stock | 321 | 321 | 500 |
| Surplus | 1,179 | 679 | 500 |
| Undivided profits | 3,978 | 4,476 | 4,856 |
| **MEMORANDA** | | | |
| Noncurrent loans and leases | 16 | 19 | 47 |
| Earning assets | 39,339 | 37,657 | 37,912 |
| Long-term assets (5+ years) | 11,358 | 5,849 | 7,069 |
| Average assets, year-to-date | 41,192 | 39,508 | 37,528 |
| Average assets, quarterly | 42,234 | 39,805 | 38,730 |
| Volatile liabilities | 9,814 | 9,836 | 9,215 |
| Insider loans | 125 | 123 | 137 |
| FHLB advances (TFR filers only) | N/A | N/A | N/A |
| Unused loan commitments | 736 | 575 | 770 |
| Restructured loans and leases | 0 | 0 | 0 |
| Quarterly mutual fund sales | 0 | 0 | 0 |
| Off-balance-sheet derivatives | 0 | 0 | 0 |

*(continued)*

EXHIBIT 1    First State Bank of Roans Prairie Balance Sheet (dollar figures in thousands) (continued)

|  | (Year-to-date) | (Year-to-date) | (Year-to-date) |
|---|---|---|---|
| **INCOME AND EXPENSE** | | | |
| *Total interest income* | *2,851* | *2,808* | *2,680* |
| *Total interest expense* | *1,502* | *1,473* | *1,372* |
| Net interest income | 1,349 | 1,335 | 1,308 |
| Provision for credit losses | 31 | 61 | 22 |
| Total noninterest income | 218 | 191 | 185 |
| Service charges on deposit accounts | 196 | 176 | 162 |
| Total noninterest expense | 834 | 805 | 723 |
| Salaries and employee benefits | 471 | 432 | 406 |
| Premises and equipment expense | 121 | 118 | 71 |
| All other noninterest expense | 242 | 255 | 246 |
| Pretax net operating income | 702 | 660 | 748 |
| Securities gains (losses) | −1 | 12 | −8 |
| Applicable income taxes | 204 | 188 | 217 |
| Extraordinary gains—net | 0 | 0 | 0 |
| **Net income** | **497** | **484** | **523** |
| Net charge-offs | 26 | 67 | 51 |
| Cash dividends | 16 | 16 | 25 |
| Net operating income | 498 | 475 | 529 |

|  | (Year-to-date) | (Year-to-date) | (Year-to-date) |
|---|---|---|---|
| **MEMORANDA** | | | |
| Average assets | 41,192 | 39,508 | 37,528 |
| Percentage of unprofitable institutions | N/A | N/A | N/A |
| Percentage of institutions with earnings gains | N/A | N/A | N/A |

|  | (Year-to-date) | (Year-to-date) | (Year-to-date) |
|---|---|---|---|
| **PERFORMANCE RATIOS** (%) | | | |
| Yield on earning assets | 7.36% | 7.45% | 7.47% |
| Cost of funding earning assets | 3.88% | 3.91% | 3.82% |
| Net interest margin | 3.48% | 3.54% | 3.64% |
| Noninterest income to earning assets | 0.56% | 0.51% | 0.52% |
| Noninterest expense to earning assets | 2.15% | 2.14% | 2.01% |
| Net operating income to assets | 1.21% | 1.20% | 1.41% |
| **Return on assets** | **1.21%** | **1.23%** | **1.39%** |
| Return on equity | 9.05% | 8.37% | 9.45% |
| Retained earnings to average equity (YTD only) | 8.76% | 8.09% | 8.99% |
| *Net charge-offs to loans* | *0.17%* | *0.50%* | *0.42%* |
| Credit loss provision to net charge-offs | 114.81% | 91.04% | 43.14% |
| Earnings coverage of net loan charge-offs | 28.19 | 10.76 | 15.09 |
| Efficiency ratio | 53.22% | 52.75% | 48.43% |
| Assets per employee (in millions) | 4.21 | 4.01 | 3.90 |
| Market to book value of securities held to maturity | N/A | N/A | N/A |
| Cash dividends to net income (ytd only) | 3.21% | 3.30% | 4.78% |

*(continued)*

EXHIBIT 1    First State Bank of Roans Prairie Balance Sheet (dollar figures in thousands)
(continued)

|  | (Year-to-date) | (Year-to-date) | (Year-to-date) |
|---|---|---|---|
| **CONDITION RATIOS (%)** | | | |
| Loss allowance to loans | 1.06% | 1.19% | 1.42% |
| Loss allowance to noncurrent loans | 1,118.75% | 921.05% | 382.98% |
| Noncurrent assets plus other real estate owned to assets | 0.04% | 0.08% | 0.14% |
| *Noncurrent loans to loans* | *0.09%* | *0.13%* | *0.37%* |
| Net loans and leases to deposits | 46.00% | 42.49% | 38.44% |
| Net loans and leases to core deposits | 63.05% | 59.62% | 53.67% |
| Net noncore funding to long-term assets | 40.20% | 38.47% | 42.64% |
| Equity capital to assets | 13.01% | 13.65% | 15.00% |
| Core capital (leverage) ratio | 13.77% | 13.50% | 15.40% |
| Tier 1 risk-based capital ratio | 28.12% | 28.58% | 34.70% |
| Total risk-based capital ratio | 28.98% | 29.51% | 35.78% |

less than $100 million in assets were unprofitable. Small banks were hurt by both declining net interest margins and lower contributions from noninterest income in 2000. However, the improvement in industry earnings was made possible by strong growth in noninterest income and by lower noninterest expenses, which outweighed a $1.3-billion decline in proceeds from securities sales.

## Legislation

The United States recently signed into law S. 900, the Gramm-Leach-Bliley Act, the historic and wide-reaching legislation that modernizes the laws governing the financial services industry. By updating old laws that created barriers among financial service providers, the financial modernization bill allows banks, securities firms, and insurance companies to enter each other's businesses. Consumers want loans at the best rates, investment services with the most choices, and money management services from efficient providers. Consumers can take advantage of one-stop shopping for products and enjoy more flexibility and options.

Additionally, by allowing banks to offer insurance services, consumers will enjoy lower costs, convenient service, and increased availability. Insurers that use independent agents for auto insurance spend 30 percent of each premium dollar on commissions, advertising, and other costs. Those that use other methods of distribution, such as selling directly to consumers, reduce those costs up to 10 percent. Also, a majority of low-to-moderate income households are either underserved or without life insurance. Banks can reach a broader market and reduce costs through branch networks and existing household relationships. The Department of Treasury estimates U.S. firms will save $15 billion per year in gained efficiencies.

The Internet is growing and gaining acceptance at astounding rates. It has taken the Internet only four years to reach an audience of fifty million. Radio and television took thirty years and thirteen years, respectively, to accomplish the same feat.

Forward-thinking bankers recognize that the Internet provides the means of driving fundamental changes in consumer perceptions of banking. A simple example was the added convenience brought to consumers by Internet banking. For community bankers that had long relied on personal service as the basis for competitive advantage, the Internet is a natural extension of their existing business strategy.

EXHIBIT 2    Comparison Report (dollar figures in thousands)

| | First State Bank Roans Prairie, TX | Anderson State Bank Anderson, TX | The National Bank of Anderson Anderson, TX |
|---|---|---|---|
| | *December 31, 2000* | *December 31, 2000* | *December 31, 2000* |
| **ASSETS AND LIABILITIES** | | | |
| Total employees (full-time equivalent) | 10 | 40 | 23 |
| **Total assets** | **$42,105** | **$133,864** | **$43,071** |
| Cash and due from depository institutions | 4,861 | 4,146 | 1,866 |
| Interest-bearing | 3,102 | 0 | 0 |
| *Securities* | *18,843* | *10,723* | *9,437* |
| Federal funds sold & reverse repurchase agreements | 700 | 9,150 | 2,025 |
| *Net loans & leases* | *16,694* | *103,799* | *27,560* |
| Loan loss allowance | 179 | 1,939 | 532 |
| Trading account assets | 0 | 0 | 0 |
| Bank premises and fixed assets | 381 | 852 | 865 |
| *Other real estate owned* | *0* | *2,055* | *99* |
| Goodwill and other intangibles | 0 | 0 | 0 |
| Mortgage servicing assets | 0 | 0 | 0 |
| All other assets | 626 | 3,139 | 1,219 |
| Total liabilities and capital | 42,105 | 133,864 | 43,071 |
| **Total liabilities** | **36,627** | **122,813** | **39,443** |
| *Total deposits* | *36,291* | *121,513* | *39,159* |
| Interest-bearing deposits | 31,894 | 111,977 | 31,170 |
| Deposits held in domestic offices | 36,291 | 121,513 | 39,159 |
| % insured (estimated) | 95.78% | 92.07% | 95.88% |
| Federal funds purchased & repurchase agreements | 0 | 0 | 0 |
| Demand notes issued to U.S. Treasury | 0 | 0 | 0 |
| Trading liabilities | 0 | 0 | 0 |
| Other borrowed funds | 0 | 0 | 0 |
| Subordinated debt | 0 | 0 | 0 |
| All other liabilities | 336 | 1,300 | 284 |
| **Equity capital** | **5,478** | **11,051** | **3,628** |
| Perpetual preferred stock | 0 | 0 | 300 |
| Common stock | 321 | 950 | 1,000 |
| Surplus | 1,179 | 9,050 | 1,008 |
| Undivided profits | 3,978 | 1,051 | 1,320 |
| **MEMORANDA** | | | |
| Noncurrent loans and leases | 16 | 50 | 883 |
| Earning assets | 39,339 | 123,672 | 39,022 |
| Long-term assets (5+ years) | 11,358 | 25,830 | 1,227 |
| Average assets, year-to-date | 41,192 | 127,443 | 44,601 |
| Average assets, quarterly | 42,234 | 130,632 | 43,878 |
| Volatile liabilities | 9,814 | 28,882 | 6,980 |
| Insider loans | 125 | 115 | 158 |
| FHLB advances (TFR filers only) | N/A | N/A | N/A |
| Unused loan commitments | 736 | 13,479 | 1,259 |
| Restructured loans and leases | 0 | 0 | 14 |
| Quarterly mutual fund sales | 0 | 0 | 0 |
| Off-balance-sheet derivatives | 0 | 0 | 0 |

EXHIBIT 3    Comparison Report

| | First State Bank Roans Prairie, TX | The National Anderson State Bank Anderson, TX | Bank of Anderson Anderson, TX |
|---|---|---|---|
| | *December 31, 2000* | *December 31, 2000* | *December 31, 2000* |
| Percentage of unprofitable institutions | N/A | N/A | N/A |
| Percentage of institutions with earnings gains | N/A | N/A | N/A |
| | *(Year-to-date)* | *(Year-to-date)* | *(Year-to-date)* |
| **PERFORMANCE RATIOS (%)** | | | |
| Yield on earning assets | 7.36% | 9.58% | 8.61% |
| Cost of funding earning assets | 3.88% | 4.17% | 3.64% |
| Net interest margin | 3.48% | 5.42% | 4.97% |
| Noninterest income to earning assets | 0.56% | 0.78% | 1.58% |
| Noninterest expense to earning assets | 2.15% | 2.76% | 4.66% |
| Net operating income to assets | 1.21% | 2.02% | 0.67% |
| **Return on assets** | **1.21%** | **2.02%** | **0.68%** |
| Return on equity | 9.05% | 22.15% | 8.59% |
| Retained earnings to average equity (YTD only) | 8.76% | −3.72% | 8.59% |
| *Net charge-offs to loans* | *0.17%* | *0.02%* | *1.79%* |
| Credit loss provision to net charge-offs | 114.81% | 0.00% | 60.73% |
| Earnings coverage of net loan charge-offs | 28.19 | 163.32 | 1.53 |
| Efficiency ratio | 53.22% | 44.51% | 71.26% |
| Assets per employee (in millions) | 4.21 | 3.35 | 1.87 |
| Market to book value of securities held to maturity | N/A | 98.70% | N/A |
| Cash dividends to net income (YTD only) | 3.21% | 116.77% | 0.00% |
| | *(Year-to-date)* | *(Year-to-date)* | *(Year-to-date)* |
| **CONDITION RATIOS (%)** | | | |
| Loss allowance to loans | 1.06% | 1.83% | 1.89% |
| Loss allowance to noncurrent loans | 1,118.75% | 3,878.00% | 60.25% |
| Noncurrent assets plus other real estate owned to assets | 0.04% | 1.57% | 2.28% |
| *Noncurrent loans* | *0.09%* | *0.05%* | *3.14%* |
| Net loans and leases to deposits | 46.00% | 85.42% | 70.38% |
| Net loans and leases to core deposits | 63.05% | 112.05% | 85.64% |
| Net noncore funding to long-term assets | 40.20% | 21.61% | 19.90% |
| Equity capital to assets | 13.01% | 8.26% | 8.42% |
| Core capital (leverage) ratio | 13.77% | 8.31% | 8.44% |
| Tier 1 risk-based capital ratio | 28.12% | 9.41% | 12.73% |

## Multigenerational Customer Base

Today, banks are faced with both the difficult task and an enormous opportunity of serving five generational cohorts. Demographics define generational cohorts by birth ranges of twenty years. They are as follows:

- Silent generation (1925–1944): 52 million
- Baby boomers (1945–1964): 76 million

- Generation X (1965–1984): 51 million
- Nexters (1985–2004): estimated 82 million

The silent generation controls a significant part of the country's discretionary spending, and its members own billions in real estate. It is estimated that they own three-quarters of the financial assets in the United States, or $10–$12 trillion in net worth, and have personal incomes of $800 billion. Civic pride, loyalty, and respect for their country characterize this generation.

The baby boom generation marked the end of the rural, agrarian lifestyle. Its members are characterized by being highly confident, team-oriented, and egocentric. They are less loyal than the silent generation. This generation is moving into its peak earning and spending years.

Clever, resourceful, technologically savvy, comfortable with change, and a general lack of loyalty—all these qualities define Generation X. This generation represents the smallest of the five generations.

The Nexters are characterized by confidence, motivation, achievement, and optimism. Its members are the authority on technology. They are estimated to be the largest generation ever.

## COMPETITION

First State Bank of Roans Prairie is located in the center of Grimes County and is only thirteen miles from Anderson. Anderson currently has three banks: (1) Anderson State Bank, (2) The National Bank of Anderson, and (3) Norwest/Wells Fargo.

### Anderson State Bank

Anderson State Bank is the strongest of the three competitors. Its performance ratios indicate that it manages to control overhead while maintaining and investing in quality assets. It is are owned and managed by a bank holding company from Chicago. Management of the holding company sets the rates on loans and deposits. A substantial portion of the loan portfolio consists of participation loans in apartment complexes. These participation loans are generally for apartment complexes in Dallas, San Antonio, or Houston. Due to the large number of participation loans, Anderson State Bank has fewer assets invested in securities and a substantially higher percent loaned out. This allows the bank to pay higher rates on its deposits since it is reinvesting the money in loans that have higher returns than securities. Anderson State has traditionally led the local competition in pricing rates on deposits.

First State Bank, on the other hand, has fewer assets invested in loans and is more heavily weighted in the securities market. Thus, paying higher rates to retain deposits has reduced its net interest margin in recent years.

### The National Bank of Anderson

The National Bank of Anderson also has a higher loan-to-deposit ratio than First State Bank of Roans Prairie (70 percent vs. 46 percent). However, National Bank's loans are mostly local loans. The higher loan portfolio also gives the bank a higher net interest margin than First State Bank. It appears, however, that the loan portfolio has grown at the expense of asset quality. This is indicated in the high delinquency and net charge-off to loans. This has drawn scrutiny from the board and examiners. Therefore, the bank has started turning some good business away in order to maintain liquidity (usually larger lines of credit).

Additionally, National Bank employs one employee for each $1.87 million in assets. This is a much higher ratio than First State Bank's, which is one employee per $4.2 million in assets. Likewise, National Bank's noninterest expense to earning assets is significantly higher than that of First State Bank and Anderson State Bank.

### Norwest/Wells Fargo

There is no need to analyze or question the financial status of Wells Fargo. Nevertheless, the mold, which it has created for its metropolitan banks, does not work in the rural communities. For instance, one must drive fifty miles from Anderson to Bryan if he or she wants to apply for a home mortgage or real estate loan. Also, the fee schedules are much higher than those of the other local competitors. Rural customers are used to convenient, courteous, low-cost service. Wells Fargo lacks the flexibility needed to remain in Anderson. A lot of customers have migrated from Wells Fargo to the other local banks.

### THE FUTURE

First State Bank of Roans Prairie wants to continue to pursue operational efficiencies through the use of technology. Management feels that by controlling overhead, it can maintain profitability in good times as well as bad. In additional, management feels that it must grow the loan portfolio in order to increase profitability. Pursuing the local rural real estate market can do this. Furthermore, management feels that it must maintain the banker–customer relationship on which it has built its reputation.

# THE AUDUBON NATURE INSTITUTE—2001

Caroline M. Fisher
Loyola University, New Orleans

www.auduboninstitute.org

The tourism industry of New Orleans was devastated by the terrorist attacks of September 11, 2001. Travel to the city declined dramatically. Conferences were canceled. Hotels that usually were booked solid had such low occupancy rates that they had to lay off workers. Restaurants that depended on the tourist trade equally felt the effects of the decline. All tourism activities dwindled to a trickle.

The Audubon Nature Institute also experienced declines in usage rates—but differentially by location. The Aquarium of the Americas and the IMAX Theatre, both located in downtown New Orleans, saw dramatic declines in admissions. Admissions to the Audubon Zoo were not down as dramatically, and the Nature Center actually saw an increase in usage.

The pattern of the declines in admissions dramatized what the Audubon Nature Institute already knew—that the downtown locations are frequented by tourists to a much greater extent than the more distant zoo and nature center. But what was usually seen as a weakness—dependency on local residents for admissions—was now a strength that helped to counteract the decline in tourism. Audubon's management needed to respond to the changes in admission patterns to keep from losing money during the last part of 2001 and to keep from having to slow down development of the Audubon Insectarium and other new ventures.

## HISTORY

Formed in 1988, the Audubon Nature Institute is a nonprofit "family of museums and parks dedicated to nature and unified with a purpose of celebrating life through nature." Its purpose of "celebrating the wonders of nature" guides its mission to:

1. provide a guest experience of outstanding quality.
2. exhibit the diversity of wildlife.
3. preserve native Louisiana habitats.
4. educate our diverse audience about the natural world.
5. enhance the care and survival of wildlife through research and conservation.
6. provide opportunities for recreation in natural settings.
7. operate a financially self-sufficient collection of facilities.
8. weave quality entertainment through guest experiences.

Ron Forman, Director of the Audubon Nature Institute, describes the essence of the Institute's purpose to be to "teach children, especially inner-city children, to love nature and to value living things." Another goal of the Institute is to contribute to the economic development of the New Orleans area by encouraging tourism, especially family tourism, and by creating jobs.

159

In 2001, the Audubon Nature Institute was in charge of (1) Audubon Zoological Garden, (2) Audubon Aquarium of the Americas, (3) Freeport-McMoRan Audubon Species Survival Center, (4) Audubon Louisiana Nature Center, (5) Entergy IMAX® Theatre, (6) Audubon Center for Research of Endangered Species, (7) Audubon Park, (8) Audubon Wilderness Park, and (9) Woldenberg Riverfront Park. It plans to open the Audubon Insectarium in 2003.

## AUDUBON ZOOLOGICAL GARDEN

The Audubon Zoo was the focus of national concern in the early 1970s, because of the well-documented stories of animals kept in conditions that were termed an "animal ghetto," "the New Orleans antiquarium," and even "an animal concentration camp."

In 1971, the Bureau of Governmental Research recommended to the Audubon Park Commission and the City Council of New Orleans a $5.6 million zoo improvement plan. The Audubon Park Commission proposed a bond issue and a property tax that was earmarked for the zoo. Voters overwhelmingly approved it, and the New Orleans City Planning Commission finally approved the master plan for the Audubon Park Zoo in 1973.

The expansion of the Audubon Park Zoo took it from fourteen to fifty-eight acres. The zoo was laid out in geographic sections according to the zoo master plan developed by the Bureau of Governmental Research, and it included: the Asian Domain, the World of Primates, the World's Grasslands, Savannah, North American Prairie, South American Pampas, and Louisiana Swamp, Additional exhibits included the Wisner Discovery Zoo, the sea lion exhibit, and Flight Cage.

The main purpose of the Audubon Park Zoo is entertainment. Many of the promotional efforts of the zoo are aimed at creating an image of the zoo as an entertaining place to go. Obviously, such a campaign is necessary to attract visitors to the zoo. Behind the scenes, the zoo also preserves and breeds many animal species, conducts research, and educates the public.

The 2000 *Annual Report* states that

*Ensuring the survival of endangered species becomes possible only when people learn about these animals and embrace efforts to save them. That's our goal every time visitors walk into our facilities. The more they come, the more they learn— and the more they want to help.*

## AUDUBON AQUARIUM OF THE AMERICAS

The Aquarium of the Americas opened in September 1990. The $40 million project, consisting of the fourteen acre Woldenberg Park and the aquarium itself, provided a logical pedestrian link between the major attractions of the Riverwalk and the Jax Brewery, two shopping centers in the French Quarter. The facility was one hundred ten thousand square feet in size and included five permanent exhibits: the Caribbean Reef, the Amazon Rainforest, the Mississippi River, the Gulf of Mexico, and Living in Water. Management of the aquarium was placed under the Audubon Nature Institute, the same organization that ran the Audubon Zoo.

Construction of Phase II of the aquarium, a $25 million project, began in 1995. It included a ten-thousand-square-foot Changing Exhibit Gallery that encompassed new tanks with 360 degree viewing, new species, and a variety of hands-on activities. The finalized aquarium was described by the *Times-Picayune,* the local newspaper, as "one of the best architecture achievements in the metro area in the past 100 years."

Besides exhibits, the aquarium has added educational shows, a summer program for students in grades seven to ten called Aquakids, and Discovery Cove, where children can see and touch aquatic species. The aquarium is also the headquarters for the Louisiana Marine Mammal and Sea Turtle Rescue program. This program is committed to the care and treatment of injured, ill, or out-of-habitat marine mammals and sea turtles.

As he championed the zoo, Forman kept the aquarium constantly changing. He initiated several temporary exhibits, including the most popular, SHARKS! The year 2000 saw the opening of a highly popular exhibit, entitled Seahorses. The Seahorse Gallery exhibit was praised by *Southern Living* as an Official Southern Travel Treasure. Summer 2001 saw the introduction of Frogs!, another exciting collection in the Changing Exhibit Gallery, which featured more than two dozen species from around the globe.

The aquarium not only has continued to attract visitors over the years with its excellent permanent and changing exhibits, but it has also received accolades for its efforts. While celebrating its tenth anniversary in 2000, the aquarium received a ranking of fourth among all U.S. zoos and aquariums in the *Places Rated Almanac*'s Family Friendly Travel Awards.

## FREEPORT-MCMORAN AUDUBON SPECIES SURVIVAL CENTER

The success of the "new" zoo and the Aquarium of the Americas inspired Forman and the Audubon Nature Institute to explore future projects. The Institute sought to remain committed to preserving endangered wildlife through the development of such projects.

The Institute designated the Westbank of New Orleans (on the west bank of the Mississippi River) as the most appropriate site for its preservation projects. In December 1993, the Freeport-McMoRan Audubon Species Survival Center (FMASSC) was dedicated in conjunction with the U. S. Fish and Wildlife Service. The Center was established to provide endangered animals a refuge where they could breed in order to boost their numbers. Located on twelve-hundred acre site, the Center initially housed such animals as the Mississippi sandhill crane and the Baird's tapir, with more arriving as the Center expanded.

## THE AUDUBON LOUISIANA NATURE CENTER

The Institute reaffirmed its commitment to education and entertainment with the acquisition of the Louisiana Nature and Science Center. The Audubon Nature Institute merged with the Society for Environmental Education in May 1994 and assumed control of the eighty-six-acre site. The stated purpose of the Center was to provide ecological and environmental science programs for the entire community.

The dedicated staff and volunteers of the Nature Center have received many honors for their environmental stewardship. In 2000, the Louisiana Wildlife Federation hailed the Nature Center as the Environmental Conservation Organization of the Year. The Louisiana Urban Forestry Council gave the Nature Center a Special Projects Award for its work in advancing conservation, environmental understanding, and urban forests. Newspapers across the state spotlighted the Nature Center's innovative Louisiana YES! Program. This annual Youth Environmental Summit (YES) brings together students, teachers, politicians, business people, and other professionals to brainstorm solutions to the state's environmental problems. The students then embark on projects in their home areas.

A new exhibit at the Nature Center in 2000 focused attention on the plight of the Louisiana black bear. An interactive display tracked the species' decline and the conservation efforts to save it. Also new in 2000 were special Family Saturdays at the Nature Center, with fun themes ranging from Vulture Culture to The Bear Essentials. The Nature Center also provides educational outreach programs to students.

## ENTERGY IMAX® THEATRE

The Institute finished construction of the highly anticipated Entergy IMAX® Theatre in October 1995. The theatre was part of the $25 million Phase II of the aquarium and was expected to receive 650,000 visitors and to earn a profit of $700,000 in its first year. The theatre the largest of its kind in the Gulf South, included 354 seats and a nearly six-story-high screen. The Institute chose *The Living Sea,* an exotic journey through coral reefs and the depths of the Central Pacific as its initial offering, and it promised a 3-D film as its subsequent selection. The forty-minute feature cost $6.50 for adults and $4.50 for children, but a combo ticket for the theatre and aquarium was offered at a reduced price of $14.00 for adults and $9.00 for children.

The movies shown at the IMAX® Theatre are changed regularly. In 2000, the theatre presented *Dolphins, Mysteries of Egypt, Everest,* and *Michael Jordan: To the Max.* Movies for 2001 included *Galápagos, Antarctica,* and *CyberWorld 3-D.* The IMAX® Theater also participates in the New Orleans Film Festival, showcasing 3-D movies.

## THE AUDUBON CENTER FOR RESEARCH OF ENDANGERED SPECIES

The Institute next constructed the Audubon Center for Research of Endangered Species (ACRES). The Research Center was to study advanced breeding techniques, animal behavior, and nutrition. The Institute opened a thirty-six-square-foot building that included labs for reproduction, molecular genetics, cryogenics, and veterinary care in the spring of 1996. Senator J. Bennett Johnston secured $19 million in federal funds for the research center, the first breeding center of its kind.

The Research Center has made an international splash with several of its research projects. First, in an unprecedented embryo transfer, a common housecat gave birth to Jazz, an African wildcat, in 1999. ACRES Director Dr. Betsy Dresser commented on the significance of this birth: "By using nonendangered species as surrogates, we can increase the number of births of endangered and rare animals." Second, the first two test-tube caracals (African wildcats) were born via in vitro fertilization using frozen sperm in 2000. The use of frozen sperm, embryos, and other genetic material of vanishing animals promises to help the scientific community preserve endangered species.

Dr. Dresser, Audubon's research head, who was responsible for the embryo transfer, earned the prestigious Chevron Conservation Award in 2000. She was praised as an internationally recognized pioneer. A local weekly newspaper, *Gambit,* named Dr. Dresser as the New Oreleanian of the Year for 2000. The Research Center was hailed in such national publications as the *Washington Post, U.S. News and World Report, Popular Science,* and *Scientific American.*

## PARKS

The Audubon Nature Institute owns and operates three free public parks: (1) Audubon Park next to the zoo in uptown New Orleans, (2) Audubon Wilderness Park on the Westbank, and (3) Woldenberg Riverfront Park on the riverfront in downtown New Orleans. The Audubon Wilderness Park features an orientation center, hiking trails, and signs posting wetland facts. This park is dedicated to preserving the natural environment of Louisiana and providing opportunities for family recreation in a natural setting. Groups such as the Boy Scouts use this park for group camping outings; reservations are handled by the Audubon Nature Center. The long-term goal for the Audubon Wilderness Park is for it to serve as a major urban park. Woldenberg Riverfront Park complements the aquarium and provides an extensive area from which the public can view the river and its traffic.

Audubon Park includes many very old oak trees, a jogging path, picnic areas, riding stables, and the Audubon Golf Course. Extensive renovation of the golf course, a resurfaced jogging track, and other improvements designed to maximize opportunity for outdoor recreation at Audubon Park were begun in 2001. After some controversial feedback, the plans for the clubhouse and parking lot for the golf course were scaled back in size.

## THE AUDUBON NATURE INSTITUTE

The Audubon Nature Institute has a twenty-four-member governing board. Yearly elections are held for six members of the board, who serve four-year terms. The board oversees the policies of the Audubon Nature Institute and sets guidelines for memberships, concessions, fundraising, and marketing. However, actual policy making and operations are controlled by the Audubon Commission, which sets zoo hours, admission prices, and so on.

Through its volunteer programs, the Audubon Nature Institute staffs many of the Audubon programs. The vast majority of the volunteers work at the zoo or the aquarium. Volunteers from the Audubon Nature Institute help with education, membership, public relations, graphics, clerical work, research, or even exhibits and animal care. In 2000, 900 volunteers provided 101,000 hours of service, valued at $1,554,390.

In 2001, a person could join the Audubon Nature Institute as a member of the zoo, the aquarium, the nature center, or any combination of the three. Annual fees for an individual are $45 for one facility, $65 for two, and $85 for all three. Participation in hands-on, behind-the-scenes, members-only events at the zoo, aquarium, and Nature Center, in addition to unlimited free admission and free parking, are benefits of membership. Members also receive discounts on tickets to the Entergy IMAX® Theater, discounts on selected merchandise in Institute gift shops, and a free subscription to *Audubon Up Close*, a quarterly publication for members only.

The effort to increase membership requires a special marketing approach for all of the Audubon facilities. Chip Weigand, Director of Marketing for the Zoo, stated,

> . . . {I}n marketing memberships we try to encourage repeat visitations, the feeling that one can visit as often as one wants, the idea that the zoo changes from visit to visit and that there are good reasons to make one large payment or donation for a membership card, rather than paying for each visit. . . . {T}he overwhelming factor is a good zoo that people want to visit often, so that a membership makes good economical sense.

*Southern Living* magazine in 2000 named Audubon Zoo among the South's favorite zoos'; *Family Fun* magazine called it one of the nation's top family-friendly zoos. *Places Rated Almanac*'s Family Friendly Travel Awards ranked the aquarium fourth among all U.S. zoos and aquariums.

The Audubon Nature Institute publishes a quarterly newsletter for members called *Audubon Up Close*. This publication received a Silver Award for design excellence from the American Institute of Graphic Arts in 2000, its first year of publication. The colorful eight-page publication is crammed full of pictures and articles about recent achievements and upcoming events at all the facilities.

## PROMOTIONAL PROGRAMS

The American Association of Zoological Parks and Aquariums reported that most zoos find that the majority of their visitors live within a single population center in close proximity to the park. Thus, in order to sustain attendance over the years, zoos must attract the same visitors repeatedly. A large number of the zoo's promotional programs and special events are aimed at doing just that.

The Audubon Nature Institute conducts a multitude of very successful promotional programs. The effect is to have ongoing parties and celebrations going on, which attract a variety of people to the zoo and other facilities (and raising additional revenue). Key among these annual events are the Zoo-To-Do; the Swamp Fest, a cajun music festival held over two weekends in October; and the Boo at the Zoo Halloween. In addition to these annual promotions, the Audubon Nature Institute schedules special family weekends throughout the year.

Many educational activities are conducted all year long. These include: (1) a Junior Zookeeper program for seventh and eighth graders, (2) a Student-Intern program that enables college students to receive zookeeper training, (3) a Swamp School for third graders, (4) the Wild Science after-school program for fifth graders, and (5) AquaKids at the Audubon Aquarium.

## ADMISSION POLICY

The average yearly attendance for a zoo may be estimated using projected population figures multiplied by a "visitor generating factor." The average visitor generating factor of fourteen zoos similar in size and climate to the Audubon Zoo was 1.34, with a rather wide range (from a low of .58 in the cities of Phoenix and Miami to a high of 2.80 in Jackson, Mississippi).

In 2001, the Audubon Nature Institute charged admission fees for all of its facilities, as indicated in Exhibit 1; all of the other nonzoo parks charged admissions fees from day one or when they became part of the Institute. However, admission is free for members and for children on school field trips. Nearly 300,000 students visited the nine facilities on such trips during 2000.

## FINANCES

The zoo's ability to generate operating funds has been credited to the dedication of the Audubon Nature Institute, continuing increases in attendance, and creative special events and programs. A history of adequate operating funds allows the zoo to guarantee capital donors that their gifts will be used to build and maintain top-notch exhibits. A comparison of the 1998, 1999, and 2000 combined statements of income and expenses for the Audubon Nature Institute is in Exhibit 2; Exhibit 3 shows the balance sheet.

### Fundraising

The Audubon Nature Institute raises funds through five major types of activities: membership, concessions, the annual fund, Adopt An Animal, Zoo-To-Do, and capital fund drives. Zoo managers from around the country come to the Audubon Park Zoo for tips on fundraising, especially to learn about the Zoo-To-Do.

EXHIBIT 1    Admission Fees

| Facility | Adults | Children | Seniors |
|---|---|---|---|
| Aquarium | $13.50 | $ 6.50 | $10.00 |
| IMAX | 7.75 | 5.00 | 6.75 |
| IMAX & Aquarium | 17.25 | 10.50 | 14.00 |
| Nature Center | 4.75 | 2.50 | 3.75 |
| Zoo | 9.00 | 4.75 | 5.75 |

*Source:* The Audubon Nature Institute.

EXHIBIT 2    Statement of Zoo Operating Income and Expenses (in thousands)

| | 2000 | % Change | 1999 | % Change | 1998 |
|---|---|---|---|---|---|
| **OPERATING INCOME** | | | | | |
| Admissions | $12,997 | −0.44% | $13,054 | −1.22% | $13,215 |
| Concessions & Catering | 6,251 | 0.79% | 6,202 | 21.01% | 5,125 |
| Membership Support | 2,413 | 13.13% | 2,133 | 3.75% | 2,056 |
| Marketing Events & PR | 211 | −35.08% | 325 | | 0 |
| Recreational & Educational Programs | 1,040 | 6.78% | 974 | −21.64% | 1,243 |
| Other | 601 | −3.06% | 620 | −22.69% | 802 |
| TOTAL OPERATING INCOME | 23,423 | 0.49% | 23,308 | 3.86% | 22,441 |
| | | | | | |
| **NON-OPERATING ITEMS*** | | | | | |
| Debt Service Funded by Operations | −895 | −4.18% | −934 | −33.71% | −1,409 |
| Dedicated Tax Millage | 2,999 | 25.27% | 2,394 | 4.36% | 2,294 |
| Interest/Endowment Income | 804 | −48.16% | 1,551 | 1.70% | 1,525 |
| Fundraising Transfer to Operations | 2,086 | −99.91% | 2,453 | 169.26% | 911 |
| TOTAL INCOME | 28,417 | −1.23% | 28,772 | 11.68% | 25,762 |
| | | | | | |
| **OPERATING EXPENSES** | | | | | |
| Operations, Maintenance, & Utilities | 6,792 | −7.12% | 7,313 | 39.45% | 5,244 |
| Curatorial & Research | 4,888 | −13.32% | 5,639 | −8.78% | 6,182 |
| Food Service, Catering, & Gift Shops | 3,856 | 8.31% | 3,560 | 27.60% | 2,790 |
| Membership | 856 | 8.35% | 790 | 34.13% | 589 |
| Recreational & Educational | 1,200 | −15.37% | 1,418 | 7.42% | 1,320 |
| Marketing & Promotions | 1,925 | −15.72% | 2,284 | 10.28% | 2,071 |
| Visitor Services & Volunteers | 1,392 | 2.65% | 1,356 | 11.97% | 1,211 |
| Administration, Personnel, & MIS | 3,920 | 3.38% | 3,792 | 5.98% | 3,578 |
| Fringe Benefits | 2,265 | 13.99% | 1,987 | 28.61% | 1,545 |
| TOTAL EXPENSES | 27,094 | −3.71% | 28,139 | 14.70% | 24,532 |
| REVENUES—EXPENSES | 1,413 | 123.22% | 633 | −48.54% | 1,230 |
| CAPITAL EXPENDITURES | 11,989 | 20.09% | 9,983 | | NA |

*Excludes capital revenues and expenditures and depreciation associated with buildings and field exhibitry.
*Source:* Audubon Nature Institute *Annual Reports* (1998, 1999, 2000).

*Adopt An Animal*

Zoo "Parents" pay a fee to "adopt" an animal, and the fee varies with the animal chosen. Zoo Parents' names are listed on a large sign inside the zoo. They also have their own celebration, Zoo Parents Day, held at the zoo annually.

*Zoo-To-Do*

Zoo-To-Do is a black-tie fundraiser held annually, with live music, food and drink, and original, high-class souvenirs such as posters or ceramic necklaces. Admission tickets, limited to three thousand, are priced starting at $150 per person. A raffle is conducted in conjunction with the Zoo-To-Do, with raffle items ranging from an opportunity to be zoo curator for a day to the use of a Mercedes-Benz for a year. Despite the rather stiff price, the Zoo-To-Do is a popular sellout every year. Local restaurants and other businesses donate most of the necessary supplies, decreasing the cost of the affair. In 1985, the Zoo-To-Do raised almost $500,000 in one night, more money than any other

EXHIBIT 3    Balance Sheet for the Audubon Nature
             Institute, All Units

|  | *December 31, 2000* |
|---|---:|
| **LIABILITIES:** | |
| **CURRENT LIABILITIES:** | |
| Accounts payable and accrued liabilities | $    4,255,480 |
| Due to (or from) the Audubon Institute, Inc. | |
| Due to other locations/funds | 2,033 |
| Total current liabilities | 4,257,513 |
| **CURRENT LIABILITIES PAYABLE FROM RA** | |
| Accrued interest payable | 174,809 |
| Revenue bonds—current portion | 840,874 |
| Limited tax bonds—current portion | 1,496,793 |
| Construction payables | 1,211,993 |
| Due to other funds | – |
| Total payable from restricted assets | 3,724,469 |
| Total current liabilities | 7,981,982 |
| **LONG-TERM LIABILITIES:** | |
| Limited tax bonds | 42,007,548 |
| Revenue bonds | 12,064,612 |
| Discounts on bond issues | (1,263,428) |
| Other | 1,001,322 |
| Total long-term liabilites | 53,810,054 |
| **TOTAL LIABILITIES** | 61,792,036 |
| **NET ASSETS—Operating accounts** | 111,293,872 |
| **TOTAL LIABILITIES & NET ASSETS** | $173,085,908 |

*(continued)*

nonmedical fundraiser in the country. In 2000, the Zoo-To-Do and the Zoo-To-Do for Kids brought in more than $1 million. The Zoo-To-Do continues to sell out annually, and it remains a major fundraiser as well as a great public relations event for the Zoo.

*Annual Fund*

The Audubon Annual Fund, used to pay for day-to-day operations at all Audubon facilities, raised a record $266,000 in 2000.

*Grants*

The Institute was awarded a $112,500 operating grant in 2000 from the Institute of Museum and Library Services, a highly esteemed national grant. The horticulture department of the Audubon Park and Audubon Zoo received a $5,000 grant from the Louisiana Urban Forestry Council to inventory the site's wealth of trees.

*Audubon Tea Room*

In 2000, the Institute increased its revenue-generating potential by opening the Jerome S. Glazer Audubon Tea Room at the Audubon Zoo. The Tea Room provides 10,000 square feet of space, which can be rented for elegant occasions such as weddings, corporate gatherings, and other special events.

EXHIBIT 3    Balance Sheet for the Audubon Nature
             Institute, All Units        **(continued)**

| | December 31, 2000 |
|---|---|
| **ASSETS** | |
| **CURRENT ASSETS:** | |
| Cash and temporary investments | $    1,132,847 |
| Accounts receivable—net | 736,165 |
| Accrued interest receivable | 31,602 |
| Inventories, at cost | 409,462 |
| Prepaid expenses | 431,079 |
| Total current assets | 2,741,155 |
| **RESTRICTED ASSETS:** | |
| Debt service accounts | 3,201,686 |
| Accounts receivable for capital improvements | 361,828 |
| Due from other funds for capital improvements | – |
| Pledges receivable | 8,870,472 |
| Endowment/funds functioning investments | 22,696,487 |
| Total restricted assets | 35,130,473 |
| **PROPERTY AND EQUIPMENT:** | |
| Land | 800,000 |
| Buildings and fixed exhibitry | 137,872,539 |
| Equipment | 15,048,061 |
| Construction in progress | 9,764,776 |
| Gross property | 163,485,376 |
| Less accumulated depreciation | (40,391,364) |
| Net property and equipment | 123,094,012 |
| **OTHER ASSETS:** | |
| Prepaid rent—DockBoard | 9,957,820 |
| Receivable under REDA | 1,493,279 |
| Unamortized bond issue costs | 669,169 |
| Total other assets | 12,120,268 |
| **TOTAL ASSETS** | $173,085,908 |

*Source:* The Audubon Nature Institute.

## Expeditions

The Institute organizes and conducts several expeditions annually. In 2000, the Institute offered three different safaris to Kenya, to Zimbabwe/Zambia/South Africa, and to Botswana. In 2001, it offered an African safari to Tanzania, an expedition to Australia, and an ecotour to Ecuador and the Galápagos Islands. For 2002, a twelve-day birding and wildlife adventure in Costa Rica is already planned. This expedition will take participants from lush rainforests to an active volcano.

## E-COMMERCE

The Audubon Nature Institute has not ignored the Internet and its opportunities. It has its own Web site, is listed on important informational Web sites, and has used eBay to raise funds for its work. The Institute's Web site is **www.auduboninstitute.org**. It uses its Web site to provide "outgoing" information, to provide a means for "incoming" information (through e-mail addresses for key Institute staff), and to sell admission tickets on line.

The Institute has also capitalized on the Web sites of others. It is listed on a number of Web sites that promote recreational activities in the New Orleans area to tourists and locals. Among these are **www.neworleans.net**, **www.neworleans.com**, **www.gambitno.com**, **www.louisianatravel.com**, and **www.nawlins.com**. In addition, using paintings created by the orangutans at the Audubon Zoo, the Audubon chapter of the American Association of Zookeepers sold orangutan-created paintings on eBay, raising money to support a wide range of conservation organizations, from the World Wildlife Fund to the Dian Fossey Gorilla Fund.

## THE NATURAL ENVIRONMENT

The Audubon Nature Institute is "dedicated to nature and unified with a purpose of celebrating life through nature." Its purpose of "celebrating the wonders of nature" guides its mission.

An indicator of the Institute's dedication to nature is the change that was made in its name in 2000. Prior to that year, it was called Audubon Institute. The word *nature* was added to its name to emphasize the central aspect of nature to the organization. The name was paired with a new logo designed to strengthen its unity of purpose—nature—and the broad scope of the organization.

Many of the efforts of the Institute to preserve and celebrate nature were described earlier. Even the zoo, contrary to the public image of most zoos, is involved in efforts to return endangered species to the wild, not just preserve a few specimens in captivity. In 2000, the zoo staff helped release Guam rails, including four chicks born at the zoo, on the island of Rota in the Pacific Ocean. This species of birds was wiped out on the island of Guam by the brown tree snake, a species accidentally introduced to Guam. The zoo also saw the birth of three baby jaguars in 2001—an endangered species from Central and South America.

## THE FUTURE

### The Audubon Insectarium

This living science museum is scheduled to open in the U.S. Custom House on Canal Street in downtown New Orleans in 2003. It will become the tenth facility operated by the Audubon Nature Institute. Ron Forman sees this museum as a way to help the economic development of the city of New Orleans by bringing local people back to Canal Street in downtown New Orleans. The zoo's Bugmobile is heralding the coming opening of the Insectarium as it travels to schools and community centers to provide outreach education.

The very popular butterfly exhibit from the zoo will be moved to the Insectarium. In this exhibit, butterflies hatch from cocoons inside a large enclosed area and fly freely around the many flowers and the visitors walking through. Another exhibit will be on termites, a major problem in the New Orleans area and throughout the southern United States.

Ron Forman is tremendously optimistic about the future of the Audubon Nature Institute, especially considering the forces opposing them. The Institute faces a rather weak New Orleans economic situation. Exhibit 4 provides facts regarding the New Orleans area. The Institute operates in a city where many attractions compete for the leisure dollar of natives and tourists. It has to vie with the French Quarter, Dixieland jazz, the Superdome, casinos—and the greatest attraction of all, Mardi Gras. The decline in tourism following the terrorist attacks of September 11, 2001, adds to the challenges facing the Institute.

## EXHIBIT 4    A Few Facts About New Orleans

**FACTS**

| | |
|---|---|
| Population | 1,337,726[1] |
| Per Capita Personal Income | $25,960[2] |
| Unemployment Rate | 5.0%[3] |
| Average Temperature | 77.42 degrees Fahrenheit[4] |
| Average Annual Rainfall | 5.125 inches[5] |
| Elevation | 25 feet (high)[6] |
| | −8 feet (low) |
| Area | 3,401 square miles of land |

**MAJOR ECONOMIC ACTIVITIES**

Tourism (7 million visitors per year)
Oil and Gas Industry
The Port of New Orleans (200 million tons of cargo/year)

**TAXES**

| | |
|---|---|
| State Sales Tax | 3.97%[7] |
| Parish (County) Sales Tax | 4.75% (Jefferson Parish)[8] |
| | 5.00% (Orleans Parish)[9] |
| State Income Tax | 2.1–2.6% on first $20,000 |
| | 3.0–3.5% on next $30,000 |
| | 6.0% on $51,000 & over |
| Parish Property Tax | Exempt first $75,000 |
| | $161.63/$10,000 (Orleans)[10] |

[1] 2000 http://quickfacts.census.gov/qfd/states/22000.html
[2] 1999 http://www.bea.doc.gov
[3] 2000 http://data.bls.gov/cgi-bin/surveymost?la+22
[4] 2001 http://www.weather.com/weather/climatology/70118
[5] 2001 http://www.weather.com/weather/climatology/70118
[6] http://mac.usgs.gov/mac/isb/pubs/booklets/elvadist/elvadist.html#50
[7] http://www.rev.state.la.us/htmlfiles/faq/faq.asp#SalesTax
[8] http://www.rev.state.la.us/taxforms/R1003.pdf
[9] http://www.rev.state.la.us/taxforms/R1003.pdf
[10] http://www.rev.state.la.us/

One proposal that the Institute is championing is a program called "Family Freedom Days." The purpose of this program is to help Louisiana residents who sustained personal or economic loss because of the wave of attacks on the United States and to encourage residents to visit local sites. Ron Forman feels strongly that people aren't getting out and having fun as much since the September 11 terrorist attacks. Each participating organization offers free admission to its facilities on a particular Saturday. The Institute offered free admission to the zoo, aquarium, and nature center on one Saturday before the end of the year 2001. Although admission was free, donations were requested to benefit relatives of the Louisiana residents who were killed in the September 11 attacks. The last time the Audubon Zoo offered free admission (January 17, 1999), attendance exceeded 38,000 for the one day. In considering this program, the staff of the Institute needs to consider its likely impacts, both short and long term, on the Institute.

Forman believes his once weak and now overwhelmingly powerful Audubon Nature Institute possesses the necessary focus and facilities to forge successfully well into the new millennium. The Audubon Nature Institute and its facilities are well-known both locally and nationally. Exhibits 5 and 6 provide information from visitor and non-visitor surveys conducted for the Institute. The Institute has loyal membership and contributor bases. The facilities are first-class. Forman sums up the present and future of the Institute by stating, "All of our exhibits are on the leading edge of what is being done; we believe the best way to educate people is through fun."

EXHIBIT 5    Audubon Zoo Visitor Survey

| | 1998 | | 1999 | |
|---|---|---|---|---|
| | *Number* | *Percent* | *Number* | *Percent* |
| First Visit to Zoo | 74 | 31% | 136 | 45% |
| Number of Visits in Last Year | | | | |
| No visits | 32 | 22 | 37 | 23 |
| 1 visit | 29 | 20 | 36 | 22 |
| 2 visits | 20 | 14 | 27 | 17 |
| 3 or more visits | 66 | 45 | 63 | 39 |
| Average Number of Visits | 6.1 | – | 4.7 | – |
| When Decided to Visit | | | | |
| Today or yesterday | 99 | 41 | 94 | 31 |
| Within the past week | 77 | 32 | 144 | 48 |
| Two weeks to one month ago | 37 | 15 | 45 | 15 |
| More than one month ago | 27 | 11 | 18 | 6 |
| Reasons for Visiting | | | | |
| Interest in animals | 145 | 61 | 109 | 36 |
| Bring children | 107 | 45 | 141 | 47 |
| Entertainment | 101 | 42 | 103 | 34 |
| Sightseeing | 79 | 33 | 116 | 39 |
| Education | 71 | 30 | 70 | 23 |
| Number of Persons in Group | | | | |
| Adults | 2.3 | – | 2.1 | – |
| Children | 1.1 | – | 1.3 | – |
| Adults (Adults Only) | | | | |
| 1 | 13 | 14 | 15 | 14 |
| 2 | 72 | 79 | 71 | 68 |
| 3 or more | 6 | 6 | 19 | 19 |
| Percentage of Total Groups | – | 39 | – | 36 |
| Average Group Size | 1.9 | – | 2.2 | – |
| Average Adult Age | 39.6 | – | 40.4 | – |
| Number of Children (Groups with Children) | | | | |
| 1 | 68 | 48 | 66 | 36 |
| 2 | 47 | 33 | 68 | 37 |
| 3 | 16 | 11 | 32 | 17 |
| 4 or more | 11 | 8 | 17 | 9 |
| Percent of Total Groups | – | 61 | – | 64 |
| Average Group Size | | | | |
| Children | 1.8 | – | 2.1 | – |
| Adults | 2.5 | – | 2.0 | – |
| Average Child Age | 6.0 | – | 6.5 | – |

*(continued)*

EXHIBIT 5    Audubon Zoo Visitor Survey                    (continued)

| | 1998 | | 1999 | |
| --- | --- | --- | --- | --- |
| | *Number* | *Percent* | *Number* | *Percent* |
| Respondent's Education | | | | |
| Some high school or less | 4 | 2 | 19 | 6 |
| High school graduate | 37 | 16 | 66 | 22 |
| Some college | 69 | 30 | 70 | 23 |
| College degree | 82 | 36 | 94 | 31 |
| Graduate degree | 37 | 16 | 52 | 17 |
| Respondent's Household Family Income | | | | |
| Less than $25,000 | 31 | 14 | 47 | 16 |
| $25,000–39,999 | 47 | 21 | 68 | 23 |
| $40,000–54,999 | 55 | 25 | 55 | 18 |
| $55,000–74,999 | 40 | 18 | 62 | 21 |
| $75,000–149,999 | 42 | 19 | 59 | 20 |
| $150,000 or more | 4 | 2 | 10 | 3 |
| Respondent's Race | | | | |
| Caucasian | 188 | 82 | 212 | 71 |
| African-American | 25 | 11 | 69 | 23 |
| Hispanic | 8 | 3 | 7 | 2 |
| Asian | 2 | 1 | 10 | 3 |
| Native American | 4 | 2 | 0 | 0 |
| Other | 3 | 1 | 1 | 0 |
| Respondent's Gender | | | | |
| Female | 137 | 62 | 179 | 61 |
| Male | 84 | 38 | 116 | 39 |

*Source:* The Audubon Nature Institute.

EXHIBIT 6    Audubon Zoo Nonvisitor
             Survey

| *Reason* | *Pleasure* | *Business* |
| --- | --- | --- |
| **WHY RESPONDENT DID NOT VISIT THE ZOO (in %)** | | |
| No time | 47% | 66% |
| Too hot | 12 | 15 |
| Other plans | 12 | 14 |
| No interest | 11 | 4 |
| Been before | 10 | 4 |

*Source:* The Audubon Nature Institute.

**EXHIBIT 7**    Audubon Nature Institute Mission Statements

## CORE VALUES (MISSION) OF THE INSTITUTE

We believe in Quality in all we do. We believe Total Quality leads to Unprecedented Success. These beliefs are reflected in our Core Values:

- *Service.* We recognize the importance of each and every guest experience and strive to make each one memorable through genuine hospitality, an attitude of caring, and careful training to ensure exceptional customer service.
- *People.* We value the great potential of each individual within the Audubon family. We stimulate initiative and maximize talent through clearly stated goals, professional training and the job support necessary to ensure individual success that exceeds expectations.
- *Stewardship.* We adhere to the highest standards in assuring the well-being of the animals and habitats under our care, and through pace-setting research and conservation and education programs, we work to preserve nature on a local, regional, national and global scale.
- *Innovation.* We enhance and encourage creativity, aggressively seeking to set new standards in all that we do, from new exhibit development to animal breeding programs.
- *Diversity.* We believe in recruiting from a diverse talent pool to build and maintain an extraordinary workforce. Our hiring and promotion practices emphasize ability and potential, eliminating barriers based on race, age, gender, sexual orientation, physical limitations, religion, ethnic background or national origin.
- *Cooperation.* Our growth and development—our every accomplishment—is made possible through a spirit of teamwork that unites our staff, galvanizes our community and ensures attainment of our mission, from educating our diverse audience to enhancing the care and survival of wildlife.
- *Leadership.* We seek to be industry role models and civic leaders, always guided by the highest professional and ethical standards, as well as an entrepreneurial spirit that recognizes selective economic development as a vehicle for advancing environmental education.
- *Stability.* Maintaining economic stability through financial self-sufficiency is paramount as we fuel our operations and strive to fulfill our ambitious vision for the future.
- *Fun.* Our celebrations of life emphasize enjoyment of the world around us. Good humor, optimism and playfulness translate into a healthy workplace—and the ideal environment for teaching others about the wonders of life and nature.

## AUDUBON PARK/AUDUBON ZOO

- *Mission Statement.* The mission of the Audubon Park/Audubon Zoo is to connect people with nature by providing superior recreational, educational, zoological and botanical experiences.

## ACRES/FREEPORT-MCMORAN AUDUBON SPECIES SURVIVAL CENTER

- *Mission Statement.* The mission of the Audubon Center for Research of Endangered Species/Audubon Freeport-McMoRan Species Survival Center is to safeguard wildlife for future generations through innovative scientific programs that accelerate reproduction and preserve the Earth's genetic heritage.

## AUDUBON LOUISIANA NATURE CENTER/AUDUBON WILDERNESS PARK

- *Mission Statement.* The mission of the Audubon Louisiana Nature Center/Audubon Wilderness Park is to lead and inspire a diverse audience to a better understanding and deeper appreciation of the natural world.

*(continued)*

---

EXHIBIT 7    Audubon Nature Institute Mission Statements                    (continued)

## AQUARIUM OF THE AMERICAS/AUDUBON ENTERGY IMAX® THEATER/WOLDENBERG RIVERFRONT PARK

- *Mission Statement.* The mission of the Aquarium of the Americas/Audubon Entergy IMAX® Theatre/ Woldenberg Riverfront Park is to inspire our audience to respect, conserve and enjoy the wonders of nature through an urban oasis offering unique aquatic exhibits, quality IMAX® films, excellent education programs and exceptional guest services.

## AUDUBON CENTRAL ORGANIZATION

- *Mission Statement.* The mission of the Audubon Central Organization is to provide Audubon facilities with an outstanding array of shared support services that facilitate doing business while achieving the mission of the overall organization.

# RIVERBANKS ZOOLOGICAL PARK AND BOTANICAL GARDEN—2002

Carolyn R. Stokes and Eugene M. Bland
**Francis Marion University**

http://www.riverbanks.org

The Riverbanks Zoo and Garden (803-779-8717), a 170-acre park located on the Lower Saluda River in Columbia, the capital of South Carolina, celebrated its new Lexington County entrance in 2001. The complex consists of the Zoological Park, with over two thousand animals in natural habits, and the Botanical Garden on a seventy-acre section devoted to woodlands, gardens, historic ruins, and plant collections. Riverbanks Zoo and Garden is a major attraction of the Columbia metropolitan area, of South Carolina, and of the entire Southeast.

Riverbanks, one of 185 accredited institutional members of the American Zoo and Aquarium Association (AZA), is recognized as being one of the best zoos in America because of it conservation efforts and recreational activities, and it has received numerous awards. Riverbanks is recognized as one of the top ten zoos in North America with respect to support for the AZA programs. The Zoo has received recognition for its captive breeding accomplishments. The Zoo received the prestigious Governor's Cup Award from the South Carolina Chamber of Commerce in 2002 as South Carolina's leading attraction. Riverbanks is recognized as one of the most visited zoos in America. In 2000, Riverbanks received a $112,000 grant from the prestigious Institute of Museum and Library Service. The Southeastern Tourism Society recently gave Riverbanks its Shining Example Award for Visual Excellence for its video, *The Birds of the World*. Riverbanks has been recognized as one of the twenty most visited zoos in the United States. For over ten years, it has averaged approximately 850,000 visitors annually (see Exhibit 1) with 25 percent coming from outside of the state.

Riverbanks' executive director, Palmer Krantz, continues to move Riverbanks into the future. The twenty-fifth anniversary year (1999) marked the launching of Zoo 2002, Riverbanks' largest expansion and renovation plan since its opening. This new construction effort costs in the neighborhood of $19 million. It is being funded with a $15 million bond referendum approved by the Richland and Lexington county governments and with donations from Riverbanks members and supporters, who provided the remaining $4 million. The Zoo 2002 project has received $17 million of the expected $19 million. It has provided funds for new animals, flora and fauna, habitats, and a new Lexington County entrance on the Botanical Garden side. The beautifully landscaped zoo and garden provide an educational and enjoyable experience for all families.

## RIVERBANKS DEVELOPMENT

The Zoo 2002 major expansion plan that began in 1999 refurbished nearly 50 percent of the zoo's core exhibit space; it also created a new entrance into the Botanical Garden. Recently completed exhibits include the gorilla compound in the Ndoki Forest, a birdhouse, and the Bird Conservation Center (a research and breeding center that allows visitors to view the bird conservation operations). The new birdhouse replaced the 1974

174

EXHIBIT 1    Riverbanks Zoo Attendance Analysis

| | Fiscal Year Ending | | |
| --- | --- | --- | --- |
| | *June 30, 2001* | *June 30, 2000* | *June 30, 1999* |
| **Paid Attendance:** | | | |
| Regular | 295,579 | 291,291 | 338,576 |
| Group | 95,008 | 112,706 | 115,458 |
| Total Paid | 390,587 | 403,997 | 454,034 |
| **Free Attendance** | | | |
| Lexington/Richland school groups | 31,016 | 32,065 | 31,631 |
| Riverbanks Society | 232,513 | 216,043 | 228,779 |
| Prepaid and Complementary | 18,751 | 15,554 | 18,445 |
| Promotional-Free Friday's | 38,077 | 29,729 | 47,855 |
| Children under three | 51,820 | 56,539 | 55,964 |
| Total free | 372,177 | 349,930 | 382,674 |
| **Total Attendance for the Year** | 762,764 | 753,927 | 836,708 |
| **Rain Days:** | | | |
| Saturdays | 5 | 5 | 11 |
| Sundays | 4 | 6 | 3 |
| Weekdays | 9 | 15 | 15 |

*Source:* Riverbanks Zoo 2001 *Annual Report.*

original birdhouse, a facility whose groundbreaking research and conservation efforts had helped to secure Riverbanks' reputation in this field. Completed in January 2002 was the Ndoki Forest elephant compound and a meerkat exhibit.

The Lexington County entrance on the botanical garden side was completed ahead of schedule in February 2001. The well-designed Lexington County entrance on the left bank of the Saluda River has a new, elaborately landscaped parking lot. This new location for the entrance is expected to increase attendance by reducing travel time for many Lexington County residents. All of these developments are in keeping with the mission (Exhibit 2) of the Riverbanks Zoological Park and Botanical Garden: "to foster an appreciation and concern for all living things."

EXHIBIT 2    Riverbanks' Mission Statement

It is our mission to foster appreciation and concern for all living things.

We are dedicated to providing:

- the highest standards of care for our animal and plant collections.
- a diverse educational and high-quality recreational experience for all Riverbanks visitors.
- all the resources at our disposal for the conservation of the earth's flora and fauna.

*Source:* Riverbanks Zoo 2001 *Annual Report,* p. 2.

Riverbanks is governed by the Riverbanks Parks Commission, supported by the Riverbanks Society, and managed by the Riverbanks staff under the leadership of Palmer E. Krantz, III, the executive director. Riverbanks is accredited by the American Association of Zoological Parks and Aquariums, and it is a member of the American Association of Botanical Gardens and Arboreta. Riverbanks, with approximately 160 employees, has one of the leading zoos in the country.

## ZOOLOGICAL PARK

The zoo uses a modern approach to exhibit design: It houses wild animals in naturalistic settings that are preferred by both animal residents and human visitors alike. The naturalistic settings at Riverbanks enable animals to enjoy living in a setting that recreates the wild, and such settings allow visitors to see the animals in a more realistic environment rather than warehoused in cages as in earlier times. At the farm, some domesticated animals are exhibited in a barn and in related settings so that visitors can view them as they would on a working farm. The zoo is home to more than 2,000 animals including 300 birds, 300 reptiles and amphibians, and 1,300 fish and invertebrates.

Major zoo attractions include an award-winning Aquarium Reptile Complex, an African Plains section, a large mammal area, a small mammal area, a sea lion exhibit, bird exhibits, a farm, and the soon-to-be completed Ndoki Forest. The Aquarium Reptile Complex (ARC), with its 55,000 gallon aquarium, has four galleries featuring animals from South Carolina, the desert, the tropics, and the Pacific Ocean. The complex is innovative: It uniquely blend's the features of a reptile habitat with those of an aquarium. The year after the ARC opened to the public in 1989, it was named one of the top three new zoo exhibits by AZA. Attendance reached 1,000,000.

The African Plains section features giraffes, rhinoceros, zebras, and ostriches in a savanna setting complete with moats. The large mammal area features tigers and lions, and the small mammal area features monkeys, tamarins, tree kangaroos, and lemurs. The sea lion exhibit presents the animals in their habitat, swimming, playing, and feeding.

In February 2001, the new birdhouse, the first major component in the Zoo 2002 expansion plan, opened with over 12,000 square-feet of exhibit space. Visitors could walk across the boardwalk to the birdhouse, where they viewed a beach filled with colorful flamingos on one side and a koi pond filled with colorful Japanese fish on the other side. Inside the well-designed birdhouse is an Asian Trek, a Savanna Exhibit, and a Penguin Coast.

The Asian Trek, with the lush foliage of a rainforest and a simulated rainstorm, is home to rhinoceros hornbills, Bali mynas, Victoria crowned pigeons, Palawan peacock pheasants, and many other beautiful birds. The Savanna Exhibit presents the African and South American birds in a safari setting under a canvas tent complete with safari equipment. Here, visitors find the Baft crusted bustard, the African bee eater, the Tavita golden weave, and troupial and blue-crowned motmots. The Penguin Coast exhibit, with more than 1,350 square feet of space, is home to the African and rock-hopper penguins. Visitors look through a 65-foot-long glass at the penguins on their rocky coast and in the water playing and diving. The Penguin Coast is one of the finest exhibits of penguins in North America. The birdhouse is user-friendly to children and features interactive activities. Other bird exhibits include Riverbanks' new Conservation Center, which allows visitors to view zoo operations, including the raising and feeding of birds, and new outdoor aviaries, which display parrots, vultures, and other birds.

Riverbanks Farm features a barn and barnyards with animals such as goats, cows, pigs, chickens, llamas, and honey bees, as well as a backyard garden. Here, visitors can view the chickens hatching from eggs and Riverbanks staff milking a cow. Visitors can also view the feedings of many animals on the farm and in other sections of the zoo.

The Ndoki Forest is the centerpiece of ZOO 2002, a $19 million expansion plan. The forest has five acres of animal exhibits, with lush plants and visitor facilities. The Ndoki Forest provides a new natural habitat for the gorilla, elephant, and meerkat exhibits. The forest also includes an African village, a pizza restaurant, and Ndoki Lodge. The lodge overlooks the elephant exhibit, seats up to 300 dinner guests, and is available for rental.

The gorilla portion of the Ndoki Forest opened in late July 2001 to large crowds. Visitors could view the gorillas from their base camp or in the Ndoki Forest. In the first month that the gorilla exhibit was open to the public, attendance was nearly 75 percent larger than during the same period in 2000. Palmer Krantz, executive director of Riverbanks, said that 79,600 people visited the four-gorilla troop from July 28 through August 21, 2001.

The Ndoki Forest elephant exhibit houses four elephants. Riverbanks uses the recently developed form of elephant management known as "protected care." Once the elephants have had time to adjust to the new environment, Riverbanks will offer an elephant show in which visitors can watch the interaction of the elephants and their keepers.

The new meerkats exhibit in the Ndoki Forest was the most challenging to design. The U.S. Department of Interior has designated this species as Injurious Wildlife, and a permit is required to display it. The permit requires that two escape-proof barriers be maintained between the meerkats and freedom. Riverbanks' first barrier will be a stainless steel wire mesh fence to prevent them from digging out. The second barrier will be either a six-foot un-climbable wall or a wall with an impassable overhang. Riverbanks, with its zoological expertise, will provide guests the opportunity to visit meerkats, animals not often seen in captivity.

In line with the missions of Riverbanks, the zoo actively participates in the Species Survival Plans (SSP) of the AZA to ensure the survival of endangered species. Many zoos participate in the program. For example, in Texas, the Houston Zoological Gardens hatched two critically endangered species, the prairie chicken and the Hawaiian thrush. Riverbanks focuses on 24 endangered species, including the golden lion tamarin, Siberian tiger, palm cockatoo, African penguin, and Bali myna. Riverbanks has received awards for successfully breeding the back howlers and the white-faced sakis. Riverbanks had the honor of being the first zoo to breed in captivity two rare birds, the toco toucan and the crimson seedcracker, and it was the first zoo in the Western Hemisphere to breed milky eagle owls, blue-billed weavers, and cinereous vultures. Riverbanks has the only pair of cinereous vultures raising their own. Riverbanks has successfully bred the endangered pine barrens tree frog in captivity, a first for this species. In 1998, Riverbanks received the Edward H. Bean Award for its long-term success with the captive breeding of Ramphastids (i.e., toucans, toucanets, aracaris).

Riverbanks' Research Department continues to strive to fulfill its mission by leading several AZA-based conservation programs, including:

**North American regional studbooks/Population Management Plans (PMPs)** for the following species:

1. Rodrigues Fruit bat
2. African lion
3. Nile hippo
4. Hawk-headed parrot
5. Golden-breasted starling
6. King cobra

7. Leaf tailed gecko
8. False gharial

**International Studbooks** for the following species:

1. Fishing cat
2. Rare leopards
3. Black howler monkey

**Species Survival Plans (SPS)** for the following species:

1. Bali myna
2. Cinereous vulture

Riverbanks uses the Zoological Park for a variety of activities, such as Migratory Bird Day (with hands-on activities), Ekekeh Day, and Fiesta a la Orilla Del Rio, and if presents culture activities of the relevant countries; it also offers educational events, such as Read Between the Lions Day. On Migratory Bird Day, visitors learn about bird banding, making birdhouses and feeders, and satellite tracking. On Ekekeh Day, Africa comes alive at Riverbanks. Visitors visit an African village, listen to African music, eat African food, and listen to African story readings. At the Fiesta a la Orilla Del Rio ("party by the banks"), visitors learn about Latin America and enjoy arts and crafts; they also see performances of folkloric music and dance from Panama, Colombia, Puerto Rico, Mexico, and Argentina. On Read Between the Lions Day, children and adults listen to animal stories read at different locations in the zoo.

## BOTANICAL GARDEN

The Botanical Garden provides visitors with a variety of settings to view the flora and fauna and a variety of opportunities to learn about them. The Botanical Garden includes a visitors center, a walled garden, an amphitheater, a river walk, woodlands trails, mill ruins with a log cabin, and an outdoor classroom. The Botanical Garden, with its new entrance on the Lexington side, now has two entrances for visitors. Visitors now may enter through the original gate in Richland County on the Zoological Park side or from the newly constructed entrance to the Garden on the Lexington side of the Saluda River.

On March 16, 2001, the new entrance opened ahead of schedule. Riverbanks Society members, Lexington County politicians, Riverbanks staff, and young children from the Saluda River Academy of the Arts attended the opening ceremonies. Young children in the Saluda River Singers, focusing on conservation, nature, and growth, sang about giving a tree room to grow during the special ceremonies.

The well-designed Lexington County entrance on the left bank of the Saluda River has a new, elaborately landscaped parking lot large enough for 250 cars, a landscaped entrance gate, and a boardwalk/bridge leading to the Botanical Garden. Visitors passing through the Lexington County entrance walk past the new Bog Garden in the entrance plaza. Then they walk along a short path through woodlands and over a wooden bridge about 35 feet above a brook bordered by plants and flowers and on up toward the entrance to a walled garden that is larger than a football field. Visitors entering the original gate walk or ride the tram up from the zoo to the Botanical Garden.

At the front of the walled garden is the visitors center, which provides guests with a gift shop featuring garden-related products, a gallery, and multipurpose spaces for functions. In the walled garden, guests will find cascade and pinwheel fountains as well as seasonal, exotic annuals; perennials; and bulbs that complement the permanent shrubbery and trees. Beside the walled garden is a terraced amphitheater and grass carpeted for seating as well as a large domed stage for cultural events, such as a zoo ballet and educational programs. At the rear of the garden is the entrance to the walking trail. Here, visitors enjoy scenic river views and the Saluda Factory Interpretive Center. The trail provides visitors a view of many trees, plants, flowers, and animals indigenous to the upper and lower parts of the state. The scenic trail in 1996 was featured on an episode of *Nature Scene*, a nationally broadcast series originating at the educational television station in South Carolina.

The Saluda Factory Interpretive Center is a woodland log cabin. This rough-hewn cabin located near the mill ruins features exhibits that assist in the interpretation of the mill ruins and the flora and fauna of the area. There is also an outdoor classroom for educational programs.

The Garden is a leading source of horticultural and botanical information in the area. Through a cooperative effort with Clemson Extension Service, the public can access information by talking with an extension agent or by using the Internet in the visitors center. The Garden also provides facilities for related activities. The Mid-Carolina Daylily Society holds its annual show and the South Carolina Native Plant Society holds its annual symposium in the Garden. The Community Concert Band has held its annual show in the amphitheater since 1983. Riverbanks was selected again in 2001 to host a Southern Living Gardening School.

## SPECIAL ATTRACTION

In 1987, Riverbanks began an event, "Lights Before Christmas," with the lighting of about 25 percent of the zoo. Each year, except during the recent construction period, more lights were added. The 2001 "Lights Before Christmas" display lit the entire zoo for the first time since the Zoo 2002 construction began. This special attraction enhances Riverbanks in December with colorful lights along walkways, in trees, on shrubbery, and in other locations. At the entrance, visitors are greeted with lighted trees containing large stars and the sound of Christmas music. There are colorful lighted images of animals, including a bear, lion, horse, deer, frog, rhino, pig, and fox. Some of the animals appear to be in motion. For example, there is an elephant spraying water over its back, an ostrich running through the woods, and bears ice skating in the Rhino Camp. Visitors on their way to the bridge pass under an arch that is artfully decorated with colorful lights, and they view numerous decorated trees and shrubs as well as a group of frogs that appear to be playing. The bridge is decorated with images of fish and other sea life.

Riverbanks is one of a number of zoos that is presenting attractions of this kind. The Winnipeg, Canada, Assiniboine Park Zoo, for example, one of the coldest zoos in the world, features the "The Lights of the Wild" and reindeer sleigh rides. The Fort Worth Zoo presents a "Zoobilee of Lights," which increased its December attendance from only 10,000 to 12,000 visitors before its introduction to over 75,000 visitors afterward.

Attendance at Riverbanks' 2001 "Lights Before Christmas" was an all-time record: 101,825. In addition to gate receipts, this event generates revenue from concessions, from carousel rides, and from new memberships. With over a million lights designed to depict animal and garden scenes, the Riverbanks' "Lights Before Christmas" has been named one of the Top 20 Events in the Southeast by the Southeast Tourism Society and one of the Top 100 Events in North America by the American Bus Association.

## RENTAL OF ZOO AND GARDEN

Riverbanks has offered members and guests the opportunity to rent various portions of the property and facilities for activities such as birthday parties and business meetings. With the completion of several new projects, Riverbanks has now increased the variety of facilities available for rental. Total revenue from all rentals has increased from approximately $74,000 in 2000 to just over $90,000 in 2001. Birthday party revenue has enjoyed a 25 percent increase in 2001 over the same time period in 2000. The revenue associated with birthday parties increased from $5,500 in 2000 to $6,900 in 2001.

The zoo offers facilities for meetings of up to 250 people during daytime hours for $500. Evening rentals can range from the bridge spanning the Lower Saluda River for $500, the entire zoo for $1,500, or the zoo and garden for $2,500. The walled garden and visitors center are available for weddings and receptions for $1,750. Rental of Riverbanks property and facilities promotes attendance by more individuals and organizations who benefit from the enjoyable and educational experience of seeing the animal exhibits and/or the flora and fauna.

## RIVERBANKS EDUCATION DEPARTMENT

The Education Department, established in 1993, works to interpret animal exhibits and plants, and to assist in learning about animal and plant worlds. The primary facility of the Education Department is the Education Center, which has two classrooms, an auditorium, and a library. Other facilities available for education programs include a classroom in the Aquarium Reptile Complex, another in Riverbanks Farm, an outdoor classroom at the Saluda Factory Interpretive Center, and the amphitheater adjacent to the Botanical Garden.

During the week, Riverbanks offers classes to groups ranging from preschool through college (see Exhibit 3). On weekends and in the summer, Riverbanks offers classes and special programs for students, scouts, teachers, and family members. Special programs include the Zoo Camp for overnight guests; a one-week day camp for kindergarten; and Winter Wednesday Series, Saturday Series, and Wildlife in the Zoo for gifted classes. Annually, over 40,000 people participate in the education programs.

## FINANCING

Individuals, businesses, and government have funded the original construction, major renovations, and expansions as well as the annual operating budget. The Riverbanks Zoological Park and Botanical Garden has an annual operating budget of over $5 million. Revenues (see Exhibit 4) from admissions and concession fees provide approximately 60 percent of the resources; funds from Richland and Lexington counties, the state of South Carolina, and federal and city grants provide approximately 30 percent; and the Riverbanks Society provides approximately 10 percent. Nationally, governments provide approximately 54 percent of the support for zoos.

Riverbanks, a nonprofit organization, uses fund accounting to report its financial position and the results of its operations. The balance sheet for the years ending June 30, 1998, to June 30, 2001, is shown in Exhibit 5.

Admission revenues are affected by weather conditions because most of the attractions are outdoors. Riverbanks earns admissions revenue directly from visitors who pay per visit or indirectly from Riverbanks Society members who pay per year for one of several different memberships. General admission fees are small. A single admission is $7.25 for adults and $4.75 for children ages three to twelve. Special prices of $6.00 for students and $5.75 for senior citizens are available. Discounts are available for groups,

EXHIBIT 3    Examples of Riverbanks Education
Programs

*Single-Grade Programs*

**Special Education**
* Animal Encounters
**Preschool and Kindergarten**
* "M" Is for Mammal
* Varmint's Garments
* Ocean Odyssey
**Grade 1**
* Survival Senses
* Whoo's There
**Grade 2**
* Hedgerows to Mole Holes
* Dinosaur Detectives

**Grade 3**
* Trunks, Tails, Spots and Scales
* Look Out Below
**Grade 4**
* Herpetology
* Good Buddies
**Grade 5**
* Nature's Cycles and Chains
* The Living Sea
**Grade 6**
* Species on the Brink
* Sea of Uncertainty

*Multigrade Programs*

**Grades 7–12**
* World of Animals and Zoos
* Careers in Zoos and Botanical Gardens
* Biodiversity
* Save Our Species

*College Level Programs*

Contact Education Department at 803–779–8717 x1113

*Source:* http://www.riverbanks.org/html/s07education/p02school.

for special activities, or on special days. Free classes are provided for Lexington and Richland County schools. Charges for special activities vary.

Additional information concerning zoo and aquarium industry financing is available at the AZA Web site, **www.aza.org.**

## RIVERBANKS SOCIETY

The Riverbanks Society, which started with 200 members in 1976, has grown to over 28,000 households today, making it one of the largest zoo societies per capita in the United States. The Society, which grew out of the private sector, provided much of the needed support prior to the opening of Riverbanks, and it plays a major role in the support of Riverbanks. It provides funds for operations, construction, and renovations, new exhibits, and special activities.

Many of the exhibits and portions of the gardens were provided by individual donations. For example, the Old Rose Garden established in the Botanical Garden as well as the new bird house and gorilla exhibits in the zoo were funded by private contributions as were other projects in previous years. A new endangered species carousel, funded by a local business, is a focal point of the children's play area. The carousel has 22 endangered species, which children can ride, and a scenic mural of other endangered species in their natural habitats.

EXHIBIT 4    Riverbanks Park Commission—General Fund Statement of Revenues,
Expenditures and Changes in Fund Balance
(for the fiscal year ended June 30, 2001)

| | Budgeted for Year | Actual Current Month | Actual Year-to-Date Current Year | Actual Year-to-Date Last Year | Ideal Remaining Percent: 0.0% Budget Remaining Amount | Percent |
|---|---|---|---|---|---|---|
| **REVENUES:** | | | | | | |
| Earned Revenues: | | | | | | |
| Admissions Net Revenue | $1,788,232 | $217,941 | $1,783,613 | $1,611,621 | $ 4,619 | 0.3% |
| Aramark Concession Fees | 600,000 | 64,064 | 598,276 | 548,992 | 1,724 | 0.3% |
| Riverbanks Society Contribution | 607,000 | 0 | 607,000 | 607,000 | 0 | 0.0% |
| Other Revenues – Page 5 | 610,607 | 88,867 | 599,584 | 563,110 | 11,043 | 1.8% |
| Total Earned Revenues | $3,605,839 | $370,872 | $3,588,453 | $3,330,723 | $17,386 | 0.5% |
| Governmental Support: | | | | | | |
| Richland County | 1,305,928 | 10,656 | 1,305,928 | 1,108,121 | 0 | 0.0% |
| Lexington County | 699,868 | 13,252 | 699,868 | 666,540 | 0 | 0.0% |
| State of South Carolina | 182,989 | 0 | 182,989 | 182,989 | 0 | 0.0% |
| Accommodations Tax Revenue | 137,500 | (38,500) | 122,500 | 128,500 | 15,000 | 10.9% |
| Total Governmental Support | 2,326,285 | (14,592) | 2,311,285 | 2,066,150 | 15,000 | 0.6% |
| Total Revenues | $5,932,124 | $356,280 | $5,899,738 | $5,416,873 | $32,386 | 0.5% |
| **EXPENDITURES BY DIVISION:** | | | | | | |
| Administrative | 1,019,797 | 239,728 | 1,058,417 | 922,288 | (38,620) | −3.8% |
| Animal Care | 2,216,994 | 272,259 | 2,182,747 | 1,924,328 | 34,247 | 1.5% |
| Botanical | 669,584 | 88,834 | 631,979 | 574,678 | 37,605 | 5.6% |
| Facility Management/Utilities | 907,518 | 95,674 | 923,417 | 869,411 | (15,899) | −1.8% |
| Public Services | 1,160,897 | 224,621 | 1,154,906 | 1,063,538 | 5,991 | 0.5% |
| Total Expenditures | 5,974,790 | 898,917 | 5,951,465 | 5,354,243 | 23,325 | 0.4% |
| Excess (deficit) of Revenue Over Expend. | (42,666) | (542,637) | (51,727) | 62,630 | | |
| Fund Balance – Beginning of Period | | | 699,273 | 639,087 | | |
| Fund Balance – End of Period | | | $ 649,989 | $ 701,717 | | |

*Source:* Riverbanks Zoo 2001 *Annual Report*

The Riverbanks Society offers reasonable annual membership fees that allow
admission for individuals or family members. The Society offers a variety of memberships for individuals and families, ranging from $29 to $125 for a standard membership
and from $250 to $1,000 for Gold Circle memberships. Types of memberships, associated benefits, and costs are shown in Exhibit 6.

Society members enjoy benefits in addition to those in the exhibits. Riverbanks
sends Society members a bimonthly newsletter and a quarterly magazine. The magazine was redesigned in 2001. Each new issue of *Riverbanks* magazine contains a feature article, timely information on zoo and garden activities, and pages devoted to
younger members. Some issues of the magazine have pictures of children with their
zoo art, word puzzles, and special children's programs and activities. This is especially appropriate since many children visit Riverbanks. Recent feedback indicates
that the new format of the magazine is a hit with members. Riverbanks arranges
tours by its staff for Society members to Africa, Australia, Peru, South America, and

EXHIBIT 5    Riverbanks Park Commission—General Fund Comparative Balance Sheets
(as of June 30, 2001 and 2000)

| | *June 30, 2001* | *June 30, 2000* | *Changes* |
|---|---|---|---|
| **ASSETS** | | | |
| Cash on Hand, on Deposit & Invested in REPO | $  746,083 | $  418,259 | $327,824 |
| Accounts Receivable – General | 129,600 | 104,460 | 25,139 |
| Accounts Receivable – Local Governments | 0 | 48,500 | (48,500) |
| Accounts Receivable – Ticket Sales | 8,515 | 4,852 | 3,863 |
| Accounts Receivable – Riverbanks Society | 118,195 | 556,747 | (438,552) |
| Due from Capital Projects Fund | 68,039 | 8,966 | 57,073 |
| Inventories – General Supplies & Animal Feed | 22,209 | 19,146 | 3,083 |
| Total Assets | 1,090,641 | 1,160,930 | (70,289) |
| | | | |
| **LIABILITIES AND FUND BALANCE** | | | |
| Current Liabilities: | | | |
| Accounts Payable | 240,234 | 278,046 | (37,812) |
| Accrued Salaries Payable | 55,008 | 41,056 | 13,952 |
| Payroll Taxes Accrued and Withheld | 0 | 339 | (339) |
| Admissions and Use Taxes Payable | 0 | 8,927 | (8,927) |
| State Ret. Contrl. Payable—Employer & Employee | 45,132 | 40,272 | 4,860 |
| Due to Riverbanks/Aramark Invest. Fund | 53,489 | 0 | 53,489 |
| Deferred Revenue – Consign. Tickets/Wild Weeks | 45,484 | 90,575 | (45,091) |
| Total Liabilities | 439,347 | 459,215 | (19,868) |
| Fund Balance | | | |
| Reserved for: | | | |
| Inventories – General Supplies & Animal Feed | 22,209 | 19,146 | 3,063 |
| Operating Cushion | 590,000 | 590,000 | 0 |
| Major Repairs and Renovation | 0 | 0 | 0 |
| Endowed Funds – Phelps | 33,833 | 32,395 | 1,438 |
| Unreserved, Undesignated (Deficit) | 5,252 | 60,175 | (54,923) |
| Total Fund Balance | 651,294 | 701,716 | (50,422) |
| Total Liabilities and Fund Balance | 1,090,641 | 1,160,931 | (70,289) |

*Source:* Riverbanks Zoo 2001 *Annual Report*

other places across the globe. The members get the opportunity to travel to each animal's country and to learn from a Riverbanks professional as they tour the natural habitats of animals.

## FUTURE

The zoo and botanical garden industry always faces difficulties due to the fact that the live animals and plants are exposed to the elements; the uncertainty of the economy and competition are also concerns. The recent downturn in the economy has reduced the tax receipts of many states, including South Carolina, thus leading to budget cuts. The terrorist attacks on September 11, 2001, have resulted in greater competition for charitable donations and greater concerns about security, a development which is motivating many to seek recreation closer to home.

Many attractions in South Carolina may increase competition for the entertainment dollar and time of tourists and local residents. Myrtle Beach, a popular entertainment and

## EXHIBIT 6    Riverbanks Society Memberships

**STANDARD MEMBERSHIPS**

*Individual—$29*

FREE admission for 1 adult named on card PLUS 4 guest passes
One free admission to "Lights before Christmas,"
Free admission to 100 other zoos, *Riverbanks* magazine and newsletter, discounts in gift shops and education programs, members only events, preview of exhibits

*Individual Plus—$39*

Benefits of Individual Membership PLUS permanent guest option, six guest passes

*Family/Grandparent—$49*

Benefits of Individual Membership PLUS admission for children/grandchildren 18 years and under, six free passes

*Family Plus—$64*

Benefits of Family/Grandparent Membership PLUS 12 free passes, early bird enrollment in Wild Weeks Summer Camp, unlimited free admission to "Lights Before Christmas," and 4 free carousel tokens

*Patron—$125*

Benefits of Family Plus Membership PLUS permanent guest option, duplicate membership card, subscription to *Wildlife Conservation*

**GOLD CARD MEMBERSHIPS**

*Curators' Circle—$250*

Benefits of Patron Membership PLUS 16 free passes and private Gold Circle events

*Director's Circle—$500*

Same benefits as Curators' Circle PLUS escorted behind-the-scenes tours, *Satch's Scoop* newsletter, 25% discount on facility rentals

*Benefactor—$1,000*

Same benefits as Director's Circle PLUS VIP tours and events

*Source:* http://www.riverbanks.org/html/society_membership.html.

shopping destination, is home to Ripley's Aquarium, which is located at Broadway at the Beach, and many other forms of entertainment. Charleston, famous for its historic district, is home to the South Carolina State Aquarium, the CSS *Hunley* (the Confederate submarine credited with being the first submarine to sink a ship), and Patriot's Point (museum site of the aircraft carrier USS *Yorktown* and several other naval vessels). Columbia, the capital city, is home to the SC State Museum and other attractions.

By the end of 2002, the zoo's renovation should be complete and visitors should be enjoying the new renovations, including the new bird house, Lemur Island, Ndoki Forest (with the gorilla compound), and elephant and meerkat habitats. Riverbanks, which provides an attractive educational and recreational environment where both adults and children can enjoy and learn about our world of animals, flora, and fauna at very reasonable prices, should continue to be one of the top attractions in South Carolina.

# CARNIVAL CORPORATION—2002

**Mike Keeffe, John K. Ross, III, and Bill Middlebrook**
**Southwest Texas State University**

CCL

www.carnivalcorp.com

Carnival Corporation is the largest cruise line in the world, and it is considered to be the leader and innovator in the cruise travel industry. Carnival has grown from two converted ocean liners to an organization with two cruise divisions and a chain of Alaskan hotels and tour coaches. Corporate revenues for fiscal 2001 reached $4.5 billion, with net income from operations of $962 million. Carnival has several "firsts" in the cruise industry; more than 1 million passengers carried in a single year and the first cruise line to carry 5 million total passengers by fiscal 1994. Currently, its overall market share of the cruise travel industry stands at approximately 40%.

The Carnival Corporation CEO and chairman, Micky Arison, and the Carnival Cruise Lines president and COO, Bob Dickinson, are prepared to maintain the company reputation as the leader and innovator in the industry. The two men have assembled one of the newest fleets catering to cruisers, with the introduction of several superliners built specifically for the Caribbean and Alaskan cruise markets, and they expect to invest over $3.6 billion in new ships by the year 2004.

Additionally, the company has expanded its Holland America Lines fleet to cater to more established cruisers and plans to add five of the new ships to its fleet in the premium cruise segment. Carnival also acquired 100 percent ownership of Costa Cruise Lines on September 29, 2000. Strategically, Carnival Corporation seems to have made the right moves at the right time, sometimes in direct opposition to industry analysts and cruise trends.

Cruise Lines International Association (CLIA), an industry trade group, has tracked the growth of the cruise industry for over twenty-five years. In 1970, approximately 500,000 passengers took cruises for three consecutive nights or more, reaching a peak of 6.66 million passengers in 2000, an average annual compound growth rate of approximately 9 percent. By the end of 2000, CLIA estimates that there were 164 ships with 165,000-berth capacity, which is projected to grow to 206 ships in 2004. CLIA expects the number of cruise passengers to continue to grow and the competition to intensify between cruise operators.

Carnival has exceeded the recent industry trends: Over the 1996 to 2001 period, it has achieved a growth rate of 50 percent in the number of passengers carried. The company's passenger capacity increased by 10,150 berths during 2001. Additional capacity will be added with the delivery of several new cruise ships already on order. By the summer of 2002, the company expects to have some 56,858 passenger capacity, a 44.1 percent growth over the 1998 period.

Even with the growth in the cruise industry, the company believes that cruises represent only 2 percent of the applicable North American vacation market, defined as individuals who travel for leisure purposes on trips of three nights or longer and who spend at least one night in a hotel. The Boston Consulting Group, in a 1989 study, estimated that only 5 percent of all individuals in the North American target market have taken a cruise for leisure purposes, and it estimated the market potential to be in excess of $50 billion. Carnival Corporation (in 2000) believes that only 12 percent of the North American population has ever cruised. Various cruise operators, including Carnival Corporation, have based their expansion and capital spending programs on the possibility of capturing part of the 88 percent of the North American population that has yet to take a cruise vacation.

## HISTORY

In 1972, Ted Arison, backed by American Travel Services, Inc., purchased an aging ocean liner from Canadian Pacific Empress Lines for $6.5 million. The new AITS subsidiary, Carnival Cruise Line, refurbished the vessel from bow to stern and renamed it the *Mardi Gras* to capture the party spirit. (Also included in the deal was another ship later renamed the *Carnivale*.) The company start-up, however, was not promising. On the first voyage, the *Mardi Gras,* with over three hundred invited travel agents aboard, ran aground in Miami harbor. The ship was slow and guzzled expensive fuel, limiting the number of ports of call and lengthening the minimum stay of passengers on the ship to break even. Arison then bought another, older vessel from Union Castle Lines to complement the *Mardi Gras* and the *Carnivale,* and he named it the *Festivale.* To attract customers, Arison began adding diversions on board, such as planned activities, a casino, nightclubs, discos, and other forms of entertainment designed to enhance the shipboard experience.

Carnival Corporation is expanding through internally generated growth as evidenced by the number of new ships on order (see Exhibit 1). Additionally, Carnival seems to be willing to continue with its external expansion through acquisitions if the right opportunity arises.

## THE CRUISE PRODUCT

Ted and Mickey Arison envisioned a product in which classical cruise elegance along with modern convenience could be had at a price comparable to land-based vacation packages sold by travel agents. Carnival's all-inclusive package, when compared to resorts or to a theme park such as Walt Disney World, is often priced below these destinations, especially when the array of activities, entertainment, and meals are considered.

A typical vacation on a Carnival cruise ship starts when the bags are tagged for the ship at the airport. Upon arriving at the port of embarkation, passengers are ferried by air-conditioned buses to the ship for boarding, and luggage is delivered by the cruise ship staff to the passenger's cabin. Waiters wander the ship, offering tropical drinks against the background sound of a Caribbean rhythm, while the cruise staff orients passengers to the various decks, cabins, and public rooms. In a few hours (most ships sail in the early evening), dinner is served in the main dining rooms, where, the wine selection rivals the finest restaurants and the variety of main dishes is designed to suit every palate. Diners can always order double portions if they decide not to save room for the variety of desserts and after-dinner specialties.

After dinner, cruisers can choose between many forms of entertainment, including live music, dancing, nightclubs, and a selection of movies; or they can sleep through the midnight buffet until breakfast. (Most ships have five or more distinct nightclubs.) During the night, a daily program of activities arrives at each passengers' cabin. The biggest decisions to be made for the duration of the vacation will be what to do (or not do), what to eat and when (there are usually eight separate serving times, not including the twenty-four-hour room service), and when to sleep. Service in all areas, from dining to housekeeping, is upscale and immediate. The service is so good that a common shipboard joke says that if you leave your bed during the night to visit the head (sea talk for

## EXHIBIT 1    Carnival and Holland America Ships Under Construction

| Ship | Expected Service Date (1) | Shipyard | Passenger Capacity (2) | Estimated Total Cost (3) |
|---|---|---|---|---|
| **CARNIVAL:** | | | | |
| Carnival Pride (4) | 12/01 | Masa-Yards | 2,124 | $    375 |
| Carnival Legend | 8/02 | Masa-Yards | 2,124 | 375 |
| Carnival Conquest | 12/02 | Fincantieri | 2,974 | 500 |
| Carnival Glory | 8/03 | Fincantieri | 2,974 | 500 |
| Carnival Miracle | 4/04 | Masa-Yards | 2,124 | 375 |
| Carnival Valor | 11/04 | Fincantieri | 2,974 | 500 |
|     Total Carnival | | | 15,294 | 2,625 |
| **HOLLAND AMERICA:** | | | | |
| Zuiderdam | 12/02 | Fincantieri | 1,848 | 410 |
| Oosterdam | 7/03 | Fincantieri | 1,848 | 410 |
| Newbuild | 5/04 | Fincantieri | 1,848 | 410 |
| Newbuild | 11/05 | Fincantieri | 1,848 | 410 |
|     Total Holland America | | | 7,392 | 1,640 |
| **COSTA:** | | | | |
| Costa Mediterranea | 7/03 | Masa-Yards | 2,114 | 335 |
| Costa Fortuna | 1/04 | Fincantieri | 2,720 | 390 |
| Costa Magica | 12/04 | Fincantieri | 2,720 | 390 |
|     Total Costa | | | 7,554 | 1,115 |
| **CUNARD:** | | | | |
| Queen Mary | 12/03 | Chantiers de l'Atlantique | 2,620 | 780 |
| Newbuild | 2/05 | Fincantieri | 1,968 | 410 |
|     Total Cunard | | | 4,588 | 1,190 |
|     Total | | | 34,828 | $6,570 |

*Source:* Carnival's 2001 *Annual Report,* p. 81.

bathroom), your cabin steward will have made the bed and placed chocolates on the pillow by the time you return.

After the cruise, passengers are transported back to the airport in air-conditioned buses for the flight home. Representatives of the cruise line are on hand at the airport to help cruisers meet their scheduled flights. When all amenities are considered, most vacation packages would be hard-pressed to match Carnival's per diem prices which range from $112 to $250 per person/per day, depending on accommodations. (Holland America and Seabourn are higher, ranging from $157 to $624 person/per day.) Occasional specials allow for even lower prices, and special suite accommodations can be had for an additional payment.

## CARNIVAL OPERATIONS

Carnival Corporation, headquartered in Miami, is composed of Carnival Cruise Lines; Holland America Lines, which includes Windstar Sail Cruises as a subsidiary; Holland America Westours; Westmark Hotels; Airtours; Costa; Seabourn; Gay Line of

Alaska and Seattle; and the newly created Cunard Line Limited. Carnival Cruise Lines, Inc., is a Panamanian corporation, and its subsidiaries are incorporated in Panama, the Antilles, the British Virgin Islands, Liberia, and the Bahamas. The ships are subject to inspection by the U.S. Coast Guard for compliance with the Convention for the Safety of Life at Sea (SOLAS), which requires specific structural requirements for the safety of passengers at sea, and by the U.S. Public Health Service for sanitary standards. The company is also regulated in some aspects by the Federal Maritime Commission.

At its helm, Carnival Corporation is led by the CEO and chairman of the board, Micky Arison, and by the Carnival Cruise Lines president and COO, Bob Dickinson. Mr. A. Kirk Lanterman is the president and CEO of the Holland America Cruise division, which includes Holland America Westours and Windstar Sail Cruises. (A listing of corporate officers is presented in Exhibit 2.)

The company's product positioning stems from its belief that the cruise market is actually comprised of three primary segments, with different passenger demographics, passenger characteristics, and growth requirements. The three segments are the contemporary, premium, and luxury segments. The contemporary segment is served by Carnival ships for cruises that are seven days or shorter in length and that feature a casual ambiance. The premium segment, served by Holland America, serves the seven-day-and-longer market and appeals to more affluent consumers. The luxury segment, while considerably smaller than the other segments, caters to experienced cruisers for seven-day-and-longer sailings and is served by Seabourn. Specialty sailing cruises are provided by Windstar Sail Cruises, a subsidiary of Holland America.

Corporate structure is built around the "profit center" concept and is updated periodically, when needed, for control and coordination purposes. The cruise subsidiaries of Carnival give the corporation a presence in most of the major cruise segments and provide for worldwide operations.

Carnival has always placed a high priority on marketing in an attempt to promote cruises as an alternative to land-based vacations. It wants customers to know that the ship itself is the destination and the ports of call are important, but secondary, to the cruise experience. Education and the creation of awareness are critical to corporate mar-

## EXHIBIT 2    Corporate Officers of Carnival Corporation

| Name | Age | Position |
|---|---|---|
| Richard D. Ames | 54 | Vice President-Audit Services |
| Micky Arison | 52 | Chairman of the Board of Directors and Chief Executive Officer |
| Gerald R. Cahill | 50 | Senior Vice President-Finance and Chief Financial Officer |
| Pamela C. Conover | 46 | President and Chief Operating Officer of Cunard Line Limited |
| Robert H. Dickinson | 59 | President and Chief Operating Officer of Carnival and Director |
| Kenneth D. Dubbin | 48 | Vice President-Corporate Development |
| Pier Luigi Foschi | 54 | Chairman and Chief Executive Officer of Costa Cruises, S.p.A. |
| Howard S. Frank | 60 | Vice Chairman of the Board of Directors and Chief Operating Officer |
| Ian J. Gaunt | 50 | Senior Vice President-International |
| A. Kirk Lanterman | 70 | Chairman of the Board of Directors, President, and Chief Executive Officer of Holland America Line-Westours Inc. and Director |
| Arnaldo Perez | 42 | Vice President, General Counsel and Secretary |
| Lowell Zemnick | 58 | Vice President and Treasurer |

*Source:* Carnival's 2001 *Annual Report,* p. 33.

keting efforts. Carnival was the first cruise line to successfully break away from traditional print media and to use television to reach a broader market. Even though other lines have followed Carnival's lead in selecting promotional media and approximate Carnival's budget in total advertising expenditures, the organization still leads all cruise competitors in advertising and marketing expenditures.

Carnival wants to remain the leader and innovator in the cruise industry, and works to accomplish this goal with sophisticated promotional efforts and by trying to gain the loyalty of former cruisers, by refurbishing ships, by varying activities and ports of call, and by being innovative in all aspects of ship operations. Management intends to build on the theme of the ship as a destination, given its past success with this promotional effort.

## FINANCIAL PERFORMANCE

The consolidated financial statements for Carnival Cruise Lines, Inc., are shown in Exhibits 3 and 4, and selected financial data are presented in Exhibit 5.

By the end of fiscal 2001, Carnival had outstanding long-term debt of $2.9 billion. According to the Internal Revenue Code of 1986, Carnival is considered a "controlled foreign corporation (CFC)" since 50 percent of its stock is held by individuals who are residents

---

EXHIBIT 3    Carnival Corp. Consolidated Statements of Operations (in thousands, except earnings per share)

| | Years Ended November 30, | | |
| --- | --- | --- | --- |
| | *2001* | *2000* | *1999* |
| **REVENUES** | $4,535,751 | $3,778,542 | 3,497,470 |
| Costs and Expenses | | | |
| Operating | 2,468,730 | 2,058,342 | 1,862,636 |
| Selling and administrative | 618,664 | 487,403 | 447,235 |
| Depreciation and amortization | 372,224 | 287,667 | 243,658 |
| Impairment charge | 140,378 | | |
| | 3,599,996 | 2,833,412 | 2,553,529 |
| Operating Income Before (Loss) Income From Affiliated Operations | 935,755 | 945,130 | 943,941 |
| (Loss) Income From Affiliated Operations, Net | (44,024) | 37,828 | 75,758 |
| **OPERATING INCOME** | 891,731 | 982,958 | 1,019,699 |
| Nonoperating Income (Expense) | | | |
| Interest income | 34,255 | 16,506 | 41,932 |
| Interest expense, net of capitalized interest | (120,692) | (41,372) | (46,956) |
| Other income, net | 108,649 | 8,460 | 29,357 |
| Income tax benefit (expense) | 12,257 | (1,094) | (2,778) |
| Minority interest | | | (14,014) |
| | 34,469 | (17,500) | 7,541 |
| **NET INCOME** | $ 926,200 | $ 965,458 | $1,027,240 |
| Earnings Per Share: | | | |
| Basic | $1.58 | $1.61 | $1.68 |
| Diluted | $1.58 | $1.60 | $1.66 |

*Source:* Carnival's 2001 *Annual Report,* p 69.

EXHIBIT 4    Carnival Corp. Consolidated Balance Sheets (in thousands, except par value)

| | November 30, | |
|---|---|---|
| | *2001* | *2000* |
| **ASSETS** | | |
| Current Assets | | |
| | $ 1,421,300 | $ 189,282 |
| Short-term investments | 36,784 | 5,470 |
| Accounts receivable, net | 90,763 | 95,361 |
| Inventories | 91,996 | 100,451 |
| Prepaid expenses and other | 113,798 | 158,918 |
| Fair value of hedged firm commitments | 204,347 | |
| Total current assets | 1,958,988 | 549,482 |
| Property and Equipment, Net | 8,390,230 | 8,001,318 |
| Investments in and Advances to Affiliates | | 437,391 |
| Goodwill, less Accumulated Amortization of | 651,814 | 701,385 |
| $117,791 and $99,670 | | |
| Other Assets | 188,915 | 141,744 |
| Fair Value of Hedged Firm Commitments | 373,605 | |
| | $11,563,552 | $9,831,320 |
| **LIABILITIES AND SHAREHOLDERS' EQUITY** | | |
| Current Liabilities | | |
| Current portion of long-term debt | $    21,764 | $  248,219 |
| Accounts payable | 269,467 | 332,694 |
| Accrued liabilities | 298,032 | 302,585 |
| Customer deposits | 627,698 | 770,425 |
| Dividends payable | 61,548 | 61,371 |
| Fair value of derivative contracts | 201,731 | |
| Total current liabilities | 1,480,240 | 1,715,294 |
| Long-Term Debt | 2,954,854 | 2,099,077 |
| Deferred Income and Other Long-Term Liabilities | 157,998 | 146,332 |
| Fair Value of Derivative Contracts | 379,683 | |
| Commitments and Contingencies (Notes 7 and 8) | | |
| Shareholders' Equity | | |
| Common stock; $.01 par value; 960,000 shares authorized; | | |
| 620,019 and 617,568 shares issued | 6,200 | 6,176 |
| Additional paid-in capital | 1,805,248 | 1,772,897 |
| Retained earnings | 5,556,296 | 4,884,023 |
| Unearned stock compensation | (12,398) | (12,283) |
| Accumulated other comprehensive loss | (36,932) | (75,059) |
| Treasury stock; 33,848 and 33,087 shares at cost | (727,637) | (705,137) |
| Total shareholders' equity | 6,590,777 | 5,870,617 |
| | $11,563,552 | $9,831,320 |

*Source:* Carnival's 2001 *Annual Report*, p. 68.

of foreign countries and its countries of incorporation exempt shipping operations of U.S. citizens from income tax. Because of its CFC status, Carnival expects that all of its income (with the exception of U.S. source income from the transportation, hotel, and tour businesses of Holland America) will be exempt from U.S. federal income taxes at the corporate level.

EXHIBIT 5    Carnival Selected Financial Data

|  | Revenues | Operating Income (Loss) |
|---|---|---|
| **2001** | | |
| Cruise | $4,357,942 | $   958,273 |
| Tour | 229,483 | (10,357) |
| Affiliated operations (d) | | (44,024) |
| Intersegment elimination | (51,674) | |
| Corporate (e) | | (12,161) |
| | $4,535,751 | $   891,731 |
| **2000** | | |
| Cruise | $3,578,372 | $   957,226 |
| Tour | 259,662 | 7,664 |
| Affiliated operations | | 37,828 |
| Intersegment elimination | (59,492) | |
| Corporate (e) | | (19,760) |
| | $3,778,542 | $   982,958 |
| **1999** | | |
| Cruise | $3,286,701 | $   947,452 |
| Tour | 271,828 | 10,403 |
| Affiliated operations | | 75,758 |
| Intersegment elimination | (61,059) | |
| Corporate (e) | | (13,914) |
| | $3,497,470 | $1,019,699 |

*Source:* Carnival's 2001 *Annual Report,* p. 86.

The primary financial consideration of importance to Carnival management involves the control of costs, both fixed and variable, for the maintenance of a healthy profit margin. Carnival has the lowest breakeven point of any organization in the cruise industry (ships break even at approximately 60 percent of capacity) due to operational experience and economies of scale. Unfortunately, fixed costs, including depreciation, fuel, insurance, port charges, and crew costs, which represent more than 33 percent of the company's operating expenses, cannot be significantly reduced in relation to declines

EXHIBIT 6    Carnival's Revenues and Assets by Region

|  | 2001 | 2000 | 1999 |
|---|---|---|---|
| Revenues: | | | |
| United States | $ 3,489,913 | $3,180,667 | $2,934,492 |
| Foreign | 1,045,838 | 597,875 | 562,978 |
| | $ 4,535,751 | $3,778,542 | $3,497,470 |
| Assets: | | | |
| United States | $ 2,040,145 | $   680,897 | $1,063,963 |
| Foreign | 9,523,407 | 9,150,423 | 7,222,392 |
| | $11,563,552 | $9,831,320 | $8,286,355 |

*Source:* Carnival's 2001 *Annual Report,* p. 87.

in passenger loads and aggregate passenger ticket revenue. (Major expense items are air fares [25–30 percent], travel agent fees [10 percent], and labor [13–15 percent]. Increases in these costs could negatively affect the profitability of the organization.

## PRINCIPLE SUBSIDIARIES

### Carnival Cruise Lines

At the end of fiscal 2001, Carnival operated 16 ships, with a total berth capacity of 41,192. Carnival principally operates in the Caribbean and has an assortment of ships and ports of call serving the three, four, and seven-day cruise markets.

Each ship is a floating resort and includes a full maritime staff, shopkeepers and casino operators, entertainers, and a complete hotel staff. Approximately 14 percent of corporate revenue is generated from shipboard activities such as casino operations, liquor sales, and gift shop items. At various ports of call, passengers can also take advantage of tours, shore excursions, and duty-free shopping at their own expense.

Shipboard operations are designed to provide maximum entertainment, activities, and service. The size of the company and the similarity in design of the new cruise ships have allowed Carnival to achieve various economies of scale, and management is very cost-conscious.

Although the Carnival Cruise Lines division is increasing its presence in the shorter-cruise markets, its general marketing strategy is to use three, four, or seven-day, moderately priced cruises to fit the time and budget constraints of the middle class. Shorter cruises can cost less than $500 per person (depending on accommodations), but up to roughly $3,000 per person in a luxury suite on a seven-day cruise (costs include port charges). (Per diem rates for shorter cruises are slightly higher, on average, than per diem rates for seven-day cruises.) Average rates per day are approximately $180, excluding gambling, liquor and soft drinks, and items of a personal nature. Guests are expected to tip the cabin steward and waiter at a suggested rate of $3 per person/per day, and the busboy at $1.50 per person/per day.

Some 99 percent of all Carnival cruises are sold through travel agents, who receive a standard commission of 10 percent (15 percent in Florida). Carnival works extensively with travel agents to help promote cruises as an alternative to a Disney or European vacation. In addition to training travel agents from nonaffiliated travel/vacation firms to sell cruises, a special group of employees regularly visits travel agents posing as prospective clients. Travel agents who specify a Carnival cruise before other options receive $100 on the spot. In calendar year 2000, Carnival took reservations from about twenty-nine thousand of the approximately forty-five thousand travel agencies in the United States and Canada, and no one travel agency accounted for more than 2 percent of Carnival revenues.

On-board service is labor intensive, employing help from some fifty-one nations—mostly developing countries—with reasonable returns to employees. For example, waiters on the *Jubilee* can earn approximately $18,000 to $27,000 per year (base salary and tips), significantly greater than could be earned in their home countries for similar employment. Waiters typically work ten hours per day, with approximately one day off per week for a specified contract period (usually three to nine months). Carnival records show that employees remain with the company for approximately eight years and that applicants exceed demand for all cruise positions. Nonetheless, the American Maritime union has cited Carnival (and other cruise operators) several times for exploitation of its crew.

## Holland America Lines

On January 17, 1989, Carnival acquired all of the outstanding stock of HAL Antillen N.V. from Holland America Lines N.V. for $625 million in cash. Carnival financed the purchase through $250 million in retained earnings (cash account) and borrowed the other $375 million from banks at .25 percent over the prime rate. Carnival received the assets and operations of the Holland America Lines, Westours, Westmark Hotels, and Windstar Sail Cruises. Holland America currently has ten cruise ships, with a capacity of 13,348 berths, but new ships are to be delivered in the future.

Founded in 1873, Holland America Lines is an upscale line (it charges an average of 25 percent more than similar Carnival cruises) with principal destinations in Alaska during the summer months and the Caribbean during the fall and winter, with some worldwide cruises of up to ninety-eight days. Holland America targets an older, more sophisticated cruiser and offers fewer youth-oriented activities. On Holland America ships, passengers can dance to the sounds of the Big Band era and avoid the discos of Carnival ships. Passengers on Holland America ships enjoy more service (the ships have a higher staff-to-passenger ratio than Carnival) and have more cabin and public space per person as well as a no tipping shipboard policy. Holland America has not enjoyed the spectacular growth of Carnival, but it has sustained constant growth in the 1980s and 1990s with high occupancy rates. The operation of these ships and the structure of the crew is similar to the Carnival cruise ship model, and the acquisition of the line gave the Carnival Corporation a presence in the Alaskan market, where it had none before.

Holland America Westours is the largest tour operator in Alaska and the Canadian Rockies, and it provides vacation synergy with Holland America cruises. The transportation division of Westours includes motor coaches, which consist of the Gray Line of Alaska, the Gray Line of Seattle, Westours motor coaches, the McKinley Explorer railroad coaches, and three-day boats for tours to glaciers and other points of interest. Carnival management believes that Alaskan cruises and tours should increase in the future due to a number of factors, including the fact that the aging population wants relaxing vacations with scenic beauty and the fact that Alaska is a U.S. destination.

Westmark Hotels consists of sixteen hotels in Alaska and the Yukon territories, and it also provides synergy with cruise operations and Westours. Westmark owns the largest group of hotels in the region, providing moderately priced rooms for the vacationer.

Windstar Sail Cruises was acquired by Holland America Lines in 1988 and consists of four computer-controlled sailing vessels with a berth capacity of 756. Windstar is very upscale and offers an alternative to traditional cruise liners, with a more intimate, activity-oriented cruise. The ships operate primarily in the Mediterranean and the South Pacific, visiting ports not accessible to large cruise ships. Although catering to a small segment of the cruise vacation industry, Windstar helps with Carnival's commitment to participate in all segments of the cruise industry.

## Seabourn Cruise Lines

In April 1992, Carnival acquired 25 percent of the capital stock of Seabourn. As part of the transaction, the company also made a subordinated secured ten-year loan of $15 million to Seabourn and a $10 million convertible loan to Seabourn. In December 1995, the $10 million convertible loan was converted by the company into an additional 25 percent equity interest in Seabourn. In 2000, the company took full ownership of Cunard Line Limited, which owns Cunard and Seabourn.

Seabourn targets the luxury market with three vessels with a capacity of two-hundred passengers per ship; each ship provides all-suite accommodations. Seabourn is considered the Rolls Royce of the cruise industry, and in 1992 it was named the "World's Best Cruise Line" by the prestigious Condé Naste Traveler's Fifth Annual Readers Choice poll. Seabourn cruises the Americas, Europe, Scandinavia, the Mediterranean, and the Far East.

### Airtours

In April 1996, Carnival acquired a 29.5 percent interest in Airtours for approximately $307 million. Airtours along with its subsidiaries is the largest air-inclusive tour operator in the world and is publicly traded on the London Stock Exchange. Airtours provides air-inclusive packaged holidays to the British, Scandinavian, and North American markets. Airtours provides holidays to approximately 5 million people per year and owns or operates thirty-two hotels, two cruise ships, and thirty-one aircraft.

Airtours operates nineteen aircraft (two additional aircraft began service in the spring of 2000) exclusively for its United Kingdom tour operators, providing a large proportion of their flying requirements. In addition, Airtours' subsidiary Premiair operates a fleet of fourteen aircraft, which provide most of the flying requirements for Airtours' Scandinavian tour operators.

Airtours owns or operates thirty-two hotels (6,500 rooms) which provide rooms to Airtours' tour operators principally in the Mediterranean and the Canary Islands. In addition, Airtours has a 50 percent interest in Tenerife Sol, a joint venture with Sol Hotels Group of Spain, which owns and operates three additional hotels in the Canary Islands that provide 1,300 rooms.

Through its subsidiary, Sun Cruises, Airtours owns and operates four cruise ships. The ships operate in the Mediterranean, the Caribbean, and around the Canary Islands, and they are booked exclusively by Airtours' tour operators.

### Costa Crociere S.p.A.

In June 1997, Carnival and Airtours purchased the equity securities of Costa from the Costa family at a cost of approximately $141 million, and they completed the purchase of the remainder of the company in September 2000. Costa is headquartered in Italy and is considered to be Europe's largest cruise line, with seven ships and a 9,200 passenger capacity. Costa operates primarily in the Mediterranean, Northern Europe, the Caribbean, and South America. The major market for Costa is southern Europe, mainly Italy, Spain, and France.

## FUTURE CONSIDERATIONS

Carnival's management will have to continue to monitor several strategic factors and issues for the next few years. The industry itself should see further consolidation through mergers and buyouts, and the expansion of the industry could negatively affect the profitability of various cruise operators. Another factor of concern to management is how to reach the large North American market, of which only 10 percent to 12 percent have ever taken a cruise.

With the industry maturing, cruise competitors have become more sophisticated in their marketing efforts, and price competition is the norm in most cruise segments. Royal Caribbean Cruise Lines has also instituted a major shipbuilding program and is successfully challenging Carnival Cruise Lines in the contemporary segment. The announcement that the Walt Disney Company was entering the cruise market with two eighty thousand ton cruise liners in 1998 could significantly affect the family cruise vacation segment.

The increasing industry capacity is also a source of concern to cruise operators. The slow growth in industry demand is occurring during a period when industry berth capacity continues to grow. The entry of Disney into the field and the ships already on order by current operators will increase industry berth capacity by over ten thousand per year through 2006, a significant increase. The danger lies in cruise operators using the price weapon in their marketing campaigns to fill cabins. If cruise operators cannot make a reasonable return on investment, operating costs will have to be reduced (affecting quality of services) to maintain profitability. This will increase the likelihood of further industry acquisitions, mergers, and consolidations. A worst case scenario would be the financial failure of weaker lines.

Still, Carnival's management believes that demand should increase well into the 2000s. Considering that only 12 percent of the population in the North American market has taken a cruise vacation, reaching more of the North American target market would improve industry profitability. Industry analysts state that the problem is that an assessment of market potential is only an educated guess. What if the current demand figures are not reflective of the future? The recessionary economic conditions in the United States coupled with travelers' reluctance to travel due to terrorist threats concern analysts.

# ROYAL CARIBBEAN CRUISES, LTD.—2002

**Lenessa E. Hawkins**
**Francis Marion University**

RCL

www.royalcaribbean.com, www.celebrity-cruises.com, www.rclinvestor.com

"Get on board because the fate of our industry is at stake and with it the fate of our country," Air Transport Association president and CEO Carol Hallett said on October 2, 2001. She further stated that safety was the number one priority to get the public traveling again. These comments were made to delegates gathered at a Cruise Industry Conference in Florida soon after the World Trade Center and Pentagon attacks on September 11, 2001. With the economy slowing and capacity increasing every day, the cruise industry now has—and continues to have—a potentially disastrous issue with which to deal: Empty cabins.

In the aftermath of the tragic events, airports were closed. Some travelers were not able to meet their ships, some were unable to disembark, and some were able to leave their ship but had no means of getting back home. An analyst predicts that cancellations alone could result in a $2 million loss in revenue by the cruise industry. Cancellations the week following the attacks totaled nearly 1,000 for Royal Caribbean Cruises, Ltd., based in Miami, Florida. The company's share price fell 40 percent, or $8.42, from $21.18 to $12.76 in the week following the attacks, and the company lost $20 million to $25 million that week alone when bookings fell to 50 percent of the prior week's totals. Immediately following the attacks, new bookings dropped by more than 50 percent over prior-year levels. But within days, booking levels began to improve, and by the first week in October, new booking levels had almost recovered to their prior-year levels.

After the September 11, 2001, attacks, Royal Caribbean Cruises, Ltd. almost immediately redeployed ships which were docked at New York ports and several overseas ports to other North American ports such as Baltimore, New Orleans, and Galveston, Texas. Cruise lines dropped cruise prices to levels that shocked veteran travel agents. Royal Caribbean Cruises increased travel agent commissions from 10 percent to 20 percent after a five-hundred employee layoff in October 2001. These attempts to keep capacity above 90 percent have pushed the industry into a pricing war. Some cruises are being booked at $99 per day, which will make it a bargain comparable to hotel rates that average the same or higher.

Royal Caribbean launched four huge new ships in 2001, comprising 9,250 new berths. Company revenues increased 9.7 percent to $3.1 billion but net income dropped sharply to $254 million.

## CRUISE INDUSTRY HISTORY

In the early 1950s, after the arrival of air transportation service between Europe and North America, large transatlantic liner companies sought an alternate use for their ships. Shipping lines renovated their large ocean liners for leisure cruising and, to appeal to the traveling public's desire for exotic travel and exploration, deployed them to more tropical climates, calmer seas, and extraordinary ports of call. The early 1970s saw the incorporation of companies such as Royal Caribbean, Norwegian Cruise Lines, Carnival Cruise Lines as well as the arrival of European-based companies such as Peninsular and Oriental (future Princess Cruises), Cunard, and Chandris (which would become Celebrity Cruises). In the next decade, the industry matured and became a solid participant in the leisure industry. As the cruise industry grew, companies built larger ships and reduced prices in order to appeal to a broader mix of passengers. In order to draw a wider audience, the companies introduced new ships that offered a variety of entertainment options such as bars, lounges, libraries, spas, workout facilities, and business centers. With the larger ships came additional capacity, which expanded the industry's passenger loads by 60 percent between 1990 and 1999.

With introduction of modern 3,000 plus passenger vessels in the Caribbean and Europe, Carnival, Royal Caribbean, and Princess Cruises have all seen an increase in their profit margins. In addition to new ship construction, better product positioning, changes in demographics, a healthy economy, and a wider range of cruise lengths and departure points also fueled swift growth in the industry. In keeping with the main marketing focus of cruise lines—namely, that the ship itself is the true destination—cruise lines offered passengers a floating resort where the amenities and conveniences rivaled that of land facilities.

Cruise passenger counts have grown in proportion to the industry's growth. The Cruise Line International Association (CLIA) predicted that North American passenger levels would surpass 7 million by year-end 2001 and these projections were indeed accurate. With the cruise industry only attracting 2 percent of the entire leisure/travel market, there is a market potential of $85 billion over the next five years.

Royal Caribbean Cruises, Ltd., like other cruise companies, is positioned for major growth in the industry. To date, only 12.3 percent of Americans have ever taken a cruise, which leaves a tremendous untapped market available for cruise lines to attract. There is an untapped market not only in the United States, but also around the world. Prior to September 11, 2001, there was a major push by leading cruise lines to expand their fleets, in order to increase capacity worldwide. Now the major cruise lines have lowered their rates in a desperate attempt to draw customers.

After the Chapter 11 bankruptcy of Renaissance Cruises and in the wake of other earnings warnings, industry analysts expect larger, financially stronger cruise companies to increase their market shares, while small, weaker companies try to survive. Occupancy rates for recent voyages of Carnival Corporation, Royal Caribbean Cruises, Ltd., and Peninsular and Oriental (P&O) Princess Cruises, PLC, were reported to be around 97.7, 97, and 92 percent, respectively, whereas the companies normally report rates of over 100 percent.

## COMPANY HISTORY

Royal Caribbean Cruises, Ltd. is a foreign corporation operating in the United States that is exempt from U.S. income tax. The company was incorporated on July 23, 1985, in the Republic of Liberia under the Business Corporation Act of Liberia, but its principal executive offices are located in Miami, Florida. The original company, Royal Caribbean International, was founded in 1968, and the maiden voyage of its first ship, *Song of Norway,* occurred on November 7, 1970. In 1971, the *Nordic Prince* joined the Royal Caribbean fleet, and the *Sun Viking* followed in 1972. Royal Caribbean pioneered the concept of air/sea vacations by flying passengers to Miami from all over North America. When demand exceeded supply, management pursued an innovative strategy by slicing two of its ships apart and adding eighty-five-foot additions to each midsection. This innovation allowed the *Song of Norway* and *Nordic Prince* to emerge larger and more streamlined—and with a wider array of amenities. Introduced in 1982, the *Song of America*, the first of a new generation of large cruise ships, featured a Viking Crown Lounge that was wrapped completely around the funnel, a design soon emulated by other cruise lines. Royal Caribbean developed a long-range expansion plan when the cruise industry boomed in the 1980s. The arrival of *Sovereign of the Seas* in 1988 signaled the beginning of a growth period that saw Royal Caribbean triple in size between 1988 and 1992. In 1991, Royal Caribbean introduced CruiseMatch 2000, the travel industry's first fully automated cruise vacation reservations system. By the end of 1991, more than 25,000 travel agent CRS (Central Reservations System) users had access to this remarkable cruise booking system.

Royal Caribbean International's second expansion program occurred between 1995 and 1998 when it ordered six Vision-class vessels ranging in size from 1,804 to 2,000 berths. Royal Caribbean sold four of its original, older vessels, which were no longer consistent with its image and marketing strategy. More recently, now in the third phase of its expansion and featuring the Voyager-class and Radiance-class vessels, Royal Caribbean launched the *Voyager of the Seas* and *Explorer of the Seas* in November 1999 and October 2000, respectively. There are three additional Voyager-class vessels on order. Delivery of *Radiance of the Seas* in March 2001 marked the debut of the first of four Radiance-class vessels on order. However, the company exercised its options and delayed the purchase of additional Radiance-class vessels in December 2000 and June 2001.

Royal Caribbean Cruises, Ltd. acquired Celebrity in July 1997. Celebrity Cruises' first capital expansion program occurred between 1995 and 1997, during which period it added three Century-class vessels and disposed of one of its three original ships. Currently engaged in its second capital expansion program, Celebrity took delivery of *Millennium* and *Infinity* in June 2000 and February 2001, respectively. Two additional Millennium-class vessels are on order. In March 2000, Royal Caribbean announced the formation of a new tour company, Royal Celebrity Tours, which offers premium land tour programs in Alaska for guests traveling under the Royal Caribbean International and Celebrity Cruises brands. Royal Caribbean also entered into a strategic alliance and joint venture (to launch a European cruise line) with First Choice Holidays PLC, one of the United Kingdom's largest tour operators. Celebrity Cruises primarily serves the premium segment of the cruise vacation market. Celebrity Cruises operates seven cruise ships with 12,294 berths, and it offers various itineraries that range from five to fifteen nights. Modern vessels, gourmet dining and service, extensive and luxurious spa facilities, large staterooms, and a high staff-to-guest ratio are hallmarks of the premium cruise vacation market.

Celebrity Cruises is expanding its fleet to provide an increasing variety of itineraries and cruise lengths, and it, therefore, has deployed a higher proportion of its fleet in seasonal markets (i.e., Alaska, Bermuda, Europe, and South America) than does the Royal Caribbean International brand. Key selling points for Celebrity Cruises are its award winning gourmet cuisine; Aquaspa (SM), billed as "The Most Sophisticated Spa at Sea"; stylish, trendy clubs; spacious luxury suites; and museum-quality contemporary art.

## INTERNAL OPERATIONS

Royal Caribbean is the world's second largest cruise company, with 25 cruise ships that have 45,854 berths. Both Royal Caribbean International and Celebrity Cruises offer a wide array of shipboard activities, services, and amenities, including swimming pools, sun decks, beauty salons, exercise and massage facilities, lounges, bars, showtime entertainment, retail shopping, and cinemas. Royal Caribbean ships offer a selection of destinations throughout the world: Alaska, Australia, the Bahamas, and Canada. As seen in the segmented data presented in Exhibit 1, Royal Caribbean's revenues earned from non-American consumers decreased from 82 percent in 2000 to 70 percent of total revenues in 2001.

Royal Caribbean International's volume cruise vacation market is categorized into two segments: contemporary and premium. The Royal Caribbean International brand operates 19 cruise ships with 39,182 berths, offering many itineraries that range from two to sixteen nights and include destinations worldwide. Along with varying itineraries, Royal Caribbean International also offers a variety of shore excursions at each port of call, multiple options for on-board dining, entertainment, and other on-board activities. Key selling points for Royal Caribbean International are it spectacular ships, choice itineraries, consistent quality, and on-board programs.

In 2000, Royal Caribbean Cruises, Ltd. formed sales and marketing alliances in the United Kingdom and Europe with an investment in First Choice Holidays PLC, one of the United Kingdom's largest integrated tour operators. Royal Caribbean also entered into a joint venture with First Choice Holidays to launch a European cruise line. First Choice Holidays PLC brings a large distribution base, several well-known brand outlets, and a new distribution technology to the alliance. Royal Caribbean provides special training and promotional material to assist with the distribution of both the Royal Caribbean International and Celebrity Cruises brands in the United Kingdom. The new cruise brand, called Island, is set to target the European mass market. The *Viking Serenade* has been slated to be the first ship to be operated by the new cruise line. It will be renamed and then deployed out of the Mediterranean in the summer and the Caribbean in the winter.

In 2001, Royal Caribbean also established a partnership with Abercrombie & Kent (A&K) a top-ranked tour and safari outfitter in Europe. A&K will be providing pre- and postcruise land tours for interested cruise guests. These strategies will help Royal Caribbean Cruises to gain market share in the land tour market. Land tours are vacation packages that feature travel between various destinations by tour bus, railcar, and other forms of land transportation.

After assessment and encouragement from travel partners and guests regarding a need for land-based tour opportunities, Royal Caribbean announced a new tour company in March 2000, Royal Celebrity Tours. This new company was created to enhance vacation products in Alaska by offering premium land-tour programs for guests traveling on Royal Caribbean Cruises or Celebrity Cruises brands.

According to Royal Caribbean's vision statement, the company's goal is "to empower and enable our employees to deliver the best vacation experience to our guests, thereby generating superior returns for our shareholders, and enhancing the well-being of our communities." After the resignation of Richard Sasso, former president of

EXHIBIT 1    Royal Caribbean Cruises, Ltd.—Domestic vs. Global Revenue (%)

| Years | 2001 | 2000 | 1999 | 1998 |
|---|---|---|---|---|
| United States | 70% | 82% | 83% | 84% |
| All other countries | 30% | 18% | 17% | 16% |

*Source:* Royal Caribbean's 2001 *Annual Report.*

Celebrity Cruises, Royal Caribbean's organizational structure looks like the organizational chart presented in Exhibit 2, when Jack L. Williams was named president of both Royal Caribbean International and Celebrity Cruises.

Royal Caribbean has pursued expansion in spite of taking on a high debt load to finance the purchase of both new ships and their latest acquisitions. Royal Caribbean Cruises, Ltd. is heavily leveraged, with a long-term debt of over 5.4 billion. The consolidated balance sheet in Exhibit 3 provides more information.

## Natural Environment

As the result of several violations of various cruise lines, member cruise lines of the International Council of Cruise Lines (ICCL) must meet or exceed their recycling and waste discharge guidelines, beginning July 1, 2001. Alaskan legislators are considering a tax of $50 per cruise ship passenger as well. Most cruise lines have accepted the new guidelines because they have already started adopting ways to combat the problems, but all oppose the new tax by Alaskan legislators.

Royal Caribbean Cruises has significantly improved its image. In 1999, the company was fined $18 million and pled guilty to twenty-one felony counts for dumping oil and dangerous chemicals into the ocean and for illegally storing hazardous wastes. In January 2000, Royal Caribbean agreed to pay Alaska $3.5 million for dumping toxic chemicals and oil-contaminated water into the state's waters. Today, Royal Caribbean is a leader in innovative improvements in its approach to environmental concerns. Royal Caribbean Cruises is the first cruise line to invest in $32 million gas turbine engines. These engines produce almost smokeless emissions. Two Celebrity Cruises ships treat gray water using a new $1.8 million Rochem system of reverse osmosis. Royal Caribbean is *required* to discharge treated black water at least four nautical miles from shore, but it has adopted an even *stricter* discharge standard: It will not discharge wastes any closer than twelve nautical miles from shore. This "Above and Beyond Compliance" approach,

---

EXHIBIT 2    Royal Caribbean Cruises, Ltd. Organizational Chart—2001

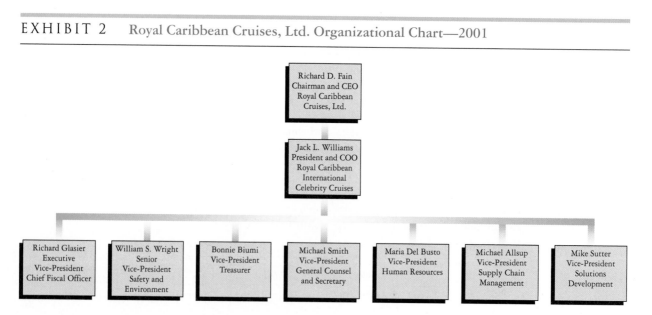

*Source:* Adapted from Royal Caribbean's 2001 *Annual Report*, p. 52.

EXHIBIT 3    Consolidated Balance Sheets (*in thousands, except per-share data*)

| | As of December 31, | |
| --- | --- | --- |
| | *2001* | *2000* |
| **ASSETS** | | |
| **Current Assets** | | |
| Cash and cash equivalents | $  727,178 | $  177,810 |
| Trade and other receivables, net | 72,196 | 53,609 |
| Inventories | 33,493 | 30,115 |
| Prepaid expenses and other assets | 53,247 | 49,185 |
| Total current assets | 886,114 | 310,719 |
| **Property and Equipment**—at cost less accumulated depreciation and amortization | 8,605,448 | 6,831,809 |
| **Goodwill**—less accumulated amortization of $138,606 and $128,192, respectively | 278,561 | 288,974 |
| **Other Assets** | 598,659 | 396,963 |
| | $10,368,782 | $7,828,465 |
| **LIABILITIES AND SHAREHOLDERS' EQUITY** | | |
| **Current Liabilities** | | |
| Current portion of long-term debt | $  238,581 | $  109,926 |
| Accounts payable | 144,070 | 158,143 |
| Accrued expenses and other liabilities | 283,913 | 200,900 |
| Customer deposits | 446,085 | 443,411 |
| Total current liabilities | 1,112,649 | 912,380 |
| **Long-Term Debt** | 5,407,531 | 3,300,170 |
| **Other Long-Term Liabilities** | 92,018 | — |
| **Commitments and Contingencies (Note 12)** | | |
| **Shareholders' Equity** | | |
| Common stock ($.01 par value; 500,000,000 shares authorized; 192,310,198 and 192,122,088 shares issued) | 1,923 | 1,921 |
| Paid-in capital | 2,045,904 | 2,043,111 |
| Retained earnings | 1,731,423 | 1,576,921 |
| Accumulated other comprehensive loss | (16,068) | — |
| Treasury stock (475,524 and 435,180 common shares at cost) | (6,598) | (6,038) |
| Total shareholders' equity | 3,756,584 | 3,615,915 |
| | $10,368,782 | $7,828,465 |

*Source:* Royal Caribbean's 2001 *Annual Report,* p. 39.

among other strategies, has earned Royal Caribbean the Greater Miami Chamber of Commerce's 2001 Environmental Business Practices Award.

E-Commerce

Royal Caribbean's Web sites enable visitors to book travel, explore destinations, and view media presentations. In 2000, Royal Caribbean International was the first cruise line to install Internet centers, Royal Caribbean Online, on its fleet of ships. Celebrity Cruises will follow with Online@CelebrityCruises by the end of 2001. Royal Caribbean has introduced Web sites developed by eCompanyStore for the purchase of branded apparel and accessories. Visitors may follow links from the company's Web sites to purchase items that until now were only available on board the ships. Travel agents and other visitors may purchase items for incentives and promotions as well.

## EXTERNAL AFFAIRS

The cruise industry is the fastest growing segment of the travel industry and has experienced 1,000 percent growth since 1970. Nearly 88 percent of North Americans have never been on a cruise. With 6.91 million North American cruisers in the year 2001, cruise lines offer something for everyone. Newly designed cruise ships are larger and more efficient. Higher revenues are realized by the configuration of cabins and public spaces. With 70 more cruise ships under construction or on order, with deliveries by 2006, the worldwide fleet of cruise ships could then carry 17 million passengers annually.

Royal Caribbean expects to increase its share of the market by preparing itself for the influx of supply. Several markets overseas have been studied for new cruise routes, such as France, Italy, and Germany. The United Kingdom is now the second largest cruise market in the world after North America. Europe and the Mediterranean were the fastest growing cruise regions during 2000, accounting for 15 percent of all cruises. Fifty percent of all adults dream of taking a cruise, with the highest interest exhibited by the emerging baby boomer category. The target market consists of passengers under the age of fifty-five.

Travel agencies supply the cruise industry with a distribution system. Travel agents are paid a commission on bookings by cruise lines. Cruise sales are now in second place behind air ticket sales in generation of income and profits for many agents. Travel agents sell over 95 percent of all cruises, according to the CLIA. Generating a high repeat rate, cruises are profitable to sell. Agencies that place an emphasis on selling cruises and on training personnel are the most successful and productive. Good relations with travel agencies enhance the growth of the cruise industry.

Currently, there has been an increase of bookings via the Internet. Some 60.5 million consumers are expected to use the Internet to make travel plans in 2001, up from 25 million in 1996, according to the Travel Industry Association of America. In 2002, that number is expected to increase to 71.9 million. Twenty percent of those making plans will actually make a purchase for travel online. Of those 20 percent, 44 percent are ages 18 to 34 and 48 percent are ages 35 to 54.

Public demand for travel/leisure options is directly influenced by the economic situation of travelers. With job cuts and an uncertainty regarding the recession, Americans are searching for more affordable ways to spend their vacations. Some travelers are choosing to make short day trips or to stay at home during their vacation in order to cut back on spending. The cruise lines compete with other travel alternatives, such as land-based resorts and touring destinations, for consumers' disposable spending dollars. The cruise industry is particularly cyclical as well, with peak demand during the summer months.

EXHIBIT 4    Royal Caribbean's Selected Statistical Information (unaudited)

|  | 2001 | 2000 | 1999 |
|---|---|---|---|
| Guests Carried | 2,438,849 | 2,049,902 | 1,704,034 |
| Guest Cruise Days | 15,341,570 | 13,019,811 | 11,227,196 |
| Occupancy Percentage | 101.8% | 104.4% | 104.7% |

*Source:* Royal Caribbean's 2001 *Annual Report*, p. 29.

## EXHIBIT 5    Royal Caribbean's Fleet Expansion

Our current fleet expansion program encompasses three distinct vessel designs known as the Voyager-class, Millennium-class and Radiance-class. Since 1999, we have taken delivery of three Voyager, three Millennium and one Radiance class vessels. We currently operate 22 ships with 45,854 berths. We have six ships on order. The planned berths and expected delivery dates of the ships on order are as follows:

| Vessel | Expected Delivery Date | Berths |
|---|---|---|
| **Royal Caribbean International** | | |
| Voyager-class: | | |
| *Navigator of the Seas* | 1st Quarter 2003 | 3,114 |
| *Mariner of the Seas* | 1st Quarter 2004 | 3,114 |
| Radiance-class:[1] | | |
| *Brilliance of the Seas* | 3rd Quarter 2002 | 2,100 |
| *Serenode of the Seas*[2] | 4th Quarter 2003 | 2,100 |
| *Jewel of the Seas*[2] | 2nd Quarter 2004 | 2,100 |
| **Celebrity Cruises** | | |
| Millennium-class: | | |
| *Constellation* | 2nd Quarter 2002 | 2,034 |

[1]We have two options on Radiance-class vessels with delivery dates in the third quarters of 2005 and 2006.
[2]These two ships are committed to the new southern European joint venture with P&O Princess.
*Source:* Royal Caribbean's 2001 *Annual Report,* p. 30.

As seen in the weeks following the World Trade Center and Pentagon attacks, terrorist attacks, war, and political uprisings directly affect the cruise industry. If consumers do not feel safe or have qualms about their travel options, they will choose to stay at home or seek alternatives as precautions.

## Competitors

### Carnival

Carnival is the largest and most profitable cruise company in the world. Carnival owns Carnival Cruise Lines, Holland America Line, Costa Cruises, Cunard Line, Seabourn Cruise Line, and Windstar Cruises. The company's cruise lines operate forty-four ships with voyages from two to seventeen days in length—from a variety of North American homeports to the Bahamas, the Caribbean, Mexican Riviera, Alaska, Hawaii, the Panama Canal, New England, the Canadian Maritimes, Bermuda, and Europe.

Carnival uses an exclusive marketing alliance established in October 1998, called "The World's Leading Cruise Lines" (WLCL), as a means of communicating its message regarding its highly diversified, global cruise product. This product capitalizes on the unique attributes and amenities of the company's six distinct member lines: Carnival, Holland America, Windstar, Seabourn, Cunard, and Costa. The WLCL's fleet currently consists of 43 vessels totaling more than 61,000 lower berths. The company's brands are positioned to appeal to each of the three major sectors of the vacation market—contemporary, premium, and luxury. Carnival operates fourteen cruise ships that cruise in the Caribbean and the Mexican Riviera. Holland America operates nine cruise ships that cruise in Alaska, the Caribbean, and Europe. Windstar operates four luxury, sail-powered vessels that cruise primarily in the Caribbean, Europe, and Central America. Cunard and Seabourn operate two and six luxury cruise vessels, respectively, to worldwide destinations. Holland America markets sightseeing tours both separately and as part of Holland America Westours cruise/tour packages.

During 2000, Carnival completed the acquisition of Costa Crociere S.p.A. Miami-based Carnival (the NYSE symbol is CCL) has enlisted the help of Garrigan Lyman Group (GLG) to design a new and highly interactive Web site under its multi-cruise-line brand name, World's Leading Cruise Lines www.leaderships.com. The site allows the company to present its six diverse cruising brands in a unique one-stop manner, giving visitors a taste of the wide range of cruising experiences that are available. Not only has Carnival expanded its online marketing strategy, but it is also one of the first cruise lines to initiate a television marketing campaign. GLG created an innovative "concierge" function for the WLCL site that automatically leads visitors through a series of questions about their cruise plans, ranging from budgets to recreation, and then recommends the cruise lines best suited to the vacation they have in mind.

Carnival is strong financially, with a debt-to-equity ratio of 0.38, a current ratio of 0.94, and a return on equity (ROE) of 16.4. Revenues were $3.779 billion in fiscal year 2000, an increase of 8 percent over 1999's $3.50 billion. Net income was $965.5 million in fiscal year 2000, a decline of 6 percent from 1999's net income of $1.03 billion. The total number of guests served increased by 12.8 percent in 2000, to 2.7 million. Carnival's shipbuilding program has been accelerated. Carnival Corporation had ordered sixteen new ships by the end of 2000, with delivery dates scheduled over the next five years at a total cost of $7 billion. Its European cruise business has been expanded to help position the company for future growth in the worldwide market.

### Princess Cruises

P&O Princess Cruises, a spin-off of the Peninsular and Oriental Steam Navigation Company (NYSE: POC), is a global cruise and tour company that offers a premium-style cruise experience that appeals to a wide variety of travelers. One of the three largest cruise companies in the world, P&O Princess Cruises (the NYSE stock symbol is POC) consists of Princess Cruises in North America, P&O Cruises and Swan Hellenic in the United Kingdom, Seetours and AIDA in Germany, and P&O Cruises in Australia. P&O operates eighteen ships on 150 different itineraries, calling at nearly 260 ports around the globe, and serves more than 600,000 passengers annually. It is a leading provider of cruises to Alaska, the Caribbean, Europe, the Panama Canal, the Mexico Canal, the South Pacific, South America, Hawaii/Tahiti, Asia, India, Africa, the Holy Land, Canada/New England, and other exotic destinations. Princess Cruises owns four riverside wilderness lodges, with a fifth under construction, plus a fleet of UltraDome railcars and luxury motor coaches that take passengers through the heart of the forty-ninth state. Princess additionally operates cruise tours in China, Australia, Africa, India, Europe, the Canadian Rockies, and the eastern United States.

P&O began a major new marketing campaign in January 2001—"Princess . . . where I belong." Targeted principally at the experienced traveler and creating a sense of community, the campaign seeks to position P&O as the cruise line that focuses on individual choice and customized cruise experiences. P&O entered into an alliance with AOLTime Warner in October 2000 to enhance its direct marketing capabilities and market to approximately 27 million AOLTime Warner and CompuServe customers worldwide. P&O has revamped its Web site, www.princesscruises.com, to include a booking engine for travel agents, a "wedding cam," and options for choosing shore excursions when booking a cruise.

P&O Princess Cruises is moderately strong financially, with a debt-to-equity ratio of 0.52, a current ratio of 0.45, and an ROE of 10.66. Profits were $276.7 million in fiscal year 2000, compared to $310.8 million in 1999. Operating cash flow in 2000 was $532.3 million, compared to $310.8 million in 1999. In 2000, passenger cruise days increased by 22 percent to over 8.7 million. The introduction of *Golden Princess* in May 2001 marked the first of six new ships to be introduced over the next four years.

## CONCLUSION

Coincidentally, Richard Fain, CEO of Royal Caribbean Cruises, Ltd., and Peter Ratcliffe, CEO of Princess Cruises, met on September 11, 2001, to discuss a merger between the two companies. In November 2001, the companies announced their intention to merge to create the world's largest cruise line, with sixty-one thousand berths and forty-one total ships. Royal Caribbean and Princess Cruises together would hold 40.2 percent of the market worldwide, based on the number of berths. There were mixed opinions on the soundness and timing of the decision given the economic recession and the 30 percent drop in U.S. cruise reservations since the start of bombings in Afghanistan. At the same time, some analysts are confident that the intended merger is a good move for both companies in spite of the uncertainty of the industry.

In spite of an uncertain future in the cruise industry, Royal Caribbean continues to pursue aggressive measures to remain competitive in the global market. Royal Caribbean has taken decisive steps to diversify and join competitors and other companies with core competitive advantages from which it can benefit. The proposed merger with Princess Cruises, if successful, will enable the company to gain market share and surpass Carnival Cruise Lines as the leader in the global cruise market. Increased capacity, global recession, and warring nations are three primary threats of the cruise industry. Will cruise lines be able to survive these threats until world conditions change? Will they be able to attract consumers to their floating paradises through competitive pricing and enticing marketing campaigns? Should Royal Caribbean Cruises, Ltd. diversify further into land-based products for uncertain travelers who are unwilling to fly but just want to get away?

## REFERENCES

www.almaco.cc
http://corporate.ir.net
www.cruising.org
www.e-travelnews.com
www.finance.yahoo.com
http://FirstSearch.oclc.org
http://www.forbes.com

http://investor.stockpoint.com
www.rccl.com
*The Wall Street Journal*
http://web6infotrac.galegroup.com/itw/
    informanarc
*USA Today*
http://yahoo.marketguide.com

# CENTRAL UNITED METHODIST CHURCH—2002

Robert T. Barrett
Francis Marion University

www.centralmethodist.net

In the aftermath of the terrorist attack in New York City and Washington, D.C., U.S. citizens are becoming more and more aware of the need to seek out positive forces in the world. As people come to grips with the tragedy, they are frequently turning to religious organizations for support. Church attendance and memberships are swelling, in part due to this brush with reality.

Central United Methodist Church, located at the heart of downtown Florence, South Carolina, is a vibrant and growing church. This growth over the past few years has primarily resulted from the influx of young families. These young families are having babies, so the church programming thrust is increasingly centered on children and youth ministries. The church is in the final stages of a building project that has greatly increased the size of the physical facility. Focus now turns to the development and management of programs that minister to the needs of this changing congregation.

## MISSION STATEMENTS

### The United Methodist Church

The mission of the church is to make disciples of Jesus Christ. Local churches provide the most significant arena through which disciple-making occurs. The statement that follows was taken from the Disciplines of the United Methodist Church.

> ### Central United Methodist Church
> Central United Methodist Church exists to serve and glorify God as revealed in Jesus Christ by making disciples through worship, fellowship, education and service to the Church and the community.

## CENTRAL UNITED METHODIST CHURCH—PAST AND PRESENT

Central United Methodist Church was established in the late 1800s and moved to its present site at the corner of Irby and Cheves streets in 1913. Through a variety of land and property acquisitions since 1913, Central's main campus has grown to include approximately two hundred feet of frontage on Irby Street and three hundred feet of frontage on Cheves Street. With its downtown location, a limited number of acquisition possibilities remain available to Central. In the mid-1900s, Central had the opportunity to purchase a house that was adjacent to church property for a cost of $30,000. The church turned down this opportunity, and the owner sold the property to a group which developed a hotel and cafeteria on the property. After the hotel failed, the church was able to buy the property in 1980 for $100,000. In 1984, Central purchased a building adjacent to the property that serves as both the primary facility for the youth ministry and the location of other Sunday school classes. Central continues to actively seek property for building and parking purposes.

## Church Property

In addition to the main church campus in the downtown Florence location at Cheves and Irby streets, Central United Methodist Church owns a large tract of land just outside of Florence, named Camp Sexton (after the donor), and a Boy Scout hut a few miles from the main church property. Most church programs are held at the downtown location. A summer camp for children is held for several weeks at Camp Sexton. Camp Sexton hosts special programs during the year and Sunday afternoon swim sessions for church members during the summer. The church sponsors Boy Scout troop meetings weekly in the Boy Scout hut.

The church sanctuary seats approximately 400 people. Attendance averages for the two Sunday morning services are shown for the past thirteen years in Exhibit 1. The sanctuary overflows for performances of the Masterworks Choir, the Christmas Eve services, Easter and Mothers Day Sunday services, and large funerals and weddings.

## New Facilities

After an extensive study of programs and facilities by a Long Range Planning committee, the church decided to embark on a building project to expand the physical plant and to enhance the programming possibilities. The efforts began in the late 1990s with a capital fundraising campaign. Pledges in excess of $2 million and collections of half of the pledges allowed the church to obtain a loan for the remainder of the $5 million project and to finalize the architectural designs and begin construction.

Central United Methodist Church is now in the final stages of this building project. Pictures of the new facility can be viewed on its Web site (**www.centralmethodist.net**). With the completion of the building project, church capacity will be increased by almost one-third. The new building provides high-quality space for infants, toddlers, and older children. One program that has taken full advantage of the new facility is the Mother's Morning Out program. This program was once cramped by space limitations, but the new building has allowed it to grow and to satisfy the needs of church families.

### EXHIBIT 1    Central United Methodist Church Membership and Attendance Levels

| Year | Church Membership | Average Worship Attendance | Sunday School Membership | Average Attendance |
|------|-------------------|----------------------------|--------------------------|--------------------|
| 2001 | 1,976 | 637 | 1,992 | 330 |
| 2000 | 1,944 | 609 | 1,913 | 334 |
| 1999 | 1,901 | 604 | 1,872 | 333 |
| 1998 | 1,899 | 617 | 1,757 | 443 |
| 1997 | 1,874 | 593 | 1,399 | 325 |
| 1996 | 1,863 | 589 | 1,572 | 322 |
| 1995 | 1,866 | 590 | 1,416 | 380 |
| 1994 | 1,855 | 551 | 1,376 | 331 |
| 1993 | 1,826 | 522 | 1,206 | 323 |
| 1992 | 1,801 | 523 | 1,111 | 308 |
| 1991 | 1,797 | 523 | 1,088 | 338 |
| 1990 | 1,795 | 540 | 1,091 | 336 |
| 1989 | 1,800 | 534 | 1,048 | 342 |

*Source:* Central United Methodist Church.

The Davis Christian Life Center, named for the former minister who pushed the church to begin the building project and his wife, is an excellent facility for larger informal programs. The tile-floored facility has a full-length basketball court that is flanked by a raised stage for music programs, the annual talent show, and other church fellowship programs. The very popular Wednesday Night Supper program, now scheduled in the Davis Life Center, has drawn over three hundred members and averaged over two hundred attendees, up a full 33 percent over previous years when the smaller fellowship hall had seating limitations. The new Christian Life Center has truly made growth possible.

The facility expansion not only provided new space for children and the new multipurpose facility, but it also allowed existing space to be reallocated for other pressing needs. Adult groups moved into renovated classrooms that had previously housed children's Sunday school classes. A beautiful welcoming/commons area was located where members and visitors enter from a new parking lot. Many feel that this area makes the church much more open, inviting, and warm to newcomers. Handicap access to the sanctuary was greatly improved, particularly in this new commons area. The church has initiated the Igniting Ministries program, which is designed to help members reach out to visitors. Greeters meet and welcome newcomers in the commons area.

## Membership Profile and Contributions

Exhibit 1 shows the membership levels for Central for twelve recent years, along with average attendance levels for the Sunday morning worship (two services) and the Sunday school. Approximately 23 percent of the members are younger than 10 years of age (note that young people on rolls prior to joining the church formally in seventh grade are only considered to be "Preparatory Members"), approximately 12 percent are in the 11-to-20 year age bracket, approximately 16 percent are in the 21-to-30 year age bracket, approximately 14 percent are in the 31-to-40 year age bracket, approximately 12 percent are in both the 41-to-50 and 51-to-60 year age brackets, and the remaining 11 percent are age 61 or older. Note that over 60 percent of the members are younger than 40, with 35 percent of this group being classified as children and youth. Another interesting breakdown of church membership shows that approximately 60 percent of the members are married, with a bulk of the remaining 40 percent being in the children and youth age brackets. This demonstrates the commitment of the membership to strong family values. In a time of declining memberships in churches across the country, Central has been able to maintain membership and participation levels.

Exhibit 2 gives information on contributions to the operating budget, to the building fund, and to the category labeled "Building Fund Extra," which is for designated project gifts. Contributions have steadily increased in recent years. Church budgets in excess of $800,000 were overpledged (and collected) in the late 1990s. However, with more and more contributions going to the building fund to pay for the new building, the operating budget has suffered. Pledges to the operating budget have been down since the startup of the capital campaign, and the church has had to scramble to meet the operating budget obligations.

## Church Property and the Annual Budget

Exhibit 3 gives the value of property owned by Central and debt owed by Central over the period of twelve recent years. The value of church property has grown, while debt service has continued to decline over recent years. The annual budget for 2002 is given in Exhibit 4.

EXHIBIT 2    Central United Methodist Church Contributions

| Year | Operating Budget | Building Fund | Building Fund Extra |
|---|---|---|---|
| 2001 | $1,174,367.00 | — | — |
| 2000 | $ 997,187.00 | — | — |
| 1999 | $ 968,110.00 | $614,814.00 | $104,133.72 |
| 1998 | $ 868,987.00 | $592,400.00 | $ 75,108.00 |
| 1997 | $ 820,610.00 | $145,231.33 | $ 6,464.75 |
| 1996 | $ 830,009.91 | $131,661.41 | $ 7,251.00 |
| 1995 | $ 734,799.03 | $133,602.07 | $ 26,527.24 |
| 1994 | $ 691,713.08 | $125,171.98 | $ 1,589.50 |
| 1993 | $ 631,750.74 | $110,831.43 | $ 2,204.50 |
| 1992 | $ 587,278.22 | $115,747.47 | $ 3,810.77 |
| 1991 | $ 561,148.50 | $120,976.75 | $ 8,635.50 |
| 1990 | $ 518,341.80 | $102,735.34 | $ 38,221.41 |
| 1989 | $ 499,069.64 | | |

*Source:* Central United Methodist Church.

## FLORENCE, SOUTH CAROLINA

Founded in 1850, Florence historically was and remains a railroad city. Florence is located in a region of South Carolina called the Pee Dee, named after a tribe of Indians who inhabited the area. The local Chamber of Commerce touts Florence as the trade, industrial, medical, transportation, cultural, financial, and educational center of the Pee Dee. Located where Interstate I-95 and I-20 intersect, Florence sees many travelers headed north to New York, south to Florida, east to Myrtle Beach, and west to the Appalachian Mountains.

EXHIBIT 3    Central United Methodist Church Assets and Debt

| Year | Value of Church Campus Property | Parsonage & Furniture | Other Assets | Debt |
|---|---|---|---|---|
| 2001 | $14,224,880 | $436,290 | $ 630,931 | $2,183,943 |
| 2000 | $12,365,340 | $495,000 | $1,138,347 | $ 970,000 |
| 1999 | $ 9,376,600 | $475,000 | $2,737,150 | $ 0 |
| 1998 | $ 9,298,340 | $457,900 | $2,143,500 | $ 0 |
| 1997 | $ 8,880,000 | $421,000 | $ 918,000 | $ 0 |
| 1996 | $ 8,223,700 | $432,700 | $ 476,997 | $ 103,100 |
| 1995 | $ 8,223,700 | $432,700 | $ 476,997 | $ 188,000 |
| 1994 | $ 8,223,700 | $432,500 | $ 535,625 | $ 206,105 |
| 1993 | $ 6,944,000 | $213,500 | $ 320,000 | $ 388,271 |
| 1992 | $ 7,492,875 | $313,000 | $ 380,000 | $ 458,166 |
| 1991 | $ 7,492,875 | $313,000 | $ 380,000 | $ 467,532 |
| 1990 | $ 7,492,875 | $313,000 | $ 380,000 | $ 27,348 |
| 1989 | $ 6,107,068 | $314,000 | $ 380,000 | $ 526,000 |

*Source:* Central United Methodist Church.

EXHIBIT 4  Central United Methodist Annual Budget, 2002

| Accounts | Annual Budget (This Year) |
|---|---|
| **EXPENSES** | |
| **SALARIES** | |
| 005001 – PASTOR | $ 70,600.00 |
| 005002 – ASSOCIATE PASTOR | $ 28,900.00 |
| 005003 – DIRECTOR CHILDREN'S MINIST | $ 35,000.00 |
| 005004 – DIRECTOR YOUTH MINISTRIES | $ 15,900.00 |
| 005005 – DIRECTOR ADULT MINISTRIES | $ 22,280.00 |
| 005006 – ADMINISTRATIVE SECRETARY | $ 20,000.00 |
| 005007 – STAFF SECRETARY | $ 16,940.00 |
| 005008 – COMMUNICATIONS DIRECTOR | $ 18,030.00 |
| 005010 – FACILITIES MANAGER | $ 26,000.00 |
| 005011 – CUSTODIAN-NIGHT | $ 13,395.00 |
| 005012 – CUSTODIAN-DAY | $ 13,395.00 |
| 005013 – CUSTODIAN/MAID | $ 15,475.00 |
| 005014 – MAINTENANCE PERSONAL | $ 17,639.00 |
| 005015 – MUSIC DIRECTOR/ORGANIST | $ 50,750.00 |
| 005016 – CHILDREN'S MUSIC DIRECTOR | $ 6,170.00 |
| 005017 – HANDBELL DIRECTOR | $ 2,429.00 |
| 005018 – CHILDREN'S ACCOMPANIST | $ 3,625.00 |
| 005019 – CAMP SEXTON DIRECTOR | $ 9,200.00 |
| 005021 – VISITOR FOR CHURCH | $ 8,000.00 |
| 005022 – DIRECTOR OF YOUNG ADULT MIN. | $ 5,100.00 |
| 005025 – BUSINESS MANAGER | $ 26,500.00 |
| 005030 – NURSERY WORKERS PAID | $ 17,160.00 |
| 005031 – CAMP SEXTON SUMMER STAFF | $ 13,500.00 |
| 005057 – FACILITY/CUSTODIAL ASSIST | $ 0.00 |
| 005070 – SALARY CONTINGENCY | $ 5,000.00 |
| **Total SALARIES** | $460,988.00 |
| **ALLOWANCES** | |
| 005101 – PASTOR REIMBURSEMENT | $ 3,000.00 |
| 005102 – ASSOCIATE MINISTER REIMBU | $ 3,000.00 |
| **CONTINUING EDUCATION** | |
| 005110 – PASTOR'S CONTINUING EDUCA | $ 400.00 |
| 005111 – ASSOCIATE MINISTER CONTIN | $ 600.00 |
| 005112 – DIR CHILDREN MINIS CONTIN | $ 600.00 |
| 005113 – MUSIC DIR/ORGANIST CONTIN | $ 800.00 |
| 005114 – CHILDREN'S CHOIR DIR CONT | $ 200.00 |
| 005115 – OFFICE STAFF CONTINUING E | $ 1,200.00 |
| 005116 – HANDBELL DIR CONTIN EDUCA | $ 200.00 |
| 005117 – ADULT DIRECTOR CONT EDUCA | $ 600.00 |
| 005118 – YOUTH DIRECT CONTINU EDUC | $ 600.00 |
| 005119 – BUSINESS ADMINISTRATOR CONT EDUC | $ 600.00 |
| **Total CONTINUING EDUCATION** | $ 5,800.00 |
| **SOCIAL SECURITY** | |
| 005122 – LAY EMPLOYEES SOCIAL SECU | $ 26,210.00 |
| **Total SOCIAL SECURITY** | $ 26,210.00 |
| **HOSPITALIZATION** | |
| 005133 – MUSIC DIR/ORG HOSPITALIZA | $ 1,200.00 |
| **Total HOSPITALIZATION** | $ 1,200.00 |
| **UTILITIES** | |
| 005140 – PASTOR UTILITIES | $ 7,500.00 |

*Source:* Central United Methodist Church.

The city of Florence has more than 33,000 residents, a total that is projected to double by the year 2010. Florence County has 122,000 residents, and it projects growth to 130,000 by 2010. Florence has churches of all denominations. Within three miles of the downtown location of Central United Methodist Church are Baptist, Presbyterian, Lutheran, Episcopal, and other Methodist churches. In the city of Florence, there are five Methodist churches. Many other churches have chosen to locate in areas on the outskirts of town. Thus, as the population of Florence grows, there is increased "competition" for parishioners.

## CHURCH ORGANIZATION

### Church Staff

Central United Methodist Church is served by a staff of twenty-three. The senior pastor acts as the chief administrative officer of this staff. Other primary staff members include one associate pastor, a music director, a part-time director of children's ministries, a part-time director of adult ministries, a part-time director of young adult ministries, and a part-time director of youth ministries. Clerical and custodian assistants make up most of the remaining staff positions. The church has adopted a strategy of successfully using part-time staff. The benefits of using a part-time staff are apparent in efficiencies and quality of service. This strategy allows the church to hire a person who is skilled in a particular function for the limited amount of time needed for that job. Salaries of these key personnel are presented in Exhibit 5. One change that will happen in the near future is that the half-time director-of-children's-ministries position will become a full-time position. This move will better allow the church to meet the needs of this growing sector of the congregation.

Central United Methodist Church has moved aggressively into Internet communication. The Web site (**www.centralmethodist.net**) is updated on a regular basis. The Web site has pages describing many of the church committees. The senior minister sends a weekly e-mail newsletter to church members, keeping them apprised of church programs and important church news as well as providing a weekly devotional thought. Church committees are informed of meeting schedules and agendas through e-mail. Church members contact staff members with concerns and news via the Web.

EXHIBIT 5    Central United Methodist Church, Salary for Key Personnel

|  | 1999 Annual Budget | 2000 Annual Budget | 2001 Annual Budget |
|---|---|---|---|
| Pastor | $65,156 | $68,413 | $69,042 |
| Associate Pastor | $26,476 | $29,132 | $37,240 |
| Director of Children's Ministries | $14,239 | $15,662 | $16,131 |
| Director of Youth Ministries | $13,726 | $14,137 | $15,550 |
| Director of Adult Ministries | $14,239 | $15,662 | $21,840 |
| Director of Young Adult Ministries | $   0 | $   0 | $  4,500 |
| Business Manager | $   0 | $24,000 | $25,500 |
| Administrative Secretary | $18,211 | $18,939 | $19,507 |
| Staff Secretary | $   0 | $   0 | $16,940 |
| Financial Secretary | $21,118 | $17,500 | $   0 |
| Music Director/Organist | $41,419 | $43,489 | $50,000 |
| Building/Property Superintendent | $18,287 | $18,287 | $25,000 |

*Source:* Central United Methodist Church.

### Volunteer Structure

Like most churches, much of the church's work is carried out by volunteers. The committee structure that helps to govern and carry out church programs is headed by the Administrative Board. Under the current structure, all committees report on a bimonthly basis to the Administrative Board. The key committees are listed below along with the primary functions of each.

- *The Board of Trustees* is primarily responsible for the maintenance, upkeep, and repair of the buildings and grounds of the church property.
- *The Finance Committee* must approve all expenditures and all fundraising initiatives/ideas of groups in the church.
- *The Council on Ministries* is the key programming organization of the church, consisting of several committees that develop and implement church programs. See Exhibit 5 for a list of the committees and councils that report to the Council on Ministries, along with their annual budgets.
- *The Staff/Parish Relations Committee* handles all church personnel-related issues.

People are busy. Many want to support the ministries and missions of the church, but they want their efforts to be efficient. Some members have expressed a concern with the current church structure. A problem with the current administrative structure is that many of the church volunteers serve on multiple committees that hear the same reports several times. An example should demonstrate the extent of the problem. The chair of the Outreach Committee helps a subcommittee plan for the building of the Habitat for Humanity house sponsored by the church. This subcommittee reports the plans to the full Outreach Committee. The chair then makes this report a part of the report to the Council on Ministries. The chair finally presents this report to the Administrative Board. Thus, the chair presents this report to four groups. Members of other committees may hear the same report several times.

As the building project comes to its conclusion, the church now turns to two pressing issues. A primary reason for increasing and updating church space was that many new families with young children were joining the church. It is not unusual to baptize several babies each month of the year. As the membership mix continues to become younger, program expansion and support of that program expansion become crucial to the life of the church. Streamlining the organization that supports this program is also important. See the organizational chart in Exhibit 6.

## CHARGE TO THE ADMINISTRATIVE BOARD

The senior minister would like the church to consider streamlining the program coordination structure. A resolution presented to the Administrative Board at a recent meeting follows:

> *From the Program Staff: We recommend that a committee of not more than ten be named by the Administrative Board to study the church structure which will best serve Central's Ministry and Mission needs. The study should include investigating other churches' size and a thorough examination of Central's Mission Statement so that the structure is designed to implement our mission. This committee should report {its} findings to the Administrative Board at its late spring meeting.*

The senior minister also provided the board a copy of the church standard from the *Book of Disciplines* of the United Methodist Church.

**EXHIBIT 6**    Organizational Chart Central United Methodist Church

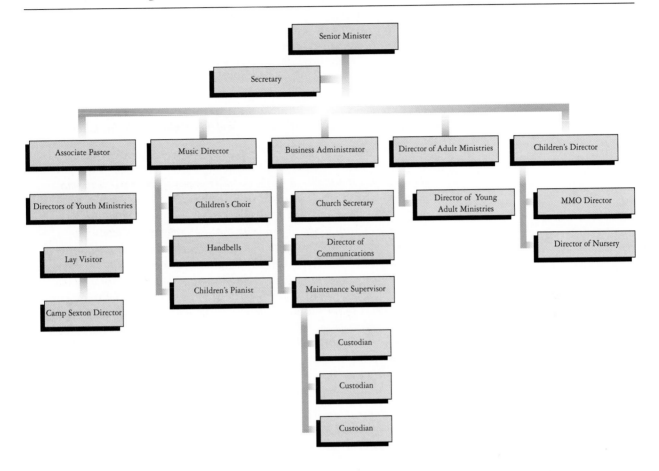

## Section VI. Organization and Administration

242. *Primary Tasks*—*The local church shall be organized so that it can pursue its primary task and mission in the context of its own community— reaching out and receiving with joy all who will respond; encouraging people in their relationship with God and inviting them to commit to God's love in Jesus Christ; providing opportunities for them to seek strength and growth in spiritual formation; and supporting them to live lovingly and justly in the power of the Holy Spirit as faithful disciples.*

*In carrying out its primary task, it shall be organized so that adequate provision is made for the basic responsibilities: (1) planning and implementing a program of nurture, outreach and witness for persons and families within and without the congregation; (2) providing for effective pastoral and lay leadership; (3) providing for financial support, physical facilities, and the legal obligations of the church; (4) utilizing the appropriate relationships and resources of the district and annual conferences; (5) providing for the proper creation, maintenance, and disposition of documentary record material of the local church; and (6) seeking inclusiveness in all aspects of its life.*

**243. *Organization*—***The basic organizational plan for the local church shall include provision for the following units: a charge conference, a church council, a committee on pastor-parish relations, a board of trustees, a committee on finance, a committee on lay leadership, and such other elected leaders, commissions councils, committees, and task forces as the charge conference may determine. Every local church shall develop a plan for organizing its administrative and programmatic responsibilities. Each local church shall provide a comprehensive program of nurture, outreach, and witness, along with leadership training, and the planning and administration of the congregation's organizational and temporal life, in accordance with the mission of The United Methodist Church.*

1.  *The church council and all other administrative and programmatic structures of the local church shall be amenable to the charge conference. The church council shall function as the executive agency of the charge conference.*

2.  *Alternative plans may be developed in accordance with the provisions of paragraph 246.2. Such alternatives include nurture, outreach and witness ministries; administrative council; or administrative board/council on ministries.*

3.  *Members of the church council shall be persons of genuine Christian character who love the church, are morally disciplined, are committed to the mandate of inclusiveness in the life of the church, are loyal to the ethical standards of The United Methodist Church set forth in the Social Principles, and are competent to administer its affairs. It shall include youth members chosen according to the same standards as adults. All shall be members of the local church, except where central conference legislation provides otherwise. The pastor shall be the administrative officer and, as such, shall be an ex officio member of all conferences, boards, councils, commissions, committees, and tasks forces, unless otherwise restricted by the Disciplines.*

**244. *Information Technology*—***Each local church, as it creates or maintains computerized information and data, is strongly encouraged to confer with its annual conference for recommendations and guidelines as it relates to information technology.*

## YOUR TASK

Help the church and the senior pastor develop an administrative programming structure that best fits the mission of the church. Try to develop the structure such that volunteers are not overly taxed with duplicate meetings. Take into consideration the structures used by other churches of similar size. Also keep in mind the suggestions/recommendations of The United Methodist Church. A helpful Web site will be **www.umc.org**. (Other Web sites are **www.centralmethodist.net** and **www.umc.org**.)

# ELKINS LAKE BAPTIST CHURCH—2002

Paul R. Reed, William B. Green, and Diane J. Green
**Sam Houston State University**

www.elbc.com

Comfortably dressed in his denim fatigues and leaning back in his captain's chair surrounded by the extensive library collection that fills his modest-sized office, Dr. Hugghins thought back to 1990 when he became pastor of Elkins Lake Baptist Church (ELBC). When he was "called" to be the ELBC pastor, the church had 487 members who were cramped into a small facility. Now, on the first of September, some eleven years later, church membership has grown to 722, and the church has moved to a new and much larger location. With this growth have come new challenges, and its pastor and members are today faced with issues that were not contemplated in 1990. Is the membership willing to accept the lifestyle and ideas of a newer, younger, and more liberal group of potential members that make up the community? Is the pastor equipped to lead the members of such a broad-based following? Will the fact that the membership is growing enable the church to fund the continued growth of the physical plant and the operating costs? Will ELBC be able to continue to function without a strategic plan? Should ELBC consider the idea of abandoning the Elkins Lake name in hopes of attracting a broader-based membership?

These and other questions seemed to multiply quickly as issues facing ELBC flowed through Dr. Hugghins' mind. No doubt, Hugghins will rely on his library and personal contacts to find some guidance or to find answers to these questions. However, it will take more than one man to deal with these issues.

## EXTERNAL ENVIRONMENT

### History

Elkins Lake Baptist Church was organized as a new church during a meeting in the Elkins Lake subdivisions clubhouse in 1970. For the next two years, while a sanctuary was being constructed, the new church met in a variety of locations. Initially its members met in the basement of the Elkins Lake clubhouse, where the clubhouse bar was located. Shortly thereafter, the church reached an agreement with the leadership of First Christian Church (Disciples of Christ), who allowed it to use the First Christian Church sanctuary. Churchgoers met at 8:00 on Sunday mornings and again each Sunday evening, since First Christian Church did not schedule a Sunday evening service. Because of scheduling conflicts, the new church moved into some vacant office space in the Huntsville National Bank office building for a few months. In 1972, the group was able to occupy its new building on the south side of Huntsville on State Highway 75. The facility was easily visible from Interstate 45 and from the Elkins Lake subdivision just across Interstate 45. Over the next fourteen years, the church membership grew to the point where it became necessary to build a new sanctuary on the Highway 75 site—or to search for a new location.

215

**EXHIBIT 1**    Huntsville's Southern Baptist Church Locations

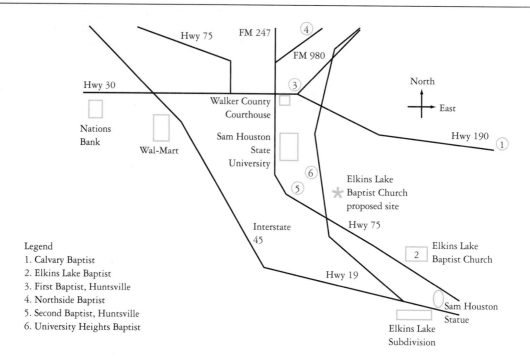

Legend
1. Calvary Baptist
2. Elkins Lake Baptist
3. First Baptist, Huntsville
4. Northside Baptist
5. Second Baptist, Huntsville
6. University Heights Baptist

In 1986, the church membership decided to relocate and voted to purchase a 9.5-acre tract located on Highway 19 on the south side of Huntsville (see Exhibit 1). This location would provide considerable room for growth, and it more centrally located the church within the city of Huntsville, Texas. The land was purchased for $225,000, and it was funded by a bank loan and the church's building fund.

In 1995, the church held a groundbreaking ceremony, and the following March, construction of the new building began. Only the trees that had to be removed were cut, and the revenue generated by the timber sales was applied toward construction costs. Additional funds came from a $620,000 bank loan, collateralized by personal guarantees from church members, and from a bond program, which raised $160,000 from its members. The bonds were repaid when the old church building and property were sold for $300,000. The remaining proceeds from the sale were used to reduce the bank note.

In March 1997, the church moved to its current location on Highway 19 and shortly thereafter acquired an additional 12.5 acres of adjoining land. The new facility included 6,527 square feet of sanctuary space; 1,890 square feet of offices and library space; 7,067 square feet of classroom space; and 2,314 square feet of kitchen, bathrooms, and miscellaneous space; as well as paved parking for 115 vehicles. Additional, spillover parking for about ten vehicles is available on an unpaved portion of the property. The sanctuary is very modern and functional. Interlocking chairs, rather than the kinds of pews that are commonly associated with Southern Baptist churches, were used. The sanctuary space is designed for use as a multifunctional space; it can be converted to nonworship space by simply taking the chairs apart and clearing the floor. Rather than the typical stained glass, the sanctuary windows provide a scenic view of the property, which overlooks a small creek. The Sunday morning service is somewhat nontraditional in that there are no altar flowers or children's sermon. Because many members of ELBC come from church communities where these features were important, these nontraditional features of the sanctuary and the service bother some parishioners. To these more traditional members, a church is just not a Southern Baptist Church without the stained glass, pews, altar flowers, and children's sermon. Conversely, a young family not steeped in Southern Baptist tradition and looking for a church home might consider Elkins Lake Baptist Church a fashionable place of worship.

Temporary buildings were moved from the old church to the present site to be utilized until additional classroom space could eventually be built. Two more temporary buildings were recently acquired to accommodate the growing religious-education space needs. Each of the new buildings has the capacity to hold two classrooms, with twenty people to a classroom. However, lack of space continues to be a problem. Classes have to be held in both the sanctuary and the regular classrooms. When questioned about the shortage of educational space and a possible date for beginning the next stage of construction, Hugghins cleverly remarked, "It is not about running an organization with a lot of amenities. It is about teaching people the word of God—and that can be done in living rooms." Hugghins would feel at home proclaiming "the word" in a large sanctuary, a small office, or in home living rooms. However, Hugghins does have individuals examining funding alternatives, and there are plans to add one more temporary building to the site soon.

## Local Area

Huntsville is located along Interstate 45, approximately 70 miles north of Houston and 170 miles south of Dallas/Fort Worth. Bryan/College Station is located 54 miles to the west on Highway 30. When Interstate 45 was constructed in the 1960s, the highway was located about a mile west of Huntsville. During the ensuing 40 years, the geometric center of the town has gravitated toward the interstate. This movement of the town toward the interstate should continue since the city of Huntsville has recently begun construction of a wastewater treatment facility and a north-south arterial on the west side on Interstate 45. This additional infrastructure should stimulate development on the west side of town.

Huntsville, the county seat of Walker County (with a 2000 population of 61,758), in many respects is a typical east Texas county seat, which serves as the trade center for the county and the surrounding rural population. Huntsville, however, is also home to Sam Houston State University (SHSU) and is the headquarters for the Texas Department of Criminal Justice (TDCJ), the largest state agency and the only agency not headquartered in Austin. In addition to the administrative headquarters, five prison units are located within the Huntsville city limits, and two other prison units are located in the county about ten miles north of town. The 2000 census placed the population of Huntsville at 35,078. In addition to the local citizens, the population totals include 8,904 inmates housed in the prisons and all university students residing in Huntsville. TDCJ employs approximately 7,771 personnel to staff the system's administrative headquarters and the seven area prisons. Student enrollment at the university was 12,997 students during the fall 2001 semester, an increase of 5.2% from the fall 2000 semester. Housing data for the fall 2001 semester are not available, but for the fall 2000 semester, 43 percent of the students lived on campus or in the Huntsville/Walker County community. The remaining 57 percent of the students commuted from outside Walker County. The university employs 2,169 faculty and staff. Employment in these two institutions is quite stable. Because the prison population has grown statewide, the local TDCJ administrative staff has also grown. Additional employment is supported by the city, county, school district, Huntsville Memorial Hospital, and by the typical small service, retail, and light industry-type firms present in the community.

Criminal activity in Huntsville is similar to other college towns located in rural communities. In 2000, there were 3,336 reported offenses. Included among those offenses were 921 reported thefts, 314 cases of criminal mischief, 251 cases of public intoxication, 23 cases of disorderly conduct, and 119 cases of DWI. Many of the Sam Houston State University students come from the Houston metropolitan area and find the recreational and social activities available in Huntsville limited.

On the immediate west side of the city, there are three residential communities, the largest being the Elkins Lake subdivision. Elkins, as it commonly called, was originally developed as a retirement community for those who wished to live in a rural setting, but one with the amenities of metropolitan Houston nearby. Elkins originally contained approximately 2,200 home sites. There are about 1,100 homes in Elkins, but because some homes were built on two lots and because other lots, on account of the terrain, can't be developed, less than one-half of the home sites are available for development. During the past several years, the average age of an Elkins Lake resident has declined as more working families with children have purchased homes. Today, only half of the residents of Elkins Lake are retired. Elkins Lake Baptist Church draws a disproportionate number of its members from the Elkins area. Nearly 7 percent of the residents of Elkins are members of ELBC. So the membership has become younger as more young families from Elkins join the church. Spring Lake and Westridge, the other two residential subdivisions, have been "built out" since the late 1980s.

## Competition

There are 76 churches, including 15 associated with the Southern Baptist Convention, in Walker County. The 15 Southern Baptist churches have a combined resident membership of 5,641, a Sunday school enrollment of 4,066, and average Sunday school attendance of 1,625. While the resident Baptist membership represents about 15 percent of the nonprison population, on any given Sunday less than 5 percent of the general population is in attendance in the Baptist churches in Walker County. Less than 30 percent of the residents of Huntsville are members of a local church.

ELBC, which is affiliated with the Southern Baptist Convention, faces its strongest membership competition from five other Southern Baptist churches in Huntsville. However, during the last few decades, families have become increasingly willing to select a church on the basis of factors other than "brand name." Location, youth and children's programs, activities for singles, "praise services," and other factors have become increasingly important considerations in church selection.

Dr. Hugghins has served ELBC longer than any of the other pastors. Occasionally, the Baptist preachers get together for discussions, and four of the churches come together annually for Bible study. Hugghins has an off-and-on relationship with the local Ministerial Alliance, an organization composed of all the ministers in town, not just those of the Baptist faith. The main function of the Ministerial Alliance is to organize and promote a community Thanksgiving service. The service is held in a different church each year, with the most recently employed pastor delivering the Thanksgiving message. Three of the other Southern Baptist churches are located in central Huntsville. ELBC is located on the southern perimeter, and the other two churches are on the northern and eastern perimeter of town. Assorted data from the Southern Baptist churches of Huntsville are presented in Exhibits 2 through 7.

## EXHIBIT 2    Huntsville Southern Baptist Churches, Membership

| Church | 2000 | 1999 | 1998 | 1997 | 1996 | 1995 | 1994 |
|--------|------|------|------|------|------|------|------|
| Calvary Baptist | 588 | 609 | 623 | 779 | 665 | 674 | 646 |
| Elkins Lake Baptist | 727 | 698 | 799 | 776 | 719 | 708 | 651 |
| First Baptist | 2,426 | 2,464 | 2,455 | 2,481 | 2,496 | 2,468 | 2,415 |
| Northside Baptist | N/A | 1,093 | 1,015 | 949 | 825 | 635 | 532 |
| Second Baptist | 1,028 | 997 | 1,007 | NA | 983 | 986 | 1,006 |
| University Heights Baptist | 1,810 | N/A | 1,650 | 1,602 | 1,554 | 1,515 | 1,677 |

*Source:* Tyron Evergreen Baptist Association.

## EXHIBIT 3    Huntsville Southern Baptist Churches, Receipts

| Church | 2000 | 1999 | 1998 | 1997 | 1996 | 1995 | 1994 |
|--------|------|------|------|------|------|------|------|
| Calvary Baptist | $ 170,193 | $171,426 | $271,988 | $210,151 | $233,732 | $248,724 | $202,314 |
| Elkins Lake Baptist | $ 433,928 | $455,823 | $522,869 | $346,074 | $357,174 | $317,229 | $255,922 |
| First Baptist | $1,304,814 | $885,618 | $833,406 | $812,551 | $788,394 | $776,039 | $672,594 |
| Northside Baptist | N/A | $289,440 | $356,862 | $301,737 | $249,936 | $221,000 | $181,280 |
| Second Baptist | $ 409,154 | $231,766 | $152,869 | NA | $110,195 | $159,632 | $115,963 |
| University Heights Baptist | $ 710,562 | N/A | $409,942 | $915,620 | $660,947 | $453,675 | $407,454 |

*Source:* Tyron Evergreen Baptist Association.

## EXHIBIT 4    Huntsville Southern Baptist Churches, A.M. Worship Service Attendance

| Church | 2000 | 1999 | 1998 | 1997 | 1996 | 1995 | 1994 |
|--------|------|------|------|------|------|------|------|
| Calvary Baptist | 150 | 300 | NA | 170 | 132 | 170 | 300 |
| Elkins Lake Baptist | 211 | 203 | 228 | 207 | 210 | 278 | 192 |
| First Baptist | 406 | 245 | 300 | 384 | 417 | 464 | 474 |
| Northside Baptist | N/A | 350 | 350 | 375 | 325 | 275 | 225 |
| Second Baptist | 175 | 175 | 135 | NA | 84 | 80 | 95 |
| University Heights Baptist | 550 | N/A | 550 | 600 | 500 | 500 | 500 |

*Source:* Tyron Evergreen Baptist Association.

## EXHIBIT 5    Huntsville Southern Baptist Churches, Sunday School Enrollment

| Church | 2000 | 1999 | 1998 | 1997 | 1996 | 1995 | 1994 |
|--------|------|------|------|------|------|------|------|
| Calvary Baptist | 157 | 197 | 251 | 213 | 223 | 297 | 351 |
| Elkins Lake Baptist | 404 | 388 | 407 | 393 | 421 | 424 | 398 |
| First Baptist | 800 | 777 | 997 | 1,034 | 1,094 | 1,139 | 1,066 |
| Northside Baptist | N/A | 226 | 292 | 290 | 292 | 260 | 176 |
| Second Baptist | 144 | 168 | 80 | NA | 109 | 131 | 128 |
| University Heights Baptist | 1,111 | N/A | 979 | 942 | 940 | 942 | 1,064 |

*Source:* Tyron Evergreen Baptist Association.

EXHIBIT 6    Huntsville Southern Baptist Churches, Total Young Adult Sunday School
             Enrollment (Ages 18–34)

| Church | 2000 | 1999 | 1998 | 1997 | 1996 | 1995 | 1994 |
|--------|------|------|------|------|------|------|------|
| Calvary Baptist | 21 | 35 | 35 | 34 | 57 | 47 | 42 |
| Elkins Lake Baptist | 96 | 126 | 126 | 90 | 77 | 117 | 51 |
| First Baptist | 126 | 67 | 229 | 300 | 292 | 237 | 156 |
| Northside Baptist | N/A | 60 | 34 | 49 | 57 | 56 | 12 |
| Second Baptist | 16 | 19 | 17 | NA | 8 | 0 | 12 |
| University Heights Baptist | 256 | N/A | 347 | 275 | 143 | 155 | 119 |

*Source:* Tyron Evergreen Baptist Association.

EXHIBIT 7    Huntsville Southern Baptist Churches, Value of Church Property

| Church | 2000 | 1999 | 1998 | 1997 | 1996 | 1995 | 1994 |
|--------|------|------|------|------|------|------|------|
| Calvary Baptist | $ 650,000 | $ 650,000 | $ 650,000 | $ 650,000 | $ 650,000 | $ 650,000 | $ 650,000 |
| Elkins Lake Baptist | $2,085,400 | $2,400,000 | $1,250,000 | $1,600,000 | $ 800,000 | $ 800,000 | $ 800,000 |
| First Baptist | $4,473,000 | $4,426,700 | $4,473,000 | $4,472,909 | $4,600,000 | $4,600,000 | $4,472,909 |
| Northside Baptist | N/A | $1,500,000 | $1,500,000 | $1,500,000 | $1,500,000 | $1,500,000 | $ 265,000 |
| Second Baptist | $1,235,000 | $1,235,000 | $2,000,000 | NA | $1,275,000 | $1,275,000 | $1,275,000 |
| University Heights Baptist | N/A | N/A | $2,800,000 | $2,800,000 | $1,700,000 | $1,700,000 | $1,700,000 |

*Source:* Tyron Evergreen Baptist Association.

## INTERNAL ENVIRONMENT

Elkins Lake Baptist Church is incorporated under the state laws of Texas and tends to
operate under a constitution and bylaws. It follows the Southern Baptist doctrine, which
tends to follow the literal descriptions and teachings of the Bible.

### Personnel and Organized Committees

Besides Dr. Hugghins, ELBC has two other full-time staff members—a youth director
and a financial secretary—and ten part-time employees. Three part-time employees,
including a choir director, organist, and pianist, are in charge of the music program.
Three interim educational directors, an education secretary, two nursery school workers,
and a custodian make up the remainder of the part-time staff. The church also heavily
depends on volunteers from the membership to provide services (ministries) ranging
from singing in the choir, teaching classes, parenting programs, and providing nursery
care to acting as a substitute pianist. The church is always looking for volunteers to
undertake new ministries as new opportunities for ministry emerge.

The ELBC has for several years considered adopting a formal personnel policy manual, but this manual has remained in draft form and has never been adopted. One result
of this lack of action is that there are no formal guidelines for committees. Hugghins
feels that revisions need to be made to the church constitution, but he has not initiated
any changes because he feels the controversy created would exceed the benefit of such
changes. For example, he would prefer a constitution that makes no gender references.
He also thinks that the duties of the committees should not be specifically outlined in
the constitution in order to create more of a here-is-what-matters, go-and-do-it attitude.

He believes that it should be made clear to each committee what is important, and the committee, in turn, should be empowered to handle what needs to be done.

The church treasurer and the Finance and Budget Committee direct the church's financial affairs. The records are maintained and reported by the financial secretary. The annual budget is established through a process requiring the various committees and pastor to present their respective needs and anticipated expenditures for the coming year. Revenue projections are adjusted for attendance trends. When the budget is finalized, it is presented to the membership for vote. (Financial statements are shown in Exhibit 8.)

The pastor looks to a panel of deacons for general policy guidance, but he is given great latitude in exercising control over the church's affairs. There are a total of 29 deacons (and five deacon emeritis) who serve three-year terms. The pastor and his deacons use a participative management style. Normally, the pastor confers with the deacons before recommending a policy change to the membership, who then finalize the decision by majority vote.

## The Pastor's Outlook

When Hugghins came to Elkins Lake Baptist Church, he assumed that it was a progressive church. Several facts had led him to this conclusion: the church's method of providing a music ministry, the fact that the education director was a woman, the fact that the preceding pastor was well-educated, and the fact that Huntsville was a university town. Within a month of his arrival, Hugghins began to see that the membership was more conservative than he anticipated. But he still believes ELBC to be the most diverse Baptist church in town.

## EXHIBIT 8    ELBC Financial Statement

| | As of December 31, | | | | | | |
|---|---|---|---|---|---|---|---|
| | *1994* | *1995* | *1996* | *1997* | *1998* | *1999* | *2000* |
| **BANK BALANCES** | | | | | | | |
| Checking | $ 5,511 | $ 10,766 | $ 5,000 | $ 30,538 | $ 17,193 | ($ 1,408) | $ 7,787 |
| Building Fund | 36,534 | 28,922 | 94,121 | 56,369 | 29,561 | 17,857 | 3,749 |
| Cert. of Deposit | | 32,500 | 79,709 | 30,000 | 20,378 | 49,003 | 25,000 |
| Special/Design. | | | | | 26,884 | 51,275 | 102,354 |
| Total Receipts, Year to Date | 255,922 | 317,229 | 357,174 | 346,074 | 522,869 | 455,823 | 433,928 |
| Projected Budget Needs | 270,286 | 227,148 | 278,388 | 320,382 | 422,877 | 454,321 | 460,565 |
| Percentage of Collections Over Expenses (Under) | (94.69%) | 139.66% | 128.30% | 108.02% | 123.65% | 100.3% | (94.22%) |
| **EXPENDITURES** | | | | | | | |
| 100 Missions | $ 42,621 | $ 55,384 | $ 54,447 | $ 61,200 | $ 63,562 | $ 77,683 | $ 68,884 |
| 200 Personnel | 135,252 | 145,417 | 136,255 | 159,583 | 174,808 | 201,226 | 206,878 |
| 300 Music Ministry | 2,608 | 3,902 | 3,205 | 3,564 | 3,278 | 5,340 | 4,357 |
| 400 Education Ministry | 8,821 | 11,255 | 8,594 | 10,826 | 18,871 | 11,300 | 24,867 |
| 500 College and Youth | 2,743 | 3,783 | 1,054 | 2,841 | 1,762 | 15,300 | 7,388 |
| 600 Church Administration | 14,061 | 15,318 | 15,666 | 20,874 | 19,982 | 22,300 | 23,725 |
| 700 Building and Equipment | 24,599 | 23,856 | 28,110 | 30,313 | 42,956 | 38,900 | 42,238 |
| 800 Debt Retirement | 18,732 | 18,863 | 17,186 | 18,715 | 82,957 | 82,224 | 82,228 |
| 900 Miscellaneous | 412 | 431 | 227 | 458 | 1,402 | | |
| Total Expenditures | $249,849 | $278,209 | $264,744 | $308,374 | $409,578 | $454,323 | $460,565 |

*Source:* Elkins Lake Baptist Church.

Hugghins, a relatively liberal man for a Southern Baptist preacher, would like to see the church move toward a more "modern Southern Baptist atmosphere," which would include female deacons and ministers, a less literal interpretation of the Bible, and increased pastoral authority. He is well read and regularly quotes authors of other denominations, causing some members to criticize him for not quoting more Baptist authors in his sermons.

Hugghins recognizes that Huntsville is strategically located for considerable growth possibilities. Because of the availability of land and the existing community infrastructure, he is convinced that ELBC is situated to fill the church needs of those looking for a modern, progressive Baptist church. Hugghins feels that ELBC's primary growth will come from members bringing friends to church. But growth can also come from follow-up visits to visitors who just "show up."

A few members, including some large contributors, were lost to more conservative churches over the years. One former member feels not only that Hugghins is "too modern," but also that he likes to do "things his own way, and this is not particularly what the members want." Some members feel that Dr. Hugghins should consider a change in style and take a more conservative approach. For a time during the mid-1990s, Hugghins found himself the subject of a controversy between the old versus new members—as well as old versus new ideas. He feels that he has not found a common element to deal with everyone (i.e., old members, new members, Elkins residents, and non-Elkins residents), but most of the dissidents have now left and found a church that better suits their religious views.

Originally, the target market for Elkins Lake Baptist Church was a retired, upper-middle-class individual. At present, the target group is shifting toward the working middle class. Only 19 percent of the current members are retired, whereas 67 percent are families with children. One individual, who has been a member for over twenty years, feels that the target market has changed, although this person doesn't recall this ever being openly stated or even discussed.

Hugghins has found that some long-time members are resistant to new members, their ideas, and their more liberal ways. Hugghins quotes a co-worker trying to explain to a long-time member, "It's not all about you. We need to think about what is best for the member as a whole and not what makes them 'most comfortable.'"

Hugghins fears that some misperceptions may occur because of the name, Elkins Lake Baptist Church. He is afraid that non-members will feel that the church is for members of the Elkins Lake subdivision only—and for the upper-middle class of Huntsville. He has toyed with the idea of renaming the church.

One of Hugghins' concerns is how the church responds to those young adults who "dropped out of church" during their formative years, but who are now married, have families, and feel the need to have their families involved in church. "Unfortunately," says Hugghins, "these dropouts just stopped [being] religious many years ago. For some, their last meaningful religious experience was singing songs with a guitar around a campfire at church camp. Now they are adults [but] with the religious mindset of a teenager. How the church responds to their needs will be a real challenge."

## Outreach Programs

ELBC has developed several outreach programs to attract new members, especially young families and children. Hugghins considers the active and visible ministries with leadership from the congregation to be a real asset for the church. A Sunday morning Bible study is conducted at the Elkins Lake clubhouse for those individuals looking for a more interactive worship session. Approximately fifteen individuals from various denominations regularly attend this Bible study.

ELBC also has a presence on the Sam Houston State University's campus. ELBC is affiliated with the Baptist Student Union (BSU) and holds lunches and services twice a year in a facility on campus. ELBC also works with the Walker County Jail and the Gulf Coast Trade Center (GCTC), a facility working for the rehabilitation of juvenile delinquents. The church regularly holds two classes at the GCTC to reach these troubled youths. In addition, the church supports various missions; for example, it is a sponsor church for the First Heritage Church in Houston. The church also makes its presence known at retirement facilities to bring the word of God to elderly individuals who are immobile. It is important to mention that all of these outreach programs are staffed by volunteers from the church.

## Marketing

Dr. Hugghins is quite proud of ELBC's marketing efforts, which consist of a weekly radio broadcast of the Sunday morning service, newspaper advertisements, two thirty-second radio advertisements during each Huntsville High School home football game, and seasonal radio greetings during the Christmas season. Hugghins occasionally authors an inspirational column that the local paper eagerly publishes. The Baptist Student Union promotes the ELBC on the SHSU campus with flyers about special events and announcements concerning the activities of the church.

ELBC has two signs located near the front of the property. One is a textured concrete ground sign, parallel to Highway 19, that is four feet high and five feet wide and is located between the two entrances. The sign, which provides only the church and pastor's name, is difficult to see because of the foliage, and it is also hard to read because the lettering is small and colored in shades of gray. During the past year, the church erected a new elevated sign that is perpendicular to the highway, is much more visible, and is easy to read for southbound drivers. This sign, colored in red and blue with a white background, contains the name of the church, an arrow pointing toward its location, and times of service.

Although the church is located on busy State Highway 19, buildings are located on the reverse slope of a hill that is away from the highway. The front portion of the building site is covered with large pine trees, allowing motorists to pass by without noticing the church. During the next five years, the Texas Department of Transportation is expected to make Highway 19 a four-lane divided highway, which will make it impossible for southbound traffic to turn into the church property; but if a feeder road is constructed, as is currently planned, accessibility to the property will be enhanced.

## Preparing for Future Growth

Southern Baptists have long held to the strategy of going to Sunday school from early childhood through adolescence. Therefore, great emphasis is usually placed in properly designing and utilizing educational space. Two rules of thumb are normally used: (1) to provide approximately forty-five square feet of floor space per person and (2) to maintain an average Sunday-school attendance of more than 80 percent of a church's capacity. The "80% Rule" also stands true for worship services (see Exhibit 9).

Hugghins has also utilized today's technology. He had a Web site developed that is fully operational for the church to serve as a forum that informs both members of the church and also potential members of the goings-on of the church and any special events. The pastor recognizes how fast things are changing and wants ELBC to keep up. "But is the church ready to follow?" he wonders.

EXHIBIT 9    Sunday School/Worship Attendance by Month for Elkins Lake Baptist Church

| | 1998 | | 1999 | | 2000 | | 2001 | |
|---|---|---|---|---|---|---|---|---|
| Month | Sunday School Attendance | Church Attendance | Sunday School Attendance | Church Attendance | Sunday School Attendance | Church Attendance | Sunday School Attendance | Church Attendance |
| Jan. | N/A | 204 | 183 | 243 | 179 | 208 | 175 | 221 |
| Feb. | N/A | 235 | 188 | 226 | 182 | 224 | 186 | 221 |
| March | N/A | 308 | 170 | 201 | 169 | 210 | 172 | 216 |
| April | N/A | 274 | 161 | 261 | 164 | 225 | 171 | 250 |
| May | N/A | 251 | 158 | 208 | 168 | 215 | 148 | 191 |
| June | N/A | 247 | 158 | 235 | 163 | 208 | 156 | 189 |
| July | N/A | 217 | 151 | 176 | 171 | 215 | | |
| Aug. | N/A | 261 | 171 | 219 | 185 | 243 | | |
| Sept. | N/A | 229 | 184 | 204 | 175 | 217 | | |
| Oct. | N/A | 251 | 180 | 219 | 173 | 209 | | |
| Nov. | N/A | 218 | 160 | 204 | 173 | 216 | | |
| Dec. | N/A | 216 | 172 | 218 | 148 | 187 | | |

*Source:* Elkins Lake Baptist Church newsletter, *The Window.*

## BIBLIOGRAPHY

Elkins Lake Baptist Church. *Constitution and Bylaws.*

Elkins Lake Baptist Church. *The Window* (1997, 1998, 1999, 2001).

Huntsville Police Department. *Consolidated Monthly Report* (December 2000).

Huntsville—Walker County Chamber of Commerce. *Community/Economic Profile for 2001.* <http://chamber.huntsville.tx.us/economy.html>

Judicial District Community Supervision and Corrections Department. *Fiscal Year 1998 Annual Report.* Author, no date.

Tyron Evergreen Baptist Association of Texas. Minutes of the 91st Annual Session (Conroe, Texas, 1994).

Tyron Evergreen Baptist Association of Texas. Minutes of the 92nd Annual Session (Conroe, Texas, 1995).

Tyron Evergreen Baptist Association of Texas. Minutes of the 93rd Annual Session (Conroe, Texas, 1996).

Tyron Evergreen Baptist Association of Texas. Minutes of the 94th Annual Session (Conroe, Texas, 1997).

Tyron Evergreen Baptist Association of Texas. Minutes of the 95th Annual Session (Conroe, Texas, 1998).

Tyron Evergreen Baptist Association. 1999 *Book of Reports*, 98th Annual Session (Conroe, Texas, 1999).

Tyron Evergreen Baptist Association. 2000 Book of Reports, 99th Annual Session (Conroe, Texas, 2000).

U.S. Census Bureau. State and County *Quick Facts* (Walker County, TX: <http://quickfacts.census.gov/qfd/>).

# WINN-DIXIE STORES, INC.—2002

Brian Kinard
**Mississippi State University**

WIN

www.winn-dixie.com

*Forty or fifty years ago, grandmother telephoned in a daily grocery order to a neighborhood market. It was delivered to her kitchen door later that same day. She was billed monthly.*

*It was fairly common in those days. It was called progress.*

*Cars, suburbia and "super" markets put an end to it. That was also called progress (Lind, 2000, Para. 1–2).*

Organized in Florida on December 26, 1928, Winn-Dixie Stores, Inc. is one of the nation's largest food retailers and one of the largest supermarket chains in the southeastern region of the United States. With over 1,000 stores in fourteen states, Winn-Dixie's (WD) retail stores sell groceries, meats, seafood, fresh produce, deli/bakery products, pharmaceutical products, and general merchandise items. WD also offers broad lines of merchandise and services, such as company-operated photo labs and in-store banks operated by independent third parties.

Winn-Dixie Stores, Inc. has found out recently that "winning *Dixie*" is not easy. For the past three years, the company has faced a steady decline in sales and market share. In fact, in order to fend off the new competition of mass merchandisers-turned-grocers Wal-Mart and Kmart, WD has remodeled and sometimes closed unprofitable locations. Underperforming assets were a drain on the organization, so by abandoning them, WD has lowered overall company costs. These restructuring and remodeling expenditures, costing approximately $550 million, has significantly raised WD's long-term debt. This combination of declining sales, higher debt, and the events associated with September 11, 2001, could harm WD further. In fact, to save on administrative costs, WD announced in September 2001 that there would be a shift from monthly to quarterly dividend payments. These decisions, coupled with lower than expected earnings and a plummeting stock price, have left investors skeptical about the future of the company.

## HISTORY

In 1914, William M. Davis ran a small general store in Burley, Indiana. Davis' store, typical of a country town general store in that day, carried a selection of merchandise and operated on a charge and deliver basis. Then one day, another merchant came to town and opened a cash-and-carry grocery store down the street. Soon, the new merchant had the cash and Mr. Davis was left with the "carry." Quick to see the advantages of this new method of merchandising, Davis purchased a grocery store in 1925 and brought his family to Miami, Florida.

Davis died in 1934, and his four sons assumed active management of the business. Each of the brothers in his own way contributed to WD's solid growth: A. D.'s strength was in merchandising, J. E.'s was in finance and investment, Austin was a troubleshooter, and Tine had the personality for public relations and for pioneering new divisions. Following the progressive principles set by their father, his sons saw the business

226  BRIAN KINARD

grow; and then in 1939, the four brothers purchased control of the 78 Winn & Lovett stores located in Florida and Georgia. In 1944, headquarters were established in Jacksonville, Florida, and the chain assumed the Winn & Lovett name.

After World War II, many retail chains in the Southeast began to join up with the Davis brothers. The company became Winn-Dixie Stores, Inc. in 1955. In 1967, eleven stores were acquired in Nassau and Freeport in the Bahamas, and in 1976, the retail assets of Kimbell, Inc. were acquired, adding Buddies and Foodway retail stores and facilities in the Southwest.

In 1995, WD acquired 25 Thriftway food and drug stores in the Greater Cincinnati, Ohio, area. The death of A. D. Davis on June 11, 1995, brought an end to WD's founding generation of Davis brothers. Chairman A. Dano Davis carries the Davis family legacy into its third generation. Winn-Dixie Stores, Inc., like many other large American businesses, has grown steadily from modest beginnings, due in large part to its strong leadership and the combined efforts of many people working together as a team (Winn-Dixie Stores, Inc., 2001).

## CORPORATE MISSION STATEMENT

Winn-Dixie's mission statement states:

*Winn-Dixie's mission is to innovate and implement a better and more efficient way of meeting the changing needs of our customers. Winn-Dixie strives to employ customer-oriented associates and provide them with the opportunity for training and promotion, while offering pay, benefits and working conditions equal to or better than those generally available in the food industry. Winn-Dixie deals fairly with customers, associates and suppliers in order to merit their continued patronage and support. The company supports civic and charitable efforts for the betterment of the communities in which we live and work. Winn-Dixie operates a financially sound business by energetically increasing sales and controlling expenses, for the purpose of earning a reasonable return for all who have an interest in the growth of our Company. By fulfilling the above commitment, we will ensure our future growth and profitability (Winn-Dixie Stores, Inc., 2001).*

## CORPORATE VISION STATEMENT

Winn-Dixie's vision statement, as provided in its 2001 *Annual Report* (p. 6), states:

*Winn-Dixie's vision is to be the best supermarket operator in the neighborhood, as well as the most efficient food operator in the industry.*

## EXTERNAL ISSUES

### September 11, 2001

In the wake of the September 11, 2001, terrorist attacks on the United States, the world economy has continued to decelerate, led by the U.S. economic slowdown. Asia has been weakened by the slowdown in exports to the United States, while Japan seems headed back into a recession. This is the first concerted world slowdown since the 1974–1977 period (Wyss, 2001). This slowdown in the economy could actually be good news for WD and other traditional grocers, as market share lost to restaurants and convenience stores during the economic growth period may now be regained. Consumer spending patterns are likely to change, since more individuals will be watching their budgets and will start preparing more traditional meals at home.

## Food Industry Issues

During 2000, U.S. grocery sales grew by 3.4 percent, reaching $570 billion. U.S. grocery business operators are becoming much more efficient by offering better product merchandising, consolidating, and making better use of capital by relocating, renovating, and expanding existing stores ("Supermarket and Drug Store Industry," 2001).

As of June 27, 2001, Winn-Dixie had completely implemented the restructuring program that was announced in April 2000, according to the *Annual Report* (2001). In an effort to lower costs, WD closed 112 stores as well as certain manufacturing and distribution centers, all of which had been underperforming assets. WD revamped and reformatted store layouts for more than half the stores in the chain, resizing key departments to increase profitability. Not only do these renovations enhance store physical looks, but they also appeal to consumers who prefer to buy clean and well-designed products. These restructuring initiatives improve the retail stores' look and increase overall operational efficiency. In fact, WD is currently saving approximately $400 million a year, having completed the restructuring expenditures of $552.2 million by the end of fiscal 2001.

### New Competition, More Acquisition

The grocery industry is now facing the new threat of supercenter and club store concepts. Wal-Mart, Kmart, and Target are learning the grocery business and are now formidable competitors in the retail grocery industry. Wal-Mart Supercenter grocery sales, 30 percent of total store sales, have reached $17.1 billion, making it the fourth largest food retailer in the U.S. (Griffith, 2001). To combat this threat, WD has acquired regional grocery chains in growing markets.

Acquiring existing chains is usually cheaper than building new units. Mergers and acquisitions substantially lower the risk involved in organizational expansion into new markets, as prior customer knowledge is readily available with little market research. Faster organizational expansion is possible through acquisitions, whereas mergers often tend to lower operating costs through shared marketing/advertising, manufacturing, and distribution facilities. Cost/benefit analyses are necessary in an industry in which pennies actually do matter. Intense competition among supermarkets for the consumer dollar is best demonstrated in profit margins that continue to be around 1 cent on each dollar of sales. That's right—one solid cent! That means that $100 in sales would produce a mere $1 in profit. According to the Food Marketing Institute, for fiscal years 1999 and 2000, the industry's after-tax net profit reached 1.18 percent, as seen in Exhibit 1. In fact, over the last decade, supermarket industry profits have averaged a mere 0.89 percent a year.

Acquisitions will play a key role in WD's strategy in 2002. Since January 2000, WD has acquired nine Gooding's supermarkets in the Orlando area, a core market that offers the potential for sales growth. Also, WD acquired 68 stores and 32 fuel centers owned by Mississippi-based Jitney-Jungle. The acquired store base, which is served by two of WD's existing distribution centers, has been easily integrated into the existing division structure. On September 5, 2001, WD changed the name of 48 Jitney-Jungle stores to Winn-Dixie, as a result of the positive customer reaction to the WD brand products and WD brand beef. Gooding's and Jitney-Jungle join a family of brands that also include Winn-Dixie, Save Rite, ThriftWay, and City Markets (Winn-Dixie Stores, Inc., 2001). Competition continually affects the grocery industry, and these measures were a necessity if WD was to stay competitive. This cutthroat competition is reflected in Exhibit 2, which shows that six companies have fallen from the top ten since 1980. This table clearly indicates how Winn-Dixie, falling from fifth in 1980 to tenth in 2000, has been affected by the impact of mass-merchandisers that have entered the market.

EXHIBIT 1    Net Profit as a Percentage of Sales

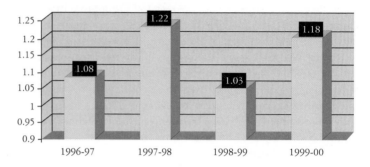

Net Profit as a Percentage of Sales

*Source: FMI Annual Financial Review* (1999–2000), p. 18.

## INDUSTRY TRENDS

### Online Sales

According to figures released by eMarketer, "Online grocery sales will climb to $33.6 billion by the year 2002, an increase of 3360 percent versus 1998." eMarketer also predicts that "online groceries will achieve a penetration rate of 15–20 percent of U.S. households by the year 2007." Are these numbers actually achievable? Apart from the convenience of online shopping, there is a technological factor, which puts new tools in the hands of shoppers. Online grocery shoppers can now sort and compare by price and nutritional value, making it possible to tilt previously brand-loyal consumers to cheaper options. However, it's difficult to predict the success of these Internet grocers because of the heavy capital requirements necessary to compete. Companies need to invest heavily in a delivery infrastructure to compete with traditional supermarket chains. A typical problem for these companies is same-day local delivery, which usually reflects 10 to 12 percent of the total grocery bill (**www.economy.com**). The current low volume and

EXHIBIT 2    Top Ten Supermarket Companies

| 1980 | 1990 | 2000 |
|---|---|---|
| Safeway | American | Kroger |
| Kroger | Kroger | Wal-Mart Supercenters |
| A&P | Safeway | Albertson's |
| Lucky | A&P | Safeway |
| Winn-Dixie | Winn-Dixie | SUPERVALU |
| American | Albertson's | Ahold USA |
| Jewel | Penn Traffic | Fleming |
| Grand Union | SGC | Delhaize America |
| Albertson's | Publix | Loblaw |
| Supermarket Gen. | Ahold USA | Winn-Dixie |

*Source: Supermarket News* (2001).

usage by consumers make operating these types of companies very expensive, and the current prognosis suggests that the future is bleak.

## "Super" Growth

Supercenter growth is expected to continue well into the future. Exhibit 3 depicts the projected growth of supercenters through 2005. Consumers are embracing the idea of shopping for packaged grocery items at a general merchandise store such as Super Wal-Mart, Big-K, and SuperTarget. Competing on the basis of price and service, WD has been able to hold on by increasing customer service and in-store services to complement the grocery shopping experience. Grocers, including WD, are starting to place small banking centers within stores, where customers can fill out loan forms or do other banking tasks. This win-win strategy potentially increases the foot traffic for a grocery retailer, while increasing financial transactions for the bank.

## Where's the Loyalty?

Supermarket chains have increased the introduction of private brand labels to compete with national brands in an effort to target price-sensitive customers. In light of the economic downturn, price-conscious consumers are more wary of overspending than previously. Purchases of store or lower-priced brands, instead of national brands, decreased one percentage point from 1999. More than half of all consumers—51 percent—are buying private brand labels "every time" or "fairly often" when they shop ("Spending and Saving Money," 2001).

WD has an opportunity to capitalize on this trend. The WD product line carries higher profit margins than the comparable national brands; at the same time, such lines promote customer loyalty. WD has one of the leading store-brand programs in the industry. WD Chek soda, for example, holds a leading position in several markets, outselling some prominent national brands (Winn-Dixie Stores, Inc., 2001).

## INTERNAL ISSUES

### New Look, New Ideas

A pleasant customer shopping experience heavily depends on clean, well-stocked, customer-friendly retail stores. Creating a new look for WD stores is a top priority for senior management. WD's store base has been revitalized—more than 60 percent of the stores are new or have been remodeled in the past five years. Nearly 50 percent of the stores have been improved in the past year alone. WD is already achieving increasingly accurate inventory tracking and greater purchasing leverage because of the new centralized procurement

| EXHIBIT 3 | Projected Number of Supercenters by 2005 |
|---|---|
| Wal-Mart | 1,400 |
| Kmart | 200 |
| Meijer | 180 |
| Fred Meyer | 180 |
| SuperTarget | 60 |
| TOTAL | 2,020 |

*Source:* Griffith (2001).

system. New concepts will be added, such as pet centers, soft drink and snack centers, house-hold cleaning sections, and baby-needs centers. New growth opportunities range from pharmacy operations in stores to fuel centers, such as those acquired as part of Jitney-Jungle. Also, WD has several profitable liquor stores in operation and holds additional liquor licenses for future expansion. By aggressively building new and larger locations, remodeling and enlarging existing locations, and offering an expanded line of merchandise and services, WD seeks continued growth (Winn-Dixie Stores, Inc., 2001).

On October 3, 2001, WD unveiled a multimillion dollar ad campaign—the "Real Deal"—to communicate a new brand position. The Real Deal is a part of the company's continuous initiative to increase brand awareness and market share. The campaign addresses WD core competencies of offering real good food, to real good people, at a real good price. This effort reflects a committed approach in the transformation of the company to the new WD.

### Areas of Operations

As indicated in Exhibit 4, WD currently operates supermarket and Marketplace super-stores in Florida, Georgia, North and South Carolina, Alabama, Mississippi, Louisiana, Kentucky, Ohio, Tennessee, Indiana, Virginia, Texas, and Oklahoma. WD also operates twelve City Markets and Winn-Dixie Stores in the Bahamas. In addition, WD operates twenty facilities that produce or process company products as follows: coffee, tea and spices, carbonated and noncarbonated drinks, crackers, corn snacks and cookies, frozen pizza, sausage, luncheon and smoked meats, mayonnaise and salad dressings, preserves and peanut butter, and eggs and dairy products (Winn-Dixie Stores, Inc., 2001).

### Financial Overview

Winn-Dixie's 1997–2001 balance sheets are provided in Exhibit 5. Note that the company took on $697 million in long-term debt in 2001.

### EXHIBIT 4    Store Locations

| State | Total | Winn-Dixie | Marketplace | Thriftway | Jitney-Jungle | Sack & Save | City Meat Markets | Buddies | Save Rite |
|---|---|---|---|---|---|---|---|---|---|
| Florida | 436 | 61 | 372 | | | | | | 3 |
| Alabama | 118 | 39 | 74 | | 5 | | | | |
| North Carolina | 109 | 53 | 56 | | | | | | |
| Georgia | 94 | 13 | 81 | | | | | | |
| Louisiana | 79 | 18 | 60 | | 1 | | | | |
| Texas | 71 | 14 | 56 | | | | | 1 | |
| Mississippi | 69 | 7 | 12 | | 42 | 8 | | | |
| South Carolina | 62 | 24 | 38 | | | | | | |
| Kentucky | 40 | 6 | 29 | 5 | | | | | |
| Virginia | 28 | 10 | 18 | | | | | | |
| Ohio | 17 | | | 17 | | | | | |
| Bahamas | 12 | 3 | | | | | 9 | | |
| Tennessee | 12 | 4 | 8 | | | | | | |
| Oklahoma | 5 | 4 | 1 | | | | | | |
| Indiana | 1 | | 1 | | | | | | |
| Total | 1,153 | 256 | 806 | 22 | 48 | 8 | 9 | 1 | 3 |

*Source:* Winn-Dixie Stores, Inc. (2001).

EXHIBIT 5    WINN-DIXIE STORES, INC. Annual Balance Sheet
(in millions, except book value per share)

| | June 30, | | | | |
|---|---|---|---|---|---|
| | 2001 | 2000 | 1999 | 1998 | 1997 |
| **ASSETS** | | | | | |
| Cash & Equivalents | 121.06 | 29.57 | 24.74 | 23.56 | 14.12 |
| Receivables | 109.15 | 107.42 | 188.31 | 146.16 | 175.68 |
| Notes Receivable | 0.00 | 0.00 | 0.00 | 0.00 | 0.00 |
| Inventories | 1,198.60 | 1,141.40 | 1,425.09 | 1,404.91 | 1,249.21 |
| Other Current Assets | 170.37 | 193.51 | 159.83 | 161.14 | 148.96 |
| **Total Current Assets** | **1,599.20** | **1,471.92** | **1,797.99** | **1,735.79** | **1,587.97** |
| Net Property & Equipment | 1,146.65 | 1,034.49 | 1,222.63 | 1,169.84 | 1,128.68 |
| Investments & Advances | 0.00 | 0.00 | 128.52 | 38.78 | 88.08 |
| Other Noncurrent Assets | 0.00 | 0.00 | 0.00 | 0.00 | 0.00 |
| Deferred Charges | 106.14 | 166.44 | 0.00 | 22.62 | 22.13 |
| Intangibles | 92.87 | 18.79 | 0.00 | 0.00 | 0.00 |
| Deposits & Other Assets | 96.79 | 55.43 | 0.00 | 101.66 | 94.55 |
| **Total Assets** | **3,041.67** | **2,747.09** | **3,149.14** | **3,068.71** | **2,921.41** |
| **LIABILITIES & SHAREHOLDERS' EQUITY** | | | | | |
| Notes Payable | 0.00 | 235.00 | 465.00 | 420.00 | 380.00 |
| Accounts Payable | 599.85 | 575.87 | 662.17 | 660.53 | 604.03 |
| Current Portion Long-Term Debt | 4.29 | 0.00 | 0.00 | 0.00 | 0.00 |
| Current Portion Capital Leases | 3.27 | 2.84 | 2.75 | 2.90 | 3.02 |
| Accrued Expenses | 373.96 | 367.63 | 331.20 | 339.86 | 312.41 |
| Income Taxes Payable | 24.29 | 85.60 | 10.73 | 12.11 | 32.92 |
| Other Current Liabilities | 144.23 | 154.59 | 75.46 | 71.77 | 60.22 |
| **Total Current Liabilities** | **1,149.90** | **1,421.55** | **1,547.32** | **1,507.20** | **1,392.61** |
| Mortgages | 0.00 | 0.00 | 0.00 | 0.00 | 0.00 |
| Deferred Taxes/Income | 49.02 | 0.00 | 0.00 | 0.00 | 0.00 |
| Convertible Debt | 0.00 | 0.00 | 0.00 | 0.00 | 0.00 |
| Long-Term Debt | 697.41 | 0.00 | 0.00 | 0.00 | 0.00 |
| Noncurrent Capital Leases | 28.95 | 32.23 | 38.49 | 48.58 | 54.03 |
| Other Noncurrent Liabilities | 344.71 | 425.46 | 152.25 | 144.04 | 137.28 |
| Minority Interest (Liabilities) | 0.00 | 0.00 | 0.00 | 0.00 | 0.00 |
| **Total Liabilities** | **2,270.01** | **1,879.25** | **1,738.06** | **1,699.83** | **1,583.92** |
| **SHAREHOLDERS' EQUITY** | | | | | |
| Preferred Stock | 0.00 | 0.00 | 0.00 | 0.00 | 0.00 |
| Common Stock (Par) | 140.46 | 140.83 | 148.57 | 148.53 | 148.88 |
| Capital Surplus | 0.00 | 0.00 | 0.00 | 0.00 | 0.00 |
| Retained Earnings | 634.69 | 727.00 | 1,259.59 | 1,220.35 | 1.188.62 |
| Other Equity | (3.50) | 0.00 | 2.90 | 0.00 | 0.00 |
| Treasury Stock | 0.00 | 0.00 | 0.00 | 0.00 | 0.00 |
| Total Shareholders' Equity | 771.65 | 867.83 | 1,411.07 | 1,368.88 | 1,337.49 |
| **Total Liabilities & Shareholders' Equity** | **3,041.67** | **2,747.09** | **3,149.14** | **3,068.71** | **2,921.41** |
| Total Common Equity | 771.65 | 867.83 | 1,411.07 | 1,368.88 | 1,337.49 |
| Average Shares | N/A | 145.79 | 148.24 | 150.04 | 150.29 |
| Book Value per Share | 5.49 | 6.01 | 9.49 | 9.22 | 8.98 |

*Source:* Zack's Investment Research (2001).

The annual income statement for Winn-Dixie Stores, Inc. is depicted in Exhibit 6. Sales for fiscal 2001, a 52-week year, were $12.9 billion, compared to fiscal 2000's $13.7 billion (also a 52-week year), and fiscal 1999's $14.1 billion (a 53-week year). This reflects a decrease of 5.8 percent for fiscal 2001, a decrease of 3.1 percent for fiscal 2000, and an increase of 3.8 percent in 1999. Sales decreased largely as a result of the elimination of unprofitable sales departments, the elimination of unprofitable sales items in remaining departments, and a reduction in the number of 24-hour stores. WD has substantially completed its planned store retrofits, resulting in labor savings and other efficiencies. The store retrofits have enhanced WD's competitive position and may positively affect WD's sales during fiscal 2002.

As a percentage of sales, gross profit margins were 26.8 percent, 27.2 percent, and 27.6 percent in fiscal 2001, 2000, and 1999, respectively. Gross profit dollars have decreased in the current year partially as a result of the closing of 112 stores as part of management's restructuring plan. In addition, gross profit has been negatively affected by the elimination of high gross-profit, yet unprofitable, sales departments (Winn-Dixies Stores, Inc., 2001).

## PUTTING THE CUSTOMER FIRST

Delivering what the customer wants represents the future of WD. Customer service, attractive pricing, and modern store environment play vital roles in delivering a positive

EXHIBIT 6    WINN-DIXIE STORES, INC. Annual Income Statement
(in millions except earnings per share data)

| | June 30, | | | | |
|---|---|---|---|---|---|
| | *2001* | *2000* | *1999* | *1998* | *1997* |
| Sales | 12,903.37 | 13,697.54 | 14,136.50 | 13,617.48 | 13,218.71 |
| Cost of Goods | 9,449.34 | 10,057.70 | 10,335.59 | 9,993.56 | 9,902.86 |
| **Gross Profit** | **3,454.02** | **3,639.84** | **3,800.91** | **3,623.91** | **3,315.85** |
| Selling & Admin. & Depr. & Amort. Expenses | 3,180.29 | 3,609.24 | 3,593.65 | 3,374.90 | 3,093.77 |
| **Income after Depreciation & Amortization** | **273.74** | **30.60** | **207.26** | **249.02** | **222.09** |
| Nonoperating Income | (147.24) | (290.38) | 94.37 | 97.31 | 119.43 |
| Interest Expense | 52.84 | 42.62 | 5.15 | 28.53 | 22.08 |
| Pretax Income | 73.64 | (302.41) | 296.48 | 317.79 | 319.44 |
| Income Taxes | 28.33 | (73.51) | 114.14 | 119.17 | 115.00 |
| Minority Interest | 0.00 | 0.00 | 0.00 | 0.00 | 0.00 |
| Investment Gains/Losses (+) | 0.00 | 0.00 | 0.00 | 0.00 | 0.00 |
| Other Income/Charges | 0.00 | 0.00 | 0.00 | 0.00 | 0.00 |
| **Income from Continuous Operations** | **45.31** | **(228.89)** | **182.33** | **198.62** | **204.44** |
| Extras & Discontinued Operations | 0.00 | 0.00 | 0.00 | 0.00 | 0.00 |
| **Net Income** | **45.31** | **(228.89)** | **182.33** | **198.62** | **204.44** |
| **DEPRECIATION FOOTNOTE** | | | | | |
| Income Before Depreciation & Amortization | 457.29 | 287.27 | 499.67 | 579.42 | 513.32 |
| Depreciation & Amortization (Cash Flow) | 183.55 | 256.67 | 292.41 | 330.40 | 291.24 |
| Income After Depreciation & Amortization | 273.74 | 30.60 | 207.26 | 249.02 | 222.09 |
| **EARNINGS PER SHARE DATA** | | | | | |
| Average Shares | N/A | 145.79 | 148.24 | 150.04 | 150.29 |
| Diluted EPS Before Nonrecurring Items | 0.99 | 0.52 | 1.23 | 1.33 | 1.36 |
| **Diluted Net EPS** | **0.33** | **(1.57)** | **1.23** | **1.33** | **1.36** |

*Source:* Zack's Investment Research (2001).

WD shopping experience. These efforts are focused on delivering total customer satisfaction and low price leadership. In response to the customer's need for one-stop shopping, WD continues to move to larger stores in centralized locations. By increasing square footage, WD is able to surround the customer with more departments and more time-saving choices in such service center areas as seafood, floral, pharmacy, deli, bakery, international wines and cheeses, banking, ATMs, photo processing, postage stamps and money orders. WD's satellite communications system enables all locations to be networked more efficiently, thus allowing associates to spend less time on paperwork and more time assisting customers (Winn-Dixie Stores, Inc., 2001).

WD has introduced new training programs in customer service, food safety, and sanitation. New programs to measure customer satisfaction and to provide reward and recognition for top-performing employees also have been put into place. One example is the empowerment of store managers and division management, allowing them to act aggressively to meet local customer needs. The company has initiated the FIRST class customer service program, which is aimed at rewarding employees for providing exceptional customer service. Improvements in labor productivity have also been made through flex scheduling so that more associates are available to interact with customers, thus shortening waiting lines at peak hours (Winn-Dixie Stores, Inc., 2001).

## Constant Community Commitment

Being a good corporate citizen and a good neighbor in the communities in which the company operates has been a part of the WD philosophy and commitment since its beginning in 1928. During the 1999 and 2000 fiscal years, the company contributed over $10 million in support of local community efforts. The following are just a few of the countless ways in which WD and its associates strive to make a difference:

### Even-It-Up

WD's Even-It-Up program provides an opportunity for its customers to donate small change from their grocery orders to support nonprofit organizations. WD is currently donating these proceeds to the disaster relief fund related to the terrorist attacks in New York City and Washington, D.C.

### Education

Every year, WD awards college scholarships to qualified associates and their dependents to further their education. Currently, over four hundred students are on WD scholarships. WD's Youth Management Day program demonstrates an investment in the future of the company's associates.

### Natural Environment

WD is concerned about both solid waste and preserving the environment for future generations. WD's goal is to constantly find ways to reduce, reuse, and recycle solid waste. WD works within the industry and with public and private environmentally responsible institutions to promote responsible recycling. The corporate programs include the recycling of paper, plastics, and other materials; ongoing evaluation of procedures, costs, and areas for improvement is a part of these programs.

### Health

The WD Hope Lodge is a $1 million commitment made by WD and its associates to establish the American Cancer Society/Winn-Dixie Hope Lodge Center in Gainesville, FL. The Lodge provides a nurturing, homelike residence where cancer patients and their families traveling away from home during treatments can stay at no charge (Winn-Dixie Stores Inc., 2001).

## A Strong Foundation

WD takes great pride in the contributions that each associate makes toward keeping the company on the cutting edge. WD's strength lies in the family of more than 120,000 loyal and productive associates. Additionally, WD subscribes to a promotion-from-within policy and believes in a drug-free workplace. WD has a long history and tradition, one that that was founded on the premise that people make the difference (Winn-Dixie Stores Inc., 2001). Exhibit 7 reflects the organizational structure of the company, with focused management over geographic regions, as well as product lines.

## Future Considerations

WD has opportunities to capitalize on current trends over the next few years. The economic slowdown will force many customers back into grocery stores for more traditional meals, causing more price-conscious buying behavior, which is beneficial to corporate branded products. In order to stay competitive, WD may need to continually acquire

---

**EXHIBIT 7    Directors and Management**

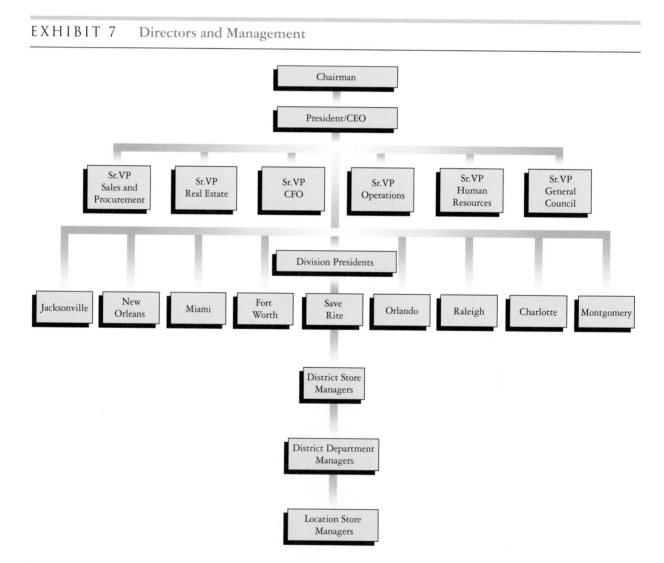

*Source:* Adapted from Winn-Dixie's 2001 *Annual Report.*

and expand operations of retail grocery chains in performing market areas. Mergers and acquisitions may be the only means of competing in a mass-merchandising environment.

For a future acquisition opportunity, WD could look at the Indianapolis, Indiana-based grocery retailer, Marsh Supermarkets, Inc. Marsh operates 93 supermarkets and 179 Village Pantry convenience stores in central Indiana and western Ohio. Marsh offers products and services comparable to WD's, and store locations can easily be serviced by WD's current distribution center in Louisville, Kentucky. An industry leader in technology, Marsh is currently one of the industry's best performing companies. Acquiring Marsh could enhance brand awareness and grow current market share.

Traditional grocers such as WD may find it difficult to compete merely on price with mass-merchandisers, but intangible benefits, such as exceptional customer service, should be stressed as a high priority. The institution of customer service programs, such as FIRST, should be continuously reviewed and measured to ensure that first-class customer service is maintained. Currently, such customer service in mass-merchandise locations is lacking.

Finally, WD needs to continue to improve its marketing campaigns, which seem to have been less than productive in years past, in order to induce more shopping behavior within the company's market area. These new initiatives should encompass the entire organization, not just the physical aspect of the organization. The new "Real Deal" WD campaign should be just that: a real change in products and services, which produce real measurable outcomes that make a real difference.

## REFERENCES

www.economy.com
Economy.Com Network. "Retail Stores: Grocery and Drug." (2001). http://www.economy.com/research

www.fmi.org
Food Marketing Institute. "Competition and Profit." (2001). http://www.fmi.org/facts_figs/Competitionandprofit.pdf

Food Marketing Institute. "Spending and Saving Money." (2001). http://www.fmi.org/facts_figs/spendingandSavingMoney.pdf

Griffith, Tom. "The U.S. Retail Food Industry: 2001 Format Update." Willard Bishop Consulting (2001, June). http://www.bishop-consulting.com/edge_jun_01.cfm

Lind, Robin. "Online Grocery Shopping Is Growing and Ripening." WebPointers Online (2000). http://www.webpointers.com/groc99.html

"Online Grocery Sales to Increase 3360% by Year 2002." Advanced E-Commerce Home Shopping Solutions (2000). http://www.emarketer.com

"Supermarket and Drug Store Industry," U.S. Business Reporter (2001). http://www.acitivemediaguide.com/ddrugstore_industry.htm

Winn-Dixie Stores, Inc., Annual Report (2001). http://www:winn-dixie.com/company/annualreport/main.asp http://www.winn-dixie.com

Wyss, David. "U.S. Economic Forecast: The Big Engine That Could," Standard & Poor's (2001). http://www.sanp.com/Forum/MarketAnalysis/Articles/082301_bigengine.html

Zack's Investment Research, Winn-Dixie Annual Income Statement and Balance Sheet, E-Line Financials (2001). http://lada.zacks.com

# STRICTLY ROOTS NATURAL HAIR CARE SALON—2002

Paul R. Reed, Anthony Williams, Valerie Muehsam, and
Donald Bumpass
Sam Houston State University

Jhamella Bolade has a hairy situation on her hands and she loves every minute of it. As she reclines in one of her hair styling stations and reflects over her recent business success, she can't help being a little anxious about her salon's future. Bolade is the owner and operator of Strictly Roots Natural Hair Care Salon (713-529-5017), which specializes in braiding and locking of the hair of African Americans in the greater Houston, Texas, area. Although her salon has been open for less than nine months, business is really booming, and Bolade wouldn't have it any other way. Bolade does not apply any permanents, nor does she apply any chemicals at her salon because this would violate her natural hair-care philosophy. Bolade even makes her own natural hair-care product, which is known as Strictly Roots Anointing Oil.

Bolade could not have secured a better location for her salon. It is located in the Third Ward area of Houston, an area that is experiencing an economic comeback and is located not very far from the downtown area. The salon is surrounded by several other businesses that attract African American customers, including a Caribbean restaurant named the Reggae Hut, the Naturally Yours Pharmacy and Health Food Store, and the D&B African Village Art Gallery. While there is limited available parking space at this location, Strictly Roots' clients and the neighboring businesses do not seem to mind.

Bolade would like to take advantage of Strictly Roots success by opening her second natural hair-care salon, which she plans to call Strictly Roots Too. Finding time to pursue this goal will be difficult since she also wants to return to college so that she can earn her bachelor's degree in business administration; she also needs time to increase the production of her anointing oil. To further complicate matters, Bolade is also the proud mother of two preschool-aged children. Finally, Bolade must always be prepared for the ever-present threat that one of her independent stylists will resign his or her post in order to open his or her own salon.

## STRICTLY ROOTS' HISTORY

Bolade was born in New York City as Yvette Talley 32 years ago. She began braiding hair at the age of 13, and it was during this period in her career that she learned the Egyptian palm-rolling method of locking hair. Unlike traditional methods of locking hair, which involves tying and twisting, the Egyptian method requires stylists to lock a client's hair by rolling the hair in their palm to transform the hair into permanent locks. She eventually became a licensed master braider and loctition in the state of New York. After perfecting her natural hair sculpting techniques in New York, she left her Harlem home and worked at salons in Atlanta, Chicago, and Los Angeles. In 1987, Bolade matriculated as a college student at nearby Texas Southern University, which is located in the Third Ward area of Houston, Texas. Bolade began sculpting the hair of her classmates to earn spending money while she studied journalism, a profession in which her mother earned a living.

Formal business operations in Houston began in 1990, when Bolade decided to return to the career which she enjoyed the most. Bolade worked out of her home for several years until the birth of her first child. It was at this point that she decided that her home was no longer a good place to sculpt hair and that it was important to move her personalized consultations out of her home and into a more appropriate place of business. Shortly after making this decision, Bolade rented space at the Cut-N-Shine Barbershop, also located in the Third Ward. It was here, in the African American-friendly atmosphere which was surrounded by other business that offered services similar to Strictly Roots cultural ideals, that Bolade's business began to really take off. She began to pass out flyers to market her services and developed plans to construct her own Web site. When the news came that a Cut-N-Shine neighboring business was vacating some lease space, Bolade immediately secured the square footage and opened Strictly Roots.

## STRICTLY ROOTS' SERVICES

Strictly Roots is in the business of pampering its clients' hair roots via a holistic approach to hair care. Her salon specializes in braids, dreadlocks, twists, and natural hair-care styles for African Americans. In one of her professionally designed color flyers, Bolade states that "natural hair is virgin hair, not altered by chemical or thermal services. Natural hair care, in turn, is the process by which the hair service enhances that natural state." Her holistic approach to hair care can take hours to complete and recognizes the integrated balance between the body, mind, and spirit. The services provided are gentle and wholesome, and they are corrective and nurturing to the entire body. Environmentally safe products (nontoxic) are a part of the services. Products made of plants, fruits, vegetables, herbs, or essential oils are used during these therapeutic services. The reference of these services is consistent with Bolade's anointing oil.

The service begins with a personalized consultation with the client, during which the stylist tries to ascertain the hairstyle that's desired. The stylist then assesses the client's immediate hair-care needs and recommends the most appropriate process in which these needs can be matched with a desired hairstyle. The client's hair is then washed thoroughly and slowly dried. Once dried, the client's hair is twisted, braided, or locked. If the client's hair is very short, then it will probably be twisted in a fashionable manner until it is long enough to be braided. If the client's hair does not grow much longer than its twisted length, then it will be maintained in this manner.

If the client's hair is long enough to be braided, then a more complicated hair-sculpting process takes place. If the client wants dreadlocks, then the stylist will use the Egyptian palm-rolling method and lock the hair. Unlike the temporary twisting or braiding of hair, once the client's hair is locked, it is transformed and permanent. The dreadlocks hair appears matted, somewhat unclean, cannot be combed, and must be cut if the client desires a different hairstyle.

## STRICTLY ROOTS' CULTURE AND ORGANIZATIONAL STRUCTURE

Strictly Roots fosters an environment that encourages the native African experience. All of Bolade's stylists are strongly encouraged to assume a native African name which will be referred to when the stylist is sculpting hair at the salon. The salon currently accommodates up to five independent stylists at one time and has regular operating hours of 10:00 A.M. to 8:30 P.M., Tuesday through Saturday. The independent stylist must pay a $65 weekly booth fee and abide by Bolade's price listing for the various services. All income earned after the weekly booth fee is paid belongs to the stylist. Bolade currently does not have a wage-earning administrative assistant and relies on one of her long-time independent stylists to act in this capacity. This will be a problem until she develops a financial strategy to address this issue while she actively pursues other personal and professional goals.

Since the process of twisting, braiding, and locking hair is very time-consuming, independent stylists are allowed to set their own schedules: Walk-ins are routed to their stylists if they are established clients; if not, they are assigned a stylist based on the client's needs and the stylist's sculpting ability. All independent stylists must adhere to Bolade's natural hair-care philosophy if they are to continue to provide services at the salon. By enforcing this philosophy, Bolade can honestly make the claim that Strictly Roots is "Houston's Only Natural Hair-Care Salon."

The city of Houston is the fourth largest city in the United States. In 1990, Houston's 28 percent black population, or 457,990, placed it sixth among American cities in terms of the size of its black population. Preliminary 2000 U.S. Census results show that the African American population in Houston has grown approximately 45 percent to 709,432. Other reports show that approximately 15 percent of African Americans made over $30,000 annually during this period. As a result, there are more potential clients with more expendable income.

The hairstyles created at Strictly Roots are most popular among younger African Americans. Many young people idolize the many musical rappers and professional athletes who wear the hairstyles. Bolade even has some celebrity-clients who come to her for consultations, including local Houston rappers and professional NBA basketball players. Bolade would like to grow her business by capitalizing on her current celebrity clientele and by luring players on the startup Houston Texans football franchise once the team begins play.

Unfortunately, the hairstyles are not so readily accepted in the corporate environment. Many people think that individuals who wear such hairstyles may be abusing illegal drugs, may be engaging in some form of international crime, or may not be concerned about their overall appearance. The opportunity to expand the salon's base of clients still remains positive, however, since the Houston area has a large number of African American high school students as well as many college students who attend the University of Houston, Texas Southern University, Houston Baptist University, and Rice University.

## STRICTLY ROOTS' ANOINTING OIL PRODUCT

Strictly Roots' Anointing Oil was designed to meet Bolade's desire to provide environmentally safe products as a part of her services. The anointing oil has the potential to bring in additional revenues if she can begin to meet her demand for the product. Bolade's current cost to produce twenty-four jars of anointing oil is approximately $50.00, or $2.08 per jar. Production time to produce the oil is approximately two hours. A jar of anointing oil sells for $9.00, yielding a net profit of $6.92. Average sales of anointing oil are only twenty-four jars per month, resulting in $166.08 profit a month—or $1,992.96 annually.

Bolade is having problems meeting the demand for the anointing oil for several reasons. She currently lacks an established schedule for producing the oil; she has no formalized production staff to produce the oil; and to have the oil produced by a contract vender may result in lost revenues for Bolade. Also, if a contract vendor produces the product, then Bolade would have to reveal her processing secrets and ingredients, which could result in a loss of her competitive edge. In addition to her own clients, there are independent businesspeople who would love to acquire the secret of Bolade's anointing oil. These people would like to make a direct profit themselves instead of paying Bolade's $9.00-per-jar price and then marking up the price of the jars in order to earn a small profit. One retailer has openly suggested that he could retain the services of a chemist to break down the compounds of the anointing oil and have the product produced under his company's name since the oil is not patented. Nonetheless, Bolade is resisting these advances and plans to increase the production of her oil internally in the near future.

## STRICTLY ROOTS' COMPETITION

There are several cosmetology schools in the greater Houston area. Each graduating class has individuals who aspire to own their own salons someday. As mentioned earlier, this is a constant threat for small salons like Strictly Roots. This problem is magnified by the fact that Strictly Roots has a specific market niche that has allowed it to become an immediate success in the Houston market. Bolade experienced this threat directly on two different occasions when two of her former independent stylists left their booths at Strictly Roots so that they could open their own natural hair-care salons. The competition is intensified by the fact that both of these salons were opened within a two-block radius of Strictly Roots (see Exhibit 2). These salons are named Back to Natural, Soul Scissors, and Hyde & Jojo's. A brief summary of these salons follows.

### Soul Scissors

Soul Scissors was launched in June 1997 and is owned and operated by Troy Julian. In addition to cutting hair, Soul Scissors sells acid jazz compact discs, T-shirts, African art, essential oils, and incenses. The salon provides services in a converted gasoline station approximately two blocks from Strictly Roots. The salon has a functional Web site at **www.soulscissors.com**.

The salon and African art store also has a natural hair-care specialist on-site whose name is Georgette Johnson. Johnson, a former independent stylist at Strictly Roots, is a self-proclaimed loctition who states that she specializes in dreadlocks, twists, braids, corn-rows, and other natural hair-care styles. Although Johnson originally lured some of Strictly Roots clients away from Bolade, many of these customers have since returned.

### Back to Natural

There is yet another salon within a two-block radius of Strictly Roots, Back to Natural, and it is owned and operated by Keesha Eniyi. Eniyi is also a former Strictly Roots independent stylist who branched out on her own after learning the core processes of the natural hair-care philosophy. Her salon is located slightly off Almed Blvd. between Strictly Roots and Soul Scissors. However, Back to Natural has neither a functional Web site on the Internet nor any products that would rival Strictly Roots Anointing Oil. Eniyi is a relentless businesswoman who is determined to carve out her share of the natural hair-care market.

### Hyde & Jojo's

This particular natural hair-care salon is located approximately twenty miles away from Strictly Roots in the Alief area of Houston, Texas, and it is owned and operated by individuals native to Jamaica. Hyde & Jojo's specializes in locking hair and has a huge following of island natives who currently reside in the Houston area. Bolade would have trouble gaining market share on these potential customers and accepts this healthy rivalry that may hold future alliances.

### Strictly Roots' Finances

Strictly Roots has been quite profitable during its first few months in business. Bolade charges $65.00 to braid or lock a client's hair. Hair maintenance is also an additional $65.00 per visit. Despite the turmoil of opening the business, the anointing oil production problems, and the departure of two of her most promising independent stylists, the salon has been able to turn a respectable profit. Bolade experienced a $23,593 increase in revenues for the year 2000, but then a $6,742 decline in 2002. Although Bolade's overall cost of goods sold increased over 50 percent, most of this can be attributed to the leasing and utilities costs related to Strictly Roots versus the booth fee she paid while providing services at the Cut-N-Shine Barbershop. Likewise, her net income increased by 32 percent, from $25,351 in 1999 to $42,671 in 2000. Net income to 2002 declined to $35,929. Bolade currently has no long-term debt, nor does her company have large account receivables or payables. Strictly Roots financial summary can be found in Exhibits 1 and 2.

## STRICTLY ROOTS' FUTURE

Bolade will need to decide in which direction she will move her business over the next few years. Although the business has done well over the past several months, Bolade has not experienced a full year of operations at her current location. What makes things even more interesting is the fact that Bolade may have to raise her weekly booth fee to offset lost profits resulting from a slowing economy, rising utility costs, and rising gasoline prices. It is uncertain how her independent stylists will react to such an increase, and there is still the ever-present threat that some of the stylists may depart the salon to open their own businesses.

EXHIBIT 1    Strictly Roots Consolidated Balance Sheet

|  | March 31, 2002 | March 31, 2001 | March 31, 2000 |
|---|---|---|---|
| **CURRENT ASSETS** | | | |
| Cash and cash equivalents | $1,890.00 | $2,035.00 | $ 700.00 |
| Accounts receivable | — | — | — |
| Inventory | $ 327.00 | $ 186.00 | $ 73.00 |
| Other current assets | $ 461.00 | $ 345.00 | $ 94.00 |
| **Capital Assets** | $4,014.00 | $3,250.00 | $ 467.00 |
| Total Assets | $6,692.00 | $5,816.00 | $1,334.00 |
| **CURRENT LIABILITIES** | | | |
| Accounts payable | $ 562.00 | $ 219.00 | $ 163.00 |
| Taxes payable | $ 429.00 | $ 567.00 | — |
| Notes payable | $1,073.00 | — | — |
| **Long-Term Debt** | — | — | — |
| **SHAREHOLDERS' EQUITY** | | | |
| Retained Earnings | $4,628.00 | $5,030.00 | $1,171.00 |
| Total liabilities and shareholders' equity | $6,692.00 | $5,816.00 | $1,334.00 |

*Source:* Strictly Roots' Company Report.

EXHIBIT 2    Strictly Roots' Income Statement

| For the year ended | March 31, 2002 | March 31, 2001 | March 31, 2000 |
|---|---|---|---|
| Revenues | $47,681.00 | $52,393.00 | $28,800.00 |
| Cost of services | $ 7,527.00 | $ 6,960.00 | $ 3,120.00 |
| Selling, marketing, and administration | $ 3,305.00 | $ 2,050.00 | $   300.00 |
| Amortization | $   268.00 | $   145.00 | $    29.00 |
| Income from operations | $36,581.00 | $43,238.00 | $25,351.00 |
| Investment income | — | — | — |
| Income before taxes | $36,581.00 | $43,238.00 | $25,351.00 |
| Provision for income taxes | $   652.00 | $   567.00 | — |
| Net Income | $35,929.00 | $42,671.00 | $25,351.00 |

Source: Strictly Roots' Company Report.

Bolade will need to secure a reliable administrative assistant who can be trusted to supervise the daily salon operations while she increases the production of Strictly Roots Anointing Oil and opens Strictly Roots Too. Pursuing either of these goals will be twice as difficult for this single mother of two, who plans to return to college for her bachelor's degree.

# THE CLASSIC CAR CLUB OF AMERICA—2002

Matthew C. Sonfield
Hofstra University

www.classiccarclub.org

The Classic Car Club of America, Inc. (CCCA) was formed in 1952 by a small group of enthusiasts interested in the luxury cars of the late 1920s and 1930s. The CCCA phone number is 847-390-0443 and their e-mail address is **www.classiccarclub@aol.com** Certain high-priced, high-quality, and limited-production cars were designated as "Classic Cars," and the period of 1925 to 1942 was chosen as the "Classic Era." It was felt that cars built prior to 1925 had not yet reached technical maturity and that after World War II, the quality of most so-called luxury cars had succumbed to the economic pressures of mass production. Some pictures of Classic Cars are provided in Exhibit 1.

Over the years, the list of CCCA-recognized Classic Cars was modified and expanded, and the time period was extended to 1948 to include certain pre-WWII models that continued in production for a few years after the war. All cars included on the list were of considerably higher price and quality than the mass-production cars of this era, and most had original prices in the $2,000 to $5,000 range. (This was a considerable amount of money at that time; in 1930, a Ford Model A [*not* a Classic Car] sold new for about $450.) Some of the most luxurious Classic Cars, such as the American Duesenberg, the English Rolls-Royce, the French Hispano-Suiza, and the Italian Isotta-Fraschini, sold new in the $10,000 to $20,000 range! Exhibit 2 lists those cars recognized as Classic Cars by the CCCA in 2002.

The mission statement of the CCCA, as stated in its legal by-laws, states:

> *The purposes for which the club is founded are: for the development, publication and interchange of technical, historical and other information for and among members and other persons who own or are interested in fine or unusual foreign or domestic motor cars built between and including the years 1925 and 1948, and distinguished for their respective fine design, high engineering standards and superior workmanship, and to promote social intercourse and fellowship among its members; and to maintain references upon and encourage the maintenance, restoration and preservation of all such Classic Cars.*

## THE COLLECTOR CAR HOBBY

The collector car hobby in the United States is a broad and wide-reaching activity involving a large number of Americans. Basically, a "collector car" is any automobile owned for purposes other than normal transportation. The most widely read collector car hobby magazine, *Hemmings Motor News,* had an average circulation of about 250,000 in 2001. Another magazine, *Car Collector,* estimates that nearly 1 million Americans are engaged in the old-car hobby. However, a figure of 500,000 to 750,000 would probably be a more conservative estimate of the number of Americans engaged in this hobby.

*Collector car* is a loose term, ranging from turn-of-the-century "horseless carriages" to currently built but limited-production cars, such as Italian super-sports cars. Naturally, owners of collector cars enjoy the company of other individuals with similar

EXHIBIT 1    Classic Cars

1926 Duesenberg (above); 1934 Rolls Royce (top right); 1941 Packard (right).
*Source:* The Classic Car Club of America, Inc.

interests, and thus a wide variety of car clubs exist to suit almost any particular segment of this vast hobby. The largest of these clubs, the Antique Automobile Club of America, caters to owners of virtually all cars twenty-five years old or older, and it has a membership of more than sixty thousand. In contrast, the CCCA has a much narrower collector-car focus and, thus, far fewer members.

## CCCA ORGANIZATION AND ACTIVITIES

When the CCCA's 2001 fiscal year ended on December 31, 2001, the club had 5,918 members, as indicated below. (Exhibit 3 gives a comparison of membership figures for recent years.)

| | |
|---|---|
| Active (regular membership—2002 dues @ $45/year) | 4,425 |
| Associate (for spouses, no publications—$7/year) | 1,204 |
| Life (after ten years, one-time fee of $800) | 217 |
| Life Associate (spouse of Life—$80) | 69 |
| Honorary (famous car designers, etc.) | 3 |
| | 5,918 |

CCCA members receive a variety of benefits from their membership. A magazine, *The Classic Car*, is published four times a year. High in quality and highly respected by automotive historians, it features forty-eight pages or more of articles and photos of Classic Cars. A CCCA *Bulletin* is also published eight times a year, and it contains club and hobby news, technical columns, and members' and commercial ads for Classic Cars, parts, and related items. A further publication is the club's *Handbook and Directory*, published annually. It contains a current listing of members and the Classic Cars they own,

EXHIBIT 2    CCCA-Recognized Classic Cars

| | | |
|---|---|---|
| A.C. | Excelsior* | Mercer |
| Adler* | Farman* | M.G.* |
| Alfa Romeo | Fiat* | Minerva* |
| Alvis* | FN* | N.A.G.* |
| Amilcar* | Franklin* | Nash* |
| Armstrong-Siddeley* | Frazier-Nash* | Packard* |
| Aston Martin* | Georges Irat* | Peerless |
| Auburn* | Graham* | Peugot* |
| Austro-Daimler | Graham-Paige* | Pierce-Arrow |
| Ballot* | Hispano-Suiza* | Railton* |
| Bentley* | Horch | Raymond Mays* |
| Benz* | Hotchkiss* | Renault* |
| Blackhawk | Hudson* | Reo* |
| B.M.W.* | Humber* | Revere |
| Brewster* | Invicta | Roamer* |
| Brough Superior* | Isotta-Fraschini | Rochet Schneider* |
| Bucciali* | Itala | Rohr* |
| Bugatti | Jaguar* | Rolls-Royce |
| Buick* | Jensen* | Ruxton |
| Cadillac* | Jordan* | Squire |
| Chenard-Walcker* | Julian* | S.S. and S.S. Jaguar* |
| Chrysler* | Kissell* | Stearns-Knight |
| Cord | Lagonda* | Stevens-Duryea |
| Cunningham | Lanchester* | Steyr* |
| Dagmar* | Lancia* | Studebaker* |
| Daimler* | La Salle* | Stutz |
| Darracq* | Lincoln* | Sunbeam* |
| Delage* | Lincoln Continental | Talbot* |
| Delahaye* | Locomobile* | Talbot-Lago* |
| Delaunay Belleville* | McFarlan | Tatra* |
| Doble | Marmon* | Triumph* |
| Dorris | Maserati* | Vauxhall* |
| Duesenberg | Maybach | Voisin |
| Du Pont | Mercedes | Wills St. Claire |
| Elcar* | Mercedes-Benz* | Willys-Knight* |

*Indicates that only certain models of this make are considered Classic. Some other 1925–1948 custom-bodied cars not listed above may be approved as Classic upon individual application.
*Source:* The Classic Car Club of America, Inc.

EXHIBIT 3    Selected CCCA Membership Data (at end of fiscal year)

| | *2001* | *2000* | *1999* | *1998* | *1997* |
|---|---|---|---|---|---|
| Active Members | 4,425 | 4,198 | 4,138 | 4,182 | 4,164 |
| Associate Members | 1,204 | 1,113 | 1,078 | 1,077 | 996 |
| Life Members | 217 | 215 | 213 | 207 | 205 |
| Life Associate Members | 69 | 69 | 70 | 69 | 66 |
| Honorary Members | 3 | 3 | 3 | 3 | 5 |
| Total | 5,918 | 5,598 | 5,502 | 5,538 | 5,436 |

*Source:* The Classic Car Club of America, Inc.

so that club members can locate other members who own similar cars or live nearby. Commercial car-related advertisements are solicited for this *Handbook and Directory,* and its cost is fully paid for by these advertisements. Advertisements also cover some of the costs of the magazine and bulletin.

The CCCA also sponsors three types of national events each year. The annual meeting in January includes business meetings and a car judging meet and is held in a different location in the United States each year. In the spring and summer, a series of "Grand Classic" judging meets are held simultaneously in ten to twelve locations around the country, with a total of four hundred to six hundred Classic Cars being exhibited and judged. At CCCA judging meets, cars are evaluated by a point system that takes into account the quality and authenticity of restoration and the general condition of the car, both mechanically and cosmetically. CCCA judging meets are not usually publicized to the general public, and access to view the cars is generally restricted to club members and their guests only.

Each year, the club sponsors several "Classic CARavans" in various parts of the United States and Canada. The CARavan is a tour in which members in as many as one hundred Classic Cars join together in a week-long planned itinerary. Every few years, a cross-country CARavan that lasts for several weeks is run.

The annual meeting, Grand Classics meets, and CARavans are designed to be financially self-supporting, with attending members paying fees that cover the costs of the events.

The CCCA has members who have volunteered to be technical advisers available to assist other members. Furthermore, the club makes available for sale to members certain club-related products, such as hats, ties, shirts, and umbrellas with a Classic Car design. In still another member-oriented venture, the CCCA in 1990 and 2001 commissioned the publications editor to edit two 750-page hardcover books (*The Classic Car* and *The Classic Era*), which were composed of members' photos and stories of their Classic Cars and of the time period in which they were built. These books were published by the club and sold to members and through bookstores to the general public, and they have brought in additional revenue to the CCCA.

The CCCA also maintains a World Wide Web site (**www.classiccarclub.org**). This attractive Web site provides a wide range of information about the club and about Classic Cars. At this site, one can join the club, buy the club's books, see many Classic Cars, and find much more. As of late 2001, the site had received more than one hundred thousand hits.

The club is managed by a fifteen-member board of directors, with a president, vice presidents, treasurer, secretary, and so on. All are club member volunteers (from all over the United States) who have shown a willingness and ability to help run the CCCA, and who have been elected by the total membership to three-year terms of office. They are not reimbursed for their expenses, which include attending eight board meetings each year, most of which are held at club headquarters in a club-owned office condominium in Des Plaines, Illinois (a site chosen because of its central location within the United States and its close proximity to Chicago's main airport). Another member volunteers as executive administrator and oversees the club's employees and its daily operations. The only paid employees of the club are a full-time office secretary, a part-time clerical worker, and the publications editor, who is a freelance automotive writer/editor. An organization chart of the CCCA is shown in Exhibit 4.

In addition to belonging to the national CCCA, the majority of members also pay dues and belong to a local CCCA regional chapter. In 2002, there are twenty-six regions throughout the United States (see Exhibit 5). Each region sponsors a variety of local activities for members and their Classic Cars and also publishes its own magazine or newsletter. Many of the regions also derive revenues from the sale of Classic Car replacement parts, service items, or clothing, offered to all members of the national club.

**EXHIBIT 4**     2002 CCCA Organization Chart

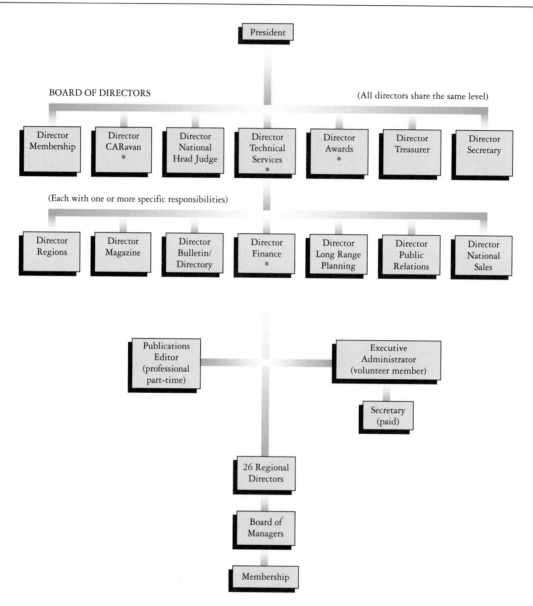

*This director chairs a committee for this functional responsibility, composed of other directors and members.
*Source:* The Classic Car Club of America, Inc.

Legally separate from the CCCA and its regions, a Classic Car Club of America Museum also exists. It occupies space as part of a larger old car museum in Hickory Corners, Michigan, and it displays a variety of Classic Cars that have been donated to it. The CCCA Museum, unlike the CCCA itself, is eligible to receive tax-deductible gifts of money and property (such as cars). Although the CCCA has granted the museum the right to use the CCCA name, the museum has a separate board of trustees and is run totally apart from the club. Because of this legal separation, the club's directors do not

EXHIBIT 5    Classic Car Club Regions

| | |
|---|---|
| Arizona | North Texas |
| Chesapeake bay (MD) | Northern California |
| Colorado | Ohio |
| Delaware Valley (PA) | Oil Belt (OK) |
| Dixie | Oregon |
| Florida | Pacific Northwest (WA) |
| Gold Coast (So. FLorida) | Rio Grande |
| Greater Illinois | San Diego/Paim Springs |
| Indiana | Southern California |
| Lone Star (Texas) | Spirit of St. Louis |
| Metropolitan (NY, NJ, So. CT) | Upper Midwest (MN) |
| Michigan | Western Pennsylvania |
| New England (MA, ME, NH, No. CT, RI, VT) | Wisconsin |

have the authority to make strategic decisions for the museum; nor can be museum's performance and finances directly benefit the club.

## CURRENT CONCERNS THAT FACE THE CCCA

While the officers and directors of the CCCA believe the club to be strong, both financially and in its value to its members, a variety of concerns about the future exists. One concern involves the use of the word *Classic* as it refers to collector cars. While the CCCA uses this term to denote the specific listing of 1925 to 1948 luxury cars that the club has designated as "Classic Cars," many other collector car hobbyists use the term more loosely to refer to any collector car which they see as special. Thus, one can find the word *Classic* used to describe 1928 Fords and 1955 Chevrolets. While the CCCA cannot legally protect and limit the hobby's use of *Classic*, the club has legally registered the terms *Full Classic* (a CCCA-designated Classic Car with its original body and motor) and *Modified Classic* (a Classic Car chassis with a replica body or incorrect motor). In its publications and publicity, the CCCA now refers to its members' cars as "Full Classics," and it is hoped that this trademark registration and usage will help to protect the term *Classic* as used by the club.

Another concern is the continuing effect of rising costs upon the club's ability to maintain its current level of services and benefits to members. In particular, the costs of both its publications and its headquarters (i.e., the office administration) have risen considerably over the years. The board of directors has responded by both watching costs carefully and by raising annual dues several times (from $10 in the 1960s to an increase in 2001 to $45 per year), but it recognizes that certain cost increases, while unavoidable, may result in a loss of members. (Financial statements are provided in Exhibits 6 and 7.)

One way to overcome this problem is to increase the number of members and thus create greater revenues for the club. (The number of members has risen only slightly in recent years. See Exhibit 3.) The directors know that many Classic Car owners do not belong to the CCCA. While CCCA members listed about seventy-five hundred Classic Cars in the most recent *Handbook and Directory*, no one really knows how many Classic Car owners are *not* in the club. Club efforts in recent years to increase membership have been targeted at these Classic Car-owning non-CCCA members. Letters have been sent to past members who failed to renew their CCCA membership (about 5 percent to 10 percent each year), region officers have contacted local non-CCCA members known to

EXHIBIT 6    CCCA Statements of Receipts and Disbursements (Cash Flow Basis)

| | FY2001 | FY2000 | FY1999 |
|---|---|---|---|
| **RECEIPTS** | | | |
| Active Membership Dues (dues received for current FY) | $ 18,462 | $ 25,116 | $ 17,302 |
| Prepaid Active Dues (dues received for next FY) | 177,603 | 159,561 | 152,440 |
| Associate Membership Dues | 1,008 | 1,099 | 712 |
| Prepaid Associate Dues | 7,425 | 7,425 | 6,830 |
| Life Memberships | 3,600 | 2,500 | 6,400 |
| Life Associate Memberships | 180 | 0 | 240 |
| Publications Sales | 1,558 | 2,793 | 2,912 |
| Awards Income (member registration fees for meets, etc.) | 12,977 | 10,530 | 10,831 |
| Caravan Income | 27,640 | 27,485 | 14,500 |
| National Sales Items | 9,045 | 7,310 | 6,253 |
| Insurance Income (from regions) | 4,225 | 3,397 | 3,540 |
| Book Income | 67,716 | 128,494 | 988 |
| Advertising Income—Bulletin | 25,228 | 26,890 | 28,205 |
| Advertising Income—Magazine | 2,000 | 2,500 | 1,465 |
| Advertising Income—Directory | 15,750 | 23,100 | 16,550 |
| Interest Income | 7,005 | 9,884 | 11,902 |
| Miscellaneous Income | 6,182 | 14,794 | 10,852 |
| TOTAL RECEIPTS | 387,604 | 452,878 | 291,922 |
| **DISBURSEMENTS** | | | |
| Membership Expense (recruitment) | 6,543 | 6,506 | 13,059 |
| Annual Meeting Expense | 10,792 | 8,944 | 2,015 |
| Awards Expense (meets, etc.) | 22,933 | 15,032 | 23,085 |
| Caravan Expense | 21,474 | 21,969 | 7,895 |
| National Sales Items | 12,261 | 4,888 | 1,725 |
| Book Expense | 40,599 | 251,231 | 11,061 |
| Bulletin Editor Fee | 10,221 | 13,244 | 13,537 |
| Bulletin Printing | 43,587 | 49,675 | 35,922 |
| Magazine Editor Fee | 10,000 | 10,092 | 10,700 |
| Magazine Printing | 78,163 | 85,457 | 81,004 |
| Directory Printing | 16,325 | 15,586 | 15,045 |
| General Administration (supplies, postage telephone, etc.) | 19,252 | 38,438 | 29,755 |
| Office (wages, condo expense) | 58,021 | 57,009 | 36,106 |
| Insurance | 8,936 | 6,909 | 8,366 |
| Professional Services | 6,424 | 8,832 | 5,445 |
| Miscellaneous Expenses | 7,253 | 3,607 | 7,727 |
| TOTAL EXPENSES | 372,784 | 597,419 | 302,447 |
| EXCESS RECEIPTS OVER DISBURSEMENTS (DEFICIT) | $ 14,820 | ($144,541) | ($ 10,525) |

Note: Certain unusual one-time receipts and disbursements omitted
*Source:* The Classic Car Club of America, Inc.

own Classic Cars, mailings have been sent to Classic Car-owning individuals found in directories of other old car clubs, articles about CCCA activities as well as a few paid advertisements have been placed in various old car hobby magazines, and membership ads have been placed in single-marque car clubs (such as the Packard club) in return for allowing those clubs to place their membership ads in the CCCA's publications.

Furthermore, while some CCCA members do not own Classic Cars, most do, for much of the pleasure of belonging to the club derives from participating in the various

EXHIBIT 7    CCCA Balance Sheets

|  | FY2001 | FY2000 | FY1999 | FY1998 | FY1997 | FY1996 |
|---|---|---|---|---|---|---|
| ASSETS |  |  |  |  |  |  |
| Bank Balance | $ 20,500 | $ 35,815 | $ 25,550 | $ 30,957 | $ 8,685 | $ 28,970 |
| Investments (at cost) (money market funds, govt. notes, etc.) (includes life membership fund) | 389,959 | 291,215 | 322,992 | 293,019 | 385,700 | 256,743 |
| Office Condominium | 166,636 | 148,071 | 151,968 | 154,698 | 84,968 | 84,968 |
| TOTAL ASSETS | 577,095 | 475,101 | 500,510 | 478,674 | 479,353 | 370,681 |
| LIABILITIES | 0 | 0 | 0 | 0 | 0 | 0 |
| OWNERS' EQUITY | $577,095 | $475,071 | $500,510 | $478,674 | $479,353 | $370,681 |

*Source:* The Classic Car Club of America, Inc.

activities with a Classic Car. Thus, while Classic Car enthusiasts who do not own a Classic Car might also be appropriate targets for CCCA new-membership recruitment efforts, the primary focus has been on people who currently own a Classic Car.

Currently, very few CCCA members live outside the United States. About 2 percent of all members live in Canada, and less than 2 percent live outside of North America (mainly in western Europe). While countries beyond the United States might be good targets for membership recruitment efforts, the club's directors have never been able to determine whether this is the case, and no formal attempts at international recruitment have ever been made.

The club's membership recruitment efforts have only been moderately successful. While new members have offset the annual 5 to 10 percent attrition rate, total membership has risen only slightly in recent years. Yet unless the listing of recognized Classic Cars is expanded, the number of Classic Cars in existence is fixed, and with it, by and large, so too is the number of Classic Car owners.

There are varying opinions within the CCCA with regard to expanding the current listing of Classic Cars, and there are two directions for such an expansion. One way is to add makes and/or models to the current 1925 to 1948–year limits. Another way is to add cars built before 1925 or after 1948.

Several times in recent years, the board of directors has voted to add additional models of existing Classic makes to the CCCA's 1925 to 1948 listing (for example, by adding a Packard model line slightly lower in original price to already-listed Packard model lines of the same year). Also, a few lesser-known makes of this time period have been added (such as the American Elcar and the French Georges Irat), but only a handful of these cars still exist. These additions have drawn a mixed reaction from the membership. Some members feel that such additions dilute the meaning of "Classic Car," while most other members seem to support the directors' decisions—or have no strong opinion.

More controversial is the issue of expanding the listing to before 1925 or after 1948. In a 1999 membership survey, many members supported going earlier. They argued that many luxury car models of the early 1920s were virtually identical to CCCA-recognized 1925 Classics—and, therefore, these cars should also be recognized as "Classic." Other members believe that certain high-quality pre-1925 cars should be added to the "Classic" listing, even if they are not identical to their 1925 counterparts.

In the same survey, a somewhat smaller group of members favored a post-1948 expansion, again some wanting to add only cars identical to already-recognized 1948 models and others wanting different but equally high-quality post-1948 cars. An additional argument for adding post-1948 cars is that it might add new and younger members to the CCCA. It is argued that the club is currently not attracting young members, and this is because younger people are less able to afford the cost of a Classic Car and are also unable to "identify" with a 1925 to 1948 car the way they can with a car of the 1950s or 1960s. Current prices of Classic Cars vary greatly, depending upon the make of car, its condition, and type of body. Also, it is true that many current CCCA members own Classic Cars because of nostalgia for cars of their youth.

The issue of an aging CCCA membership is supported by the numbers. In 1983, 21 percent of all members responding to a membership survey were under forty-five years of age. In 1999, only 6 percent were under forty-five. In 1983, 22 percent were sixty-five or older; in 1999, that percentage had increased to 44 percent. Clearly, the club's membership is aging. Yet the total number of club members has held fairly steady. So is an aging membership a threat to the CCCA or just a changing characteristic of the club?

The CCCA's board of directors is struggling with the issues of expanding beyond the current 1925 to 1948 "Classic Car" limits. While changes might add new (and perhaps younger) members and more dues revenues, the club's mission and focus might be diluted by any expansion. Would a broader focus and listing of accepted "Classics" reduce the attraction of the club to its existing members, who have many other old car clubs to choose from?

Beyond the board's concerns about the meaning and usage of the term *Classic Car* and the future financial strength of the club, there is also a concern about the use of members' Classic Cars and the nature of CCCA activities. As previously mentioned, the values of Classic Cars have risen significantly over the years. In 1952, when the club was founded, most people viewed Classic Cars as simply "old cars," and they could generally be bought for a few hundred to a few thousand dollars. Today, many view Classic Cars as major investment items, with professional dealers and auctions a significant factor in the marketplace. While some less exotic and unrestored Classic Car models can be found for under $15,000, most sell for $20,000 to $75,000, and the most desirable Classic Cars (convertible models with custom bodies, twelve and sixteen cylinder engines, etc.) can sell for $100,000 and more. (A very small number of especially exotic and desirable Classic Cars have sold in the $250,000 to $1,000,000 range, and a 1929 Bugatti Royale reportedly sold in 1987 for over $9.8 million!) Furthermore, judging meets have become very serious events, with awards and high scores adding significantly to a Classic Car's sales value. Thus, many highly desirable and/or top scoring Classic Cars are now hardly driven at all, and they are transported in enclosed trailers to and from judging meets. While most Classic Car owners still enjoy driving their cars—and the CCCA CARavans continue to be highly popular among club members—some members yearn for the old days when there was less emphasis on judging and on a car's value, and when CCCA members would drive and park their Classic Cars anywhere.

Still another concern of some members involves the possibility of a greater stress in future years on the conservation of gasoline in this country. If the country did focus more seriously on its high usage of gasoline, how would the public view Classic Cars and the collector-car hobby in general? Would the ownership and driving of cars for nontransportation purposes be considered unpatriotic or wasteful?

## MEMBERSHIP SURVEYS

In response to these various concerns, the CCCA Board of Directors established a Long Range Planning Committee to study issues about the future of the club and to make recommendations to the board. In 1983, in 1991, and again in 1999, a membership questionnaire was sent to all members along with their membership renewal material. The response rate to each survey was excellent. Exhibit 8 presents a summary of the 1999 survey findings.

## FUTURE DIRECTION OF THE CCCA

As the club's 2002 fiscal year progresses, the CCCA Board of Directors is studying these and other issues. Some issues seem more important than others and deserve more immediate attention. While the survey clarifies some of the opinions of the members, the board does not view this survey as a ballot, one that obligates the board to follow the majority preference in every question area.

Beyond the specific concerns discussed here, the officers and directors of the club simply want to do a good job. Their fellow members have elected them to keep the club strong and to improve it further. They want to be proactive as well as reactive; they want to be imaginative in their strategic management activities as well as to respond to concerns and issues already raised.

Together for their regular Board of Directors meeting in early 2002, the fifteen officers and directors of the CCCA ask themselves the following questions:

1. What are the various criteria we should consider when making strategic decisions for the club? How do we balance financial objectives and nonfinancial objectives? Which are primary and which are secondary?

2. How important are and how should we deal with rising costs to the club?

3. If we are forced to choose between raising dues or lowering the services provided to the members, which takes priority?

4. Should the club be offering more services to its members, even if this requires an increase in dues?

5. Is expansion of the listing of recognized Classic Cars desirable?

6. Which is preferable: adding cars within the 1925 to 1948 time period, or adding cars of earlier or later years? What are the pros and cons of these alternatives?

---

EXHIBIT 8    Classic Car Club of America 2002 Membership Survey Responses Summary

---

1. Thirty-two percent of the member (1,766 members) responded to the survey.
2. There is a continued aging of the membership, as well as the number of years of individuals' membership.
   Seventy-eight percent of the members are 55 years or older.
   The average age is 63.
   Seventy-eight percent of the members have been club members for 5 years or more.
   Sixty percent have been members for more than 10 years.
3. Members own an average of 3 Classic Cars.
   Members own an average of 2 other collector cars.
4. Seventy-six percent of the members belong to a CCCA Region.
5. Seventy-two percent of the members attended a national CCCA event in the past 3 years.
6. Members belonged to an average of 4 other car clubs.
7. Seventy-four percent of members rated the CCCA as "best" or "better than most" in comparison to other car clubs.
8. Sixty-six percent rated the CCCA Grand Classic judging meets "good" to "excellent." (31% had no opinion).
9. Thirty-one percent rated the annual meetings as "good" to "excellent." (64% had no opinion).
10. Eighty-one percent rated *The Classic Car* magazine as "excellent," an additional 16% rated it "good."
11. Sixty-nine percent rated the *CCCA Bulletin* as "excellent"; an additional 27% rated it "good."
12. Within the 1925–1948 time period, 44% favored keeping the listing of accepted Classic Cars as-is; 41% favored expanding the list to include additional 1925–1948 cars.
13. Regarding the possibility of expanding the 1925–1948 time period: 20% favored retaining the current 1925–1948 time period; 16% favored accepting certain pre-1925 cars but no post-1948 cars; 13% favored accepting certain post-1948 cars but no pre-1925 cars; 38% favored accepting certain pre-1925 cars *and* certain post-1948 cars; 13% gave no answer; answered "don't know," or gave inconsistent responses.

7. How important is it to increase the number of members in the club? What are some alternative ways to increase membership?

8. How serious is the aging membership of the club? How can younger people be attracted to the CCCA? How important is this? What specific strategies could be adopted to accomplish this goal?

9. Are there other possible sources of revenue to the club? What might some be?

10. How important is protecting the term *Classic Car*? What else can the CCCA do to further such protection?

11. Are there other long-range issues or concerns that the club has not yet addressed?

# HARLEY-DAVIDSON, INC.—2002

**Richard A. Cox**
**Francis Marion University**

HDI

www.harley-davidson.com

There is something about the power of this brand and this company that intrigues us all. Whether you are a rider or an investor—or whether you are just interested—you have to admit that the way this company connects with its customers truly sets Harley-Davidson apart. Harley-Davidson has customers who are very passionate about their products. The name Harley-Davidson and its logo no doubt represent symbols of American individualism and even a bit of American rebelliousness. Everyone has seen at least one person with the famous Harley Bar & Shield logo tattooed on his or her arm. What is it about this company that would cause someone to want to be associated with it in such a permanent way? Is it the people and events that draw riders to Harley-Davidson? The company sponsors rides and rallies everywhere from Daytona to Houston—or even in international cities like Saint-Tropez, Sungwoo, and Lillehammer. From Mexico to Mount Fuji or from Austria to Australia, riders today can experience Harley at events in more than one hundred countries.

For some riders, however, the thrill may just be the back roads and just riding alone on a lazy Saturday afternoon. Others could have been lured in by the distinctive sound of a Harley-Davidson. Even the Harley Web site roars. No other motorcycle has the same sound as the company's legendary V-twin. The famous uneven rumble or "potato, potato, potato" sound has survived for generations and is as distinctive as the customers who ride the bikes. Whatever the reason, this type of loyalty has helped Harley-Davidson to survive against fierce international competition and maintain a strong financial performance.

In 2001, Harley-Davidson delivered record revenue and earnings for the sixteenth consecutive year. As shown in Exhibit 1, Harley's net sales for 2001 totaled $3.36 billion, a 15.7 percent increase over 2000. Net income was 437.7 million, up 25.9 percent from 2000. The company has experienced a compound annual growth rate in its stock price of over 40 percent since going public in 1986. Harley's 2001 balance sheet is provided in Exhibit 2.

## HISTORY

In 1903, what was to become a legendary motorcycle company was formed in the Davidson family's backyard. The Davidson brothers, William D., Walter, Arthur, and William S. Harley, made their first motorcycle there. In 1909, Harley-Davidson introduced its first V-twin engine. This engine is still the company standard to this day.

During World War I, Harley-Davidson supplied the military with some 20,000 motorcycles. During this time, there were major advancements in the design of motorcycles, and Harley was the leader. However, a decade after the war ended, the Great Depression devastated the motorcycle industry. Only Harley-Davidson and Indian (Hendee Manufacturing) survived through the 1930s.

In 1941, World War II called, and Harley-Davidson answered with more than 90,000 motorcycles. After the war, demand for motorcycles exploded, and Harley-Davidson added

EXHIBIT 1    Consolidated Statement of Income (in thousands, except per share amounts)

| Years ended December 31, | 2001 | 2000 | 1999 |
|---|---|---|---|
| Net sales | $3,363,414 | $2,906,365 | $2,452,939 |
| Cost of goods sold | 2,183,409 | 1,915,547 | 1,617,253 |
| Gross profit | 1,180,005 | 990,818 | 835,686 |
| Financial services income | 181,545 | 140,135 | 132,741 |
| Financial services interest and operating expense | 120,272 | 102,957 | 105,056 |
| Operating income from financial services | 61,273 | 37,178 | 27,685 |
| Selling, administrative and engineering expense | (578,777) | (513,024) | (447,512) |
| Income from operations | 662,501 | 514,972 | 415,859 |
| Gain on sale of credit card business | — | 18,915 | — |
| Interest income, net | 17,478 | 17,583 | 8,014 |
| Other, net | (6,524) | (2,914) | (3,080) |
| Income before provision for income taxes | 673,455 | 548,556 | 420,793 |
| Provision for income taxes | 235,709 | 200,843 | 153,592 |
| Net income | $437,746 | $ 347,713 | $ 267,201 |
| Basic earnings per common share | $1.45 | $1.15 | $.88 |
| Diluted earnings per common share | $1.43 | $1.13 | $.86 |
| Cash dividends per common share | $ .12 | $ .10 | $.09 |

*Source:* Harley's 2001 *Annual Report,* p. 55.

additional facilities in Milwaukee in 1947. That same year, the company began selling what was to become the classic black leather motorcycle jacket. After Indian closed in 1953, Harley-Davidson was the sole American motorcycle manufacturer for the next 46 years (**www.harley-davidson.com**). Harley ended family ownership in 1965 with a public offering. Only four years later, the company merged with the American Machine and Foundry Company (AMF), a longtime producer of leisure products.

By the early 1970s, the Japanese were importing huge numbers of lower-priced motorcycles into the United States. Japanese firms were able to capture a large portion of Harley's market share. Because it had expanded production so quickly, Harley was also having quality problems. In 1981, thirteen of Harley's senior executives purchased the business from AMF. The company then convinced President Ronald Reagan, by relying on a recommendation from the International Trade Commission (ITC), to impose additional tariffs on imported heavyweight Japanese motorcycles that were 700cc or larger for five years, starting in 1983. Then in 1986, Harley-Davidson, Inc. became publicly held for the first time since 1969. That same year, Harley regained its place at the top of the U.S. superheavyweight market, beating out Honda. The next year, the company asked the ITC to remove the tariffs one year early. This move made both business and American history, and President Reagan praised the company as an "American success story." Harley's U.S. market share continued to grow, and the company was listed on the New York Stock Exchange in 1987. The company had not only survived a difficult time, but some would say that it became an American icon.

## CORPORATE MISSION STATEMENT

Harley's mission statement as provided in the company's 2001 *Annual Report* says, "We fulfill dreams through the experiences of motorcycling, by providing to motorcyclists and to the general public an expanding line of motorcycles, branded products and services in selected market segments."

EXHIBIT 2    Consolidated Balance Sheets (in thousands, except share amounts)

| December 31, | 2001 | 2000 |
|---|---|---|
| **ASSETS** | | |
| Current assets: | | |
| Cash and cash equivalents | $ 439,438 | $ 419,736 |
| Marketable securities | 196,011 | — |
| Accounts receivable, net | 118,843 | 98,311 |
| Current portion of finance receivables, net | 656,421 | 530,859 |
| Inventories | 181,115 | 191,931 |
| Deferred income taxes | 38,993 | 28,280 |
| Prepaid expenses & other current assets | 34,443 | 28,147 |
| Total current assets | 1,665,264 | 1,297,264 |
| Finance receivables, net | 379,335 | 234,091 |
| Property, plant, and equipment, net | 891,820 | 754,115 |
| Goodwill, net | 49,711 | 54,331 |
| Other assets | 132,365 | 96,603 |
| | $3,118,495 | $2,436,404 |
| | | |
| **LIABILITIES AND SHAREHOLDERS' EQUITY** | | |
| Current liabilities: | | |
| Accounts payable | $ 194,683 | $ 169,844 |
| Accrued expenses and other liabilities | 304,376 | 238,390 |
| Current portion of finance debt | 217,051 | 89,509 |
| Total current liabilities | 716,110 | 497,743 |
| Finance debt | 380,000 | 355,000 |
| Other long-term liabilities | 158,374 | 81,707 |
| Postretirement health care benefits | 89,912 | 80,666 |
| Deferred income taxes | 17,816 | 15,633 |
| Commitments and contingencies | | |
| Shareholders' equity: | | |
| Series A junior participating preferred stock, none issued | — | — |
| Common stock, 324,340,432 and 321,185, 567 shares issued in 2001 and 2000, respectively | 3,242 | 3,210 |
| Additional paid-in capital | 359,165 | 285,390 |
| Retained earnings | 1,833,335 | 1,431,017 |
| Accumulated other comprehensive income (loss) | (13,728) | 308 |
| | 2,182,014 | 1,719,925 |
| Less: | | |
| Treasury stock (21,550,923 and 19,114,822 shares in 2001 and 2000, respectively), at cost | (425,546) | (313,994) |
| Unearned compensation | (185) | (276) |
| Total shareholders' equity | 1,756,283 | 1,405,655 |
| | $3,118,495 | $2,436,404 |

*Source:* Harley's 2001 *Annual Report.*

## CORPORATE VISION STATEMENT

Harley's vision statement is as follows:

> *Harley-Davidson is an action-oriented, international company, a leader in its commitment to continuously improve {its} mutually beneficial relationships with*

*stakeholders (customers, suppliers, employees, shareholders, government, and society). Harley-Davidson believes the key to success is to balance stakeholders' interests through the empowerment of all employees to focus on value-added activities.*

## HARLEY DIVISIONS

Harley-Davidson is divided into two segments: (1) motorcycles and related products and (2) financial services. The motorcycles and related products segment designs, manufactures, and sells motorcycles, motorcycle parts, accessories, and general merchandise. The financial services segment consists of Harley's wholly owned subsidiary, Harley-Davidson Financial Services, Inc (HDFS). HDFS provides financial service programs to Harley and Buell dealers and consumers in the United States and Canada. Note in Exhibit 3, the organizational chart for the company, that Harley's management is centered on these two divisions.

The average purchaser of a U.S. Harley-Davidson motorcycle is a married male in his mid-forties, with a household income of approximately $77,700. Over two-thirds of the sales of Harley-Davidson motorcycles are to buyers with at least one year of higher education beyond high school, and 30 percent have college degrees. Only about 9 percent of Harley's U.S. retail motorcycle sales are to women. Repeat business is strong as about 45 percent of motorcycle purchasers owned a Harley previously.

Harley's heavyweight class of motorcycles is divided into four segments: standard, performance, touring, and custom. The standard segment emphasizes simplicity and cost, and the performance segment emphasizes handling and acceleration. The touring segment for the company focuses on comfort for long-distance travel. Harley-Davidson pioneered this segment of the heavyweight market. Harley's custom segment gives owners the opportunity to customize their bikes.

Harley-Davidson makes twenty-four models of Harley-Davidson touring and custom heavyweight motorcycles, with retail prices ranging from about $6,000 to $20,000. The prices of Harley's custom bikes on the high end can be as much as 50 percent more than its competitors' custom motorcycles. The custom segment makes up the highest number of Harley's sold and demands a higher price because of its features, styling, and high resale value.

Harley has one custom model that is priced competitively with comparable motorcycles available in the market—the 883cc Sportster. This model serves as sort of an introduction bike for new Harley-Davidson customers. The company's surveys of retail purchasers indicate that over 75 percent of the purchasers of its Sportster model have previously owned competitive-brand motorcycles, are new to the sport of motorcycling, or have been out of the sport for five or more years. The company also has research indicating that more than 92 percent of its motorcycle customers intend to repurchase. Harley is hoping that the purchasers of the lower-priced Sportster models will be tempted to purchase a higher-priced custom model the next time around.

The Buell motorcycle line serves the standard and performance segments of the market. Buell sells four heavyweight performance models, with retail prices ranging from $8,795 to $13,700. The company also introduced the Buell Blast in 2000 for the standard market, with a price tag of about $4,395. The Blast is smaller and lighter than the other motorcycles offered by Buell. The bike also has a single cylinder engine as opposed to the trademark V-engine configuration. The company's studies indicate that almost half of Buell Blast purchasers have never owned a motorcycle before, and over 50 percent are women. Harley-Davidson bought a minority interest in Buell, a sport bike company, in 1992 and finished buying the remaining interest in 1998. Production of the new Buell Firebolt XB9R began in 2001.

EXHIBIT 3    Harley Davidson's Organization Chart

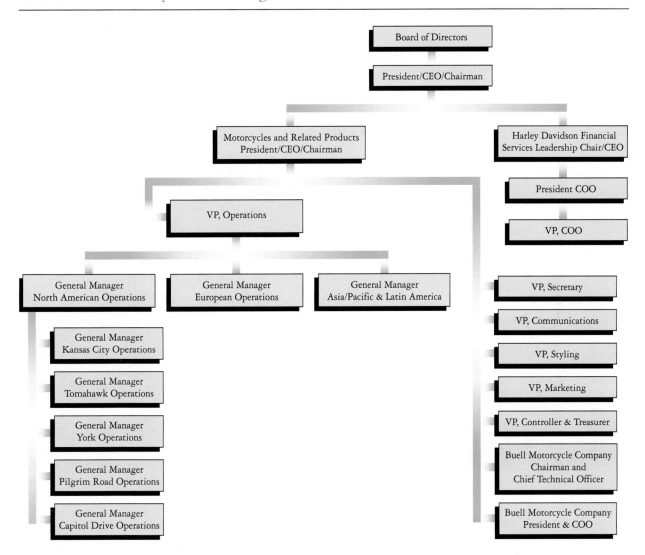

Harley-Davidson Financial Services (HDFS) has in 2001 helped over 87,000 retail buyers with the purchase of a new or used Harley. HDFS also offers wholesale financing, with services including floorplan and open account financing of motorcycles and accessories. In addition, the company often makes real estate loans, computer loans, and showroom remodeling loans to many dealers. In the United States and Canada, where these services are offered, they were used by about 97 percent of all dealers.

Note in Exhibit 4 that the financial services division had a great year during 2001; operating income increased 64.8 percent—to 61 million. The ability of HDFS to offer a package of wholesale and retail financial services is a major competitive advantage. HDFS can compete based on convenience, service, terms, and price. The financial services segment can also rely on its strong dealer relations and industry experience to compete for both the company's wholesale and retail finance businesses. HDFS finances

EXHIBIT 4    Operations Relating to the Financial Services Segment (in thousands)

|  | 2000 | 1999 | 1998 |
|---|---|---|---|
| Interest income | $ 71,414 | $ 78,502 | $ 65,203 |
| Securitization and servicing fee income | 42,257 | 36,378 | 24,380 |
| Other income | 26,464 | 17,861 | 13,339 |
| Total income | 140,135 | 132,741 | 102,922 |
| Interest expense | 30,354 | 28,686 | 24,008 |
| Provision for credit losses | 9,919 | 17,919 | 10,338 |
| Operating expenses | 62,684 | 58,451 | 48,365 |
| Total expenses | 102,957 | 105,056 | 82,711 |
| Operating income from financial services | $ 37,178 | $ 27,685 | $ 20,211 |

*Source:* Harley's 2001 *Annual Report*, p. 37.

about 25 percent of new Harley-Davidson motorcycles retailed in the U.S. The main competitors for the retail and wholesale businesses of HDFS are local and regional financial institutions.

## MARKETING AND DISTRIBUTION

Harley-Davidson has approximately 630 independently owned full-service dealerships in the United States. The marketing efforts are divided between dealer promotions, customer events, magazine and direct mail advertising, and public relations. Harley also sponsors racing activities and special promotional events, and it participates in all major motorcycle consumer shows and rallies. The Harley Owners Group (H.O.G), which was founded in 1983, currently has approximately 660,000 members worldwide and is the industry's largest company-sponsored motorcycle enthusiast organization (**www.hog.com**). The Buell Riders' Adventure Group (BRAG) was also formed in recent years and has grown to approximately 10,000 members. Both H.O.G and BRAG sponsor events, including national rallies and rides, across the United States and around the world for motorcycle enthusiasts.

A major marketing initiative for Harley in 2003 will be the celebration of its 100th anniversary. The company plans to have a rolling birthday party lasting more than a year. The party will circle the globe with a series of traveling festivals lasting two to three days at a time. In July 2002, the Open Road Tour began in North America and then moved south to Mexico. The tour will jump continents to Australia and Japan before wrapping up with a couple of events in Europe in the summer of 2003.

Harley-Davidson is one of the most admired and recognized companies in the world today. Recently, the company has attempted to create an increased awareness of the Harley-Davidson brand name among the nonriding public and to provide a wide range of products for enthusiasts by licensing the Harley-Davidson name. The company has licensed the production and sale of T-shirts, jewelry, small leather goods, toys, and other products. The company also licenses the Harley-Davidson name to two cafes, one located in New York and one in Las Vegas. As can be seen in Exhibit 5, general merchandise sales went up 12.5 percent to $163.9 million in 2001.

Harley has also created an Academy of Motorcycling for those interested in learning to ride a motorcycle. The Academy, which is called "Rider's Edge," introduced more than one thousand aspiring motorcyclists to the sport in 2000. Those riders learned aboard the new single-cylinder Buell Blast. The participating dealers are creating new customers

EXHIBIT 5    Motorcycle Unit Shipments and Net Sales (dollars in millions)

| | 2001 | 2000 | Increase (Decrease) | % Change |
|---|---|---|---|---|
| Motorcycle Unit Shipments | | | | |
| Harley-Davidson® motorcycle units | 234,461 | 204,592 | 29,869 | 14.6% |
| Buell® motorcycle units | 9,925 | 10,189 | (264) | (2.6) |
| Total motorcycle units | 244,386 | 214,781 | 29,605 | 138% |
| Net Sales | | | | |
| Harley-Davidson motorcycles | $   2,630.1 | $   2,246.4 | $    383.7 | 17.1% |
| Buell motorcycles | 61.9 | 58.1 | 38 | 6.6 |
| Total motorcycles | 2,692.0 | 2,304.5 | 387.5 | 16.8% |
| Motorcycle Parts and Accessories | 507.3 | 447.9 | 59.4 | 13.3 |
| General Merchandise | 163.9 | 151.4 | 12.5 | 8.2 |
| Other | .2 | 2.6 | (2.4) | (92.3) |
| Total Motorcycles and Related Products | $   3,363.4 | $   2,906.4 | $    457.0 | 15.7% |

*Source:* Harley's 2001 *Annual Report*, p. 42.

today that could lead to lifelong relationships. Harley dealers are serious about the future success of Harley-Davidson; almost half of all U.S. dealers have opened new retail stores or completed major renovations to their existing facilities in the past three years.

Harley has an online catalog featuring its genuine motor accessories and motor-clothes. In addition to browsing and making a wish list, customers can actually purchase these products at the Web site. The orders are then distributed to local dealers who can ship the products directly or hold the items for pick-up. More than 5 million visitors surfed through the e-commerce area during the year.

## INTERNATIONAL SALES

Harley-Davidson faces some unique competitive challenges in international markets. In Europe, for example, it must consider the unique tastes of many individual countries that together represent a market about the size of the U.S. market. Also, the European Union's motorcycle noise standards are lower than those of the Environmental Protection Agency (EPA). This causes research and development costs related to motorcycle noise emissions to be higher for motorcycles produced for the European market.

Another challenge for Harley is the fact that the European heavyweight motorcy-cle market is made up of 74 percent of the standard and performance segments. Harley has only recently started to compete in the performance market with the addition of its Buell motorcycles. As can be seen in Exhibit 6, the European market had 293,400 new registrations in 2000, down 4.3 percent from 306,700 in 1999. Harley ended 2001 with a 6.7 percent share of the European heavyweight market, down from 7.4 percent in 2000. The company has had difficulty growing its market share in European markets. In the European region, there are about 350 Harley-Davidson dealerships.

Harley finished 2001 with a 20.4 percent share of the Asia/Pacific heavyweight market, up from 19.5 percent in 2000. It is now easier than previously to obtain a heavy-weight motorcycle driver's license in Japan. While total market registrations in the Asia/Pacific decreased 1.0 percent in 2001, Harley registrations were up 3.7 percent over 1999. In 2001, lawmakers in Japan scrapped a widely unpopular law that restricted the speed to 48 mph (80 kph) on expressways (see **www.japanauto.com/autotrends**). The revision, the first in thirty-five years, boosts the speed to 62 mph (100 kph). The

EXHIBIT 6    Worldwide Heavyweight Motorcycle Registration Data (Engine Displacement of 651+cc) (units in thousands)

|  | 2000 | 1999 | 1998 |
|---|---|---|---|
| **NORTH AMERICA**[1] |  |  |  |
| Total market new registrations | 363.4 | 297.9 | 246.2 |
| Harley-Davidson® new registrations | 164.0 | 142.1 | 116.1 |
| Buell® new registrations | 4.3 | 4.0 | 3.3 |
| Total company registrations | 168.3 | 146.1 | 119.4 |
| Total company market share % | 46.3% | 49.0% | 48.5% |
| **EUROPE**[2] |  |  |  |
| Total market new registrations | 293.4 | 306.7 | 270.2 |
| Harley-Davidson new registrations | 19.9 | 17.8 | 15.7 |
| Buell new registrations | 1.9 | 2.1 | 1.6 |
| Total company registrations | 21.8 | 19.9 | 17.3 |
| Total company market share % | 7.4% | 6.5% | 6.4% |
| **JAPAN/AUSTRALIA**[3] |  |  |  |
| Total market new registrations | 62.7 | 63.1 | 69.2 |
| Harley-Davidson new registrations | 12.2 | 11.6 | 10.3 |
| Buell new registrations | .7 | .7 | .5 |
| Total company registrations | 12.9 | 12.3 | 10.8 |
| Total company market share % | 20.5% | 19.6% | 15.6% |
| **TOTAL** |  |  |  |
| Total new registrations | 719.5 | 667.7 | 585.6 |
| Harley-Davidson new registrations | 196.1 | 171.5 | 142.1 |
| Buell new registrations | 6.9 | 6.8 | 5.4 |
| Total company registrations | 203.0 | 178.3 | 147.5 |
| Total company market share % | 28.2% | 26.7% | 25.2% |

[1]Includes the United States and Canada. Data provided by the Motorcycle Industry Council.
[2]Includes Austria, Belgium, France, Germany, Italy, The Netherlands, Spain, Switzerland, and the United Kingdom. Data provided by Giral S.A.
[3]Data provided by JAMA and ABS.

Japanese Automobile Manufacturers Association (JAMA) reported that an American-based research firm expects motorcycle sales to rise 30 percent as a result of the changes. There are currently about 213 Harley-Davidson outlets serving eight country markets in the Asia/Pacific region (see Exhibit 7).

In 1998, the company opened a new assembly facility in Manaus, Brazil, the first such operation outside the United States. The facility imports U.S.-made components for final assembly in Brazil. This will increase the availability of Harley's motorcycles in Brazil, and it will reduce duties and taxes, making them more affordable to a larger group of Brazilian customers. In the past, only the wealthy in Brazil could afford a Harley because of the steep import tariffs. The facility currently assembles fewer than one thousand motorcycles per year.

In 2001, international sales were 597.0 million, up 20.0 percent from 2000. The motor company exported about 20.3 percent of its Harley-Davidson motorcycles in 2001, down slightly from the 22.4 percent reported in 2000.

EXHIBIT 7    Geographic Information (in thousands)

|  | 2001 | 2000 | 1999 |
|---|---|---|---|
| Net sales: | | | |
| United States | $2,766,391 | $2,320,991 | $1,915,631 |
| Europe | 301,729 | 285,372 | 274,737 |
| Japan | 141,181 | 148,684 | 135,589 |
| Canada | 96,928 | 93,352 | 80,271 |
| Other foreign countries | 57,185 | 57,966 | 46,711 |
|  | $3,363,414 | $2,906,365 | $2,452,939 |
| Long-lived assets: | | | |
| United States | $1,021,946 | $ 856,746 | $ 775,764 |
| Other foreign countries | 33,234 | 27,844 | 8,948 |
|  | $1,055,180 | $ 884,590 | $ 784,712 |

*Source:* Harley's 2001 *Annual Report,* p. 81.

## COMPETITION

The U.S. and international heavyweight (651+cc) motorcycle market is highly competitive. Some of Harley's major competitors have larger financial and marketing resources and are more diversified. For example, only about half of the sales of Yamaha Motor Company are motorcycles. Competition in the heavyweight motorcycle market is based on price, quality, reliability, styling, and customer preference. Harley-Davidson does not emphasize price in its heavyweight bikes partly because the resale prices for used Harley-Davidson motorcycles are generally higher than that of its competitors.

Since 1986, Harley has led the industry in domestic sales of heavyweight motorcycles. As shown in Exhibit 8, Harley's share of the U.S. heavyweight (651+cc) market was 47.4 percent in 2000, down from 50.2 percent in 1999. The company believes this decline was due to its ongoing capacity constraints. However, Harley's share is still significantly greater than its largest competitor in the domestic market, Honda, which had an 18.6 percent market share in 2000. During 2000, the worldwide heavyweight market grew 7.8 percent, while retail registrations for Harley-Davidson's motorcycles grew 13.8 percent. Note in Exhibit 6 that this netted the company a worldwide heavyweight market share of 28.2 percent, up from 26.7 percent in 1999.

A new potential domestic threat for Harley-Davidson in recent years is Polaris. Polaris, an American snowmobile/ATV manufacturer, started production of its Victory motorcycles on July 4, 1998. The company is planning to introduce three more models in 2002, and all are priced below the average price of a Harley (see **www.polarisindustries.com**). The company has more than three hundred dealers in the United States, and in 2000, it expanded into Canada, United Kingdom, and Australia, with plans for future expansion. While current sales volumes for Polaris motorcycles are not significant in comparison to Harley-Davidson, the threat that Polaris may gain a piece of the domestic market is very real. Polaris finished 2000 with retail sales of motorcycles up 50 percent, to about $20 million. Motorcycles currently represent only about 1 percent of overall sales at Polaris. The president of Polaris, Tom Tiller, stated in a February 2001 press release, "We are in the motorcycle business for the long-term and remain confident in Victory's ability to contribute to profitable growth for Polaris" (**www.americanmotor.com/news**).

EXHIBIT 8   Market share of U.S. Heavyweight Motorcycles[1]
(Engine Displacement of 651+cc)

| | Year Ended December 31, | | | | |
|---|---|---|---|---|---|
| | *2000* | *1999* | *1998* | *1997* | *1996* |
| **NEW U.S. REGISTRATIONS (THOUSANDS OF UNITS):** | | | | | |
| Total market new registrations | 338.0 | 275.6 | 227.1 | 190.2 | 165.7 |
| Harley-Davidson® new registrations | 155.9 | 134.5 | 109.1 | 93.5 | 79.9 |
| Buell® new registrations | 4.2 | 3.9 | 3.2 | 1.9 | 1.7 |
| Total Company new registrations | 160.1 | 138.4 | 112.3 | 95.4 | 81.6 |
| **PERCENTAGE MARKET SHARE:** | | | | | |
| Harley-Davidson motorcycles | 46.1% | 48.8% | 48.1% | 49.2% | 48.2% |
| Buell motorcycles | 1.3 | 1.4 | 1.4 | 1.0 | 1.0 |
| Total Company | 47.4 | 50.2 | 49.5 | 50.2 | 49.2 |
| Honda | 18.6 | 16.4 | 20.3 | 18.5 | 18.8 |
| Suzuki | 9.4 | 9.4 | 10.0 | 10.1 | 8.7 |
| Kawasaki | 9.1 | 10.3 | 10.1 | 10.4 | 12.2 |
| Yamaha | 8.4 | 7.0 | 4.2 | 5.4 | 5.9 |
| Other | 7.1 | 6.7 | 5.9 | 5.4 | 5.2 |
| Total | 100.0% | 100.0% | 100.0% | 100.0% | 100.0% |

[1] Motorcycle registration and market share information has been derived from data published by the Motorcycle Industry Council for the years 1997-2000 and from data published by R.L. Polk & Co. for 1996.

In November 2001, Suzuki Motor Corporation and Kawasaki Heavy Industries, Ltd. formed a strategic alliance in the areas of product development, design, engineering, and manufacturing of motorcycles (see **www.suzukicycles.com**). The alliance is expected to strengthen both companies' global motorcycle businesses. Each company will continue to use its own brand insofar as marketing and sales will not be combined. Note in Exhibit 8 that when combined, the market share of Suzuki and Kawasaki rivals that of Honda, Harley's number one competitor in the United States. Harley will have to address this new competitive threat, since the alliance of these two firms will certainly strengthen their efforts to gain more of Harley's coveted domestic market for heavyweights.

## STRATEGIC PLAN FOR SUSTAINABLE GROWTH

The company announced on September 19, 2001, that it plans to move the assembly operation of its "Dyna Glide" family of motorcycles to its facility in Kansas City, Missouri. This was done as part of its continuing effort to narrow the gap between supply and demand. All Dyna Glide models are currently assembled in York, Pennsylvania, and this part of its business represents around 15 percent of total production. The company also announced on July 11, 2001, that it plans to build a new $145 million, 350,000 square-foot assembly plant in York on the site of its existing manufacturing facility. The president of the motor company feels that this new facility, coupled with the movement of production between the plants, will provide strong and flexible manufacturing capabilities.

Harley plans to continue to increase its motorcycle production to be able to sustain its annual double-digit growth rate for units shipped. The company has plans to expand its operations in Tomahawk, Wisconsin, and at its product development center in

Milwaukee. Harley produced and sold 234,461 Harley-Davidson motorcycles in 2001, up 14.6 percent from the 204,592 shipped in 2000. As recently as 1999, the company had envisioned reaching an annual production target of 200,000, but not until the year 2003. Harley may have underestimated the growth in the demand for its bikes, the growth in the worldwide heavyweight market, and in its ability to increase production.

The Buell division sold 9,925 motorcycles in 2001, down 264 units from 2000. This was due in part to a shift in sales emphasis from the new Buell Blast to the heavyweight Buell cycle.

## THE FUTURE

Domestically, Harley has the kind of name recognition and brand loyalty that is the envy of the industry. Could it ever develop a similar customer relationship abroad? Recognizing that part of the Harley image was built on tradition, how can Harley stay true to the things (and people) that helped to make it what it is and still grow as it has in the past few years?

Prepare a three-year strategic plan for Harley-Davidson. Address the specific issues of international growth opportunities in European countries as well as domestic competitive threats from Honda and the new alliance of Suzuki and Kawasaki. Examine the strengths of the Harley-Davidson brand along with the continuing weakness of ongoing capacity constraints. Imagine you are Chairman and CEO Jeffery L. Bleustein and have the task of leading this company as it prepares to meet the growing demand for its motorcycles in the coming years. What specific actions would you take? Should your recommendations be financed with debt or equity? Develop pro-forma financial statements to assess the impact of your changes.

# WINNEBAGO INDUSTRIES—2002

John G. Marcis
**Coastal Carolina University**
Eugene M. Bland
**Francis Marion University**

WGO

www.winnebagoind.com

Saving money is nice, but it is not the real reason why people travel in a motor home. Motor homing is just plain fun. Motor homers are an adventurous lot—they like to go, see, and do. Florida residents have replaced Californians as the most active motor home campers. New Yorkers are third on the "most on the go" list. Recreational vehicle (RV) owners say that they not only save money when camping but also can avoid the bother of having to stop for restaurants and bathrooms.

Motor home traveling is purported to be much less expensive than traveling by car or plane and staying in a motel. Motor homers stop when there is something to see and do. They often spend summers where it is cool and winters where it is warm. In fact, industry advertisements tout the RV lifestyle with this slogan: "Wherever you go, you're always at home."

Winnebago Industries, Inc. is a leading manufacturer of motor homes. Company revenues for the fiscal year ended August 25, 2001, decreased to $681.83 million, compared to $753.38 million in 2000. Motor home shipments (Class A and Class C) during fiscal 2001 were 9,076 units, a decrease of 1,440 units, or 13.7 percent, compared to fiscal 2000. However, market share increased to 18.9 percent of the Class A and C motor home market in 2001, compared to 17.0 percent for the same period in calendar 2000. The company builds quality products with state-of-the-art computer-aided design and manufacturing systems on automotive-style assembly lines. Although Winnebago competes with Fleetwood and Coachmen, the name Winnebago is considered synonymous with the term *motor home*.

Winnebago was founded in 1958 and has always been headquartered in Forest City, Iowa (515-582-3535). The company's common stock is listed on the New York, Chicago, and Pacific Stock Exchanges, and it is traded under the symbol WGO. Options for Winnebago's common stock are traded on the Chicago Board Options Exchange. Winnebago's home page can be accessed at **http://www.winnebagoind.com**, and corporate press releases are available through Company New On-Call at **www.prnewswire.com/cnoc/exec/menu/105967**.

Winnebago Industries is financially stable. The firm owns its land, buildings, and equipment, and it has no long-term debt. The firm has an enviable cash balance, which provides the company with the opportunity for future growth. Winnebago ended fiscal 2001 as the number one motor home retail sales company for the first time in 20 years. The company improved its market share by 10 percent in 2001 from 2000.

## EARLY MOTOR HOMING

The first motor home was built in 1915 to take people from the Atlantic Coast to San Francisco. It had wooden wheels and hard rubber tires. It was promoted as having all the comforts of an ocean cruiser. By the 1920s, the house car had become a fixture in the United States and a symbol of freedom. All kinds of house cars could be seen traveling across America's dirt roads. They ranged from what looked like large moving cigars to two-story houses with porches on wheels. But these house cars featured poor weight distribution, poor insulation, and poor economy. From the 1930s to the 1950s, they gave way in popularity to the trailer.

In the mid-1950s, motor homes were called motorized trailers. They were overweight, underpowered, and poorly insulated, but they were still a vast improvement over the house cars of the 1920s. In the 1960s, motor homing became much more popular, largely as a result of the innovations of Winnebago. From Forest City, Iowa, where the company was founded in 1958, Winnebago has set the pace for all new developments in motor homes. The Winnebago name became a household word. Buyers of motor homes were asked, "When will your Winnebago be delivered?"

## CORPORATE PROFILE

### Corporate Mission Statement

Winnebago's motto is "Quality Is a Journey—Not a Destination." From the beginning, the company recognized the critical roles played by employees, customers, and dealers in the total quality process. The significance of quality to the firm is evidenced by its Mission Statement, its Statement of Values, and its Statement of Guiding Principles, which are provided in Exhibit 1.

### Production Facilities

Winnebago has major production facilities in Forest City, Iowa. Currently, over twenty buildings at this location fill more than 2 million square feet (approximately sixty acres under roof) and contain the company's manufacturing, maintenance, and service operations. There are also satellite-manufacturing facilities at Hampton and Lorimor, Iowa. These two facilities add another seven hundred thousand square feet of manufacturing space. All corporate facilities in Forest City are located on approximately 784 acres of land that is owned by Winnebago.

Winnebago has three nine-hundred-foot assembly lines for final assembly of motor homes. Statistical process control is practiced at Winnebago and has enhanced the quality of its van products. As a motor home moves down the assembly line, quality control is carefully monitored. Units are taken randomly from the line for a thorough examination. The performance of every RV is tested before it is delivered to a dealer's lot. The company makes sure that all of its motor home components meet or exceed federal and durability standards. Some of the tests routinely performed include lamination strength, appliance performance, chip resistance, vibration, drop, salt spray, and crash tests.

## RESEARCH AND DEVELOPMENT

Winnebago uses computer technology to design its motor homes. The company has a state-of-the-art, computer-aided design/computer-aided manufacturing (CAD/CAM) system. This system aids in the production of low-cost sheet metal parts, new paint lines for steel and aluminum parts, and modifications of assembly equipment.

One of Winnebago's product-testing facilities at Forest City houses some of the most sophisticated technology being used in the RV industry (such as a high- and low-temperature chamber for subjecting parts to extreme temperatures and high stress).

## EXHIBIT 1    Winnebago Industries, Inc. Mission Statement

**MISSION STATEMENT**

Winnebago Industries, Inc. is a leading manufacturer of recreation vehicles (RVs) and related products and services. Our mission is to continually improve our products and services to meet or exceed the expectations of our customers. We emphasize employee teamwork and involvement in identifying and implementing programs to save time and lower production costs while maintaining the highest quality values. These strategies allow us to prosper as a business with a high degree of integrity and to provide a reasonable return for our shareholders, the ultimate owners of our business.

**VALUES**

How we accomplish our mission is as important as the mission itself. Fundamental to the success of the Company are these basic values we describe as the four P's:

**People**—Our employees are the source of our vast strength. They provide our corporate intelligence and determine our reputation and vitality. Involvement and teamwork are our core human values.

**Products**—Our products are the end result of our team's efforts, and they should be the best in meeting or exceeding our customers' expectations worldwide. As our products are viewed, so are we viewed.

**Plant**—The Company believes its plant is the most technologically advanced in the RV industry. We continue to review facility improvements that will increase the utilization of our plant capacity and enable us to build the best quality product for the investment.

**Profitability**—Profitability is the ultimate measure of how efficiently we provide our customers with the best products for their needs. Profitability is required to survive and grow. As our respect and position within the marketplace grows, so will our profit.

**GUIDING PRINCIPLES**

**Quality comes first**—To achieve customer satisfaction, [we must make] the quality of our products and services . . . be our number one priority.

**Customers are central to our existence**—Our work must be done with our customers in mind, providing products and services that meet or exceed the expectations of our customers. We must not only satisfy our customers, we must also surprise and delight them.

**Continuous improvement is essential to our success**—We must strive for excellence in everything we do: in our products, in their safety and value, as well as in our services, our human relations, our competitiveness, and our profitability.

**Employee involvement is our way of life**—We are a team. We must treat each other with trust and respect.

**Dealers and suppliers are our partners**—The Company must maintain mutually beneficial relationships with dealers, suppliers, and our other business associates.

**Integrity is never compromised**—The Company must pursue conduct in a manner that is socially responsible and that commands respect for its integrity and for its positive contributions to society. Our doors are open to all men and women alike without discrimination and without regard to ethnic origin or personal beliefs.

*Source:* Winnebago Industries, 1999 *Annual Report,* p. 21.

## PRODUCT LINE

In 1997, the board of directors elected Ronald D. Buckmeier to the position of vice president of product development. The new product development team implemented a process to develop new products and to maximize production efficiencies. This system involves a cross-functional approach for the design and manufacture of RVs, and it streamlines the production process. Nearly every one of the sixty product series have either been dramatically redesigned or introduced as a completely new product since the 1997 offerings.

Winnebago manufactures three principal kinds of recreational vehicles, as indicated in Exhibit 2: Class A Motor Homes, Class B Van Campers, and Class C Motor Homes (Mini). Class A motor homes are constructed on a chassis that already has the engine and drive components attached. They range in length from twenty-three to

EXHIBIT 2    Motor Home Product Classification

Class A Motor Homes

These are conventional motor homes constructed directly on medium-duty truck chassis which include the engine and drive train components. The living area of the driver's compartment is designed and produced by Winnebago Industries. Class A motor homes from Winnebago Industries include Winnebago Brave, Adventurer, Chieftain, and Journey; Itasca Sunrise, Suncruiser, Sunflyer, and Horizon; and Ultimate Advantage and Freedom.

Class B Van Campers

These are panel-type trucks to which sleeping, kitchen, and toilet facilities are added. These models also have a top extension to provide more headroom. Winnebago Industries converts the EuroVan Camper, which is distributed by Volkswagen of America and Volkswagen of Canada.

Class C Motor Homes (Mini)

These are minimotor homes built on a van-type chassis onto which Winnebago Industries constructs a living area with access to the driver's compartment. Class C motor homes from Winnebago industries include Winnebago Minnie and Minnie Winnie; Itasca Spirit and Sundancer; and Rialta.

*Source:* Winnebago Industries, 2001 *Annual Report,* p. 16.

thirty-seven feet and can sell for more than $250,000. Class A motor homes include the Winnebago Adventurer, Brave, Chieftain, and Journey; the Itasca Suncruiser, Sunrise, Sunflyer, and Horizon; and the Ultimate Advantage and Freedom, as indicated in Exhibit 3. Although the Winnebago Adventurer and Itasco Suncruiser are popular, the Winnebago Brave and Itasca Sunrise models are the company's top-selling vehicles. As of August 25, 2001, the backlog for orders for Class A and Class C motor homes was nearly 1,600 units (compared to only 1,355 in August of 2000, an 18 percent increase).

Winnebago's Class B van campers are actually conventional vans manufactured by Ford, General Motors, and Daimler-Chrysler that are custom tailored by Winnebago with special interiors, exteriors, windows, and vents. In many American households, van campers are replacing the family car as the vehicle of choice. These vehicles can tum a long family trip from an ordeal into a pleasant adventure. Winnebago manufactures the EuroVan Camper conversion for Volkswagen of America and Volkswagen of Canada. Class B van campers are seventeen feet in length.

Class C motor homes are constructed on a van chassis; the driver's compartment is accessible to the living area. These motor homes are compact and easy to drive. They range from twenty-one to twenty-nine feet in length and have five popular floor plans. Typical options of a Class C vehicle include six feet of headroom, shower, stove, sink, refrigerator, and two double beds. Winnebago's Minnie Winnie vehicle is the most popular Class C motor home in the country. The company's Itasca Sundancer and Itasca Spirit also are popular.

Winnebago introduced two new Class A models (the Winnebago Sightseer and the Itasca Sunova) and two new Class C models (the Winnebago Vista and the Itasca Sunstar) for the 2002 model year. The Sightseer and the Sunova are entry-level, wide-body, basement-style models with many standard features typically found as options on many competitive units in this price class. Although the Vista and Sunstar models are built in classic Class C design, they are unique in that they are fuel-efficient motor homes built on a heavy duty front-wheel-drive chassis.

---

**EXHIBIT 3    Winnebago Family Tree**

Winnebago Industries manufactures four brands of Class A and C motor homes. Listed below are the band names and model designations of the company's 2000 product line.

| Winnebago | Itasca | Rialta | Ultimate |
|---|---|---|---|
| –Vista | –Spirit | –Rialta | –Ultimate Advantage |
| –Minnie | –Sundancer | | –Ultimate Freedom |
| –Minnie Winnie | –Sunrise | | |
| –Brave | –Suncruiser | | |
| –Adventurer | –Sunflyer | | |
| –Chieftain | –Horizon | | |
| –Journey | –Sunstar | | |
| –Journey DL | | | |
| –Sightseer | –Sunova | | |

**OTHER RELATED PRODUCTS:**

Winnebago Conversion Vehicles—Licensed truck and van conversions manufactured and marketed by Choo Choo Customs Group, Inc.
Winnebago Park Homes—Licensed products manufactured and marketed by Chariot Eagle, Inc.
Winnebago Tents—Licensed products manufactured and marketed by Avid Outdoor.

*Source:* Winnebago Industries, 2001 *Annual Report,* p. 16.

## Marketing

Consumer research reveals that the demographics for motor home buyers are undergoing a change. Traditionally, buyers have been "woofies" ("well-off older folks" defined as people over fifty years of age with discretionary available income) with time to enjoy leisure travel and outdoor recreation. According to research, an individual in the United States is turning fifty every 7.5 seconds, thus contributing an additional 350,000 people per *month* to that prime target market. Available demographic information indicates that this trend will continue for the next thirty years.

The peak selling seasons for RVs has historically been spring and summer. Class A and Class C motor homes are marketed under the Winnebago and Itasca brand names and were sold in the United States and, to a limited extent, in Canada and other foreign countries through a network of approximately 340 dealers in 2001; this is up from 325 in 1994.

Winnebago Industries believes it has the most comprehensive service program in the RV industry. With the purchase of any new Class A or Class C motor home (except the Rialta, which has a 24-month, 24,000-mile warranty), Winnebago offers a comprehensive 12-month/15,000-mile warranty, a 3-year/36,000 mile warranty on sidewalls and slide-out room assemblies, and a 10-year fiberglass roof warranty. Winnebago features a 2-year/24,000-mile warranty on the Rialta. Winnebago also instituted a toll-free hotline at which experienced service advisers respond to inquiries from prospective customers and expedite and resolve warranty issues. Every owner of a new Winnebago motor home receives free roadside assistance for twelve months.

## RECENT YEARS

Winnebago celebrated its 40th anniversary in 1998, which was a banner year for both production and revenue. Although the motor home industry had a good year overall, Winnebago outperformed the motor home industry by 12 percent during the first nine months of the calendar year. Revenues were a record $525.1 million for the fiscal year (compared with $438.1 million for the 1997 fiscal year). Income from continuing operations for the year reflected a nearly fourfold increase from the previous fiscal year. In December 1998, Winnebago had a sales order backlog of over three thousand units, the largest in the company's history.

Winnebago's good fortune continued through 2000. Unit production increased about 27.2 percent (from $525.1 million to $667.7 million) between 1998 and 1999 and an additional 12.8 percent (to $753.3 million) between 1999 and 2000. However, RV sales fell approximately 17 percent during the first six months of 2001. This decline in sales was due to a number of factors: wavering consumer confidence in the national economy, a weakening national economy, and a dramatic spike in the prices of gasoline and diesel fuel. In an attempt to sell the existing inventory, manufacturers and dealers started to offer sales incentives, which put pressure on operating margins. Consequently, Winnebago's revenues for the fiscal year ended August 25, 2001, were $681.8 million, compared with revenues of $753.4 million for the previous fiscal year. Moreover, the economic uncertainty introduced since the terrorist attacks of September 11, 2001, further cloud the fiscal picture of leisure-related activities like RVing.

## WINNEBAGO'S EXTERNAL ENVIRONMENT

Winnebago's motor homes can attract a low-frills buyer who wants the most stripped-down RV, the person with expensive tastes who wants the ultimate in RV luxury—and

EXHIBIT 4    Net Revenues By Major Product Class (Unaudited)
(dollars in thousands)

|  | Fiscal Year Ended[1] | | | | |
|---|---|---|---|---|---|
|  | *Aug. 25, 2001* | *Aug. 26, 2000* | *Aug. 28, 1999* | *Aug. 29, 1998* | *Aug. 30, 1997* |
| Motor homes (Class A & Class C) | $630,017 | $695,767 | $619,171 | $474,954 | $387,161 |
|  | 92.4% | 92.4% | 91.5% | 89.0% | 86.9% |
| Other recreation vehicle revenues[2] | 17,808 | 18,813 | 16,620 | 19,222 | 21,159 |
|  | 2.6% | 2.5% | 2.5% | 3.6% | 4.7% |
| Other manufactured products revenues[3] | 29,768 | 34,894 | 38,225 | 37,133 | 35,881 |
|  | 4.4% | 4.6% | 5.6% | 7.0% | 8.1% |
| Total manufactured products revenues | 677,593 | 749,474 | 674,016 | 531,309 | 444,201 |
|  | 99.4% | 99.5% | 99.6% | 99.6% | 99.7% |
| Finance revenues[4] | 4,241 | 3,908 | 2,995 | 2,076 | 1,420 |
|  | .6% | .5% | .4% | .4% | .3% |
| Total net revenues | $681,834 | $753,382 | $677,011 | $533,385 | $445,621 |
|  | 100.0% | 100.0% | 100.0% | 100.0% | 100.0% |

(1) All fiscal years in the table contained 52 weeks.
(2) Primarily recreation vehicle related parts, EuroVan Campers (Class B motor homes), and recreation vehicle service revenue.
(3) Primarily sales of extruded aluminum, commercial vehicles, and component products for other manufacturers.
(4) WAC revenues from dealer financing.
*Source:* Winnebago Industries, 2001 *Annual Report,* p. 39.

**EXHIBIT 5** Consolidated Statements of Income (in thousands, except per-share data)

| | Year Ended | | |
|---|---|---|---|
| | August 25, 2001 | August 26, 2000 | August 28, 1999 |
| Revenues: | | | |
| Manufactured products | $677,593 | $749,474 | $674,016 |
| Dealer financing | 4,241 | 3,908 | 2,995 |
| Total net revenues | 681,834 | 753,382 | 677,011 |
| Costs and expenses: | | | |
| Cost of manufactured products | 587,330 | 640,488 | 574,603 |
| Selling | 25,423 | 25,118 | 24,321 |
| General and administrative | 13,607 | 17,122 | 14,105 |
| Total costs and expenses | 626,360 | 682,728 | 613,029 |
| Operating income | 55,474 | 70,654 | 63,982 |
| Financial income | 3,754 | 3,338 | 2,627 |
| Income before income taxes | 59,228 | 73,992 | 66,609 |
| Provision for taxes | 15,474 | 25,593 | 22,349 |
| Income before cumulative effect of change in accounting principle | 43,754 | 48,399 | 44,260 |
| Cumulative effect of change in accounting principle, net of taxes | (1,050) | — | — |
| Net income | $ 42,704 | $ 48,399 | $ 44,260 |
| Earnings per common share (basic): | | | |
| Income before cumulative effect of change in accounting principle | $ 2.11 | $ 2.23 | $ 1.99 |
| Cumulative effect of change in accounting principle | (0.05) | — | — |
| Income per share (basic) | $ 2.06 | $ 2.23 | $ 1.99 |
| Earnings per common share (diluted): | | | |
| Income before cumulative effect of change in accounting principle | $ 2.08 | $ 2.20 | $ 1.96 |
| Cumulative effect of change in accounting principle | (.05) | — | — |
| Income per share (diluted) | $ 2.03 | $ 2.20 | $ 1.96 |
| Weighted average shares of common stock outstanding: | | | |
| Basic | 20,735 | 21,680 | 22,209 |
| Diluted | 21,040 | 22,011 | 22,537 |

*Source:* Winnebago Industries, 2001 *Annual Report,* p. 34.

everyone in between. RVs can be purchased or rented. Many families unable to buy a mobile home rent one to take on vacation. As the baby boomers age and approach retirement, many of them will consider selling their primary residences, purchasing and moving into a motor home, and traveling to any point they desire in North America.

The motel and hotel industries have been experiencing an oversupply of available rooms, which has resulted in low rates for rooms. Compared to the cost of owning/renting and operating an RV, the costs of staying in a motor home versus a motel are about the same if not a bit lower in favor of the motel. Motor home sales historically increase whenever travel, tourism, and vacationing gain in popularity. The converse is also true.

There are about 122,000 campsites in U.S. state parks, including 4,500 that are maintained by the U.S. Forest Service and 100 in the national parks system. In addition, there are more than 15,000 private campgrounds and over 1,620 county parks. Winnebagos can access nearly all of these sites.

## EXHIBIT 6    Consolidated Balance Sheets (dollars in thousands)

|  | August 25, 2001 | August 26, 2000 |
|---|---|---|
| Assets |  |  |
| Current assets: |  |  |
| Cash and cash equivalents | $ 93,779 | $ 51,443 |
| Receivables, less allowance for doubtful accounts | 20,183 | 32,045 |
| ($244 and $1,168, respectively) |  |  |
| Dealer financing receivables, less allowance for doubtful accounts | 40,263 | 32,696 |
| ($117 and $27, respectively) |  |  |
| Inventories | 79,815 | 85,707 |
| Prepaid expenses | 3,604 | 3,952 |
| Deferred income taxes | 6,723 | 7,675 |
| Total current assets | 244,367 |  |
| **Property and equipment, at cost:** |  | 213,518 |
| Land | 1,029 | 1,138 |
| Buildings | 45,992 | 45,219 |
| Machinery and equipment | 82,182 | 78,099 |
| Transportation equipment | 5,482 | 5,414 |
|  | 134,685 | 129,870 |
| Less accumulated depreciation | 88,149 | 84,415 |
| Total property and equipment, net | 46,536 | 45,455 |
| Investment in life insurance | 22,223 | 21,028 |
| Deferred income taxes | 21,495 | 19,044 |
| Other assets | 7,412 | 8,050 |
| **Total assets** | $342,033 | $307,095 |
| Liabilities and Stockholders' Equity |  |  |
| **Current liabilities:** |  |  |
| Accounts payable, trade | $ 30,789 | $ 26,212 |
| Income taxes payable | 4,938 | 8,790 |
| Accrued expenses: |  |  |
| Accrued compensation | 13,730 | 13,924 |
| Product warranties | 8,072 | 8,114 |
| Insurance | 4,567 | 5,384 |
| Promotional | 3,181 | 3,145 |
| Other | 4,842 | 4,675 |
| Total current liabilities | 70,119 | 70,244 |
| Postretirement health care and deferred compensation benefits | 64,450 | 61,942 |
| Contingent liabilities and commitments |  |  |
| **Stockholders' equity:** |  |  |
| Capital stock common, par value $.50; authorized 60,000,000 shares, | 12,943 | 12,939 |
| issued 25,886,000 and 25,878,000 shares, respectively |  |  |
| Additional paid-in capital | 22,261 | 21,994 |
| Reinvested earnings | 234,139 | 195,556 |
|  | 269,343 | 230,489 |
| Less treasury stock, at cost | 61,879 | 55,580 |
| Total stockholders' equity | 207,464 | 174,909 |
| **Total liabilities and stockholders' equity** | $342,033 | $307,095 |

*Source:* Winnebago Industries, 2001 *Annual Report,* pp. 22–23.

## EXHIBIT 7    Business Segment Information (dollars in thousands)

For the years ended August 25, 2001, August 26, 2000 and August 28, 1999, the Company's segment information is as follows:

| | Recreation Vehicles & Other Manufactured Products | Dealer Financing | General Corporate | Total |
|---|---|---|---|---|
| **2001** | | | | |
| Net revenues | $677,593 | $ 4,241 | $    — | $681,834 |
| Operating income (loss) | 52,120 | 4,102 | (748) | 55,474 |
| Identifiable assets | 175,343 | 40,856 | 125,834 | 342,033 |
| Depreciation and amortization | 7,158 | 5 | 217 | 7,380 |
| Capital expenditures | 8,974 | 19 | 96 | 9,089 |
| **2000** | | | | |
| Net revenues | $749,474 | 3,908 | $    — | $753,382 |
| Operating income (loss) | 67,252 | 3,892 | (490) | 70,654 |
| Identifiable assets | 191,501 | 33,508 | 82,086 | 307,095 |
| Depreciation and amortization | 6,375 | 4 | 243 | 6,622 |
| Capital expenditures | 14,412 | — | 136 | 14,548 |
| **1999** | | | | |
| Net revenues | $674,016 | $ 2,995 | $    — | $677,011 |
| Operating income (loss) | 60,435 | 4,085 | (538) | 63,982 |
| Identifiable assets | 181,951 | 25,439 | 78,499 | 285,889 |
| Depreciation and amortization | 5,507 | 4 | 237 | 5,748 |
| Capital expenditures | 11,463 | 18 | 96 | 11,577 |

Operating income of the dealer financing segment reflects a $1,100,000 repayment of a previously fully reserved receivable.
*Source:* Winnebago Industries, 2001 *Annual Report,* p. 36.

## COMPETITORS

Twelve firms account for 80 percent of the RV industry's volume. In addition to Winnebago Industries, some of the other major publicly held firms in the industry are Rexhall Industries, Mallard Coach, Kit Manufacturing, Harley-Davidson, and Skyline Corporation. The following is a list of major motor home competitors:

| Company | Headquarters Location |
|---|---|
| Fleetwood Enterprises, Inc. | Riverside, California |
| Coachmen Industries, Inc. | Elkhart, Indiana |
| Mark III Industries, Inc. | Ocala, Florida |
| Jayco, Inc. | Middlebury, Indiana |
| Glaval Corp. | Elkhart, Indiana |
| Newmar Corp. | Nappanee, Indiana |
| Monaco Coach Corp. | Junction City, Oregon |
| Tiffin Motor Homes, Inc. | Red Bay, Alabama |

Throughout the 1990s, Fleetwood Enterprises was first in sales, followed by Coachmen, and then Winnebago Industries. However, in early 2001, Winnebago became the industry leader in Class A and Class C retail motor home sales. It achieved the number one position in the industry with an 18.8 percent market share, compared to its 17.1 percent market share twelve months earlier.

## INDUSTRY OUTLOOK

Calendar year 2000 was not a good year for the RV industry. Specifically, conventional motor home volume was down 27 percent, folding camping trailer sales declined 22 percent, and truck camper sales were down 8 percent. The poor year for the industry was due to the combined effects of a slowing national economy, faltering consumer confidence in the national economy, and relatively high gas prices nationally. Over the long term, recent demographic changes bode well for the growth of the industry. The number of people over the age of fifty is growing and should continue to grow at a similar rate.

# AVON PRODUCTS, INC.—2002

**James Camerius**
**Northern Michigan University**

AVP

www.avon.com

On September 13, 2001, Andrea Jung, chairman of the board and chief executive officer of Avon Products, Inc., announced that the Avon Products Foundation would make a donation of $1 million of corporate funds to the American Red Cross in greater New York to help victims and their families recover from the September 11, 2001, terrorist attacks. She said, "There are no words that can express our sorrow for the victims and their families. As a company that touches the lives of people in many personal ways, we want to do whatever we can to aid the relief efforts and provide direct assistance to families." This contribution was later expanded to include a fund that would direct financial aid to educational institutions, after-school programs, and children's programs that provide counseling, safety education, child-care, and other related services.

The days that followed the terrorist attacks were difficult and challenging. Jung reflected on the attacks and the overall weak consumer spending trends that had developed as she sat down at her desk in her executive office in New York on the morning of September 25, 2001. Since September 11, Avon's stock had fallen 10 percent. The combined threats of additional terrorism and global economic recession were a primary concern. Economists were predicting rising unemployment, lower business profits, decreased discretionary spending, and a general retrenchment by businesses and consumers. And the firm's revenues could be hit hard insofar as many of the big overseas markets, such as Argentina and Brazil, faced economic decline. She felt encouraged when notified that Avon's business had returned quickly to near-normal levels.

Jung assumed the position of president and chief executive officer of Avon Products, Inc. on November 4, 1999. At the age of forty-one, she became the first woman to lead Avon in that position in the company's history, and she was one of the few Fortune 500 women CEOs. On September 6, 2001, she also assumed the additional post of chairman of the board of directors.

Jung had expected the appointment and was aware of the awesome responsibility of the position. Avon enjoyed a global reputation stemming largely from its formidable worldwide network of independent sales agents. But the effectiveness of the sales force had waned in the years prior to her appointment as chief executive officer as the company grappled with how best to sell cosmetics, jewelry, and apparel to an increasingly sophisticated customer and with how to compete against other mass merchandisers. Balance sheet and income statement data for Avon is shown in Exhibits 1 and 2.

## AVON PRODUCTS

Avon is the world's largest direct-selling organization and merchandiser of beauty and beauty-related products. From corporate offices in New York City, Avon markets product lines to women in 143 countries through 3.5 million independent sales representatives who sold primarily on a door-to-door or direct-selling basis. Total sales in 2001 were $5.95 billion.

Avon's product line includes skin care items, makeup, perfume fragrances for men and women, and toiletries for bath, hair care, personal care, hand and body care, and sun care. It also includes an extensive line of fashion jewelry, apparel, gifts, and collectibles. Recognizable brand names such as Anew, Skin-So-Soft, Avon Color, Advance Techniques, and Avon Wellness are featured. There are approximately six hundred items in the product line. Internationally, the company's product line is marketed primarily at moderate price points. The marketing strategy emphasizes department store quality at discount store prices. Global marketing efforts resulted in a number of highly successful global "power" brands in the areas of cosmetics, skin care, and fragrance (i.e., products such as Anew, Avon Color, Avon Basics, and the recently introduced Anew Retroactive).

Avon is also the world's largest manufacturer and distributor of fashion jewelry, and it markets an extensive line of gifts and collectibles. The product line also includes watches, shoes, purses, CDs, videos, toys, and a wide array of other products from around the world. The major categories and subcategories of products are shown in Exhibit 3.

## THE EARLY YEARS

In the late 1800s, David McConnell, a door-to-door book salesman, had an idea he believed would encourage women to buy his books. Following a common trade practice of the period, he gave prospective customers a gift of perfume to arouse their interest. Before long, he discovered that the perfume was more popular than the books. He formed a new firm, which he called the California Perfume Company. "I started in a space scarcely larger than an ordinary kitchen pantry," McConnell noted in 1900. "My ambition was to manufacture a line of goods superior to any other and take those goods through canvassing agents directly from the laboratory to the consumer." McConnell based his business upon several factors: (1) products sold directly to the consumer, (2) an image of the company that captured the beauty and excitement of the state of California, and (3) a national network of sales agents he had organized during his years as a bookseller.

In the early 1950s, the sales representatives' territories were reduced in size, a strategy that led to a quadrupling of the sales force and increased sales sixfold over the next twelve years. Avon advertisements appeared on television for the first time during this period. The famous slogan "Ding Dong, Avon Calling" was first used in 1954.

In 1960, total sales were $1.5 million, international sales were $8.2 million, and the company consisted of 6,800 employees and 125,000 sales representatives. Sales continued to grow dramatically throughout the 1960s. By 1969, total sales had grown to $558.6 million, international sales were $193.1 million, and the firm had 20,800 employees and over 400,000 sales representatives. Manufacturing plants, distribution centers, and sales branches were opened throughout the world as part of an expansion program.

In 2000, Avon increased its research and development budget 46 percent to get the newly developed "blockbuster" products to market faster. Normally, Avon spends at least three years developing new products, but Janice Teal, head of R&D, recalls Jung saying to her, "You've got two years. I need a breakthrough, and that's the goal."

Avon's strategy also includes making the direct-selling system more relevant to the contemporary woman. This strategy meant providing more meaningful career opportunities as well as harnessing technology to make Avon more user friendly for the sales representatives. "If Avon stops adding numbers of active representatives, the fuel and the lifeblood of the business slows down," Jung suggested. A new motivation and recruiting program was implemented as part of the strategic plan.

EXHIBIT 1    Consolidated Balance Sheets (in millions, except share data)

| | December 31, | |
| --- | --- | --- |
| | *2001* | *2000* |
| **ASSETS** | | |
| **Current assets** | | |
| Cash, including cash equivalents of $381.8 and $23.9 | $  508.5 | $  122.7 |
| Accounts receivable (less allowance for doubtful accounts of $45.1 and $39.2) | 519.5 | 499.0 |
| Income tax receivable | — | 95.2 |
| Inventories | 612.5 | 610.6 |
| Prepaid expenses and other | 248.6 | 218.2 |
| Total current assets | 1,889.1 | 1,545.7 |
| **Property, plant and equipment, at cost** | | |
| Land | 49.4 | 53.0 |
| Buildings and improvements | 664.0 | 659.5 |
| Equipment | 841.2 | 810.6 |
| | 1,554.6 | 1,523.1 |
| Less accumulated depreciation | 779.7 | 754.7 |
| | 774.9 | 768.4 |
| Other assets | 529.1 | 512.3 |
| Total assets | $3,193.1 | $2,826.4 |
| **LIABILITIES AND SHAREHOLDERS' (DEFICIT) EQUITY** | | |
| **Current liabilities** | | |
| Debt maturing within one year | $    88.8 | $  105.4 |
| Accounts payable | 404.1 | 391.3 |
| Accrued compensation | 145.2 | 138.2 |
| Other accrued liabilities | 338.2 | 251.7 |
| Sales and taxes other than income | 108.8 | 101.1 |
| Income taxes | 375.9 | 371.6 |
| Total current liabilities | 1,461.0 | 1,359.3 |
| Long-term debt | 1,236,3 | 1,108.2 |
| Employee benefit plans | 436.6 | 397.2 |
| Deferred income taxes | 30.6 | 31.3 |
| Other liabilities (including minority interest of $29.0 and $30.7) | 103.2 | 95.2 |
| Commitments and Contingencies | | |
| Share repurchase commitments | — | 51.0 |
| **SHAREHOLDERS' (DEFICIT) EQUITY** | | |
| Common stock, par value $.25—authorized: | | |
| 800,000,000 shares; issued 356,312,680 and 354,535,840 shares | 89.1 | 88.6 |
| Additional paid-in capital | 938.0 | 824.1 |
| Retained earnings | 1,389.9 | 1,139.8 |
| Accumulated other comprehensive loss | (489.5) | (399.1) |
| Treasury stock, at cost—119,631,574 and 116,373,394 shares | (2,002.1) | (1,869.2) |
| Total shareholders' (deficit) equity | (74.6) | (215.8) |
| Total liabilities and shareholders' (deficit) equity | $3,193.1 | $2,826.4 |

*Source:* Avon's 2001 *Annual Report,* p. 39.

## EXHIBIT 2    Consolidated Statements of Income (in millions, except per-share data)

| | Years ended December 31, | | |
| --- | --- | --- | --- |
| | *2001* | *2000* | *1999* |
| Net sales | $5,952.0 | $5,673.7 | $5,289.1 |
| Other revenue | 42.5 | 40.9 | 38.8 |
| Total revenue | 5,994.5 | 5,714.6 | 5,327.9 |
| Costs, expenses and other: | | | |
| Cost of sales | 2,220.1 | 2,122.7 | 2,031.5 |
| Marketing, distribution and administrative expenses | 2,932.1 | 2,803.2 | 2,641.8 |
| Contract settlement gain, net of related expenses | (25.9) | — | — |
| Asset impairment charge | 23.9 | — | — |
| Special charge | 94.9 | — | 105.2 |
| Operating profit | 749.4 | 788.7 | 549.4 |
| Interest expense | 71.1 | 84.7 | 43.2 |
| Interest income | (14.4) | (8.5) | (11.1) |
| Other expense, net | 27.0 | 21.5 | 10.7 |
| Total other expenses | 83.7 | 97.7 | 42.8 |
| Income from continuing operations before taxes, minority interest and cumulative effect of accounting changes | 665.7 | 691.0 | 506.6 |
| Income taxes | 230.9 | 201.7 | 204.2 |
| Income before minority interest and cumulative effect of accounting changes | 434.8 | 489.3 | 302.4 |
| Minority interest | (4.5) | (4.2) | — |
| Income from continuing operations before cumulative effect of accounting changes | 430.3 | 485.1 | 302.4 |
| Cumulative effect of accounting changes, net of tax | (0.3) | (6.7) | — |
| Net income | $ 430.0 | $ 478.4 | $ 302.4 |
| Basic earnings per share: | | | |
| Continuing operations | $    1.82 | $    2.04 | $    1.18 |
| Cumulative effect of accounting changes | — | (.03) | — |
| | $    1.82 | $    2.01 | $    1.18 |
| Diluted earnings per share: | | | |
| Continuing operations | $    1.79 | $    2.02 | $    1.17 |
| Cumulative effect of accounting changes | — | (.03) | — |
| | $    1.79 | $    1.99 | $    1.17 |

*Source:* Avon's 2001 *Annual Report,* p. 38.

## COMPETITION

Competition in the direct-selling industry consists of a few large, well-established firms and many small organizations that sell about every product imaginable, including toys, animal food, collectibles, plant care products, clothing, computer software, and financial services. In addition to Avon, the dominant companies include Mary Kay (cosmetics), Amway (home maintenance products), Shaklee Corporation (vitamins and health foods), Encyclopaedia Britannica (reference books and learning systems), Tupperware (plastic dishes and food containers), Electrolux (vacuum cleaners), and Fuller (brushes and household products). Avon is substantially larger in terms of sales representatives, sales volume, and resources than Mary Kay Cosmetics, Inc., its nearest competitor in direct sales.

Headquartered in Dallas, Texas, Mary Kay's product line includes more than two hundred products in eight categories: facial skin care, color cosmetics, nail care, body

EXHIBIT 3     Avon Product Line

**SKIN CARE PRODUCTS**

Anew: Age management skin care
Avon Skin Care: Specific skin care concerns
Basics: Affordable, easy to use skin care
Clearskin: Acne-fighting products
Moisture Therapy: Dry skin care products

**MAKEUP**

Avon Color: Basic global cosmetics brand
Beyond Color: Anti-aging line
Hydra Finish: Sheer and natural cosmetics
Perfect Wear: Transfer-proof, long-wearing products
Color Trend: Global, trendy, chic colors at low prices

**HAIR CARE**

Advance Techniques: Alternative hair-care products
Herbal Care: Natural global botanical products

**FRAGRANCES** (includes one new product introduction each year)

**BATH**

Skin-So-Soft: Bath oil, bug repellent, and sunscreen
Naturals: Moisturizing cleansers
Aromatherapy: Candles, creams, lotions, bath products
Footworks: Foot care line
Avon Bubble Bath: In assorted fragrances
Milk Made: Vitamin enriched items for bath and body

**JEWELRY** (fashion, classic, and seasonal)

**APPAREL** (watches, shoes, and purses)

**GIFT LINE** (collectibles, toys, and unique gifts)

*Source*: Company records

care, sun protection, fragrances, men's skin care, and dietary supplements. Mary Kay is a privately held company whose wholesale sales for 2000 were approximately $1.2 billion; this translates to more than $2.5 billion in sales at the retail level. Since opening its first international venture in Australia in 1971, Mary Kay, Inc. has expanded and is now sold in thirty-seven countries worldwide.

Several other firms, such as Procter & Gamble Co., Unilever NV, Revlon, Inc., Estee Lauder, and France's L'Oreal sell cosmetics and personal care products primarily through department stores and mass merchandisers, and they are considered important competitors in the marketplace. Revlon, whose image varies by product line, had built a multibillion dollar business by buying out old established lines like Max Factor, Charles of the Ritz, Germain Monte, Diane Von Furstenberg, and Almay. Some international firms, such as Shiseido, Japan's biggest cosmetics maker, are experimenting with beauty service centers in the United States and other countries. The centers offer free lessons on massage techniques and information on how to apply makeup. Shiseido found that many customers who visited such centers soon made a purchase in the department stores where Shiseido products were sold.

## INTERNATIONAL EXPANSION

For the three years ended 2001, 2000, and 1999, the company derived approximately 60 percent of both its consolidated net sales and consolidated pretax income from the operations of its international subsidiaries (see Exhibit 4). Total international sales in 2001 were $3.68 billion, compared to Avon North America sales of $2.27 billion. Total international operating profit in 2001 was $707.1 million, compared to Avon North American profit of $380.2 million. The international operations of the company are divided into four geographic regions: (1) North America region, which includes Canada, Puerto Rico, and the United States; (2) Latin American region, which includes Brazil, Mexico, Argentina, and Venezuela; (3) Pacific region, which includes the Philippines, Thailand, Japan, New Zealand, Australia, and China; and (4) the European region, which comprises the United Kingdom, Central Europe, and Russia.

Avon management feels that it is time to reevaluate and map out the long-term future of the firm's beauty businesses on a global level. Senior management realizes that the traditional Avon system of door-to-door house calls worked wonderfully in developing nations. The company has direct investments in fifty-three markets and through distributorships, specially appointed representatives, and licensees in 143 countries, including a significant presence in Egypt, Greece, and Saudi Arabia.

Enormous growth opportunities exist in countries with huge populations such as China, Indonesia and India. In Eastern Europe, management is excited about the potential in Poland, Czech Republic, Slovakia, and Hungary. In the Pacific Rim area, countries like Vietnam, Cambodia, and Laos are targeted as market opportunities.

The second area of potential growth is to continue to emphasize direct selling in the emerging and developing markets of Latin America, the Pacific Rim, and other areas. In those markets, the retail infrastructure is undeveloped, especially in the interiors of those countries. The Avon representative provides consumers with an opportunity to buy a wide range of quality products at acceptable prices. In some developing markets, where access to quality goods has been particularly prized, Avon's direct selling method opened up unprecedented prospects for women. In China, for example, women are so eager for Avon products that a projected six-month inventory of lotion sold out in only two weeks.

Growth in the markets of Central and Eastern Europe are considered Avon's primary opportunities for growth by management in the new millennium. Avon Russia rebounded in 2000, reversing a downturn in 1999 that followed the 1998 Russian economic crisis. Local sales nearly doubled, driven by a more than 60 percent growth in units and a nearly 30 percent rise in the number of active sales representatives. Russia also returned to profitability following an operating loss in 1999. Several new initiatives, such as a drive to improve operating efficiency, the introduction of several new products, and revised marketing management structures, were introduced in 2000.

The number of people buying from Avon in markets like the United States had been dwindling by 2 to 3 percent per year for about twelve years. "We applied all the tried-and-true stimuli to our direct-selling system: changes in recruiting, incentives, commissions, brochures, and more," suggested Preston when he was CEO. "We had some success. But we didn't stop the decline of customer purchasing activity." Management felt growth would come if it were to update the direct-selling channel.

## EXHIBIT 4    Avon's Segment Financial Data

| | 2001 Net Sales | 2001 Operating Profit (Loss) | 2000 Net Sales | 2000 Operating Profit (Loss) | 1999 Net Sales | 1999 Operating Profit (Loss) |
|---|---|---|---|---|---|---|
| **A.** | | | | | | |
| North America | | | | | | |
| U.S. | $2,016.7 | $ 373.4 | $1,894.9 | $ 343.5 | $1,809.3 | $329.3 |
| U.S. Retail* | 13.9 | (25.9) | 8.5 | (4.5) | 3.4 | (2.7) |
| Other† | 242.6 | 32.7 | 244.5 | 29.2 | 237.6 | 34.5 |
| Total | 2,273.2 | 380.2 | 2,147.9 | 368.2 | 2,050.3 | 361.1 |
| International | | | | | | |
| Latin America North‡ | 966.3 | 251.6 | 848.8 | 215.2 | 731.7 | 181.6 |
| Latin America South‡ | 933.3 | 175.9 | 992.0 | 200.3 | 909.0 | 184.9 |
| Latin America | 1,899.6 | 427.5 | 1,840.8 | 415.5 | 1,640.7 | 366.5 |
| Europe | 1,009.6 | 167.0 | 885.6 | 129.5 | 878.0 | 126.2 |
| Pacific | 771.4 | 112.6 | 799.4 | 117.8 | 720.1 | 102.1 |
| Total | 3,680.6 | 707.1 | 3,525.8 | 662.8 | 3,238.8 | 594.8 |
| Total from operations | 5,953.8 | 1,087.3 | 5,673.7 | 1,031.0 | 5,289.1 | 955.9 |
| Global expenses | (1.8) | (242.5) | — | (242.3) | — | (255.3) |
| Contact settlement gain, net of related expenses | — | 25.9 | — | — | — | — |
| Asset impairment charge | — | (23.9) | — | — | — | — |
| Special and non-recurring charges§ | — | (97.4) | — | — | — | (151.2) |
| Total | $5,952.0 | $ 749.4 | $5,673.7 | $ 788.7 | $5,289.1 | $549.4 |

*Includes U.S. Retail and Avon Center.
†Includes operating information for Canada and Puerto Rico.
‡Latin America North primarily includes the markets of Mexico, Venezuela, and Central America. Latin America South primarily includes the markets of Brazil, Argentina, Chile, and Peru. Avon's operations in Mexico reported net sales for 2001, 2000, and 1999 of $620.7, $555.6 and $471.6, respectively. Avon's operations in Mexico reported operating profit for 2001, 2000, and 1999 of $154.8, $136.0, and $115.1, respectively.
§The $97.4 is included in the Consolidated Statements of Income as a Special charge ($94.9) and as inventory write downs in Cost of sales ($2.5).
*Source:* Avon's 2001 *Annual Report,* p. 24.

For a number of years, Avon management considered Japan to be one of the most significant trouble spots for the firm. The sluggish Japanese economy, combined with intense pricing pressure as well as operating issues, contributed to Avon Japan's disappointing performance. However, at the end of 2000, growth was driven by a 10 percent increase in orders and units. Japan's operating profit climbed 24 percent for the year. Contributing to Japan's results were several highly successful promotions, including the distribution of over 30 million flyers supported by newspaper ads. New initiatives, such as Japan's Avon Lady retail shops and the use of the Internet consumer Web site, resulted in significant new customer growth.

## GLOBAL MARKETING

Satisfying the subtleties and intricacies of customer demand around the world means that a firm's business varies from country to country and market to market. In the United States, for example, Avon tested Avon Select, an early direct marketing program, to enable customers to buy Avon products in various settings. Customers could order

## B.

| Sales | 2001 | 2000 | 1999 |
|---|---|---|---|
| Beauty* | $3,730.5 | $3,533.9 | $3,220.8 |
| Beauty Plus† | 1,233.7 | 1,174.6 | 1,061.6 |
| Beyond Beauty‡ | 987.8 | 965.2 | 1,006.7 |
| Total net sales | $5,952.0 | $5,673.7 | $5,289.1 |

*Beauty includes cosmetics, fragrances, and toiletries.
†Beauty Plus includes fashion jewelry, watches and apparel and accessories.
‡Beyond Beauty includes home products, gift and decorative and candles.

## C.

| Total Assets | 2001 | 2000 | 1999 |
|---|---|---|---|
| North America | | | |
| U.S. | $ 638.9 | $ 640.0 | $ 536.9 |
| U.S. Retail* | 29.2 | 12.0 | 13.3 |
| Other† | 119.1 | 116.2 | 101.2 |
| Total | 787.2 | 768.2 | 651.4 |
| International | | | |
| Latin America North‡ | 334.6 | 292.9 | 248.9 |
| Latin America South | 277.8 | 310.7 | 294.1 |
| Latin America | 612.4 | 603.6 | 543.0 |
| Europe | 512.3 | 451.3 | 415.4 |
| Pacific | 393.9 | 399.8 | 411.2 |
| Total | 1,518.6 | 1,454.7 | 1,369.6 |
| Corporate and other | 887.3 | 603.5 | 507.6 |
| Total assets | $3,193.1 | $2,826.4 | $2,528.6 |

*Includes U.S. Retail and Avon Centre.
†Includes Canada and Puerto Rico.
‡Avon's operations in Mexico reported total assets at December 31, 2001, 2000, and 1999 of $211.0, $189.9, and $157.4, respectively.

## D.

| Capital Expenditures | 2001 | 2000 | 1999 |
|---|---|---|---|
| North America | | | |
| U.S. | $ 26.4 | $ 67.6 | $ 39.2 |
| U.S. Retail* | 7.5 | .1 | .4 |
| Other† | 6.4 | 8.6 | 8.7 |
| Total | 40.3 | 76.3 | 48.3 |
| International | | | |
| Latin America North‡ | 20.5 | 17.5 | 37.6 |
| Latin America South | 15.4 | 24.6 | 15.8 |
| Latin America | 35.9 | 42.1 | 53.4 |
| Europe | 42.0 | 47.1 | 39.6 |
| Pacific | 11.9 | 13.4 | 33.6 |
| Total | 89.8 | 102.6 | 126.6 |
| Corporate and other | 25.2 | 14.6 | 28.5 |
| Total capital expenditures | $155.3 | $193.5 | $203.4 |

‡Avon's operations in Mexico reported capital expenditures for 2001, 2000, and 1999 of $13.9, $11.7, and $32.1, respectively.
Source: Avon's 2001 Annual Report, pp. 55–57.

products via any one of four methods: (1) through an Avon representative, (2) by mail though special select catalogs, (3) by the 1-800-FOR-AVON telephone number, or (4) by fax.

The traditional door-to-door method, with the Avon lady as the homemakers' friend and beauty consultant, made the company the world's largest cosmetics firms and the number-one direct seller. The approach was viewed as expensive (the salesperson got a 20 to 50 percent commission), and there were the problems associated with hiring, training, managing, and motivating the sales force. Avon recently strengthened its traditional direct-selling channel through a program called Sales Leadership, a business model designed to attract and retain sales representatives through initiatives focused on business and beauty training. Each representative who signs up for the leadership program gets a percentage of the sales of every representative she recruits and every representative that the recruit herself recruits—and so on down through three "generations" of Avon representatives.

In September 2001, Avon announced that it had reached an agreement with the JCPenney Co. to set up shops called Becoming within retail stores operated by the firm. The shops would be built around an an assisted open-selling concept, which allows customers to browse racks that feature the Becoming brand. Each shop has six areas featuring color cosmetics, skin care, fragrance, aromatherapy, mother-and-baby beauty products, and nutritional products for active lifestyles. Becoming was designed specifically with one thought in mind: to avoid cannibalizing core Avon lines and the business done by traditional Avon sales representatives. It is priced and designed to target shoppers in mass department and specialty stores. The line is priced between mass marketed lines such as L'Oreal Paris and 10 percent to 15 percent below the entry-level department store brands. Avon had also initially planned to launch Becoming at Sears, Roebuck & Company stores, but Sears announced in July that it would stop selling cosmetics, claiming that it was a drain on profits. The in-store concept is "not without risk, but with great opportunity," said Jung. "It's a giant step." The firm used panels of sales representatives as a sounding board to design the centers and to determine the products the center will stock.

In addition to retail stores, Avon is continuing to test a direct-mail catalog, which would allow customers to bypass the Avon representative and place orders themselves. The success of a mail order catalog will depend greatly upon Avon's ability to manage its mailing and customer lists, to control inventory carefully, to offer quality merchandise, and to project a distinctive customer-benefiting image. In a limited test of a catalog, Avon has reached a more upscale customer who placed an average order of $40, more than double that of orders placed through the regular Avon sales brochure.

## GROWTH STRATEGIES

Upgrading the Avon global image is considered by management to be extremely important. One important element of the image upgrade was the announcement of a global advertising strategy. By consolidating worldwide advertising, Avon management feels it can expand its global presence and communicate a more unified brand image throughout its international markets (to view a recent organizational chart, see Exhibit 5). In 2000, management increased advertising expenditures by 50 percent to more than $90 million, and it created Let's Talk, the company's first-ever global advertising campaign. Let's Talk television and print advertisements featured young sports professionals who serve as role models. A new global product line of women's health and well-being products called Avon Wellness was part of this image program. It was aimed at expanding the definition of beauty to encompass inner health as well as outward appearance, and it featured vitamins and nutritional supplements as well as various exercise, fitness, and stress relief items. The image campaign also featured the corporate line, "The Company for Women."

In September 2000, Avon revolutionized its direct sales approach by plugging its U.S. representatives into a marketing tool called youravon.com that empowered them with the technology of the World Wide Web. As e-representatives, they had a global reach and the technological advantage of the Internet that enabled them to direct sales and establish customer relationships. The company also opened kiosks, called Avon Centers, in about forty high-traffic shopping malls. The centers were designed to display an upscale beauty image, showcase the company's beauty brands, and encourage customer trials of products. The centers were modeled after similar initiatives in Malaysia, the Philippines, Taiwan, Spain, Chile, Venezuela, and Mexico. They were small but attractive 400- to 600-square-foot environments that added significantly to the company's retail presence in locations where retail and direct selling had a history of being able to coexist.

EXHIBIT 5    Avon Products, Inc., Organization Chart (2002)

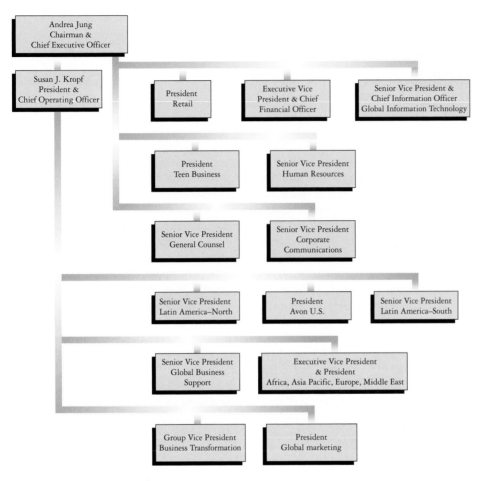

*Source:* Avon Products, Inc.

## CONCLUSION

Avon is part of a fiercely competitive industry. The company experienced 2001 operating profit declines in a number of countries including Poland, South Africa, and the entire Pacific region.

CEO Jung needs to put in place a solid strategy for the 2002–2004 time period, including clear recommendations and support of pro forma financial statements. Let's say she asks you, as an outside management consultant, to perform this work for Avon. Do the best job that you can to explain what your strategy would be.

# REVLON, INC.—2002

**M. Jill Austin**
**Middle Tennessee State University**

REV

www.revlon.com

The vision of Revlon is to "provide glamour, excitement and innovation to consumers through high-quality products at affordable prices." Net sales for 2001 decreased by $126.3 million (8.7 percent) to $1,321.5 million (compared to $1,447.8 million in 2000), and operating income in 2001 was $16.1 million, up from $15.9 million in 2000. Revlon products are sold in 175 countries around the world, with sales outside the United States accounting for approximately 41 percent of sales in 2000.

Product categories for the company include skin care, cosmetics, personal care, fragrance, and professional products. Some of the company's most recognized brand names include Revlon, Ultima, ColorStay, Almay, Charlie, Flex, Mitchum, and Jean Naté. Successful products developed recently by the company include Revlon Skinlights, Revlon High Dimension Haircolor, Almay Kinetin Skincare Advanced Anti-Aging products, and Absolutely Fabulous Lipcream. Exhibit 1 shows the company products in each business category.

It is the long-term mission of Revlon to emerge as the dominant cosmetics and personal care firm in the twenty-first century by appealing to young/trendy women, health conscious women (skin care), and older women with its variety of brands.

## HISTORY

Revlon, Inc. was formed in 1932 with a $300 investment by two brothers, Charles and Joseph Revson, and by Charles Lachmann. Charles Lachmann was a nail polish supplier who is most notably remembered for his contribution of the "l" in the Revlon name. Charles Revson was the primary force behind the success of Revlon until his death in 1968. In the early years, Revson developed a near monopoly on beauty parlor sales by selling his nail polish door-to-door at salons. He expanded into the lipstick market with the slogan "Matching Lips and Fingertips." Some of the landmark advertising campaigns directed by Revson included "Fatal Apple" and "Fire & Ice." Revson was a hard taskmaster, expecting the same whole-life devotion of his workers that he gave to Revlon. He sometimes held meetings until two in the morning, called employees at home to discuss business, cursed out employees, and pretended to fall asleep during some presentations.

The company started with only one product—nail enamel. Revlon nail enamel was manufactured with pigments instead of the dyes typically used in this type of manufacturing. This approach allowed Revlon to market a large number of color options to consumers relatively quickly. It took the three company founders just six years to transform their small nail enamel company into a multimillion-dollar organization. This successful collaboration launched one of the most recognizable brands and companies in the world.

Originally, Revlon offered its nail enamels through a limited distribution system in which professional salons carried the products. However, as the 1930s progressed, the products were distributed widely in select drugstores and department stores. As the

EXHIBIT 1    Revlon, Inc. Products and Business Categories

| BRAND | COSMETICS | SKIN CARE | FRAGRANCES | PERSONAL CARE PRODUCTS |
|---|---|---|---|---|
| Revlon | Revlon, ColorStay, Revlon Age Defying, Super Lustrous, Absolutley Fabulous, Moon Drops, Skinlights, Line & Shine, Shine Control Mattifying, New Complexion, High Dimension, Super Top Speed, Illuminance, Wet/Dry, EveryLash, StreetWear | Vitamin C Absolutes, Revlon Absolutes, Eterna 27 | Charlie, Ciara, Fire & Ice, Absolutely Fabulous | Flex, Outrageous, Aquamarine, Mitchum, Lady Mitchum, ColorStay, Colorsilk, Frost & Glow, Jean Naté, Revlon Beauty Tools, High Dimension, Almay |
| Almay | Almay, Time-Off, Amazing, One Coat, Organic Fluoride Plus Beyond Powder, Skin Stays Clean | Almay Kinetin, Almay MilkPlus | | |
| Ultima | Ultima, Beautiful, Nutrient, Wonderwear, Pucker & Pout Ultimate Edition, Full Moisture, Glowtion | Glowtion, Vital Radiance, CHR, Light Captor-C | | |
| Significant Regional Brands | Jeanne Gatineau, Cutex | Jeanne Gatineau | | Bozzano, Juvena |

*Source:* Revlon's 2001 *Annual Report,* p. 3.

world entered WWII, Revlon contributed to the war effort by providing first aid kits and dye markers for the U.S. Navy. After the war, Revlon expanded its product lines with the introduction of manicure and pedicure instruments (a natural complement to the nail enamel products). Revlon management recognized global demand potential and began offering company products in a number of new markets. Stock was first offered in the company in 1955. The 1960s were associated with the American Look campaign designed to introduce the All-American girl to the world cosmetics market via well-known U.S. models. Further identifying with the changing role of women in the market and society, the Charlie fragrance line was introduced in the early 1970s. Sales for this extremely popular line surpassed $1 billion by 1977.

After the death of Charles Revson, Michel Bergerac took control of the company. He built up the pharmaceutical side of the business. By 1985, two-thirds of Revlon's sales were health care products such as Tums and Oxy acne medications, and the company was losing ground in cosmetics. Millionaire Ronald Perelman made five offers to purchase Revlon and eventually took over the company for $1.8 billion in a leveraged buyout. Perelman returned the company to its roots and sold off the health care product lines. He refocused the company to make it an internationally known manufacturer and seller of cosmetics and fragrances. Perelman took the company private in 1987 by buying the stock from all of the public shareholders. A subsidiary of MacAndrews & Forbes stills holds 83 percent of the outstanding shares of Revlon, and Perelman is chairman and chief executive officer of MacAndrews & Forbes Holdings, Inc. The company was taken public in 1996 and is traded on the New York Stock Exchange (NYSE).

In September 1996, Revlon was given approval to manufacture, distribute, and market Revlon products in China, and the first manufactured goods rolled off the production line in December 1996. The company acquired Bionature S.A., a South American manufacturer of hair and personal care products in 1997. The completion of acquisitions in South America increased distribution and manufacturing capabilities in these markets.

## PRESENT CONDITIONS

The company has struggled in recent years and has debt of nearly $2 billion. Since October 1998, sales have fallen significantly in the United States and in countries such as Russia and Brazil, causing declines in total sales in 1998, 1999, 2000, and 2001. In an effort to reduce expenses, the company's worldwide professional products line was sold for $315 million in March 2000, and two months later, the Argentina brand Plusbelle was sold for $46 million. In November 2000 the company closed three manufacturing plants and reduced its workforce by 1,115 employees (14 percent of the workforce) in an effort to improve efficiency. A review of net sales by geographic area and product type indicates that sales in both areas have suffered in recent years (see Exhibit 2).

Even with these financial difficulties, Revlon is the number one brand in the U.S. mass market for color cosmetics. The company continues to launch new products and reintroduce some of its mature brands. The thirty-three-year-old Ultima II brand was reintroduced in 2001, and Charlie perfume was reintroduced in 2002. The new product Skinlights was launched in the United Kingdom in 2001, and in 2002 the company's Charlie perfume will be marketed to United Kingdom teenagers. Revlon spent $12.5 million advertising its new Absolutely Fabulous lip cream in 2001.

## DEMOGRAPHIC AND SOCIAL TRENDS

The cosmetics and personal care industry is affected by two major changes in the demographic composition of the United States: the aging population and the change in proportions of racial and ethnic populations. Aging baby boomers make up a sig-

EXHIBIT 2    Net Sales by Geographic Area and Product Category (in millions)

|  | *1999* | *2000* | *2001* |
|---|---|---|---|
| **GEOGRAPHIC AREA** | | | |
| United States | $ 908.4 | $ 842.8 | $ 852.2 |
| Canada | $ 46.4 | $ 53.0 | $ 48.8 |
| International Ongoing Operations | 815.1 | $ 443.6 | $ 404.1 |
| A. Europe and Africa | — | $ 175.7 | $ 160.2 |
| B. Latin America | — | 142.4 | 131.9 |
| C. Far East | — | 125.6 | 112.0 |
| **PRODUCT CATEGORY** | | | |
| Cosmetics, Skin Care, and Fragrances | 881.2 | 908.2 | $ 859.4 |
| Personal Care and Professional | 828.7 | 539.6 | 462.1 |
| TOTAL Net Sales | $1,709.9 | $1,447.8 | $1,321.5 |

*Source:* Revlon, Inc. 2001 *Form 10K*, p. 88.

nificant proportion of the adult U.S. population. The seventy-five million Americans born between 1946 and 1964 are a significant market for the cosmetics/personal care industry. The aging of the population has been coupled with a mini-baby boom. Many baby boomers have high levels of disposable income and are brand loyal consumers. In addition, it appears that baby boomers' consumption patterns and rates have not necessarily changed as they have aged. The number of people in the mature market (fifty-five and older) also continues to increase in number. Many of these consumers are wealthier and more willing to spend than ever before. Additionally, women in the mature age group remain active in the workforce for longer periods of time than in the past. Another market segment of interest to cosmetics companies is the U.S. teen market (ages twelve to nineteen) since this group was estimated to number 15.2 million in 2001.

The ethnic/racial makeup of the American population is shifting. While African Americans represents the largest minority segment (36 million in 2000), the Hispanic American segment is the fastest growing segment and is projected to be the largest minority segment in the United States by the year 2010, with approximately 40.5 million individuals. The result is that the non-Hispanic white share of the U.S. population is expected to decline to 68 percent by the year 2010. The Asian American population is also growing rapidly. International sales of cosmetics/skin care products are also affect by ethnic/racial issues. There are significant opportunities for companies in Asian countries (60 percent of the world's population). The youthful, increasingly affluent Latin American countries also represent a growth opportunity. Since the majority of personal care products are currently sold in the United States, Japan, and Canada, as well as in the European countries (less than 20 percent of the world's population), the potential for sales of personal care products around the world is excellent.

Other social and demographic issues that may affect the industry include consumers' concerns about product safety and animal testing by cosmetics companies. Increasingly, cosmetics/personal care is not an industry for women only; men purchase personal care products such as skin creams and hair care products/dyes, and many men are trying cosmetics in an effort to improve their appearance. The market for hair coloring has expanded because teenagers and adults want more vibrant coloring options.

## ECONOMICS ISSUES

U.S. economic growth began to slow in 2001, and consumer confidence declined beginning in the fall of 2000. After the terrorist attacks on the World Trade Center in New York City and the Pentagon on September 11, 2001, consumer confidence continued to falter. In addition, American consumers now have significant credit card debt. Because of this debt, consumers may elect not to purchase some expensive or nonessential products. In addition, many baby boomers are saving for their children's college or caring for older parents and may be unwilling to spend significant dollars on items such as expensive cosmetics.

International economics provides unique challenges for companies in the cosmetics/skin-care industry. Many emerging economies in Asia and Eastern Europe are eager to have mass marketers situate operations in their countries, but operating situations are generally uncertain. Countries such as Brazil and Mexico have experienced hyperinflation for several years. The economies in Japan, Latin America, and many European countries have also slowed in recent years. High inflation, the strength of the dollar in international markets, and the fluctuation of foreign currency exchange rates all pose difficulties for companies operating in international markets.

## COMPETITION

Competition is intense in the cosmetics/skin care industry. In the past, the retail cosmetics industry was dominated by sales of cosmetics in specialty stores and department stores, with beauty consultants providing service. Today, large numbers of women prefer purchasing these items at drugstores, supermarkets, mass volume retailers such as Kmart and Wal-Mart; from door-to-door sellers such as Avon; and on the Internet. Revlon's major competitors include Procter & Gamble; Avon Products; Estee Lauder Companies, Inc.; L'Oreal; and Unilever. Recent entrants into the color cosmetics market include Oil of Olay (Procter & Gamble) and Neutrogena (Johnson & Johnson). The cosmetics and skin care industry is expected to be a $200 billion business worldwide by 2003.

Other competitors include small companies, such as Urban Decay; specialty stores, such as Bath and Body Works, Body Shop, and H$_2$O; and retailers selling their own brands, such as Benneton, Banana Republic, and Victoria's Secret. Competition for the African American market is also increasing, with brands such as Fashion Flair and cosmetics lines launched by Iman and Patti LaBelle. A discussion of major competitors of Revlon, Inc. follows.

## PROCTER & GAMBLE

Procter & Gamble (P&G) is a multinational company offering products in a wide range of categories, including personal care, cosmetics, fragrances, hair care, and skin care. Some of the P&G products not in the cosmetics/skin care industry include diapers, baking mixes, bleach, dish care products, juice, laundry products, oral care products, and peanut butter. The company operates in more than seventy countries.

Revlon faces competition from P&G in a number of product categories. P&G offers hair care products through its Pantene, Vidal Sassoon, and Ivory brands. P&G skin care lines include Oil of Olay, Noxzema, and Clearasil. Fragrance lines sold by P&G include Giorgio, Hugo Boss, Old Spice, Venezia, and Wings. The P&G cosmetics line includes Cover Girl, Max Factor, and Oil of Olay. In 2001, beauty care products contributed $7.3 billion to revenue and $972 million to profit for P&G.

In 1999, the singer Brandy was hired to promote Cover Girl products, and the company spent $100 million to introduce new Cover Girl products. Currently, Faith Hill and Queen Latifah promote Cover Girl products. Selected financial information for Procter & Gamble is shown in Exhibit 3.

### L'Oreal

L'Oreal is the world's largest cosmetics firm. During the 1990s, the company enjoyed double-digit growth. L'Oreal acquired Maybelline, one of its leading competitors, in

EXHIBIT 3    Financial Information for Procter & Gamble (in millions)

|  | 2000 | 2001 |
|---|---|---|
| Net Sales | $39,951 | $39,244 |
| Operating Income | 5,954 | 4,736 |
| Net Earnings | 3,542 | 2,922 |
| Total Debt | 22,079 | 22,377 |
| Long-Term Debt | 9,012 | 9,797 |

*Source:* www.pg.com

1996 for $758 million. This move was an attempt to strengthen its position in the U.S. market. L'Oreal previously held only a 7.5 percent share of the market, but the acquisition of Maybelline made L'Oreal the number two cosmetics firm in the United States. L'Oreal competes with Revlon in the area of cosmetics (L'Oreal, Maybelline, and Helena Rubenstein), hair care (L'Oreal and Redken), and fragrances (Vanderbilt and Ralph Lauren Perfumes). In 1998, L'Oreal acquired Soft Sheen, an ethnic hair care business and introduced a quick dry nail polish called Jet-Set. From 1997 to 1999, Maybelline sales almost doubled ($320 million to $600 million), and sales outside the United States during these years accounted for 50 percent of total sales. Some of the advertising spokespersons for the company are Milla Jovovich, Jessica Alba, and Sarah Michelle Gellar. Financial information for L'Oreal is shown in Exhibit 4.

## Unilever

Unilever is an Anglo-Dutch firm that until recently has been noted as a manufacturer of soap/detergent products and food products. The company also manufactures personal care products. Some of the Unilever brands include mass skin care (Ponds, Vaseline, Pears, Hazeline), hair care (Organics, Sunsilk, Clinic, Gloria), mass perfume (Brute, Impulse, Denim, Axe/Lynx, Rexoral/Reward), and prestige fragrance lines (Elizabeth Arden, Calvin Klein, Elizabeth Taylor, Karl Lagerfeld, and Chloe). Unilever now markets seven of the top ten fragrance products in the United States, including Obsession, White Diamonds, Passion, Black Pearls, and Eternity.

The company is a world leader in prestige fragrances and leads the hair care market in Africa, the Middle East, Latin America, and Asia/Pacific. Its skin care products lead the market in North America, Africa, Latin America, Asia/Pacific, and the Middle East. Financial results for Unilever are shown in Exhibit 5.

## Avon Products, Inc.

Avon is the number one direct seller of cosmetics and beauty products in the world. Its direct sales force number 3 million people in 139 countries. Some brand names for Avon products include Avon Color, Avon Skin Care, Anew, and Skin-So-Soft. In 2001, Avon began selling vitamins and nutritional supplements. Avon also sells jewelry, gift items, lingerie, and casual clothing. Venus and Serena Williams were hired in February 2001 to promote Avon products in the "Dream big . . . let's talk Avon" advertising campaign.

The company's products can be purchased through its Internet site **www.avon.com**, but 98 percent of Avon revenue is generated by sales representatives. In an attempt to address the concerns of sales representatives that Internet sales would

---

EXHIBIT 4    Financial Information for L'Oréal
(converted to U.S. $ in millions)

|  | 1998 | 1999 | 2000 |
|---|---|---|---|
| Revenue | $13,417.4 | $10,824.8 | $11,931.2 |
| Operating Income | 1,688.5 | 1,315.3 | 1,450.8 |
| Net Income | 838.6 | 701.5 | 967.8 |
| Total Assets | 12,298.5 | 10,719.5 | 12,838.2 |
| Long-Term Debt | 682.6 | 523.1 | 784.0 |

*Source*: **www.hoovers.com**

EXHIBIT 5    Financial Information for Unilever
(converted to U.S. $ in millions)

|  | 1999 | 2000 |
|---|---|---|
| Revenue | $43,635.8 | $44,813.0 |
| Operating Profit | 4,582.8 | 3,110.0 |
| Net Income | 3,165.1 | 1,041.0 |
| Total Assets | 28,023.6 | 54,285.0 |
| Long-Term Debt | 2,845.0 | 12,306.0 |

*Source:* www.hoovers.com

take away their livelihood, Avon is allowing sales representatives to have their own Web sites. Avon posted sales of $5.7 billion in 2000. Selected financial information is provided in Exhibit 6.

### Estée Lauder

The Estée Lauder Companies, Inc. manufactures and markets cosmetics, fragrances, and skin care products. Some of the company's cosmetics/skin care brands include Estee Lauder and Clinique. Fragrances are sold under the brands Beautiful and White Linen. In addition, Estee Lauder holds the worldwide license for fragrances and cosmetics with the brand names Tommy Hilfiger and Donna Karan (DKNY). In 1998, the company acquired jane, a color cosmetics line targeted toward young women, and Aveda, a prestige brand of products for hair care. The company also has an investment in MAC (Make-Up Art Cosmetics, Limited). Stila Cosmetics, Inc., a Los Angeles-based company known for ecofriendly packaging, was acquired in 1999. Other Estée Lauder brands include Bobbi Brown Essentials, Aramia, Prescriptives, and Origins. Estée Lauder has sales in more than one hundred countries. In 1999, the company rehired model Karen Graham, known as the face of Estée Lauder, to be in advertisements for Resilience Lift products, which are targeted to mature women. Selected financial information for Estée Lauder is shown in Exhibit 7.

### INTERNAL FACTORS FOR REVLON, INC.

#### Organization/Management

About 1990, then-Chairman Levin led the company in recruiting a strong team of experienced managers who would work to achieve leadership in the cosmetics/skin care industry. It was about this same time that Revlon developed its vision to "provide glam-

EXHIBIT 6    Financial Information for Avon Products (in millions)

|  | 1998 | 1999 | 2000 |
|---|---|---|---|
| Net Sales | $5,212.7 | $5,289.1 | $5,714.6 |
| Gross Profit | 3,159.7 | 3,257.6 | 3,591.9 |
| Net Income | 270.0 | 302.4 | 478.4 |
| Total Assets | 2,433.5 | 2,528.6 | 2,826.4 |
| Long-Term Debt | 201.0 | 701.4 | 1,108.2 |

*Source:* www.avon.com and http://www.hoovers.com

**EXHIBIT 7**    Financial Information for Estée Lauder Companies, Inc. (in millions)

|  | 1999 | 2000 | 2001 |
|---|---|---|---|
| Net Sales | $3,961.5 | $4,366.8 | $4,608.1 |
| Gross Profit | 3,061.6 | 3,394.7 | 3,635.8 |
| Net Income | 272.9 | 314.1 | 305.2 |
| Total Assets | 2,746.7 | 3,043.3 | 3,218.8 |
| Long-Term Debt | 422.5 | 418.4 | 410.9 |

*Source:* www.hoovers.com

our, excitement, and innovation to consumers through high-quality products at affordable prices." The company set up the Revlon Learning Center and developed training programs to communicate its strategic principles to employees. Training provided a means for ensuring that the company's teamwork approach remained effective. In 1994, Revlon established the Charlie Awards to recognize the efforts of employees whose accomplishments significantly affected Revlon. A number of these awards are given to deserving employees each year.

At the core of the Revlon organization is its belief in individual values and the integrity of the firm and its actions. Revlon and its employees are active in supporting women's health programs and other community efforts. In the last decade, Revlon has spent $25 million on services and research that help women. One of the events that Revlon sponsors is the Revlon Run/Walk in Los Angeles. This event has raised millions of dollars for the Revlon/UCLA Women's Cancer Research Center. In 1998, the company established a partnership with the National Council of Negro Women to help support wellness programs for African American women.

## Marketing

The primary customers for Revlon products are large mass merchandisers and chain drug stores. Some of the major retail customers are Walgreens, Wal-Mart, Target, Kmart, CVS, Drug Emporium, Eckerds, Rite Aid, and JC Penney. Revlon provides point-of-sale displays and samples for these stores. In addition, the *Revlon Report* is distributed with the merchandise worldwide (and in magazines). The *Report* provides information about the company's products and the rebates/coupons that are offered. Revlon's products are also sold through its Web site (www.revlon.com).

Advertising continues to be one of the primary areas of promotion spending by Revlon. The company made a strategic decision in 2001 to hire outside advertising agencies to handle promotional efforts for Revlon. Revlon managers hired two firms—Kirshenbaum, Bond & Partners and Deutsch—to develop marketing ideas for the company's products. Longtime Revlon spokesperson Cindy Crawford, one of the most recognizable faces in the cosmetics world, promoted Revlon products for eighteen years. In 2001, however, the company decided to discontinue Crawford's contract, and it hired four relatively unknown models to promote the company's brands. Some of the company's recent promotions include the "Capture the Glow" and "It's fabulous being a woman" campaigns. In the summer of 2001, Revlon teamed with Absolut Vodka and W Hotels to promote its Absolutely Fabulous products. Parties for models and celebrities were held in Los Angeles, New York, Chicago, and Atlanta and were used to promote Absolutely Fabulous on Revlon's Web site. Revlon's advertising and promotion expenses were $272.9, $268.7, and $352.2 million in 2001, 2000, and 1999, respectively.

New product development continues to be a primary objective of Revlon even in bad financial times. Revlon spent $24 million and $27 million on research and development efforts for new products in 2000 and 2001, respectively, and employed 160–200 people respectively in this effort. In addition to development efforts, Revlon has plans to revitalize some of its long-established products. Revlon is updating the Charlie perfume for the company's 70th anniversary in 2002. Charlie will be available in three bottle designs and will be sold in gift boxes in Wal-Mart, CVS, and Target stores.

### Manufacturing/Distribution

Globalization of the company's manufacturing and distribution efforts has enabled the company to consolidate its production facilities. This consolidation and coordination between markets has provided increased operating efficiency and better use of capital assets. The number of production facilities has been reduced and centralized to cover core regions. Currently, the company has production facilities in Oxford, North Carolina, and Irvington, New Jersey. Production facilities are also located in Venezuela and South Africa. Several of the company's plants have ISO-9002 certification, thus signifying the company's commitment to quality-manufacturing standards. Planning for long-term growth includes a focus on and utilization of top-notch production facilities and distribution systems.

### Financial Conditions

Significant financial issues affect the company's operations. Long-term debt at the end of 2001 was almost $2 billion. This debt represents several years of debt problems for Revlon. Jobs lost to restructuring in 1999, 2000, and 2001, respectively, were 1,213, 403, and 1,697. Costs associated with these restructurings include employee severance, personnel benefits, and factory/warehouse/office costs.

Ron Perelman sold a large amount of his Golden State Bancorp stock in October 2001 to provide cash so Revlon could pay off junk bonds that were due. Note in Exhibit 8 (statements of operations) that sales decreased in the 1999–2001 period and that the company had net losses all three years. According to the balance sheet information in Exhibit 9, current assets, total assets, and current liabilities decreased from 2000 to 2001.

## FUTURE OUTLOOK

As Revlon, Inc. deals with its debt problems and tries to continue its strategy of innovation, product development, and globalization, several issues must be considered:

1. Should Revlon concentrate its efforts on international markets?
2. Should Revlon diversify its operations or develop joint ventures with other cosmetics companies?
3. What role does innovation play in the strategic planning of Revlon, Inc.? Which specific types of innovation might Revlon use?
4. What role should branding play in the future growth strategies of Revlon?
5. How will competitive reactions affect Revlon's future plans?
6. What is the impact of social trends and economic trends on companies in the cosmetics/skin care industry?
7. What plans should Revlon, Inc. develop to pay off long-term debt?

# EXHIBIT 8   Revlon, Inc. and Subsidiaries Consolidated Statements of Operations
(dollars in millions, except per-share data)

| | Year Ended December 31, | | |
| --- | --- | --- | --- |
| | *2001* | *2000* | *1999* |
| Net sales | $    1,321.5 | $    1,447.8 | $    1,709.9 |
| Cost of sales | 544.2 | 574.3 | 726.3 |
| Gross profit | 777.3 | 873.5 | 983.6 |
| Selling, general and administrative expenses | 723.1 | 803.5 | 1,155.4 |
| Restructuring costs and other, net | 38.1 | 54.1 | 40.2 |
| Operating income (loss) | 16.1 | 15.9 | (212.0) |
| Other expenses (income): | | | |
| Interest expense | 140.5 | 144.5 | 147.9 |
| Interest income | (3.9) | (2.1) | (2.8) |
| Amortization of debt issuance costs | 6.2 | 5.6 | 4.3 |
| Foreign currency losses (gains), net | 2.2 | 1.6 | (0.5) |
| Loss (gain) on sale of product line, brands and facilities, net | 14.4 | (10.8) | 0.9 |
| Miscellaneous, net | 2.7 | (1.8) | — |
| Other expenses, net | 162.1 | 137.0 | 149.8 |
| Loss before income taxes and extraordinary item | (146.0) | (121.1) | (361.8) |
| Provision for income taxes | 4.1 | 8.6 | 9.1 |
| Loss before extraordinary item | (150.1) | (129.7) | (370.9) |
| Extraordinary item – early extinguishment of debt, net of tax | (3.6) | — | — |
| Net loss | $    (153.7) | $    (129.7) | $    (370.9) |
| Basic and diluted loss per common share: | | | |
| Loss before extraordinary item | $    (2.87) | $    (2.49) | $    (7.12) |
| Extraordinary items | (0.07) | — | — |
| Net loss per common share | $    (2.94) | $    (2.49) | $    (7.12) |
| Weighted average number of common shares outstanding: | | | |
| Basic and diluted | 52,199,349 | 52,166,980 | 52,073,558 |

*Source:* Revlon's 2001 *Annual Report*, p. 37.

# EXHIBIT 9   Revlon, Inc. and Subsidiaries Consolidated Balance Sheets
(dollars in millions, except per share data)

| | *December 31,* *2001* | *December 31,* *2000* |
| --- | --- | --- |
| **ASSETS** | | |
| Current assets: | | |
| Cash and cash equivalents | $   103.3 | $    56.3 |
| Marketable securities | 2.2 | — |
| Trade receivables, less allowances of $15.4 and $16.1, respectively | 203.9 | 220.5 |
| Inventories | 157.9 | 184.8 |
| Prepaid expenses and other | 45.6 | 66.1 |
| Total current assets | 512.9 | 527.7 |
| Property, plant and equipment, net | 142.8 | 221.7 |
| Other assets | 143.4 | 146.3 |
| Intangible assets, net | 198.5 | 206.1 |
| Total assets | $   997.6 | $1,101.8 |

*(continued)*

EXHIBIT 9    Revlon, Inc. and Subsidiaries Consolidated Balance Sheets
             (dollars in millions, except per share data)                    (continued)

|  | December 31, 2001 | December 31, 2000 |
|---|---|---|
| **LIABILITIES AND STOCKHOLDERS' DEFICIENCY** | | |
| Current liabilities: | | |
| Short-term borrowings – third parties | $    17.5 | $    30.7 |
| Accounts payable | 87.0 | 86.3 |
| Accrued expenses and other | 281.3 | 310.7 |
| Total current liabilities | 385.8 | 427.7 |
| Long-term debt – third parties | 1,619.5 | 1,539.0 |
| Long-term debt – affiliates | 24.1 | 24.1 |
| Other long-term liabilities | 250.9 | 217.7 |
| Stockholders' deficiency: | | |
| Preferred stock, par value $.01 per share; 20,000,000 shares authorized, 546 shares of Series A Preferred Stock issued and outstanding | 54.6 | 54.6 |
| Preferred stock, par value $.01 per share; 20,000,000 shares authorized, 4,333 shares of Series B Convertible Preferred Stock issued and outstanding | — | — |
| Class B Common Stock, par value $.01 per share; 200,000,000 shares authorized, 31,250,000 issued and outstanding | 0.3 | 0.3 |
| Class A Common Stock, par value $.01 per share; 350,000,000 shares authorized, 20,516,135 and 20,115,935 issued and outstanding, respectively | 0.2 | 0.2 |
| Capital deficiency | (201.3) | (210.3) |
| Accumulated deficit since June 24, 1992 | (1,075.4) | (921.7) |
| Accumulated other comprehensive loss | (61.1) | (29.8) |
| Total stockholders' deficiency | (1,282.7) | (1,106.7) |
| Total liabilities and stockholders' deficiency | $  997.6 | $1,101.8 |

*Source*: Revlon's 2001 *Annual Report*, p. 36.

## REFERENCES

Byrnes, Nanette. "Avon—The New Calling," *Business Week* (September 18, 2000): 136.

Davis, Riccardo. "Revlon to Shut Plant, Ax 900 Jobs in Valley," *The Arizona Republic* (November 2, 2000): A1.

Edmondson, Gail. "The Beauty of Global Branding," *Business Week* (June 28, 1999): 70.

Fairclough, Gordon. "Revlon Takes Down 'For Sale' Sign, As Shares Sink 34%," *The Wall Street Journal* (October 4, 1999): B6.

Grossman, Andrea. "Teens, Males Boost Color Sales," *Drug Store News* (November 23, 1998): 53.

Klepacki, Laura. "Revlon Builds Brand Foundation," *Brandmarketing* (March 1999): 6.

Klepacki, Laura. "Ultima Plans a Makeover," *Women's Wear Daily* (December 15, 2000): 10.

Mack, Ann. "Casting Call," *Adweek Southwest* (April 9, 2001): 16.

"Market Undergoes Sea Change," *MMR* (June 25, 2001): 9.

Revlon, Inc. 1996 and 1998 *Annual Reports*.

"Revlon Resorts to Cuts," *Cosmetic Insider's Report* (November 8, 1999): 2.

Sandler, Linda and Yumiko Ono. "Revlon's Makeup Fails to Hide Some Frowns as Investors Wonder if Perelman Will Pay Debt," *The Wall Street Journal* (December 2, 1997).

Spears, John. "Revlon to Shed 120 Jobs in Shift to U.S.," *The Toronto Star* (October 25, 2000).

Tode, Chantal. "Beauty Advertising Puts on a New Face," *Brandmarketing* (May 1999): 66.

www.avon.com
www.pg.com
www.revlon.com
www.unilever.com

# PILGRIM'S PRIDE CORPORATION—2002

James L. Harbin
Texas A & M University—Texarkana

CHX

www.pilgrimspride.com

Headquartered in Pittsburg, Texas, Pilgrim's Pride Corporation (903-855-1000) is engaged in the production, processing, and marketing of fresh chicken and further processed and prepared chicken products. It is the second-largest further processing chicken company in the United States and the third-largest domestic chicken producer and fourth-largest turkey producer. In Mexico, it is the second-largest chicken company. Its prepared foods are sold throughout the United States; and its fresh chickens are sold regionally in the central, southwestern, and western United States and Northern and Central Mexico. Additionally, the company exports approximately 12 percent of its product line to overseas markets such as Russia and eastern Europe.

Among the many companies that Pilgrim's serves are Wal-Mart, KFC, PepsiCo., Kraft, Nestlé, Wendy's, Grandy's, Burger King, Church's, Chili's, and Long John Silver. At year-end 2001, Pilgrim's employed nearly 22,500 people and processed more than 2.5 billion pounds of chicken. Pilgrim's net income declined annually from $65, to $52, to $41 million in 1999 to 2000 to 2001.

Lonnie "Bo" Pilgrim, one of a family of seven children raised during the Great Depression, took his concern from a small farm-supply store fifty years ago to a corporation producing more than $2.2 billion in 2001 sales.

Pilgrim's remarkable growth has taken place in a commodity industry in which, every year for the past fifty years, economists have been predicting doom and gloom. Citing industry sales as an indicator, experts have also deduced that the chicken industry has finally matured. The big question facing Pilgrim's today is whether it can continue to grow in an industry undergoing increased consolidation through additional marketing techniques, further cost curtailment, increased integration (gaining control over supplies and distribution), improved genetics and growing techniques.

## BO PILGRIM'S BACKGROUND AND PHILOSOPHY

Bo Pilgrim's story is a classic one of deprivation and determination and then success. Born in northwest Texas in 1928, he was the fourth of seven children. His father died when Bo was nine, and he left home at twelve to live with his grandmother.

His entrepreneurial spirit had early roots. One of his first goals in life, he says, was "to be able to buy a soda when I wanted it. My father would, on occasion, give me money for a cold drink, but only after I had finished some work he wanted done for it." He learned at an early age that he could buy his own soft drinks. He bought sodas from his father's general merchandise store and sold them at a profit to the local factory workers. He later peddled newspapers, raised chickens and hogs, hauled gravel, picked peas and cotton, and sacked groceries—all before he turned eighteen.

He likens business to "a game, even a war." Commenting on how he spends his time, he says, "I spend one-third of my working days dealing with the government, one-third with lawyers, and the remaining one-third of my time is spent constructively."

He commented, "Today, we don't appreciate how much we have and how easy it is to get things. I'm definitely hooked on the free enterprise system." He added, "In fact, when I visited with President Reagan, I reminded him that the chicken and the egg industry has never had any kind of subsidy. I also shared my belief that the government should not be in the business of protecting the inefficient."

On entrepreneurship, Pilgrim said, "It is more than just shooting from the hip. A company has four resources—people, dollars, time, and facilities. Our company's objective is to gain optimum use of these four through planning, building pride, and rewarding your employees."

When asked about his secret of success, Bo responded, "Take your abilities, season them with experience on the job, and combine that with drive and motivation, and you will be successful. The way to make a difference in your life is to make that mind-boggling decision not to be average."

Most Texans know Bo as the chicken king who wears a Pilgrim's hat in his television commercials. Visitors to corporate headquarters get parking spaces marked with a picture of a chicken and the words "Pullet her in." The first-floor lobby walls are festooned with more than three hundred samples of memorabilia of Pilgrim and his company—wooden thank-you plaques, framed newspaper clippings, and photographs of him with prominent politicians. In the second-floor executive office suite, representations of chickens are everywhere—there are ceramic chickens, oil paintings of chickens, photographs of chickens, and stuffed chickens.

## HISTORY

Because commodity chicken down cycles had almost bankrupted Pilgrim's twice over the years, the company has increasingly emphasized value-added and branded products, including its chill-pack and further processed and prepared food lines. In the late 1980s, Pilgrim's spent $25 million on a facility for preparing chickens. Such products generate higher prices per pound, exhibit lower price volatility, and result in higher and more consistent profit margins than non-value-added products, such as whole ice-pack chicken.

In order to crack the food service business with processed and prepared chicken, Pilgrim's had to price its products below Tyson Foods, Inc. (its chief competitor) at a loss. The company also had to spend approximately $6 million to $8 million a year on advertising, promotion, and supermarket-slotting allowances to entice this business.

Pilgrim's Pride lost about $50 million over three years trying to enter the prepared chicken market. In fiscal 1988, the company lost a net $8 million on $506 million in sales. "I never envisioned how difficult it would be," Bo said. "It was like getting on the wrong ski lift, you might wish you hadn't done it, but there was no other way to get back down." Disgruntled investors dumped the stock, which had just had an initial public offering in January 1987. The value of Bo Pilgrim's stake shrank by 76 percent to $61 million.

Pilgrim's finally turned the corner with a strategic retreat from the supermarkets and a major advance into the food service market. Retail products now account for a mere 2 percent of Pilgrim's prepared chicken sales. In food service, Pilgrim's positioned itself as an alternative to Tyson, aiming at those customers who are leery of being too dependent on one supplier. "A lot of buyers gave us information to help us duplicate the products they were buying from Tyson," Pilgrim says. With over forty of the country's largest restaurant chains as customers, the company now has been able to raise its prices to be in line with Tyson.

## MISSION

A large group of Pilgrim's employees representing all areas of the company recently met to brainstorm the company's direction, vision, and mission. Many in the group were afraid that rather than developing a mission, they might end up with a mission statement. The difference, according to Monty Henderson, then president and CEO, was "that a mission statement becomes very wordy and usually winds up as a long paragraph or two that no one—not even the authors—can remember and usually winds up in a file somewhere. A mission, by contrast, is known by everyone, practiced daily by everyone, and becomes a way of life."

After much discussion about the business, the customers, and the competition, the group came to a consensus that Pilgrim's vision is "to achieve and maintain leadership in each product and service that we provide." To achieve this goal, the group felt that its mission was summed up as follows: "Our job is customer satisfaction . . . every day." Because of the increased emphasis on the international market, Pilgrim's later amended its vision: "To be a world class chicken company—better than the best."

## COMPETITION

Pilgrim's competes with other integrated chicken companies and to a lesser extent with local and regional poultry companies that are not fully integrated. The primary competitive factors in the chicken industry include price, product line, and customer service. Although its products are competitively priced and generally supported with in-store promotions and discount programs, the company believes that product quality, brand awareness, and customer service are the primary methods through which it competes. Pilgrim's believes that it has only one competitor (Tyson) with a more complete line of value-added products.

Tyson, the number-one poultry processor (with 2000 sales of about $8 billion), generates 24 percent of the U.S. poultry production. Gold Kist has 10 percent, Perdue Farms has 8 percent, and Pilgrim's and Conagra Poultry each have approximately 6 percent.

Tyson's strategy has been one of many acquisitions over the past decade. It acquired Hudson Foods, Inc. for $682 million in 1997. At that time, Hudson had 5 percent of the market. In 1988, *The Wall Street Journal* reported that Tyson would acquire Pilgrim's for approximately $162 million, but the deal fell through. In 2001, Tyson acquired IBP Inc., the world's largest producer of fresh beef and pork, in an approximate $3 billion-plus deal. IBP had $16.9 billion in 2000 sales. Tyson, with the IBP acquisition, has about 28 percent of the U.S. beef market, 24 percent of the chicken market, and 18 percent of the pork market.

"Our marketing strategy for success is simple—segment, concentrate, dominate. We identify a promising market segment, concentrate our resources in it, and ultimately gain for Tyson Foods a dominate share of that segment," stated a recent Tyson annual report. "Our customers include all of the nation's top 50 food service distributors, 88 of the top 100 restaurant chains, 100 of the top retail supermarket chains, and every major wholesale club."

## MEXICO

Pilgrim's plants are geographically located to serve over 75 percent of the Mexican market. Its business strategy for Mexico calls for using its U.S. management expertise to solidify its position as the most efficient operator in Mexico and, at the same time, to develop a strong consumer and trade franchise for the Pilgrim's Pride brand. With the Mexican market maturing at an accelerated rate and customers increasingly selecting

298 JAMES L. HARBIN

value-added products, it appears that Pilgrim's entry is particularly timely. Pilgrim's sales in Mexico rose to $323 million in 2001, an increase from its 1996 sales of $228 million to $323 million in 2000.

## THE BROILER INDUSTRY

Before the 1950s, farmers were reluctant to undertake chicken farming because investments in buildings, equipment, feed, chicks, and other inputs could easily be lost due to disease or natural calamities. Chicken feed suppliers recognized that they could increase their own sales by extending credit to farmers, enabling them to remain in business while they paid off their debts. This risk-sharing arrangement spurred chicken production and eventually evolved into the kind of grower-contracting arrangements that are now common to all poultry production. Meanwhile, the feed suppliers integrated further into slaughter and processing operations, which are the integrated chicken firms of today.

Through contracting arrangements, integrated chicken firms accept much of the risk of chicken growing in exchange for greater control over both the quality and quantity of the birds. Usually, the firm provides company-owned chicks and feed, while the contract farmer provides the housing and labor and then returns the fully grown chickens to the firm for processing. The firm, typically, pays a pre-established fee per pound for live broilers plus a bonus or penalty for performance relative to other chicken farmers.

Vertical integration in the poultry industry was listed as one of top ten events having the greatest impact on the meat industry during the twentieth century. Other top ten events pertinent to the poultry industry were the passage of the Federal Meat Inspection Act (1906), the development of refrigerated rail cars and trucks and the national interstate highway system, the growth of fast-food chains, and the passage of both the Humane Slaughter Act (1958) and the Poultry Products Inspection Act (1957).

### Profitability

Industry profitability is primarily a function of the consumption of chicken and competing meats and the costs of feed grains. Historically, the broiler industry operated on a fairly predictable cycle of about three years: a year of good profits, followed by a year of expanded output and declining profits, followed by a year of losses and production cuts.

The chicken companies have spent much of their energy trying to escape the commodity cycle through marketing and further processing. Frank Perdue, with his classic commercials, was the first to demonstrate that a company could charge a premium for a brand name bird. Today, the biggest producers all play the brand-loyalty game. This leaves the chicken producers in an odd situation: They are commodity concerns trying to behave like consumer-products companies. As Prudential-Bache's John McMillin foretold in the 1980s, "The 1990s chicken industry will be better capitalized, more competitive—and less profitable." That prediction came true.

Industry profitability can be significantly influenced by feed costs, which are influenced by a number of factors unrelated to the broiler industry, including legislation that provides discretion to the federal government to set price and income supports for grain. Historically, feed costs have averaged approximately 50 percent of total production costs of non-value-added products and have fluctuated substantially with the price of corn, milo, and soybean meal. By comparison, feed costs typically average approximately 25 percent of total production costs of further processed and prepared chicken products such as nuggets, fillets, and deli products; as a result, increased emphasis on sales of such products by chicken producers reduces the sensitivity of earnings to feed cost movements.

Although feed costs may vary dramatically, the production costs of chicken are not as severely affected by changing feed ingredient prices as are the production costs of beef and pork. Chickens require approximately two pounds of dry feed to produce one pound of meat, compared to cattle and hogs, which require approximately seven and three pounds, respectively, of feed.

## Problems

Across the southeastern United States, where 85 percent of the country's chickens are processed, the poultry industry often suffers from bad publicity. Chicken processing plants are said to be dirty, rotten meat is reaching the market; salmonella-tainted chickens are poisoning people, and the chicken growers who contract with the processors are being ripped off. Ross Perot publicly lambasted Bill Cinton's gubernatorial record by saying that the Arkansas poultry business is "not an industry of tomorrow."

The industry's biggest worry may be microscopic in physical size. Chickens in battery farms (and those in farmyards) often live in their own dung, which in turn encourages the growth of bacteria such as salmonella which in turn contaminate the meat during processing. About 6 million Americans are made ill by such bacteria every year, and about 1,300 die. Scientists at the Centers for Disease Control say chickens may be the cause of up to half of those cases.

The industry's high-tech, fast-paced production lines, which can process some 200,000 birds a day at a single plant, heighten fecal contamination. Bacteria often spread among birds as they speed along conveyors from hot collective baths through wet mechanical feather pickers to tanks of cold water. Partly to hold down the price of poultry, the industry has not tried to produce cleaner chickens, but it relies instead on consumers to cook the meat thoroughly.

The trend toward larger plant sizes raises several public policy issues. The volume of animal waste is but one concern. Critics contend that the need to reduce production costs comes at the expense of worker safety. Conditions on the production line can be tough. Repetitive motion from such tasks as pulling out chicken guts can cause disabling injuries. Employees frequently spend shifts in either a freezing cooler or 95-degree heat. "The industry has one foot in the twenty-first century when it comes to chickens, but [it] left one foot back in the nineteenth century when it comes to people," stated Bob Hall, research director for the Institute for Southern Studies, a labor-funded advocacy group in Durham, North Carolina. Poultry is a highly labor intensive industry.

Consolidation has resulted in a highly centralized and vertically integrated industry in which the five top players control 55 percent of American production. As a result, the country has been carved up into regional buying monopolies, and each region's dominant processor can dictate terms to the growers. The vast majority of growers receive only short-term contracts from the processors, with no formal assurances of long-term business relationships. Farmers are at a distinct disadvantage when negotiating contract terms since they are financially unable to risk falling into disfavor with the processors.

A report from the Texas Commissioner of Agriculture concluded that although "the grower makes a substantial capital investment and takes most of the risk, he or she is not sharing in the success of the industry." In some cases, growers have received as little as $579 in annual income per 20,000-bird-capacity chicken house.

The processors defend their practices. Industry spokespeople point out that growers are guaranteed a price for adult chickens, typically about 3.5 cents to 4 cents a pound. Thus, the processors contend, growers are sheltered from much of the risk of the volatile chicken market. Bill Roenigk, spokesperson for the National Broiler Council, a processor trade group, says studies have shown that chicken farmers' average return on investment is 5 percent, which is higher than the return in many other agriculture operations.

## CHANGING DEMAND AND SUPPLY

Before 1970, most poultry bought by consumers was whole chickens and turkeys, and the export business was almost nonexistent. It would have been difficult to find a restaurant or fast-food outlet selling chicken sandwiches or nuggets. Deboned chicken breasts did not exist. Today, exports account for almost one-sixth of U.S. poultry production, and consumers are confronted with an endless variety of chicken products.

Per capita poultry consumption jumped from 34 pounds in 1960 (a level that was about 50 percent of the beef total) to 96 pounds in 1999—nearly 40 percent higher than beef consumption. The USDA estimates that chicken consumption will increase at a 3 percent compounded annual growth rate into the future. Consumption in Mexico is 38 pounds per capita, and it is projected to grow by 10 percent per year.

The major factors influencing this growth are consumer awareness of the health and nutritional characteristics of chicken, the price advantage of chicken relative to red meat, and the convenience of further processed and prepared chicken products. This growth has been enhanced by new product forms and packaging that increase convenience and product versatility. A larger, more affluent, mobile population has created a demand for more convenient foods. People are willing to trade dollars for time, and the industry has cashed in by providing value-added products.

Chicken firms have further segmented the market by observing that Americans are willing to pay much higher prices for white meat breasts than for dark meat thighs and drumsticks. They have also learned—and benefited—from the fact that overseas countries provide a market for low-value parts (chicken feet, tails, wingtips, gizzards) at a higher price than Americans are willing to pay.

The poultry sector isn't solely chicken; it also includes turkey, duck, goose, and quail. But the poultry industry in America is chicken-driven. Chicken nuggets account for about 10 percent of total U.S. broiler output and showed chicken companies what could happen if they went beyond selling what are called, in the trade, "feathers-off, guts-out birds."

Chicken, priced pound-per-pound, is one-third the cost of beef and one-half the cost of pork. Non-value-added chickens are selling for less than they did in 1923, when Mrs. Wilmer Steele of Ocean View, Delaware, sold what chicken historians say was the nation's first flock of commercial broilers for 62 cents a pound. Why is chicken cheaper than the competition? The answer has to do with the fact that a chicken is highly efficient at converting feed to flesh. As noted, to produce a pound of meat, a chicken consumes less than two pounds of feed, compared with six or seven pounds for a cow and three for a pig.

Also, a chicken doesn't live long. The shorter a creature's life cycle, the quicker its generations can be manipulated genetically. Chicken breeders have steadily developed birds that grow bigger on less feed in less time. Breeders may be approaching the limits of practicality on this score; modern chickens have "put on so much weight that they have some real problems mating," said Walter Becker, professor emeritus of genetics and cell biology at Washington State University.

Furthermore, chickens don't graze. Raising cattle requires an investment in land; raising chickens doesn't. Chickens used to need to run around in the sun; otherwise, they would develop a vitamin D deficiency and rickets. But in the 1920s, poultry producers solved the vitamin D problem by adding cod-liver oil to chicken feed. Since then, they have been able to raise thousands of chickens in confinement, allowing about 0.7 square foot per bird.

## THE FUTURE

During the next few years, per capita consumption of chicken could more than double throughout the world.

In the domestic market; fewer and fewer meals consumed at home are made from scratch. In 1999, Americans spent approximately $970 million a day eating out. With 70 percent of mothers working outside of the home and 40 percent of consumers not knowing what they will eat as late as four o'clock in the afternoon, meal planning and preparation take a back seat to convenience and eating out.

Concern for healthy food may be slackening. Some say nutrition is on the back burner, with taste the big thing. One analyst recently commented, "A few years back, when everyone was concerned about health and diet, the fast-food restaurants started wringing fat from hamburgers, but sales dropped because they had less and less flavor. So restaurants took bacon and slapped slices of that on the sandwiches, and sales took off like gangbusters." The increasing size of meals served in restaurants is but another sign that fat may be back.

Pilgrim's acquired WLR Foods, Inc. on January 27, 2001, expanding into the Mid-Atlantic region. WLR Foods was the seventh-largest poultry company in the United States. One analyst described the WLR deal as pricey (Pilgrim's paid about twice per share what WLR stock was trading at when the deal was announced). Another described WLR as a company "going nowhere fast" that will benefit from being absorbed by a bigger and more competitive player. He went on to say "that the last thing this industry needs is more capacity, so you have to congratulate (Pilgrim's) management for choosing this route to grow, which doesn't add to the industry's overcapacity problems."

Although the acquisition created synergistic opportunities and a chance to establish a presence in the nation's Mid-Atlantic region, Pilgrim's is faced with integration challenges combined with a more leveraged situation. There has long been pressure on management to improve margins and stock performance (see Exhibits 1–3 for details).

EXHIBIT 1    Pilgrim's Pride Corporation and Subsidiaries September 29, 2001
(in thousands)

| | Fiscal Year Ended | | |
| --- | --- | --- | --- |
| | September 29, 2001<br>(52 weeks) | September 30, 2000<br>(52 weeks) | October 2, 1999<br>(53 weeks) |
| **Net Sales to Customers:** | | | |
| Chicken and Other Products: | | | |
| United States | $1,652,199 | $1,192,077 | $1,102,903 |
| Mexico | 323,678 | 307,362 | 254,500 |
| Sub-total | 1,975,877 | 1,499,439 | 1,357,403 |
| Turkey | 238,835 | — | — |
| Total | $2,214,712 | $1,499,439 | $1,357,403 |
| **Operating Income:** | | | |
| Chicken and Other Products: | | | |
| United States | $    78,096 | $    45,928 | $    88,177 |
| Mexico | 12,157 | 34,560 | 21,327 |
| Sub-total | 90,253 | 80,488 | 109,504 |
| Turkey | 4,289 | — | — |
| Total | $    94,542 | $    80,488 | $  109,504 |
| **Depreciation and Amortization:**[b] | | | |
| Chicken and Other Products: | | | |
| United States | $    38,155 | $    24,444 | $    23,185 |
| Mexico | 11,962 | 11,583 | 11,351 |
| Sub-total | 50,117 | 36,027 | 34,536 |
| Turkey | 5,273 | — | — |
| Total | $    55,390 | $    36,027 | $    34,536 |
| **Total Assets:** | | | |
| Chicken and Other Products: | | | |
| United States | $  764,073 | $  496,173 | |
| Mexico | 247,681 | 209,247 | |
| Sub-total | 1,011,754 | 705,420 | |
| Turkey | 203,941 | — | |
| Total | $1,215,695 | $  705,420 | |
| **Capital Expenditures:**[a] | | | |
| Chicken and Other Products | | | |
| United States | $    80,173 | $    69,712 | |
| Mexico | 29,425 | 22,417 | |
| Sub-total | 109,598 | 92,129 | |
| Turkey | 3,034 | — | |
| Total | $  112,632 | 92,129 | |

(a) Excludes business acquisition cost of $239,539, incurred in connection with the acquisition of WLR Foods on January 27, 2001.

(b) Includes amortization of capitalized financing costs of approximately $0.9 million, $1.2 million, and $1.1 million in fiscal years 2001, 2000, and 1999, respectively.

*Source:* Pilgrim's Pride, 2001 *Annual Report,* p. 65.

EXHIBIT 2    Consolidated Statements of Income Pilgrim's Pride Corporation
(in thousands, except per-share data)

| | Three Years Ended September 29 | | |
| --- | --- | --- | --- |
| | *2001* | *2000* | *1999* |
| Net Sales | $2,214,712 | $1,499,439 | $1,357,403 |
| Cost and Expenses: | | | |
| Cost of sales | 2,000,762 | 1,333,611 | 1,171,695 |
| Selling, general and administrative | 119,408 | 85,340 | 76,204 |
| | 2,120,170 | 1,418,951 | 1,247,899 |
| Operating Income | 94,542 | 80,488 | 109,504 |
| Other Expenses (Income): | | | |
| Interest expense, net | 30,775 | 17,779 | 17,666 |
| Foreign exchange (gain) loss | 122 | (152) | (50) |
| Miscellaneous, net | 351 | 75 | 984 |
| | 31,248 | 17,702 | 18,600 |
| Income Before Income Taxes and Extraordinary Charge | 63,294 | 62,786 | 90,904 |
| Income Tax Expense | 21,263 | 10,442 | 25,651 |
| Income Before Extraordinary Charge | 42,031 | 52,344 | 65,253 |
| Extraordinary Charge, Net of Tax | 894 | — | — |
| Net Income | $41,137 | $52,344 | $65,253 |
| Income per Common Share Before Extraordinary Charge—Basic and Diluted | $1.02 | $1.27 | $1.58 |
| Extraordinary Charge, Net of Tax | (.02) | — | — |
| Net Income per Common Share-Basic and Diluted | $1.00 | $1.27 | 1.58 |

See Notes to Consolidated Financial Statements.
*Source:* Pilgrim's Pride, *Annual Report,* p. 5.

EXHIBIT 3    Consolidated Balance Sheets Pilgrim's Pride Corporation
(in thousands, except share and per-share data)

| | September 29, 2001 | September 30, 2000 |
|---|---|---|
| **ASSETS** | | |
| **Current Assets:** | | |
| Cash and cash equivalents | $   20,916 | $  28,060 |
| Trade accounts and other receivables, less allowance for doubtful accounts | 95,022 | 50,286 |
| Inventories | 314,400 | 181,237 |
| Other current assets | 12,934 | 9,387 |
| Total Current Assets | 443,272 | 268,970 |
| **OTHER ASSETS** | 20,067 | 18,576 |
| **Property, Plant and Equipment:** | | |
| Land | 36,350 | 26,137 |
| Buildings, machinery and equipment | 929,922 | 565,034 |
| Autos and trucks | 53,264 | 48,187 |
| Construction-in-progress | 71,427 | 68,743 |
| | 1,090,963 | 708,101 |
| Less accumulated depreciation | 338,607 | 290,227 |
| | 752,356 | 417,874 |
| | $1,215,695 | $705,420 |
| **LIABILITIES AND STOCKHOLDERS' EQUITY** | | |
| **Current Liabilities:** | | |
| Accounts payable | $   151,265 | $105,078 |
| Accrued expenses | 83,558 | 34,704 |
| Current maturities of long-term debt | 5,099 | 4,657 |
| Total Current Liabilities | 239,922 | 144,439 |
| **LONG-TERM DEBT, LESS CURRENT MATURITIES** | 467,242 | 165,037 |
| **Deferred Income Taxes** | 126,710 | 52,496 |
| **Minority Interest in Subsidiary** | 889 | 889 |
| **Commitments and Contingencies** | — | — |
| **STOCKHOLDERS' EQUITY:** | | |
| Preferred stock, $.01 par value, authorized 5,000,000 shares; none issued | — | — |
| Common stock–Class A, $.01 par value, authorized 100,000,000 shares; and 13,794,529 shares issued and outstanding in 2001 and 2000, respectively; | 138 | 138 |
| Common stock – Class B, $.01 par value, authorized 60,000,000 shares; 27,589,250 issued and outstanding in 2001 and 2000 | 276 | 276 |
| Additional paid-in capital | 79,625 | 79,625 |
| Retained earnings | 302,758 | 264,088 |
| Accumulated other comprehensive income (loss) | (297) | — |
| Less treasury stock, 271,100 shares | (1,568) | (1,568) |
| Total Stockholders' Equity | 380,932 | 342,559 |
| | $1,215,695 | $705,420 |

*Source:* Pilgrim's Pride, 2001 *Annual Report,* p. 50.

# H.J. HEINZ COMPANY—2002

**Henry Beam**
**Western Michigan University**

HNZ

www.heinz.com

H.J. Heinz Company is a worldwide provider of processed food products and nutritional services. Headquartered in Pittsburgh, Pennsylvania, it has 45,000 employees, and markets more than 5,700 varieties of food products in more than 200 countries. It has manufacturing facilities in 21 countries. Heinz reported sales of $9.43 billion and net income of $478 million in the fiscal year ending May 2, 2001. In addition to ketchup, its original and best-known product, Heinz's product mix includes steak sauces, pet food, baby food, frozen potatoes, snacks, pasta, tuna, nutrition drinks, and soup. While the company's diversified product line makes it difficult for Heinz to have a succinct mission statement, its CEO, William R. Johnson, says, "Our mission is to have a bottle of ketchup on every table, everywhere."

## HISTORY

In 1869, Henry J. Heinz formed a partnership with his friend, L.C. Noble, to sell grated horseradish fresh from his family's garden in western Pennsylvania. The firm soon moved to Pittsburgh and continued to grow until the overextended enterprise was forced into bankruptcy by the banking panic of 1875. Heinz paid all related debts before founding a new business, F. & J. Heinz, with his cousin and brother that same year. In its first year, the company produced pickles, horseradish, and what would become a world-renowned product—bottled ketchup. By 1888, Heinz gained financial control of the company as well, changing the name to H.J. Heinz.

Heinz put his ketchup in the familiar narrow-necked bottle to make it easier to pour and to reduce the amount of contact with air, which darkened the sauce. In 1895, a 17-ounce "Imperial Bottle" of ketchup was introduced with a delicately embossed symmetrical shape to appeal to higher-end hotels, restaurants, and upper-income families. A succession of prepared products followed. Heinz had discovered that most people were willing to let someone else take over a share of their kitchen operations and that a pure product of superior quality would find a ready market if properly packaged and promoted.

While traveling on a New York City elevated train in 1896, Heinz saw a shoe store sign advertising "21 styles." He liked the phrase and came up with the slogan "57 varieties" to describe what his company produced. The H.J. Heinz Company already produced more than 57 varieties, but Heinz stuck with the phrase because he liked the sound of the number 57. Heinz then drew a streetcar ad featuring the slogan. The public latched onto the slogan, which is displayed on the Heinz label to this day. In 1910, Heinz printed a small dark-green pickle on the bottom of the keystone label to further product recognition. The pickle remains a key element of the Heinz label today.

When Henry Heinz died in 1919, he was succeeded by his son Howard, who continued to grow the business internally. The company was run by H.J. Heinz II from 1941 to 1966. By the end of the 1940s, Heinz and ketchup went together naturally. As stated in a 1949 issue of the *Saturday Evening Post*, "Heinz ketchup, although not the first commercial ketchup, has led the American market for so long that it has determined the shape of almost all ketchup bottles because the public just naturally recognizes that shape as ketchup." The H.J. Heinz Company went public in 1946 after 77 years as a privately held firm.

In 1958, Heinz began to grow through acquisitions in Europe and Mexico as well in the United States. In the 1980s, Heinz became a leader in the nutrition and wellness field with the purchase of Weight Watchers and as a result of its development, into a global brand. The company also built major production bases in Spain, Portugal, and New Zealand. In 1998, William R. Johnson assumed the position of president and CEO from Dr. O'Reilly, becoming only the sixth CEO in the firm's long history. Today, H.J. Heinz Company is one of the largest publicly held food companies in the United States, as shown in Exhibit 1. Its major competitors are Campbell Soup, ConAgra, and Nestlé.

## PRODUCT CATEGORIES

Heinz has organized its products into six core categories in which it seeks global leadership. Products with the leading market share position in their respective markets generate about two-thirds of the company's sales.

### Ketchup, Condiments, and Sauces

Ketchup, condiments, and sauces, Heinz's largest segment, saw sales increase 4 percent in 2001 to $2.54 billion.

#### Ketchup

Heinz ketchup has always been the company's flagship brand. The company is the world's largest buyer of tomatoes, a key ingredient for its ketchup and related products, such as steak and barbecue sauce. Each year, the company processes more than 2 million tons of tomatoes and sells over $1 billion of ketchup worldwide. In the United States, it holds market-share highs of 57 percent in dollars and 51 percent in volume.

EXHIBIT 1    The Top Ten Publicly Held Food Companies in 2000 (in millions)

| Company | Sales | Net Income | Major Brands/Products |
|---|---|---|---|
| Archer Daniels | 14,283 | 281 | Agricultural commodities and products |
| Bestfoods[1] | 8,637 | 717 | Mazola, Hellman's, Skippy, Thomas |
| Campbell Soup | 6,424 | 766 | Campbell's, Pepperidge Farm, Godiva, Healthy Request |
| ConAgra Foods | 24,594 | 696 | Grocery products, Healthy Choice, agricultural products |
| Diageo plc[2,3] | 18,246 | 618 | Pillsbury, Green Giant, Burger King, Smirnoff, Guinness |
| General Mills[3] | 6,246 | 567 | Wheaties, Betty Crocker, Bisquick, Hamburger Helper |
| Group Danone | 13,415 | 688 | Dannon, Lee & Perrins sauces, Evian, Galbani cheese |
| H.J. Heinz | 9,300 | 882 | Heinz ketchup, Star-Kist, Ore-Ida, Ken-L Ration |
| Hershey | 3,971 | 333 | Hershey's, Reese's, Cadbury's, Kit-Kat |
| Kellogg | 6,984 | 549 | Corn Flakes, Rice Krispies, Special K, Pop Tarts |

[1]Formerly CPC International; acquired by Unilever in October 2000.
[2]Created in the December 1997 merger of Grand Metropolitan plc and Guinness plc.
[3]General Mills acquired the Pillsbury unit of Diageo in July 2000.
*Sources: Value Line Investment Survey* and **www.hoovers.com**.

In its 2000 *Annual Report,* Heinz stated that it would focus on making ketchup its primary growth vehicle in the United States and abroad. Heinz is focusing its global advertising campaign on increasing the consumption of ketchup by teenagers. Children ages six to twelve are the largest consumers of ketchup, followed closely by twelve to eighteen year olds. Households with children consume over twice as much ketchup as households without children. In 2001, Heinz introduced its colorful EZ Squirt kids' ketchup that comes in green and purple colors as well as the traditional tomato red. The squeezable bottle has a narrow opening that allows children to draw and write on their food.

Ketchup is used in many different ways around the world. It is eaten with pasta in Sweden, with rice in Venezuela, and with fish and chips in the United Kingdom. Heinz built a ketchup factory in China to supply its emerging market there for prepared foods. Annual per capita ketchup consumption in selected countries is shown in Exhibit 2. Heinz has set a goal "to make Heinz ketchup as ubiquitous as Coca-Cola. Everywhere fast-food is sold—whether in Asia, Africa, Europe, or the Americas—Heinz ketchup will be there, too." Global ketchup consumption is expected to increase about 6 percent annually.

Heinz's ketchup faces challenges from salsa and private ketchup brands. Introduced to American consumers over fifty years ago, salsa includes an array of sauces that include picante, enchilada, taco, and other chili-based sauces that appeal particularly to younger consumers. Salsa now outsells ketchup in some retail stores, indicating the changing nature of American tastes. Large food retailers such as A&P, Jewel, and Kroger offer lower cost, private label ketchup which competes directly with Heinz ketchup. Private label brands can be sold for less because there are no promotion or advertising costs associated with them.

EXHIBIT 2    Annual per capita Ketchup Consumption in Selected Countries, All Brands (in U.S. dollars)

| Country | Ketchup Consumption |
|---|---|
| Sweden | $4.00 |
| Australia | 2.50 |
| United States | 2.20 |
| Canada | 2.20 |
| Germany | 1.70 |
| United Kingdom | 1.60 |
| Poland | 1.40 |
| Japan | 1.40 |
| France | 1.20 |
| Russia | 0.90 |
| Thailand | 0.70 |
| Malaysia | 0.60 |
| Brazil | 0.40 |
| Indonesia | 0.40 |

*Source:* Heinz's 1999 *Annual Report,* p. 7.

In 2001, Heinz acquired Vlasic pickles from Vlasic Foods International, which was in bankruptcy proceedings. Vlasic has about 25 percent of the $1.1 billion pickle, pepper, and relish categories, compared to about 3 percent for Heinz prior to the acquisition. A Heinz news release commented, "The addition of Vlasic pickles, a venerable brand with a history of excellence, quality and market innovation, will provide another condiment category with a number one brand for Heinz."

### Food Service

Heinz's food service segment is the largest supplier of prepared foods to restaurants, diners, cafeterias, and other away-from-home eating places. Products include packets of ketchup and salad dressing and frozen soup concentrate. U.S. families spend about 50 cents of every food dollar on meals outside the home, up from about 33 cents twenty-five years ago. Sales of this segment, over $1 billion annually, were severely affected by the events of September 11, 2001, as people cut back on travel and were reluctant to dine in public places.

### Sauces

Heinz has expanded its offering of sauces by acquiring such brand names as Open Pit barbeque sauce, Mr. Yoshida's Fine Sauces, and Boston Market HomeStyle Gravies. Heinz also has a licensing agreement to market Jack Daniel's Grilling Sauces. Sauces are typically sold in the same aisle of the store as ketchup.

### Frozen Meals/Snacks

This segment includes Weight Watchers Smart Ones frozen entrees; Boston Market frozen meals; Bagel Bites frozen snacks, pasta, and potatoes; and Alden Merrell premium priced frozen desserts. Sales of this category increased 26 percent to $1.96 billion in 2001. The introduction of Boston Market HomeStyle Meals was very successful, as sales reached $130 million in the first full year of national distribution.

The Ore-Ida unit, with sales of $1 billion in 2001, includes retail and specialty frozen foods. Its principal product is frozen potatoes that are sold to fast-food chains, but it also sells a wide variety of frozen potato products in supermarkets. Ore-Ida has over half of the frozen potato market. It also makes the popular Tater Tots, which are formed from the slivers of potato that remain when a square section is sliced out to be made into French fried potatoes. A successful new Ore-Ida product is Bagel Bites pizza-topped snacks.

### Tuna and Seafood

Heinz's Star-Kist division is the world's largest processor of canned tuna, a high-quality, low-cost, low-fat source of protein. Star-Kist's global sales of tuna and seafood were $1.04 billion in 2001, little changed from the previous year. It introduced a single-serving pouch of tuna in the spring of 2001 as an alternative to canned tuna. The vacuum sealed pouch, available in three and seven ounce sizes, provides firmer, fresher-tasting tuna. Star-Kist advertising features icons Charlie the Tuna and Morris the Cat.

Heinz operates modern, automated canneries in the Pacific and Indian Oceans, in Africa, and in Europe. Tuna prices fell to record low levels in 2001, and Heinz closed its tuna and fishing operations in Puerto Rico.

## Quick-Serve Meals/Soups

Heinz's Quick-Serve meal segment, which includes soup, beans, and pasta, had sales of $1.22 billion in 2001. Heinz is the leading soup brand in the United Kingdom, Canada, Australia, and New Zealand. Heinz U.K. launched Fridge Door Soup, which is packaged in one-liter plastic bottles that are designed for storage on refrigerator doors. In Europe, Heinz introduced fast and convenient microwavable soup and baked beans products.

Heinz is the country's largest producer of private-label soup, with a nearly 90 percent share of the private-label market. Overall, Heinz has less than a 10 percent share of the total U.S. soup market. Campbell Soup Company is by far the largest producer of brand name canned soups in the United States, with a market share of nearly 75 percent of the $2.5 billion U.S. canned soup market. Heinz made a major attempt to enter the brand-name soup business in 1970 but failed because it wasn't able to adequately fund national media advertising. Instead, it decided to withdraw from the brand-name soup market in United States and concentrate on its private-label business.

## Pet Products

Pet products had sales of $1.15 billion in 2001 and offers a broad range of cat and dog foods. Heinz's 9-Lives cat food is the market leader. Its dog food brands include Kibbles'n Bits, Gravy Train, Cycle, Ken-L Ration, and Jerky Treats. Heinz, Ralcorp, and Nestlé-Alpo each have about 20 percent of the domestic pet food business. Heinz recently introduced several pet food products, including Pup-Peroni Nawsomes, soft and chewy treats that are packed in a tennis ball container and Meaty Bone Savory Bites, crunchy treats with soft centers flavored with beef, chicken, or peanut butter. Heinz has about a third of the high-margin pet treats market.

## Infant Feeding

Sales of Heinz's jarred baby foods, cereals, formulas, juices, and biscuits were $971 million in 2001. Heinz's market share in the United States is significantly behind that of industry leader Gerber (a division of Novartis, a Swiss firm) but ahead of Beechnut (a division of Ralcorp Holdings). However, Heinz is the market leader outside the United States. It has over half of the infant food market in Australia, Canada, Italy, New Zealand, and the United Kingdom, and it is working to expand its infant feeding business in eastern Europe, Russia, India, and China.

## FINANCE

Highlights of H.J. Heinz Company's performance for the last two years are given in Exhibit 3. Heinz has increased its dividend every year since 1967. Heinz's financial statements are given in Exhibits 4 and 5. Heinz's net income was unusually high in 2000 because of the $465 million gain it recorded for the sale of its Weight Watchers storefront business. Business segment information is given in Exhibits 6 and 7. Advertising costs for fiscal years 2001, 2000, and 1999 were $404 million, $374 million, and $374 million, respectively. Like many other multinational companies, Heinz has been adversely affected by the strength of the dollar. In recent years, exchange rates have reduced Heinz sales by about $1.1 billion when international sales are translated into U.S. dollars for reporting purposes.

EXHIBIT 3    H.J. Heinz Company and Subsidiaries Consolidated Balance Sheets
(in thousands)

|  | May 2, 2001 | May 3, 2000 |
|---|---|---|
| **ASSETS** | | |
| CURRENT ASSETS: | | |
| Cash and cash equivalents | $  138,849 | $  137,617 |
| Short-term investments, at cost which approximates market | 5,371 | 16,512 |
| Receivables (net of allowances: 2001—$15,075 and 2000—$18,697) | 1,383,550 | 1,237,804 |
| Inventories: | | |
| Finished goods and work-in-process | 1,095,954 | 1,270,329 |
| Packaging material and ingredients | 312,007 | 329,577 |
|  | 1,407,961 | 1,599,906 |
| Prepaid expenses | 157,801 | 171,599 |
| Other current assets | 23,282 | 6,511 |
| Total current assets | 3,116,814 | 3,169,949 |
| PROPERTY, PLANT, AND EQUIPMENT: | | |
| Land | 54,774 | 45,959 |
| Buildings and leasehold improvements | 878,028 | 860,873 |
| Equipment, furniture and other | 2,947,978 | 3,440,915 |
|  | 3,880,780 | 4,347,747 |
| Less accumulated depreciation | 1,712,400 | 1,988,994 |
| Total property, plant, and equipment, net | 2,168,380 | 2,358,753 |
| OTHER NONCURRENT ASSETS: | | |
| Goodwill (net of amortization: 2001—$334,907 and 2000—$312,433) | 2,077,451 | 1,609,672 |
| Trademarks (net of amortization: 2001—$118,254 and 2000—$104,125) | 567,692 | 674,279 |
| Other intangibles (net of amortization: 2001—$157,678 and 2000—$147,343) | 120,749 | 127,779 |
| Other noncurrent assets | 984,064 | 910,225 |
| Total other noncurrent assets | 3,749,956 | 3,321,955 |
| Total assets | $9,035,150 | $8,850,657 |
| **LIABILITIES AND SHAREHOLDERS' EQUITY** | | |
| CURRENT LIABILITIES: | | |
| Short-term debt | $1,555,869 | $  151,168 |
| Portion of long-term debt due within one year | 314,965 | 25,407 |
| Accounts payable | 962,497 | 1,026,960 |
| Salaries and wages | 54,036 | 48,646 |
| Accrued marketing | 146,138 | 200,775 |
| Accrued restructuring costs | 134,550 | 125,704 |
| Other accrued liabilities | 388,582 | 358,738 |
| Income taxes | 98,460 | 188,672 |
| Total current liabilities | 3,655,097 | 2,126,070 |
| LONG-TERM DEBT AND OTHER LIABILITIES: | | |
| Long-term debt | 3,014,853 | 3,935,826 |
| Deferred income taxes | 253,690 | 271,831 |
| Nonpension postretirement benefits | 207,104 | 208,958 |
| Other | 530,679 | 712,116 |
| Total long-term debt and other liabilities | 4,006,326 | 5,128,731 |

(continued)

## EXHIBIT 3    H.J. Heinz Company and Subsidiaries Consolidated Balance Sheets
(in thousands)                                                    **(continued)**

|  | May 2, 2001 | May 3, 2000 |
|---|---|---|
| **SHAREHOLDERS' EQUITY:** | | |
| Capital stock: | | |
| Third cumulative preferred, $1.70 first series, $10 par value | 126 | 139 |
| Common stock, 431,096,485 shares issued, $0.25 par value | 107,774 | 107,774 |
|  | 107,900 | 107,913 |
| Additional capital | 331,633 | 304,318 |
| Retained earnings | 4,697,213 | 4,756,513 |
|  | 5,136,746 | 5,168,744 |
| Less: | | |
| Treasury shares, at cost (82,147,565 shares at May 2, 2001 and 83,653,233 shares at May 3,2000) | 2,922,630 | 2,920,471 |
| Unearned compensation relating to the ESOP | 3,101 | 7,652 |
| Accumulated other comprehensive loss | 837,288 | 644,765 |
| Total shareholders' equity | 1,373,727 | 1,595,856 |
| Total liabilities and shareholders' equity | $9,035,150 | $8,850,657 |

Source: Heinz's 2001 *Annual Report,* pp. 44–45.

## EXHIBIT 4    H.J. Heinz Company and Subsidiaries Consolidated Statements of Income
(in thousands, except per-share amounts)

|  | Fiscal year ended | | |
|---|---|---|---|
|  | May 2, 2001 (52 Weeks) | May 3, 2000 (53 Weeks) | April 28, 1999 (52 Weeks) |
| *Sales* | $ 9,430,422 | $ 9,407,949 | $ 9,299,610 |
| Cost of products sold | 5,883,618 | 5,788,525 | 5,944,867 |
| Gross profit | 3,546,804 | 3,619,424 | 3,354,743 |
| Selling, general and administrative expenses | 2,564,450 | 2,350,942 | 2,245,431 |
| Gain on sale of Weight Watchers | – | 464,617 | – |
| *Operating income* | 982,354 | 1,733,099 | 1,109,312 |
| Interest income | 22,692 | 25,330 | 25,082 |
| Interest expense | 332,957 | 269,748 | 258,813 |
| Other (income)/expense, net | (969) | 25,005 | 40,450 |
| Income before income taxes and cumulative effect of accounting changes | 673,058 | 1,463,676 | 835,131 |
| Provision for income taxes | 178,140 | 573,123 | 360,790 |
| Income before cumulative effect of accounting changes | 494,918 | 890,553 | 474,341 |
| Cumulative effect of accounting changes | (16,906) | – | – |
| *Net income* | $ 478,012 | $ 890,553 | $ 474,341 |
| **PER COMMON SHARE AMOUNTS:** | | | |
| Income before cumulative effect of accounting changes—diluted | $ 1.41 | $ 2.47 | $ 1.29 |
| Income before cumulative effect of accounting changes—basic | $ 1.42 | $ 2.51 | $ 1.31 |
| Net income—diluted | $ 1.36 | $ 2.47 | $ 1.29 |
| Net income—basic | $ 1.37 | $ 2.51 | $ 1.31 |
| Cash dividends | $ 1.545 | $ 1.445 | $ 1.3425 |
| Average common shares outstanding—diluted | $351,041,321 | $360,095,455 | $367,830,419 |
| Average common shares outstanding—basic | $347,758,281 | $355,272,696 | $361,203,539 |

Source: Heinz's 2001 *Annual Report,* p.43.

EXHIBIT 5    Heinz's International vs. Domestic Income Before Taxes (in thousands)

|  | 2001 | 2000 | 1999 |
|---|---|---|---|
| Domestic | $116,126 | $ 805,464 | $427,089 |
| Foreign | 556,932 | 658,212 | 408,042 |
| Total Income Before Taxes | $673,058 | $1,463,676 | $835,131 |

*Source:* Heinz's 2001 *Annual Report,* p. 57.

## GROWTH THROUGH ACQUISITIONS AND LICENSING

The food industry is mature, and most of Heinz's major brands date back to before World War II. Heinz has had little success developing new products with large sales potential. While cost cutting can increase earnings, it does not add to sales. Thus, Heinz has sought to increase sales and earnings by making acquisitions or divesting units with low margins.

In the 1990s, Heinz made major acquisitions or entered into licensing agreements that complemented its pet food business (from Quaker Oats in 1995), its food service business (from Borden in 1994), its seafood business (John West Foods U.K. in 1997), and its frozen entrees business (Boston Market licensing arrangement, 1999). Heinz has also divested itself of peripheral businesses, such as its Hubinger corn milling unit (1991), its Italian confectionery business (1994), its Near East specialty rice business (1994), its bakery products unit (1998), and its storefront Weight Watchers business (1999).

Acquisitions are an ongoing part of Heinz's strategy. Here are some of Heinz's acquisitions in 2001:

- Poland: acquired several popular ready-meal brands
- France: acquired Comexo, a leading maker of high quality sauces sold to French restaurants and caterers
- Northern Europe: acquired the CSM Food Division of CSM Nederland NV, a leading food company in the Netherlands, Belgium, and Luxembourg
- South Africa: acquired John West Foods South Africa, a maker of branded seafood and canned and bottled spices and fruit
- United States: acquired Borden Food Company's pasta sauces and dry bouillon and soup businesses, including the Classico and Wyler's brands, Alden Merrell frozen desserts, Vlasic pickles, and Open Pit and Jack Daniel's barbeque sauces.

Heinz sold its All American Gourmet and Budget Gourmet brands of frozen foods to focus on its faster growing frozen entree brands.

## CEO WILLIAM R. JOHNSON

In November 1998, William R. Johnson, then forty-eight, became president and COO while his predecessor as president and COO, Dr. Anthony O'Reilly, retained his position as chairman of the Board of Directors. Bill Johnson joined Heinz in 1982 after working for two other food processing firms, Ralston Purina and Anderson Clayton. He made his mark at Heinz by successfully cutting costs in the tuna and pet food businesses. He instituted "price-based costing," whereby he determined first what consumers were willing to pay and then drove costs down to provide adequate margins at that selling price.

# EXHIBIT 6    Heinz's By-Segment Financial Data (in thousands)

| | Fiscal year ended | | | |
|---|---|---|---|---|
| | *May 2, 2001*<br>*(52 Weeks)* | *May 3, 2000*<br>*(53 Weeks)* | *May 2, 2001*<br>*(52 Weeks)* | *May 3, 2000*<br>*(53 Weeks)* |
| | *Net External Sales* | | *Intersegment Sales* | |
| North American Grocery & Food Service | $4,146,538 | $4,124,060 | $ 38,198 | $ 37,987 |
| North American Frozen | 1,125,396 | 1,023,915 | 12,660 | 12,782 |
| Europe | 2,746,870 | 2,583,684 | 3,657 | 2,687 |
| Asia/Pacific | 1,087,330 | 1,196,049 | 3,376 | 2,853 |
| Other Operating Entities | 324,288 | 480,241 | – | 2,526 |
| Nonoperating | – | – | (57,891) | (58,835) |
| Consolidated Totals | $9,430,422 | $9,407,949 | $ – | $ – |
| | *Operating Income (Loss)* | | *Operating Income (Loss) Excluding Special Items* | |
| North American Grocery & Food Service | $ 487,013 | $ 694,449 | $ 876,205 | $ 875,268 |
| North American Frozen | 83,964 | 152,018 | 202,012 | 181,511 |
| Europe | 388,647 | 364,207 | 518,009 | 502,302 |
| Asia/Pacific | 96,123 | 124,125 | 147,599 | 177,454 |
| Other Operating Entities | 49,284 | 540,155 | 37,958 | 32,255 |
| Nonoperating | (122,677) | (141,855) | (99,060) | (102,337) |
| Consolidated Totals | $ 982,354 | $1,733,099 | $1,682,723 | $1,666,453 |
| | *Depreciation and Amortization Expense* | | *Capital Expenditures* | |
| North American Grocery & Food Service | $ 127,123 | $ 133,471 | $ 190,254 | $ 171,295 |
| North American Frozen | 37,589 | 36,480 | 20,768 | 79,575 |
| Europe | 90,106 | 81,802 | 140,780 | 127,595 |
| Asia/Pacific | 26,288 | 28,871 | 46,166 | 60,795 |
| Other Operating Entities | 8,117 | 13,066 | 4,716 | 8,495 |
| Nonoperating | 9,943 | 12,793 | 8,615 | 4,689 |
| Consolidated Totals | $ 299,166 | $ 306,483 | $ 411,299 | $ 452,444 |
| | *Identifiable Assets* | | | |
| North American Grocery & Food Service | $3,775,052 | $3,711,691 | | |
| North American Frozen | 797,943 | 882,225 | | |
| Europe | 3,130,680 | 2,781,238 | | |
| Asia/Pacific | 912,515 | 1,085,491 | | |
| Other Operating Entities | 208,267 | 187,684 | | |
| Nonoperating | 210,693 | 202,328 | | |
| Consolidated Totals | $9,035,150 | $8,850,657 | | |

*Source:* Heinz's 2001 *Annual Report,* p. 67.

EXHIBIT 7    Heinz's Revenues By Product (in thousands)

| | Fiscal year ended | |
|---|---|---|
| (Unaudited) | May 2, 2001 (52 Weeks) | May 3, 2000 (53 Weeks) |
| Ketchup, condiments, and source | $2,537,294 | $2,439,109 |
| Frozen foods | 1,961,267 | 1,561,488 |
| Tuna | 1,035,302 | 1,059,317 |
| Soups, beans, and pasta meals | 1,220,348 | 1,197,466 |
| Infant/nutritional foods | 973,004 | 1,041,401 |
| Pet products | 1,151,011 | 1,237,671 |
| Other | 552,196 | 871,497 |
| Total | $9,430,422 | $9,407,949 |

| | Net External Sales | |
|---|---|---|
| Fiscal year ended | May 2, 2001 (52 Weeks) | May 3, 2000 (53 Weeks) |
| United States | $4,911,689 | $4,848,125 |
| United Kingdom | 1,459,492 | 1,314,550 |
| Other | 3,059,241 | 3,245,274 |
| Total | $9,430,422 | $9,407,949 |

Source: Heinz's 2001 Annual Report, p. 68.

When Johnson took office, Heinz had been criticized by stock market analysts for several years for not doing as much as it could to increase earnings in an environment of low inflation and virtually no growth. Sensitive to such criticisms, Johnson quickly took steps to improve Heinz's competitive position. He created the Frozen Foods division by merging Ore-Ida frozen potato products with Weight Watchers Gourmet Foods, created a unified headquarters in Pittsburgh for Heinz's $5-billion North American food business, and entered into a licensing agreement with Boston Market to market its frozen meals. Under the agreement, Heinz would make and sell packaged food products, including frozen dinner entrees, bearing the Boston Market name.

One of Johnson's most significant decisions was to sell the Weight Watchers International weight control business that O'Reilly had acquired in 1977 and built into the world's largest weight control system. The Weight Watchers storefront business was sold because it did "not fit strategically with Heinz. The skills required to manage this retail business are not synergistic with our core competencies." Heinz retained its Weight Watchers Smart Ones line of frozen meals, desserts, and breakfast items. An organization chart for Heinz is given in Exhibit 8.

## THE FUTURE

Under CEO Johnson, Heinz has made acquisitions to fill out its product lines, streamlined its organizational structure, and invested heavily in new plants and automated equipment. Looking to the future, Johnson wants Heinz to focus on increasing sales, which have been stalled at just over the $9 billion mark since 1997. It will attempt to do this by aligning its product offerings with consumer trends, such as the demands for more convenient ways to eat food on the go and organic foods.

**EXHIBIT 8**    Organization Chart for H.J. Heinz Company

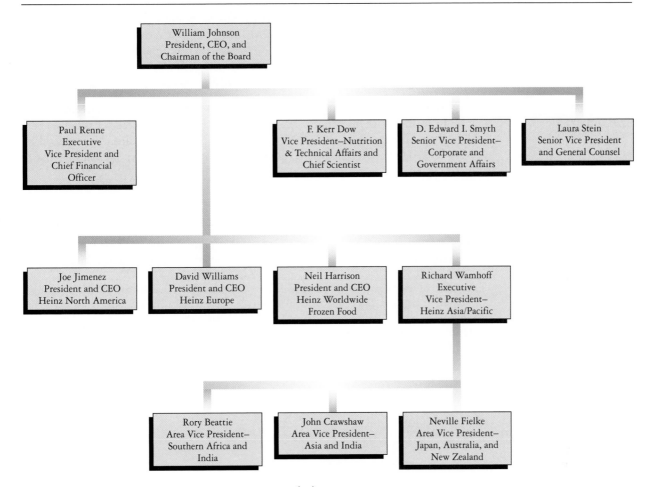

*Source:* Adapted from H.J. Heinz Company Web site (**www.heinz.com**).

The son of a former professional head football coach, Johnson stresses the importance of sports marketing in Heinz's future. Heinz Frozen Food has obtained endorsements from such eminent athletes as skateboarder Tony Hawk (Bagel Bites), former NBA star Larry Bird (Boston Market), and figure skater Kristi Yamaguchi (Smart Ones). Heinz acquired the naming rights for the new Pittsburgh Steeler's football stadium and called it Heinz Field. NFL football is the most popular sport in the United States, attracting over 100 million television viewers each week. Heinz Field will generate millions of media impressions for the Heinz brand, at a cost of less than $3 million per year, or about the price of a single Super Bowl television spot.

Heinz set up a new category, organic and functional foods, to run parallel to its six core food product categories. It will emphasize the development of organic and functional foods to take advantage of consumers' increasing interest in nutritional food. According to Johnson, "The category is growing at a 15 to 20 percent rate in the United States and is expected to expand in Europe at 25 percent annually over the next four years."

Johnson closed his remarks in the 2001 Heinz *Annual Report* as follows:

*Heinz remains a fundamentally sound business with great brands, strong cash flow, good dividend yield and extensive global reach. People will always have to eat, and our premium brands, innovative marketing and aggressive strategies for profitable growth should position us well over the next three to five years. The tech-stock fervor and megamerger mania have cooled, leaving a stock market hungry for value, which we are committed to delivering to our loyal shareholders.*

While Johnson has made major changes at Heinz, the board of directors is not entirely satisfied with his performance insofar as the price of Heinz stock has fallen about 25 percent since he became CEO. In August 2001, the board of directors increased his salary by $70,000, to $976,000, to keep it competitive with the pay of other food industry CEOs, but it decreased his bonus from $1,776,864 to $724,857.

---

## REFERENCES

Creswell, Julie. "Bottled Up." *Fortune* (September 18, 2000): 195–196, 200, 202, 204, 206.

Dienstag, Eleanor Foa. *In Good Company: 125 Years at the Heinz Table* (Warner Books, 1994).

"Heinz CEO Takes It in the Bonus." CBS Market Watch (August 3, 2001).

"Heinz Puts Its Money Where the Young Mouths Are." *The New York Times* (September 12, 2001).

Morrow, Matt and Rekha Balu. "Corporate Icons Are a Hard Act to Follow, As Successors Discover." *The Wall Street Journal* (April 29, 1999).

# HERSHEY FOODS CORPORATION—2002

**Forest David**
**Mississippi State University**

HSY

www.hersheys.com

Have you ever been to Hershey, Pennsylvania, the home of Hershey Foods Corporation? Known as Chocolate Town, USA, the air in this city actually smells like chocolate. There you can walk down Chocolate Avenue, see sidewalks lit with lights in the shape of Hershey Kisses, visit the Hershey Zoo, and see the chocolate kiss tower in Hershey Park. Hershey's Chocolate World is America's most popular corporate visitor's center.

Hershey has grown from a one-product, one-plant operation in 1894 to a $4.2 billion company producing an array of quality chocolate, nonchocolate, and grocery products. The company markets confectionery and grocery products in over ninety countries worldwide. Hershey's prominent products are chocolate and nonchocolate confectionery products consisting of bar goods, bagged items, and boxed items. Hershey grocery products include baking ingredients, peanut butter, chocolate drink mixes, dessert toppings, and beverages. Hershey markets these products under more than fifty different brands, such as Hershey Bar, Mr. Good Bar, Reese's, Kit Kat, Kisses, and Mounds. Hershey introduced no new products in the year 2000.

In 2002, Hershey remains behind M&M Mars in the confectionery market. Previously the largest candy maker, Hershey has slipped below Mars in market share. Almost 90 percent of Hershey's sales are generated in domestic markets. Hershey remains inexperienced in, ineffective in, and uncommitted to markets outside the United States, Mexico, and Canada, even though the candy industry has globalized. Mars, Borden, Nestlé, and other competitors all have a growing and effective presence in international markets. Analysts question whether Hershey can continue to survive as a domestic producer of candy while its competitors gain economies of scale and learn how to sell in world markets. Shareholders are becoming concerned too. Net income in 2001 decreased $127.4 million, or 38 percent, from 2000.

Sales to Wal-Mart stores are about 12 percent of Hershey's total revenues amounting to $819, $710, and $685 million in 2001, 2000, and 1999, respectively. Hershey needs a clear strategic plan to guide future operations and decisions. Company sales overall were up 8 percent in 2001 over 2000, and the company increased its dividend payout for the twenty-sixth seventh consecutive year.

According to its mission statement, Hershey is "to be a focused food company in North America and selected international markets and a leader in every aspect of [the] business."

## HISTORY

Milton Hershey's love for candy-making began with a childhood apprenticeship under candy maker Joe Royer of Lancaster, Pennsylvania. Hershey was eager to own a candy-making business. After numerous attempts and even bankruptcy, he finally gained success in the caramel business. Upon seeing the first chocolate-making equipment at the Chicago Exhibition in 1893, Hershey envisioned endless opportunities for the chocolate industry.

By 1901, the chocolate industry in America was growing rapidly. Hershey's sales reached $662,000 that year, creating the need for a new factory. Mr. Hershey moved his company to Derry Church, Pennsylvania, a town that was renamed Hershey in 1906. The new Hershey factory provided a means of mass-producing a single chocolate product. In 1909, the Milton Hershey School for Orphans was founded. Mr. and Mrs. Hershey could not have children, so for many years the Hershey Chocolate Company operated mainly to provide funds for the orphanage. Hershey's sales reached $5 million in 1911.

In 1927, the Hershey Chocolate Company was incorporated under the laws of the state of Delaware and listed on the New York Stock Exchange. That same year, 20 percent of Hershey's stock was sold to the public. Between 1930 and 1960, Hershey went through rapid growth; the name Hershey became a household word. The legendary Milton Hershey died in 1945.

In the 1960s, Hershey acquired the H.B. Reese Candy Company, which makes Reese's Peanut Butter Cups, Reese's Pieces, and Reese's Peanut Butter Chips. Hershey also acquired San Giorgio Macaroni and Delmonico Foods, both pasta manufacturers. In 1968, Hershey Chocolate Corporation changed its name to Hershey Foods Corporation. Between 1976 and 1984, William Dearden served as Hershey's chief executive officer. An orphan who grew up in the Milton Hershey School for Orphans, Mr. Dearden diversified the company to reduce its dependence on fluctuating cocoa and sugar prices.

In the 1970s, Hershey acquired Y&S Candy Corporation, a manufacturer of licorice-type products such as Y&S Twizzlers, Nibs, and Bassett's Allsorts. The company also purchased Procino-Rossi, a pasta company, and Skinner Macaroni Company. During the 1980s, Hershey acquired A. B. Marabou of Sweden as well as the Dietrich Corporation, maker of Luden's Throat Drops, Luden's Mellomints, Queen Anne chocolate covered cherries, and 5th Avenue candy bars. It also acquired the Canadian confectionery (chocolate and nonchocolate candy) and snack nut operations of Nabisco Brands Ltd. Hershey acquired Peter Paul/Cadbury's U.S. candy operations, which gave it new products, such as Mounds, Almond Joy, York Peppermint Pattie, Cadbury Dairy Milk, Cadbury Fruit & Nut, Cadbury Caramello, and Cadbury Creme Eggs. Hershey received the rights to market the Peter Paul products worldwide.

Hershey purchased Nacional de Dulces (NDD) and renamed it Hershey Mexico, which today produces, imports, and markets chocolate products for the Mexican market under the Hershey brand name. In 1996, Hershey acquired Leaf North America in order to achieve market share leadership in North America in nonchocolate confectionery candies. In December 2000, Hershey purchased the breath freshener mints and gum businesses of Nabisco to obtain such products as Ice Breakers, Breath Savers, Bubble Yum and Fruit Stripe gum. On March 12, 2001, R.H. Lenny was elected president and chief executive officer of Hershey after previously serving as a division president with Nabisco. Hershey divested its Ludens throat drops business in 2001.

## INTERNAL AFFAIRS

### North American Operations

Hershey does not make public an organizational chart, but titles of executives suggest that Hershey operates from a centralized, functional structure with no divisional presidents. This type of structure would be somewhat unusual for an organization of Hershey's size, since it is more common for large companies to be decentralized in some manner. Another indication of the functional structure is that Hershey does not provide for its shareholders' financial data by segment, such as geographic region or product, again implying centralized control and accountability. In the late 1990s, Hershey operated with two divisions: Hershey North America and Hershey International.

Hershey's Mexico, Canadian, and U.S. operations generate about 90 percent of total company sales. Hershey's North American manufacturing operations are located in the following cities: Hershey, Pennsylvania; Oakdale, California; Stuarts Draft, Virginia; Lancaster, Pennsylvania; Robinson, Illinois; Smith Falls, Ontario, Canada; and Guadalajara, Mexico.

Hershey's North American operations produce an extensive line of chocolate and nonchocolate products that are sold in the form of single bars, bagged goods, and boxed items. These products are marketed under more than fifty brand names, and they are sold in over 2 million retail outlets in the United States, including grocery wholesalers, chain stores, mass merchandisers, drugstores, vending companies, wholesale clubs, convenience stores, and food distributors.

The U.S. confectionery market is growing only 2 percent annually in sales volume. The nonchocolate segment, which accounts for about one-third of the overall sweets market, is growing 5 percent annually, whereas the chocolate segment is growing at 1 percent. Hershey has only 4 percent of the nonchocolate confectionery market, while the leader is RJR Nabisco with 18 percent. RJR's Life Savers and Gummy Life Savers compete with Hershey's Amazin' Fruit Gummy Bears. Confectionery is the largest segment of the $52 billion U.S. snack market. Candy and gum represent 31 percent of this market.

Hershey recently established a new eastern distribution center near Hershey, Pennsylvania, to go with its refurbished southeastern distribution center near Atlanta, Georgia.

## International Operations

Hershey's international operations have been a trouble spot, and they contributed zero profits to the company's 2000 bottom line. It is not clear what the profit contribution was in 2001. Hershey exports confectionery and grocery products worldwide. Europeans have the highest per-capita chocolate consumption rates in the world, but Hershey has no plans to overtake or even threaten Nestlé or Mars in Europe. In the Far East, Hershey has signed licensing agreements both with Selecta Dairy Products (to manufacture Hershey's ice cream products in the Philippines) and with Kuang Chuan Dairy in Taiwan (to manufacture Hershey's beverages). Hershey has introduced its products into Russia, the Philippines, and Taiwan. Overall in the Far East, however, Hershey is not planning a sustained effort due to the perceived high political and economic risks coupled with its own lack of experience in that area.

## Social Responsibility

Hershey Foods Corporation is committed to the values of its founder, Milton S. Hershey, a man possessing the highest standard of quality, honesty, fairness, integrity, and respect. The firm makes annual contributions of cash, products, and services to a variety of national and local charitable organizations. Hershey is the sole sponsor of the Hershey National Track and Field Youth Program. Hershey also makes contributions to the Children's Miracle Network, a national program benefiting children's hospitals across the United States.

The corporation operates the Milton Hershey School, whose mission is to provide full-time care and education (including all costs) for disadvantaged children, mainly orphans. The school currently cares for over one thousand boys and girls in grades kindergarten through twelve. The Hershey School Trust owns over 75 percent of all Hershey Corporation's common stock.

## Research and Development

Hershey engages in research and development activities in order to develop new products, improve the quality of existing products, and improve and modernize production processes. As shown here, the company has steadily decreased its research and development expenditures:

| Year | Research and Development |
|------|--------------------------|
| 1998 | $28.6 million |
| 1999 | $26.7 million |
| 2000 | $25.4 million |
| 2001 | $26.5 million |

## Finance

Hershey's 2001 financial statements are given in Exhibits 1 and 2. Note that Hershey's long-term debt is $876 million and net income has declined annually since 1999.

## Marketing

Hershey's marketing strategy is focused on maintaining the consistently superior quality of its products; mass distribution and the best possible consumer value in terms of price and weight are also features of its strategy. The company devotes considerable resources to the identification, development, testing, manufacturing, and marketing of new products. Hershey has developed a distribution network from its manufacturing plants; distribution centers and field warehouses are strategically located throughout the United States, Canada, and Mexico.

EXHIBIT 1    Hershey Foods Corporation Consolidated Statements of Income
(In thousands except per-share amounts)

| For the years ended December 31, | 2001 | 2000 | 1999 |
|---|---|---|---|
| Net Sales | $4,557,241 | $4,220,976 | $3,970,924 |
| Costs and Expenses: | | | |
| Cost of sales | 2,665,566 | 2,471,151 | 2,354,724 |
| Selling, marketing and administrative | 1,269,964 | 1,127,175 | 1,057,840 |
| Business realignment and asset impairments | 228,314 | — | — |
| Gain on sale of business | (19,237) | — | (243,785) |
| Total costs and expenses | 4,144,607 | 3,598,326 | 3,168,779 |
| Income before Interest and Income Taxes | 412,634 | 622,650 | 802,145 |
| Interest expense, net | 69,093 | 76,011 | 74,271 |
| Income before Income Taxes | 343,541 | 546,639 | 727,874 |
| Provision for income taxes | 136,385 | 212,096 | 267,564 |
| Net Income | $ 207,156 | $ 334,543 | $ 460,310 |
| Net Income Per Share—Basic | $1.52 | $ 2.44 | $ 3.29 |
| Net Income Per Share—Diluted | $ 1.50 | $ 2.42 | $ 3.26 |
| Cash Dividends Paid Per Share: | | | |
| Common Stock | $ 1.165 | $ 1.08 | $ 1.00 |
| Class B Common Stock | 1.050 | .975 | .905 |

*Source:* Hershey's 2001 *Annual Report,* p. 16.

EXHIBIT 2    Hershey Foods Corporation Consolidated Balance Sheets
(in thousands)

| December 31, | 2001 | 2000 |
|---|---|---|
| **ASSETS** | | |
| **Current Assets:** | | |
| Cash and cash equivalents | $ 134,147 | $ 31,969 |
| Accounts receivable—trade | 361,726 | 379,680 |
| Inventories | 512,134 | 605,173 |
| Deferred income taxes | 96,939 | 76,136 |
| Prepaid expenses and other | 62,595 | 202,390 |
| Total current assets | 1,167,541 | 1,295,348 |
| **Property, Plant and Equipment, Net** | 1,534,901 | 1,585,388 |
| **Intangibles Resulting from Business Acquisitions, Net** | 429,128 | 474,448 |
| **Other Assets** | 115,860 | 92,580 |
| Total assets | $3,247,430 | $3,447,764 |
| | | |
| **LIABILITIES AND STOCKHOLDERS' EQUITY** | | |
| **Current Liabilities:** | | |
| Accounts payable | $ 133,049 | $ 149,232 |
| Accrued liabilities | 462,901 | 358,067 |
| Accrued income taxes | 2,568 | 1,479 |
| Short-term debt | 7,005 | 257,594 |
| Current portion of long-term debt | 921 | 529 |
| Total current liabilities | 606,444 | 766,901 |
| **Long-term Debt** | 876,972 | 877,654 |
| **Other Long-term Liabilities** | 361,041 | 327,674 |
| **Deferred Income Taxes** | 255,769 | 300,499 |
| Total liabilities | 2,100,226 | 2,272,728 |
| **Stockholders' Equity:** | | |
| Preferred Stock, shares issued: none in 2001 and 2000 | — | — |
| Common Stock, shares issued: 149,517,064 in 2001 and 149,509,014 in 2000 | 149,516 | 149,508 |
| Class B Common Stock, shares issued: 30,433,808 in 2001 and 30,441,858 in 2000 | 30,434 | 30,442 |
| Additional paid-in capital | 3,263 | 13,124 |
| Unearned ESOP compensation | (15,967) | (19,161) |
| Retained earnings | 2,755,333 | 2,702,927 |
| Treasury—Common Stock shares, at cost: 44,311,870 in 2001 and 43,669,284 in 2000 | (1,689,243) | (1,645,088) |
| Accumulated other comprehensive loss | (86,132) | (56,716) |
| Total stockholders' equity | 1,147,204 | 1,175,036 |
| Total liabilities and stockholders' equity | $3,247,430 | $3,447,764 |

*Source:* Hershey's 2001 *Annual Reports,* p. 17.

Hershey has steadily increased its advertising expenses, which were $193.3 million, $161.6 million, $164.9 million, and $187.5 million in 2001, 2000, 1999, and 1998, respectively. Hershey changes the prices and weights of its products to accommodate changes in manufacturing costs, the competitive environment, and profit objectives, while at the same time maintaining consumer value. The last standard candy bar price increase was implemented in December 1995, resulting in a wholesale price increase of approximately 11 percent on its standard and king-size candy bars, which are sold in the United States.

Per-capita candy sales in the United States have increased by 7.1 percent from 1997–2002. Americans spend over $21 billion a year on sweets. Upscale candy items such as Mars' Dove Promises are selling well. People are eating more ethnic foods today than ten years ago, which means more garlic and flavor. Breath-freshener–type candies are selling well in response to this eating trend.

Conventional wisdom in the candy industry is that a person rarely selects the same candy bar twice in a row; consequently, product variety is crucial to success. Marketing issues relative to health, nutrition, and weight consciousness are important. The media Hershey uses most often for advertising are network television, followed by syndicated television, spot television, magazines, and network and spot radio.

Confectionery sales are generally lowest during the second quarter of the year and highest during the third and fourth quarters, due largely to the holiday seasons. Hershey generates about 20 percent of its annual sales during the second quarter and 30 percent of its annual sales during the fourth quarter.

## GLOBAL ISSUES

The most significant raw material used in the production of Hershey's chocolate products is cocoa beans. This commodity is imported principally from West African, South American, and Far Eastern equatorial regions. West Africa accounts for approximately 65 percent of the world's crop. Cocoa beans are not uniform, and the various grades and varieties reflect the diverse agricultural practices and natural conditions found in the many growing areas. Hershey buys a mix of cocoa beans to meet its manufacturing requirements. Because demand remained low worldwide, due partly to worsening economic conditions, cocoa prices in 2000 and 2001 remained near historic lows.

Hershey's second most important commodity for its domestic chocolate and confectionery products is sugar. Due to import quotas and duties that are imposed to support the price of sugar, sugar prices paid by U.S. users are currently substantially higher than prices on the world sugar market. Hershey also uses a large amount of peanuts, almonds, and dairy products.

The chocolate/cocoa products industry is SIC 2066, while candy/confectionery is SIC 2064. The main distribution channels for chocolate are grocery, drug, and department stores as well as vending machine operators. Almost all of these distributors are local, regional, or national; only a few are multinational. Although chocolate producers have not yet developed globally uniform marketing programs, the situation is changing. European unification extended grocery and department store channels of distribution. For example, Safeway, a U.S. grocer chain, now operates stores in Canada, the United Kingdom, Germany, and Saudi Arabia. As global channels of distribution become more available for chocolate manufacturers, global marketing uniformity will become more prevalent in the industry. Global cultural convergence is accelerating the need for more global marketing uniformity in the confectionery industry. Hershey's competitors are taking advantage of this globalization trend.

The confectionery industry is characterized by high manufacturing economies of scale. Hershey's main chocolate factory, for example, occupies more than 2 million square feet, is highly automated, and contains heavy equipment, vats, and containers. It is the largest chocolate plant in the world. High manufacturing costs in any industry encourage global market expansion, globally standardized products, and globally centralized production.

The confectionery industry is also characterized by high transportation costs for moving milk and sugar, the primary raw materials. This fact motivates companies such as Hershey to locate near their sources of supply. Since milk can be obtained in large volumes in many countries, chocolate producers have many options when locating plants. Also, producing chocolate is not labor-intensive; nor does it require highly skilled labor.

Industry analysts expect the candy industry to continue to grow. Consumption of chocolate, according to industry analysts, is closely related to national income, although the Far East is an exception to this rule. Candy consumption varies in the major markets of the developed nations. Americans consume about 22 pounds of candy annually per person, and Europeans consume about 27 pounds of candy per person.

Chocolate accounts for about 54 percent of all candy consumed. Northern Europeans consume almost twice as much chocolate per capita as Americans. In the European countries, the citizens of Switzerland, Norway, and the United Kingdom consume the most chocolate, while those of Finland and Italy consume the least. The Japanese also consume very little chocolate—about 1.4 kilos per capita. Throughout Asia and southern Europe, there is a preference for types of sweets other than chocolate, partly because of the high incidence of lactose intolerance (difficulty in digesting dairy products).

## COMPETITORS

The $10-billion U.S. confectionery industry is composed of six major competitors that control nearly 70 percent of the market: Hershey, M&M Mars, Brach & Brock, Nestlé of Switzerland, RJR Nabisco, and Leaf Inc. The remaining 30 percent is divided among many local and regional candy manufacturers. Nabisco recently introduced a line of SnackWell's low-, no-, and fat-free candies in three flavors—raisin dips, chocolate chews, and caramel nut clusters.

Based in Switzerland, Nestlé clearly has an edge internationally, insofar as it is the world leader in many food categories, including candy. Almost 98 percent of Nestlé's revenues come from international sales. Hershey's other competitors also do much of their business outside North America. For example, Cadbury-Schweppes obtains 50 percent of its revenues from international sales, and Mars 50 percent, whereas Hershey obtains the least with 10 percent. Hershey's two major candy competitors are Mars and Nestlé.

### Mars

Mars has a stronger presence than Hershey in Europe, Asia, Mexico, and Japan. Only one year after entering Mexico, Mars had gained 12 percent of that market. Analysts estimate Mars' worldwide sales and profits to be over $7 billion and $1 billion, respectively. Mars was successful introducing its Bounty chocolate candy into the United States without prior test marketing. Bounty was originally a European candy. Mars, unlike Hershey, uses uniform marketing globally. For example, the company's M&M candies slogan, "It melts in your mouth, not in your hands," is used worldwide. In contrast, Hershey's successful BarNone candy is named Temptation in Canada.

Mars is controlled by the Mars family through two brothers, John and Forrest, Jr. Mars is one of the world's largest, private, closely held companies. It is a secretive company, unwilling to divulge financial information and corporate strategies. Unlike Hershey, Mars has historically relied upon extensive marketing and advertising expenditures, rather than on product innovation, to gain market share. Mars has been repackaging, restyling, and reformulating its leading brands, including Snickers, M&M's, Milky Way, and 3 Musketeers, but that strategy is now being supplemented with extensive product development. New Mars products include Bounty, Balisto, and PB Max. The company also successfully developed and marketed frozen Snickers ice cream bars. The product was so successful that it dislodged Eskimo Pie and Original Klondike from the number-one ice cream snack slot without any assistance from promotional advertising. Mars has world-class production facilities in Hackettstown, New Jersey; from that plant, it ships products worldwide. In addition, it has manufacturing plants in Mexico and in several European locations.

Mars entered the Russian market in 1992 and today virtually owns the chocolate market there. Hershey is trying to gain a presence in Russia and China, but so far, it is struggling.

### Nestlé

With annual sales of $7.3 billion in the United States and having recently acquired Carnation, Nestlé is the largest food company in the world. Nestlé's U.S. operations are headquartered in Glendale, California (818-549-6000). With corporate headquarters in Vevey, Switzerland (021-924-2111), Nestlé is a major competitor in Europe, the Far East, and South America. Nestlé sells products in over 360 countries on five continents, many in the developing nations. It is the world's largest instant coffee manufacturer, with Nescafe the dominant product. Nestlé also produces and markets chocolate and malt drinks, and it is the world's largest producer of milk powder and condensed milk.

Nestlé's chocolate and confectionery products carry some popular brand names, including Callier, Crunch, and Yes. With the acquisition of Rowntree, additional notable brands were added to the product line, including Smarties, After Eight, and Quality Street. The Perugina division produces Baci. Through the RJR Nabisco acquisition, Nestlé acquired Curtiss Brands, a U.S. confectionery producer of such products as Baby Ruth and Butterfinger. Nestlé manufactures chocolate in twenty-three countries, particularly in Switzerland and Latin America. Each factory is highly automated, employing an average of 250 people.

Another major product concentration for Nestlé is frozen foods and other refrigerated products. Findus in Europe and Stouffer in the United States represent the bulk of the group's frozen food sales, with well-known brands such as Lean Cuisine. Nestlé also manufactures a fast-developing range of fresh pasta and sauces in Europe and the United States under the name Contadina.

## CONCLUSION

Hershey's global market share in the chocolate confectionery industry is only 10 percent, lowest among its competitors. A major strategic issue facing Hershey today is where, when, and how to best expand geographically. Perhaps Hershey should expand into the Far East, since the economies of those countries are growing so rapidly. China and India are huge untapped markets. Malaysia, Indonesia, Vietnam, and Thailand also are untapped. Should Hershey wait for Mars and Nestlé to gain a foothold in those countries?

Firms are becoming more and more environmentally proactive in their manufacturing and service delivery processes. Environmentally responsible firms market themselves and their products as being "green-sensitive." Concern for the natural environment is an issue Hershey should address before competitors seize the initiative. Developing environmentally safe products and packages, reducing industrial waste, recycling, and establishing an environmental audit process are strategies that could benefit Hershey.

Some analysts contend that Hershey's functional structure is an ineffective design. Would a divisional structure by product be more effective? The product divisions could be chocolate, nonchocolate, and grocery. Or would a divisional structure by geographic region be more effective? Can you recommend an improved organizational design that could enhance Hershey's lackluster international operations?

Should Hershey acquire firms in other foreign countries? Analysis is needed to identify and place a value on specific acquisition candidates. In developing an overall strategic plan, what recommendations would you present to CEO Kenneth Wolfe? Should Hershey diversify more into nonchocolate candies, since that segment is growing most rapidly? Should a new manufacturing plant be built in Asia or in Europe?

Design a global marketing strategy that could enable Hershey to boost its exports of chocolate. Should Hershey increase its debt further or dilute ownership of its stock further to raise the capital needed to implement your recommended strategies? Develop pro forma financial statements to fully assess and evaluate the impact of your proposed strategies.

# BOEING—2002

Carolyn R. Stokes and Arthur S. Boyett
Francis Marion University

BA

www.boeing.com

The Boeing Company (312-544-2000), newly headquartered in Chicago, Illinois, is the largest aerospace firm in world, as measured by total sales, and the world's leading manufacturer of commercial aircraft, having cornered, on average, more than 60 percent of the market for the last twenty years. It is the world's leader in military aircraft, and the largest contractor for NASA. Boeing is one of the largest U.S. exporters, with about $18 billion in sales to foreign countries in 2000 (see Exhibit 1). Boeing has four major segments: (1) commercial aircraft, (2) military aircraft and missiles, (3) space and communications, and (4) customer and commercial Financing. Jetliners currently in production include the families of the Boeing 717, 737, 747, 757, 767, and 777 models. Boeing manufactures helicopters, military aircraft, electronic systems, and missiles; and it provides communication services for aerospace related activities and is a major contractor in the space station.

The aerospace industry was greatly affected by the events of September 11, 2001, when the United States was attacked by terrorists who had highjacked four commercial airliners. Two of the aircraft were flown into the Twin Towers of the World Trade Center in New York City, one aircraft was flown into the Pentagon in Washington, D.C., and the other crashed in Pennsylvania. For the first time in U.S. history, all air traffic was grounded. With new high-security measures in place, airports gradually reopened but with fewer flights and fewer passengers. Airlines, the major customer of Boeing's commercial jets, are laying off workers and ordering fewer aircraft. The U.S. president and Congress declared war on the terrorists, and the United States and its allies went to Afghanistan to hunt down the terrorist networks that had killed thousands of U.S. citizens. In this war of "Enduring Freedom," the military is depreciating its aircraft and is using up its arsenal of weapons. The U.S. intelligence community is using state of the art technological equipment, such as the satellites that Boeing produces.

Boeing, led by Chairman and CEO Philip M. Condit and President and COO Harry C. Stonecipher (see Exhibit 2), had revenues of $58.1 billion in 2001, compared to revenues of $51.3 billion in 2000. In the Military Aircraft and Missile Systems segment, Boeing recorded net earnings of $1.34 billion on sales of $12.4 billion in 2001. Growth in world air traffic is still projected to average 4.7 percent annually over the next twenty years, with much of the increase coming from Asian markets. With improved cost management and well-designed aircraft, Boeing should remain a major competitor in the aerospace industry. Boeing is in an aerospace environment that will be facing declining demand for some commercial aircraft in the near future and possible increasing demand for additional defense and space contracts due to the replacement needs for aircraft and missiles that are being used in the "Enduring Freedom" effort. Boeing's three fundamental goals are to run healthy core businesses, leverage strengths into new products, and service and open new frontiers. The company needs a clear strategic plan for the future.

# EXHIBIT 1    The Boeing Company and Subsidiaries Sales by Geographic Area (in millions)

| | Year ended December 31, | | |
|---|---|---|---|
| | *2000* | *1999* | *1998* |
| Asia, other than China | $ 5,568 | $10,776 | $14,065 |
| China | 1,026 | 1,231 | 1,572 |
| Europe | 9,038 | 9,678 | 8,646 |
| Oceania | 887 | 942 | 844 |
| Africa | 542 | 386 | 702 |
| Non-U.S. Western Hemisphere | 559 | 461 | 701 |
| United States | 33,701 | 34,519 | 29,624 |
| Total Sales | $51,321 | $57,993 | $56,154 |

*Source:* www.boeing.com.

## COMMERCIAL AIRCRAFT

With the attack on the United States on September 11, airline demand for new aircraft is uncertain. Boeing recognized that demand had been softening even before the September 11 attack and had already reduced the amount of time required to produce a Boeing 737 from thirty thousand labor hours to under ten thousand labor hours. Boeing's backlog of orders dropped from $86.9 billion in 1998 to $73.0 billion in 1999, before rising to $89.8 in 2000. Backlogs have averaged about $85.7 billion over the past five years. Boeing worked to solve any possible delays in production by rapidly ramping up the production process. The increased production rate helped to keep the backlog of orders under $90.0 billion. For two decades, Boeing has averaged over a 60 percent share of the world market for commercial jets. In 2000, customers announced orders for 611 jetcraft, as compared to 391 in 1999. However, by the middle of November 2001, Boeing had received only 284 gross orders. Even with the decline in orders from Asian

# EXHIBIT 2    The Boeing Leadership

**TOP MANAGEMENT**

Philip M. Condit, Chairman of the Board and Chief Executive Officer
Harry C. Stonecipher, President and Chief Operation Officer

*Source:* www.boeing.com.

**OPERATING MANAGEMENT**

Alan R. Mulally, Senior VP of Boeing and President, Commercial Airplanes Group
Gerald E. Daniels, Senior VP of Boeing and President, Military Aircraft and Missile Systems Group
James F. Albaugh, Senior VP of Boeing and President, Space and Communications Group
James F. Palmer, Senior VP of Boeing and President, Boeing Capital Corporation
Scott Carson, Senior VP of Boeing and President, Connexion by Boeing$^{SM}$
John B. Hayhurst, Senior VP of Boeing and President, Air Traffic Management
Laurette T. Koeller, Senior VP of Boeing and President, Shared Services Group
David O. Swain, Senior VP of Engineering & Technology and President, Phantom Works

*Source:* www.boeing.com.

markets, approximately 34 percent of Boeing's 2000 airline sales were from non-U.S. carriers, down from 40 percent in 1999 and 47 percent in 1998.

As of December 2000, Boeing's expected number of commercial jet transport deliveries for 2000 was approximately 489, down from the 620 aircraft delivered in 1999. However, Boeing's production has greatly increased from the 274 jetcraft in 1997 and 269 in 1996. The backlogs, possible increases in military orders for aircraft, and possible returns to normal passenger demand following the September 11 attack may push production levels upward in 2002.

In March 2001, Boeing unveiled its new Sonic Cruiser, a high-speed aircraft expected to cost $10 billion to develop. The new plane, designed to fly just below the sound barrier and cut airtime by 20 percent, marks the emergence of a high-speed family that is directly derived from a supersonic transport design. The Sonic Cruiser family will replace the 767 family. Boeing expects the Sonic Cruiser to be completed in either 2006 or 2008. Boeing could use a new aircraft to compete with Airbus's new model.

Boeing's commercial airjet segment currently produces the new 717 family, together with the 737, 747, 757, 767, and 777 families. The MD-95 was redesigned as the new Boeing 717, and the other MD aircraft were phased out of production by the end of 2001. Boeing's commercial airjet development has focused on the 717, 777, and the 737 families, as well as on the long-range derivatives of the 767, 747, and 777. The new 717, originally the MD-95, was originally delivered in 1999. This 717-200 responds to the need for a one-hundred seat regional jet. Boeing had received a total of 151 orders by the end of 2000 and had delivered 44 aircraft by the end of 2000. However, Boeing had a net loss of 14 orders for the first three quarters of 2001.

Boeing is pleased with the response to the Boeing 777 family that was originally put into service in 1995. The 777 was developed to meet the need for a more efficient, comfortable, and high-capacity capacity jet. The 777-200 and 777-300 series along with their recently launched extended range derivatives can seat from 305 to 550 passengers, and the two aircraft have ranges from 5,925 to 8,861 miles. According to the results of a Boeing survey, three out of four passengers preferred the Boeing 777. Boeing had received a total of 563 orders and had delivered 316 aircraft by the end of 2000.

The smallest member of the Boeing jetliner family is the 737; it is the best-selling aircraft of all time, with 4,783 orders and 3,857 deliveries by the end of 2000. The 737 family, developed for short-to-medium range flights, is designed for greater range and speed, and it complies with new noise and emission standards. The 600, 700, 800, and 900 members of the 737 family have outsold all aircraft in their market. The 737 family includes two Boeing business jets, both derivatives of the 737-700 and 737-800 members. Boeing received 117 orders for all 737s in 2000.

The Boeing 757 and 767 are medium-capacity, fuel-efficient twinjets that meet FAA requirements for extended-range operations. The 757 can carry 194 passengers as far as 4,500 nautical miles. In 1999, Boeing introduced the 757-300, which has 20 percent more seating and 10 percent lower per-seat operating costs than the 757-200. The 757-300 can carry 289 passengers up to 3,990 nautical miles. Boeing received 1,027 orders and had delivered a total of 948 by the end of 2000.

The 767 is larger, carrying about 260 passengers in mixed-class configurations, and the range of some versions exceeds 6,000 nautical miles. The 767-200 can carry 181 to 224 passengers, and its range is 7,618 miles; the 767-300, which comes in an extended-range version, can carry 20 percent more passengers than the 200 version. The first deliveries of the extended-range version of the 767 were to Delta and Continental in August 2000. The 767-400ER can carry 304-375 passengers up to

6,501 miles. In 2000, Boeing committed to production of a longer-range version of the 767-400ER.

The flagship of the Boeing aircraft family, the 747-400, can carry 568 passengers more than eight thousand nautical miles, and it offers airline customers the lowest seat-mile costs of any twin-aisle commercial jetcraft in the world. The new extended-range version has a range of 8,850 miles. The 747-400 has both an all-cargo as well as a Combi model for passengers and freight. The Boeing 747 freight aircraft is in great demand at Narita, Tokyo's international airport, which handles more than 1.5 million tons of freight per year, more than any other airport in the world. Almost 80 percent of the jets using Narita are Boeing 747s. The 747-400F gives Boeing's airline customers the ability to carry twenty tons more payload on the routes they fly than the 747-200 freighters, or its customers can carry the same payload eight hundred nautical miles farther. Boeing had received orders for 1,338 and it had delivered a total of 1,261 by the end of 2000.

The company reported the following key financial information for the commercial aircraft segment for the most recent three years (numbers are all in millions of dollars):

|  | 2001 | 2000 | 1999 | 1998 |
|---|---|---|---|---|
| Revenues | $ 35,056 | $ 31,171 | $ 38,475 | $ 36,998 |
| Operating income | 2,632 | 2,736 | 2,082 | (148) |
| Assets | 11,479 | 9,800 | 8,075 | 11,003 |
| Liabilities | 7,579 | 7,972 | 6,135 | 6,907 |
| Research & Development costs | 858 | 574 | 585 | 1,021 |
| Contractual backlog of orders | 75,850 | 89,780 | 72,972 | 86,057 |

Source: www.boeing.com.

## Competition in Commercial Aircraft

The European Aeronautic Defense and Space Co. (EADS), which was formed in 2000 from aerospace groups in Germany, France, and Spain, remains Boeing's most formidable competitor in the commercial aircraft industry. Daniel Michaels in his November 14, 2001, *Wall Street Journal* article, "Airbus Faces Adjustment in Output as Demand Falls," states that EADS's revenue over the last nine months of 2001 was 30 percent higher than the total that was recorded in the same period a year earlier. Airbus originally planned to deliver 320 planes in 2001. Some analysts expect Airbus deliveries to outpace Boeing deliveries by the end of the decade. However, many industry analysts expect that Airbus will have to cut production to as low as 290 planes—and possibly as low as 250 planes.

## Customer Service

Boeing provides regional world centers for proactive, value-added maintenance, parts, and training. Boeing acquired Continental Graphics, a specialist in airline information systems, and Jeppensen Sanderson, Inc., the leader in in-flight information services, to better support customers. The maintenance and modification market is about $90 billion annually, and Boeing is working to increase its 4 percent share. Boeing is providing ready access to parts and training programs using the Web and ED-ROM technologies. Customers access parts information on the Web site **MyBoeingFleet.com**. Information on the availability of parts, maintenance, engineering, and operational data are provided on this Web site for customers.

## BOEING FRONTIERS

### Connexion by Boeing<sup>SM</sup>

Connexion by Boeing$^{SM}$ is a dynamic breakthrough consumer and commercial airline service that will provide air travelers an unparalleled array of high-speed data communication services via a space-based network. The venture's strategic focus is on providing television and high-speed real-time Internet services to commercial airlines, business jets, and government customers. Boeing, leading the airborne broadband communications frontier, has excelled at blending creative innovation with large-scale integration. Boeing's competency in satellite systems, commercial aircraft construction, and high-speed critical data transfer methodology gives it a competitive advantage that no narrow-band provider can match. Currently, a prototype of the service is available on some Boeing business jets. According to a June 14, 2001, article in the *Wall Street Journal* by J. Lynn Lunsford, Boeing has signed a letter of intent to enter into a joint venture with Delta Air, United, and American for the Connexion by Boeing$^{SM}$ service. Boeing, the major shareholder, will share the revenue with the airlines, and it will be responsible for the overall management of the operation. Connexion by Boeing$^{SM}$ is an example of a new frontier that was developed by using the company's core strengths.

### Air Traffic Management

Boeing is developing an Air Traffic Management (ATM) system to replace the current ground-based program. The proposed ATM would integrate today's separate control, communications, navigation, surveillance, and weather services into a single, seamless Common Information Network (CIN). The new ATM will rely primarily on Global Positioning Satellites (GPSs). The system should be relatively inexpensive and easy to install on older aircraft, both those of Boeing and Airbus. Boeing's new planes already come equipped with the technology that allows them to fly from place to place without ground control. According to a May 17, 2001, *Wall Street Journal* article by J. Lynn Lunsford, United Parcel Service Inc.'s UPS Airlines and FedEx Corp.'s Federal Express have already been using an early satellite version to improve operations at large hubs. According to Bois and Sweatman in an October 2001 article in *Interavia Business & Technology*, the ATM is designed to supplement, expand, and eventually supersede the FAA's Operational Evolution Plan, which should be ready by 2010. Boeing projects that its ATM could be ready within eight years. As the air travel and air freight business increases, the current ground-based system becomes more overloaded. The proposed new Boeing ATM program may be the answer. However, the new program will require the cooperation of all stakeholders in the airline industry to be successful.

### Aircraft and Missile Systems

Boeing is a major player in the field of military aircraft and missiles whose biggest customer is the U.S. Department of Defense. Boeing also sells to foreign governments under licenses granted by the U.S. government to its allies.

This segment of the company produces tactical fighters, trainers, helicopters, military transports, tankers, strike missiles, and special purpose planes. It also provides aerospace support products and services. The biggest programs in this industry segment are the C-17 Globemaster transport program and the F/A-18E/F Super Hornet fighter program. The segment also includes the F/A-18C/D Hornet, AH-64 Apache, F-22 Raptor, F-15 Eagle, V-22 Osprey, and CH-47 Chinook programs.

The company reported the following key financial information for the military aircraft and missile systems segment for the most recent years (numbers are all in millions of dollars):

|                                | 2001 | 2000 | 1999 | 1998 |
|--------------------------------|------|------|------|------|
| Revenues                       | $12,451 | $12,197 | $12,220 | $12,990 |
| Operating income               | 1,346 | 1,271 | 1,193 | 1,283 |
| Assets                         | 2,477 | 3,321 | 3,206 | 3,506 |
| Liabilities                    | 1,612 | 1,189 | 1,080 | 743 |
| Research and development cost  | 258 | 257 | 264 | 304 |
| Contractual backlog of orders  | 17,630 | 17,113 | 15,691 | 17,007 |

*Source:* www.boeing.com.

The company states that "The basic strategy of the . . . segment is to provide competitive products and services in every selected market . . . [and] to provide integrated product and service solutions that best meet customer needs."

The U.S. Department of Defense has pledged to examine its weapon systems and to modernize many of them, which would appear to mean that 2001 and future years continue to be bright for this segment of the company. One such innovation is the use of unmanned, reusable aircraft to fly bombing missions. These craft combine some of the best features of missiles with those of manned aircraft: (1) the aircraft loses no people if shot down and (2) the aircraft delivers its payload and returns the delivery system for reuse, unlike missiles, which destroy the delivery system with the payload.

Two major events in late 2001 may have a significant impact on this segment:

1. The September 11 destruction of the World Trade Center and part of the Pentagon, which triggered the U.S. military attacks on Afghanistan, seem to indicate that the government will be procuring additional military hardware and services in the years to come. Discussions are reported to be taking place both in Congress and in the Defense Department that could result in additional purchases of transport planes and tankers that are built from converted 767 commercial aircraft. Boeing's military aircraft and missiles segment is poised to benefit from those additional purchases.

2. The Department of Defense announced on October 26, 2001, that it had chosen Lockheed-Martin as the prime contractor to produce the Joint Strike Fighter, which is being designed to replace aging aircraft in several U.S. and U.K. military services—as well as in the arsenals of several NATO allies. Analysts project that the contract will be worth at least $200 billion in revenues—and may be worth up to $1 trillion—for Lockheed-Martin. Boeing was in the final stage of the competition, and it had expected to obtain at least a part of the final award, but the contract was granted as a "winner take all" award to Lockheed-Martin. Boeing may still benefit by subcontracting some of the components of the project from Lockheed-Martin. It is not uncommon for the winner of such a contract to subcontract various components of such a large program. It is being reported that some members of Congress are discussing legislation to require splitting the contract between Lockheed and Boeing.

## SPACE AND COMMUNICATIONS

The space and communications segment, which is the newest and smallest of the significant segments, seems to be the fastest growing. The four major areas of operations in this segment are launch services, information and communication, human space flight and exploration, and missile defense and space control.

The 767 AWACS is a flying, all-weather surveillance, command, communications, and control system installed in a 767 commercial aircraft. The system is used by the military to monitor and control attack aircraft in offensive engagements and to warn those aircraft of enemy response by either airplanes or missiles. AWACS systems were also used, following the September 11 attack on the World Trade Center and the Pentagon, to enforce the order that all flights over U.S. territory be grounded. The Pentagon is reported to be considering modernizing its fleet of AWACS craft, in part due to the terrorist attacks of September 11.

Boeing's president recently set a goal of making Boeing "number 1 in space." Boeing has Delta programs that produce rocket boosters used by NASA and some private satellite-launch groups to put satellites into orbit and to launch other space-related activities. The Delta III is still undergoing tests. Some of the tests have resulted in spectacular failures, but the company is not likely to lose money on the program because its government contracts are "cost-plus" contracts.

The company reported the following key financial information for the space and communications segment for the most recent years (numbers are all in millions of dollars):

|  | 2001 | 2000 | 1999 | 1998 |
|---|---|---|---|---|
| Revenues | $10,364 | $ 8,039 | $ 6,831 | $ 6,889 |
| Operating income | 619 | (323) | 415 | 248 |
| Assets | 10,299 | 9,629 | 4,245 | 3,149 |
| Liabilities | 3,123 | 2,903 | 1,350 | 1,452 |
| Research and development costs | 526 | 526 | 492 | 570 |
| Contractual backlog of orders | 13,111 | 13,707 | 10,585 | 9,832 |

*Source:* www.boeing.com.

The prospects for this segment are quite varied. The launch services sector is dependent on NASA and on the commercial satellite launch market. This is a highly competitive area. The information and communication services sector is positioned to experience rapid growth. For its governmental customers, Boeing offers airborne mission systems, space systems, and satellite systems; and for commercial customers, the company offers satellite manufacturing, hybrid network systems, and telecommunications. The human space flight sector expects relatively flat growth over the next ten years. Boeing's activities will include completing existing contracts for the International Space Station and operations and maintenance on the space shuttle program.

### Financing

Customer and commercial financing segment revenues are made up primarily of interest from the financing of receivables and lease income from equipment leased to others under operating leases. A major expense of the segment is depreciation on the equipment leased. No interest expense on debt incurred by the company is included in the calculation of segment income. (The interest and debt expense for the company is reported as a single amount on the income statement. It is not allocated to the segments.)

The revenues from the segment were $863 million, $758 million, $771 million, and $612 million for the years 2001, 2000, 1999, and 1998, respectively. Comparable net earnings were $596 million, $494 million, $426 million, and $249 million for the same four years. The segment employed assets of $9.646 billion, $6.959 billion, $6.004 billion, and $5.751 billion; and it had liabilities of $351 million, $240 million, $228 million, and $301 million in 2001, 2000, 1999, and 1998, respectively.

This segment is likely to continue to grow as long as airline companies and others need additional airplanes. Because of the high cost of purchasing a commercial aircraft, many of Boeing's customers will opt for either financing the purchase or leasing the aircraft from the company. This should provide a steady source of revenue for this segment. As long as interest rates are low, the segment can make a good profit.

## CONCLUSION

In 2001, Boeing's net income increased to $2,827 million (see Exhibits 3 and 4). Even following the attack on the United States on September 11, in each of the four major segments of the company, there were still some favorable factors. The war effort, "Enduring Freedom," has reduced our nation's supply of aircraft, missiles, and other aerospace products, thereby requiring repletion of these products by Boeing and other manufacturers. The airline passenger business is expected to increase over the next twenty years at an

EXHIBIT 3    The Boeing Company Consolidated Statements of Operations
(in millions except per-share data)

| | Year ended December 31, | |
| --- | --- | --- |
| | *2001* | *2000* |
| Sales and other operating revenues | $58,198 | $51,321 |
| Cost of products and services | 48,778 | 43,712 |
| | 9,420 | 7,609 |
| Equity in income from joint ventures | 93 | 64 |
| General and administrative expense | 2,389 | 2,335 |
| Research and development expense | 1,936 | 1,441 |
| In-process research and development expense | | 557 |
| Gain on dispositions, net | 21 | 34 |
| Share-based plans expense | 378 | 316 |
| Special charges due to events of September 11, 2001 | 935 | |
| Earnings from operations | 3,896 | 3,058 |
| Other income, principally interest | 318 | 386 |
| Interest and debt expense | (650) | (445) |
| Earnings before income taxes | 3,564 | 2,999 |
| Income taxes | 738 | 871 |
| Net earnings before cumulative effect of accounting change | 2,826 | 2,128 |
| Cumulative effect of accounting change, net | 1 | |
| Net earnings | $ 2,827 | $ 2,128 |
| Basic earnings per share | $ 3.46 | $ 2.48 |
| Diluted earnings per share | $ 3.41 | $ 2.44 |
| Cash dividends paid per share | $ 0.68 | $ 0.56 |

*Source:* www.boeing.com.

EXHIBIT 4   Boeing Company Annual Balance Sheet
(in millions except for per-share items)

|  | 2001 | 2000 | 1999 |
|---|---|---|---|
| Cash & Equivalents | 633.0 | 1,010.0 | 3,354.0 |
| Short Term Investments | — | — | 100.0 |
| Cash and Short Term Investments | 633.0 | 1,010.0 | 3,454.0 |
| Trade Accounts Receivable, Net | 5,156.0 | 5,519.0 | 3,453.0 |
| Other Receivables | — | — | — |
| Total Receivables, Net | 5,156.0 | 5,519.0 | 3,453.0 |
| Total Inventory | 6,920.0 | 6,852.0 | 6,539.0 |
| Prepaid Expenses | — | — | — |
| Other Current Assets | 3,497.0 | 3,132.0 | 2,266.0 |
| **Total Current Assets** | 16,206.0 | 16,513.0 | 15,712.0 |
| Property/Plant/Equipment–Gross | — | — | — |
| Accumulated Depreciation | (12,369.0) | (12,156.0) | (11,874.0) |
| Property/Plant/Equipment, Net | 8,459.0 | 8,814.0 | 8,245.0 |
| Goodwill, Net | 6,443.0 | 5,214.0 | 2,233.0 |
| Intangibles, Net | — | — | — |
| Long Term Investments | — | — | — |
| Other Long Term Assets | 17,235.0 | 12,136.0 | 9,957.0 |
| **Total Assets** | 48,343.0 | 42,677.0 | 36,147.0 |
| Accounts Payable | 13,872.0 | 12,312.0 | 11,269.0 |
| Accrued Expenses | — | — | — |
| Notes Payable/Short Term Debt | — | — | 200.0 |
| Current Port. LT Debt/Capital Leases | 1,399.0 | 1,232.0 | 552.0 |
| Other Current Liabilities | 5,215.0 | 5,383.0 | 1,635.0 |
| **Total Current Liabilities** | 20,486.0 | 18,927.0 | 13,656.0 |
| Long Term Debt | 10,866.0 | 7,567.0 | 5,980.0 |
| Capital Lease Obligations | — | — | — |
| **Total Long Term Debt** | 10,866.0 | 7,567.0 | 5,980.0 |
| **Total Debt** | 12,265.0 | 8,799.0 | 6,732.0 |
| Deferred Income Tax | 177.0 | 0.0 | 172.0 |
| Minority Interest | — | — | — |
| Other Liabilities | 5,989.0 | 5,163.0 | 4,877.0 |
| **Total Liabilities** | 37,518.0 | 31,657.0 | 24,685.0 |
| Redeemable Preferred Stock | — | — | — |
| Preferred Stock–Non Redeemable, Net | — | — | — |
| Common Stock | 5,059.0 | 5,059.0 | 5,059.0 |
| Additional Paid-In Capital | 1,975.0 | 2,693.0 | 1,684.0 |
| Retained Earnings (Accum. Deficit) | 14,340.0 | 12,090.0 | 10,487.0 |
| Treasury Stock–Common | (8,509.0) | (6,221.0) | (4,161.0) |
| Other Equity | (2,040.0) | (2,601.0) | (1,607.0) |
| **Total Equity** | 10,825.0 | 11,020.0 | 11,462.0 |
| **Total Liability & Shareholders' Equity** | 48,343.0 | 42,677.0 | 36,147.0 |
| Shares Outs.–Common Stock | 837.6 | 875.5 | 909.5 |
| **Total Common Shares Outstanding** | 837.6 | 875.5 | 909.5 |
| **Total Preferred Stock Shares Outs.** | — | — | — |
| Employees (actual figures) | 186,900.0 | 198,000.0 | 197,000.0 |
| Number of Common Shareholders (actual figures) | — | — | — |

*Source:* http://investor.stockpoint.com.

EXHIBIT 5    The Boeing Company Segment Information

A. Sales and Other Operating Revenues

| Year ended December 31, | 2001 | 2000 |
|---|---|---|
| Commercial Airplanes | $35,056 | $31,171 |
| Military Aircraft and Missile Systems | 12,451 | 11,924 |
| Space and Communications | 10,364 | 8,039 |
| Customer and Commercial Financing | 863 | 728 |
| Other | 365 | 303 |
| Accounting differences/eliminations | (901) | (844) |
| | $58,198 | $51,321 |

B. Net Earnings (Loss) Before Cumulative Effect of Accounting Change

| Year ended December 31, | 2001 | 2000 |
|---|---|---|
| Commercial Airplanes | $ 2,632 | $ 2,736 |
| Military Aircraft and Missile Systems | 1,346 | 1,245 |
| Space and Communications | 619 | (243) |
| Customer and Commercial Financing | 596 | 516 |
| Other | (388) | (76) |
| Accounting difference/eliminations | (368) | (442) |
| Share-based plans expense | (378) | (316) |
| Unallocated expense | (163) | (362) |
| Earnings from operations | 3,896 | 3,058 |
| Other income, principally interest | 318 | 386 |
| Interest and debt expense | (650) | (445) |
| Earnings before taxes | 3,564 | 2,999 |
| Income taxes | 738 | 871 |
| | $ 2,826 | $ 2,128 |

C. Research and Development

| Year ended December 31, | 2001 | 2000 |
|---|---|---|
| Commercial Airplanes | $ 858 | $ 574 |
| Military Aircraft and Missile Systems | 258 | 257 |
| Space and Communications | 526 | 526 |
| Other | 294 | 84 |
| | $ 1,936 | $ 1,441 |

*(continued)*

average annual rate of 4.7 percent, with the air cargo business expected to double over the same period. The space and communications market is looking forward to significant increases in the commercial market.

In the face of the expected business environment, prepare a strategic plan for CEO Philip M. Condit and COO Harry C. Stonecipher. Keep in mind that according to the 2000 *Annual Report,* Boeing's plan for the near, medium, and long-term future is to "create converging and ever-increasing streams of value—for customers and shareholders."

EXHIBIT 5    The Boeing Company Segment Information   (continued)

D. Assets at December 31,

|  | 2001 | 2000 |
|---|---|---|
| Commercial Airplanes | $11,479 | $ 9,800 |
| Military Aircraft and Missile Systems | 2,477 | 3,035 |
| Space and Communications | 10,299 | 9,629 |
| Customer and Commercial Financing | 9,646 | 6,856 |
| Other | 1,290 | 389 |
| Unallocated | 13,152 | 12,968 |
|  | $48,343 | $42,677 |

E. Capital Expenditures, Net

|  | 2001 | 2000 |
|---|---|---|
| Commercial Airplanes | $    207 | $    237 |
| Military Aircraft and Missile Systems | 99 | 25 |
| Space and Communications | 362 | 438 |
| Customer and Commercial Financing | 1 | 7 |
| Other | 32 | 40 |
| Unallocated | 367 | 185 |
|  | $ 1,068 | $    932 |

*Source:* **http://www.boeing.com.**

## REFERENCES

Bois, and Sweatman. *Intervaia Business and Technology* (October 2001).

Lunsford, J. Lynn. *Wall Street Journal* (June 14, 2001).

Lunsford, J. Lynn. *Wall Street Journal* (May 17, 2001).

Michaels, Daniel. "Airbus Faces Adjustment in Output as Demand Falls." *Wall Street Journal* (November 14, 2001).

# LOCKHEED MARTIN CORPORATION—2002

**K. Todd Ellison**
**Francis Marion University**

LMT

www.lockheedmartin.com

On September 11, 2001, the United States suffered a tremendous loss when terrorists viciously attacked the mainland of the United States using hijacked commercial aircraft. As the second largest company in the defense, intelligence, and aerospace industry, Lockheed Martin Corporation, previously suffering from government defense funding cuts, now faced (and continues to face) tremendous new opportunities. As the builder of many of the best-known military aircraft and rocket systems, such as the C-5A, C-130, F-16, F-22, F-117 aircraft and the Atlas, Titan, and Trident rocket systems, Lockheed Martin products are leading the war on terrorism. Lockheed Martin also produces many lower visibility high-tech products and services that possess intelligence-gathering capabilities. Lockheed Martin handles the operation of many federal and state government data processing and communications systems, including many post office, air traffic control, and social services systems. Lockheed Martin's stated vision is "to be the world's best advanced technology systems integrator."

## HISTORY

Lockheed Aircraft Company was formed in 1926 by Allan Loughead, Malcolm Loughead, and Fred Keeler after the Loughead (name was later changed to Lockheed) brothers had previously experienced several unsuccessful forays into the aircraft manufacturing business. The company's first aircraft, the Vega, was designed by the future founder of the Northrup Corporation, John Northrup. Amelia Earhart was flying a Vega when she became the first woman to fly solo across the Atlantic. Wiley Post flew a Lockheed Vega during his around-the-world solo flight.

Robert Gross, Carl Squier, and Lloyd Stearman purchased Lockheed Aircraft Corporation in 1932. The Lockheed Electra, the first successful pressurized commercial aircraft, was developed in the 1930s. Lockheed continued to produce many famous aircraft, including the P-38 Lightning of WWII fame, the P-80 Shooting Star, and the F-104 Starfighter, as well as spy planes such as the U-2 (1955) and the SR-71 Blackbird (1964). The C5-A Galaxy, C-130 Hercules, and C-141 Starlifter military cargo aircraft as well as the L-1011 Tristar passenger airliner were also produced by Lockheed.

In the 1960s and 1970s, Lockheed suffered many financial setbacks, including C-5A cost overruns, cancellation of the Cheyenne helicopter program, and cost problems associated with the L-1011 passenger jet. Additional problems arose in the 1970s when Lockheed became involved in a corporate bribery scandal, which led to revisions in antibribery laws. Government loans were required in 1971 to save the company from bankruptcy. In 1992, Lockheed entered an agreement to provide satellites for Motorola's Iridium phone project.

Glenn Martin founded the Glenn L. Martin Aircraft Company in 1912 and in 1916 merged with the company founded by the Wright Brothers. The twin-engine Martin MB-2 was used by General Billy Mitchell to demonstrate the potential of air bombardment. In the 1930s, Martin built the M-130 Clipper flying boat, which became famous as the Pan Am Clipper. Martin produced the B-26 bomber during World War II.

Martin produced missiles, electronics, and nuclear systems during the 1950s. In an attempt to diversify in 1961, Martin merged with the chemical and construction material company American-Marietta Company to become Martin Marietta. Martin Marietta developed the Titan II rocket in the 1960s. Other Martin Marietta projects included the Viking Mars lander, the MX missile, and the external fuel tanks for the space shuttle. Martin Marietta was forced to sell off many of its businesses in 1982 after it acquired $1 million of debt fending off a takeover attempt from Bendix Corporation. In 1992, Martin Marietta purchased the aerospace operations of General Electric.

Lockheed Martin was formed in 1995 when Lockheed acquired Martin Marietta. These two companies seemed to be an ideal match since Lockheed was a major builder of military aircraft while Martin Marietta was a strong force in defense electronics. Lockheed Martin paid $7.6 billion in 1996 to acquire the majority of the electronics giant Loral Corporation. The merger of Lockheed and Martin Marietta and many of Lockheed Martin's early acquisitions allowed Lockheed Martin to achieve a high degree of vertical integration in many of its businesses. This development could be seen in the way the electronics and systems integration business that was acquired with the purchase of Loral complemented the defense electronics business of Martin Marietta.

In 1996, Lockheed Martin sold its defense systems and armament systems businesses to General Dynamics. L-3 Communications was formed in 1997 when Lockheed Martin spun off portions of ten technology units not deemed to be part of the core business. Lockheed Martin offered to buy Northrop Grumman for $11.6 billion in 1997, but the deal collapsed in 1998 when the U.S. government indicated it had antitrust problems with the deal.

By 1998, acquisitions and mergers had resulted in a 185 percent increase in the number of core competencies in Lockheed Martin's technology profile, with only 15 percent of the competencies being duplicated as a result of acquisitions. Lockheed Martin has achieved a high degree of vertical integration in military aircraft, avionics, airframes, and space vehicles.[1]

## INTERNAL CONDITION

In 2000, Lockheed Martin completed the purchase of 49 percent of the satellite network company COMSAT for $1.7 billion. The remainder of COMSAT cannot be purchased without government approval. COMSAT is an entity that acts as an interface between U.S. communications companies and INTELSAT, an international agency that controls the majority of the world's communications satellites.

Lockheed Martin now operates approximately 440 facilities, most of which are located in the United States. The company has used its own information technology to generate internal networks to facilitate the sharing of information and technology. In this respect, Lockheed Martin operates as a virtual enterprise. Although some economies of scale could be achieved by combining divisions, Lockheed Martin believes innovation may be better promoted by small organizations working independently while remaining electronically interconnected to the rest of the organization.

Lockheed Martin has made several attempts to lower costs and improve profitability. Lockheed Martin Aeronautical Systems (LMAS) embraced the "lean" or Toyota production system in 1997. Lockheed's goal is to have the Toyota system fully in place in four years. This appears to be a rather ambitious goal since GE required twelve years to accomplish the same task.[2]

Lockheed Martin is organized into four principal sectors: systems integration, space systems, aeronautics, and technology services. Lockheed Martin's financial statements are shown in Exhibits 1–4. The company's earnings have been in decline in recent years.

## Systems Integration

This segment is engaged in the design, development, and integration of complex systems for global defense, civil government, and commercial markets. Core businesses include undersea warfare, surface warfare, and land surveillance systems; tactical

---

**EXHIBIT 1**    Lockheed Martin Corporation Consolidated Statement of Operations
(In millions, except per-share data)

| | Year ended December 31, | | |
| --- | --- | --- | --- |
| | *2001* | *2000* | *1999* |
| **Net sales** | $23,990 | $24,541 | $24,999 |
| Cost of sales | 22,447 | 22,881 | 23,346 |
| Earnings from operations | 1,543 | 1,660 | 1,653 |
| Other income and expenses, net | (655) | (409) | 344 |
| | 888 | 1,251 | 1,997 |
| Interest expense | 700 | 919 | 809 |
| Earnings from continuing operations before income taxes, extraordinary items and cumulative effect of change in accounting | 188 | 332 | 1,188 |
| Income tax expense | 109 | 714 | 459 |
| Earnings (loss) from continuing operations before extraordinary items and cumulative effect of change in accounting | 79 | (382) | 729 |
| Discontinued operations | (1,089) | (42) | 8 |
| Extraordinary loss on early extinguishments of debt | (36) | (95) | — |
| Cumulative effect of change in accounting | — | — | (335) |
| **Net (loss) earnings** | $ (1,046) | $  (519) | $   382 |
| Earnings (loss) per common share: | | | |
| Basic: | | | |
| Continuing operations before extraordinary items and cumulative effect of change in accounting | $   0.18 | $  (0.95) | $  1.91 |
| Discontinued operations | (2.55) | (0.10) | 0.02 |
| Extraordinary loss on early extinguishments of debt | (0.08) | (0.24) | — |
| Cumulative effect of change in accounting | — | — | (0.93) |
| | $  (2.45) | $  (1.29) | $  1.00 |
| Diluted: | | | |
| Continuing operations before extraordinary items and cumulative effect of change in accounting | $   0.18 | $  (0.95) | $  1.90 |
| Discontinued operations | (2.52) | (0.10) | 0.02 |
| Extraordinary loss on early extinguishments of debt | (0.08) | (0.24) | — |
| Cumulative effect of change in accounting | — | — | (0.93) |
| | $  (2.42) | $  (1.29) | $  0.99 |

*Source:* Lockheed's 2001 *Annual Report,* p. 51.

---

**EXHIBIT 2**    Lockheed Martin Corporation
Consolidated Balance Sheet (in millions)

| | December 31, | |
| --- | --- | --- |
| | *2001* | *2000* |
| **ASSETS** | | |
| Current assets: | | |
| Cash and cash equivalents | $   912 | $  1,505 |
| Receivables | 4,049 | 3,986 |
| Inventories | 3,140 | 3,805 |
| Deferred income taxes | 1,566 | 1,213 |
| Assets of businesses held for sale | 638 | 2,332 |
| Other current assets | 473 | 498 |
| Total current assets | 10,778 | 13,339 |
| Property, plant and equipment, net | 2,991 | 2,941 |
| Investments in equity securities | 1,884 | 2,433 |
| Intangible assets related to contracts and programs acquired | 939 | 1,073 |
| Goodwill | 7,371 | 7,479 |
| Prepaid pension cost | 2,081 | 1,794 |
| Other assets | 1,610 | 1,367 |
| Total Assets | $27,654 | $30,426 |
| **LIABILITIES AND STOCKHOLDERS' EQUITY** | | |
| Current liabilities: | | |
| Accounts payable | $  1,419 | $  1,106 |
| Customer advances and amounts in excess of costs incurred | 5,002 | 4,697 |
| Salaries, benefits and payroll taxes | 1,100 | 978 |
| Income taxes | 63 | 519 |
| Current maturities of long-term debt | 89 | 882 |
| Liabilities of businesses held for sale | 387 | 467 |
| Other current liabilities | 1,629 | 1,653 |
| Total current liabilities | 9,689 | 10,302 |
| Long-term debt | 7,422 | 9,065 |
| Post-retirement benefit liabilities | 1,565 | 1,647 |
| Deferred income taxes | 992 | 790 |
| Other liabilities | 1,543 | 1,462 |
| Total Liabilities | 21,211 | 23,266 |
| Stockholders' equity: | | |
| Common stock, $1 par value per share | 441 | 431 |
| Additional paid-in capital | 2,142 | 1,789 |
| Retained earnings | 3,961 | 5,199 |
| Unearned ESOP shares | (84) | (115) |
| Accumulated other comprehensive loss | (17) | (144) |
| Total stockholders' equity | 6,443 | 7,160 |
| Total Liabilities and Stockholders' Equity | $27,654 | $30,426 |

*Source:* Lockheed's 2001 *Annual Report*, p. 53.

EXHIBIT 3    Lockheed's Financial Data by Business Segment
(in millions)

|  | 2001 | 2000 | 1999 |
|---|---|---|---|
| **Net sales** | | | |
| Systems Integration | $ 9,014 | $ 9,647 | $ 9,570 |
| Space Systems | 6,836 | 7,339 | 7,285 |
| Aeronautics | 5,355 | 4,885 | 5,499 |
| Technology Services | 2,763 | 2,649 | 2,574 |
| Corporate and Other | 22 | 21 | 71 |
|  | $23,990 | $24,541 | $24,999 |
| **Operating profit (loss)** | | | |
| Systems Integration | $    836 | $    583 | $    880 |
| Space Systems | 405 | 401 | 506 |
| Aeronautics | 416 | 343 | 247 |
| Technology Services | 130 | 82 | 137 |
| Corporate and Other | (899) | (158) | 227 |
|  | $    888 | $  1,251 | $  1,997 |

*Source:* Lockheed's 2001 *Annual Report,* p. 72.

missiles, air defense systems, and fire control and sensor systems; information superiority systems; simulation and training systems; air traffic management systems; aerospace systems and platform integration; business system solutions; and distribution technologies, which includes automated material handling solutions for postal systems and commercial customers.

The total for 2000's net sales of the systems integration segment showed an increase of 1 percent over 1999's figure, and it increased 3 percent between 1998 and 1999. The increases are a result of volume increases in the segment's naval electronic and surveillance systems product line and in its electronic platform integration activities. Net sales also increased in the segment's missiles and air defense product line, primarily as a result of the Theater High Altitude Area Defense (THAAD) program's movement into the engineering, manufacturing and development (EMD) phase. These increases were partially offset by a reduction in net sales related to the AES and control systems businesses, reductions that were primarily due to the divestiture of these businesses in 2000.

Operating profit for the systems integration segment increased by 2 percent both in 2000 (compared to 1999) and in 1999 (compared to 1998). In 2000, the previously mentioned volume increases in the segment's naval electronic and surveillance systems product line and in its electronic platform integration activities contributed to the increase in operating profit from 1999. This increase was partially offset by a decline in operating profit related to the AES and control systems businesses, declines that were due to their divestiture in 2000.

## Space Systems

This segment is engaged in the design, development, engineering and production of civil, commercial, and military space systems. Major product lines include spacecraft, space launch vehicles, and human space systems; their supporting ground systems and

**EXHIBIT 4**    Lockheed's Net Sales by Customer Category (in millions)

|  | 2001 | 2000 | 1999 |
|---|---|---|---|
| **U.S. Government** | | | |
| Systems Integration | $ 6,952 | $ 6,855 | $ 7,017 |
| Space Systems | 5,956 | 5,932 | 6,069 |
| Aeronautics | 3,437 | 2,784 | 2,979 |
| Technology Services | 2,269 | 2,120 | 2,033 |
| Corporate and Other | — | — | — |
|  | $18,614 | $17,691 | $18,098 |
| **Foreign governments** [a] [b] | | | |
| Systems Integration | $ 1,790 | $ 2,231 | $ 2,125 |
| Space Systems | 94 | 79 | 188 |
| Aeronautics | 1,899 | 2,061 | 2,501 |
| Technology Services | 104 | 116 | 106 |
| Corporate and Other | — | 1 | — |
|  | $ 3,887 | $ 4,488 | $ 4,920 |
| **Commercial(b)** | | | |
| Systems Integration | $ 272 | $ 561 | $ 428 |
| Space Systems | 786 | 1,328 | 1,028 |
| Aeronautics | 19 | 40 | 19 |
| Technology Services | 390 | 413 | 435 |
| Corporate and Other | 22 | 20 | 71 |
|  | $ 1,489 | $ 2,362 | $ 1,981 |

[a] Sales made to foreign governments through the U.S. Government are included in the foreign governments category above.
[b] Export sales, included in the foreign governments and commercial categories above, were approximately $4.1 billion, $5.2 billion and $5.7 billion in 2001, 2000 and 1999, respectively.
*Source:* Lockheeds' 2001 *Annual Report,* p. 74.

services; and strategic fleet ballistic missiles. In addition to its consolidated business units, this segment has investments in joint ventures that are principally engaged in businesses which complement and enhance other activities of the segment.

Net sales of the space systems segment declined by 1 percent in 2000 (compared to 1999), and by 16 percent in 1999 (compared to 1998). In 2000, net sales declined due to both volume declines in military, civil, and classified satellite activities, and to decreased ground systems activities. There was also an additional decline related to reduced volume in government launch vehicle programs. These declines were partially offset by increased volume on commercial space activities as well as by an increase in various other space system activities.

Operating profit for the segment declined by 28 percent in 2000 (compared to 1999), and it declined by 48 percent in 1999 (compared to 1998). Continued market and pricing pressures on commercial space programs, increased investment in certain launch vehicle programs, and reduced margins on commercial satellites reduced 2000 operating profit by approximately $180 million (compared to 1999).

## Aeronautics

This segment is engaged in the design, research and development, and production of combat and air mobility aircraft, surveillance/command systems, reconnaissance systems, platform systems integration, and advanced development programs. Major products and programs include the F-16 multirole fighter; the F-22 air-superiority fighter; the C-130J tactical airlift aircraft; support for the C-5, F-117 and U-2 aircraft; and the Joint Strike Fighter concept demonstration program.

Net sales of the aeronautics segment declined by 11 percent in 2000 (compared to 1999), after having increased by 1 percent in 1999 (compared to 1998). Approximately 95 percent of the decline in 2000 net sales is attributable to declines in F-16 fighter aircraft and C-130J airlift aircraft sales and deliveries. These declines more than offset increases in net sales related to the F-22 fighter aircraft program. The 1999 increase consisted of $715 million in increased sales related to C-130J program activities but was offset by a $717 million decline in F-16 sales and deliveries. The remaining increase was attributable to increased sales on various other aircraft programs.

Operating profit for the segment increased by 39 percent in 2000 (compared to 1999), after having decreased by 62 percent in 1999 (compared to 1998).

## Technology Services

This segment provides a wide array of management, engineering, scientific, logistic, and information services to federal agencies and other customers. Major product lines include e-commerce, enterprise information services, software modernization and data center management for the Department of Defense and for civil government agencies; engineering, science, and information services for NASA; aircraft and engine maintenance and modification services; operation, maintenance, training, and logistics support for military and civilian systems; launch, mission, and analysis services for military, classified, and commercial satellites; and research, development, engineering, and science in support of nuclear weapons stewardship and naval reactor programs.

Net sales of the technology services segment increased by 3 percent in 2000 (compared to 1999), and by 17 percent in 1999 (compared to 1998). The increases in 2000 net sales consist of increases in various federal technology services programs, including the Consolidated Space Operations contract and the Rapid Response contract. These increases were partially offset by a decline in volume on aircraft maintenance and logistics contracts and on certain defense and science energy services contracts due to program completions.

Operating profit for the segment increased by 17 percent in 2000 (compared to 1999), and by 1 percent in 1999 (compared to 1998). The increase in 2000 was primarily attributable to various federal technology services programs, including the impact of the volume increases discussed earlier, and to the increased profitability of certain information services contracts, as well as to the improved performance on certain aircraft maintenance and logistics contracts.

## COMPETITORS AND EXTERNAL FACTORS

Boeing leads the industry and had 2001 revenues of $58,198 million. Lockheed Martin was second in revenues in 2001 with $23,990 million. Other industry leaders include United Technologies, Raytheon, Allied Signal, and British Aerospace. All of the industry leaders are diversified and have employed various strategies to enhance the survivability of their companies in the tenuous environment that defense contractors have operated in since the end of the Cold War.

According to *Aviation Week & Space Technology*'s "Best Managed Aerospace Performance" rankings, British Aerospace is ranked first, United Technologies is ranked third, Allied Signal is ranked eighth, Boeing is ranked fourteenth, Raytheon is ranked seventeenth, and Lockheed Martin is ranked eighteenth. This ranking compares aerospace companies' performances based on 25 financial ratios and allocates scores based on asset utilization, productivity, and financial stability.[3]

Boeing, since acquiring McDonald Douglas, has a very strong diversified position in both civil and military aerospace. The civilian aircraft portion of Boeing's business, despite European competition from Airbus, helps to add international sales revenues to Boeing's revenue stream. International sales for Boeing accounted for 47 percent of its sales in 2000, while U.S. government sales accounted for 70 percent of Lockheed Martin's sales in 2000. Additionally, while commercial aircraft sales accounted for 63 percent of Boeing's sales, foreign and domestic government sales accounted for 89 percent of Lockheed Martin's sales. Boeing is a strong competitor of Lockheed Martin in the satellite systems market.

United Technologies is noted for building Pratt and Whitney jet engines and Sikorsky helicopters. United Technologies adopted a diversification strategy in the 1970s when it acquired Otis Elevator and Carrier. As a result of this diversification strategy, the bulk of United Technologies sales are split between Carrier (27 percent), Otis (22 percent), and Pratt & Whitney (30 percent); flight systems, such as Sikorsky and Hamilton Sunstrand (10 percent), and automotive parts (11 percent), add to the mix. Also, approximately 44 percent of United Technologies' income is derived from international operations.

British Aerospace, another strong competitor of Lockheed Martin, is similar to Lockheed Martin in that 72 percent of its sales come from its defense unit. However, British Aerospace owns 20 percent of Airbus Industries, which produces commercial aircraft and generates the remaining 28 percent of British Aerospace sales. With the acquisition of Marconi Electronic Systems, British Aerospace will become a stronger competitor. In contrast to Lockheed Martin, British Aerospace derives only 11 percent of its sales from its home country, the United Kingdom. The bulk of the balance of British Aerospace sales are generated in the Middle East (38 percent), Europe (23 percent), the United States and Canada (13 percent), and the Far East, including Australia (14 percent). It has one advantage over Lockheed Martin in military sales in that it can sell military equipment to current and former Commonwealth nations without the government scrutiny that Lockheed Martin faces when it attempts to sell military products outside the United States. An additional aid to foreign military sales comes from the subsidiaries and affiliates in which British Aerospace participates in other countries. These include (in addition to Airbus) such companies as Eurofighter Jagdflugzeug of Germany (33 percent ownership), Matra Bae Dynamics of France (50 percent), Panavia Aircraft of Germany (43 percent), Saab-BAe Grippen of Sweden (50 percent), and Asia Pacific Training and Simulation in Singapore (63 percent). Additionally, British Aerospace is a primary member of Lockheed Martin's Joint Strike Fighter development team.

Late in 1999, the aerospace division of DaimlerChrysler combined with Aerospatiale Matra to form the aforementioned European Aeronautic, Defense, and Space (EADS). EADS will have combined revenues of approximately $23 billion and will become the third largest aircraft and defense business behind Boeing and Lockheed. EADS will also have an 80 percent stake in Airbus Industries. This merger will cause renewed Pentagon concerns that the major European and American defense contractors will become competitors instead of partners in the worldwide arms sales business. These concerns include worries about the interoperability of NATO weapons systems developed separately as competitive systems by U.S. and European defense companies. Another concern involves mergers that increase the probability that U.S and European defense agencies will limit purchases to those items produced by their own countries' companies.[4]

One of the observations about Lockheed Martin's competitors is that most of them have in some way managed to avoid becoming dependent on a single market (i.e., Lockheed Martin's dependence on the U.S. government) for survival. Lockheed Martin's competitors have achieved this independence from a single market by either diversification of products or diversification of customer base. Lockheed Martin's alliance with the U.S. military has enabled Lockheed Martin to develop cutting edge technologies, but the same alliance fosters government restrictions that prohibit Lockheed Martin from taking full advantage of the technologies in the worldwide marketplace. This same issue keeps Lockheed Martin from exploiting many of the advantages it has in the satellite and command, control, communications, and intelligence ($C^3I$) arenas. Lockheed Martin has acquired saleable skills in $C^3I$, which are desired for many domestic and foreign civilian business applications, but sales have been mainly to the military, to the FAA, to the Postal Service, to social services, and to other government agencies.

It should be noted that most current aerospace products are developed and constructed from products produced by numerous defense and aerospace companies. As an example, an Apache helicopter has a Boeing airframe, Lockheed Martin electro-optics, a Lockheed Martin and Northrop Grumman radar system, and General Electric engines. Military and civilian aerospace products employ this systems approach to the design and construction of most products. This translates into a situation in which most products are produced by a lead contractor who has multiple system and subsystem partners.[5]

As a lead contractor, Lockheed competes primarily against U.S. companies for U.S. defense sales, while it competes against international and U.S. companies for defense sales in foreign countries. In the commercial satellite launching and operation business, commercial aviation business, and software business, Lockheed must compete with international companies. As an additional constraint, Lockheed faces government scrutiny to ensure that it does not transfer technology to a customer who will wittingly or unwittingly use it for military purposes against the United States or one of its allies.

## RECENT DEVELOPMENTS

Until late 2001, Lockheed Martin's outlook for the future was gloomy at best. With a failing economy, government defense budget cuts, elimination of the X-33 (space shuttle replacement) project, and satellite failures, Lockheed Martin was struggling. However, every cloud has a silver lining. The September 11, 2001, attacks that propelled the United States into a sustained war effort has substantially changed the Lockheed Martin outlook. Lockheed Martin's stock price soared following the attack due to the proposed increases in national security spending. As a result of the war on terrorism, Lockheed is projecting 2002 earnings to increase by 20 percent. As if the war on terrorism were not enough to give Lockheed Martin the boost it was looking for, it has also been awarded the largest defense contract ever. On October 26, 2001, Lockheed Martin was awarded a contract potentially amounting to over $200 million over the next century. The contract is to build the supersonic, stealth aircraft dubbed the Joint Strike Fighter, now also known as the F-35. The F-35 will replace thousands of aging aircraft flown by the United States, the United Kingdom, and allied countries. Although the competition for the contract was fierce, Lockheed Martin emerged on top and will be adding over 9,000 jobs as a result. Lockheed has full control over the project and may subcontract portions as desired.

## CONCLUSION

Before September 11, 2001, Lockheed Martin was a company struggling with its identity and facing a challenging future. After surviving the defense industry consolidation of the 1990s, Lockheed Martin seemed to be not only having trouble maintaining its core defense business, but also seemed to be unable to take advantage of the civilian technologies it had acquired in an attempt to diversify. Lockheed Martin had had little success growing revenues and income, was holding $12 billion in debt that had been acquired during takeover activity, and had sales and revenue problems due to quality and cost control problems associated with many of its products. The terrorist attacks on the United States, the current war on terrorism, and the receipt of the largest defense contract ever awarded for the F-35, seem to nearly eliminate Lockheed Martin's problems and certainly give the firm a much needed breath of fresh air. Lockheed Martin must take advantage of these opportunities by continuing to focus on fixing its weaknesses and capitalizing on its strengths.

## REFERENCES

ADVANI, R.N., M. ANDERSON, S. BOWLING, D. DOANE, and E.B. ROBERTS "Technology Strategy in Defense Industry Acquisitions: A Comparative Assessment of Two Giants." *International Journal of Technology Management,* 15 no. 8 (1998): 781–804.

BOYLE, ALAN. "Lockheed Wins Huge Fighter Contract" (October 26, 2001). **www.msnbc.com/news646985**

COLE, J. "CEO at Lockheed Martin Is Only Top Official Still Remaining." *The Wall Street Journal* (November 1, 1999): A4.

COLE, J. "Lockheed Plans to Streamline Operations." *The Wall Street Journal* (September 28, 1999): A3, A8.

COLE, J., A.M. SQUEO, and T.E. RICKS. "Specter of F-22 Funding Cut Skews Lockheed's Recovery Plans." *The Wall Street Journal* (July 26, 1999): A4.

"Daimler and Aerospatiale Matra Agree to Combine Their Aerospace Businesses—European Firms' Accord Will Create No. 3 Firm in Aircraft and Defense." *The Wall Street Journal* (October 15, 1999): A3, A4.

Lockheed Martin Corporation, 2000 *Annual Report.*

NEWMAN, R.J. "The Air Up There—If You Build Them, Will They Fly?" *U.S. News and World Report* (November 8, 1999): 38.

POPE, H. "Turks Vow to Spend Heavily as Military Expands—Arms Fair Popular as U. S. Firms See Major Opportunities." *The Wall Street Journal* (October 5, 1999): A21.

RICKS, T.E. and A.M. SQUEO. "Air Force Says F-22 Funding Cut May Hurt Programs, Contractors." *The Wall Street Journal* (July 27 1999): A4.

SQUEO, A.M. "Boeing Is Awarded Contract to Make Imagery Satellites." *The Wall Street Journal* (September 8, 1999): B14.

SQUEO, A.M. "Review of Lockheed Unit's Woes Cites Poor Oversight and Quality Control." *The Wall Street Journal* (September 9, 1999): A16.

VELOCCI, A.L. "U.K. Industry Rewarded by Focusing on 'Basics'." *Aviation Week and Space Technology* (May 31, 1999): 45–55.

VELOCCI, A.L. "Lockheed Martin Faces Long, Painful Recovery." *Aviation Week and Space Technology* (November 8, 1999): 30–33.

## NOTES

1. R.N. ADVANI, M. ANDERSON, S. BOWLING, D. DOANE, and E.B. ROBERTS, "Technology Strategy in Defense Industry Acquisitions: A Comparative Assessment of Two Giants," *International Journal of Technology Management* 15, no. 8 (1998): 781–804.

2. ALAN BOYLE, "Lockheed Wins Huge Fighter Contract" (October 26, 2001). **www.msnbc.com/news646985**.

3. A.L. VELOCCI, "U.K. Industry Rewarded by Focusing on 'Basics,'" *Aviation Week and Space Technology* (May 31, 1999): 45–55.

4. "Daimler and Aerospatiale Matra Agree to Combine Their Aerospace Businesses—European Firms' Accord Will Create No. 3 Firm in Aircraft and Defense," *The Wall Street Journal* (October 15, 1999): A3, A4.

5. H. POPE, "Turks Vow to Spend Heavily as Military Expands—Arms Fair Popular as U.S. Firms See Major Opportunities," *The Wall Street Journal* (October 5, 1999): A21.

# DELL COMPUTER CORPORATION—2002

Nicole Seminario
**Francis Marion University**

DELL

www.dell.com

The events of September 11, 2001, thrust the United States and the global economy into recession. The full impact of this tragedy arises from at least three factors:

1. Consumer confidence could plummet, dragging down consumer spending, which represents two-thirds of the gross domestic product (GDP). Just a 3 percent drop in consumption during the last quarter of 2001 would cause growth to contract at an 8 percent annual rate.

2. The war on terrorism could raise prices and weaken the economy, a development that occurred during the Persian Gulf War. Political moves and economic stimulus options that could be provided by the Federal Reserve and the government are unclear. Demand for goods, technology, and stocks have already tumbled.

3. Corporate failures in leading industries, such as finance and transportation, could further impair the economy. These industries are critical because they facilitate trade and investment in other sectors.

Just six hours after the terrorist attacks, a securities firm crippled by the attacks ordered 200 new PCs from Dell Computer. A surge of orders soon turned into a flood, and Dell immediately stepped up production at its plant in Austin, Texas. Dell has been running its factories day and night since the attacks to satisfy increased demand. A week after the attacks, Dell reported selling more than 24,000 servers, laptops, and desktop computers to replace equipment lost in the attacks. The company sent hundreds of technicians to Manhattan and Washington, D.C., converted three 18-wheel trucks into mobile technology support-and-installation facilities, and chartered an airliner to fly parts from Taiwan to its Texas factory.

Dell positioned itself to fill requests from the Pentagon, from businesses affected by the Trade Center attacks, and from disaster-management groups in Washington and New York City. Computer industry analysts agreed that Dell would probably benefit most immediately because of its flexible and quick manufacturing. Further declines in aggregate demand for computers are, however, likely to overshadow repair-related demand.

Dell Computer produces desktop computers, notebook computers, enterprise systems, refurbished systems, and third-party peripherals and software; its services include consulting, installation, Internet access, and systems integration. Dell's customers include large corporations, the government, healthcare and educational institutions, as well as individuals and small-to-medium sized businesses.

Dell competes with Compaq Computer, which has been acquired by Hewlett-Packard, to be the leading PC maker worldwide. Dell has achieved a competitive advantage over its rivals with a build-to-order approach, a direct sales approach, and an attractive price. Dell's built-to-order boxes allow for lower inventories, lower costs, and higher profit margins, all of which allow the company to compete in price wars that characterize the computer sector.

Dell's revenue for fiscal year 2002 was $31.1 billion, down from $31.9 billion in 2001, based on global market share estimates. At the end of the third quarter of 2001, figures showed that worldwide sales of PCs were down by more than 11 percent, but Dell was the bright spot in the computer sector, insofar as it was the only company to improve sales. Dell's sales increased $4.23 million and its market share increased to 13.8 percent. However, after enjoying average annual sales increases of almost 60 percent during the 1990s, Dell's revenue growth has slowed considerably, and for the first time in the company's history, employees are being laid off. Dell has approximately 40,000 regular employees; 27,000 are located in the United States, and 13,000 are located in other countries.

## HISTORY

Michael Dell founded Dell Computer in 1984, at the age of twenty-one, in his dorm room at the University of Texas in Austin with a simple vision and business concept. He believed that personal computers could be built to order and sold directly to customers. When Dell started operations, it used the direct-to-consumer strategy because of Compaq's dominance in the PC retail channel. Initially, Dell started with a mail order and phone order system.

Michael Dell believed that his approach to the PC business had two advantages. First, bypassing distributors and retailers let him eliminate the markups of resellers. Second, built-to-order machines greatly reduced the costs and risks associated with carrying large stocks of parts, components, and finished goods. While Dell sometimes struggled during its early years as it tried to refine its strategy, build an adequate infrastructure, and establish market credibility against better-known rivals, its build-to-order and direct-sale approach proved appealing to growing numbers of customers in the mid-1990s as global PC sales rose to record levels. Dell's strategy gave the company a substantial cost and profit margin advantage over rivals that manufactured PCs in volume and that kept their distributors and retailers stocked with ample inventories.

Dell's approach of selling personal computer systems directly to customers demonstrates that the company has a better understanding of its customers' needs, and it thus strives to make it easier for customers to choose, purchase, and support their computing environments. Today, Dell is enhancing and broadening the fundamental competitive advantages of its direct model by increasingly applying the efficiencies of the Internet to its entire business. Approximately half of Dell's sales are Web-based, approximately half of the technical support activities occur online, and approximately three-quarters of its order-status transactions occur online. Dell pioneered direct telephone sales of computers after noticing the increased sophistication of the consumer, who was buying computers sight unseen. Dell exemplifies leadership and vision with a keen eye on execution. Dell has set up systems that are the envy of other computer manufacturers. Warehousing, supply chain integration, and build-to-order manufacturing with quick customer fulfillment give Dell the edge in what has turned into a commodity business.

Yet Dell lacks the product line and service breadth of Hewlett-Packard, or IBM, and it has no in-house repair capabilities. Also, Dell can see that its performance is affected by the global economic recession. Worldwide sales of PCs fell for the first time in fifteen years in the second quarter 2001 and were down another 11 percent in the third quarter. Dell is striving to avoid other threats too, such as the continuously changing consumer demands, rapid technological advancement, aggressive pricing wars, and the strong brand name of competitors such as IBM.

## INTERNAL ISSUES

### Vision and Mission Statements

Dell's current vision statement stresses its strength:

> *It's the way we do business. It's the way we interact with the community. It's the way we interpret the world around us—our customers' needs, the future of technology, and the global business climate. Whatever changes the future may bring, our vision—Dell Vision—will be our guiding force.*

Dell's current mission statement is as follows:

> *Dell's mission is to be the most successful Computer Company in the world at delivering the best customer experience in markets we serve. In doing so, Dell will meet customer expectations of:*

- *Highest quality.*
- *Leading technology.*
- *Competitive pricing.*
- *Individual and company accountability.*
- *Best-in-class service and support.*
- *Flexible customization capability.*
- *Superior corporate citizenship.*
- *Financial stability.*

### Organizational Structure

Headquartered in Round Rock, Texas, Dell Computer is managed on a geographic basis. The three geographic segments are the Americas; Europe, the Middle East, and Africa; and Asia-Pacific as illustrated in Exhibit 1. The Americas segment, based in Round Rock, covers the United States, Canada, South America, and Latin America, and it represented 71 percent of the company's revenue and 81 percent of its profits in fiscal year 2001. The European segment, based in Bracknell, the United Kingdom, covers the European countries and also some countries in the Middle East and Africa. This segment represented 21 percent of the company's revenue and 13 percent of the company's profit in fiscal 2001. The Asia-Pacific segment covers the Pacific Rim, including Japan, Australia, and New Zealand, and it is based in Singapore. This segment represented 8 percent of Dell's revenue and 6 percent of the total profits.

Dell has offices in more than 30 countries, with manufacturing facilities located in or around Austin, Texas; Nashville, Tennessee; El Dorado do Sul, Brazil; Limerick, Ireland; Penang, Malaysia; and Xiamen, China.

### Natural Environment

Dell provides information on environmental programs and accomplishments through annual environmental reports. Product-specific environmental attributes are available through environmental data sheets provided to customers upon request. Dell has implemented environmental management systems (EMS) at eleven manufacturing sites around the world. These systems help Dell to identify the environmental impact of its products and processes and to set achievable targets for improving environmental performance. The objective of Dell's EMS is to integrate environmental performance into overall business management so that environmental goals are seen to be as important as quality or financial

EXHIBIT 1    Dell Computer Corporation's Organizational Chart
(Probable)

*Source:* Dell Computer Internal Report.

goals. Elements of the EMS include an environmental policy, planning, implementation and operation, checking and corrective action, and management review. These elements complement the ISO 9002 quality systems already established at Dell's manufacturing sites. The EMS allows all employees to participate in improving Dell's environmental performance. Dell has a corporate policy that guides the company and its employees in their handling of environmental issues. Dell's environmental policy has the following objectives:

- Comply with the law.
- Prevent waste and pollution.
- Design products with the environment in mind.
- Continually improve and communicate our performance.
- Be a responsible neighbor.

### E-commerce

Dell runs one of the world's leading Internet sites at **www.dell.com:** during the second quarter of year 2001, this site trafficked 500 million page-views. Dell sells more than $50 million worth of products a day, which translates into annual sales of goods and services over the Internet of $18.3 billion. Dell's $1.2 billion in earnings 2002 were largely attributed to e-business. The Web gives Dell the following benefits:

- It increases its margins and revenues. The Web has replaced Dell's customer call center, thus eliminating the need for many sales representatives and technical support staff. Phone and material costs are lower and the sales process is faster.
- Via the Web, customers choose computers and price them without sending faxes. This makes it easier to price and compare configurations.
- Web demographics show that a high percentage of users are young professionals who already are computer literate and are comfortable with a computer, as demonstrated by the fact that they use it to link up with the Web.

- Dell provides internal virtual Web stores within large corporate Intranets to aid in the purchasing process.

Finance

Dell's financial statements are presented in Exhibits 2, 3, and 4.

Note that Dell has managed to achieve impressive net income growth, increasing 14 percent from 1999 to 2000 and 30 percent in the 2000–2001 period. These gains have come at the direct expense of its rivals. Because Dell is the low-cost producer, it has led the way in an industry price-war, increasing its market share at the expense of competitors. However Dell's net income in 2002 declined almost 50 percent.

EXHIBIT 2    Dell Computer Corporation (DELL) Annual Income Statement (in millions except for per-share items)

|  | 52 Weeks Ending 02/01/02 | 52 Weeks Ending 02/02/01 | 52 Weeks Ending 01/28/00 |
|---|---|---|---|
| Revenue | 31,168.0 | 31,888.0 | 25,265.0 |
| Other Revenue | — | — | — |
| Total Revenue | 31,168.0 | 31,888.0 | 25,265.0 |
| Cost of Revenue | 25,661.0 | 25,445.0 | 20,047.0 |
| Gross Profit | 5,507.0 | 6,443.0 | 5,218.0 |
| Selling/General/Administrative Expenses | 2,784.0 | 3,193.0 | 2,387.0 |
| Research & Development | 452.0 | 482.0 | 374.0 |
| Depreciation/Amortization | — | — | — |
| Interest Expense (Income), Net Operating | — | — | — |
| Unusual Expense (Income) | 482.0 | 105.0 | 194.0 |
| Other Operating Expenses | — | — | — |
| Total Operating Expense | 29,379.0 | 29,225.0 | 23,002.0 |
| Operating Income | 1,789.0 | 2,663.0 | 2,263.0 |
| Interest Expense, Net Non-Operating | — | — | — |
| Interest/Investment Income, Non-Operating | — | — | — |
| Interest Income (Expense), Net Non-Operating | (58.0) | 531.0 | 188.0 |
| Gain (Loss) on Sale of Assets | — | — | — |
| Other, Net | — | — | — |
| Income Before Tax | 1,731.0 | 3,194.0 | 2,451.0 |
| Income Tax | 485.0 | 958.0 | 785.0 |
| Income After Tax | 1,246.0 | 2,236.0 | 1,666.0 |
| Minority Interest | — | — | — |
| Equity In Affiliates | — | — | — |
| Net Income Before Extra. Items | 1,246.0 | 2,236.0 | 1,666.0 |
| Accounting Change | 0.0 | (59.0) | — |
| Discontinued Operations | — | — | — |
| Extraordinary Item | — | 0.0 | 0.0 |
| Net Income | 1,246.0 | 2,177.0 | 1,666.0 |
| Preferred Dividends | — | — | — |
| Income Available to Common Excl. Extra. Items | 1,246.0 | 2,236.0 | 1,666.0 |
| Income Available to Common Incl. Extra. Items | 1,246.0 | 2,177.0 | 1,666.0 |
| Basic/Primary Weighted Average Shares | 2,602.0 | 2,582.0 | 2,536.0 |
| Basic/Primary EPS Excl. Extra. Items | 0.479 | 0.866 | 0.657 |

Source: http://investor.stockpoint.com

EXHIBIT 3    Dell Computer Corporation (DELL) Annual Balance Sheet
(in millions except for per-share items)

| | As of 02/01/02 | As of 02/02/01 | As of 01/28/00 |
|---|---|---|---|
| Cash & Equivalents | 3,641.0 | 4,910.0 | 3,809.0 |
| Short Term Investments | 273.0 | 525.0 | 323.0 |
| Cash and Short Term Investments | 3,914.0 | 5,435.0 | 4,132.0 |
| Trade Accounts Receivable, Net | 2,636.0 | 2,895.0 | 2,608.0 |
| Other Receivables | — | — | — |
| Total Receivables, Net | 2,636.0 | 2,895.0 | 2,608.0 |
| Total Inventory | 278.0 | 400.0 | 391.0 |
| Prepaid Expenses | — | — | — |
| Other Current Assets | 1,049.0 | 996.0 | 550.0 |
| **Total Current Assets** | 7,877.0 | 9,726.0 | 7,681.0 |
| Property/ Plant/ Equipment – Gross | — | — | — |
| Accumulated Depreciation | — | (538.0) | (375.0) |
| Property/ Plant/ Equipment, Net | 826.0 | 996.0 | 765.0 |
| Goodwill, Net | — | 0.0 | 0.0 |
| Intangibles, Net | — | — | — |
| Long Term Investments | 4,373.0 | 2,418.0 | 2,721.0 |
| Other Long Term Assets | 459.0 | 530.0 | 304.0 |
| **Total Assets** | 13,535.0 | 13,670.0 | 11,471.0 |
| Accounts Payable | 5,075.0 | 4,286.0 | 3,538.0 |
| Accrued Expenses | 2,444.0 | 2,492.0 | 1,654.0 |
| Notes Payable/ Short Term Debt | — | — | — |
| Current Port. LT Debt/ Capital Leases | — | — | — |
| Other Current Liabilities | — | — | — |
| **Total Current Liabilities** | 7,519.0 | 6,778.0 | 5,192.0 |
| Long Term Debt | 520.0 | 509.0 | 508.0 |
| Capital Lease Obligations | — | — | — |
| **Total Long Term Debt** | 520.0 | 509.0 | 508.0 |
| **Total Debt** | 520.0 | 509.0 | 508.0 |
| Deferred Income Tax | — | — | — |
| Minority Interest | — | — | — |
| Other Liabilities | 802.0 | 761.0 | 463.0 |
| **Total Liabilities** | 8,841.0 | 8,048.0 | 6,163.0 |
| Redeemable Preferred Stock | — | — | — |
| Preferred Stock – Non Redeemable, Net | — | — | — |
| Common Stock | — | 4,795.0 | 3,583.0 |
| Additional Paid-In Capital | — | — | — |
| Retained Earnings (Accum. Deficit) | — | 839.0 | 1,260.0 |
| Treasury Stock – Common | — | — | — |
| Other Equity | 4,694.0 | (12.0) | 465.0 |
| **Total Equity** | 4,694.0 | 5,622.0 | 5,308.0 |
| **Total Liability & Shareholders' Equity** | 13,535.0 | 13,670.0 | 11,471.0 |
| Shares Outs. – Common Stock | 2,599.0 | 2,601.0 | 2,575.0 |
| **Total Common Shares Outstanding** | 2,599.0 | 2,601.0 | 2,575.0 |
| **Total Preferred Stock Shares Outs.** | — | — | — |
| Employees (actual figures) | 34,600.0 | 40,000.0 | 36,500.0 |
| Number of Common Shareholders (actual figures) | — | 34,830.0 | 34,781.0 |

*Source:* http://investor.stockpoint.com

EXHIBIT 4    Dell Computer Corporation Financial Segment Data (in millions)

|  | Fiscal Year Ended | | |
|---|---|---|---|
|  | February 2, 2001 | January 28, 2000 | January 29, 1999 |
| **GEOGRAPHIC SEGMENTS** | | | |
| **New Revenue** | | | |
| Americas | $22,871 | $17,879 | $12,420 |
| Europe | 6,399 | 5,590 | 4,674 |
| Asia-Pacific and Japan | 2,618 | 1,796 | 1,149 |
| Consolidated New Revenue | $31,888 | $25,265 | $18,243 |
| **PRODUCT GROUPS** | | | |
| **Net Revenue** | | | |
| Desktop Computers | $15,452 | $13,568 | $10,979 |
| Notebook Computers | 8,572 | 5,847 | 3,859 |
| Enterprise Systems | 5,511 | 3,828 | 2,193 |
| Other | 2,353 | 2,022 | 1,212 |
| Totals | $31,888 | $25,265 | $18,243 |

*Source:* Dell's 2001 *Annual Report.*

## Marketing

Dell's customers include large corporations, government agencies, healthcare and educational institutions, small businesses, and individuals. Dell uses comparable sales and marketing approaches across its customer groups. Within each region, the sales and marketing forces are divided among the various customer groups in order to meet each customer group's specific needs.

Dell divides its customers into three groups: relationship, transactional, and Internet.

- *Relationship Customers*—This segment includes Dell's large corporate customers, as well as governmental, healthcare and educational institutions, and small-to-medium businesses. Dell maintains a field sales force throughout the world to call on its Relationship Customers and prospects.
- *Transactional Customers*—Dell has many customers among individuals and small-to-medium sized businesses. Dell markets its products and services to these customers by advertising on the Internet and television, in trade and general business publications, and by mailing a broad range of direct marketing publications, such as promotional pieces, catalogs, and customer newsletters.
- *Internet Customers*—Through Dell's World Wide Web site at **www.dell.com**, customers can access a wide range of information about Dell product and service offerings, configure and purchase systems online, and access volumes of support and technical information.

## Manufacturing

Dell manufactures its computer systems in six locations: Austin, Texas; Nashville, Tennessee; El Dorado do Sul, Brazil (Americas); Limerick, Ireland (Europe, Middle East, and Africa); Penang, Malaysia (Asia-Pacific and Japan); and Xiamen, China (China). The manufacturing process at Dell's worldwide manufacturing facilities comprises the assembly, testing, and quality control of its computer systems. Parts, components, and subassemblies purchased from suppliers are tested and held to quality standards. Because of its build-to-order manufacturing process, Dell quickly produces customized computer systems, achieves rapid inventory turnover, and reduced inventory levels. These attributes lessen Dell's exposure to the risk of declining inventory values. Another advantage of this flexible manufacturing process is that Dell can incorporate new technologies or components into its product offerings quickly. To ensure a defect-free product, Dell performs tests along the process and on the final products.

## EXTERNAL ISSUES

### Competition

The level of competition facing Dell is formidable; Hewlett-Packard and IBM are its chief rivals. Gateway and Apple Computer also compete with Dell for their place in the PC market. Analysts expect that in the short-term, in the wake of the HP-Compaq merger, Dell will benefit because those firms will struggle to integrate their operations. Dell is already claiming to have gained new customers who have switched from the Compaq label due to uncertainty about the brand's future. Longer term, however, Compaq and HP together will have strengths that Dell does not have, especially on the service side, and IBM is already very powerful.

The combined HP-Compaq Company is now the market-share leader, with 16.8 percent. Dell presently leads the industry in market share with 13.8 percent, and it is also leading the way in an industry price war, taking market share from its competitors in the process. For the second quarter of 2001, Dell increased its market share by 20.2 percent; during the same period, one-time market leader Compaq saw its market share decline by 14.4 percent, which left with a current market share of 10.4 percent. HP lost 8.5 percent, leaving it with 6.4 percent of the market; and IBM lost 6.9 percent, which left it with a current market share of 6.6 percent.

Among the factors that make Dell an appealing choice for PC buyers, are the following factors:

- Its build-to-order approach
- Its attractive price
- Its strong understanding of customer preferences and requirements
- The close working relationships it has forged with customers
- Its ability to save customers money
- Its direct sales approach

Dell encounters aggressive competition in all aspects of its business. Competing on the basis of price, technology availability, performance, quality, reliability, service, and support, Dell could maintain profitability by reducing operating expenses and by continuing to leverage its lean inventory model to rapidly realize the benefit of component price declines.

EXHIBIT 5    Dell Computer Corporation Top Competitors

| | | | | As of September 10, 2001 | | | |
|---|---|---|---|---|---|---|---|
| | Dell Computer | Compaq | Hewlett-Packard | IBM | | | |
| **Key Numbers** | | | | | | | |
| Annual Sales ($ in millions) | 31,888 | 42,383 | 48,782 | 88,396 | | | |
| Employees | 40,000 | 94,600 | 88,500 | 316,303 | | | |
| Market Value ($ in millions) | 58,772.30 | 17,532.90 | 34,770.00 | 167,535.6 | | | |

| | Dell Computer | Compaq | Hewlett-Packard | IBM | Industry | Market |
|---|---|---|---|---|---|---|
| **Profitability** | | | | | | |
| Gross Profit Margin | 20.25% | 26.55% | 27.68% | 42.31% | 20.87% | 45.29% |
| Pretax Profit Margin | 9.49% | (1.14%) | 6.19% | 13.31% | 5.14% | 6.70% |
| Net Profit Margin | 4.51% | (0.79%) | 2.95% | 9.36% | 3.29% | 3.75% |
| Return on Equity | 26.70% | – | 9.80% | 37.70% | 13.70% | 8.30% |
| Return on Assets | 11.10% | (1.3%) | 4.10% | 10.00% | 6.90% | 1.60% |
| Return on Invested Capital | 24.40% | (2.5%) | 8.20% | 20.40% | 12.50% | 4.30% |

| | Dell Computer | Compaq | Hewlett-Packard | IBM | Industry | Market |
|---|---|---|---|---|---|---|
| **Valuation** | | | | | | |
| Price/Sales Ratio | 1.8 | 0.43 | 0.74 | 1.86 | 1.38 | 2.42 |
| Price/Earnings Ratio | 40.3 | – | 25.93 | 20.61 | 54.08 | 60.49 |
| Price/Book Ratio | 10.7 | 1.49 | 2.47 | 7.5 | 5.73 | 5.37 |
| Price/Cash Flow Ratio | 24.27 | 15.92 | 9.52 | 12.53 | 29.5 | 25.05 |

| | Dell Computer | Compaq | Hewlett-Packard | IBM | Industry | Market |
|---|---|---|---|---|---|---|
| **Operations** | | | | | | |
| Inventory Turnover | 65.7 | 14.5 | 6.4 | 10.8 | 63.7 | 8.9 |
| Days Cost of Goods Sold in Inventory | – | – | 57 | 33 | 6 | 40 |
| Asset Turnover | 2.6 | 1.6 | 1.4 | 1.1 | 2 | 0.5 |
| Net Receivables Turnover Flow | 12.1 | 5.6 | 6.1 | 3.4 | 11.7 | 7.7 |
| Effective Tax Rate | 29.70% | – | 20.50% | 29.70% | 35.90% | 43.40% |

*Source*: www.hoovers.com.

## Global Issues

Economies around the globe are in recession. The U.S. economy, which has a tremendous impact on the rest of the world, was growing at the slowest rate in ten years prior to the September 11 attacks on the World Trade Center, and it has since been thrust into a recession.

The PC market is in trouble. Worldwide shipments of personal computers fell in the second quarter of 2001, the first year-on-year decline since 1986 according to reports published by International Data Corp and Gartner Dataquest (July 2001). International sales fell 2 percent, to approximately 30 million units. Of great concern was an unanticipated slowdown of sales in Japan, a market with strong growth potential because PC penetration is relatively low there. The Japanese market had seen 30 percent growth in 2000, but it had a largely flat second quarter of 2001. The world PC market is likely to continue to be flat to negative into 2002. Dell Computer is the only PC maker managing to increase sales while the rest of the top five companies all suffered declines. Gateway announced the closing of its UK operations in September 2001.

CONCLUSION

Dell Computer is a strong company; it is the PC industry leader. Dell has also positioned itself as the industry low-cost producer, placing it in the position to weather the current decline in the market demand for PCs. Dell is using its low-cost advantage to engage the industry in a price war that is squeezing the profits out of the competition and at the same time growing its own market share in a shrinking market.

A recent strategy that should help Dell continue to grow and outperform the rest of the industry is the introduction of a standardized low-price PC. The low-price PC should help Dell continue to take market share from the competition.

# HEWLETT-PACKARD COMPANY—2002

**Fred David**
**Francis Marion University**

HPQ

www.hewlett-packard.com

Hewlett-Packard (HP) was incorporated in 1947 as the successor to a partnership founded in 1939 by William Hewlett and David Packard. In May 1998, HP changed its state of incorporation from California to Delaware. In late 2001, HP acquired Compaq Computer Company to become the largest computer company in the world. HP today has approximately 145,000 employees worldwide, and business presence and services capability in more than 160 countries. The HP mission statement pre- and post merger remains unchanged as follows:

> *To invent technologies and services that drive business value, create social benefit and improve the lives of customers—with a focus on affecting the greatest number of people possible.*

In fiscal year 2001 (ended October 31, 2001), HP reported revenues of $45.2 billion, while in fiscal year 2001 (ended December 31, 2001), Compaq reported revenues of $33.6 billion. Special synergies created by this huge computer industry merger are as follows:

- Number 1 globally in Windows and UNIX servers
- Number 1 globally in enterprise storage
- Number 1 globally in imaging and printing
- Number 1 globally in personal computers
- Number 1 globally in management software
- Number 3 IT services provider in the industry

Headquartered in Palo Alto, California, HP's chief executives are Carleton S. (Carly) Fiorina, Chairman and CEO and Michael Capellas, President.

## ORGANIZATIONAL STRUCTURE

Prior to the Compaq merger, HP operated in three basic segments: Imaging and Printing Systems, Computing Systems, and Information Technology (IT) Services. Exhibit 1 reveals HP's revenues and earnings by segment for 2001, 2000, and 1999. Note that only the IT segment had increasing revenues for 2001 while all three divisions had declining earnings. HP's revenues broken down by geographic area are provided in Exhibit 2. Note that HP revenues declined both in the United States and outside the U.S. in 2001. Exhibit 3 provides HP's various headquarter locations around the world. Note that Geneva, Switzerland and Hong Kong, China are important cities for HP.

The new post-merger HP operates in the following four segments described as follows:

## EXHIBIT 1    Hewlett-Packard Company Segment Financial Data (in millions)

The following table presents financial information for each reportable segment as of and for the years ended October 31:

| | Imaging and Printing Systems | Computing Systems | IT Services | All Other | Total Segments |
|---|---|---|---|---|---|
| **2001:** | | | | | |
| Net revenue from external customers | $19,447 | $17,482 | $7,599 | $1,010 | $45,538 |
| Intersegment net revenue | — | 289 | — | — | 289 |
| Total net revenue | $19,447 | $17,771 | $7,599 | $1,010 | $45,827 |
| Earnings (loss) from operations | $ 1,987 | $ (450) | $ 342 | $ (321) | $ 1,558 |
| Depreciation expense | $ 227 | $ 82 | $ 508 | $ 14 | $ 831 |
| Inventory | $ 3,495 | $ 1,337 | $ 337 | $ 35 | $ 5,204 |
| **2000:** | | | | | |
| Net revenue from external customers | $20,462 | $20,329 | $7,139 | $1,511 | $49,441 |
| Intersegment net revenue | 6 | 324 | 11 | 45 | 386 |
| Total net revenue | $20,468 | $20,653 | $7,150 | $1,556 | $49,827 |
| Earnings (loss) from operations | $ 2,666 | $ 1,007 | $ 474 | $ (92) | $ 4,055 |
| Depreciation expense | $ 298 | $ 76 | $ 445 | $ 7 | $ 826 |
| Inventory | $ 3,475 | $ 1,665 | $ 377 | $ 182 | $ 5,699 |
| **1999:** | | | | | |
| Net revenue from external customers | $18,512 | $16,837 | $6,240 | $1,250 | $42,839 |
| Intersegment net revenue | 38 | 558 | 64 | 6 | 666 |
| Total net revenue | $18,550 | $17,395 | $6,304 | $1,256 | $43,505 |
| Earnings (loss) from operations | $ 2,364 | $ 988 | $ 494 | $ (112) | $ 3,734 |
| Depreciation expense | $ 479 | $ 73 | $ 408 | $ 4 | $ 964 |
| Inventory | $ 2,810 | $ 1,539 | $ 336 | $ 178 | $ 4,863 |

*Source:* HP's 2001 *Annual Report,* p. 81.

- **Enterprise Systems Group (ESG)**, led by Peter Blackmore, executive vice president. ESG focuses on providing the key technology components of enterprise IT infrastructure to enhance business agility—including enterprise storage, servers, management software and a variety of solutions.

## EXHIBIT 2    Hewlett-Packard Company Geographic Financial Data (in millions)

**GEOGRAPHIC INFORMATION**

Net revenue and net property, plant and equipment, classified by major geographic areas in which HP operates, were as follows:

| | Years ended October 31, | | |
|---|---|---|---|
| | 2001 | 2000 | 1999 |
| **Net revenue:** | | | |
| U.S. | $18,833 | $21,528 | $18,883 |
| Non-U.S. | 26,393 | 27,342 | 23,488 |
| Total | $45,226 | $48,870 | $42,371 |

*Source:* HP's 2001 *Annual Report,* p. 83.

## EXHIBIT 3    HP Locations Around the World

### HEADQUARTERS OF GEOGRAPHIC OPERATIONS

| *Latin America* | *Europe, Africa, Middle East* | *Asia Pacific* |
|---|---|---|
| Miami, Florida | Geneva, Switzerland | Hong Kong |

### PRODUCT DEVELOPMENT AND MANUFACTURING

| *Americas* | *Europe* | *Asia Pacific* |
|---|---|---|
| Cupertino, Costa Mesa, Mountain View, Palo Alto, Roseville, San Diego, Santa Clara, Santa Monica, Sunnyvale and Woodland, California | Grenoble and Isle D'Abeau, France | Melbourne, Australia |
| Fort Collins and Greeley, Colorado | Boeblingen, Germany | Shanghai, China |
| Boise, Idaho | Dublin, Ireland | Bangalore, India |
| Mt. Laurel, New Jersey | Amsterdam and Amersfoort, The Netherlands | Komiya, Japan |
| Corvallis, Oregon | Barcelona, Spain | Singapore |
| Memphis and Nashville, Tennessee | Bristol, United Kingdom | Taiwan |
| Austin, Texas | | |
| Chester, Richmond and Sandston, Virginia | | |
| Vancouver, Washington | | |
| Aguadilla, Puerto Rico | | |
| Sao Paulo, Brazil | | |
| Guadalajara, Mexico | | |

### HEWLETT-PACKARD LABORATORIES
Palo Alto, California
Grenoble, France
Bangalore, India
Haifa, Israel
Tokyo, Japan
Bristol, United Kingdom

*Source:* HP's 2001 *Annual Report,* p. 12.

- **Imaging and Printing Group (IPG)**, led by Vyomesh Joshi ("VJ"), executive vice president. HP is the leading provider of printing and imaging solutions for both business and consumers. IPG includes printer hardware, all-in-ones, digital imaging devices such as cameras and scanners, and associated supplies and accessories. It is also expanding into the commercial printing market.

- **HP Services (HPS)**, led by Ann Livermore, executive vice president. HP Services is a premier IT services team with 65,000 professionals around the globe. HPS offers guidance, know-how and a comprehensive portfolio of services to help customers realize measurable business value from their IT investment.

- **Personal Systems Group (PSG)**, led by Duane Zitzner, executive vice president. PSG focuses on providing simple, reliable and affordable personal computing solutions and devices for home and business use, including desktop and notebook PCs, workstations, thin clients, smart handhelds and personal devices.

- In addition to the four business groups, **HP Labs**, led by Dick Lampman, senior vice president, provides a central research function for the company. HP Labs is focused on inventing new technologies that change markets and create business opportunities. (**www.hewlett-packard.com**)

## Financial Matters

HP's net revenue for 2001 declined 7 percent to $45.2 billion. U.S. revenue in 2001 declined 13 percent to $18.8 billion, while international revenue decreased just 3 percent to $26.4 billion. HP's 2001 income statements and balance sheets are provided in Exhibits 4 and 5 respectively.

HP's research and development expense as a percentage of net revenue was 5.9 percent in 2001 compared to 5.4 percent in 2000 and 5.8 percent in 1999. On advertising, HP spent $1.0 billion, $1.1 billion, and $1.3 billion in 2001, 2000, and 1999 respectively.

## CONCLUSION

CEO Fiorina needs a clear strategic plan for the coming three years. Major competitors such as IBM, Dell Computer, Apple Computer, and Gateway are looking for weakness in the new HP. These competitors are using relentless price cutting, shortened product life cycles, mass advertising, and promotions to cripple HP to the extent possible. Develop a proposed three-year strategic plan for HP.

EXHIBIT 4    Hewlett-Packard Company Consolidated Statement of Earnings

*For the years ended October 31*
*In millions, except per share amounts*

| | 2001 | 2000 | 1999 |
|---|---|---|---|
| **Net revenue:** | | | |
| Products | $37,498 | $41,653 | $36,113 |
| Services | 7,325 | 6,848 | 5,960 |
| Financing income | 403 | 369 | 298 |
| Total net revenue | 45,226 | 48,870 | 42,371 |
| **Cost of sales:** | | | |
| Products | 28,370 | 30,343 | 25,436 |
| Services | 4,870 | 4,470 | 4,284 |
| Financing interest | 234 | 233 | 168 |
| Total cost of sales | 33,474 | 35,046 | 29,888 |
| Gross margin | 11,752 | 13,824 | 12,483 |
| **Operating expenses:** | | | |
| Research and development | 2,670 | 2,634 | 2,440 |
| Selling, general and administrative | 7,259 | 7,063 | 6,225 |
| Restructuring charges | 384 | 102 | — |
| Total operating expenses | 10,313 | 9,799 | 8,665 |
| Earnings from operations | 1,439 | 4,025 | 3,818 |
| Interest and other, net | 171 | 356 | 345 |
| Net investment (losses) gains | (455) | 41 | 31 |
| Litigation settlement | (400) | — | — |
| (Losses) gains on divestitures | (53) | 203 | — |
| Earnings from continuing operations before extraordinary item, cumulative effect of change in accounting principle and taxes | 702 | 4,625 | 4,194 |
| Provision for taxes | 78 | 1,064 | 1,090 |
| Net earnings from continuing operations before extraordinary item and cumulative effect of change in accounting principle | 624 | 3,561 | 3,104 |
| Net earnings from discontinued operations | — | 136 | 387 |
| Extraordinary item—gain on early extinguishment of debt, net of taxes | 56 | — | — |
| Cumulative effect of change in accounting principle, net of taxes | (272) | — | — |
| Net earnings | $   408 | $ 3,697 | $ 3,491 |
| **Basic net earnings per share:** | | | |
| Net earnings from continuing operations before extraordinary item and cumulative effect of change in accounting principle | $   0.32 | $   1.80 | $   1.54 |
| Net earnings from discontinued operations | — | 0.07 | 0.19 |
| Extraordinary item—gain on early extinguishment of debt, net of taxes | 0.03 | — | — |
| Cumulative effect of change in accounting principle, net of taxes | (0.14) | — | — |
| Net earnings | $   0.21 | $   1.87 | $   1.73 |
| **Diluted net earnings per share:** | | | |
| Net earnings from continuing operations before extraordinary item and cumulative effect of change in accounting principle | $   0.32 | $   1.73 | $   1.49 |
| Net earnings from discontinued operations | — | 0.07 | 0.18 |
| Extraordinary item—gain on early extinguishment of debt, net of taxes | 0.03 | — | — |
| Cumulative effect of change in accounting principle, net of taxes | (0.14) | — | — |
| Net earnings | $   0.21 | $   1.80 | $   1.67 |
| Weighted average shares used to compute net earnings per share: | | | |
| Basic | 1,936 | 1,979 | 2,018 |
| Diluted | 1,974 | 2,077 | 2,105 |

*Source:* HP's 2001 *Annual Report*, p. 45.

## EXHIBIT 5    Hewlett-Packard Company Consolidated Balance Sheet

| October 31<br>In millions, except par value | 2001 | 2000 |
|---|---|---|
| **ASSETS** | | |
| Current assets: | | |
| Cash and Cash equivalents | $ 4,197 | $ 3,415 |
| Short-term investments | 139 | 592 |
| Accounts receivable, net | 4,488 | 6,394 |
| Financing receivables, net | 2,183 | 2,174 |
| Inventory | 5,204 | 5,699 |
| Other current assets | 5,094 | 4,970 |
| Total current assets | 21,305 | 23,244 |
| Property, plant and equipment, net | 4,397 | 4,500 |
| Long-term investments and other assets | 6,882 | 6,265 |
| Total assets | $32,584 | $34,009 |
| **LIABILITIES AND STOCKHOLDERS' EQUITY** | | |
| Current liabilities: | | |
| Notes payable and short-term borrowings | $ 1,722 | $ 1,555 |
| Accounts payable | 3,791 | 5,049 |
| Employee compensation and benefits | 1,477 | 1,584 |
| Taxes on earnings | 1,818 | 2,046 |
| Deferred revenue | 1,867 | 1,759 |
| Other accrued liabilities | 3,289 | 3,204 |
| Total current liabilities | 13,964 | 15,197 |
| Long-term debt | 3,729 | 3,402 |
| Other liabilities | 938 | 1,201 |
| Commitments and contingencies | | |
| Stockholders' equity: | | |
| Preferred stock, $0.01 par value (300 shares authorized; none issued) | — | — |
| Common stock, $0.01 par value (9,600 and 4,800 shares authorized at October 31, 2001 and 2000, respectively; 1,939 and 1,947 shares issued and outstanding at October 31, 2001 and 2000, respectively) | 19 | 19 |
| Additional paid-in capital | 200 | — |
| Retained earnings | 13,693 | 14,097 |
| Accumulated other comprehensive income | 41 | 93 |
| Total stockholders' equity | 13,953 | 14,209 |
| Total liabilities and stockholders' equity | $32,584 | $34,009 |

Source: HP's 2001 *Annual Report,* p. 46.

# STRYKER CORPORATION—2002

**Henry H. Beam**
**Western Michigan University**

SYK

www.strykercorp.com

Stryker Corporation is a leading maker of specialty surgical and medical products based in Kalamazoo, Michigan. Although not yet a household name, Stryker is one of America's most consistently profitable growth companies. In 2001, Stryker posted record sales of $2.6 billion and net income of $267 million. After John Brown became chairman in 1977, Stryker achieved 20 percent or more annual earnings-per-share growth every year until 1998, a remarkable record. In December 1998, Stryker took a strategic detour to take advantage of a unique opportunity to acquire Howmedica, the orthopedic division of Pfizer, which enabled the company to nearly double its size. CEO Brown commented, "When we acquired Howmedica, we announced our intention to get to be back at 20 percent or better net earnings growth. Not only did the company get back on the 20 percent track in 2000, but we did so with profit growth that makes up for the strategic detour of 1998 and 1999. With this return to the Stryker "Gold Standard," we have delivered the equivalent of 24 years of growth at the rate of 20 percent or higher." Stryker's consistent success has not gone unnoticed by Wall Street, where its stock is increasingly on the recommended list of leading brokerage firms.

All this growth comes from making products that people hope they never have to use—but are glad to have available when they need them. Stryker develops, manufactures, and markets a wide variety of surgical products and specialty hospital beds that are sold primarily to physicians and hospitals throughout the world. Stryker also provides outpatient physical therapy services in the United States.

In the 1950s and 1960s, Stryker's reputation was enhanced by good publicity about some of its unique products. Roy Campanella, the Brooklyn Dodger baseball star who had been paralyzed from injuries received in an automobile accident in 1958, was cared for on Stryker equipment. *Life* magazine did a story about the Tennessee American Legion buying a Circ-O-Lectric Hospital Bed for Sergeant Alvin York, the World War I Medal of Honor winner who had become an invalid by the early 1960s. When Senator Edward Kennedy suffered a back injury in a plane crash in 1964, he was cared for on a Stryker turning frame and was later moved to a Circ-O-Lectric Hospital Bed, both of which were pictured in national magazines during his recovery. More recently, former First Lady Barbara Bush has had Osteonics hip replacements. Such favorable publicity has enhanced the image of the company in the public's eye.

## HISTORY

The Stryker corporation takes it name from its founder, Dr. Homer Stryker, a remarkable man in many respects. After serving briefly in World War I, Stryker earned his medical degree from the University of Michigan in 1925, chose orthopedics as his specialty, and located his medical practice in Kalamazoo, Michigan. Throughout his life, he liked to fiddle with gadgets. During the early years of his medical practice, Stryker invented a mobile hospital bed and a cast-cutting saw. The mobile bed had a frame that pivoted from side to side so physicians could position injured patients for treatment while keeping them immobile. He won a contract to supply the army with his beds during World War II and was soon running a small business as well as a medical practice. The contract was terminated when the war ended in 1945, but the business continued.

Dr. Stryker wrote about how he invented the cast-cutting saw:

> *In 1943, the removal of a large cast was a tedious process for me and an unpleasant one at best for the patient. In search of a better way, I observed that if a small circular blade with sharp teeth was pressed firmly against the skin, or the soft cast padding used to protect the skin, and then moved back and forth, no more than an eighth of an inch of skin would move with the saw teeth and neither the skin or the padding and skin would be cut.*
>
> *However, if I took the same blade and pressed against a plaster cast and moved it back and forth with the same stroke and pressure, it would cut the plaster. I took a 1/20th horsepower electric grinder, replaced the grinding stone with a two-inch diameter saw blade and designed and attached a mechanism which would convert the rotation of the saw to oscillation, with the teeth oscillating about an eight of an inch at about 18,000 oscillations per minute. When completed, the instrument was tested by removing a cast at the hospital. I was able to remove the cast without disturbing the patient, in about one-fourth the time previously required.*

This is typical of how Stryker used his creativity to improve the products that physicians used to treat their patients. The rapid acceptance of the cast cutter by physicians and hospital beds by the army convinced Stryker that he had more than a part-time business on his hands. In 1946, the Orthopedic Frame Company was incorporated, with Dr. Stryker as its sole shareholder. Stryker continued with his medical practice, where he continued to develop pioneering surgical techniques. His business grew rapidly. His son Lee joined him in the business in 1955 after earning a bachelor's degree in business administration from Syracuse University. Lee's business sense balanced his father's desire to use the company as an outlet for his inventive talents.

In 1964, the company changed its name to the Stryker Corporation. New products came regularly, and sales reached $4.7 million in 1966. Although Stryker's medical equipment manufacturing business would make him wealthy, he gave away hundreds of ideas and techniques free of charge to other physicians, who passed them on to their patients. Stryker retired from his company in 1969. The company continued to grow under the guidance of Lee Stryker until his tragic death in an airplane crash in Wyoming in July 1976. Later that year, John Brown became president of Stryker.

Brown graduated from Auburn University in 1957 with a bachelor of science degree in chemical engineering. Prior to becoming president of Stryker, Brown held management positions with Ormet Corporation, Thiokol, and Bristol-Myers Squibb, where he was president of a subsidiary. Brown took charge of a firm with sales of $23 million and net income of $1.5 million. He swiftly took steps to decentralize the company, creating the autonomous divisional structure it has today. When he realized that salespeople were quitting because the compensation system had been changed from commissions to salaries and bonuses only, he restored commissions as the dominant form of compensation for salespeople. He also established goals of 20 percent growth in sales and earnings per share a year, every year. At the time, nearly 70 percent of Stryker's sales were coming from hospital beds. Building on the strength of the Stryker name with hospitals, Brown added hip implants and medical video cameras, and he strengthened the line of power surgical tools.

Acquisitions have played an important part in Stryker's growth. In 1996, Stryker purchased Osteo Holdings AG for $45.5 million. Osteo, based in Switzerland, produces a broad variety of high-quality trauma products. Stryker saw the acquisition of Osteo as a way to enter the $1 billion global trauma market. In December 1998, Stryker acquired Howmedica, the orthopedic unit of Pfizer, for $1.65 billion in cash. Howmedica makes a wide variety of innovative products for the orthopedic market, including craniofacial trauma products through Leibenger, a German company it had purchased in 1996. At the time of its acquisition, Howmedica had sales of $850 million. At Stryker's 1999 annual meeting, a smiling John Brown gave his rationale for the Howmedica acquisition. "We did it to gain a better position in the marketplace. Bigger is better. We decided a boutique player would have a hard time in this marketplace in the years ahead."

Stryker continues to make niche acquisitions, such as the Neptune fluid and smoke waste management system used in operating rooms; Colorado Biomedical, which makes the Colorado Micro Needle used in precision electrosurgery; and Image Guided Technologies, which makes three-dimensional optical measurement devices used in image-guided surgery.

Although located mainly in Kalamazoo, Michigan, Stryker also leases facilities in other U.S. cities, France, Germany, Ireland, Switzerland, Canada, and Puerto Rico. Officers, directors, and the Stryker family trust own about a third of the shares. Stryker's financial statements are shown in Exhibits 1 through 2.

## THE U.S. HEALTHCARE INDUSTRY

The U.S. healthcare system is highly diverse. Healthcare providers deliver many different kinds of services in a wide variety of settings: acute-care, inpatient general hospitals; specialty hospitals; free-standing ambulatory clinics and surgical centers; nursing homes; and patients' homes (via home healthcare services). Despite a growing proportion of elderly people in the U.S. population, hospital admission rates have declined for the past decade and are expected to continue to decline in the future. In contrast, outpatient volume has increased due to restricted reimbursement policies for inpatient care and the development of diagnostic and therapeutic procedures that do not require inpatient settings. According to the American Hospital Association, over half of all surgeries performed at community hospitals are done on an outpatient basis, up from about 20 percent ten years ago.

The United States is the global leader in the production of medical equipment and supplies, accounting for about half of the $140 billion worldwide medical device industry. Export growth in recent years has benefited from the demand for sophisticated diagnostic equipment and from the growing emphasis on the provision of quality healthcare services in countries worldwide.

Business conditions throughout the hospital industry are becoming tougher as a result of the expanding influence of managed-care plans such as health maintenance organizations (HMOs) and as a result of the constraints on reimbursement from both the federal government and insurance companies. Moreover, the number of hospitals in the United States has been declining for nearly two decades. With about a third of all hospital beds in the United States considered to be excess capacity, the fast pace of industry consolidations is likely to continue. As purchasing decisions in the 1980s and 1990s shifted away from physicians to hospitals and buying alliances, producers of medical equipment were increasingly forced to demonstrate the cost effectiveness of their products. About 60 percent of all medical device purchases in the United States are now made by managed-care buyers, and that figure is expected to increase to 80 percent in five years.

EXHIBIT 1    Consolidated Statements of Earnings
Stryker Corporation and Subsidiaries
(in millions, except per share amounts)

| | Years ended December 31 | | |
|---|---|---|---|
| | 2001 | 2000 | 1999 |
| Net sales | $2,602.3 | $2,289.4 | $2,103.7 |
| Cost of sales | 963.8 | 815.2 | 989.7 |
| Gross profit | 1,638.5 | 1,474.2 | 1,114.0 |
| Research, development and engineering expenses | 142.1 | 122.2 | 105.2 |
| Selling, general and administrative expenses | 985.4 | 885.6 | 808.4 |
| Acquisition-related and restructuring charges (credits) | 0.6 | (1.0) | 18.9 |
| | 1,128.1 | 1,006.8 | 932.5 |
| Other expense (income): | | | |
| Interest expense | 67.9 | 96.6 | 122.6 |
| Intangibles amortization | 38.4 | 34.7 | 33.9 |
| Other | (1.6) | 1.2 | (4.8) |
| | 104.7 | 132.5 | 151.7 |
| Earnings before income taxes and extraordinary item | 405.7 | 334.9 | 29.8 |
| Income taxes | 133.9 | 113.9 | 10.4 |
| Earnings before extraordinary item | 271.8 | 221.0 | 19.4 |
| Extraordinary loss, net of income taxes | (4.8) | — | — |
| Net earnings | $ 267.0 | $ 221.0 | $ 19.4 |
| Basic earnings per share of common stock: | | | |
| Before extraordinary item | $ 1.38 | $ 1.13 | $ .10 |
| Extraordinary loss | ($.02) | — | — |
| Net earnings | $ 1.36 | $ 1.13 | $ .10 |
| Diluted earnings per share of common stock: | | | |
| Before extraordinary item | $ 1.34 | $ 1.10 | $ .10 |
| Extraordinary loss | ($.02) | — | — |
| Net earnings | $ 1.32 | $ 1.10 | $ .10 |

Source: Stryker's 2001 Annual Report, pp. 36–37.

## STRYKER'S ORGANIZATION

Following the Howmedica acquisition, Stryker has organized itself into five major product divisions: Howmedica Osteonics, MedSurg Equipment, Physiotherapy, International, and BioTech/Spine/Trauma. An approximate organization chart is given in Exhibit 3.

### Howmedica Osteonics

The Howmedica Osteonics division produces a variety of both total and partial hip and knee implants. It is a combination of the former Stryker Osteonics division and the Howmedica acquisition and is now the company's largest division. With sales of $1.44 billion in 2001, it is Stryker's largest unit, accounting for 55 percent of its sales.

Every year, about five hundred thousand people in the United States and a comparable number abroad, most of them elderly, undergo joint replacement surgery to regain some of their previous mobility. Most hip and knee replacements result from osteoarthritis (a condition affecting the aged in which joints become painful and mobility is

EXHIBIT 2   Consolidated Balance Sheets Stryker Corporation and Subsidiaries
(in millions, except per-share amounts)

| | December 31 | |
| --- | --- | --- |
| | 2001 | 2000 |
| **ASSETS** | | |
| **Current Assets** | | |
| Cash and cash equivalents | $ 50.1 | $ 54.0 |
| Accounts receivable, less allowance of $36.3 ($28.8 in 2000) | 332.1 | 343.7 |
| Inventories | 399.8 | 392.1 |
| Deferred income taxes | 171.5 | 168.7 |
| Prepaid expenses and other current assets | 39.6 | 38.5 |
| Total current assets | 993.1 | 997.0 |
| **Property, Plant and Equipment** | | |
| Land, buildings and improvements | 287.6 | 211.9 |
| Machinery and equipment | 469.3 | 444.0 |
| | 756.9 | 655.9 |
| Less allowance for depreciation | 312.9 | 277.8 |
| | 444.0 | 378.1 |
| **Other Assets** | | |
| Goodwill, less accumulated amortization of $58.5 ($40.3 in 2000) | 434.3 | 470.6 |
| Other intangibles, less accumulated amortization of $74.5 ($53.2 in 2000) | 368.0 | 368.7 |
| Deferred charges, less accumulated amortization of $205.5 ($154.1 in 2000) | 102.1 | 99.3 |
| Deferred income taxes | 60.4 | 84.0 |
| Other | 21.7 | 33.1 |
| | 986.5 | 1,055.7 |
| | $2,423.6 | $2,430.8 |
| **LIABILITIES AND STOCKHOLDERS' EQUITY** | | |
| **Current Liabilities** | | |
| Accounts payable | $ 108.5 | $ 94.1 |
| Accrued compensation | 128.5 | 115.2 |
| Acquisition-related reorganization reserves and liabilities | 9.5 | 56.8 |
| Income taxes | 75.1 | 33.6 |
| Accrued expenses and other liabilities | 210.1 | 181.7 |
| Current maturities of long-term debt | 1.7 | 136.0 |
| Total current liabilities | 533.4 | 617.4 |
| **Long-Term Debt, Excluding Current Maturities** | 720.9 | 876.5 |
| Other Liabilities | 113.1 | 82.0 |
| Stockholders' Equity | | |
| Common stock, $.10 par value: | | |
| Authorized—500.0 shares | | |
| Outstanding—196.7 shares (195.9 in 2000) | 19.7 | 19.6 |
| Additional paid-in capital | 83.2 | 64.3 |
| Retained earnings | 1,120.7 | 873.4 |
| Accumulated other comprehensive loss | (167.4) | (102.4) |
| Total stockholders' equity | 1,056.2 | 854.9 |
| | $2,423.6 | $2,430.8 |

*Source:* Stryker's 2001 *Annual Report,* p 35.

**EXHIBIT 3**    Approximate Organization Chart for Stryker Corporation

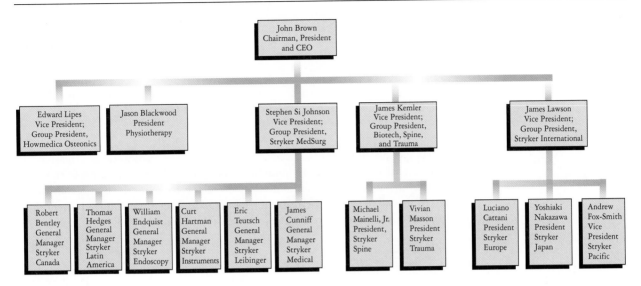

*Source:* Adapted from Stryker Corporation, 2001 *Annual Report.*

impaired) and rheumatoid arthritis (a disease that destroys cartilage at the joint's surface). Orthopedic research has led to the development of a broad array of prosthetic equipment and related devices, including digital cameras. Recent innovations include porous hip and knee replacements, which allow bone to grow directly into the metal implant.

### MedSurg Equipment

The MedSurg (medical and surgical) division has four major components: Stryker Endoscopy, Stryker Instruments, Stryker Leibenger, and Stryker Medical. With sales of $978 million in 2001, this division accounted for 39 percent of Stryker's sales. Each MedSurg unit competes against medical equipment subsidiaries of large firms (e.g., DePuy of Johnson & Johnson, Hill-Rom of Hillenbrand Industries) as well as independent firms, such as Biomet, Midas Rex, U.S. Surgical, and Zimmer.

#### Stryker Endoscopy

This division makes a broad range of medical video imaging equipment and instruments for arthroscopy and general surgery. In an endoscopic (less invasive) surgical procedure, the surgeon removes or repairs damaged tissue through several small punctures rather than through an open incision. Patients experience reduced trauma and pain, less time in the hospital, and a quicker return to health. Less invasive removal of the gallbladder requires a single day in the hospital, followed by a week of convalescence. Traditional gallbladder surgery, by contrast, meant four to eight days in the hospital and a month's convalescence.

Imaging technology plays a crucial role in endoscopic procedures. Stryker is a leader in medical video imaging systems. Through pioneering engineering work, Stryker miniaturized a three-chip video camera (with a separate computer chip for each primary color) and became the first company to offer the surgeon a broadcast-quality image. This division also makes digital cameras to assist with endoscopic procedures.

*Stryker Instruments*

This division produces a wide range of operating room equipment that is utilized primarily in orthopedic procedures, such as bone saws and drills. It is a market leader for battery-powered heavy-duty surgical instruments. Its Stryker 940 cast removal system is the newest version of Dr. Stryker's original cast cutter.

*Stryker Leibenger*

Stryker Leibenger is a leading maker of surgical instruments and products primarily used for head, neck, and hand surgery. Its headquarters are in Germany.

*Stryker Medical*

It produces specialty stretchers and beds, which facilitate the transportation, transfer, and treatment of patients within the hospital. It has designed a line of innovative stretchers as a result of a close analysis of hospital needs, focusing on reducing the number of patient transfers (from bed to stretcher to operating table and back again) that must be performed in a hospital. It also produces accessories such as bedside stands and overbed tables.

## Physiotherapy Associates

The Physiotherapy Associates division operates outpatient rehabilitation centers in over twenty states and the District of Columbia. Following orthopedic or neurological injury, the centers provide physical, occupational, and speech therapy to help speed a patient's return to work or full activity. With sales of $147 million in 2000, this division accounted for 6 percent of Stryker's sales. In the outpatient physical therapy market, Stryker's principal competitors are independent practices and hospital-based services. Competition is also provided by national rehabilitation companies such as HealthSouth, NovaCare/RCI, and Rehability.

## Stryker Spine

Stryker Spine is a new division that provides both implants and instruments to assist in the repair of the human spine. An estimated ten thousand spinal injuries occur each year in the United States, nearly half of which are related to automobile and motorcycle accidents. About one-third of all spine procedures are fusions, in which surgeons seek to stop painful motion in the back by fusing unstable vertebrae. The spinal market is estimated to be in excess of $1 billion, and it is growing at a rate of 20 percent per year.

## INTERNATIONAL OPERATIONS

In the early 1990s, Stryker sought to improve the distribution of its products internationally by investing in Matsumoto, the largest Japanese distributor of orthopedic, general surgery, and emergency care products. In addition to Stryker products, Matsumoto also distributed devices from other leading American and European medical device makers. Shortly after Stryker took a majority ownership position in Matsumoto in 1995, several medical instrument companies stopped distributing through Matsumoto because they felt uncomfortable with Stryker's majority stake. As a result, Matusmoto saw sales of non-Stryker products fall by over 50 percent from 1995 to 1996. In 1999, Stryker purchased the remaining shares of Matsumoto stock, bringing its direct ownership to 100 percent. Matsumoto is now called Stryker Japan and accounts for about 13 percent of Stryker's sales. Its major competitor in Japan is Zimmer Holdings, a former Bristol Myers-Squibb unit that had sales of $1.04 billion and net income of $176 million in 2000. Zimmer designs and markets orthopedic products such as reconstructive implants and fracture management devices. Products include the NexGen knee implant series and the Versys system for hips. International sales are about 40 percent of Zimmer's total sales, with Japan accounting for about half of that market.

Stryker Europe and Stryker Pacific (all except Japan) comprise Stryker's other international operations. Segment data on Stryker's international sales is given in Exhibits 4 and 5.

## MANUFACTURING AND R&D

Stryker's manufacturing processes consist primarily of precision machining, metal fabrication, assembly operations, and the investment (precision) casting of cobalt chrome and finishing of cobalt chrome and titanium. The principal raw materials used by the company are stainless steel, aluminum, cobalt chrome, and titanium alloys. In all, purchases from outside sources are about half of the company's total cost of sales.

Many of the company's products and product improvements have been developed internally. The company maintains close working relationships with physicians and medical personnel in hospitals and universities who assist in product research and development. Research and development is under the direct control of the operating divisions, where it can be focused on specific markets. Stryker seeks to obtain patent protection on its products whenever possible. It currently holds over 1,500 patents worldwide on products it has developed.

Twice in the last three years, a Stryker manufacturing facility has been named one of America's best manufacturing plants. In 1998, *Industry Week* named Howmedica Osteonics, located in Allendale, New Jersey, as one of the top ten manufacturing plants in the United States. Then in 2000, the Stryker Instruments manufacturing facility in Kalamazoo, Michigan, was similarly honored by *Industry Week*. All of the plant's workforce participates in self-directed work teams. More than 99 percent of all finished products meet quality requirements at initial inspection, and 98 percent of all deliveries are made on time. Business segment sales are given in Exhibit 6.

## STRYKER'S CORPORATE CULTURE

Since John Brown became CEO, Stryker has developed a distinctive corporate culture that is sometimes described as "a lot like being in the Marine Corps," although senior executives try to downplay that image. Sayings representing Stryker's core beliefs are prominently written on walls in lobbies and cafeterias. One of the most common, "First

EXHIBIT 4    Stryker's Domestic/International and Product Line Sales Information

| | Net Sales (in millions) | | | Percentage Change | |
|---|---|---|---|---|---|
| | *2001* | *2000* | *1999* | *2001/00* | *2000/99* |
| Domestic/international sales | | | | | |
| Domestic | $1,688.4 | $1,408.2 | $1,228.4 | 20% | 15% |
| International | 913.9 | 881.2 | 875.3 | 4 | 1 |
| Total net sales | $2,602.3 | $2,289.4 | $2,103.7 | 14 | 9 |
| Product line sales | | | | | |
| Orthopedic Implants | $1,442.5 | $1,313.0 | $1,248.2 | 10 | 5 |
| MedSurg Equipment | 978.9 | 829.1 | 733.5 | 18 | 13 |
| Physical Therapy Services | 180.9 | 147.3 | 122.0 | 23 | 21 |
| Total net sales | $2,602.3 | $2,289.4 | $2,103.7 | 14 | 9 |

*Source:* Stryker's 2001 *Annual Report,* p. 27.

### EXHIBIT 5    Stryker's Geographic Data

The Company's areas of operation outside of the United States, Japan and Europe principally include the Pacific, Canada, Latin America and the Middle East.

|  | Net Sales | Long-Lived Assets |
|---|---|---|
| **Year ended December 31, 2001** | | |
| United States | $1,688.4 | $ 780.7 |
| Europe | 414.5 | 455.6 |
| Japan | 266.5 | 94.1 |
| Other foreign countries | 232.9 | 39.7 |
|  | $2,602.3 | $1,370.1 |
| **Year ended December 31, 2000** | | |
| United States | $1,408.2 | $ 715.4 |
| Europe | 380.5 | 472.9 |
| Japan | 280.1 | 119.3 |
| Other foreign countries | 220.6 | 42.2 |
|  | $2,289.4 | $1,349.8 |
| **Year ended December 31, 1999** | | |
| United States | $1,228.4 | $ 746.7 |
| Europe | 416.8 | 498.5 |
| Japan | 266.7 | 143.1 |
| Other foreign countries | 191.8 | 39.1 |
|  | $2,103.7 | $1,427.4 |

*Source:* Stryker's 2001 *Annual Report,* p. 57.

be best, then be first," refers to the competitive corporate philosophy established by Dr. Stryker that Stryker should first make the best products and then seek market leadership for those products.

Although there are no time clocks visible in Stryker facilities, employees wear scanning ID cards that keep track of when they arrive for work and when they leave. Lunch time is restricted to thirty minutes, just enough time to eat in the company cafeteria. Given the pressure of the 20 percent annual increase in earnings-per-share goal, the workweek for white collar workers is typically between fifty and sixty hours. It is common for executives to work evenings or on weekends. In return for their hard work ethic, employees are encouraged to share in the company's prosperity through a generous stock purchase plan. Employees can contribute up to 14 percent of their earnings to purchase Stryker stock. The company will match the first 8 percent contributed by the employees. None of the company's employees are covered by collective bargaining agreements.

Most of the company's products are marketed in the United States directly to more than 7,500 hospitals and to doctors and other healthcare facilities. The company maintains dedicated sales forces for each of its principal product lines to provide focus and a high level of expertise to each medical speciality served. The domestic sales force is compensated in large part by commissions. According to CEO Brown, "The beauty of commissions is there's no cap. The more the individual sells, the more he makes. The most ambitious and driven salespeople thrive in a commission environment." Stryker has been referred to as a "salesperson's paradise," where top performers can earn $200,000 or more a year. Hourly workers can earn pay increases or bonuses for meeting quality objectives. Nevertheless, some employees find Stryker's growth-oriented culture to be too demanding and leave to work for other companies.

# EXHIBIT 6     Stryker's Sales and Other Financial Information by Business Segment

| | Orthopedic Implants | MedSurg Equipment | Other | Total |
|---|---|---|---|---|
| **Year ended December 31, 2001** | | | | |
| Net sales | $1,442.5 | $978.9 | $180.9 | $2,602.3 |
| Interest income | — | — | 2.2 | 2.2 |
| Interest expense | — | — | 67.9 | 67.9 |
| Depreciation and amortization expense | 129.6 | 34.6 | 7.8 | 172.0 |
| Acquisition-related and restructuring charges (credits) | 0.8 | (0.2) | – | 0.6 |
| Income taxes (credit) | 111.1 | 54.5 | (31.7) | 133.9 |
| Segment earnings (loss) before extraordinary item | 197.7 | 115.5 | (41.4) | 271.8 |
| Extraordinary loss, net of income taxes | — | – | (4.8) | (4.8) |
| Segment net earnings (loss) | 197.7 | 115.5 | (46.2) | 267.0 |
| Total assets | 1,737.6 | 574.6 | 111.4 | 2,423.6 |
| Capital expenditures | 133.5 | 21.6 | 6.8 | 161.9 |
| **Year ended December 31, 2000** | | | | |
| Net sales | 1,313.0 | 829.1 | 147.3 | 2,289.4 |
| Interest income | — | — | 4.1 | 4.1 |
| Interest expense | — | — | 96.6 | 96.6 |
| Depreciation and amortization expense | 132.8 | 29.6 | 6.2 | 168.6 |
| Acquisition-related and restructuring charges (credits) | (1.8) | 0.5 | 0.3 | (1.0) |
| Income taxes (credit) | 112.7 | 50.5 | (49.3) | 113.9 |
| Segment net earnings (loss) | 174.1 | 103.4 | (56.5) | 221.0 |
| Total assets | 1,739.1 | 588.2 | 103.5 | 2,430.8 |
| Capital expenditures | 56.5 | 19.1 | 5.1 | 80.7 |
| **Year ended December 31, 1999** | | | | |
| Net sales | 1,248.2 | 733.5 | 122.0 | 2,103.7 |
| Interest income | — | — | 4.2 | 4.2 |
| Interest expense | — | — | 122.6 | 122.6 |
| Depreciation and amortization expense | 128.2 | 29.1 | 5.5 | 162.8 |
| Additional cost of sales for inventory stepped-up to fair value | 170.6 | 27.6 | — | 198.2 |
| Acquisition-related and restructuring charges | 9.5 | 9.4 | — | 18.9 |
| Income taxes (credit) | 43.9 | 21.8 | (55.3) | 10.4 |
| Segment net earnings (loss) | 30.8 | 68.0 | (79.4) | 19.4 |
| Total assets | 1,916.5 | 559.1 | 104.9 | 2,580.5 |
| Capital expenditures | 48.3 | 23.5 | 4.6 | 76.4 |

*Source:* Stryker's 2001 *Annual Report,* p. 56.

A manager at Stryker Instruments made the following connection between Stryker's culture and its success: "There is nothing particularly special about what we do from a manufacturing standpoint, in comparison to our competitors. The difference is in our culture. We aren't the only smart guys out there, but we do have the most highly defined, tangibly strong culture. And that is what, above all, we need to protect."

## THE FUTURE

Stryker has prospered for more than twenty years under the direction of John Brown. Despite its past success, Stryker may find it increasingly difficult to make its target of 20 percent earnings growth every year. First, most of Stryker's major markets have shown annual growth rates of 5 percent or less over the last few years. This means Stryker's divisions need to grow more rapidly than the market segments in which they compete in order to meet the 20-percent-per-year growth goal. Second, mergers and acquisitions within the healthcare sector will probably continue at a rapid pace. This could lead to the emergence of larger and more powerful buying groups, such as Novation, that could put increased pressure on the suppliers of medical equipment, such as Stryker, to reduce the cost of their products. Third, Stryker faces a nimble new competitor in Zimmer, recently spun off from Bristol-Myers Squibb. Zimmer competes directly with Stryker in many of its product lines in the United States and abroad. Finally, employees may tire of the high-pressure Stryker culture and look for less stressful jobs with other companies.

Stryker does have some opportunities available to it to help make its growth goals. One opportunity is to use its strong financial position to continue making selected acquisitions to enter new markets, as it did when it entered the trauma business in 1996 with its acquisition of Osteo Holdings; or it can increase its share of existing markets, as it did with its 1998 acquisition of Howmedica. A second opportunity for growth is to add centers to its Physical Therapy Services division. Each center averages $400,000 in revenue per year. A third opportunity would be to place increased emphasis on Stryker Biotech, its corporate research and development laboratory. One of its promising products is Stryker's OP-1 bone growth protein, designed to help with difficult-to-heal fractures and spinal fusions. OP-1 has been under development for several years and is awaiting Food and Drug Administration (FDA) approval.

Stryker has seen many changes as it has grown from a $23 million company when John Brown became CEO to over $2.6 billion in sales today. It will probably see as many more in the next twenty years. However, as long as John Brown is CEO, one aspect of the Stryker culture that isn't likely to change is the expectation that every employee will do his or her best to help earnings increase 20 percent a year, every year.

## QUESTIONS

- How much longer can John Brown realistically expect its sales and earnings per share to continue to grow at 20 percent every year now that Stryker's sales are more than $2 billion?
- Should salary be a component of the compensation system for the sales force?
- Should Stryker soften the no nonsense corporate culture it has developed under John Brown?
- Are adequate steps being taken to identify a successor for John Brown when he retires?
- Would a merger with Zimmer be in Stryker's best interests?

## REFERENCES

Brewer, Geoffrey. "20 Percent—Or Else!" *Sales and Marketing Management* (November 1994): 67–72.

Purdum, Traci. "Employee Involvement Contributes to Rapid Productivity Gains at Surgical-Tool Maker," *Industry Week* (October 16, 2000): 109–110.

Royal, Weld. "America's Best Plants: Stryker Corporation, Allendale, N.J.," *Industry Week* (October 19, 1998): 72–74.

Willis, Clint. "Super Chiefs: Six CEOs Who Consistently Make Companies Great and Investors Wealthy," *Worth* (September 1997): 60.

# BIOMET, INC.—2002[1]

Satish P. Deshpande
Western Michigan University

BMET

www.biomet.com

On September 11, 2001, the world witnessed one perhaps the most devastating attacks ever on the United States. The terrorist attacks in New York and Washington, D.C., delivered a stunning blow to an already deteriorating U.S. economy. Equities lost $1.2 trillion in value in the immediate aftermath of the tragedy. One of the sectors that many investors are looking at as a safe haven to invest their money is the healthcare sector, an industry relatively impervious to a slowing economy.

Biomet, Inc. operates in the musculoskeletal products business segment of the healthcare sector which is a $6.445 billion product market in the United States (see Exhibit 1). The company is a specialty manufacturer, designer, and marketer of orthopedic products, including reconstructive and fixation devices, electrical bone growth stimulators, orthopedic support devices, operating room supplies, general surgical instruments, and arthroscopy products. Biomet has its corporate headquarters in Warsaw, Indiana, and manufacturing facilities in eighteen worldwide locations. The company and its subsidiaries distribute products primarily aimed at musculoskeletal medical specialists who work in the fields of both surgical and nonsurgical therapy in over one hundred countries, and it employs over forty-four hundred people worldwide.

Biomet reported record sales for its fiscal year ending May 31, 2001. For the fiscal year 2001, sales increased 12 percent to $1.03 billion. This includes the impact of foreign currency fluctuations and discontinued products, which reduced sales by $31.4 million and $9.3 million respectively. Net income increased 14 percent to $197.5 million. Revenues reflect the continued market penetration of the reconstructive, fixation, spinal, and other product lines of the company. The fourth quarter of fiscal year 2001 was Biomet's sixteenth consecutive quarter of 15 percent or greater growth in earnings.

Orthopedic implant manufacturers have faced increasing pressure to contain their costs as hospitals seek various ways to limit expensive inventories. Burdensome regulations, expensive product liability, and managed care have led many manufacturers to develop and manufacture their products abroad. On the other hand, the Food and Drug Administration (FDA) has come under increasing public and political pressure to speed up the approvals of drugs and medical devices. In Senate hearings, the FDA has been attacked for failing to provide timely access to new medical technology. Congressional leaders in the past have called for privatization of the governmental agency. The federal government in response has announced a number of steps to ease restrictions. These are positive signals for Biomet.

## HISTORY

Biomet, Inc. was incorporated in 1977 in Indiana by Dane A. Miller, Niles L. Noblitt, Jerry Ferguson, and Ray Harroff. Miller is president and chief executive officer of Biomet, and Mr. Noblitt is board chairman. Miller, as well as several other key managers, worked at the Zimmer Division of Bristol-Myers before forming their own company.

The company initially sold orthopedic support products through ten distributors. Biomet entered the reconstructive device market in the early 1980s when it introduced a titanium alloy-based hip system. Biomet further enhanced its reputation with a number of technological advances in hip replacement systems as well as in a total knee replacement. Biomet was founded on the premise that major orthopedic companies, which were primarily divisions of large pharmaceutical companies, had neglected a service orientation approach to orthopedic surgeons' needs. Through a dedication to high levels of service and a variety of innovative products, Biomet has rapidly penetrated the growing market for orthopedic products.

In 1992, Biomet purchased Walter Lorenz Surgical Instruments, Inc. (Lorenz Surgical) for $19 million. Lorenz Surgical, based in Jacksonville, Florida, was a leading marketer of oral-maxillofacial products used by oral surgeons. Its product offerings include orthognathic instruments (used for jaw alignment), craniofacial instruments (used to treat severe skull deformities), rigid fixation systems, TMJ instruments, exodontial instruments, and a transmandibular implant system. These products were principally used to correct deformities, to assist in the repair of trauma fractures, and for cosmetic applications.

In 1994, Biomet purchased Kirschner Medical Corporation of Maryland for $38.9 million ($13.3 million over the fair value). Kirschner, as does Biomet, produced joint replacements for hips, knees, and shoulders, along with fracture fixation products. Kirschner was a market leader in shoulder implants. Kirschner also produced braces, supports, splints, and cast materials. It had four manufacturing plants in the United States and one in Spain. During fiscal year 1996, Kirschner's orthopedic operations were consolidated into Biomet, eliminating duplicative administrative and overhead expenses. During the same period, Biomet Europe was established to coordinate manufacturing, development, and sales activities in Europe. In early 1998, Biomet entered into a joint venture agreement with Merck KgaA, a pharmaceutical and chemical company located in Darmstadt, Germany. Under this agreement, both companies joined their European orthopedic and biomaterials business operations to form Biomet Merck. Biomet also formed an alliance with Selective Genetics, Inc. during the fourth quarter of fiscal year 1999 to develop gene therapy products for the musculoskeletal market.

In late 1999, Biomet acquired Implant Innovation Inc ("3i"), a worldwide leader in the dental reconstructive implant market in a stock-for-stock exchange in which 7.8 million shares were issued for all issued and outstanding shares of 3i. Subsequently in late 2000, Biomet, through its subsidiary EBI, acquired Biolectron, Inc. for $90 million in cash. Biolectron's products are aimed at the spinal fusion, fracture healing, and arthroscopy markets.

Today, 60 percent of the company's business is in reconstructive devices, and almost 75 percent of the company's business is domestic. Biomet consists of six different strategic business units, encompassing over fifteen hundred sales representatives worldwide. They are:

- **Biomet-Warsaw,** which is the principal strategic business unit in the United States. The product line includes a comprehensive line of reconstructive devices and internal fixation devices. Products are sold through a 451-person, distributor-based sales network.

- **Arthrotek,** which is the company's sports medicine division. Arthrotek offers a complete line of arthroscopy products, including resorbable arthroscopic fixation products. These products are primarily distributed through two hundred Biomet/ Arthrotek sales outlets representing sixty-four independent distributorships.

- **Electro-Biology, Inc.** (EBI), which is the market leader in the electrical stimulation and external fixation market segments. EBI also offers products in the spinal and orthopedic support market segments. Its products are sold through the division's direct 422-person sales force.

- **Lorenz Surgical**, which is a pioneer in the craniomaxillofacial market segment. The Lorenz product line includes the industry's first resorbable craniomaxillofacial fixation system. Its products are sold through its own distributor network, which encompasses ninety independent sales representatives in the United States.

- **Implant Innovations, Inc.**, which is the second largest manufacturer in the $250 million domestic market and the third largest competitor in the $740 million worldwide market for dental reconstructive implants. Its products in the United States are sold through 52 direct sales representatives. In international markets, 3i distributes its products through approximately 50 direct sales representatives and 24 independent distributors.

- **BioMer C.V.**, which is a 50/50 joint venture between Biomet, Inc. and Merck KGaA, a German chemical and pharmaceutical company. The partnership significantly expands Biomet's presence in the European marketplace while providing the company with worldwide access to key biomaterials technologies. A direct sales force of 396 sales representatives and 56 service agencies throughout Europe sells the joint product lines.

## COMPETITORS

Two major changes took place in the orthopedic industry at the end of 1998. In November 1998, Johnson & Johnson acquired DePuy, Inc., and in December 1998, Stryker Corp. acquired Howmedica, Inc. As shown in Exhibit 1, the 2001 musculoskeletal products market in the United States is estimated to be nearly $6.445 billion. Reconstructive devices make up nearly 40 percent of the orthopedic market. Exhibit 2 provides detailed information on the reconstructive market in the United States. This $2.52 billion market segment includes total hip, knee, and shoulder replacements. The hip market is estimated to be $1.08 billion and is growing 10 to 12 percent annually. The $1.34 billion knee market is estimated to be growing at an annual rate of 12 to 14 percent. The shoulder market is estimated around $70 million, with an 8 percent annual growth rate.

According to Exhibit 3, Johnson & Johnson/DePuy and Stryker/Howmedica are the leaders in the reconstructive field, with each controlling around 23 percent of the market. Zimmer is the third-largest and Biomet is the fourth-largest participant, with a share of 14 percent of the market. Growth in the reconstructive market has been attributed to better products and techniques that improve surgical outcomes, cost-effective techniques, and demographics. Recent products last longer and require less surgical time in the operating room, thereby lowering costs. People today are living longer, which accounts for the expanded patient pool. Life expectancies have increased by approximately 5 percent over the past two decades. Male life expectancy has increased to 71 years, while female life expectancy has increased to 78 years. Of the estimated 37 million Americans who suffer from arthritis, approximately 14 million of them (38 percent) are between the ages of 45 and 64. A more active lifestyle, according to Biomet officials, has led to joint replacement at younger ages. Likewise, the pool of people 75 and over is increasing. Clearly, demographics are favorable for Biomet.

The general population growth rate from 1989 to 2010 is projected to be only 14 percent. But the 55–74 year sector is expected to grow 40 percent between 1997 and 2010, an increase of 16 million people. The over-75 population is expected to

EXHIBIT 1    2001 U.S. Musculoskeletal Products Market $6.445 billion
(Biomet estimates in millions)

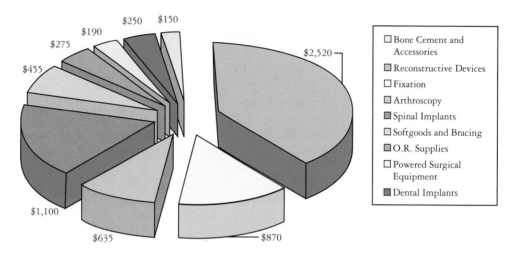

- Bone Cement and Accessories
- Reconstructive Devices
- Fixation
- Arthroscopy
- Spinal Implants
- Softgoods and Bracing
- O.R. Supplies
- Powered Surgical Equipment
- Dental Implants

*Source:* Biomet 2001 *Annual Report.*

grow by 16 percent to 18 million people over the same period. The over 65 population segment accounts for more than two-thirds of total healthcare expenditures. Competition in the implant market is based primarily on service and product design, while competition in the sale of generic internal fixation devices tends to be based more on price. Purchasing decisions for hospitals are being made increasingly through buying groups that are able to negotiate price discounts from the manufacturers.

Two additional factors squeezing profits are (1) the higher utilization of lower-priced implants for the elderly, who require less functionality and longevity of implants; and (2) the fact that surgeons are becoming more cooperative with hospital administrators and are narrowing their choices of products, thereby allowing hospitals to deal with fewer manufacturers.

EXHIBIT 2    2001 U.S. Orthopedic Reconstructive Products Market
$2.52 billion (Biomet estimates in millions)

- Shoulders
- Hips
- Knees
- Other

*Source:* Biomet 2001 *Annual Report.*

## EXHIBIT 3    2001 U.S. Reconstructive Device Market Shares $2.52 billion

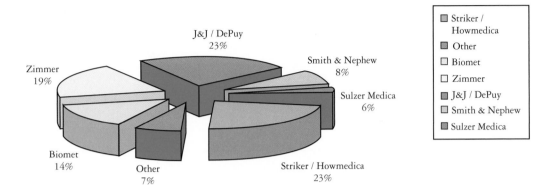

*Source:* Biomet 2001 *Annual Report.*

## PRODUCTS

Biomet's products are divided into four groups: Reconstructive Products, Fixation Products, Spinal Products, and Other Products. Exhibit 4 gives sales by product group for three fiscal years ended May 31: 1999, 2000, and 2001.

### Reconstructive Products

Biomet's net sales of reconstructive devices worldwide increased around 6 percent during fiscal year 2001 to more than $614 million. These devices replace joints that have deteriorated either from diseases such as arthritis or through injury. Reconstructive joint surgery involves modification of the area surrounding the affected joint and insertion of one or more manufactured joint components. Biomet's primary reconstructive products concern the hip, knee, and shoulder, although the company can produce peripheral joints for the wrist, elbow, finger, or large toe. A hip prosthesis consists of a femoral head, neck, and stem manufactured in a variety of head sizes, neck lengths, stem lengths, and configurations. Hip sales are expected to increase by 20 percent in the United States and 12 percent worldwide in first quarter of 2002 (fiscal year 2002). The $M^2a$ Taper Metal-on-Metal Articulation System, specially designed for young active patients, continues to experience increased market acceptance in the United States. The minimally invasive Repicci II Unicondylar Knee and the Ascent Total Knee System drive Biomet's market-leading knee performance in the United States. In addition, the AGC Total Knee System was introduced in 1983 and has shown excellent long-term clinical results. The product features left and right femoral components, matching tibial components, and appropriately sized patella components for resurfacing. Biomet's various major knee systems, with their variety of options, are one of the most versatile and comprehensive available in the orthopedic market. Knee sales are expected to increase by 18 percent in the United States and 19 percent worldwide in the first quarter of 2002. Biomet has also a Patient-Matched-Implant (PMI) services group, which designs, manufactures, and delivers one-of-a-kind reconstructive and trauma devices for orthopedic surgeons. The company acquired a patent in 1990 that allows a physician to create, prior to surgery (through the use of CT or MRI data), electronic 3-D models that are then translated into a PMI design for manufacture.

EXHIBIT 4    Biomet's Sales of Reconstructive Devices
Years Ended May 31 (dollar amounts in thousands)

|  | 2001 | | 2000 | | 1999 | |
|---|---|---|---|---|---|---|
|  | *Net Sales* | *Percent of Net Sales* | *Net Sales* | *Percent of Net Sales* | *Net Sales* | *Percent of Net Sales* |
| Reconstructive Products | 614,308 | 60% | 580,239 | 63% | 521,365 | 63% |
| Fixation Products | 202,152 | 20% | 180,336 | 20% | 162,825 | 20% |
| Spinal Products | 91,103 | 9% | 54,119 | 6% | 45,125 | 5% |
| Other Products | 123,100 | 12% | 108,857 | 12% | 101,520 | 12% |
| Total | 1,030,663 | 100% | 923,551 | 100% | 830,835 | 100% |

*Source:* Biomet 2001 *Annual Report.*

## Fixation Products

Every year, around 7 million fractures occur in the United States. The 2001 fixation market was estimated to be $870 million, and it is growing at an estimated 7 percent per year. It includes products used to stabilize broken bones and to promote healing. Biomet's net sales in this market increased by around 12 percent to $202 million. EBI is a market leader in both the $140 million external fixation market segment (30 percent of the U.S. market) and the $135 million electrical stimulation market (70 percent of the U.S. market).

External fixation is typically used to immobilize fractured bones when traditional casting is not an option. The company introduced several new products recently, including the OptiROM Elbow Fixator, the Vision System Components, the prepackaged sterile Wristfix Distal Radius Fixator, and deformity clamps for the DynaFix Rail System.

The EBI Model Bone Healing System continues to be a market leader in the domestic electrical simulation market. This product is used on fractured bones that do not heal using normal methods. A coil connected to a battery-operated treatment unit is placed on the fracture. The system produces a pulsating electromagnetic field (PEMF) which affects the cells. Since the system is noninvasive, it poses no surgical risks and has no known side effects. The company introduced a compact version of the system during fiscal year 1998 and a lighter, more patient-friendly model in 2000. The acquisition of Biolectron, Inc. helped EBI broaden and improve its already strong product line.

With a nearly 22 percent share of the U.S. market, the company's Lorenz Surgical subsidiary is a market leader in the $130 million craniomaxillofacial fixation market. The LactoSorb Craniomaxillofacial Fixation System consists of a copolymer comparable in strength to existing titanium systems, but it is completely resorbed within nine to twelve months. This system is especially beneficial for pediatric surgical procedures, since it eliminates the need for a second surgery to remove plates and screws. During fiscal 2001, Lorenz Surgical introduced eight new products and three product enhancements to the resorbable product lines. But Biomet only has a small share of the $390 million internal fixation market.

Until 1995, Biomet held the exclusive right with Orthofix of Italy to distribute the Orthofix External Fixation System (OEFS) in the United States, which is used in trauma situations in which the bone has been fractured or crushed in many places. This system essentially allows the physician to hold in place complicated fractures of long bones when casts, rods, or plates are inappropriate. This exclusive distribution right expired in 1995. In early fiscal 1996, Biomet successfully launched the Dynafix external fixation system. On June 2, 1997, Biomet announced that it would appeal a jury verdict that was entered against it in U.S. District Court for the District of New Jersey in an action brought by Orthofix SRL against EBI and Biomet concerning events related to the expiration of the distribution agreement. The jury found that in spite of Orthofix's refusal to renew the agreement, EBI's development of the Dynafix system prior to the expiration of the contract constituted a breach of the distribution agreement. The jury awarded Orthofix $49 million in compensatory damages and $100 million in punitive damages. The jury also ruled that Orthofix breached the distribution agreement and tortiously interfered with EBI's economic relations. But only nominal damages were awarded to EBI. On June 30, 1999, Biomet announced that the appellate court virtually eliminated $50 million in punitive damages assessed against the company, which thus reduced the judgment to $49.9 million plus interest. Accordingly, Biomet recorded a $55 million special charge against pretax earnings for the quarter and year ended May 31, 1999. In 2000, the company recorded a $9 million charge to reflect the final determination of the interest element of the case.

In 2001, the company took a special charge of $26.1 million due to an appellate court's decision in the Tronzo case. The underlying dispute between Dr. Tronzo and Biomet had to do with a medical device, called an "acetabular cup," that forms the upper portion of a hip implant. Dr. Tronzo alleged that he had established a confidential relationship with Biomet for the purpose of bringing his acetabular cup design to market and that Biomet was to pay him for his invention if he could successfully obtain a patent on his invention. Dr. Tronzo claimed that Biomet failed to compensate him and, instead, took his ideas and incorporated them into its highly successful Mallory/Head cup design.

## Spinal Products

The U.S. spinal implant market is estimated to be $1.1 billion (see Exhibit 1). This fastest growing segment of the musculoskeletal products market is growing at least at 20 percent annually. Back injuries cost the society nearly $16 billion every year. Over 2 million spinal procedures were performed worldwide in 2000. Nearly half of the more than three hundred thousand vertebral fusion procedures performed in the United States every year utilize some type of instrumentation. Spinal sales increased 70 percent to $91 million during 2001. This included a 55 percent increase in spinal implant sales and a 90 percent increase in spinal stimulation sales. Currently, EBI is the fourth largest participant, with nearly 9 percent of the spinal implant market in the United States. EBI is a major player in the $155 million electrical segment of the spinal market. It also has a growing presence in the $475 million plates, screws, and rods segment. Its leading product is the SpF Spinal Fusion Stimulation System. This system uses cathodes to deliver small electrical currents to facilitate successful spinal fusions. The Biolectron acquisition provided EBI with the SpinalPak noninvasive simulation system, which offers surgeons a patient-friendly device for noninvasive stimulation.

## Other Products

Biomet's "other product" sales during fiscal 2001 were approximately $123 million. This was a 13 percent increase in the United States over the previous fiscal year. This was in great part due to Arthrotek's arthroscopy products, EBI's line of soft goods and bracing products, and the introduction of the CurvTek Bone Tunneling System.

## OPERATIONS

### Research and Development

Biomet has spent nearly $122 million on research and development from 1999–2001. A number of biomaterials projects are in progress, and they address issues like designing better implants for various applications and bone substitute materials and cements. The company is placing more emphasis on finding ways to help the body heal itself naturally. In addition, its alliance with Selective Genetics, Inc., a gene therapy company, will give it access to its technology for orthopedic indications such as spinal fusions, fracture repair, bone void filling, and tendon and ligament repair. Preclinical studies have been promising.

### International Operations

Biomet manages its business segments primarily on a geographic basis. These segments are comprised of the United States, Europe, and the category labeled "Others" (Canada, South America, Mexico, Japan, and the Pacific Rim). Biomet evaluates performance based on the operating income of each geographic unit. Exhibit 5 shows the performance of each segment. The U.S. net sales in Exhibit 5 include U.S. export sales of $37 million in 2001, $50 million in 2000, and $49 million in 1999. The decline in U.S. exports in 2001 has been attributed by the company to its acquisition of foreign distributors and a changeover to direct representation in various countries like Japan and Korea. Net sales to customers in Europe and in the "Others" category in 2001 increased 4 percent to $271 million from the previous level of $261 million in 2000.

Biomet Merck provides Biomet with the exclusive rights to Merck KGaA's current and future biomaterials-based products. Currently, with a local presence in all the major markets, it is the fourth largest orthopedic company in Europe, with 9 percent of Europe's $3.03 billion musculoskeletal market. This is partly due to the successful integration of Biomet's and Merck KGaA's operations. Currently, the joint venture has a revenue of nearly $270 million and 1,360 employees.

### Management Philosophy

Biomet prides, itself on having "the responsiveness and innovation of a small company, with the resources and market presence of a large company." In the absence of a formal vision statement, the phrase "The most responsive company in orthopedics" could be seen as an informal vision statement. On its Web site (**www.biomet.com/investors/faq.cfm**), Biomet explicitly states that it has no written mission statement. But the following statement, based on information in its annual report, may act as a mission statement:

> *The Biomet team is committed to the compassionate care of patients throughout the world. We do this by connecting, building, and nurturing long-term relationships with our customers and patients that allows us to deliver technologically advanced quality products with unsurpassed service. We are also committed to ensure that our team members have the best technology, educational tools, resources, and work environment in the industry. We believe that by connecting people, ideas, technology, products, and service, we provide a network that is critical to our patients and customers; and ultimately to the future success of the company.*

### Team Biomet

According to CEO Dane Miller, who ranks fourth out of 278 Forbes 500 CEOs in Forbes.com's First Annual Best Value Bosses list (**www.forbes.com/2001/04/26/ ceoindex.html**), the major reasons for the success of Biomet are: "(1) We remain close to the market and listen to the needs of our customers, (2) We function as a team to get the job done, and (3) Our team has creative and innovative members in place to succeed." The team concept started at Biomet in 1977 and is today an integral part of the firm's philosophy. One characteristic of the concept is that Biomet has decentralized decision making so that decisions can be made at the appropriate level. Teams are composed of employees from several functional areas (e.g., design, manufacturing, quality, and

EXHIBIT 5    Biomet's Sales by Geographic Area (in thousands)

|  | 2001 | 2000 | 1999 |
|---|---|---|---|
| **NET SALES:** | | | |
| United States | $  759,465 | $662,146 | $597,336 |
| Europe | 239,136 | 236,047 | 215,913 |
| Other | 32,062 | 25,358 | 17,586 |
|  | $1,030,663 | $923,551 | $830,835 |
| **OPERATING INCOME:** | | | |
| United States | $  251,927 | $224,385 | $159,716 |
| Europe | 34,772 | 34,841 | 22,910 |
| Other | 3,988 | 4,448 | 3,276 |
|  | $  290,687 | $263,674 | $185,902 |
| **LONG-LIVED ASSETS:** | | | |
| United States | $  204,231 | $129,978 | $121,363 |
| Europe | 109,758 | 121,350 | 113,719 |
| Other | 17,640 | 5,635 | 4,723 |
|  | $  331,629 | $256,963 | $239,805 |

*Source:* Biomet, Inc., *Biomet Inc., and Subsidiaries Notes to Consolidated Financial Statements,* 2001 *Annual Report.*

production planning). Physically, employees are located by functional areas within the facility where routine decisions are handled. Only those decisions related to large commitments of capital expenditures or changes in strategic policies require presidential or vice presidential signatures.

Communications between subsidiaries and departments is frequent and open. Members of management interact with the workers on a daily basis, in addition, there are many corporate events that foster camaraderie. When Dane Miller and his colleagues started the company, his goal was to "create an organization that could grow unencumbered by the bureaucratic structures and conservatism that [we believed] stifle initiative and creativity at many large firms." Although Miller and his colleagues keep an open door for employees, they are constantly on the shop floor talking to employees in their work setting. The team concept is stressed in company brochures and meetings. There are a Biomet Team Appreciation Day and company picnics, Christmas parties, and other special events. The quarterly in-house publication *Bio Briefs* serves as an effective communication tool to keep employees informed of corporate and product information, as well as to recognize special events such as promotions, birthdays, births, anniversaries, and so on.

Biomet's team concept offers every employee financial incentives including cash bonuses, company shares, and stock options. Insiders own approximately 17 percent of the outstanding stock. The team concept also extends to the medical profession. When patients face unusual circumstances, Biomet officials are often called upon to design specialty products. Biomet enjoys a healthy reputation in the medical profession for its "team effort." This concept, first announced in 1989, is reinforced in daily operations. In the absence of a formal organization chart, Exhibit 6 recommends an organizational chart based on titles of the officers of Biomet, Inc., which are reported in the company's Web page.

Financial Information

Consolidated financial information is given in Exhibits 7 and 8.

**EXHIBIT 6** Organizational Chart

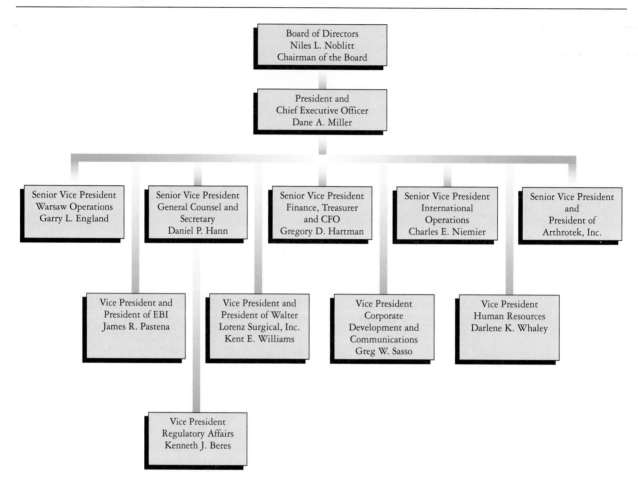

*Source:* Adapted from Information in Biomet's 2001 *Annual Report.*

## FUTURE

Prices of orthopedic devices in the United States in 2002 are expected to be up 5 percent to 6 percent. In addition, Biomet is expected to benefit from Sulzer Medica's legal problems, all of them related to hip replacement recalls. Biomet will have to continue its strategy of finding a niche such as spinal implants and stimulators and then of dominating it. With $463 million in cash and investments, the company is well positioned to make further business acquisitions. On the other hand, Biomet itself could be a target of a pharmaceutical company such as Novartis or American Home Products that wants to get into the musculoskeletal products market. The company has a Shareholders Rights Plan expiring in 2009 that protects it against any hostile takeover. In the international arena, a strong dollar could hurt U.S. exports. In addition, the company has to come up with initiatives to make an impact in the Japanese market.

## NOTES

1. The author thanks Tarkesh Veecumsee for research assistance.

# EXHIBIT 7    Consolidated Financial Information (in thousands)

## ANNUAL INCOME STATEMENT

| | Period Ending May 31, | | | |
|---|---|---|---|---|
| | 2001 | 2000 | 1999 | 1998 |
| Total Revenue | $1,030,663 | $ 920,582 | $ 757,414 | $651,405 |
| Cost of Revenue | $ 296,063 | $ 278,382 | $ 229,727 | $202,235 |
| Gross Profit | $ 734,600 | $ 642,200 | $ 527,687 | $449,170 |
| Operating Expenses | | | | |
| Research and Development | $ 43,020 | $ 40,208 | $ 35,472 | $ 36,120 |
| Sales, General and Administration | $ 374,793 | $ 326,618 | $ 265,565 | $232,944 |
| Nonrecurring Items | ($26,100) | ($11,700) | ($55,000) | $ 0 |
| Operating Income | $ 290,687 | $ 263,674 | $ 171,650 | $180,106 |
| Additional income/expense items | $ 24,099 | $ 20,211 | $ 15,810 | $ 24,032 |
| Earnings Before Interest and Tax | $ 314,786 | $ 283,885 | $ 187,460 | $204,138 |
| Interest Expense | $ 4,110 | $ 3,193 | $ 1,114 | $ 341 |
| Earnings Before Tax | $ 310,676 | $ 280,692 | $ 186,346 | $203,797 |
| Income Tax | $ 105,906 | $ 99,738 | $ 62,527 | $ 79,071 |
| Minority Interest | ($7,224) | ($7,183) | ($7,458) | $ 0 |
| Net Income—Continuing Operations | $ 197,546 | $ 173,771 | $ 116,361 | $124,726 |
| Net Income | $ 197,546 | $ 173,771 | $ 116,361 | $124,726 |
| Net Income Applicable to Common Shareholders | $ 197,546 | $ 173,771 | $ 116,361 | $124,726 |

## ANNUAL BALANCE SHEET

| | Period Ending May 31, | | | |
|---|---|---|---|---|
| | 2001 | 2000 | 1999 | 1998 |
| Total Current Assets | $ 968,379 | $ 789,628 | $ 681,708 | $570,792 |
| Total Assets | $1,489,311 | $1,218,448 | $1,067,956 | $848,739 |
| Total Liabilities | $ 343,125 | $ 275,125 | $ 292,009 | $181,321 |
| Total Equity | $1,146,186 | $ 943,323 | $ 775,947 | $667,418 |

*Source:* www.biomet.com

EXHIBIT 8    Biomet, Inc. & Subsidiaries Consolidated Balance Sheets
(in thousands, except per-share data)

| | At May 31, | |
| --- | ---: | ---: |
| | 2001 | 2000 |
| **ASSETS** | | |
| Current assets: | | |
| Cash and cash equivalents | $ 235,091 | $ 213,606 |
| Investments | 52,627 | 34,129 |
| Accounts and notes receivable less allowance for doubtful receivables | 324,848 | 249,792 |
| (2001—$13,420 and 2000—$8,241) | | |
| Inventories | 277,601 | 240,162 |
| Deferred and refundable income taxes | 48,982 | 25,811 |
| Prepaid expenses and other | 29,230 | 26,128 |
| Total current assets | 968,379 | 789,628 |
| Property, plant, and equipment: | | |
| Land and improvements | 13,877 | 14,572 |
| Buildings and improvements | 92,459 | 88,103 |
| Machinery and equipment | 219,554 | 196,619 |
| | 325,890 | 299,294 |
| Less, accumulated depreciation | 140,139 | 116,037 |
| Property, plant, and equipment, net | 185,751 | 183,257 |
| Investments | 175,430 | 159,533 |
| Intangible assets, net of accumulated amortization (2001—$23,183 and 2000—$20,580) | 8,848 | 9,100 |
| Excess acquisition costs over fair value of acquired net assets, net of | 134,835 | 60,654 |
| accumulated amortization (2001—$32,952 and 2000—$22,869) | | |
| Other assets | 16,068 | 16,276 |
| Total assets | $1,489,311 | $1,218,448 |
| | | |
| **LIABILITIES & SHAREHOLDERS' EQUITY** | | |
| Current liabilities: | | |
| Short-term borrowings and current maturities of long-term obligations | $ 62,734 | $ 70,546 |
| Accounts payable | 21,008 | 25,612 |
| Accrued income taxes | 31,085 | 17,288 |
| Accrued wages and commissions | 33,030 | 24,224 |
| Accrued litigation | 26,100 | – |
| Other accrued expenses | 67,865 | 43,773 |
| Total current liabilities | 241,822 | 181,443 |
| | | |
| Deferred federal income taxes | 5,783 | 5,386 |
| Other liabilities | 423 | 423 |
| Total liabilities | 248,028 | 187,252 |
| Minority interest | 95,097 | 87,873 |
| Commitments and contingencies | | |
| Shareholders' equity: | | |
| Preferred shares, $100 par value: Authorized 5 shares; none issued | – | – |
| Common shares, without par value: Authorized 500,000 shares; issued | 108,918 | 85,086 |
| and outstanding 2001–269,124 shares and 2000—266,480 shares | | |
| Additional paid-in capital | 48,732 | 41,451 |
| Retained earnings | 1,044,564 | 866,011 |
| Accumulated other comprehensive loss | (56,028) | (49,225) |
| Total shareholders' equity | 1,146,186 | 943,323 |
| Total liabilities and shareholders' equity | $1,489,311 | $1,218,448 |

*Source:* www.biomet.com

# PLAYBOY ENTERPRISES, INC.—2002

**Kay Lawrimore-Belanger**
**Francis Marion University**

PLA

www.playboyenterprises.com

Hugh M. Hefner created the first edition of *Playboy* magazine at his family's kitchen table in 1953, launched the magazine with $600 of his own cash, and created an organization which reported $307.7, $347.8, and $241.2 million in revenue in 1999, 2000, and 2001—in a disturbing downward trend. Headquartered in Chicago, Illinois, Playboy Enterprises, Inc. (PEI), (312-751-8000) is an international multimedia entertainment company that publishes editions of *Playboy* magazine around the globe; operates *Playboy* TV and the *Spice* networks; distributes programming via home video and DVD globally; licenses the *Playboy* and *Spice* trademarks internationally for consumer products; and operates Playboy.com. *This is not your father's Playboy!*

Playboy's current mission statement states:

> Playboy *is a preeminent international media and entertainment company with a worldwide recognized brand and many windows of opportunity to expand the* Playboy *franchise and develop other related entertainment franchises globally by leveraging* Playboy's *strengths of publishing, brand management, and marketing.*

## COMPANY STRATEGY

Christie Hefner, Playboy's CEO, has consistently described the company's strategy as being one of leveraging the magazine brand into the higher-growth, higher-margin electronic entertainment businesses. In 1998, the CEO announced the goal of having a $1 billion market capitalization by 2003, up from the 1998 $423 million.

## MANAGEMENT

In 1971, HMH Publishing Company, Inc. was consolidated under the name Playboy Enterprises, Inc. (PEI) and made its initial public offering at $23.50 per share. Since the beginning, Hugh Hefner has maintained control by holding 70 percent of the voting shares. Christie Hefner, Hugh Hefner's daughter, was named chair of the board and CEO in 1988 at the age of 29. As stated in the September 1999 issue of *Chief Executive*, "Christie didn't have CEO experience when she started, and she tried doing some things that didn't work in terms of bringing in the wrong people and putting people in the wrong places. As she got experience, she also got good at bringing people in who know what they're doing and then letting them alone to do their jobs." Corporate officers included Hugh Hefner as the founder and editor-in-chief; Christie Hefner as the chairman of the board and chief executive officer; Carr as president of the Publishing Group and publisher; English as president of Entertainment Group; Saunders as president of the Casino Gaming Group; Vaickus as president of the Product Marketing Group; and nine others. The executive group officers included the Publishing Group, the Entertainment Group, Playboy Online, the Product Marketing Group, the Casino

Gaming Group, and the Playboy Foundation. None of the approximately 650 employees in its Chicago, New York, and Los Angeles office locations are represented by collective bargaining agreements.

## FINANCIAL STATUS

When Playboy Enterprises, Inc. first went public on the New York Stock Exchange in 1971, its stock certificate featured a reclining nude. Some 20,000 people purchased a single share of PEI stock just to get a copy of the certificate. In June 1990, recapitalization created two classes of stock: PLA, the common nonvoting stock, and PLAA, the voting stock. Both are traded on the New York Stock Exchange and the Pacific Stock Exchange. Although the company's certificates no longer feature a nude female, there were 19.4 million PLA shares and 4.9 million PLAA shares outstanding as of December 31, 2000.

PEI's net revenues in 2001 fell to $291.2 million, and the company posted a net loss of $33.5 million, compared with a $47.6 million loss in 2000.

## ORGANIZATION

The financial statements in Exhibit 1 for PEI indicate five divisions: Publishing, Entertainment, Playboy Online, Catalog, and Licensing Businesses.

### Publishing

The Publishing group includes the publication of *Playboy* magazine, other domestic publishing businesses (including specials, calendars, books, and new media), and the licensing of international editions of *Playboy* magazine. PEI considers *Playboy* magazine to be the "heart and soul" of the company.

The magazine's editorial vitality, diversity, and cultural connection are evident in the fiction, articles, investigative reporting, interviews, celebrity profiles, and entertainment and service features that are monthly staples of the publication. Regular columns on politics, books, movies, music, style, men, women, and relationships reflect contemporary social and cultural issues and further the magazine's ongoing dialogue with its readers. With a paid circulation of about 3.15 million in the United States and about 5 million worldwide, the magazine has maintained its position as the world's leading monthly magazine for men, with a circulation greater than the combined circulations of *Rolling Stone*, *GQ*, and *Esquire*. However, this 3.15 million circulation is about half of what it was in the 1970s. The magazine's revenues were $105 million in the fiscal year ending in June 1997; $105.3 million in June 1996; and $104.4 million in June 1995. The magazine's revenues for the fiscal year ending in December were $106.8 million in 1998, $107.8 million in 1999, and $110.5 million in 2000; and $102.7 million in 2001.

During the 1960s, the magazine relied upon newsstand sales, but now about 70 percent of its total sales are from subscriptions. Direct mail campaigns, online promotions and television advertising campaigns are used to attract new subscribers. The price of a one-year subscription depends on the source of the subscription and the length of time the subscription has been sold. Subscription copies are distributed by second-class mail. Presorting and other methods lower the cost. During October 2001, the online promotion for subscribing was $1 per issue.

# EXHIBIT 1    PEI's Results of Operations

|  | Fiscal Year Ended 12/31/01 |
|---|---|
| **Net revenues** | |
| Entertainment | |
| Domestic TV networks | $ 86.6 |
| International TV | 17.0 |
| Worldwide home video | 9.6 |
| Movies and other | 0.6 |
| Total Entertainment | 113.8 |
| Publishing | |
| Playboy magazine | 102.7 |
| Other domestic publishing | 15.5 |
| International publishing | 9.9 |
| Total Publishing | 128.1 |
| Playboy Online | 27.5 |
| Catalog | 11.0 |
| Licensing Businesses | 10.8 |
| Total net revenues | $291.2 |
| **Net loss** | |
| Entertainment | |
| Before programming expense | $ 67.3 |
| Programming expense | (37.4) |
| Total Entertainment | 29.9 |
| Publishing | 1.8 |
| Playboy Online | (21.7) |
| Catalog | (0.4) |
| Licensing Businesses | 2.6 |
| Corporate Administration and Promotion | (19.7) |
| Total segment income (loss) | (7.5) |
| Restructuring expenses | (3.8) |
| Gain (loss) on disposals | (0.9) |
| Operating income (loss) | (12.2) |
| **Nonoperating income (expense)** | |
| Investment income | 0.8 |
| Interest expense | (14.0) |
| Minority interest | (0.7) |
| Equity in operations of PTVI and other | (0.7) |
| Playboy.com registration statement expenses | — |
| Legal settlement | — |
| Other, net | (1.5) |
| Total nonoperating expense | (16.1) |
| Loss from continuing operations before income taxes and cumulative effect of change in accounting principle | (28.3) |
| Income tax benefit (expense) | (1.0) |
| Loss from continuing operations before cumulative effect of change in accounting principle | (29.3) |
| Gain on disposal of discontinued operations (net of tax) | — |
| Loss before cumulative effect of change in accounting principle | (29.3) |
| Cumulative effect of change in accounting principle (net of tax) | (4.2) |
| Net loss | $ (33.5) |

*(continued)*

EXHIBIT 1    PEI's Results of Operations                         (continued)

| | Fiscal Year Ended 12/31/01 |
|---|---|
| Basic and diluted income (loss) per common share | |
| Income (loss) before cumulative effect of change in accounting principle | |
|    From continuing operations | $(1.20) |
|    From discontinued operations (net of tax) | — |
| Total | (1.20) |
| Cumulative effect of change in accounting principle (net of tax) | (0.17) |
| Net loss | $(1.37) |

*Source*: PEI's 2001 *Annual Report,* pp. 15–17.

The number of issues sold in retail outlets varies from month to month, depending on the cover, the pictorials, and the editorial features. As each issue goes on sale, PEI receives a cash advance based on estimated sales. Retail outlets return unsold issues to wholesalers, who shred the returned magazines and report the returns via affidavit. The national distributor settles with PEI based upon the actual number sold compared to the forecasted number. The 1995 sales were affected by the December issue which featured Farrah Fawcett and set a six-year sales record. Fiscal 1997 did not have a blockbuster issue, and sales fell 10 percent. In 1998, the two top-selling issues featured Cindy Crawford and Olympic gold medal figure skater Katarina Witt. Extraordinary sales for the April 1999 issue were due to its feature on Rena Mero, the World Wrestling Federation champion. The November 2000 issue featured World Wrestling Federation star Chyna, and it was the strongest seller in more than ten years. According to *Crain's New York Business,* PEI is considering launching a Spanish-language version of the magazine for the growing Hispanic market in the United States in 2002.

According to Publishers Information Bureau, total magazine ad revenue for the first half of 2001 dropped 2.9 percent, to $8.0 billion. Over the same period, ad pages for all magazines slipped 11 percent, to 121,772. Five of the twelve major ad categories—technology; retail; media and advertising; financial, insurance, and real estate; and automotive are spending less on advertising. Advertising expenditures declined about 40 percent during 2001 in all media platforms. *Mediaweek Magazine Monitor* reported that for the first eight months of 2001, ads for *Playboy* magazine slipped 6.3 percent, to 340 pages, from the prior year. PEI relies on advertising for less than 10 percent of its revenue; hence, it is less affected by the ad decline than most other magazines in the publishing industry.

To attract advertisers, the U.S. version of *Playboy* magazine is published in fifteen advertising editions: eight regional, two state, four metro, and one upper-income zip-coded edition. Advertising pages peaked at 1,434 in 1988 and declined to 660 in 1993, 595 in 1994 and 1995, and 569 in 1996. (In those years, the fiscal year ended in June.) After 1997, the fiscal year ended on December 31, and the advertising pages were 601 in 1998, 640 in 1999, and 674 in 2000. During 2000, for the top three hundred U.S. magazines, ad pages grew 7.9 percent, and there was a 13 percent growth in ad revenue. *Playboy* magazine reported a 13 percent gain in advertising revenue during 2000. The magazine attracted forty-one new advertisers in 2000, including Datek, ESPN, MGM Samsung, Showtime, THQ, and Toshiba. A significant portion of the advertising revenue comes from companies selling tobacco products. In 1996, the U.S. Food and Drug Administration announced a regulation restricting publication of tobacco advertisements. PEI contends that *Playboy* qualifies as an "adult publication" and is therefore exempt from the regulation.

Net advertising revenues of the U.S. edition of *Playboy* magazine for the fiscal year ended June 30 in 1997, 1996, 1995, 1994, and 1993, respectively, were $28.4 million, $27.4 million, $27.6 million, $28.0 million, and $30.4 million. Advertising revenue for the fiscal year ended December 1998, 1999, and 2000, respectively, was $30.8 million, $33.9 million, and $38.4 million.

### International Publishing

In partnership with other publishing companies, international editions of *Playboy* are produced worldwide. Overseas editions retain the distinctive style, look, and tone of the U.S. edition, and they include the work of the specific nation's writers and artists. During 2000, PEI published these international editions (dates represent the year *Playboy* was first published for these markets): Brazil (1975), Croatia (1997), Czech Republic (1991), France (1973), Germany (1972), Greece (1985), Hungary (1999), Italy (1972), Japan (1975), The Netherlands (1983), Norway (1997), Poland (1992), Romania (1999), Russia (1995), Slovakia (1997), Spain (1978), and Taiwan (1990). PEI has equity interest in only one country, Poland, in which PEI owns a majority interest. Argentina, Australia, Mexico, South Africa, Sweden, and Turkey had been licensed at one time. The terms of licensing vary but typically are for three or five years, have a guaranteed minimum royalty, and apply a formula for computing additional royalty based upon circulation and advertising revenue. Brazil, Germany, and Japan have typically accounted for 55 percent of the licensing revenues from overseas editions.

Christie Hefner says, "There is no cookie cutter for doing business overseas. In some countries, we've found the best way to get in is with small partners who are entrepreneurial." In Russia, the partner is a woman who established the first functional periodical distribution system in Russia and used the distribution system to start a daily paper, a woman's magazine, and then *Playboy*.

### Entertainment—Domestic TV Networks

PEI considers the Entertainment Group to be the company's earnings driver. PEI's growth strategy consists of taking the brand value of *Playboy* and investing in higher-margin, higher-growth electronic businesses. This strategy resulted in an operating loss of $7.3 million in the fiscal year ending June 1995; a profit of $9.2 million in the fiscal year ended in June 1996; a profit of $18.3 million in the fiscal year ending in June 1997; and profits of $26.1 million, $44.37 million, and $25.3 million in the fiscal years ending in December 1998, 1999, and 2000, respectively. PEI's TV network reaches approximately 32 million U.S. and Canadian cable and direct-to-home satellite households. The CEO and chairman of PEI often says that Playboy Enterprises is about being sexy, not primarily about sex. However, the launching of three XXX-edited, digital pay-per-view networks under the *Spice* brand in 2001 and the purchase of three XX-rated pay-per-view video networks for $70 million in July 2001 may indicate that the attitude is shifting to hardcore-porn play.

In 2001, the company acquired the television assets of Califa Entertainment Group, including the explicit Hot Network and the cable-edited adult service, the Hot Zone, for $70 million. Note that investors seemed to like the move because on the day after the announcement, PEI's stock price rose 13 percent to close at $19.75, up $2.25 from the previous close. New Frontier Media, a competitor, rose 3 cents to $2.64. Showtime Event Television reports that the adult pay-per-view market generated about $409 million in 2000, surpassing the $394 million generated by other pay-per-view events.

In 1982, PEI introduced Playboy Television, available only by monthly subscription. The Playboy Networks Worldwide president, Jim English, reported in 2001 that the company had no plans to change the programming or rate card for the networks. PEI is encouraging operators to market a full range of options to consumers: VOD, pay-per-view and subscriptions. In 1999, a twenty-four-hour Spanish-language network was launched within the United States that reaches about 3 million homes on the EchoStar service. Exhibit 2 provides select data concerning cable households.

## EXHIBIT 2    PEI's Consolidated Statements of Operations
(in thousands, except per-share amounts)

| | Fiscal Year Ended 12/31/01 | Fiscal Year Ended 12/31/00 | Fiscal Year Ended 12/31/99 |
|---|---|---|---|
| Net revenues | 291,226 | $307,722 | $347,817 |
| Costs and expenses | | | |
| Cost of sales | (240,691) | (265,369) | (277,448) |
| Selling and administrative expenses | (58,050) | (55,385) | (56,390) |
| Restructuring expenses | (3,776) | (3,908) | (1,091) |
| Gain (loss) on disposals | (955) | (2,924) | 1,728 |
| Total costs and expenses | (303,472) | (327,586) | (333,201) |
| Operating income (loss) | (12,246) | (19,864) | 14,616 |
| Nonoperating income (expense) | | | |
| Investment income | 786 | 1,519 | 1,798 |
| Interest expense | (13,970) | (9,148) | (7,977) |
| Minority interest | (704) | (125) | (92) |
| Equity in operations of PTVI and other | (746) | (375) | (13,871) |
| Playboy.com registration statement expenses | — | (1,582) | — |
| Legal settlement | — | (622) | — |
| Other, net | (1,447) | (1,202) | (904) |
| Total nonoperating expense | (16,081) | (11,535) | (21,046) |
| Loss from continuing operations before income taxes and cumulative effect of change in accounting principle | (28,327) | (31,399) | (6,430) |
| Income tax benefit (expense) | (996) | (16,227) | 862 |
| Loss from continuing operations before cumulative effect of change in accounting principle | (29,323) | (47,626) | (5,568) |
| Gain on disposal of discontinued operations (net of tax) | — | — | 233 |
| Loss before cumulative effect of change in accounting principle | (29,323) | (47,626) | (5,335) |
| Cumulative effect of change in accounting principle (net of tax) | (4,218) | — | — |
| Net loss | (33,541) | (47,626) | $ (5,335) |
| Basic and diluted weighted average number of common shares outstanding | 24,411 | 24,240 | 22,872 |
| Basic and diluted income (loss) per common share | | | |
| Income (loss) before cumulative effect of change in accounting principle | | | |
| From continuing operations | (1.20) | $ (1.96) | $ (0.24) |
| From discontinued operations (net of tax) | — | — | 0.01 |
| Total | (1.20) | $ (1.96) | (0.23) |
| Cumulative effect of change in accounting principle (net of tax) | (0.17) | — | — |
| Net loss | (1.37) | $ (1.96) | $ (0.23) |

*Source*: PEI's 2001 *Annual Report*, pp. 28–29.

In May 2000, PEI won a major battle when the U.S. Supreme Court struck down a law that enabled cable operators to block signals from sexually explicit channels during the day. Section 505 had prohibited broadcast of adult-oriented networks from 6 A.M. until 10 P.M. daily, unless expensive blocking equipment was installed in cable homes. Christie Hefner estimated that the $5 million annual revenue decline in 1999 was the result of Section 505. The court ruling provides PEI with an opportunity to increase its subscriber base, because more viewers have easier access to the programming.

Digital cable television offers more channels and provides a secure, fully scrambled signal. Christie Hefner estimates that PEI reaches 12 million analong and 4.5 million U.S. cable digital households. During 2001, many operators were slow to accept the ultra-explicit content due to concerns about the community's reaction. AT&T said that the MSO was not interested in the *Spice Platinum* services.

During the fall of 2001, PEI completed a deal with Directrix, Inc. that makes PEI an anchor tenant in Directrix's West Coast Digital Operations and Studio Center for a fifteen-year term. This reduces technical costs and increases capacity to produce original programming.

*International TV*

In 1995, PEI entered into its first international television programming agreement when it established a joint-venture with Flextech plc to offer *Playboy Television* to the United Kingdom. In 1998, PEI introduced Playboy TV and AdulTVision networks in Spain and Portugal. Playboy TV Latin America was the fastest-growing international network in 1998. In early 1999 Playboy TV-Gmbtt Germany received a license for cable and DTH carriage in Germany. During 2000, PEI programming was available in 26.3 million households in 46 countries and 13 languages.

In 1999 the Entertainment group and the Cisneros Television Group formed Playboy TV International (PTVI). PEI owns 20 percent of PTVI. This joint venture provided a significant amount of capital and a management team that was knowledgeable about the global TV industry. PTVI owns and operates existing *Playboy* and *Spice* networks worldwide, excluding the United States and Canada, and creates additional international networks.

Recognizing that the international markets differ in the restrictions of pornography (for instance, the United Kingdom and Ireland have stricter restrictions than Germany, Portugal, and Russia), PTVI varies its programs within the different countries. In February 2001, PTVI announced that the company and Venevision International, a subsidiary of the Cisneros Group, would coproduce its first Spanish-language erotic telenovela. The plan is to subdistribute the telenovela in Europe, except for Spain and Portugal. During August 2001, PTVI announced the exclusive agreement with film production company Solar Entertainment to launch a network in the Philippines that expands PTVI's presence in the Asian market.

PEI expands its international network by entering into exclusive multiyear multiproduct output agreements with overseas pay television distributors. Licenses differ, but typically PEI receives license fees for programming and for the use of the logo and trademark. PEI has equity agreements with channels in the United Kingdom, Japan, and Latin America. Separate distribution agreements allow for U.S. home video products, with dubbing or subtitling into local languages, to be sold in countries in South America, Europe, Australia, Asia, and Africa. High sales in South Korea contributed to higher revenue and profit contribution.

*Worldwide Home Video, Movies, and Other*

Following the style, quality, and focus of *Playboy* magazine, Playboy home videos are distributed via video (including Blockbuster Video), music, and other retail stores. In 2000, working with Image Entertainment, Inc., the company also released all 21 new home video titles on DVD, and 16 reached Billboard's top 40 video sales chart. PEI's videos are sold in more than 55 countries and territories. In 1998, the Entertainment Group created Alta Loma Productions to produce programming for broadcast by other networks. About 150 to 200 hours of programming and about 80 movies are produced each year. During the fall of 2001, a deal with Image Entertainment Inc. to distribute DVDs and videos in the United States and Canada was announced.

## Playboy Online

Christie Hefner reports that the company's profit centers will shift from print and publishing into the electronic area. With plans to be profitable in 2002, the online division has experienced three years of losses—$6.5 million in 1998, $9.06 million in 1999 and $25.2 million in 2000. The first three quarters of 2001 indicate another year of no profit. Hefner recently stated, "We are working on growing the online business and running it as efficiently as possible. Our strategic focus is to convert more of our visitors to purchasers via Playboy Cyber Club, e-commerce and gaming." The company said that to achieve its goal of converting visitors to subscribers at a faster rate, it is moving more of its content to the pay site, launching a new look for the homepage, and hiring a new head of marketing. PEI recently announced that it had entered into a five-year relationship with ACTV Inc. to support its Web- and TV-based interactive content. Hefner believes that online opportunities offer the same advantage of leveraging as the television business. As fixed costs are spread across a larger consumer base to generate higher revenue, operating margins rise. PEI think that most of the cost structure for the e-commerce business has occurred and that with revenues expected to grow, the e-commerce division will become the most valuable.

The e-division for PEI includes Playboy.com, PlayboyStore.com, CyberSpice.com, Rouze.com, Auctions.Playboy.com, SpiceTV.com, and Cyber Club. PEI's homepages on the World Wide Web provide four sources of revenue: advertising, shopping, subscriptions, and pay-per-view. Playboy.com was launched in 1994 and attracted ten thousand visitors on the first day. In 2001, when it had visitors from 163 countries, it attracted 1,490,000 visitors in January 2001 alone. During 1998, traffic on the site was more than 75 million page-views a month. In September 1999, the traffic on the site increased to 90 million page-views per month. During January 2000, the site had 1,157,000 visitors and in January 2001 it has 1,490,000 visitors. The majority of online visitors are in the 18–34 age group and do not read the magazine.

Cyber Club members (who belong to the online subscription site) pay as much as $60 a year for access to photo archives, chat sessions, and live Webcasts from the Hefner mansion. The number of subscribers increased to 88,500 during the third quarter of 2001. PlayboyStore.com provided the fastest-growing revenue stream in 2000 by offering thirty-one hundred items. The top-selling product categories included apparel, lingerie, jewelry, and collectibles.

During 2001, an Internet gaming division was established. During 2001, PEI joined the $3 billion online gambling industry by partnering with other companies. Christie Hefner said that PEI wants to partner with companies that are leaders and have the expertise in their fields and that also possess a gaming license in a favorable tax environment. With Ladbrokes eGaming Limited, it now has a site that offers a full range of sports wagering, allowing international consumers to bet on U.S. and international sports. With Penn National Gaming Inc., it now has a site that allows online wagering for parimutuel horseracing. Additionally, it has a site that offers a virtual casino, with more than fifty games; and it also has a site that offers free games, including fantasy sports leagues. PEI expects online gaming to account for 5 to 10 perent of the Web site's revenue. Note that News Corp., Viacom/CBS, software giant Microsoft, and the Virgin Group have been exploring ways to enter the e-gaming industry.

In November 2001, PEI announced a two-year licensing agreement to host the Web site with Korea Telecom Hitel Co. Ltd. to publish a Korean edition of *Playboy*. PEI chose Korea for an international Web site because of its Internet-savvy population. Earlier in 2001, the first international site was announced for Germany.

## Catalog

PEI's catalog business includes Collector's Choice Music, *Spice* and *Playboy*. PEI's catalog revenues were $75.4 million for the fiscal year ending on June 30, 1997, $71.1 million in 1996, and $61.4 million in 1995. Revenues were $74.4 million for the fiscal year ending in December 1998, $60.3 million in 1999, and $32.4 million in 2000. During 2001, the company was seeking a buyer for Collector's Choice Music.

The Playboy catalog offers fashions and accessories, home videos, gifts, calendars, art products, back issues of the magazine, and newsstand specials. Introduced in 1994, the music catalog Collector's Choice Music features more than 8,000 titles in CD and cassette formats from a wide assortment of music categories: classical, pop, rock, rhythm and blues, jazz, and country. It also offers an extensive library of hard-to-find recordings. The first *Spice* brand-extension effort was introduced in 1999 with a catalog offering more than seventeen hundred video, CD-ROM, and DVD titles.

### *Product Marketing/Licensing*

The consumer products division reported sales of $235 million in 2000. The company considers licensed products to be a key growth area. The name *Playboy* and the rabbit head design are among the most recognized trademarks in the world. The company leverages the power of its brand recognition, design expertise, art collection, and loyal customer base to develop and market apparel, accessories, and other products to consumers worldwide. Merchandise is sold in approximately 2,500 U.S. specialty stores and hundreds of international retail outlets, and it is available online. In total, more than 5,000 Playboy-branded products are sold in approximately 100 countries and territories worldwide. PEI is one of the top-selling fashion brands in China, with more than 400 retail outlets and shops-in-shops.

In 1997, to capture the cigar craze, PEI formed an agreement with a world's top cigar producer, Consolidated Cigar Corporation. The cigar line is sold in restaurants, cigar bars, golf course shops, nightclubs, and wine and liquor stores. Single tubed cigars were introduced in 1998. During 1998, PEI licensed Titan Motorcycle Co. of America to produce 102 motorcycles, licensed Zippo to produce lighters, and licensed Los Angeles-based California Sunshine Activeware, Inc. to produce apparel. In 1999, PEI signed a master license agreement with Mitsui & Company, Ltd. to produce and sell products and establish a freestanding Japanese *Playboy* boutique. A trend-forward fashion licensing program was introduced in the United States during the summer of 1999. In early 2000, a master license was signed with Sario Far East Company to establish a Femlin line in Japan. Early in 2001, the mail order specialist Damart and PEI signed a cross-marketing agreement to attract a younger market. PEI and Cedco Publishing signed a licensing agreement in February 2001 to produce stationery products, content-driven lifestyle books, and calendars. During the summer of 2001, PEI announced a licensing agreement with Twelve-Twenty Productions LLC to create, produce, and market a line of limited-edition fine art prints under the banner "Uniquely Playmates." Between six and nine editions a year are planned to be released. PEI plans to target department stores in the United States (but *not* Sears) and sign a master licensing agreement for Italy or Europe with Fiorucci during 2002. In October 2001, Bally Gaming and Systems entered into a licensing agreement with PEI for a series of interactive casino gaming devices featuring the trademarks, art, and images of the PEI brand. The games are scheduled for release and installation in casinos in 2002.

Products are marketed in North America, Europe, Asia, Australia, and South America, primarily through mass merchants and other retail outlets, by licensees under exclusive license agreements that authorize the manufacture, sale, and distribution of products in a designated territory. Royalties are based on a fixed or variable percentage of the licensee's total new sales, in some cases against a guaranteed minimum. Asia has contributed the majority of the royalties earned from licensing PEI's trademarks.

## Other Business: Casinos

The Playboy Casino at Hotel des Roses on the Greek island of Rhodes was opened in the spring of 1999. Christie planned to establish similar partnerships with as many as ten casinos in resorts such as Las Vegas and overseas by 2004. In 2002, the company was still seeking partners.

## IMAGE

The popularity of the Playboy name stems from its association with fun, sexiness, and quality. The words *aspiration, adventurous,* and *romantic* are a few of the many characteristics that define the Playboy customer. Overseas, the Playboy logo benefits from its strong identification with Western freedoms, American lifestyle, and a desire for "the good life." However, many investors argue that PEI is involved in peddling pornography and will thus not invest. Christie Hefner replies to the pornography concern with the following statement: "For those people who enjoy reading *Playboy*, there's no dichotomy in the fact the magazine has an erotic component and an intellectual, humorous, and celebrity component; that is the world that we live in." It has been said by industry observers that she agreed to the purchase of the hardcore-porn operation with great reluctance.

## PUBLIC AFFAIRS

PEI established the Playboy Foundation in 1965 to provide financial support for organizations that were dedicated to the protection of civil rights and civil liberties, that promoted First Amendment rights and freedom of expression, and also supported research and education on human sexuality and reproductive rights. Since 1965, the foundation has contributed more than $12 million. *Playboy* magazine provides free advertising space to nonprofit groups such as the Nature Conservancy, The National Veterans Legal Services Program, and the Special Olympics. A basic tenet of the Playboy Philosophy is that the First Amendment is the keystone to all other rights. Playboy established the Hugh M. Hefner First Amendment Awards in 1979 to honor individuals who have championed freedom of expression.

## EXHIBIT 3    PEI's Consolidated Balance Sheets (in thousands, except share data)

| | Dec. 31, 2001 | Dec. 31, 2000 |
|---|---|---|
| **ASSETS** | | |
| Cash and cash equivalents | $ 4,610 | $ 2,534 |
| Marketable securities | 3,182 | 3,443 |
| Receivables, net of allowance for doubtful accounts of $6,406 and $5,994, respectively | 41,846 | 45,075 |
| Receivables from related parties | 12,417 | 7,575 |
| Inventories, net | 13,962 | 20,700 |
| Deferred subscription acquisition costs | 12,111 | 12,514 |
| Other current assets | 7,857 | 9,568 |
| Total current assets | 95,985 | 101,409 |
| Receivables from related parties | 50,000 | 57,500 |
| Property and equipment, net | 10,749 | 11,532 |
| Programming costs | 56,213 | 55,454 |
| Goodwill, net of accumulated amortization of $7,349 and $4,761, respectively | 112,338 | 87,260 |
| Trademarks, net of accumulated amortization of $17,726 and $14,701, respectively | 52,185 | 52,585 |
| Distribution agreements acquired, net of accumulated amortization of $2,199 | 26,301 | — |
| Other noncurrent assets | 22,469 | 22,748 |
| Total assets | $426,240 | $388,488 |
| **LIABILITIES** | | |
| Financing obligations | $ 8,561 | $ 3,922 |
| Financing obligations to related parties | 15,000 | 5,000 |
| Acquisition liability | 21,023 | — |
| Accounts payable | 19,293 | 25,295 |
| Accounts payable to related parties | 169 | 718 |
| Accrued salaries, wages and employee benefits | 8,717 | 8,915 |
| Deferred revenues | 47,913 | 41,898 |
| Deferred revenues from related parties | 8,382 | 4,397 |
| Other liabilities and accrued expenses | 18,453 | 16,861 |
| Total current liabilities | 147,511 | 107,006 |
| Financing obligations | 73,017 | 89,328 |
| Financing obligations to related parties | 5,000 | 5,000 |
| Acquisition liability | 41,079 | — |
| Deferred revenues from related parties | 44,350 | 50,875 |
| Net deferred tax liabilities | 5,313 | 4,679 |
| Other noncurrent liabilities | 28,445 | 17,415 |
| Total liabilities | 344,715 | 274,303 |
| **SHAREHOLDERS' EQUITY** | | |
| Common stock, $0.01 par value | | |
| Class A voting – 7,500,000 shares authorized; 4,864,102 and 4,859,102 issued, respectively | 49 | 49 |
| Class B nonvoting – 30,000,000 shares authorized; 19,930,142 and 19,647,048 issued, respectively | 199 | 196 |
| Capital in excess of par value | 123,090 | 120,519 |
| Accumulated deficit | (36,925) | (3,384) |
| Unearned compensation restricted stock | (3,019) | (2,713) |
| Accumulated other comprehensive loss | (1,869) | (482) |
| Total shareholders' equity | 81,525 | 114,185 |
| Total liabilities and shareholders' equity | $426,240 | $388,488 |

*Source:* PEI's 2001 *Annual Report*, pp. 30–31.

EXHIBIT 4    PEI's Selected Financial Data (in thousands, except per share amounts, number of employees and ad pages)

|  | Fiscal Year Ended 12/31/01 | Fiscal Year Ended 12/31/00 |
|---|---|---|
| Long-term financing obligations as a percentage of total capitalization | 49% | 45% |
| Number of common shares outstanding | | |
| Class A voting | 4,864 | 4,859 |
| Class B nonvoting | 19,666 | 19,407 |
| Number of full-time employees | 610 | 686 |
| Selected operating data | | |
| Playboy magazine ad pages | 618 | 674 |
| Cash investments in Company-produced and licensed entertainment programming | $37,254 | $33,061 |
| Amortization of investments in Company-produced and licensed entertainment programming | $37,395 | $33,253 |
| Playboy TV networks household units (at period end) | | |
| DTH | 18,100 | 15,400 |
| Cable digital | 10,300 | 3,200 |
| Cable analog addressable | 7,800 | 11,000 |
| Movie networks household units (at period end) | | |
| DTH | 35,300 | – |
| Cable digital | 25,300 | 8,400 |
| Cable analog addressable | 17,000 | 16,200 |

*Source:* PEI's 2001 *Annual Report,* p. 15.

EXHIBIT 5    PEI's Networks Available to Household Units (in millions)

Revenues from domestic TV networks for 2001 increased $12.2 million, or 16%, and profit contribution increased $9.8 million. These increases were primarily due to the Califa acquisition described above and an increase in Playboy TV revenues.

|  | Dec. 31, 2001 | Dec. 31, 2000 |
|---|---|---|
| Playboy TV (1) | | |
| DTH | 18.1 | 15.4 |
| Cable digital | 10.3 | 3.2 |
| Cable analog addressable | 7.8 | 11.0 |
| Movie Networks (1) (2) | | |
| DTH | 35.3 | – |
| Cable digital | 25.3 | 8.4 |
| Cable analog addressable | 17.0 | 16.2 |

(1) Each household unit is defined as one household carrying one given network per carriage platform. A single household can represent multiple household units if two or more of the Company's networks and/or multiple platforms (i.e., analog and digital) are available to that household.
(2) Includes additional networks in connection with the Califa acquisition in July 2001.
*Source:* PEI's 2001 *Annual Report,* p. 18.

EXHIBIT 6    PEI's Financial Information by Reportable Segment
(in thousands)

| | Fiscal Year Ended 12/31/01 | Fiscal Year Ended 12/31/00 |
|---|---|---|
| **Net revenues (1)** | | |
| Entertainment | $113,833 | $100,955 |
| Publishing | 128,139 | 139,870 |
| Playboy Online | 27,499 | 25,291 |
| Catalog | 10,986 | 32,360 |
| Licensing Businesses | 10,769 | 9,246 |
| **Total** | **$291,226** | **$307,722** |
| Loss from continuing operations before income taxes and cumulative effect of change in accounting principle | | |
| Entertainment | $29,921 | $25,287 |
| Publishing | 1,776 | 6,881 |
| Playboy Online | (21,673) | (25,199) |
| Catalog | (453) | 54 |
| Licensing Businesses | 2,614 | 887 |
| Corporate Administration and Promotion | (19,700) | (20,942) |
| Restructuring expenses | (3,776) | (3,908) |
| Gain (loss) on disposals | (955) | (2,924) |
| Investment income | 786 | 1,519 |
| Interest expense | (13,970) | (9,148) |
| Minority interest | (704) | (125) |
| Equity in operations of PTVI and other | (746) | (375) |
| Playboy.com registration statement expenses | – | (1,582) |
| Legal settlement | – | (622) |
| Other, net | (1,447) | (1,202) |
| **Total** | **$ (28,327)** | **$(31,399)** |
| **EBITDA** | | |
| Entertainment | $ 75,506 | $ 64,307 |
| Publishing | 2,336 | 7,498 |
| Playboy Online | (19,693) | (23,497) |
| Catalog | (427) | 180 |
| Licensing Businesses | 2,823 | 1,084 |
| Corporate Administration and Promotion | (16,616) | (18,865) |
| Restructuring expenses | (3,776) | (3,908) |
| Gain (loss) on disposals | (955) | (2,924) |
| **Total** | **$ 39,198** | **$ 23,875** |
| Depreciation and amortization | | |
| Entertainment | $ 45,585 | $ 39,020 |
| Publishing | 560 | 617 |
| Playboy Online | 1,980 | 1,702 |
| Catalog | 26 | 126 |
| Licensing Businesses | 209 | 197 |
| Corporate Administration and Promotion | 3,544 | 3,249 |
| **Total** | **$ 51,904** | **$ 44,911** |

*(continued)*

EXHIBIT 6    PEI's Financial Information by Reportable Segment
(in thousands)                                    (continued)

| | Fiscal Year Ended 12/31/01 | Fiscal Year Ended 12/31/00 |
|---|---|---|
| Identifiable assets | | |
| Entertainment | $ 317,848 | $ 267,142 |
| Publishing | 49,219 | 56,191 |
| Playboy Online | 4,463 | 7,675 |
| Catalog | 1,244 | 3,797 |
| Licensing Businesses | 4,732 | 5,003 |
| Corporate Administration and Promotion | 48,734 | 48,680 |
| Total | $ 426,240 | $ 388,488 |

(1) Net revenues include revenues attributable to foreign countries of approximately $48,522, $50,165, and $71,495 in 2001, 2000, and 1999, respectively. Revenues from individual foreign countries were not material. Revenues are generally attributed to countries based on the location of customers, except product licensing royalties where revenues are attributed based upon the location of licensees. In 1999, revenues from PTVI exceeded 10% of the Company's total net revenues. See Note (C) Playboy TV International, LIC Joint Venture.
*Source:* PEI's 2001 *Annual Report,* pp. 51–52.

CONCLUSION

Consider the following:

- Which of PEI's divisions should receive the greatest emphasis and resources?
- How can PEI improves its corporate image among critics who contend that its business is obscene, pornographic, and unethical?
- Should PEI continue its international expansion? If yes, which new countries should be targeted?
- Should PEI make a major acquisition in the near future to begin publishing other magazines, such as *Cosmopolitan, Woman's Day, Ladies' Home Journal, Gentlemen's Quarterly,* or *Esquire?*
- Should PEI continue its e-commerce expansion? If yes, develop a strategy for expansion.
- How much is the company worth today?
- Develop a three-year strategic plan for PEI.

# THE READER'S DIGEST ASSOCIATION, INC.—2002

**Robert Shane**
**Francis Marion University**

RDA, RDB, RDT

www.readersdigest.com

Who has the largest single subscription magazine on the planet? Reader's Digest! Respected for its editorial creativity and direct marketing expertise, Reader's Digest Association (RDA) is heralded as the global leader in magazine publishing, direct marketing, books, recorded music collections, and home videos. The editorial mission is concentrated in the areas "home, family, health, finance and faith," the areas that "inform, enrich, entertain and inspire" customers. The flagship *Reader's Digest* magazine is published in 48 editions and 19 languages and reaches more than 100 million readers each month in virtually every area of the globe. The company's global operations include the publication of special interest magazines, do-it-yourself books, and home entertainment audio and video products. Likewise, the company actively uses the Internet, strategic alliances, and its global data centers to implement its product offerings. This vast distribution network generated revenues of $2,518 million in fiscal year 2001, an increase from $2,485 million in fiscal year 2000 and $2,459 million in 1999. Net income for 2001 was $132.1 million, a decrease from 2000's $144.7 million and 1999's $151.9 million.

Since 1998, Reader's Digest has been implementing a strategic plan to reverse previously declining revenues. These strategies have included:

- Expanding its presence in five areas of intense consumer interest—health, home, family, finance, and faith.
- Selling nonpublishing products and services in those areas.
- Continued geographic expansion.
- Developing new marketing channels.
- Broadening the customer base to include younger customers.
- Producing more products for older customers, focusing on the growing 50+ age demographic.
- Integrating the Internet into all of its businesses.

These strategic plans have resulted in an expanded international presence, increased numbers of strategic alliances, and a corporate realignment of operating segments.

## HISTORY

In 1922, DeWitt and Lila Wallace published the first five thousand copies of *Reader's Digest* from their Greenwich Village apartment. These copies were sold exclusively by mail for 25 cents. The first publication contained thirty-one carefully selected articles, including "The Future of Poison Gas," "Wanted: Motives for Motherhood," and "Advice from a President's Physician." Today, substantial portions of the selections in *Reader's*

*Digest* are original articles written by staff writers or freelance writers. The remaining articles are selected from existing published sources.

In 1929, *Reader's Digest* appeared on newsstands for the first time, and despite the Depression, sixty-two thousand copies were sold. Six years later, circulation passed the 1 million mark. In 1938, the magazine published its first international edition in the United Kingdom. Since that time, magazine publication has expanded to other countries and areas, including Latin America, Sweden, Australia, Belgium, Canada, Denmark, Finland, France, Germany, Italy, Norway, South Africa, and Switzerland.

In the 1950s, Reader's Digest launched its *Condensed Books* series, today known as *Select Editions,* in the United States and Canada. This series of books consists of previously published works which are pared down into a "condensed" version for quicker reading. During this period of the company's development, paid advertising would also appear for the first time in the magazines. In 1958, the company purchased its first computer. Today, it operates two Global Data Centers and has expanded its use of the Internet.

In the 1960s, Reader's Digest revolutionized direct marketing by introducing its easy-to-enter sweepstakes. The Quality School Program (QSP) was founded and is one of the largest fundraising organizations of its kind. This organization helps over twenty five thousand schools and youth groups in the United States and Canada. The company also has an alliance with The World's Finest Chocolate company, which has been combined with QSP to expand this program by combining the like operations.

DeWitt Wallace died in 1981 at the age of 91, and three years later, Lila Wallace, his wife and the other co-founder of *Reader's Digest,* died at the age of 94. Several years later, Reader's Digest entered the video business with *Why We Fight*. The company also acquired its first special interest magazine. Today's magazine lineup includes *The Family Handyman, American Woodworker, New Choices: Living Even Better After 50, Moneywise, Walking,* and *Benchmark*. In 1988, *Household Hints and Handy Tips* sold more than 1.2 million copies within thirty days in the United States.

Reader's Digest stock was first publicly traded on the New York Stock Exchange as RDA, a nonvoting stock in 1990; RDB was listed in 1992 as a voting stock. The fortieth international edition was launched in Russia and increased the publication to sixteen languages. The Reader's Digest Video, *Great National Parks, II*, won the first of five Emmy Awards. A direct response television commercial was launched for *The Family Handyman's Helpful Hints*. One hundred twenty-five thousand paid orders were received as a result of the advertisement. In 1996, Reader's Digest established a Web site; a Thai edition was published; and later, Australia, Hong Kong, India, Korea, Malaysia, New Zealand, the Philippines, Singapore, and Taiwan editions were launched.

In 1998, Thomas O. Ryder was appointed chairman and chief executive officer, and he "initiated a four-phase strategy, including global reengineering and growth initiatives to build on [the company's] fundamental strengths and create long-term opportunities." During this time, a public hybrid equity offering of 11.8 million shares of Trust Automatic Common Exchange Securities was completed. This offering enabled six charitable organizations to combine a portion of their Reader' Digest Class A nonvoting common stock. The new issues trade under the ticker symbol RDT. The U.S. Postal Service honored DeWitt and Lila Wallace for their philanthropic and cultural contributions with a postage stamp as part of the Great American series. In 1999, the company acquired Books Are Fun, Ltd., a leading display marketer of books and gifts. In 2000 and 2001, Reader's Digest continued the strategic plan cited earlier.

## INTERNAL ISSUES

The world economy had been in decline since early 2001. However, most of the company's strategic planning goals had been surpassed. *Reader's Digest* magazine is published in 48 distinct editions and 19 languages. The company has more than 30 Web sites worldwide. Computerized technology has enabled the company to maintain a list of prospective customers. This list consists of over 57 million households and has been recognized as one of the largest direct response lists in the United States.

Reader's Digest has formed alliances to leverage the Internet business with WebMD for health advice, Merk-MedCo for online discount prescription services, and Vanguard for investment services. Elizabeth G. Chambers, who heads Reader's Digest's business development efforts, said, "This alliance is an important part of a corporate growth strategy to leverage our brand, direct marketing expertise, and consumer databases to bring high quality financial services to customers around the world."[1] The company's other alliances in the United States include arrangements with GE Capital Assurance, Torchmark Corporation, Pethealth Inc., Physicians Mutual Insurance Company, and First USA. Internationally, the growing partner list includes AIG, AXA, GE Sovac, ING, Manulife Financial, and SCI International.

### Organizational Structure

In the fourth quarter of 2001, the company began reporting financial information under a new structure to reflect new segment operations. The four segments are North American Books and Home Entertainment (BHE), U.S. magazines, International Businesses, and New Business Development. Exhibit 1 reflects a proposed organizational chart for this structure.

### Mission Statement

Reader's Digest does not have a prescribed mission statement. However, the company's fundamental values are outlined in its written Code of Conduct. This code serves as a guide to the employees of Reader's Digest, who are quite diverse. The code addresses business ethics, employee relations, and environmental protection. A proposed mission statement for Reader's Digest might state:

> *Reader's Digest is a global leader in the publishing industry. We publish magazines, books, home entertainment products and provide various product offerings through our strategic partners to inform, enrich, inspire, and entertain people of all ages and cultures. We are dedicated to the success of* Reader's Digest *as a worldwide competitor and operate under a strong code of ethics. Our philosophy is to produce a quality product at a fair price. We are making and will continue to make significant investments*

---

EXHIBIT 1    Proposed Organizational Chart

*in management information systems and the Internet in order to improve our operating efficiencies and increase the level of customer services. We have established quality relationships and believe that our name, image, and reputation provide us a significant competitive advantage. We are committed to contributing to the economic strengths of the countries in which we conduct business. We will continue our efforts of recruiting, developing, rewarding, and retaining personnel who are dedicated and highly skilled professionals.*

### Operating Segments

During the fourth quarter of fiscal 2001, reporting segments began to reflect a new internal management organization. These segments include North American Books and Home Entertainment, U.S. Magazines, International Businesses, and New Business Development. A summary of operating segment results is provided in Exhibit 2.

### North American Books and Home Entertainment

North American Books and Home Entertainment products consist of *Reader's Digest Select Editions*, series books, general books, recorded music collections and series, home video products and series, and Reader's Digest Young Families and Reader's Digest Children's Publishing products. These products are mostly sold by direct mail. Books and gifts are also sold through the Books Are Fun subsidiary. These products are displayed at schools and businesses. RDA has a direct marketing policy that allows a customer to return any book or home entertainment product for a refund, either before or after payment. Sales of Books and Home Entertainment products are seasonal, with most occurring in the fall and winter, especially during the Christmas season. The books in the category Digest Select Editions, formerly known as "Condensed Books," consist of a series of condensed versions of current popular fiction. Select

### EXHIBIT 2    Summary of Operating Segment Results

|  | Years ended June 30, | | |
|---|---|---|---|
|  | *2001* | *2000* | *1999* |
| Revenues | | | |
| North American Books and Home Entertainment | $  719 | $  704 | $  584 |
| U.S. Magazines | 652 | 580 | 603 |
| International Businesses | 1,093 | 1,146 | 1,239 |
| New Business Development | 54 | 55 | 33 |
| Total revenues | $2,518 | $2,485 | $2,459 |
| Operating profit (loss) | | | |
| North American Books and Home Entertainment | $   71 | $   90 | $   39 |
| U.S. Magazines | 77 | 89 | 105 |
| International Businesses | 116 | 118 | 28 |
| New Business Development | (17) | (40) | (5) |
| Segment operating profit | 247 | 257 | 167 |
| Other operating items | (18) | (3) | (38) |
| Total operating profit | $  229 | $  254 | $  129 |

Editions books are published in 15 languages and are marketed in the United States, Canada, and 28 other countries. Up to six volumes are printed in the United States and Canada each a year, while some versions are published in four or five volumes a year. Select Editions generated revenues for North American Books and Home Entertainment of $97.7 million in fiscal 2001, $102.5 million in fiscal 2000, and $99.6 million in fiscal 1999.

Two types of series books are published—reading series and illustrated series. The reading series books are printed in four languages and are marketed in the United States, Canada, and nine other countries. These series include The World's Best Reading selections, which consists of full-length editions of classic works of literature. The illustrated series are printed in eight languages and are marketed in the United States, Canada, and 14 other countries. Series books generated revenues for North American Books and Home Entertainment of $30.1 million in fiscal 2001, $28.8 million in fiscal 2000, and $29.2 million in fiscal 1999.

The General Books category consists primarily of reference books, cookbooks, how-to and do-it-yourself books, and children's books. Books handle subjects such as history, travel, religion, health, nature, and the home, and they are published in 19 languages and marketed in the United States, Canada, and 35 other countries. General books generated revenues for North American Books and Home Entertainment of $85.4 million in fiscal 2001, $103.7 million in fiscal 2000, and $148.2 million in fiscal 1999. Most copies of a general book are sold through initial bulk promotional mailings, but they are also sold through subsequent promotions, through catalog sales, and through sales inserts in mailings for other Reader's Digest products. General books are also distributed for retail sale in stores through independent distributors.

Reader's Digest music collections are sold on compact disks and cassettes in the United States, Canada, and 29 other countries. Music includes various styles, such as classical, pop, jazz, and local folk. Approximately 20,000 selections are available. These products are also licensed to third parties for retail sales or for movie synchronization. The company is a member of the Recording Industry Association of America in the United States, and it has received 51 gold, platinum, and multiplatinum certificates. In several other countries, the company is a member of the International Federation of the Phonographic Industry. Music products generated revenues for North American Books and Home Entertainment of $79.9 million in fiscal 2001, $80.4 million in fiscal 2000, and $105.2 million in fiscal 1999.

Video products are marketed through direct response channels in the United States, Canada, and 22 other countries. In some countries, they are also sold through retail outlets. Several original programs have won awards of excellence, including five Emmy awards and, in 2001, four Crystal Awards of Excellence and a Cine Golden Eagle Award. Reader's Digest entered into a multiyear agreement with CBS Productions to develop television movies and miniseries based on the personal dramas chronicled in *Reader's Digest;* four scripts are currently in production. Strategic initiatives include growth into Latin America and Eastern Europe. Home video products generated revenues for North American Books and Home Entertainment of $56.1 million in fiscal 2001, $77.5 million in fiscal 2000, and $96.6 million in fiscal 1999.

Additional products are offered through Books Are Fun, Ltd., a wholly owned subsidiary which sells premium-quality books and gift items at discount prices by display marketing those products on-site at schools and businesses in all 50 states of the United States and Canada using book fairs and similar displays. Book categories include best-selling novels, cookbooks, children's books, education, sports, hobby, nature, travel, and self-help titles. Nonbook categories include music, videos, and gift items, such as jewelry and art. Reader's Digest Young Families subsidiary sells products, primarily in the United States, for children up to age eight and primarily through direct mail and telemarketing. Products include interactive books, such as *Sesame Street ABCs* and *Elmo's Neighborhood,* and videos, such as *The Country Mouse* and *The City Mouse.* The Children's Publishing subsidiary produces books, games, and other products for children up to age twelve for retail sale as well as through direct marketing through *Reader's Digest* (mail, telemarketing, display marketing, company catalogs, etc.) and the Internet. Products include Barbie, Disney (Winnie the Pooh and classic Disney characters), Hasbro (Tonka and Play-Doh), and Fisher-Price (Little People), and they have been translated into 28 languages and are marketed in the United States, Canada, Europe, South America, Australia, and Asia.

Total revenues for North American Books and Home Entertainment increased 2 percent in 2001 to $719 million, compared with $704 million in 2000 and $584 million in 1999. Operating profits for North American Books and Home Entertainment decreased 21 percent in 2001 to $71 million, compared with $90 million in 2000 and $39 million in 1999.

*U.S. Magazines*

The U.S. Magazines group publishes and markets, primarily through direct marketing, *Reader's Digest* magazine and several special interest magazines in the United States. In addition, U.S. Magazines sells its magazines and other magazines and products through youth fundraising campaigns of QSP, Inc. *Reader's Digest* magazine is sold in the United States and Canada and in 45 editions and 19 languages outside the United States and Canada. The U.S.-English edition of *Reader's Digest* has the largest paid circulation of any U.S. magazine, other than those automatically distributed to all members of the American Association of Retired Persons. This is based upon an audit report issued by the Audit Bureau of Circulation, Inc. *Reader's Digest* editions in the United States include an English-language edition and a Spanish-language edition entitled *Selecciones.* Large print and braille editions are available for the sight impaired and the blind.

Approximately 69 percent of total U.S. fiscal 2001 revenues for *Reader's Digest* were generated by circulation revenues and 31 percent by advertising revenues. Approximately 66 percent of total U.S. fiscal 2001 revenues for the special interest magazines were generated by circulation revenues and 34 percent by advertising revenues. Approximately 95 percent of the U.S. paid circulation of *Reader's Digest* consists of subscriptions. The balance consists of single-copy sales. Special interest magazines are sold by subscription and at newsstands. Independent contractors are licensed to publish *Reader's Digest* in India, Italy, Korea, South Africa, and Turkey, thus creating a broad global presence. These magazines are sold primarily through direct marketing. Independent contractors publish each edition in the United States.

Reader's Digest publishes several special interest magazines: *The Family Handyman, New Choices: The Magazine for Your Health, Money and Travel*™, and *American Woodworker.* Reader's Digest ceased publication of *Walking* magazine after the September/October 2001 issue. Other magazines include *Moneywise,* a magazine devoted to helping families manage their finances, in the United Kingdom; *Receptar,* a leading Czech do-it-yourself and gardening monthly magazine, and *Krizovky,* a Czech entertainment puzzle magazine. Special interest magazines are promoted in *Reader's Digest* through foreign contractor customer lists. Exhibit 3 shows circulation and advertising information for magazines for fiscal 2001 and 2000.

EXHIBIT 3    Summary of Circulation Rate Bases and Advertising for Reader's Digest

| Magazine Title | Circulation Rate Base | | # of Advertising Pages Carried | |
|---|---|---|---|---|
| | 2001 | 2000 | 2001 | 2000 |
| Reader's Digest—U.S.: English edition | 12,500,000 | 12,500,000 | 1,155 | 1,131 |
| Reader's Digest—Canada: English and French | 1,255,300 | Note 1 | 1,651 | Note 1 |
| Reader's Digest—Other: international | 9,415,757 | 11,225,633 | 9,103 | 12,460 |
| Reader's Digest Large Edition for Easier Reading | 500,000 | 463,000 | 169 | 153 |
| American Woodworker | 325,000 | 325,000 | 397 | 324 |
| The Family Handyman | 1,100,000 | 1,100,000 | 599 | 131 |
| New Choices: The Magazine for Your Health, Money and Travel™ | 600,000 | 600,000 | 431 | 494 |
| Selecciones | 250,000 | 210,000 | 262 | 247 |
| Walking | 650,000 | 650,000 | 388 | 435 |
| Moneywise | 97,182 | 104,000 | 760 | 712 |
| Receptar | 97,182 | Note 1 | 30 | Note 1 |
| Krizovky | 50,000 | Note 1 | 289 | Note 1 |

Note 1—Not specifically reported for 2000.
*Source:* Information obtained from Reader's Digest 2001 and 2000, 10K Report filings.

*Reader's Digest* and the special interest magazines are also sold in the United States and Canada through Quality Service Programs (QSP) and QSP, Inc., respectively. QSP helps schools and youth groups prepare fundraising campaigns in which magazine subscriptions, music and video products, books, and food and gifts are sold. QSP derives its revenues from the sale of products through fundraising organizations. World's Finest Chocolate, Inc. (a company and a product) is also offered through QSP via a long-term licensing agreement. In March 2000, QSP entered into an alliance agreement with Schoolpop, Inc., an online fundraiser that enables online shoppers to contribute funds to schools. Revenues for QSP products increased 53 percent in 2001, compared with the prior year, primarily due to higher sales of food and gift items from the integration of the products and sales force of World's Finest Chocolate. In June 2001, Quality Service Programs acquired **eFundraising.com**, which uses the Internet to enhance fundraising activities. The company **eFundraising.com** uses proprietary software that enables students to send e-mail messages about their schools or youth groups' fundraising activities to family and friends. The e-mail directs the recipients to the school or youth group's Web site, where they may purchase magazine subscriptions and a variety of gift and food products.

The Web site, **rd.com**, and some thirty other sites tie the company and its strategic partners to the Internet. Web sites offer various formats, such as audio, graphic, text and video enhancements, interactive discussions and reader involvement, and additional content relating to *Reader's Digest*.

Total revenues for U.S. Magazines increased 12 percent in 2001 to $652 million, compared with $580 million in 2000 and $603 million in 1999. The operating profit for U.S. Magazines declined 14 percent in 2001 to $77 million, compared with $89 million in 2000 and $105 million in 1999, with the majority of the operating profit continuing to be provided by QSP. Declining revenues and profits have been attributed to the increased testing of new subscription sources, the planned reductions in subscription rate bases, the higher costs associated with the fulfillment of a major outsourcing project, and the lower profits for the special interest magazines due to industrywide softness in certain advertising sectors particular to these magazines.

*International Businesses*

International Businesses operates outside of the United States and Canada (see Exhibit 4). Many of the products discussed in the other two operating segments are marketed and sold globally. Product offerings are adjusted to reflect the specific languages, cultures, and beliefs.

Many international editions of *Reader's Digest* have the largest paid circulation for monthly magazines both in the individual countries and in the regions in which they are published. For most international editions of *Reader's Digest,* subscriptions comprise almost 90 percent of the circulation. The balance is attributable to newsstand and other retail sales. Approximately 83 percent of total international fiscal 2001 revenues for *Reader's Digest* were generated by circulation revenues and 17 percent by advertising revenues. Revenues for the five International Businesses segments Select Editions, Series Books, General Books, Music Products, and Home Videos are as follows:

- Select Editions—$161.0 million in 2001, $163.5 million in 2000, and $154.4 million in 1999
- Series Books—$96.8 million in 2001, $92.7 million in 2000, and $96.3 million in 1999
- General Books—$330.8 million in 2001, $340.3 million in 2000, and $359.2 million in 1999
- Music Products—$186.4 million in 2001, $197.1 million in 2000, and $240.4 million in 1999
- Home Video Products—$79.5 million in 2001, $81.4 million in 2000, and $96.4 million in 1999

Total revenues for International Businesses segment declined 5 percent in 2001 to $1,093 million, compared with $1,146 million in 2000 and $1,239 million in 1999. However, excluding the adverse effect of foreign currency translation, revenues actually increased 4 percent in 2001. Operating profit for International Businesses declined 2 percent in 2001 to $116 million, compared with $118 million in 2000 and $28 million in 1999. Excluding the adverse effect of foreign currency translation, operating profit increased 14 percent in 2001. This segment generated approximately 43 percent of 2001 revenues and 47 percent of the operating profits.

**EXHIBIT 4    Global Subsidiaries of the International Business**

| | |
|---|---|
| Argentina | Hong Kong |
| Australia | Japan |
| Austria | Mexico |
| Belgium | Netherlands |
| Brazil | New Zealand |
| Chile | Norway |
| Colombia | Peru |
| Czech Republic | Philippines |
| Denmark | Poland |
| England | Portugal |
| Finland | Russia |
| France | Spain |
| Germany | Sweden |
| Hungary | Switzerland |
| Italy | Thailand |

*New Business Development*

New Business Development has been formed with several leading insurance companies to offer insurance products to customers globally. Partners include American International Group, Inc., Torchmark Corporation, GE Capital Assurance Company, Physicians Mutual Insurance Company, Pethealth Inc., Allianz, AXA, ING Direct, and Manulife Financial. These products include life, health, homeowners, long-term care, and pet insurance as well as hospital indemnity products. They are marketed and sold through a combination of direct mail, telemarketing, advertising in magazines, the Internet, and other marketing channels. The insurer underwrites and administers the products, provides customers and claims services, and covers marketing costs. Reader's Digest provides expertise in research and test design, database management and targeting, and promotion creation and production. Credit Products include an agreement with First USA, a subsidiary of Bank One Corporation, to market a Reader's Digest-branded credit card to customers in the United States. Under the agreement, First USA launched a Reader's Digest Platinum MasterCard in April 2000. First USA administers the credit cards. GE Capital Assurance Company and its subsidiaries market loan products internationally in France and Germany and with the Bank of Scotland in the United Kingdom. In June 2001, an alliance was formed with The Vanguard Group under which Vanguard will offer its mutual funds and other financial services, such as brokerage, financial planning, asset management, and trust services, to customers in the United States.

Other new international business developments include the publication of *Moneywise* magazine, the **Moneywise.co.uk** Web site, and Benchmark, Ltd., a publisher of quarterly investment guides distributed in Hong Kong, Taiwan, and Singapore in English and Chinese. Benchmark publishes twelve issues per year, with a fiscal 2001 annual circulation of approximately 20,000, and it operates the Web site **asiafunds.com**.

Health-services marketing involves an alliance with Twinlab Corporation, a leading U.S.-based vitamin manufacturer and marketer, to market vitamins, minerals, and supplements to *Reader's Digest* customers in the United States and Europe. Products are marketed principally through direct mail, through advertising in *Reader's Digest* and on both companies' Web sites. Twinlab is responsible for manufacturing and fulfilling the products. The arrangement includes both revenue and cost sharing. Similar alliances exist with Vitahealth in Canada. Several vitamin catalogs are also promoted in Germany. These businesses are managed by North American Books and Home Entertainment, and their results are reported in that segment. Likewise, an agreement with McMurry Publishing, Inc., a leading independent custom publisher in the health category in the United States, delivers custom publishing services to clients in North America. Several experimental pilot programs are being tested, such as the Books Are Fun efforts in Mexico and France, a QSP pilot in the United Kingdom, a test of an Australian version of *The Family Handyman*, and the testing of Reader's Digest Young Families products in several international markets. More financial information is provided in Exhibits 4 and 5.

Gifts.com, Inc. is a subsidiary of the Good Catalog Company division, a catalog marketer of home, garden, and gift-related products, and the **Gifts.com** division, an online and catalog gift shopping service. Reader's Digest owns an 80.1 percent interest in Gifts.com, Inc., and Domain.com, Inc., an affiliate of StarTek, Inc., owns a 19.9 percent interest. The **Gifts.com** Web site and catalogs feature over 500 different products. Good Catalog Company offers over 2,000 different products through five different catalog titles, which have a total circulation of over 15 million, and through its Web site, **goodcatalog.com**. Merchandise ranges from home furnishing and decorative accents to garden, health, fitness, sports, and electronic goods, as well as children's toys, games, and crafts.

EXHIBIT 5    Reader's Digest Association, Inc. Income Statement
(in millions except per-share data)

| | Year ending June 30, | | |
| --- | --- | --- | --- |
| | *2001* | *2000* | *1999* |
| Revenues | $2,518.2 | $2,484.5 | $2458.5 |
| Product, distribution, and editorial expenses | (971.2) | (907.1) | (962.6) |
| Promotional, marketing, and administrative expenses | (1299.6) | (1320.2) | (1328.9) |
| Other operating items | (18.4) | (3.4) | (37.9) |
| Operating profit | 229.0 | 253.8 | 129.1 |
| Other (expenses) income, net | (41.2) | (19.1) | (82.6) |
| Income before provisions for income taxes | 187.8 | 234.7 | 211.7 |
| Income taxes | (55.7) | (90.0) | (85.1) |
| Income before cumulative effect of change in accounting principles | 132.1 | 144.7 | 126.6 |
| Cumulative effect of change in accounting principles for pension assets, net of tax provision of $(15.2) | 0.0 | 0.0 | 25.3 |
| **Net Income** | 132.1 | 144.7 | 151.9 |
| Basic EPS from Total Operations | $1.27 | $1.35 | $1.40 |
| Diluted EPS from Total Operations | $1.26 | $1.34 | $1.39 |

*Source:* www.readersdigest.com

Revenues from New Business Development segment declined 2 percent for 2001 to $54 million, compared with $55 million in 2000 and $33 million in 1999. Operating losses declined in 2001 to $(17) million, compared with $(40) million in 2000 and $(5) million in 1999. Revenues were lower for Gifts.com, Inc. as a result of the Good Catalog Company division's reduction in merchandise catalog promotions. This decline was partially offset by higher sales generated by the **Gifts.com** Web site and financial services alliances. Operating losses for 2001 were lower, primarily as a result of the planned reductions in marketing and development costs related to the **Gifts.com** Web site. Losses for 2000 were from marketing and startup costs for a number of ventures, primarily Gifts.com, Inc.

## EXTERNAL ISSUES

Standard & Poor's provides an interesting monthly outlook for the publishing industry. S&P indicates a number of positive occurrences within the group, including mergers and alliances involving some of the major names such as Harcourt General, Bertelsmann, Reader's Digest, Pearson plc, Scholastic Inc., and Houghton Mifflin. The industry is experiencing sharp drops in advertising. Magazine advertising declined about 8.5 percent in 2001, following a 14 percent advance for 2000. Circulation revenues should gain slowly due to higher cover prices. Single-copy sales have been trending lower for more than ten years, while the growth in the number of subscriptions has been sluggish to boot. While paper prices are stable and coming down for most grades of coated paper, postage costs for mailed subscriptions will be rising over the course of the year in response to rate hikes that went into effect in the first quarter of 2001. S&P projects consumer expenditures to reach $38.1 billion by 2003, up from $30.5 billion in 1999 and

EXHIBIT 6　Reader's Digest Association, Inc. Balance Sheet
(in millions except per-share data)

| | Year ending June 30, | |
| | 2001 | 2000 |
|---|---|---|
| **ASSETS** | | |
| Cash and cash equivalents | $35.4 | $49.7 |
| Receivables, net | 305.1 | 285.3 |
| Inventories, net | 161.6 | 120.3 |
| Prepaid and deferred promotion costs | 106.7 | 115.5 |
| Prepaid expenses and other current costs | 161.8 | 185.8 |
| Total current assets | 770.6 | 756.6 |
| Marketable securities | 10.8 | 173.5 |
| Property, plant, & equipment, net | 160.2 | 152.4 |
| Intangible assets, net | 409.8 | 438.8 |
| Other noncurrent assets | 323.7 | 208.4 |
| **Total Assets** | **$1,675.1** | **$1,729.7** |
| **LIABILITIES AND STOCKHOLDERS' EQUITY** | | |
| Loans and notes payable | $160.3 | $89.4 |
| Accounts payable | 86.4 | 104.8 |
| Short-term debt | 160.3 | 89.4 |
| Accrued expenses | 251.1 | 351.2 |
| Income taxes payable | 41.2 | 38.7 |
| Unearned revenues | 291.6 | 289.4 |
| Other current liabilities | 28.9 | 30.9 |
| Total current liabilities | 859.5 | 904.4 |
| Postretirement and postemployment benefits other than pensions | 138.7 | 142.3 |
| Unearned revenue | 54.1 | 63.8 |
| Other noncurrent liabilities | 166.6 | 144.0 |
| **Total Liabilities** | **$1,218.9** | **$1,254.5** |
| **STOCKHOLDERS' EQUITY** | | |
| Capital stock | $29.6 | $28.9 |
| Paid-in capital | 226.1 | 223.1 |
| Retained earnings | 1187.7 | 1077.5 |
| Total equity | 456.2 | 504.3 |
| Accumulated other comprehensive (loss) income | (84.6) | 31.0 |
| Treasury stock | (902.6) | (885.3) |
| **Total Liabilities & Stockholders' Equity** | **$1,675.1** | **$1,758.8** |
| Total common shares outstanding (in millions) | 102.7 | 106.0 |

*Source:* www.readersdigest.com

$32.2 billion in 2000; it also expects a 5.7 percent average annual growth rate, with net book sales likely to grow at a 5.3 percent average annual rate in the five years through 2003. Children's books have benefited from the Harry Potter series, as well as from the sale of TV show and movie tie-ins. Adult trade books will be characterized in 2001 by sluggish unit sales and greater discounting. College and professional sales are benefiting from demographics, online purchases, effective marketing, and other factors.

Two of Reader's Digest major competitors are Thomas Nelson Publishers and Time Warner, Inc. Thomas Nelson revenues increased by 12 percent in 2001 to $297.9 million. Time Inc. is part of AOL-Time Warner and is the leading US consumer magazine publisher, with more than sixty magazines in its collection. Among its well-known magazine titles are *Entertainment Weekly, People, Southern Living, Sports Illustrated, Time, People en Español, Time for Kids, Teen People, Field & Stream, Golf, Skiing,* and *Yachting.* AOL-Time Warner total revenues for 2001 were $9,202 million.

## CONCLUSION

Reader's Digest's has completed many strategic initiatives, including a number of strategic alliances which capitalize on the company's marketing capabilities. RDA has been expanding and contracting its businesses as needed in order to become a more global competitor. The company has experienced rapid growth in non-U.S. markets, while revenues suffer within the United States. The effects of the September 11, 2001, attacks on economic conditions have undoubtedly been felt by numerous businesses. Likewise, in 2002, the Euro was implemented in Europe. The Reader's Digest Web site has been improved significantly. The company is a leader in publishing and direct marketing but has experienced a flattening of revenues. A clear strategic plan is needed for the future.

## NOTES

1. Standard & Poor's 2001 Industry Report.

## REFERENCES

Comtex News Network.
Hoover's Online.
www.msnbc.com.
Reader's Digest, 2001 *Annual Report.*

www.readersdigest.com.
Standard & Poor's 2001 Industry Report.
Strategy Club Web site. Available at
    www.strategyclub.com.

# NIKE, INC.—2002

**M. Jill Austin**
**Middle Tennessee State University**

NKE

www.nike.com

> *Nike is about play. It's in everything we do and everything we make. Play is the root of every sport—and of countless other activities we undertake for the same purpose: to find joy in the arc of a ball, the swing of a club, the power of a wave . . . the simple joy of our own bodies in motion.*

These perspectives on play from the company Web site, **www.nikebiz.com**, indicate a shift in the company focus. Nike has always been a company about sports. However, the traditional definition of sport is confining, and since Nike now sells yoga, snowboarding, and outdoor gear, it seems natural for the company to broaden its definition of sport. As part of the change in focus, Nike announced a new goal in 2000: to increase the women's apparel business from 22 percent of company apparel sales to 30 percent by 2003. The company's vision and mission are shown in Exhibit 1.

CEO Phil Knight believes that for 2001 the company was more "gutsy than great." Net income in 2001 for Nike, Inc. ($589.7 million) increased by only 1.8 percent over 2000. Increases in net income from 1999 to 2000 were a much more significant 28.3 percent ($579.1 million). For fiscal year 2001, revenues at Nike increased by 5.5 percent over 2000 to $9.489 billion. Since 1997, the company's successes include maintaining the number two position in soccer (the world's number one sport), becoming a major player in the golf market, increasing its market share in Europe, and becoming known as an apparel company.

## HISTORY

Philip Knight, a dedicated long-distance runner, developed a plan to make low-cost running shoes in Japan and to sell them in the United States as part of his work toward an MBA degree at Stanford University. After graduation, Knight teamed up with Bill

EXHIBIT 1    Nike, Inc. Vision and Mission

**Vision**—"To bring inspiration and innovation to every athlete* in the world"
**Mission**—Nike, Inc. is the "largest seller of athletic footwear and athletic apparel in the world. Performance and reliability of shoes, apparel, and equipment, new product development, price, product identity through marketing and promotion, and customer support and service are important aspects of competition in the athletic footwear, apparel, and equipment industry . . . We believe we are competitive in all of these areas." The company aims to "lead in corporate citizenship through proactive programs that reflect caring for the world family of Nike, our teammates, our consumers, and those who provide services to Nike."

*Nike co-founder Bill Bowerman defined an athlete by saying, "If you have a body, you're an athlete."
*Source:* **http://nikebiz.com** and Nike, Inc. Form 10-K, 2001.

Bowerman, his former track coach at the University of Oregon, to make his plan a reality. Since Bowerman's hobby was making handcrafted lightweight running shoes, his expertise was very valuable to entrepreneur Knight. In 1964, Bowerman and Knight each contributed $500 and started Blue Ribbon Sports. Knight negotiated with a Japanese athletic shoe manufacturer, Onitsuka Tiger Co., to manufacture the shoes that Bowerman had designed. Blue Ribbon Sports shoes gained a cult following among serious runners because Knight distributed the shoes, called Tigers, at track meets.

In 1971, Blue Ribbon Sports received a trademark on its Swoosh logo, and it introduced the brand name Nike that same year. Blue Ribbon Sports parted ways with Onitsuka Tiger in 1972 and contracted with other Asian manufacturers to produce the company's shoes. Blue Ribbon Sports officially changed its name to Nike in 1978. During the late 1970s and early 1980s, Nike researchers used their technological expertise to develop several types of athletic shoes that revolutionized the industry. The company became more and more successful every year, with profits increasing steadily during this time.

In 1984, after five years of 44 percent annual growth, Nike missed the emerging market for aerobic shoes. The company had concentrated its efforts on an unsuccessful line of casual shoes. Reebok took the lead in the athletic shoe industry when it began selling large numbers of its fashion-oriented aerobic shoes to women. Nike stock prices decreased by 60 percent in 1984.

In 1990, Nike opened its first retail store, called Nike Town, in Portland, Oregon. Nike acquired Tetra Plastics (now called Nike, IHM, Inc.), the manufacturer of the plastic film in Nike's air sole shoes, in 1991 for $37.5 million. Nike purchased a cap-making company called Sports Specialties (now called Nike Team Sports, Inc.) in 1993. In 1994, the outdoor division added a new shoe called "Air Mada," and the Nike sport sandal became the top seller in the market. In 1995, Nike acquired Canstar Sports, Inc. (the world's largest hockey equipment maker) for $409 million. Canstar, now called Bauer Nike Hockey, Inc., manufactures in-line roller skates, ice skates and blades, protective gear, hockey sticks, and hockey jerseys.

## PRESENT CONDITIONS

Nike sells athletic shoes, accessories, sports equipment, and clothing for men, women, and children. The company's products are sold to approximately seventeen thousands retail accounts in the United States, including department stores, footwear stores, and sporting goods stores. Nike also sells its products through independent distributors, licensees, and subsidiaries in 140 countries around the world. Approximately thirty thousand international retail outlets sell Nike products. Nike operates a total of nineteen distribution centers in several different international markets: Asia, Canada, Latin America, Europe, and Australia. Two Nike Goddess stores, geared to women's clothing and footwear, were opened in Los Angeles in 2001. Nike purchased Impact Golf Technologies and, in 2002, will begin marketing golf clubs.

The Nike name and logo have such high consumer awareness that the company no longer includes the Nike name on its products; the "swoosh" logo is all that is needed.

Nike, Inc. operates 157 retail stores in the United States, including 81 factory outlets, 2 Nike stores, 57 Cole Haan stores, 4 employee-only stores, and 13 Nike Town stores. The company's Nike Town stores are located in major U.S. cities such as Portland, Chicago, Atlanta, New York City, Seattle, Boston, Los Angeles, and San Francisco. In 1999, Nike Town stores opened in London, England, and Berlin, Germany. Nike Town stores contain sports memorabilia, educational exhibits, basketball nets for use by customers, and Nike products. There are currently 111 Nike retail outlets outside the United States.

Almost 45 percent of total revenue in 2001 came from international sales. Non-U.S. countries that have the largest Nike business include the United Kingdom, Japan, France, Italy, Spain, Germany, and Canada. Revenues increased in all geographic categories (the United States, Europe, Asia-Pacific and the Americas) in 2001, with only the U.S. footwear segment showing a decline in sales from the previous year. Critics suggest that Nike lost ground in the U.S. footwear market because the company neglected the $60 to $90 shoe that makes up most of the industry's U.S. sales. Domestic and international revenues for Nike are shown in Exhibit 2.

The company has several recent additions to its line of businesses. The Michael Jordan collection of basketball clothing was launched in 1998. In 1999, clothing designed for young men who want the "urban look" was added to the Michael Jordan collection, and sports stars Randy Moss and Derek Jeter were hired to promote the Jordan brand. A new line called ACG (all Conditions Gear), which sells gear for snowboarding, skateboarding, surfing, and mountain biking, was launched in 1999. In 2001, the company launched **www.nikegoddess.com**, a Web site that celebrates women in sports. The company began distributing *Nike Goddess* magazines in NikeTown, Nordstrom, The Finish Line, and other retailers and as an insert in magazines such as *Sports Illustrated for Women*. Beginning in the spring of 2002, the company began selling three brands of apparel: Nike Performance (for athletes), Nike Active (gym-to-street wear), and Nike Fusion (stylish clothing made of high performance fabrics).

EXHIBIT 2    Domestic and International Revenues for Nike (in millions)

|  | 1999 | 2000 | 2001 |
|---|---|---|---|
| **USA Region** | | | |
| Footwear | $3,244.6 | $3,351.2 | $3,208.9 |
| Apparel | 1,385.3 | 1,154.4 | 1,260.3 |
| Equipment and Other | 93.8 | 226.5 | 349.8 |
| Total USA | $4,723.7 | $4,732.1 | $4,819.0 |
| **Europe Region** | | | |
| Footwear | $1,182.7 | $1,309.4 | $1,422.8 |
| Apparel | 1,005.1 | 933.9 | 976.3 |
| Equipment and Other | 68.0 | 163.7 | 185.7 |
| Total Europe | $2,255.8 | $2,407.0 | $2,584.8 |
| **Asia-Pacific Region** | | | |
| Footwear | $455.3 | $557.0 | $632.4 |
| Apparel | 366.0 | 321.0 | 374.8 |
| Equipment and Other | 23.2 | 77.1 | 102.8 |
| Total Asia Pacific | $844.5 | $955.1 | $1,110.0 |
| **Americas Region** | | | |
| Footwear | $3,35.8 | $343.9 | $359.6 |
| Apparel | 12.9 | 137.7 | 152.2 |
| Equipment and Other | 12.9 | 12.5 | 27.3 |
| Total Americas | $507.1 | $494.1 | $539.1 |
| Total Nike Brand | $8,331.1 | $8,588.3 | $9,052.9 |
| Other Brands | $445.8 | $406.8 | $435.9 |
| Total Revenues | $8,776.9 | $8,995.1 | $9,488.8 |

*Source:* Nike, Inc., *Form 10-K* (1999, 2001).

## COMPETITION

The athletic shoe industry has changed tremendously since sneakers were invented. In 1873, the sneaker was developed from India rubber and canvas material. Dunlop became the dominant seller of sneakers in 1938. Keds and PF Fliers dominated the children's market in the 1960s. Adult standard brands such as Adidas and Converse were well accepted by sports enthusiasts for years. When Nike entered the market in the late 1960s, the industry changed forever. In addition to new competition, lifestyles began to change, and companies began to contract manufacturing rather than invest in plant and equipment to manufacture their own products.

The major competitors in the industry are Nike and Reebok, who hold 37 percent and 15 percent percent market shares, respectively. Some of the other two dozen competitors in the industry include Adidas-Salomon AG, New Balance, K-Swiss, Fila, Asics, Keds, and Converse. Designer brands such as Tommy Hilfiger and Nautica have entered the athletic shoe market and provide shoes for fashion-minded young people. Fashion shoe brands, such as Vans and Skechers, that appeal to teenagers and young adults are taking some market share from the major competitors. Vans, a California company specializing in skateboarding shoes, earned $15.5 million in 2001. Skechers is endorsed by Britney Spears, and the company exceeded $1 billion in sales in 2001. The most intense competition continues to be among the two industry leaders, Nike and Reebok. The secret to success for these two competitors is that they contract out the manufacture of shoes to low-wage factories in Far East countries. This strategy allows each company to concentrate on marketing, image, and research and development.

### Reebok International, Ltd.

Reebok designs and develops athletic shoes and clothing worldwide. The company sells athletic shoes in different color combinations for aerobics, cycling, volleyball, tennis, fitness, running, basketball, soccer, walking, and children's footwear. The company diversified its offerings recently to include more types of casual shoes, sports clothing, other types of athletic shoes, and sports-related equipment. There are currently 204 Reebok stores in the United States. The company's four product divisions include Reebok, the Greg Norman Collection, Rockport, and Ralph Lauren footwear.

In the early 1980s, Reebok sold aerobic shoes primarily to women, but by the mid-1980s, large numbers of men were buying Reebok shoes too. Men now account for about half of Reebok's sales. The company's shoes are designed to make a fashion statement and are marketed to build on this image. Reebok CEO Paul Fireman believes that "Reebok is basically about freedom of expression." Reebok took the lead in revenues from Nike in 1987, but Nike regained its lead over Reebok in 1990. Despite Reebok's marketing efforts, the company continued to lose ground to Nike in the 1990s.

Reebok developed a series of marketing campaigns around sports stars in an effort to increase its market share. Some of the sports personalities who signed marketing contracts with Reebok include Julie Foudy, Venus Williams, Allen Iverson, Michael Chang, Greg Norman, and the Harlem Globetrotters. Reebok was also an early sponsor of the TV show *Survivor*. In August 2001, Reebok signed a ten-year contract with the National Basketball Association to provide all court apparel beginning with the 2004–2005 season. Sales of National Football League apparel is was greater than $125 million in 2001 and should reach $200 million in 2002. NBA Star Allen Iverson currently has a five-year, $48-million endorsement contract that is expected to be renewed by Reebok with a significant increase for the basketball star. Selected financial information for Reebok is shown in Exhibit 3.

EXHIBIT 3    Selected Financial Information for Reebok
(in millions except per-share amount)

|  | 1999 | 2000 |
|---|---|---|
| Gross Revenue | $2,899.9 | $2,865.2 |
| Net Income | 50.8 | 80.9 |
| Long-term Debt | 370.3 | 345.0 |
| Net Worth | 528.8 | 607.9 |
| Net Profit Margin (%) | 1.8 | 2.8 |
| Earnings Per Share | .89 | 1.40 |

*Source:* Value Line.

## International Competition

Competition is increasing in Europe. Adidas-Salomon AG, a German company, is the number one seller of athletic shoes in Europe and number two worldwide. Analysts believe that doing well in the European market is crucial to the continued success of companies in the athletic shoe industry. Nike sales in Europe, Asia, Canada, and Latin America increased to almost $3.8 billion in 2000 and to $4.2 billion in 2001. Reebok's total international sales were about $1.2 billion in 2000. Both Nike and Reebok hope to continue increasing their presence in the international retail market.

Adidas, the top European-owned competitor, will be fighting to maintain its 13 percent worldwide share of the competitive market for athletic shoes. Founded in 1948, Adidas outfitted such sports stars as Al Oerter (1956 Olympics) and Kareem Abdul-Jabbar (NBA). Family disputes in this family-owned company threatened its success after it gained a 70 percent market share in the United States. One brother became so angry he founded the rival company Puma. During this time, the company's U.S. market share dropped from 70 percent to 2 percent. The company was sold in 1989 for $320 million. The new owner became involved in other issues and neglected the company. By the time the current CEO took over in 1993, Adidas was losing about $100 million per year. When asked what he knew about the athletic shoe industry, CEO Robert Louis-Dreyfus replied, "All I did was borrow what Nike and Reebok were doing. It was there for everybody to see."

Adidas-Salomon AG brands include Adidas (footwear, balls, bags, and apparel), Erima (swimwear and team sport apparel), Salomon (ski equipment and apparel, hiking boots, and inline skates), Taylor Made (golf equipment), Mavic (cycle components), and Bonfire (winter sports clothing). Some of the sports stars who currently have endorsement contracts with Adidas include Kobe Bryant, Martina Hingis, Anna Kournikova, Donovan Bailey, and Peyton Manning. Selected financial information for Adidas is shown in Exhibit 4.

## ECONOMIC CONDITIONS

The U.S. athletic footwear market is growing again after slowing in the late 1990s. Sales in 1998 and 1999 were lower than previous years, but by the second half of 2000, sales levels were improving over previous years. U.S. sales rose 3.6 percent in 2000 over 1999 sales. Beginning in the fall of 2000, consumer confidence began to decline, and slow general economic growth continued through 2001. After the terrorist attack on the World Trade Center and Pentagon on September 11, 2001, the U.S. economy continued

EXHIBIT 4   Selected Financial Information for Adidas
(in millions except per-share amount)

|  | 1999 | 2000 |
|---|---|---|
| Gross Revenue | $5,391.7 | $5,494.1 |
| Net Income | 229.3 | 171.1 |
| Long-Term Debt | 1,494.9 | 1,522.9 |
| Total Assets | 3,612.7 | 3,783.8 |
| Total Equity | 684.8 | 767.7 |
| Net Profit Margin (%) | 4.3 | 3.1 |
| Earnings Per Share | – | 3.78 |

*Source:* www.hoovers.com.

to falter. Athletic shoe manufacturers have also experienced economic crises in some international markets. In 1999, for example, there were economic problems in Asia, but that economy recovered by the end of the year. In addition, the impact of foreign currency fluctuations and interest rate changes has the potential to create financial problems for athletic shoe manufacturers. The transition toward the Euro has also created some economic pressures in the European Union countries that recently converted their currencies to the Euro.

Most athletic shoe companies contract with manufacturing companies in the Far East to produce their shoes. Some of the countries that manufacture shoes for Nike, Reebok, and other companies include South Korea, Taiwan, China, Thailand, Malaysia, and Indonesia. The athletic shoe companies develop design specifications and new technology for the shoes in the United States and then send them to the factory to be produced. The primary advantage of foreign contract manufacturing is that no capital investment is required and the athletic shoe companies can operate with very little long-term debt. There are also several disadvantages to contract manufacturing. Some countries, such as Korea, that have produced large numbers of athletic shoes in the past are developing the expertise and contacts to begin producing more sophisticated electronics products and do not have available capacity to continue producing athletic shoes. Some additional disadvantages of overseas production include labor unrest, political unrest, delays caused by shipping, and unreliability of quota systems (embargoes).

## SOCIAL FACTORS

Beginning in the late 1970s, athletic shoe buyers became brand conscious, and the major competitors relied on their well-known brand names to sell their products. In recent years, consumers have changed their view of athletic footwear/clothing as fashion accessories. The ages of potential consumers present some unique challenges for athletic shoe/apparel companies. Generation Y children (born from 1979–1994) rival the size of the baby boom generation, are 60 million strong, and will be a significant market in the future. Generation Y consumers prefer fashion-oriented sportswear rather than athletic brand clothing. The Generation Y population responds differently to advertising than other generations did; this group is not swayed by glossy national advertising campaigns. It responds to truth in advertising and is more cynical and practical than other generations. Typically, Generation Y members prefer to use the Internet as a source of product information. Generation Y is an important target market for athletic shoe companies. Members of the large baby boom generation are interested in staying fit and healthy. In the 1980s, adults became obsessed with fitness, and by 1991 sales in the fitness equipment industry exceeded $30 billion. Currently, exercise is not as popular a pastime for baby boomers as it was in the early 1990s, but demand for clothing/footwear for leisure activities continues to increase for this group.

Changes in the lifestyles of girls/women will likely affect the industry. Since the mid-1990s, women have purchased more athletic shoes than men have. In addition, more girls are involved in sports today than ever before. There are currently more than 13 million women and girls who play basketball and approximately 7 million who play soccer.

## NIKE INTERNAL FACTORS

### Nike Research and Development

Nike is able to stay on the cutting edge in technology because research and development in the athletic shoe industry is largely design innovation and does not require a large investment in equipment. In 1980, the company formed the Nike Sport Research Laboratory (NSRL), which uses video cameras and traction testing devices and researches several types of concerns including children's foot morphology, "turf toe," and apparel aerodynamics. In addition, NSRL evaluates ideas that have been developed by the Advanced Product Engineering (APE) group. APE is involved in long-term product development. Shoes are created for five years in the future. This group developed cross-training shoes, the Nike Footbridge stability device, inflatable fit systems, and the Nike 180 air cushioning system. The company also uses its knowledge of technology to improve sports clothing. In June 2000, Nike introduced the Swift Suit, a full-length body suit designed to help runners keep muscles warm and reduce drag. One of the newest footwear developments is a spring-loaded shoe called Nike Shox that was introduced after sixteen years of research and development.

In addition to its laboratory work, Nike gets its designers to visit athletes to learn more about shoe technology. In 1996, the Nike staff worked with the Philadelphia 76ers to test a variety of shoes, and Nike's 1999 Air Seismic cross-trainer was the result. In 1997, Nike designers visited Mia Hamm to learn about what she expected of women's soccer shoes, and the company designed a lightweight shoe with a fiber cushion and foam. Nike continues to rely on superior technological developments to differentiate its products from competitors. Exhibit 5 indicates the major developments of Nike technology from 1990 to the present.

### Marketing

Since Nike does not actually produce shoes, the main focus of the company is creating and marketing its products. Nike positions its products as high-performance shoes designed with high-technology features. The general target market for Nike athletic shoes is males and females between the ages of eighteen and thirty-four. Nike, which recently decided to target women more aggressively, created Nike Goddess stores and began marketing more toward women who have an active lifestyle. Currently, 20 percent of Nike's sales are to women, while the industry average is 50 percent.

EXHIBIT 5     Recent Nike Technological Developments

| Date | Development | Purpose |
|------|-------------|---------|
| 1990 | Air 180 | Air cushioning in the heel and front of the shoe; heel cushion is 50 percent larger than previous models (consumer has a 180 degree view of the heel air bag) |
| 1991 | Huarache Fit Technology | Combination of neoprene and lycra spandex that provides runners with a form-fitting, supportive, and lightweight shoe |
| 1993 | Air Max Cushioning technology | Provides 30 percent more cushioning |
| 1996 | Zoom Air Cushioning | Material that is used in midsole to absorb pounding without taking away stability or speed |
| 1997 | Foamposite | Material that ensures no rough spots in the shoe |
| 1997 | Air Flightposite shoe | Dual-pigmented material with metallic hues that can be molded into a shoe |
| 2000 | Air Presto | Fashion shoes made almost entirely of stretch mesh |

Nike advertises its products in a variety of ways and targets its ads to specific groups or types of people. Advertising expenditures were $1 billion in 2001. The company continues to spend advertising dollars on TV ads during professional and college sports events, prime time programs, and late night programs. Prime-time ads are intended to reach a broad range of adults, and late night TV advertising is geared toward younger adults. Print is also a very important way to advertise Nike products. Print media such as *Sports Illustrated, People, Runner's World, Glamour, Self, Tennis, Money, Bicycling*, and *Weight Watchers* are also very important media for advertising Nike products. The company sponsored the U.S. Women's soccer team that won the 1999 World Cup and has significant sponsorships for the 2002 World Cup in Japan and Korea.

Nike sells its products online through **www.nike.com**, and Phil Knight meets with the Internet team daily. The online store sells a variety of products, including shoes, equipment, and apparel. In November 1999, the company began offering NIKEiD to its online customers. Customers can personalize their athletic shoes by selecting shoe colors and a personal ID or nickname. Nike adds a $10 fee for customization and will accept up to four hundred personalized orders each day. The company believes its online business will be an important component of its future sales. According to Phil Knight, "We absolutely believe it (Internet) is creating an entire business revolution and we truly intend to be a part of that revolution."

Some of the celebrity spokespersons for Nike include Michael Jordan, Andre Agassi, Monica Seles, Mia Hamm, Charles Barkley, Pete Sampras, Cheryl Swoopes, Marion Jones, Brandi Chastain, and Tiger Woods. Michael Jordan's Nike contract has, to date, been the most lucrative endorsement contract of all time for a professional sports player. Tiger Woods signed a reported $90 million deal in 1999 to promote Nike golf wear. In September 2000, Woods signed a five-year extension on his endorsement contract that was worth an estimated $100 million. Woods plans to begin playing with Nike clubs in 2002. Michael Jordan earned approximately $500 million in his playing career promoting products for twelve companies. In the three years after his retirement, his total endorsements have been worth $40 million. It remains to be seen whether Jordan's return to professional play will be as lucrative for Nike as it was in the past. Exhibit 6 shows some of Nike's advertising campaigns.

International marketing efforts continue. Nike has operations in 140 countries on six continents. Phil Knight says, "There's a pretty strong recognition that we'll be bigger in a couple of years outside the U.S. than inside." Nike is already number one in the overall footwear market in Spain, France, Belgium, Holland, Luxembourg, Finland, Italy, and the United Kingdom. Some of the new markets that are now being pursued include Chile, Peru, Bolivia, India, Mexico, South Africa, and several Eastern European countries. Wieden and Kennedy, the advertising agency responsible for most of Nike's ads, has opened offices in London, Tokyo, and Amsterdam so that advertising can be developed by local people to fit with local cultures.

## EXHIBIT 6    Selected Nike Advertisements

| Theme | Visual Image |
|---|---|
| "Hangtime" | An Air Jordan basketball shoe promotion features Michael Jordan and Spike Lee. |
| "Revolution" | The Beatles song "Revolution" is played, and images of sports stars were shown. |
| "Bo Knows" | The ad illustrates the range of Nike shoes (20 different sport categories). |
| "Just Do It" | The ad shows people from many walks of life exercising in Nike shoes. |
| "Multiple Bo's" | Bo Jackson meets Sonny Bono and fourteen other Bo Jacksons who represent different sports. |
| "Rock 'n' Roll Tennis" | Andre Agassi shows his tennis skills in rock video format. |
| "I am not a role model" | Charles Barkley says sports stars are not role models, but parents should be role models. |
| "Aerospace Jordan" | Cartoon characters Bugs Bunny, Looney Tunes bad guy Marvin Martin, and Michael Jordan travel to Mars. (Super Bowl XXVII) |
| "Air Swoopes" | An ad with Sheryl Swoopes introduces the Air Swoopes basketball shoe and announcing Nike sponsorship of the women's U.S. Olympic basketball team. |
| "Broad-Minded" | In an advertisement with Tiger Woods, the statement made is "We're not just canvas and leather shoes. We're big—and broad-minded." |
| "Date" | The U.S. Women's Soccer Team says, "We will take on the world as a team," and everyone on the team goes on a date with one person |
| "Two Fillings" | The U.S. Women's Soccer Team all want fillings when Brandi Chastain said she had two fillings. Each woman stands and says, "I will have two fillings." |
| "Chicks Dig the Long Ball" | Pitchers Tom Glavine and Greg Maddox try to get Heather Locklear's attention from Mark McGwire. |
| "Overjoyed" | Several Jordan-brand athletes are shown in slow motion: Randy Moss in a crowded hotel lobby and Derek Jeter surrounded by media in a locker room. |
| "Freestyle" | A group of basketball players plays to a musical soundtrack; this was part of Nike's sponsorship of the NBA All Star game. |
| "Much Respect" | A basketball music video is shown on BET and MTV2 television and www.nba.com. |
| "Why Sport? You'll Live Longer" | Suzy Hamilton (track runner) is shown sprinting away from a person wielding a chainsaw. |

## Distribution

Nike opened a 630,000-square-foot apparel distribution center in Memphis in 1992 that is called Nike Next Day. Footwear is distributed from centers in Greenland, New Hampshire; Beaverton, Oregon; Wilsonville, Oregon; and Memphis, Tennessee. Nike apparel is shipped from the Memphis distribution center. Sports specialty products are distributed from Irvine, California, and Cole Haan and Bauer products are distributed from Greenland, New Hampshire. The company operates a "Futures" ordering program that allows retailers to order up to six months in advance and be guaranteed to receive their orders within a certain time period and at a certain price.

However, retailers can receive apparel orders the next day if they place their orders by 7 P.M. the day before. Nike's automatic replenishment system provides automatic shipments to high-volume merchandisers in an effort to ensure a constant supply for retailers. Approximately $100 million in annual sales comes through the automatic replenishment system.

Knight worries that the brand will lose its image as a technically superior sports shoe if international marketing is not monitored carefully. Nike has purchased the distribution operations of many of its worldwide distributors in an attempt to control the marketing of Nike products. Some of these countries with "Nike owned" distributors include Singapore, Taiwan, Hong Kong, New Zealand, Korea, Japan, and Malaysia.

## Social Responsibility

Nike has been criticized in the past few years for employment practices at its international manufacturing sites. Some consumers are concerned about the exploitive practices of managers in some Asian countries. In 2001, for example, Indonesian factory managers making Nike products were charged with sexual harassment, physical and verbal abuse, restrictions in health services, and forced overtime. In addition, some of these managers were charged with requiring employees who misbehave or are late for work to run laps or clean toilets. Nike promises to investigate and improve inappropriate conditions wherever they exist.

The company first set up a labor practices department in 1996, and in 1998 the position vice president of social responsibility was created. In 1998, Nike joined the Fair Labor Association (FLA), a sweatshop-monitoring organization founded by a presidential task force made up of apparel manufacturers and human rights organizations. The company also belongs to the Global Alliance for Workforce and Communities (GAWC), a business group whose objective is to improve factory employees' work lives. Nike's leadership on labor initiatives in factories producing its products is shown in Exhibit 7.

In addition to its membership in FLA and GAWC, Nike has developed a process for ensuring that its factories comply with the company's code of conduct. The Nike Code of Conduct can be seen in Exhibit 8.

Nike has developed several programs that show the company's concern about social responsibility issues, and the company provides contributions to several charitable and nonprofit organizations. Some of the organizations Nike supports include the September 11 Fund, 100 Black Men of America, INROADS, Boys and Girls Clubs of America, the National Head Start Association, Habitat for Humanity, the YWCA of the United States, and the Jackie Robinson Foundation. Howard White, vice president of Marketing for the Jordan brand, conducts seminars called "Believe to Achieve" for at-risk youths. The seminars include a variety of local and national celebrity speakers from entertainment, sports, and business, and the seminars provide encouragement for youths to work toward success through vision, self-esteem, and commitment.

## EXHIBIT 7    Recent Nike Labor Initiatives

- 1997—Ambassador Andrew Young conducted an independent assessment of Nike labor practices. In response to Young's recommendations, Nike adopted a termination policy for contractors who violate the code of conduct, developed penalties for violations of the code of conduct, implemented training for managers, and established training programs for U.S. managers who will work in international markets.
- 1997—Eight weeks of training in 16 Asian cities was completed to reinforce the Nike code of conduct.
- 1997—Comprehension of the code was added to the corporate audit manual as a criterion for judgment.
- 1998—Nike joined the Fair Labor Association (FLA), a sweatshop monitoring organization founded by a presidential task force made up of apparel manufacturers and human rights organizations. Companies involved include Nike, Reebok, Liz Claiborne, and Phillips Van Heusen. Efforts to recruit other businesses to the FLA have been unsuccessful. Most of the apparel manufacturers and some retailers are joining an effort that has less stringent requirements than FLA and that has been spearheaded by the American Apparel Manufacturing Association. The group United Students Against Sweatshops (students from 100 universities) has demanded that universities withdraw support from the FLA and create a more rigorous plan for monitoring sweatshops. The student group wants companies to publicly disclose the locations of their foreign factories so that independent investigations of labor practices can occur.
- 1999—Nike joined the Global Alliance for Workers and Communities, a labor monitoring project.
- 2001—Nike began revealing the results of monitoring on its Web site on a quarterly basis.

*Source:* "Nike Puts Its Code of Conduct in the Pocket of Workers," *PR Newswire* (September 17, 1997) "Sweatshop Reform: How to Solve the Standoff," *Business Week* (May 3, 1999), and www.nikebiz.com.

N.E.A.T. (Nike Environmental Action Team) was formed in 1993. The purpose of this group is to pursue environmental initiatives and to recycle old athletic shoes and reuse them in new products. Nike recovers one hundred thousand pairs of shoes each month in its Reuse-A-Shoe program for recycling. Nike demonstrates its concern for the environment by using the recycled materials in the soles of its new shoes and by providing recycled material for sports fields/tracks. Every year, Nike recycles 5 million pounds of solid wastes. Exhibit 9 shows the life of a Nike product and Nike's environmental impact.

### Management Style/Culture

Phil Knight has created a strong culture at Nike, Inc. that is based on company loyalty and locker room camaraderie. Most corporate employees are health conscious young people and are in their thirties or younger. Knight trusts these employees to "Just Do It." In

## EXHIBIT 8    Nike, Inc. Code of Conduct

Nike, Inc. is committed to the promotion of best practices and continuous improvement in:
- Occupational health and safety, compensation, hours of work, and benefits.
- Minimizing our impact on the environment.
- Management practices that recognize the dignity of the individual, the rights of free association and collective bargaining, and the right to a workplace free of harassment, abuse, and/or corporal punishment.
- The principle that decisions on hiring, salary, benefits, advancement, termination and retirement are based solely on the ability of an individual to do his/her job.

*Source:* www.nikebiz.com.

---

**EXHIBIT 9**    The Life of a Nike Product—Natural Environmental Issues

1. **Research and Development**—Nike evaluates raw materials to reduce environmental impact (recycled materials, durable materials).
2. **Manufacturing**—The goal is to maximize product quality and minimize waste. The company does not dump the overflow of rubber from molds; instead {it grates} it into powder and {mixes} it with new rubber so it can be used. Dangerous chemicals used in the production process have been replaced with cleaner, water-based products.
3. **Retail**—Packaging has been reduced, no glues are used in the boxes, and box content includes recycled materials.
4. **Consumers**—Nike collects used shoes through its Reuse-A-Shoe program. This reduces the number of shoes in landfills.
5. **Down-Cycling**—Old athletic shoes are ground up into three materials: lights, foam, and rubber. These materials are made into new products such as carpet padding, equestrian trails, basketball courts, running tracks, and tennis courts.

*Source:* Nike, Inc., Consumer Affairs (1997).

---

the past, he often dropped out of sight for months at a time and then reemerged with some new approach for the company. His philosophy is "Play by the rules, but be ferocious. . . . It's all right to be Goliath, but always act like David." The seventy-four-acre corporate campus of Nike, Inc. provides a sense of the culture: It has wooded areas, running trails, a lake, and a fitness center. Knight believes that people should find a "sense of peace at work." Nike's organizational chart is shown in Exhibit 10.

---

**EXHIBIT 10**    Nike, Inc. Organization Chart

Some critics suggest that the Nike culture may be so strong that "entrenched" Nike employees' ideas are heard while new employees' ideas are dismissed quickly without consideration. Currently, 40 percent of the company's vice presidents have been with Nike, Inc. for less than five years. These new vice presidents have been asked to solve some serious dilemmas for Nike such as "How can the manufacturing and logistics system can be improved?" and "How can the company gain market share for its extreme sports products?"

## Finance/Accounting

During its years of rapid growth, Nike, Inc. managers encouraged free spending to develop and market company products. After cost-cutting layoffs and a search for efficiency that began in 1998, vice presidents began to spend more time making employees aware of the need for financial accountability. Each geographic region manager began receiving a profit-and-loss statement in 1998, and now compensation is partly tied to performance. Note in the income statement in Exhibit 11 that revenues for 2001 increased by 5 percent over 2000 while net income increased only 2 percent. The balance sheet (see Exhibit 12) provides information on assets and liabilities for 2000 and 2001.

## FUTURE OUTLOOK

Even with limited growth and intense competition in the athletic shoe/athletic apparel markets, Nike managers expect that the company will perform well in the future.

**EXHIBIT 11**    Nike Consolidated Statement of Income
(in millions except per-share data)

|  | Year-To-Date Ending | | |
| --- | --- | --- | --- |
|  | 5/31/01 | 5/31/00 | %Chg |
| Revenues | $9,488.8 | $8,995.1 | 5% |
| Cost of Sales | 5,784.9 | 5,403.8 | 7% |
| Gross Profit | 3,703.9 | 3,591.3 | 3% |
|  | 39.0% | 39.9% |  |
| SG&A | 2,689.7 | 2,606.4 | 3% |
|  | 28.3% | 29.0% |  |
| Interest Expense | 58.7 | 45.0 | 30% |
| Other | 34.1 | 20.7 | 65% |
| Pretax Income | 921.4 | 919.2 | 0% |
| Income Taxes | 331.7 | 340.1 | −2% |
|  | 36.0% | 37.0% |  |
| Net Income | $589.7 | $579.1 | 2% |
| Diluted EPS | $2.16 | $2.07 | 4% |
| Basic EPS | $2.18 | $2.10 | 4% |
| **Weighted Average Common Shares Outstanding:** |  |  |  |
| Diluted | 273.3 | 279.4 |  |
| Basic | 270.0 | 275.7 |  |
| Dividend | $0.48 | $0.48 |  |

*Source:* Nike, Inc., 2001 *Annual Report.*

---

### EXHIBIT 12    Nike Consolidated Balance Sheet (in millions)

|  | May 31, 2001 | May 31, 2000 |
|---|---|---|
| **Assets** | | |
| Cash & Investments | $304.0 | $254.3 |
| Accounts Receivable | 1,621.4 | 1,567.2 |
| Inventory | 1,424.1 | 1,446.0 |
| Deferred Taxes | 113.3 | 111.5 |
| Income Taxes Receivable | 0.0 | 2.2 |
| Prepaid Expenses | 162.5 | 215.2 |
| **Current Assets** | **3,625.3** | **3,596.4** |
| | | |
| Fixed Assets | 2,552.8 | 2,393.8 |
| Depreciation | 934.0 | 810.4 |
| Net Fixed Assets | 1,618.8 | 1,583.4 |
| Identifiable Intangible | | |
| Assets and Goodwill | 397.3 | 410.9 |
| Other Assets | 178.2 | 266.2 |
| **Total Assets** | **$5,819.6** | **$5,856.9** |
| | | |
| **Liabilities and Equity** | | |
| Current Long-Term Debt | $0 | $50.1 |
| Payable to Banks | 855.3 | 924.2 |
| Accounts Payable | 432.0 | 543.8 |
| Accrued Liabilities | 472.1 | 621.9 |
| Income Taxes Payable | 21.9 | 0.0 |
| **Current Liabilities** | **1,781.3** | **2,140.0** |
| | | |
| Long-Term Debt | 441.3 | 470.3 |
| Deferred Income Taxes & Other Liabilities | 102.2 | 110.3 |
| Preferred Stock | 0.3 | 0.3 |
| Common Equity | 3,494.5 | 3,136.0 |
| **Total Liabilities & Equity** | **$5,819.6** | **$5,856.9** |

*Source:* Nike, Inc., 2001 *Annual Report.*

According to Phil Knight, "This is the fourth downturn in 18 years as a public company. I said going into the 1990s that if we can get through it with only two downturns, we'll have a great decade. And I'll look forward to 2000 through 2010 coming up with the same statement." The company analyzed its 2001 activities by dividing them into "successes" and "sweat." It is likely that in the future, Phil Knight will continue to "sweat" while trying to build "successes" at Nike, Inc.

Consider the following questions regarding Nike's future:

1. Is Nike trying to supply products for too many sports? Should Nike narrow its product line in athletic shoes?
2. What types of acquisitions for Nike would you suggest to Philip Knight?
3. Should Nike begin producing some of its own products?
4. Is Nike taking the correct approach in marketing its shoes internationally?
5. What changes in product and advertising should the company pursue to appeal to the aging baby boomers? To Generation Y?
6. How can Nike maintain a competitive advantage over Reebok?

7. Is Nike responding correctly to concerns about the treatment of employees in international manufacturing facilities?
8. How can the company revitalize its U.S. footwear business?
9. Has Nike chosen the appropriate targets for new marketing efforts? Can the company be successful in gaining market share among women? Can the company be successful in the extreme sports segment of the market?

## REFERENCES

BERNSTEIN, AARON. "Sweatshop Reform: How to Solve the Standoff." *Business Week* (May 3, 1999): 186.

CHANDRASEKARAN, RAJIV. "Indonesian Workers in Nike Plants List Abuses." *The Washington Post* (February 23, 2001): E1.

"Core Passion Displaces Emotion-Added Brands." *Marketing Week* (September 2, 1999): 26.

DAWSON, ANGELA. "Swing for the Fences." *AdWeek* (May 3, 1999): 40.

ELLIOTT, STUART. "The Media Business: Advertising." *The New York Times* (April 10, 2001): C8.

GRANT, LORRIE. "Reebok Goes Toe to Toe with Nike." *USA Today* (September 4, 2001): B1.

HAMILTON, JOAN. "A Show of One's Own." *Business Week* (May 24, 1999): 62.

HIMELSTEIN, LINDA. "The Swoosh Heard 'Round the World." *Business Week* (May 12, 1997): 76.

"Insider: If the Shoe Fits, Will Nike Let You Wear It?" *Bangkok Post* (February 28, 2001).

KELLY, JANE. "Stranger than Fiction." *AdWeek* (January 4, 1999): 25.

LEE, LOUISE. "Can Nike Still Do It?" *Business Week* (February 21, 2000): 121.

NEUBRONE, ELLEN, and KATHLEEN KERWIN. "Generation Y." *Business Week* (February 15, 1999): 80.

Nike *Annual Reports* (1993, 1995, 1997, 1999, 2001).

"Team Mia." *AdWeek* (June 21, 1999): 42.

"There're Running as Fast as They Can." *Business Week* (July 12, 1999): 106.

WANG, EDWARD. "Nike Trying New Strategies for Women; Company Seeks Merger of Athletics and Fashion." *The New York Times* (June 19, 2001): C1.

WALLACE, CHARLES. "Adidas Back in the Game." *Fortune* (August 18, 1997): 176.

# REEBOK INTERNATIONAL, LTD.—2002

Carlisle P. Sampson
Francis Marion University

RBK

www.reebok.com

"Reebok, a company which strives to do what's right!" Reebok was one of the first companies to leave South Africa early in the apartheid era. On May 1, 2001, former U.S. President Carter met with Reebok Chairman Paul Fireman and Reebok's Board of Directors, to discuss the company's continuing efforts to promote human rights worldwide. Carter has served on Reebok's Human Rights Award Board of Advisors since 1989.

A possible vision statement for Reebok might define the company's goal like this: "to become the largest and most profitable athletic footwear and apparel company in the world."

A possible mission statement for Reebok might state:

*"If you don't stand for something, you'll fall for anything." We stand for human rights everywhere, equal respect and fair treatment for all people— including our employees around the globe, while providing for the athletic apparel needs of all people. We offer athletic apparel in multiple brand availability through Reebok Brand, Rockport, the Greg Norman Collection and the Ralph Lauren-Polo sport line. Through the latest technology, we are able to offer the "Defy Convention" sensation in footwear, at competitive pricing. Also, through advanced computer systems, we are consistently able to communicate the changing needs of our customers to our global divisions. Our goal is to be the leading provider of footwear and apparel at the best price and profit-level for our customer and shareholder.*

Headquartered in Stoughton, Massachusetts, Reebok is a global company engaged primarily in the design and marketing of sports and fitness products, including footwear, apparel, and products for nonathletic use. Reebok launched a new "It's a Woman's World" campaign in October 2001 to attract young women. Beginning with the 2002 season, all 32 football teams in the NFL will exclusively wear the Reebok brand. The company operates in 201 retail stores and has about 6,700 employees. Reebok's sales for 2001 increased 4.5 percent to $2,993 billion.

## HISTORY

Reebok's ancestor company, based in the United Kingdom, was founded to enable athletes to run faster. In the 1890s, the first running shoes with spikes were made by Joseph William Foster. In 1895, J.W. Foster and Sons provided shoes to international athletes. By 1958, a companion company, today recognized as Reebok, was started by two of the founder's grandsons. The company was named after an African gazelle.

In 1979, Reebok introduced three running shoes into the United States. By 1981, Reebok's sales exceeded $1.5 million. In the following year, the company introduced the first athletic shoe designed especially for women. The birth of this shoe coincided with a new fitness exercise called aerobic dance. Called the Freestyle, the shoe transformed the athletic footwear industry by encouraging aerobic exercise movement and the influx of women into sports. Products are now available in over 140 countries.

In 1992, Reebok began a transformation from a company identified principally with fitness and exercise to one equally involved in many sports. The company created a host of new footwear and apparel products for football, baseball, soccer, track and field, and numerous other sports. Reebok signed numerous professional athletes, teams, and federations to sponsorship contracts. After 20 years of spectacular growth globally, Reebok is now focused on greater accomplishments and continued innovation.

One of Reebok's most recent developments is the DMX technology, which provides superb cushioning, utilizing an active airflow system. The company's apparel products include the HYDROMOVE moisture-management system, which helps to keep athletes dry and thereby facilitates regulation of the wearer's body temperature. Reebok recently made licensing deals with the National Basketball Association (NBA). Mr. Paul Fireman, Reebok's chairman, president, and CEO, and his wife own about 20 percent of the company.

## INTERNAL FACTORS

### Organizational Structure

Although Reebok does not actually provide an organizational chart, a possible organizational structure is illustrated in Exhibit 1. Reebok is organized into six strategic business units, which include Classic Footwear (focus on lifestyle footwear); Performance Footwear (responsible for football, running, outdoor footwear, tennis, basketball, baseball, golf, cross-training, adventure and outdoor footwear); Global Apparel (responsible for fitness and sports apparel worldwide); Retail Operations (responsible for retail stores as well as for developing retail merchandise and promotional concepts); Kid's Products (focusing on children's products sold under the Reebok and Weebok brands); and Fitness (responsible for men's and women's fitness products).

Reebok operates 204 stores in the United States and consists of three subsidiaries; Rockport Company, the Ralph Lauren Footwear, and the Greg Norman Collection. The Rockport Company produces and distributes specially engineered comfort footwear for men and women worldwide. This division's product lines include performance, casual, and dress shoes that are designed to address the different aspects of consumers' lives. Rockport continues to use technologies to enhance comfort in its expanding product line, the men's Prowalker DMX. The Ralph Lauren Footwear products include the RLX collection and the Lauren collection for women. The Greg Norman Collection produces a range of men's apparel and accessories, all marketed and endorsed by golfer Greg Norman. This collection includes men's sportswear, with products ranging from leather jackets and sweaters to active wear and swimwear.

The executive officers of Reebok International can be observed from Exhibit 1.

Reebok places a strong emphasis on technology and focuses on cushioning, stability, and lightweight features. Reebok's most significant advancement is its DMX technology, which provides superb cushioning by utilizing a heel-to-foot, active airflow system that delivers cushioning when and where it is needed. In late 2000, Reebok introduced the latest iteration of its DMX technology with Viz-DMX. Reebok also introduced an enhanced version of its Traxtar shoe for children. This new "smart" technology measures a wearer's athletic performance and provides interactive feedback through a sound and light display unit in the shoe's tongue.

EXHIBIT 1    Reebok's Probable Organizational Structure

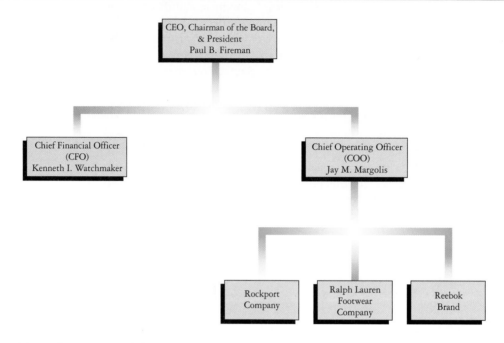

*Source:* Adapted from information in Reebok's 2001 *Annual Report*.

## Marketing

Reebok advertises through television, radio, print, and other media and utilizes its relationship with internationally recognized sport figures to maintain and enhance visibility for the Reebok brand. In early 2000, Reebok implemented product segmentation for its Classic products, which included certain new product introductions. To support this new Classic introduction, Reebok later launched a new advertising campaign featuring black and white photographs depicting both celebrities and noncelebrities wearing Classic footwear. The portraits appeared in *Vogue* and *Vanity Fair*. In addition, new relationships with two fashion boutiques, Fred Segal in Los Angeles and Gimme Shoes in San Francisco, were established. Reebok sponsored the highly successful CBS television show *Survivor,* which aired in the summer of 2000. As the exclusive title sponsor of all footwear and apparel to the show, Reebok gained significant brand exposure. Reebok also sponsored *Survivor II*, which began airing in early 2001.

Reebok continues to rely on athletic endorsements and sport sponsorships involving key athletes. In December 2000, Reebok resigned Venus Williams, winner of Wimbledon (2000), the Olympic gold medalist in both singles and doubles, and winner of both the 2000 and 2001 U.S. Open championships. This endorsement relationship reaffirms Reebok's heritage of commitment to women's sports and fitness. In its advertising campaign ("Defy Convention"), Reebok plans to showcase Venus as an icon. Other Reebok endorsements to promote the sale of its shoes are with NBA star Alan Iverson, NFL star Edgerin James, and Major League Baseball player Roger

Clemens. In soccer, Ryan Giggs, currently playing for the English league champion Manchester United, also sports Reebok boots. To gain further visibility for the Reebok brand, the company fitted 2,500 coaches, athletes, and officials in training apparel and footwear at the 2000 Summer Olympic Games in Sydney. Reebok sponsored several Olympic committees, including South Africa. Additional endorsements and sponsorships include professional tennis players Patrick Rafter and Andy Roddick.

## Finance

As indicated in Exhibit 2, for 2001 net income was $102.7 million, as opposed to net income of $80.8 million for 2000. Net sales as reported in U.S. dollars for 2001 were $2.99 billion, an increase from 2000 sales of $2.865 billion. Sales comparisons continue to be adversely affected by the weaker exchange rates of foreign currencies against the U.S. dollar.

As can be observed from Exhibit 3, footwear sales for 2001 decreased to $2.081 billion. Apparel sales in 2001 were $911.4 million, an increase from $767.2 million in 2000. Reebok's international sales of Reebok Branded products amounted to $346.1, $511, $467, and $292 million to the United Kingdom, Europe, and other countries respectively.

Rockport's sales decreased to $399.6 million in 2001 from $422.4 million in 2000, a decline of 5.4 percent. In 2001, Rockport's international revenues increased 5.2 percent. Net sales of Ralph Lauren Footwear decreased 8.8 percent to $97.3 million in 2001 from $106.7 million in 2000.

EXHIBIT 2    Reebok International Ltd. Consolidated Statements of Income (Amounts in thousands, except per-share data)

| | Year ended December 31 | | |
| --- | --- | --- | --- |
| | *2001* | *2000* | *1999* |
| **Net sales** | $2,992,878 | $2,865,240 | $2,899,872 |
| Costs and expenses | | | |
| Cost of sales | 1,894,497 | 1,779,686 | 1,783,914 |
| Selling, general and administrative expenses | 913,941 | 915,387 | 971,945 |
| Special charges | (532) | 3,289 | 61,625 |
| Interest expense, net | 17,630 | 22,126 | 40,532 |
| Other expenses, net | 11,536 | 8,947 | 13,818 |
| | 2,837,072 | 2,729,435 | 2,871,834 |
| Income before income taxes and minority interest | 155,806 | 135,805 | 28,038 |
| Income taxes | 48,300 | 49,000 | 10,093 |
| Income before minority interest | 107,506 | 86,805 | 17,945 |
| Minority interest | 4,780 | 5,927 | 6,900 |
| Net income | $ 102,726 | $ 80,878 | $ 11,045 |
| Basic earnings per share | $ 1.75 | $ 1.42 | $ .20 |
| Diluted earnings per share | $ 1.66 | $ 1.40 | $ .20 |

*Source:* Reebok's 2001 *Annual Report*, p. 39.

EXHIBIT 3    Reebok International Ltd. Net Sales

Net sales by product type are summarized below and include all brands.

|  | 2001 | 2000 | 1999 |
|---|---|---|---|
| **Net sales:** | | | |
| Footwear | $2,081,393 | $2,098,028 | $2,071,768 |
| Apparel | 911,485 | 767,212 | 828,104 |
|  | $2,992,878 | $2,865,240 | $2,899,872 |

Net sales to unaffiliated customers and long-lived assets by geographic area are summarized below:

|  | 2001 | 2000 | 1999 |
|---|---|---|---|
| **Net sales:** | | | |
| United States | $1,721,834 | $1,599,406 | $1,609,697 |
| United Kingdom | 511,426 | 514,772 | 545,562 |
| Europe | 467,207 | 462,342 | 476,695 |
| Other countries | 292,411 | 288,770 | 267,918 |
|  | $2,992,878 | $2,865,240 | $2,899,872 |
| **Long-lived assets:** | | | |
| United States | $ 152,383 | $ 142,577 | $ 167,068 |
| United Kingdom | 16,550 | 18,269 | 28,149 |
| Europe | 32,807 | 35,890 | 40,737 |
| Other countries | 8,898 | 9,387 | 11,049 |
|  | $ 210,638 | $ 206,123 | $ 247,003 |

*Source:* Reebok's 2001 *Annual Report,* p. 61–62.

## EXTERNAL FACTORS

### Research & Development

In 2001, Reebok spent $41.7 million on product research and development, compared to $49.8 million in 2000 and $55.4 million in 1999.

### E-Commerce

Use of the Internet as a distribution channel has become prominent in the apparel and footwear business. Online apparel sales exceeded $7 billion in 2001 and accounted for 3.2 percent of total apparel sales, having more than doubled since 1999.

More than 50 percent of online fashion buyers are 35 years or older, and two-thirds earn $60,000 or more annually. Reebok allows select retailers to sell Reebok and Greg Norman products to consumers through the Internet. Such e-commerce arrangements are expected to continue.

### Global Issues

The principal materials used in Reebok's footwear products are leather, nylon, and rubber. A loss of supply could temporarily disrupt production. In Europe and Great Britain, the supply of hides was recently reduced due to mad cow and foot-and-mouth diseases. This problem resulted in cost increases for the leather used in some of Reebok's footwear.

EXHIBIT 4    Reebok International Ltd Consolidated Balance Sheets
             (Amount in thousands, except per-share data)

| | December 31 | |
| --- | --- | --- |
| | *2001* | *2000* |
| **ASSETS** | | |
| Current assets: | | |
| Cash and cash equivalents | $ 413,281 | $ 268,665 |
| Accounts receivable, net of allowance for doubtful accounts (2001, $55,240; 2000, $48,016) | 383,372 | 423,830 |
| Inventory | 362,927 | 393,599 |
| Deferred income taxes | 104,280 | 101,715 |
| Prepaid expenses and other current assets | 30,835 | 37,396 |
| Total current assets | 1,294,695 | 1,225,205 |
| Property and equipment, net | 133,952 | 141,835 |
| Other non-current assets: | | |
| Intangibles, net of amortization | 76,686 | 64,288 |
| Deferred income taxes | 16,094 | 18,110 |
| Other | 21,746 | 13,608 |
| Total Assets | $1,543,173 | $1,463,046 |
| **LIABILITIES AND STOCKHOLDERS' EQUITY** | | |
| Current liabilities: | | |
| Notes payable to banks | $ 11,779 | $ 8,878 |
| Current portion of long-term debt | 97 | 13,813 |
| Accounts payable | 127,286 | 172,035 |
| Accrued expenses | 269,738 | 272,076 |
| Income taxes payable | 40,506 | 21,337 |
| Total current liabilities | 449,406 | 488,139 |
| Long-term debt, net of current portion | 351,210 | 345,015 |
| Minority interest and other long-term liabilities | 22,619 | 22,029 |
| Commitments and contingencies | | |
| Stockholders' equity: | | |
| Common stock, par value $.01; authorized 250,000,000 shares; issued shares: 98,049,605 in 2001; 96,208,558 in 2000 | 981 | 962 |
| Retained earnings | 1,453,348 | 1,301,269 |
| Less 39,010,827 shares in 2001 and 38,716,227 shares in 2000 in treasury at cost | (660,422) | (653,370) |
| Unearned compensation | (2,736) | (1,402) |
| Accumulated other comprehensive income (expense) | (71,233) | (39,596) |
| Total Stockholders' Equity | 719,938 | 607,863 |
| Total Liabilities and Stockholders' Equity | $1,543,173 | $1,463,046 |

*Source:* Reebok's 2001 *Annual Report,* p. 38.

Reebok's main suppliers are located in China and Indonesia—and thus are subject to U.S. customs duties. Duties on the footwear products range from 51 percent to 66 percent. An increase in customs duties would have a negative impact on Reebok's finances. If events should prevent Reebok from acquiring products from its suppliers in China, Indonesia, or Thailand, its operations could be disrupted until alternative suppliers could be found, and this development could have a negative financial impact. Nearly a third of Reebok's shoes are made in Indonesia. Reebok has relocated most of its non-Indonesian employees out of Indonesia because of safety concerns. If factories in Indonesia were not able to operate, it could take 30–45 days to replace a full set of molds for the bottoms of shoes that are needed to keep factories operating. Potential production slowdowns concern investors, because if prolonged, they could affect Reebok's ability to fill orders and get merchandise to retail stores. If it has to, Reebok has contingency plans it can institute, including securing excess production in China.

The European Union (EU) imposes quotas on footwear from China. If quotas are limited further, Reebok's product lines could be affected adversely, requiring sourcing from countries other than China. In addition to the quotas on China-sourced footwear, the EU has imposed antidumping duties against certain textile footwear from China and Indonesia. If the athletic footwear exemption remains in its current form, Rockport products would be subject to these duties. Reebok believes that its Reebok and Rockport trademarks and its rights to use the Greg Norman and Ralph Lauren names and logos are of great value. The company is vigilant in protecting its trademarks from counterfeiting. Loss of Reebok, Rockport, Ralph Lauren, or Greg Norman trademark rights could have a serious impact on Reebok's business.

Sales of athletic and casual footwear tend to be seasonal in nature, with the strongest sales occurring in the first and third quarters. Apparel sales also generally vary during the course of the year, with the greatest demand occurring during the spring and fall seasons.

## Competitors

Footwear competitors include Nike, Adidas, Fila, and New Balance. Apparel competitors include Nike, Adidas, Fubu, Mecca, and 2NYCE. The casual footwear market into which the Rockport product lines fall includes competitors such as Timberland, Clarks, Merrell, and Gabor. The Greg Norman line competes with Tommy Hilfiger and Nautica. The Ralph Lauren Footwear brand competes with Timberland, Tommy Hilfiger, and Gucci. Reebok International's four major competitors include Adidas-Salomon, New Balance, Fila, and Nike. Reebok currently holds the number two position behind Nike in total revenues. According to analyst John Stanley, "This industry has been as flat as a pancake for the last 9 years." From 1997–2001, Nike's market share has declined from 47 percent to 37 percent, while in the last year, Reebok's market share has increased from 12 to 15 percent.

The footwear and apparel industry is subject to rapid changes in consumer preferences. A major technological breakthrough or promotional success by one of Reebok's competitors could adversely affect its competitive position, as could a shift in consumer preferences. The athletic footwear and apparel industry has recently seen a shift away from athletic footwear to "casual" product offerings. This change of preference has adversely affected Reebok's business as well as that of some of its competitors.

In countries in which the athletic footwear market is mature, sales growth may be dependent in part on Reebok increasing its market share at the expense of its competitors. Competition for Reebok's products occurs in a variety of areas, including price, quality, product designs, brand image, marketing and promotion, and ability to meet delivery commitments to retailers. Rapid changes in consumer preference and technology in the footwear and apparel markets constitute significant risk factors for Reebok's operations.

Reebok's business is subject to changing economic conditions, including recession, inflation, general weakness in retail markets, and changes in consumer purchasing power and preferences. Adverse changes have a negative effect on Reebok. Retail sales of apparel rose by 1.5 percent in 2000. The U.S. economy slowed during the first six months of 2001. Real gross domestic product (GDP) rose 5.7 percent in the second quarter of 2000 and then slowed to a 1.3 percent increase in the third quarter and a 1.9 percent increase in the fourth. After rising 1.3 percent in the first quarter of 2001, GDP increased only 0.2 percent in the second. Prior to the terrorist attacks, the economy appeared to be hitting bottom. Since then, the economy has worsened.

## CONCLUSION

Reebok strives to "make a difference," and one official motto of Reebok has been that the company strives to become "the best, most innovative and exciting sporting goods company in the world." Reebok is currently undertaking various global restructuring activities designed to enable it to achieve operating efficiencies, improve logistics, and reduce expenses. There can be no assurance that Reebok will be able to effectively execute on its restructuring plans or that such benefits will be achieved. In the short-term, Reebok could experience difficulties in product delivery or with some of its other logistical operations as a result of its restructuring activities, and it could be subject to increased expenditures and charges due to inefficiencies resulting from such restructuring activities. Possible strategies that Reebok could embark on include streamlining its workforce and divesting operations in countries where it is most at risk. To survive in the future, Reebok needs a clear strategic plan.

## REFERENCES

www.cbs.com.

www.cnn.com.

"Economic Slowdown Takes a Toll." *Standard & Poor's Apparel and Footwear Industry Survey* (October 11, 2001): 1, 13, 20.

Jeffrey Edelman. "Reebok Gets a Boost." *Fortune* 134, no. 7 (2001): 63.

www.fortune500.com.

www.freeedgar.com.

www.msnbc.com.

www.quicken.com.

www.reebok.com.

www.strategyclub.com.

www.valueline.com.

www.wsj.com.

www.wsrn.com.

www.zacks.com.

# UST, INC.—2002

Marilyn M. Helms
Dalton State College

UST

www.ustshareholder.com

Vincent A. Gierer, Jr., CEO and chairman of the board for UST, Inc., examined the third quarter 2001 results and was pleased that the company's net earnings had increased 10.4 percent to $124.2 million, with a 7.2 percent sales increase to $417.8 million. The first nine months of 2001 saw sales increase 6.3 percent and earnings increase 8.3 percent. He reread his quote in the e-mail to the shareholders: "We experienced a strong quarter, exceeding our internal forecast and first call earnings estimates. In line with our strategic plan, all business segments have improved, and fundamentals continue to be strong for smokeless tobacco and wine. I remain confident that we will achieve our 10 percent EPS (earnings per share) growth forecast for the year." Yet with the September 11, 2001, terrorist attacks on the United States and the subsequent prolonged war and signs of a deepening recession, Gierer wondered if the external issues would hinder the firm's projected future growth. He also pondered future earnings potential given the number of pending lawsuits, increasing excise taxes in states like California, and the antitrust litigation appeal involving rival Conwood. Yet the third quarter numbers were strong, and investors remained happy and were quick to note that the company has paid cash dividends without interruption since 1912.

Favorable news came with the August 28, 2001, report that Standard & Poor's had raised UST Inc.'s long-term corporate credit and senior secured debt ratings from A– to A, as well as its senior unsecured debt from BBB+ to A– and short-term corporate credit ratings from A–2 to A–1. S & P felt that the ratings "reflect the company's moderate financial policies, solid profitability levels, and strong cash flow." Even with the S & P ratings and the strong third quarter, Gierer wondered about the company's plans for the winter of 2001. UST was planning to appeal the $1.05 billion verdict against the company in an antitrust lawsuit that had been won by its major competitor, Conwood. Could he and the company win the appeal, continue implementing their company's five-year plan, and provide superior returns to shareholders? He still remembered the initial verdict and its input on Wall Street; the company's share price had plunged $2.9375, or 15 percent, to $16.4375, a 52-week low. If the company lost the appeal, it would be a serious blow to UST and would drain the company's cash flow and possibly put its future dividends at risk.

## COMPANY PRODUCTS AND SCOPE

UST, Inc. has a company history dating to 1822, and the name U.S. Tobacco Company itself dates back to 1922. Copenhagen, UST's flagship brand, was introduced in 1822 and represents one of America's oldest trademarks; it also remains the best-selling moist, smokeless tobacco in the world. The company, based in Greenwich, Connecticut, is a holding company for four wholly owned subsidiaries: (1) United States Tobacco Company; (2) International Wine & Spirits Ltd; (3) UST Enterprises Inc.; and (4) UST

International Inc. The four groups combined employ approximately 4,800 employees. UST, through its subsidiary, U.S. Smokeless Tobacco Company (USSTC), is a leading producer and marketer of moist, smokeless tobacco products, including Copenhagen, Copenhagen Long Cut, Skoal, Skoal Long Cut, Skoal Bandits, Red Seal, and Rooster. Internationally, UST markets its products primarily in Canada, and sales have been both profitable and stable there for a number of years.

Other consumer products marketed by the company include premium wines sold nationally through the Chateau Ste. Michelle, Columbia Crest, and Villa Mt. Eden wineries as well as sparkling wine produced under the Domaine Ste. Michelle label. Other consumer products marketed by UST subsidiaries include Don Tomas and Astral premium cigars.

## COMPANY HISTORY

George Weyman, who invented Copenhagen snuff, opened a tobacco shop in Pittsburgh in 1822. Following his death in 1870, his sons took over the shop, renaming it Weyman & Bro. American Tobacco Company. A tobacco monopoly acquired Weyman & Bro. in 1905. When a Supreme Court ruling dissolved the monopoly in 1911 (finding it in violation of the Sherman Antitrust Act), the company was reorganized as Weyman-Bruton. After acquiring the United States Tobacco Company in 1921, the company took the name of the acquisition the following year. The firm introduced Skoal, a wintergreen-flavored tobacco, in 1934.

In 1965, United States Tobacco purchased the W. H. Snyder & Sons Cigar Company and later, after merging it into Wolf Brothers Cigar, renamed it House of Windsor (1981); Then it sold the company to its employees (1987). United States Tobacco entered the pipe business with the 1969 purchase of Henry, Leonard & Thomas, Inc., maker of the Dr. Grabow brand of presmoked pipes. In 1974, it added Mastercraft Pipes and bought its first winery (now called Chateau Ste. Michelle). Under Louis Bantle, who became chairman in 1973, sales of the company's snuff climbed 10 percent annually between 1974 and 1979, and by using rodeo and sports personalities as endorsers, the company expanded beyond its traditional northern markets into the Southeast and Southwest.

In the 1970s and the 1980s, the market structure of the industry began to change. Swisher International Group, Inc. and Conwood entered the market in the late 1970s. By 1980, three manufacturers sold five brands of moist snuff. Output was 26 million pounds, up from 17 million pounds in 1972. By the 1990s four manufacturers sold 28 brands. UST's share declined to 87 percent and industry output grew to 44 million pounds.

In 1983, United States Tobacco introduced Skoal Bandits, a teabag-like premeasured "dip" aimed at beginning consumers; at the time, the company denied targeting minors. Three years later, it acquired the Villa Mt. Eden and Conn Creek wineries and was incorporated as UST, a holding company for United States Tobacco.

UST's fortune fizzled in the late 1980s. Although previously excluded from the regulations imposed on cigarette makers, a $147 million case filed against the company in 1986 (Betty Ann Marsee claimed her son died of oral cancer caused by dipping Copenhagen) led to restrictions on smokeless tobacco. The suit was concluded in UST's favor in 1989, but the negative publicity led to mandatory warning notices on packaging, a ban on radio and TV advertising, and the imposition of an excise tax. Today, UST voluntarily displays the Age of Purchase Icon on print and point-of-sale ads for its products as well as on direct mailings; the message it proclaims states UST's policy of "not [being] for sale to minors." Despite the growing controversy, smokeless tobacco was the only growing segment of the industry in the early 1990s, and UST had more than 80 percent of the U.S. market. Vincent Gierer became CEO of UST in 1990.

Market growth in the industry accelerated throughout the 1990s. By 1999, there were approximately 40 brands, 24 of which were from UST's competitors. UST's share dropped to 76 percent, and total output exceeded 60 million pounds, an increase of 36 percent over 1990. By contrast, industry sales for all other tobacco products fell in the 1990s.

Allegations of nicotine manipulation in its products led the company to testify before Congress in 1994. In 1997, UST joined four other tobacco companies and paid $11.3 billion as part of Florida's settlement against the tobacco industry. It also launched discount dip Red Seal the same year. In 1998, following the tobacco industry's $206 billion settlement in several states, the company entered into a separate agreement to pay $100–$200 million over ten years for youth-targeted antismoking programs. In 1999, 34 Native American tribes filed suit in New Mexico against UST and other major tobacco companies for $1 billion of the $206 billion judgment.

In March 2000, a federal jury ordered UST to pay $1.05 billion (more than twice its 1999 profits) to competitor Conwood as a result of a 1998 antitrust lawsuit accusing UST of using unethical tactics to keep Conwood's products out of stores. UST is appealing the decision (*Hoover's Handbook of American Business, 2001*).

Today, UST is the largest U.S. manufacturer and distributor of moist chewing tobacco and snuff. CEO Gierer has an annual salary of $2,755,000. The company ranks number eight among top Republican donors, contributing some $1,927,200 from January 1990 to June 1999, as reported by Democracy Now (**http://democracynow.org/companies/ust.html**). Wine yields about 11 percent of UST's sales. The firm also makes cigars and owns Bert Grant's Ale microbrewery in Washington State. The McLane Company (a distributor owned by Wal-Mart) sells about 20 percent of UST's products. UST's profit margins (over 30 percent) are as good as Microsoft's. Its impressive returns rank among the highest of any public company, with a return on sales of 29 percent, a return on assets of 24 percent, and a return on equity of 84 percent (all in 2001).

Its tobacco division features both moist smokeless tobacco made from 100 percent American tobacco (Copenhagen, Red Seal, Rooster, Skoal, and Skoal Bandits) as well as premium cigars (Astral, Don Tomas, Habano Primero). The beverages products include craft beer (Bert Grant's Ale), premium wine (Conn Creek, Villa Mt. Eden), premium varietal wine (Chateau Ste. Michelle, Columbia Crest, Snoqualmie), and sparking wines (Domaine Ste. Michelle).

## MARKET SHARE

Of UST's $1.67 billion in total sales for 2001, $1.45 billion of this was from the smokeless tobacco segment. This was an 8 percent increase over 2000. The tobacco segment accounts for 87.5 percent of consolidated UST's sales. The wine segment had net sales of $188 million in 2001, while all other UST sales were $30.7 million. It is the leader in the smokeless tobacco market, having captured about 77 percent. This figure is down from a near 85 percent market share high in 1993. This loss shows that UST has not escaped the industry's problems. The drop also represents a 3 percent slide from 1997, when UST had a near 80 percent share of the market. Mr Gierer indicated that net volume only grew at 0.2 percent, citing slowing category growth as the reason why. The company lost one point in market share attributed to the discontinuance of some UST products.

According to the *Tobacco Report: 1998–1999*, which was issued in 2001 by the Federal Trade Commission in a report to Congress, of the five major domestic manufacturers of smokeless tobacco, UST continued to lead the industry in 1999, with 75 percent of the moist snuff market in terms of pounds sold; its closest competitor, Conwood, reportedly had 13 percent of that market. Swedish Match reportedly controlled

39 percent of the loose-leaf market in 1999; Conwood controlled 34 percent, National controlled 19 percent, and Swisher controlled 8 percent.

## SALES TRENDS BY PRODUCT SEGMENT 2001

2001

*Smokeless Tobacco*

For 2001, net sales of smokeless tobacco increased 8 percent to $1.451 billion, and gross profit increased 8.5 percent. Moist, smokeless tobacco net can sales increased 2.5 percent to 648.7 million cans in 2001. During 2001, UST introduced three new products, Copenhagen Black, Rooster Wild Berry, and Red Seal Long Cut Straight. Premium promotional can sales in 2001 were reduced by 10.4 million, or 33.6 percent for the nine-month period ending September 30, 2001; moist, smokeless tobacco net can sales increased 0.6 percent to 480.1 million cans.

*Wine Segment*

2001 wine segment revenue increased 8.2 percent to $188.9 million. Premium case sales advanced 8.8 percent, while nonpremium case sales declined. Case sales for the segment's best selling wines—Columbia Crest and Chateau Ste. Michelle—increased 13.7 and 9.3 percent respectively. Operating profit increased 22.1 percent to $21.2 million.

UST is the only wine company in the world to place five wines on *Wine Spectator*'s "Top 100 Wines of the World." In 2001, UST's Chateau Ste. Michelle Cold Creek Chardonnay was the highest ranked white wine on this prestigious list. Strong demand for premium wine in 2001 is encouraging for the company; the installation of a new president is likewise an encouraging development. Instead of expanding by acquisition, Stimson Lane will shift its focus to improving operating results by reducing costs of goods sold,

## EXHIBIT 1    UST Consolidated Statement of Earnings
### (in thousands, except per-share amounts)

| Year ended December 31 | 2001 | 2000 | 1999 |
|---|---|---|---|
| **Net Sales** | $1,670,315 | $1,547,644 | $1,512,331 |
| **Costs and Expenses** | | | |
| Cost of products sold | 312,304 | 294,802 | 276,358 |
| Excise taxes | 37,277 | 35,277 | 27,917 |
| Selling, advertising and administrative | 487,706 | 464,842 | 431,578 |
| **Total Costs and Expenses** | 837,287 | 794,921 | 735,853 |
| **Operating Income** | 833,028 | 752,723 | 776,478 |
| **Interest, net** | 33,760 | 34,288 | 13,535 |
| **Earnings Before Income Taxes** | 799,268 | 718,435 | 762,943 |
| **Income Taxes** | 307,666 | 276,549 | 293,650 |
| **Net Earnings** | $  491,602 | $  441,886 | $  469,293 |
| **Net Earnings Per Share** | | | |
| Basic | $      2.99 | $      2.71 | $      2.69 |
| Diluted | $      2.97 | $      2.70 | $      2.68 |
| **Average Number of Shares** | | | |
| Basic | 164,250 | 163,181 | 174,355 |
| Diluted | 165,682 | 163,506 | 175,114 |

*Source:* UST's 2001 *Annual Report,* p. 24.

improving top-end quality wines, and eliminating underperforming assets. By refocusing on existing operations, the wine business is expected to deliver operating profit increases in excess of 20 percent in each of the next several years, according to the 2000 Annual Report.

## MISSION AND VISION

According to U.S. Smokeless Tobacco Company's vision statement, "Our smoke-free products will be recognized by adults as the preferred way to experience tobacco satisfaction. The four key strategies to attaining this vision are breaking down barriers, improving the value equation, effectively allocating resources, and developing next-generation products." Stimson Lane's vision statement says that the company strives—"To be the leader in the ultra-premium wine segment, to elevate Washington State wines to the quality and prestige of the top wine regions of the world, and to be known for superior products, innovation, and customer focus. To realize its vision, Stimson Lane will continue to build on the significant critical acclaim it achieved in 2000."

**EXHIBIT 2**    UST Consolidated Segment Information (in thousands)

| Year ended December 31 | 2001 | 2000 | 1999 |
|---|---|---|---|
| **Net Sales to Unaffiliated Customers** | | | |
| Smokeless Tobacco | $1,450,714 | $1,343,779 | $1,309,566 |
| Wine | 188,858 | 174,472 | 174,272 |
| All other | 30,743 | 29,393 | 28,493 |
| **Net sales** | $1,670,315 | $1,547,644 | $1,512,331 |
| **Operating Profit (Loss)** | | | |
| Smokeless Tobacco | $833,185 | $768,786 | $777,122 |
| Wine | 21,212 | 17,377 | 20,234 |
| All other | (8,907) | (15,772) | (10,240) |
| **Operating profit** | 845,490 | 770,391 | 787,116 |
| Corporate expenses | (12,462) | (17,668) | (10,638) |
| Interest, net | (33,760) | (34,288) | (13,535) |
| **Earnings before income taxes** | $799,268 | $718,435 | $762,943 |
| **Identifiable Assets at December 31** | | | |
| Smokeless Tobacco | $1,268,065 | $1,120,377 | $529,518 |
| Wine | 389,243 | 342,447 | 305,447 |
| All other | 60,180 | 68,776 | 87,678 |
| Corporate | 294,214 | 114,799 | 93,005 |
| **Assets** | $2,011,702 | $1,646,339 | $1,015,648 |
| **Capital Expenditures** | | | |
| Smokeless Tabacco | $27,364 | $28,743 | $26,830 |
| Wine | 19,336 | 20,720 | 31,182 |
| All other | 246 | 522 | 939 |
| Corporate | 284 | 1,090 | 338 |
| **Capital expenditures** | $47,230 | $51,075 | $59,289 |
| **Depreciation** | | | |
| Smokeless Tobacco | $20,298 | $19,573 | $17,279 |
| Wine | 12,842 | 13,869 | 13,279 |
| All other | 914 | 1,395 | 1,534 |
| Corporate | 951 | 1,677 | 1,645 |
| **Depreciation** | $35,005 | $36,514 | $33,737 |

*Source:* UST's 2001 *Annual Report,* p. 23.

# EXHIBIT 3     UST Consolidated Statement of Financial Position
## (In thousands)

| December 31 | 2001 | 2000 |
|---|---|---|
| **Assets** | | |
| **Current assets** | | |
| Cash and cash equivalents | $ 271,969 | $ 96,034 |
| Accounts receivable | 85,423 | 82,698 |
| Inventories | 493,820 | 449,284 |
| Deferred income taxes | 16,855 | 9,907 |
| Income taxes receivable | — | 28,915 |
| Prepaid expenses and other current assets | 23,892 | 24,567 |
| Total current assets | 891,959 | 691,405 |
| **Property, plant and equipment, net** | 369,568 | 358,586 |
| **Restricted deposits** | 659,897 | 505,755 |
| **Other assets** | 90,278 | 90,653 |
| Total assets | $2,011,702 | $1,646,399 |
| **Liabilities and Stockholders' Equity** | | |
| **Current liabilities** | | |
| Short-term debt | $ 3,300 | $ 3,300 |
| Accounts payable and accrued expenses | 171,610 | 155,179 |
| Income taxes payable | 47,552 | 14,393 |
| Total current liabilities | 222,462 | 172,872 |
| **Long-term debt** | 862,575 | 865,875 |
| **Postretirement benefits other than pensions** | 81,679 | 81,677 |
| **Deferred income taxes** | 183,524 | 186,559 |
| **Other liabilities** | 80,400 | 68,844 |
| Contingencies {see note} | — | — |
| Total liabilities | 1,430,640 | 1,375,827 |
| **Stockholders' equity** | | |
| Capital stock | 101,710 | 102,372 |
| Additional paid-in capital | 635,380 | 526,996 |
| Retained earnings | 915,990 | 885,074 |
| Accumulated other comprehensive loss | (18,256) | (13,606) |
| | 1,634,824 | 1,500,836 |
| Less treasury stock | 1,053,762 | 1,230,264 |
| Total stockholder's equity | 581,062 | 270,572 |
| Total liabilities and stockholders' equity | $2,011,702 | $1,646,399 |

Source: UST's 2001 *Annual Report*, p. 25.

## PRODUCT/MARKET SHIFTS

UST Inc. seems to be benefiting from higher cigarette prices. As a maker of moist, smokeless tobacco products, UST isn't necessarily luring new consumers who don't want to pay more for cigarettes, but the company is actually winning over its own customers, who incidentally don't want to pay more for cigarettes. About 25 percent of UST's consumers also smoke cigarettes, so instead of using both, many tobacco users are moving away from higher-priced cigarettes and buying more snuff. While growth in moist snuff volume has increased, the Tobacco Merchants Association indicates that the chewing tobacco industry has been plummeting since 1988.

## PRODUCT AND FLAVOR TRENDS

Snuff is a finely ground or shredded form of tobacco, most commonly sold in small tin cans or pouches. Users put a pinch between their lower lip or cheek and gum. Snuff contains nicotine and a variety of cancer-causing chemicals that are absorbed into the blood. Because snuff is held in the mouth for minutes at a time, some argue that more of the chemicals enter the body than they would from cigarette smoking.

One of the growing trends in smokeless tobacco, besides the type of cut that is preferred (fine cut or long cut), is the preponderance toward added flavors. Mint or ice seems to be the favorite among the younger adult consumers. Changes in the smokeless tobacco market are consumer driven, and the entire smokeless market is striving to meet the changing trend. Other smokeless products that are appearing on the scene are tobacco and nicotine-free chews. These herbal snuffs are a substitute for the standard product and smokeless tobacco in general, as well as a substitute for many smokers. In mid-1995, when UST introduced its new product, the Skoal Flavor Packs, the product was marketed to "smokers who can't smoke." Skoal Bandits, a moist snuff that is packaged in portion packs similar to small tea bags, along with other smokeless products are aiding profits. In contrast to the increase in moist snuff, chewing tobacco, a longer cut tobacco sold in foil packages, has been continually losing ground.

Most competitors in the smokeless category have added a discount brand. Companies such as Conwood and Swedish Match have launched Durango, Cougar, and Southern Pride, to meet this market, which is continuing to grow. Coupled with this bargain trend, companies such as Smokey Mountain Snuff and Conwood are linking their products to sporting events as a promotional strategy.

Another factor that helps to boost the trend toward increasing sales of moist snuff is its availability within the market. This product can be purchased in locations such as supermarkets, smoke shops, mass merchandisers, and discount and convenience stores. The products can even be purchased online at retailers such as **www.freshnuff.com/orderonline.htm**. Additionally, as the number of places that people can smoke are further restricted, moist snuff sales will grow because it is easy to use anywhere. Driving the trend further is aggressive advertising, which is directed at the moist snuff segment of the market. According to the *Maxwell Report,* smokeless tobacco use in 2000 edged up 10.5 percent to 116.5 per cent million pounds versus 1999. The moist snuff category slipped 2 percent to 64.8 million pounds.

UST's newest product, Revel, was introduced in the fall of 2001 in two test markets—in Topeka, Kansas, and Youngstown, Ohio—for six months. Supporting the product launch was print advertising; direct marketing, adult sampling, and point-of-sale and retail promotions. Revel is marketed as an "Anytime, Anywhere"™ product for adults to use when they can't smoke cigarettes—for example, on airplanes, in meetings, on the factory floor, or in a shopping mall. The product is a blend of tobacco and mint flavor in a packet. Offered in both regular and mild, it differs from previous smokeless tobacco products insofar as adults who have tried it report that they feel no need to expectorate. Offered in a plastic push and flip container, each has 20 packs and is priced competitively with a pack of premium cigarettes.

Rooster has been promoted to college students in college newspapers since 2000. UST had waited one year before ending its 35-year self-imposed ban on advertising in college newspapers in 1999. Its break with the past has also generated discussions in newsrooms and on colleges campuses as students and professors have debated whether campus papers would be breaching tobacco's First Amendment rights by rejecting ads for a legal product. The campaign has had little negative response, according to advertising managers at various campus newspapers.

## MARKETING

UST is in the next phase of its "A pinch better" campaign, having launched a nearly $3 million Skoal Heavy Chevy Camero Sweepstakes effort in August 2001, which ran to the end of the year. Consumers can win a 2002 Chevrolet Camaro SS and a trip to Frank Hawley's Drag Racing School or Cobra two-way radios. Ads were placed in magazines, including *Playboy, Hot Rod*, and *Drag Race*. POP (point-of-purchase) and direct mail to 525,000 moist, smokeless tobacco users supported the campaign. Skoal recently switched from passive outdoor images after consumers requested masculine and active images more befitting the brand, said Rich Fasanelli, USSTC's VP of Marketing. The new initiative focuses on motorcycle riders, firefighters, and rugby players. Skoal also sponsors the Don Prudhomme NHRA racing team. Other marketing strategies includes special packaging to stress "outdoor adventures," mail-in sweeps for boats and trips or cash or personal navigation systems, and a "lids for gear" program that allows consumers to redeem Skoal lids for prizes such as fishing gear, knives, Cobra handheld radios, and other discounts.

## CURRENT LITIGATION

Approximately 35 cases have been filed against UST (and other tobacco manufacturers) since 1954. Only one case has been tried to a verdict, and it resulted in a unanimous jury decision in favor of UST. Most of the litigation has focused on cigarettes, and UST continues to stress the difference between cigarettes and smokeless tobacco.

UST was ordered to pay $1.05 billion to rival Conwood after a federal jury ruled that the company violated antitrust laws. After a month-long trial, the jury awarded damages, which were automatically tripled under antitrust laws. Both companies accused each other of removing display racks from stores, making under-the-table cash rebates to win retailers, and holding strategy sessions to plot ways to eliminate the other competitor from the lucrative retail-checkout market. Jurors found that UST monopolized the market by controlling prices or excluding competition or both. Conwood attorneys accused UST of spreading rumors that Conwood's snuff contained stems and was stale. Conwood also alleged that UST controlled point-of-sale advertising and often inserted its ads over Conwood's own sales displays in stores. UST hopes to have the jury's award for Conwood overturned or reversed on appeal.

UST has not escaped the class-action litigation aimed at the major domestic cigarette companies. These legal cases are geared toward the reimbursement of healthcare costs in addition to damages and other relief for smokers. While the predominance of the cases relate specifically to cigarettes, there are a few that relate directly to smokeless tobacco products like those manufactured and sold by UST.

Litigation continues to plague the smokeless tobacco industry. West Virginia has legislation pending to impose the state's first smokeless tobacco tax. The bill (SB116) would impose a 7 percent excise (or sin) tax on smokeless tobacco products. This is down from the original 25 percent tax Governor Bob Wise had proposed. Monies from the tax would be distributed to the countries. The *Charleston Daily Mail* (March 31, 2001) reported results of a study that indicated nearly half of West Virginia's teenage boys who use smokeless tobacco would quit if the price increased, but some lawmakers doubt whether a smokeless tobacco tax would help lower the relatively high percentage of West Virginian teens who use the tobacco. In males, the state ranks third in the country in smokeless tobacco use, and a 1999 Youth Risk Behavior Survey showed that West Virginian teens were twice as likely to use smokeless tobacco as other U.S. teens. Opponents of the tax want to maximize profits, while supporters of the tax want to prevent addiction and save lives. Health advocates cite scientific studies indicating that price increases are the most effective deterrent to tobacco use by youths. Retailers and wholesalers do not believe this to be true, yet they clearly believe the tax increase will hurt sales. Estimates are that approximately 12 million people in the United States use smokeless tobacco, and 3 million of these users are under 21. An estimated 2,200 young people age 11–19 try smokeless tobacco every day, and 830 become regular users. Vast regional differences are apparent, and tobacco use is highest in the South.

West Virginia could join California, which recently passed a new tax on smokeless tobacco to attempt to slash at least a third of the 100 million ounces of smokeless tobacco sold in California every year. Supporters feel the tax will deliver an extra $67 million annually to the state. Some say the tax will lead to a thriving underground racket in snuff and chewing tobacco and cheat the state of tax revenue. Moist snuff in California now costs around $8 for a can, up from about $3.

## THE SMOKELESS TOBACCO INDUSTRY

Today, the U.S. tobacco industry is an approximately $53 billion industry, with cigarettes accounting for nearly 94 percent of the total. The remaining 6 percent of usage is for cigars, moist smokeless tobacco, chewing tobacco, and snuff. The cigarette industry is quite mature and consolidated, with the top four producers accounting for approximately 72 percent of industry sales (Standard & Poor's Industry Surveys).

The smokeless tobacco industry (NAICS 312229), divided into two major areas—chewing tobacco and snuff—consists of different products. The chewing tobacco area consists of loose-leaf, moist, firm plug, and twist/roll products. The snuff group consists of dry and moist, depending on the amount of moisture added to the tobacco during manufacturing. Despite the fact that consumption patterns have shifted from loose leaf to moist snuff, there is still a large number of consumers who use both products.

Consumers of moist smokeless tobacco products are extremely brand loyal and demand product freshness. Research shows that consumers looking for a particular brand will go elsewhere if they don't find it rather than purchase another brand. Out-of-stock sales can hurt sales performance, but carrying excess inventory can result in stale products. Retailers work with suppliers to develop selections to maintain stock and to preserve product freshness.

The aggregate tobacco industry is classed with oligopolistic industries. Firms face high capital costs, hazardous antitrust and legal action, futile price-cutting, and charges of monopolistic practices if firms should try to join in a concerted action. The U.S. tobacco products industry has undergone substantial consolidation over the years. Prompted mainly by the combined challenges of declining U.S. consumption trends in a highly developed marketplace and the steady rise in legal and regulatory burdens, many manufacturers have either joined forces with competitors or perished. The increased scale needed to compete in the industry has erected very high barriers to entry.

The smokeless tobacco industry is highly concentrated in the tobacco-producing region of the United States. The five states that have the greatest number of workers in the industry are Kentucky, Tennessee, Georgia, North Carolina, and Illinois. Georgia and Illinois have replaced Virginia and Pennsylvania as leading employers of smokeless tobacco workers. Over one-half of the employment in the industry is concentrated in Kentucky. The reasons for this geographic concentration are obvious, the first being a desire to locate factories close to raw materials. Another reason is that the industry is concentrated in the area of the country that has traditionally been considered the prime market for the smokeless industry—the South.

The cigarette industry dwarfs the smokeless industry, and cigar consumption has increased among men over the age of eighteen. Magazines such as *Cigar Aficionadom, Cigar*

*Insider,* and *Smoke,* all of which are smoking lifestyle magazines, are capitalizing on the stogie's neo-cool image and drawing in luxury-goods advertisers. While its cigar operations are small, UST markets many recognized brands. This area of its business has been affected by a substantial oversupply in the marketplace, a development that has resulted from the fact that many companies flood the market in an effort to meet this neo-cool trend. UST is currently evaluating the situation to determine its prospects and alternatives.

## RETAIL DISTRIBUTION OF MOIST SNUFF

Manufacturers typically sell moist snuff to independent wholesalers that resell to retailers. By 1999, approximately 300,000 retail stores in the United States sold moist snuff, but sales volume was dominated by large chains, including mass merchandisers (e.g., Wal-Mart, 2,300 stores; Kmart, 2,160 stores), convenience stores (e.g., 7-Eleven, 2,500 stores), and supermarkets (e.g., Kroger, 2,288 stores). Conwood products are in 81 percent of all retails stores; USSTC's distribution rate is 87 percent; Swedish Match and Swisher are also widely distributed. There are no agreements between retailers and moist snuff manufacturers that force retailers to deal in the products of only one manufacturer.

In offering new products, each manufacturer must justify the retailers' allocation of space to them. About 70 to 90 percent of retailers still used separate racks provided by each moist snuff manufacturer for its own products. In the 1995–1996 period, Wal-Mart asked all manufacturers to compete in designing a single customized cabinet for the display of moist snuff products in order to provide greater uniformity, aid inventory management, and maximize shelf space efficiency. USSTC's design won. Swedish won similar competitions for exclusive rack systems in Kmart and Tom Thumb stores. Due to restrictions on self-service and theft problems, products are no longer displayed on open shelves, but they are increasingly restricted to locked cabinets and secure behind-the-counter areas.

Manufacturers offer retailer's incentive programs and rebates for providing sales data, for participating in promotional programs, or for giving a manufacturer the best placement of racks and displays. Manufacturers have sales personnel in the field, and each one visits 8 to 10 retail stores per day to routinely check racks, to check that stock is current, and to introduce new products and promotions.

## COMPETITORS AND MARKET SHARE

*The Federal Trade Commission Report to Congress for the years 1998 and 1999* (issued in 2001) indicates that of the five major domestic manufacturers of smokeless tobacco, UST continued to lead the industry in 1999 in terms of pounds sold; it has a 40.5 percent share of the total smokeless tobacco industry altogether. Published reports also indicate that Conwood's 1999 industry share was 23.8 percent, Swedish Match's was 20.5 percent, National's was 7.5 percent, and Swisher's was 6.5 percent. UST reportedly controlled 75 percent of the moist snuff market in 1999 in term of pounds sold, compared to its closest competitor, Conwood, which reportedly had 13 percent of that market. Swedish Match reportedly controlled 39 percent of the loose leaf market in 1999; Conwood controlled 35 percent, National controlled 19 percent, and Swisher controlled 8 percent. Top-selling moist snuff and fine cut tobacco brands are shown in Exhibit 4 and top-selling loose leaf chewing tobacco brands are shown in Exhibit 5.

Conwood has been privately held since the Pritzker family took the firm private in a $400 million buyout in 1985. Conwood makes Kodiak and Cougar snuff and has some 13 percent of the moist snuff market, with UST hovering between 76 and 77 percent of the market. Conwood's market share has risen steadily, from 0.0 percent to 7.6 percent during the 1979–1982 period; from 7.6 percent to 10.6 percent during the 1982–1990 period; and from 10.6 percent to 13.5 percent during the 1990–1998 period. Based in Memphis, Tennessee, Conwood is controlled through a complicated ownership scheme by Chicago's powerhouse Pritzker family.

Conwood's major brand of chewing tobacco is Levi Garrett. Taylor's Pride and Levi Garrett Plug are its moist plug brands. Kodiak and Hawken were moist snuff brands introduced in 1981. Conwood is urging Gen X males not to let peer pressure dictate their chewing preferences with regard to its newest Extreme brand, which was introduced in August 2001. It is a longer cut tobacco and features a big X stamped into a steellike background. Conwood execs chose to launch a new trademark rather than to steer its 20-year-old Kodiak brand toward young adults and in the process turn off its mature audiences.

Headquartered in Jacksonville, Florida, Swisher International, Inc. produces large cigars for the mass-market, such as Swisher Sweets, King Edward, and Optimo. It also produces BeRing, La Primadora, and Siglo 21, all of which are in the premium cigars category. These products are additions to its smokeless tobacco products line, both moist and dry snuff, under the brands Silver Creek, Redwood, and Kayak moist snuff, and the loose-leaf brands of Mail Pouch, Lancaster-Limited-Reserve, and Chattanooga Chew. This company has captured a 5 percent market share, in 1998, it experienced a 3.1 percent growth in sales and a 19.8 percent growth in net income. In 1999, this company, controlled by William Ziegler III, went private. Swisher International is in its 140th year of operations and offers smokers around the globe a full range of quality cigars and smokeless items in all price categories.

Swedish Match, formerly Pinkerton Tobacco Co. (NASDAQ: SWMAY), is owned by the car company Volvo and produces cigars, smokeless tobacco products, and pipe tobacco as well as smoking accessories such as matches and lighters. Swedish is the world's largest maker of matches and the number three producer of disposable lighters (Cricket) behind BIC and the Itochu subsidiary Tokai. Its Red Man chewing tobacco brand leads the U.S. market. Swedish Match's other tobacco offerings include pipe tobacco, snuff, and an array of cigars (it ranks number two in the world behind Altidas), including well known brands such as El Credito, Garcia y Vega, La Paz, Montague, and Tiparillo. It owns 64 percent of U.S. cigar maker General Cigar Holdings. The company makes rolling papers and filters, but it sold its cigarette division to Austria Tabak in 1999. Swedish Match's products are made in 15 countries and sold in 140 countries. The firm was founded in 1915 and is organized in five divisions—North Europe, Continental Europe, North America, Overseas, and Matches. The headquarters' offices are located in Stockholm. Its goal is to strengthen its position as a leading global player in the area of niche tobacco products, particularly in the European and North American markets, and to continue developing its position in certain selected markets in other parts of the world.

Lennart Sunden, chief executive of Swedish Match, Europe's largest producer of moist oral snuff, believes that trends appear to justify the company's decision to divest itself of its cigarette operations in 1998 and to focus on oral snuff. Although in volume terms, sales of cigarettes are declining in most developed countries due to the increased awareness of health risks and public smoking bans, London's *Financial Times* reports that sales of oral snuff are increasing in the markets where it is allowed (May 2, 2001, p. 32). Swedish Match's sales of snuff are increasing. Operating profit margins on the product were above 45 percent. With growth rates of around 20 percent and no exposure to cigarettes, the company is seen as a growth stock rather than a tobacco company.

In Sweden, where snuff consumption has been growing by around 5 percent a year, smoking has declined to less than 20 percent of the adult population. More than one in ten Swedes is a user, including the country's health minister, and Swedish Match has a market share above 90 percent in the country. Internationally, taxes on tobacco products have been hiked sharply in countries throughout the EU in recent years. Advertising prohibitions barring tobacco from British media, for example, were recently broadened to include the Internet, and a bill banning tobacco companies from maintaining databases for direct mail was making its way through Parliament before its dissolution.

However, in the United States, the company feels that it has the largest potential. Here, the market is growing by 3 percent a year, while Swedish Match's sales grew 19 percent in volume last year. Mainly through its popular Timber Wolfbrand, it now has a market share of 8 percent in volume in a market that is worth about $1.8 billion. Timberwolf was introduced in 1995, and the low-priced snuff is grossing some $115 million annually.

Outside the United States, Swedish Match is introducing its snuff products in South Africa and India, yet inside the EU, with the exception of Sweden, its sale has been banned since 1992 on health grounds. Sunden believes this ban will be lifted within a few years. On top of its extensive line of cigars and cigarillos (small cigars the size of cigarettes), the company also acquired two U.S. cigar companies, General Cigars and El Credito, which manufacture mass-market cigars and handmade premium cigars, respectively.

Like Conwood, Swedish Match has rolled out lower-priced cans of snuff that quickly make a splash in the marketplace. These low-price brands are said to be the reason UST's total share of the market during the past 10 years has fallen to 78 percent from about 90 percent. UST may face a crossroads since it has based its reputation on premium brands. Its discounted brand, Red Seal, was a costly introduction in 1999 for UST. Swedish Match also introduced Sequoia, its first premium moist snuff product which featured Cinnamon Ice and Mountain Cider flavors and a unique twist-off can. June 2001 found Swedish Match ads for the new product in *Playboy, Maxim, Hot Rod, Field & Stream, American Hunter,* and on ESPN.

## MARKETING, ETHICAL, AND HEALTH ISSUES

As with other tobacco products, there is concern over health hazards associated with chewing tobacco, the major issue being mouth cancer, which includes cancer of the cheeks and gums. As early as 1761, awareness of smokeless tobacco's harmful effects was known as English physician John Hill warned consumers of the dangers of tobacco's use. Today, the American Cancer Society and the American Dental Association oppose tobacco chewing because it stains teeth and causes gum disease and mouth infections, which can lead to cancer.

Spit tobacco poses health hazards to users, contrary to popular notions that it is a safe alternative to smoking. The various forms of spit tobacco have been found to cause mouth cancer, a disease responsible for more than 8,000 deaths annually. Aside from causing oral cancer, spit tobacco also leads to bad breath, teeth stains, gum inflammation, or periodontal disease with bone loss. The concentrated nicotine absorbed orally also accelerates the heart rate, increases blood pressure, and can heighten the risk of coronary artery problems; heart disease, period occlusive vascular and cerebrovascular diseases, as well as stroke.

Also, dry snuff sniffed through the nostrils is considered harmful since it irritates the nerves that control the sense of smell, thus diminishing one's ability to distinguish odors. Specifically, smokeless tobacco use increases the risk of oral cancer by 300 percent. In addition, elevated cholesterol levels and blood pressure are other harmful side effects. The elevated levels of blood pressure appear to result from tobacco's high sodium and sugar contents. According to the American Cancer Society, some of the major ingredients in dip and chewing tobacco are nicotine (an addictive drug), polonium 210 (nuclear waste), formaldehyde (embalming fluid), cancer-causing chemicals, and radioactive elements.

Other health problems associated with smokeless tobacco use include sickness for first-time users, cancer of the mouth and throat, leukoplakia, potential cardiovascular problems, and peptic ulcers. With the use of this variety of tobacco continuing to increase, these health problems will also increase.

Tooth staining periodontal disease, nicotine stomatitis (mouth sores), local gingival (gum) recession, leukoplakia (white patches), or other mucosal conditions are tobacco-related complications. Systematic effects such as nicotine dependence, transient hypertension (high blood pressure), and cardiovascular disease may also result from smokeless tobacco use.

## CUSTOMER DEMOGRAPHICS AND MARKETING

Chewing tobacco still remains predominantly a blue-collar, rural/suburban activity, but there has been some penetration into new urban, inner-city markets as a result of the country-western craze. The average annual income of adult consumers of moist snuff is $37,520. A study by the Department of Health and Human Services found that 19 percent of high school males use smokeless tobacco. Usage by the under-19 sector is highest in the South and the Midwest—and, in particular, in the states of Tennessee and Montana. Of student-athletes who used smokeless tobacco products, 57 percent played baseball and 40 percent played football.

Over the last 20 years, consumers have generally been attracted to lighter products in all consumption areas. It is this lighter, milder, sweeter-tasting appeal that smokeless tobacco producers are selling to customers, at least for growth products like loose-leaf and moist snuff. Consumers can enjoy a mild tobacco taste without ever lighting-up. Nationally, states have laws limiting smoking in public areas, according to Health and Human Services. Additionally, many companies have banned smoking on their premises. All of these reasons are conducive to the purchase and use of smokeless tobacco products. In addition, smokeless tobacco manufacturers have promoted their products as the most economical form of tobacco use.

Smokeless tobacco producers are now expanding their customer base into other consumer segments, including active outdoor people, sports enthusiasts, business executives, and professional people. New younger consumers, many of whom have never used any form of tobacco before, are being attracted to smokeless tobacco products, especially to moist snuff. These younger consumers like moist snuff because using this product is more socially acceptable than chewing tobacco and because snuff can be used indoors as well as outdoors insofar as one does not have to spit. Internationally, most find the practice of dipping and spitting to be gross. It is not a social custom taken up by many people.

Typical consumers are fourteen-to-eighteen-year-old boys, and most are white. Nationwide, white students are six times more likely than African Americans and three times more likely than Hispanics to use snuff. The *Courier-Journal* of Louisville, Kentucky (August 5, 2001) reported that in Kentucky, use of smokeless tobacco exceeded the overall state rate of 27.8 percent. According to former Surgeon General David Kessler, Kentucky boys are really buying a "drug-delivery system." A single 1-gram pinch of popular brands like Copenhagen and Kodiak can deliver six milligrams of nicotine—the equivalent of five Marlboro King cigarettes.

The ban on radio and television advertising of smokeless tobacco products was instituted in 1987. Additionally, manufacturers were also required to put warning labels on product packages. Furthermore, the Federal Trade Commission has proposed an amendment to the Comprehensive Smokeless Tobacco Health Education Act of 1986 to include the placement of warning labels on advertising at car races. Targets for additional labeling include cars and uniforms.

Smokeless tobacco producers use various ways to promote their products. Free-product sampling is widely used by manufacturers for new and existing products. Samples are distributed to consumers at sporting events, such as car races, concerts, gun and boat shows, and at the establishments of tobacco retailers. UST has been very successful at promoting the two largest-selling brands of moist snuff in the industry, Skoal and Copenhagen. Branded merchandise is offered by UST through its Country Western Store and concert catalog, where items are sold for a combination of cash and proofs of purchase from Skoal products. T-shirts, knives, watches, key chains, radios, Skoal silver lids, and belt buckles are a few of the branded articles available through the store. UST's sales representatives capitalize on product awareness with one-on-one product sampling to put products directly into the hands of customers. Some analysts feel that premium smokeless tobacco's hold is eroding due to value brands, which grabbed a 14.9 percent share during the second quarter of 2001 according to analyst Bonnie Herzog at Credit Suisse/First Boston. UST had avoided value lines but joined in the competition because the Red Seal brand had cut into its margins. Skoal maintained a 21.8 market share for the year ending June 10, 2001, according to ACNielsen, while Copenhagen and Kodiak slipped slightly to 34.6 percent and 11.3 percent, respectively.

## CONCLUSION

While smokeless tobacco users remain loyal to their brands and to the product category, several substitutes are entering the market that compete with nicotine-based products (rather than gum or sugared candy). Ariva is a new product that offers nicotine in a snuff-based product marketed to smokers to urge them to quit. The minty-tasting Ariva, which dissolves completely, could provide an attractive alternative to abstinence, however, as many point out. It provides a jolt of nicotine when smokers can't smoke—on airplanes, in movie theaters, or in smoke-free offices. It contains eucalyptus and mint flavorings. Star Scientific, Inc. of Chester, Virginia, makes Ariva, and it has no intention of marketing Ariva as a smoking-cessation aid due to FDA regulations.

Other substitutes include nicotine gum, nicotine patches, nasal sprays, or nicotine inhalers that deliver nicotine; there are also other tobacco-free alternatives. Although highly profitable, UST's future is uncertain. Some special concerns to consider in strategic planning are listed below:

- Will health claims and litigation against smokeless tobacco users increase?
- Should UST continue to base its reputation and fortunes on premium brands, or should it create lower-priced brands? Would lower-priced brands steal business away from Skoal and Copenhagen? Should the company abandon the lower end of the market?
- Will UST win the appeal against Conwood's antitrust case?
- Will the industry's growth be adversely affected by skyrocketing taxes and the growing stigma surrounding snuff and chewing tobacco sales in the United States?
- How can the firm attract new users and capture current and former cigarette smokers?
- Is diversification beyond wine and smokeless tobacco a key to survival? What products should be added?
- Should the company launch new brands and improve its packaging? Can snuff be made more socially acceptable? Should the company develop a nonspit product?
- Is the 10 percent EPS goal realistic?
- Should UST try to acquire a smaller competitor?

# REFERENCES

www.aap.org/advocacy/chmsmles.

www.ada.org.

*The Charleston Daily Mail* (March 31, 2001).

*Courier-Journal* (August 5, 2001).

http://democracynow.org/companies/
ust.html.

*The Federal Trade Commission Report to Congress
for the Years 1998 and 1999* (2001).

*Financial Times* (May 2, 2001): 32.

*Hoover's Handbook of American Business* (2001).

*Journal of the American Dental Association*
(September 2000).

Standard & Poor's Industry Surveys (2000).

www.swedishmatch.ch.

# COORS—2002

Stephanie Wilhelm
Francis Marion University

RKY

www.coors.com

> *Coors—It's a name that conjures up an image of cool mountain streams, clear blue skies and all that is inspiring about the Rocky Mountain West. It is a name associated with an uncompromising commitment to quality—a reputation that began more than 100 years ago and thrives to this day.*
>
> *It is the name of an ambitious 19th-century pioneer whose humble dream grew into the world's largest single-site brewery. But more than anything else, the name Coors is one held dear in the hearts of beer lovers across the country and, increasingly, around the globe. This is the story behind the name.* (**www.coors.com**)

Founded in 1872 in the foothills of the Rocky Mountains, Adolph Coors Company is ranked among the 700 largest publicly traded corporations in the United States. Coors' principal subsidiary is Coors Brewing Company, the nation's third-largest brewer. Coors' corporate headquarters and primary brewery are located in the foothills of the Rocky Mountains in Golden, Colorado, which is the world's largest brewery on a single site. Coors also has another major brewing facility in Memphis, Tennessee, as well as packaging facilities in Virginia's Shenandoah Valley near the town of Elkton, Virginia. In addition, Coors owns major aluminum can and end-manufacturing facilities near Golden and is a partner in the joint venture that operates these plants. Coors is also a partner in a joint venture that owns and operates a glass bottle manufacturing plant in Colorado. More than 90 percent of Coors U.S. production is in Golden, CO.

Throughout its history, Coors has provided consumers with high-quality malt beverages produced through an all-natural brewing process and containing the finest ingredients available. Coors produces, markets, and sells high-quality malt-based beverages. Its portfolio of brands is designed to appeal to a wide range of consumer taste, style, and price preferences. Today, the Coors portfolio consists of Coors Light—the fourth-largest-selling beer in the country—Original Coors, and more than a dozen other malt-based beverages, primarily premium and super-premium beers. Coors' beverages are sold throughout the United States and in select international markets. Coors Light has accounted for more than 70 percent of the company's sales volume in the past three years. Premium and above-premium products accounted for more than 85 percent of its total sales volume in the last three years.

Under the direction of a fourth-generation Coors, Peter Coors, the company began the 1990s by having the fastest volume growth rate in the industry and by reaching its long time goal of becoming the nation's third-largest brewer. In addition, the company started expanding internationally, eventually making its products available to consumers in Japan, Canada, Ireland, the United Kingdom, and other countries. Coors products are now sold in about 30 international markets in North America, Latin America, the Caribbean, Europe, and Asia.

Coors developed special strains of barley that it malts itself. Coors adds nothing artificial to its beers. Coors beer, on average, takes about 55 days to brew, age, finish, and package its lagers—about twice as long as its major competitors. The result is a naturally aged, stable, and smooth product. Coors beers are packaged in dark amber bottles and protective cartons to guard against light damage. Most of its beer products are kept cold throughout the brewing, packaging, and distribution process. They are then shipped cold in either insulated or refrigerated railcars and trucks. Coors gives free brewery tours in both Golden (daily except Sundays and holidays) and Memphis (Thursday through Saturday). More than 250,000 visitors tour Coors' breweries each year. Coors' net sales for 2001 were $2.43 billion, down slightly from 2000. Coors' operating income in 2001 was $151 million, up just $1.0 million from 2000. Net income for 2001 increased 12.2 percent to $123 million.

## HISTORY

Born in Barmen, Prussia, in 1847, Adolph Coors was the young German immigrant who founded Coors Brewing Company. Adolph began an apprenticeship at age fourteen at the Henry Wenker Brewery in Dortmund, Germany. Soon after he had become an apprentice at the brewing company, both of Adolph's parents died, leaving him to take care of his younger brother and sister. As an apprentice, he received clothing, food, and a place to live. It is also believed that Adolph was the brewery's nighttime bookkeeper, a job that enabled him to earn extra money.

Adolph continued to work at the Henry Wenker Brewery until the war in Germany caused him to stow away on a U.S.-bound ship at the age of 21. He arrived in Baltimore with no job and penniless, but he had a dream, like most immigrants did. Adolph's dream was to own his own brewery. Adolph traveled west through America and wound up in Naperville, Illinois; there, he was hired as a foreman at the Stenger Brewery. Apparently, the owner of the brewery, who had three daughters, saw son-in-law potential in his new foreman, but in order to avoid being pushed into marriage, Adolph continued his journey westward after two and half years.

Adolph arrived in Denver, Colorado, in 1872, and within a month, he had purchased a partnership in a Denver bottling company. Within a year, Adolph was sole owner of the company. It is said that on Sundays, Adolph roamed the foothills until he ran across an old abandoned tannery on the banks of Clear Creek.

In 1873, Adolph and Jacob Schueler, one of Adolph's bottling customers, opened "The Golden Brewery" with $18,000 from Schueler and Adolph's life savings of $2,000. Adolph died in 1929 before Prohibition ended, but one of his sons, Adolph Jr., assumed control of the brewery. In the year after Prohibition ended, the brewery produced more than 136,000 barrels of beer. Although Coors had only distributed its beer in a few isolated markets before Prohibition, the company began to expand its market to include eleven Western states once it had ended.

Since beer was viewed as important to the morale of the troops in World War II, the government allowed breweries to buy enough barley and other materials to continue brewing beer. However, the beer produced was different from the product produced before the war. The alcohol content was reduced from 4.6 percent to only 3.2 percent. Coors set aside one-half of all the beer it produced and sold it to the military. When the war finally ended, demand continued to grow, thus allowing Coors to double the amount of barrels of beer produced before the war. By 1955, Coors was producing a little more than 1 million per year barrels of beer.

Coors, along with other breweries, began to experiment with beer production by tinkering the packaging, with the sizes, and even with the types of beer produced. Before

1959, kegs and bottles were the primary means of selling beer. Then Coors introduced the first all-aluminum two-piece beverage can, along with a recycling campaign that offered one penny for every can returned to the brewery. Since the introduction of the can helped increase demand for Coors' beer, Bill Coors (a third-generation Coors) decided to develop more new technologies to use in the brewing industry. Coors also made the decision to go international in the 1970s.

Coors introduced the Coors Light brand, also known as the Silver Bullet, in 1978. In response to a national increase in the demand for beer, Coors broke ground on a new packaging facility in Virginia's Shenandoah Valley in 1985. Coors expanded again in 1990 with the purchase of a brewery in Memphis, Tennessee. Both of these locations for expansion were selected after an extensive search for water that held the same high quality characteristics as the water in Golden's Clear Creek.

In the 1990s, under the direction of Peter Coors (a fourth-generation Coors), the company became the third largest brewer in the United States and experienced the fastest volume growth rate in the industry. In addition, Coors began expanding internationally and made its products available to consumers in Canada, Ireland, Japan, the United Kingdom, as well as other smaller countries. Today, Coors' products are available in about thirty international markets.

## INTERNAL ISSUES

The Coors approach to growth at the field level is two-pronged: First, to build its big brands in locations where it has a high market share; and second, to go into high-potential markets with strong, committed local wholesaler partners. In both cases, it brings proven market-building expertise and works closely with its distributors to identify opportunities, develop clear strategies, and then execute them.

At the retail level, Coors' unique category management approach is based upon bringing value rather than just gaining shelf space. The company uses a sophisticated, objective process to help retailers sell more beer, not just its own beer. That approach builds relationships, loyalty, and, over time, sales for Coors. In 2000, Coors outpaced the U.S. industry volume growth rate for the fourth consecutive year, posted its fifth consecutive year of double-digit earnings growth, and for the sixth straight year grew Coors Light at a strong single-digit rate.

Coors experienced positive growth momentum in Puerto Rico during the second half of 2000 as a result of a new marketing strategy: It placed a stronger emphasis on Coors Light's attributes across print, outdoor, and point-of-sale media. Today, more than half the beer sold in Puerto Rico is Coors Light. Coors develops new international markets in much the same way it develops domestic ones—with highly focused strategies and strong, committed local distributor partners. Coors Light scored a win in the Canadian province of Quebec, nearly doubling its market share in 2000. Coors is constantly getting stronger through alliances and smart spending.

### Responsibility in Advertising

Coors has established its own guidelines to ensure that responsible decisions about drinking are promoted. In fact, Coors was the first brewer to incorporate alcohol awareness messages into national product advertising. Coors places advertising only where the clear majority of the audience is 21 years old or over. Coors regularly monitors all advertising placements for compliance with industry and company standards, and it publicly discloses independent audits of its television placements. To ensure compliance, when applicable, it targets television commercials to select programs: At least 60 percent of the audience must have been 21 or older in the prior reporting period. Strict internal reviews are also conducted on all advertising and marketing materials to avoid any advertising that may be misconstrued as targeted to those under 21. Coors even has a series of television ads featuring Peter Coors, Coors' CEO, which ask underage consumers not to drink and which caution adults to be responsible when they drink. As a result, Coors' advertising in the United States meets or exceeds the advertising and marketing codes of the Beer Institute and Inter-Association Task Force, thus ensuring that the company targets only adult consumers and never promotes product abuse.

## Operations

Coors' brewing facilities operate at an estimated annual average of approximately 87 percent of capacity. Annual production capacity varies due to product and packaging mix, product sourcing, and seasonality.

Coors' major facilities are shown below.

| Facility | Location | Product |
| --- | --- | --- |
| Brewery/packaging | Golden, CO | Malt beverages/packaged malt beverages |
| Packaging | Elkton, VA (Shenandoah) | Packaged malt beverages |
| Brewery/packaging | Memphis, TN | Malt beverages/packaged malt beverages |
| Can and end plants | Golden, CO | Aluminum cans and ends |
| Bottle plant | Wheat Ridge, CO | Glass bottles |
| Distribution warehouse | Anaheim, CA | Wholesale beer |
| Distribution | Meridian, ID | |
| | Denver, CO | |
| | Oklahoma City, OK | |
| | San Bernardino, CA | |
| | Glenwood Springs, CO | |

*Source:* Coor's 2001 *Annual Report.*

## Sales and Distribution

Beer in the United States must be distributed through a three-tier system consisting of manufacturers, distributors, and retailers. A national network of 517 distributors currently delivers Coors' products to U.S. retail markets. Of these distributors, 511 are independent businesses and the other six are owned and operated by one of Coors' subsidiaries. Some distributors operate multiple branches, bringing the total number of U.S. distributor and branch locations to 571 for the year ended December 31, 2000. As a result of Coors' new joint venture with Molson, Coors has an additional 350 to 400 domestic distributors that distribute Molson brands within the United States. Additional independent distributors deliver Coors products to some international markets under licensing and distribution agreements. Coors establishes standards and monitors distributors' methods of handling their products to ensure the highest product quality and freshness. Coors monitors the methods to ensure adherence to proper refrigeration and rotation guidelines for its products at both wholesale and retail locations. Distributors are required to remove Coors products from retailer outlets if they have not sold within a certain period of time.

Coors' highest volume states are California, New Jersey, New York, Pennsylvania, and Texas, which together accounted for 44 percent of the firm's total domestic volume in 2001. Coors has approximately 350 full-time salespeople throughout the United States who work closely with its distributors to assist them in implementing the industry's highest-quality practices to improve efficiency and performance. Coors' sales function is organized into two regions that manage a total of six geographic field business areas responsible for overseeing domestic sales. The company believes that this structure enables its salespeople to better anticipate wholesaler and consumer needs and to respond to those needs locally with greater speed. In addition, Coors has a team of category managers responsible for assisting leading U.S. retailers, such as large supermarket chains, in the management of their beer offerings. Coors' category managers work with retailers to enhance overall beer sales by optimizing space allocation, merchandising displays, promotional campaigns, and product distribution throughout the retailer's chain. Coors believes that its success in category management enhances its competitive position. Coors operates under a functional structure with no divisions. Only about 8 percent of Coors' 5,500 employees in the U.S. are unionized, compared with 31 percent of its 3,150 employees in the U.K.

## International Business

Coors' international volume is produced, marketed, and distributed under varying business arrangements, including export, direct investment, joint ventures, and licensing. Coors markets its products to select international markets and to U.S. military bases worldwide. Coors' malt beverages compete with numerous above premium, premium, low-calorie, popular-priced, nonalcoholic, and imported brands. National, regional, local, and international brewers produce these competing brands. Coors competes most directly with Anheuser-Busch, Inc. and the Miller Brewing Company.

### Canada

Coors is currently engaged in a partnership with Molson Inc., an alliance that is named Coors Canada and that markets Coors Light in Canada. The partnership contracts with a Molson subsidiary for the brewing, distribution, and sale of products. Coors has a 50.1 percent ownership stake in Coors Canada and Molson has a 49.9 percent ownership stake. The Coors Canada partnership contracts with a Molson subsidiary for the brewing, distribution, and sale of products. Coors Canada manages all marketing activities for Coors products in Canada. Currently, Coors Light has a market share of more than 6 percent and is now the number one light beer—and the fourth-ranked beer brand overall—in Canada.

### Puerto Rico and the Caribbean

In Puerto Rico, Coors markets and sells Coors Light to an independent local distributor. A local team of Coors employees manages marketing and promotional efforts in this market. Coors Light is the number-one brand in the Puerto Rico market, with more than a 50 percent market share in 2000. Coors also sells products in several other Caribbean markets, including the U.S. Virgin Islands, through local distributors.

### Europe

In Europe, Coors focuses its efforts on Ireland and Northern Ireland, where it markets the Coors Light brand. Additionally, Coors is currently testing Coors Light in Scotland, and it will assess the feasibility of expanding into the United Kingdom. During the fourth quarter of 2000, Coors closed its brewery and commercial operations in Spain. This brewery produced beer for Spain and other European markets. Beginning in late 2000, Coors began sourcing beer for its remaining European markets from its Memphis plant. Thomas Hardy then packages the beer for distribution under contract in the United Kingdom.

### Japan

In Japan, Coors Japan Company Ltd., which is located in Tokyo, is the exclusive importer and marketer of Coors products. Currently, the Japanese business is focused on Original Coors and Zima. Coors Japan sells Coors products to independent distributors in Japan.

### China

In China, Coors markets Original Coors beer under a licensing arrangement, one focused on select cities, with Carlsberg-Guangdong. Under this arrangement, Coors maintains representative offices that oversee the marketing of its products in China.

## Segment and Geographic Information

Coors has one reporting segment relating to the continuing operations of producing, marketing, and selling malt-based beverages. Its operations are conducted in the United States, the country of domicile, and several foreign countries, none of which is individually significant to its overall operations. Exhibit 13 reveals Coors' recent net revenues from external customers, operating income, and pretax income attributable to the United States and all foreign countries.

## Environmental Matters

Coors has a tradition of environmental responsibility; it was the company responsible for introducing the aluminum beverage can and aluminum can recycling into the United States in 1959. After facing a number of troubling environmental problems in the early 1990s, Coors responded with aggressive programs that have established comprehensive environmental management systems and that greatly reduced Coors' negative impact on the environment.

Coors, like all breweries, is subject to the requirements of federal, state, local, and foreign environmental and occupational health and safety laws and regulations. Coors continues to promote the efficient use of pollution prevention, resources, and waste reduction. It currently has several programs underway, such as recycling bottles and cans and, where practical, increasing the recycled content of product packaging materials, paper, and other supplies. Each year, Coors diverts thousands of tons of materials from landfills by recycling office paper, corrugated cardboard and paperboard, plastic banding, aluminum, and other scrap metal. Coors conducts regular, comprehensive environmental, health, and safety audits of all of its facilities. Coors is a charter member of the Colorado Pollution Prevention Partnership, a group whose members include companies, environmental organizations, the U.S. Environmental Protection Agency (EPA), and the Colorado Department of Public Health and Environment. The postconsumer recycled content of glass bottles manufactured by Coors grew from 9 percent in 1989 to about 35 percent today. The recycled content of both aluminum and corrugated materials used by Coors is about 70 percent. Most of Coors' paper packaging, which a few years ago could not be recycled, is now 90 percent recyclable.

Coors was one of the several parties named by the EPA as a "potentially responsible party" at the Rocky Flats Industrial Park site. In September 2000, the EPA entered into an Administrative Order on Consent with certain parties, including Coors, requiring implementation of a removal action. Coors' projected costs to construct and monitor the removal action are approximately $300,000. The EPA will also seek to recover its oversight costs associated with the project, costs that cannot be estimated at this time, although Coors believes it would be immaterial to its financial position.

In August 2000, an accidental spill into Clear Creek at the Golden, Colorado, facility caused damage to some of the fish population in the creek. As a result, Coors is required to pay certain fines or other costs by implementing a supplemental environmental project. Coors settled with the Colorado Department of Public Health and Environment regarding violations of its permit in the amount of $98,000 on February 22, 2001. This money was paid to the Clear Creek Watershed Foundation to construct a waste rock repository in Clear Creek County. The company has not yet settled with the Division of Wildlife for damage to the fish population, but it has proposed funding the remaining costs for construction of the waste rock repository. While Coors cannot predict its eventual aggregate cost for environmental and other related matters in which it is currently involved, Coors does believe that any payments, if required, for these matters would be made over a period of time in amounts that would not be material in any one year to its operating results or its financial or competitive position. Coors also believes that adequate reserves have been provided for losses that are probable.

## EXTERNAL ISSUES

### Competition

Coors' malt beverages compete with numerous above-premium, premium, low-calorie, popular-priced, nonalcoholic, and imported brands. National, regional, local, and international brewers produce these competing brands. Approximately 80 percent of U.S. beer shipments are attributable to the top three domestic brewers: Anheuser-Busch, Inc.; Philip Morris, Inc., through its subsidiary, The Miller Brewing Company; and Coors Brewing Company. Coors competes most directly with Anheuser and Miller, the dominant companies in the U.S. industry. Coors is currently the nation's third-largest brewer and, according to Beer Marketer's Insights estimates, it represented approximately 11.1 percent of the total 2000 U.S. brewing industry shipments of malt beverages (including exports and U.S. shipments of imports). This compares to Anheuser's 48.3 percent share and Miller's 20.6 percent share. Coors beer shipments to wholesalers increased 4.7 percent in 2000, representing the fourth consecutive year in which its shipments have outpaced industry growth by 2 percentage points or more. By comparison, Anheuser's shipments increased 2.7 percent in 2000 and Miller's declined 2.6 percent, due in part to reductions in distributor inventories. More than 85 percent of Coors unit volume was in the premium and above-premium price categories, the highest proportion among the largest domestic brewers. This product mix compares to 77 percent premium-and-above volume for Anheuser and 61 percent for Miller.

Coors continues to face significant competitive disadvantages that relate to economies of scale. Besides lower transportation costs achieved by competitors with multiple breweries, the larger brewers also benefit from economies of scale in advertising spending because of their greater unit sales volumes. In an effort to achieve and maintain national advertising exposure and grow its U.S. market share, Coors generally spends substantially more to market its beer, per barrel, than its major competitors. Although the Coors results are primarily driven by U.S. sales, international operations have increased in importance in recent years, including those in Canada, where Coors Light is the number one light beer.

Today, in 2001, the beer industry in the United States is extremely competitive. Industry volume growth has averaged less than 1 percent annually since 1991. Therefore, growing and even maintaining market share requires substantial and consistent investments in marketing and sales. In 2000, a very competitive year, domestic beer shipments increased less than 1 percent after growing 1.2 percent in 1999. In recent years, brewers have focused less on price discounting strategies and more on marketing, promotions, and innovative packaging in an effort to gain market share.

The industry's pricing environment continued to be positive in 2000, with the announcement of modest price increases on specific packages in select markets. As a result, revenue per barrel increased for major U.S. brewers during the year. However, consumer demand continued to shift away from short bottles and toward long-neck bottles, which cost significantly more to make and ship than short bottles. In addition, many raw material prices increased in 2000, including aluminum, glass, and fuel. In 2000, a significant portion of Coors incremental gross profit generated by volume growth and price increases was reinvested in packaging materials, as well as in additional marketing and sales activities.

A number of important trends continue in the U.S. beer market. The first is a trend toward lighter, more refreshing beers. The largest beer brands that grew in the U.S. market are again American-style light lagers, such as Coors Light. More than 80 percent of Coors' annual unit volume is in light beers. The second trend is toward "trading up," as consumers continued to move away from lower-priced brands to higher-priced brands, including imports. Import beer shipments rose more than 10 percent in 2000. The industry sales trends toward lighter, more upscale beers play to Coors' strengths.

The U.S. brewing industry has experienced significant consolidation in the past several years, which has removed excess capacity. Several competitors have exited the beer business, sold brands, or closed inefficient, outdated brewing facilities. The beer industry is also consolidating at the wholesaler level, a trend that continued in 2000 and generally leads to improved economics for the combining wholesalers and their suppliers. U.S. demographics continued to improve for the beer industry, with the number of consumers reaching legal drinking age continuing to increase in 2000, according to U.S. Census Bureau assessments and projections. These same projections anticipate that the 21-to-24 age group will continue to grow for virtually this entire decade. This trend is important to the beer industry because young adult males tend to consume more beer per capita than other demographic groups.

## CONCLUSION

Responsible drinking is an issue of great importance to Coors and the rest of the brewing industry. As a result, Coors is responsible for numerous policies and alcohol programs that encourage responsible drinking. Over the years, Coors has become a leader in the creation and support of initiatives aimed at preventing drunk driving, underage drinking, and other forms of alcohol abuse. Coors does not want its products to be consumed by anyone under the legal drinking age. One of Pete Coors' infamous sayings is "If you're under the legal drinking age, we'll wait for your business"—hence, the company's "21 Means 21" campaign.

Coors needs to continue growing its business and increasing profitability both domestically and internationally. Within the next three years, Coors should open new brewing facilities. By opening one facility per year in high-growth, high-margin segments, Coors should be able to increase its market share and remain at the top.

## REFERENCES

Anheuser-Busch *Annual Report* (2000).

Coors Brewing Company, *Annual Report* (2000).

CAULFIELD, KEVIN. "Coors and Ball Corporation Sign Letter of Intent For Aluminum Joint Venture" (September 6, 2001). www.coors.com/newsRelease/2001_sep6.asp.

CAULFIELD, KEVIN. "Peter H. Coors, Chairman, Coors Brewing Company, Urges Support for Tougher Drunk Driving Laws in Colorado" (March 13, 2001). Available at www.coors.com/newsReleases/2001_mar13.asp.

HEALEY, PAT. "Coors Finalizes U.S. Joint Venture with Molson" (January 2, 2001).

Available at www.coors.com/newsReleases/2001_jan2.asp.

MOOZAKIS, CHUCK. "Coors Looks For A Silver Bullet" (July 24, 2001). Available at www.internetwk.com/story/INW20010724S0005.

MURPHY, TARA. "Whassup At Anheuser-Busch" (September 27, 2001). Available at www.biz.yahoo.com.

REUTERS. "Consumers Reaching for Sweets" (November 24, 2001). Available at www.dailynews.yahoo.com.

"Which Brew For You?" *Consumer Reports* (August, 2001): 10–16.

EXHIBIT 1    Coors' Segment Financial Data (in thousands)

|  | 2001 | 2000 | 1999 |
|---|---|---|---|
| **United States and its territories** | | | |
| Net revenues | $2,353,843 | $2,331,693 | $2,177,407 |
| Operating income | $ 133,361 | $ 163,563 | $ 148,823 |
| Pretax income | $ 182,317 | $ 185,082 | $ 161,281 |
| **Other foreign countries** | | | |
| Net revenues | $ 75,619 | $ 82,722 | $ 159,077 |
| Operating income (loss) | $ 18,244 | $ (12,937) | $ (8,288) |
| Pretax income (loss) | $ 15,696 | $ (15,557) | $ (10,614) |

*Source:* Coors' 2001 *Annual Report,* p. 53.

EXHIBIT 2    Coors' Consolidated Statements of Income
(in thousands, except per-share data, for the years ended)

|  | December 30, 2001 | December 31, 2000 | December 26, 1999 |
|---|---|---|---|
| **Sales** – domestic and international | $2,842,752 | $2,841,738 | $2,642,712 |
| Beer excise taxes | (413,290) | (427,323) | (406,228) |
| **Net sales** | 2,429,462 | 2,414,415 | 2,236,484 |
| Cost of goods sold | (1,537,623) | (1,525,829) | (1,397,251) |
| Gross profit | 891,839 | 888,586 | 839,233 |
| **Other operating expenses** | | | |
| Marketing, general and administrative | (717,060) | (722,745) | (692,993) |
| Special charges | (23,174) | (15,215) | (5,705) |
| Total other operating expenses | (740,234) | (737,960) | (698,698) |
| **Operating Income** | 151,605 | 150,626 | 140,535 |
| **Other Income (expenses)** | | | |
| Gain on sales of distributorships | 27,667 | 1,000 | — |
| Interest income | 16,409 | 21,325 | 11,286 |
| Interest expense | (2,006) | (6,414) | (4,357) |
| Miscellaneous – net | 4,338 | 2,988 | 3,203 |
| Total | 46,408 | 18,899 | 10,132 |
| **Income before income taxes** | 198,013 | 169,525 | 150,667 |
| Income tax expense | (75,049) | (59,908) | (58,383) |
| **Net income** | $ 122,964 | $ 109,617 | $ 92,284 |
| **Other comprehensive income (expense), net of tax** | | | |
| Foreign currency translation adjustments | 14 | 2,632 | (3,519) |
| Unrealized (loss) gain on available-for-sale securities | 3,718 | 1,268 | (397) |
| Unrealized (loss) gain on derivative instruments | (6,200) | (1,997) | 6,835 |
| Minimum pension liability adjustment | (8,487) | — | — |
| Reclassification adjustments | (4,498) | 366 | — |
| **Comprehensive income** | $ 107,111 | $ 111,886 | $ 95,203 |
| **Net income per share – basic** | $ 3.33 | $ 2.98 | $ 2.51 |
| **Net income per share – diluted** | $ 3.31 | $ 2.93 | $ 2.46 |
| **Weighted-average shares – basic** | 36,902 | 36,785 | 36,729 |
| **Weighted-average shares – diluted** | 37,177 | 37,450 | 37,457 |

*Source:* Coors' 2001 *Annual Report,* p. 33.

## EXHIBIT 3    Coors' Consolidated Balance Sheets (in thousands)

| | December 30, 2001 | December 31, 2000 |
|---|---|---|
| **ASSETS** | | |
| **Current assets** | | |
| Cash and cash equivalents | $    77,133 | $   119,761 |
| Short-term marketable securities | 232,572 | 72,759 |
| Accounts and notes receivable | | |
| Trade, less allowance for doubtful accounts of $91 in 2001 and $139 in 2000 | 94,985 | 104,484 |
| Affiliates | 223 | 7,209 |
| Other, less allowance for certain claims of $111 in 2001 and $104 in 2000 | 13,524 | 15,385 |
| Inventories | | |
| Finished | 32,438 | 40,039 |
| In process | 23,363 | 23,735 |
| Raw materials | 41,534 | 37,570 |
| Packaging materials, less allowance for obsolete inventories of $2,188 in 2001 and $1,993 in 2000 | 17,788 | 8,580 |
| Total inventories | 115,123 | 109,924 |
| Maintenance and operating supplies, less allowance for obsolete supplies of $2,182 in 2001 and $1,621 in 2000 | 23,454 | 23,703 |
| Prepaid expenses and other assets | 21,722 | 19,847 |
| Deferred tax asset | 27,793 | 24,679 |
| Total current assets | 606,529 | 497,751 |
| Properties, at cost and net | 869,710 | 735,793 |
| Goodwill and other intangibles, less accumulated amortization of $9,049 in 2001 and $12,981 in 2000 | 86,289 | 54,795 |
| Investments in joint ventures, less accumulated amortization of $1,625 in 2001 | 94,785 | 56,342 |
| Long-term marketable securities | — | 193,675 |
| Other assets | 82,379 | 90,948 |
| Total assets | $1,739,692 | $1,629,304 |

*(continued)*

## EXHIBIT 3    Coors' Consolidated Balance Sheets (in thousands)                    (continued)

|  | December 30, 2001 | December 31, 2000 |
|---|---|---|
| **LIABILITIES AND SHAREHOLDERS' EQUITY** | | |
| **Current liabilities** | | |
| Accounts payable | | |
| Trade | $ 219,381 | $ 186,105 |
| Affiliates | 3,112 | 11,621 |
| Accrued salaries and vacations | 56,767 | 57,041 |
| Taxes, other than income taxes | 31,271 | 32,469 |
| Accrued expenses and other liabilities | 122,014 | 92,100 |
| Current portion of long-term debt | 85,000 | — |
| Total current liabilities | 517,545 | 379,336 |
| Long-term debt | 20,000 | 105,000 |
| Deferred tax liability | 61,635 | 89,986 |
| Deferred pension and postretirement benefits | 141,720 | 77,147 |
| Other long-term liabilities | 47,480 | 45,446 |
| Total liabilities | 788,380 | 696,915 |
| Commitments and contingencies | | |
| Shareholders' equity | | |
| Capital stock | | |
| Preferred stock, non-voting, no par value (authorized: 25,000,000 shares, issued and outstanding: none) | — | — |
| Class A common stock, voting, no par value (authorized, issued and outstanding: 1,260,000 shares) | 1,260 | 1,260 |
| Class B common stock, non-voting, no par value, $0.24 stated value (authorized: 200,000,000 shares; issued and outstanding: 34,689,410 in 2001 and 35,871,121 in 2000) | 8,259 | 8,541 |
| Total capital stock | 9,519 | 9,801 |
| Paid-in capital | — | 11,332 |
| Unvested restricted stock | (597) | (129) |
| Retained earnings | 954,981 | 908,123 |
| Accumulated other comprehensive income | (12,591) | 3,262 |
| Total shareholders' equity | 951,312 | 932,389 |
| Total liabilities and shareholders' equity | $1,739,692 | $1,629,304 |

*Source:* Coors' 2001 *Annual Report,* p. 34.